T0359286

A PEARSON AUSTRALIA CUSTOM BOOK

ACCT20076 Foundations of Management Accounting 2nd Edition

This custom book is compiled by Dr Ann Sardesai for CQU from:

COST ACCOUNTING: A MANAGERIAL EMPHASIS

SIXTEENTH EDITION   GLOBAL EDITION

DATAR & RAJAN

Pearson Australia
707 Collins Street
Melbourne VIC 3008

www.pearson.com.au

Project Management Team Leader:	Jill Gillies
Production Manager:	Lisa D'Cruz
Custom Portfolio Manager:	Lucie Bartonek
Production Controller:	Dominic Harman
Cover Image:	*Infra Red* by Dr Kim S. Mackenzie

Kim S. Mackenzie is an Australian author, artist and business academic. She creates semi abstract images to inspire deep reflection and understanding of complex phenomena. *Infra Red* represents electromagnetic radiation that expresses as warmth, heat and expansion, which is a useful semi-abstract metaphor to reflect the planning, control and decision making activities of management accountants in order to achieve positive and dynamic business outcomes.

ISBN: 978 1 4886 2384 4

Brief Contents

Contents

11   Decision Making and Relevant Information   446

13   Pricing Decisions and Cost Management   544

A NOTE ABOUT THE CONTENTS OF THIS CUSTOM TITLE

Welcome to **ACCT20076** *Foundations of Management Accounting* **2nd Edition**

The chapters in this custom title have been chosen specifically to meet your course requirements from *Cost Accounting: A Managerial Emphasis*, Global, 16th Edition by Horngren, Datar and Rajan. ISBN: 9781292211541.

In reading this title, please be aware that some chapters have not been included in this compilation.

The chapter numbers and page numbers throughout match the original source title, table of contents and index.

We hope you will find this custom title easy to follow and enjoyable.

About the Authors

Srikant M. Datar is the Arthur Lowes Dickinson Professor of Business Administration at the Harvard Business School, Faculty Chair of the Harvard University Innovation Labs, and Senior Associate Dean for University Affairs. A graduate with distinction from the University of Bombay, he received gold medals upon graduation from the Indian Institute of Management, Ahmedabad, and the Institute of Cost and Works Accountants of India. A chartered accountant, he holds two master's degrees and a PhD from Stanford University.

Datar has published his research in leading accounting, marketing, and operations management journals, including *The Accounting Review, Contemporary Accounting Research, Journal of Accounting, Auditing and Finance, Journal of Accounting and Economics, Journal of Accounting Research*, and *Management Science*. He has served as an associate editor and on the editorial board of several journals and has presented his research to corporate executives and academic audiences in North America, South America, Asia, Africa, Australia, and Europe. He is a coauthor of two other books: *Managerial Accounting: Making Decisions and Motivating Performance* and *Rethinking the MBA: Business Education at a Crossroads*.

Cited by his students as a dedicated and innovative teacher, Datar received the George Leland Bach Award for Excellence in the Classroom at Carnegie Mellon University and the Distinguished Teaching Award at Stanford University.

Datar is a member of the board of directors of Novartis A.G., ICF International, T-Mobile US, and Stryker Corporation and Senior Strategic Advisor to HCL Technologies. He has worked with many organizations, including Apple Computer, Boeing, DuPont, Ford, General Motors, Morgan Stanley, PepsiCo, Visa, and the World Bank. He is a member of the American Accounting Association and the Institute of Management Accountants.

Madhav V. Rajan is the Robert K. Jaedicke Professor of Accounting at Stanford University's Graduate School of Business. He is also Professor of Law (by courtesy) at Stanford Law School. From 2010 to 2016, he was Senior Associate Dean for Academic Affairs and head of the MBA program at Stanford GSB. In 2017, he will receive the Davis Award for Lifetime Achievement and Service to Stanford GSB.

Rajan received his undergraduate degree in commerce from the University of Madras, India, and his MS in accounting, MBA, and PhD degrees from Carnegie Mellon University. In 1990, his dissertation won the Alexander Henderson Award for Excellence in Economic Theory.

Rajan's research focuses on the economics-based analysis of management accounting issues, especially as they relate to internal control, capital budgeting, supply-chain, and performance systems. He has published his research in a variety of leading journals, including *The Accounting Review, Journal of Accounting and Economics, Journal of Accounting Research, Management Science*, and *Review of Financial Studies*. In 2004, he received the Notable Contribution to Management Accounting Literature award. He is a coauthor of *Managerial Accounting: Making Decisions and Motivating Performance*.

Rajan has served as the Departmental Editor for Accounting at *Management Science* as well as associate editor for both the accounting and operations areas. From 2002 to 2008, Rajan served as an editor of *The Accounting Review*. Rajan has twice been a plenary speaker at the AAA Management Accounting Conference.

Rajan has received several teaching honors at Wharton and Stanford, including the David W. Hauck Award, the highest undergraduate teaching award at Wharton. He teaches in the flagship Stanford Executive Program and is co-director of *Finance and Accounting for the Nonfinancial Executive*. He has participated in custom programs for many companies, including Genentech, Hewlett-Packard, and nVidia, and is faculty director for the Infosys Global Leadership Program.

Rajan is a director of Cavium, Inc. and iShares, Inc., a trustee of the iShares Trust, and a member of the C.M. Capital Investment Advisory Board.

Preface

Studying cost accounting is one of the best business investments a student can make. Why? Because success in any organization—from the smallest corner store to the largest multinational corporation—requires the use of cost accounting concepts and practices. Cost accounting provides key data to managers for planning and controlling, as well as costing products, services, and even customers. This book focuses on how cost accounting helps managers make better decisions, as cost accountants are increasingly becoming integral members of their company's decision-making teams. In order to emphasize this prominence in decision making, we use the "different costs for different purposes" theme throughout this book. By focusing on basic concepts, analyses, uses, and procedures instead of procedures alone, we recognize cost accounting as a managerial tool for business strategy and implementation.

We also prepare students for the rewards and challenges they face in the professional cost accounting world of today and tomorrow. For example, we emphasize both the development of analytical skills such as Excel to leverage available information technology and the values and behaviors that make cost accountants effective in the workplace.

New to This Edition

Deeper Consideration of Global Issues

Businesses today have no choice but to integrate into an increasingly global ecosystem. Virtually all aspects, including supply chains, product markets, and the market for managerial talent, have become more international in their outlook. To illustrate this, we incorporate global considerations into many of the chapters. For example, Chapter 6 describes the special challenges of budgeting in multinational companies while Chapter 23 discusses the challenges of evaluating the performance of divisions located in different countries. Chapter 22 examines the importance of transfer pricing in minimizing the tax burden faced by multinational companies. The Concepts in Action for Chapter 16 explains the importance of joint-cost allocation in creating a trade war between poultry farms in the United States and South Africa. Several new examples of management accounting applications in companies are drawn from international settings.

Increased Focus on Merchandising and Service Sectors

In keeping with the shifts in the U.S. and world economy, this edition makes great use of merchandising and service sector examples, with corresponding de-emphasis of traditional manufacturing settings. For example, Chapter 10 illustrates linear cost functions in the context of payments for cloud computing services. Chapter 20 highlights inventory management in retail organizations and uses an example based on a seller of sunglasses. Chapter 21 incorporates a running example that looks at capital budgeting in the context of a transportation company. Several Concepts in Action boxes focus on the merchandising and service sectors, including achieving cost leadership at Trader Joe's (Chapter 1), using activity-based costing to reduce the costs of health care delivery at the Mayo Clinic (Chapter 5), reducing fixed costs at Twitter (Chapter 2), and analyzing operating income performance at Best Buy (Chapter 12) and web-based budgeting at 24 Hour Fitness (Chapter 6).

Greater Emphasis on Sustainability

This edition places significant emphasis on sustainability as one of the critical managerial challenges of the coming decades. Many managers are promoting the development and implementation of strategies to achieve long-term financial, social, and environmental performance as key imperatives. We highlight this in Chapter 1 and return to the theme in several subsequent chapters. Chapter 12 discusses the benefits to companies from measuring social and environmental performance and how such measures can be incorporated in a balanced scorecard. Chapter 23 provides several examples of companies that mandate disclosures and evaluate managers on environmental and social metrics. A variety of chapters, including Chapters 2, 4, 6, 10, 13, 15, and 21, contain material that stress themes of recognizing and accounting for environmental costs, energy independence and the smart grid, setting stretch targets to motivate greater carbon reductions, using cost analysis, carbon tax, and cap-and-trade auctions to reduce environmental footprints, and constructing "green" homes in a cost-effective manner.

Focus on Innovation

We discuss the role of accounting concepts and systems in fostering and supporting innovation and entrepreneurial activities in firms. In particular, we discuss the challenges posed by recognizing R&D costs as period expenses even though the benefits of innovation accrue in later periods. In Chapter 6, we describe how companies budget for innovation expenses and develop measures to monitor success of the innovation efforts delinked from operational performance in the current period. Chapter 11 presents the importance of nonfinancial measures when making decisions about innovation. Chapter 13 stresses that innovation starts with understanding customer needs while Chapter 19 discusses process innovations for improving quality.

New Cutting-Edge Topics

The pace of change in organizations continues to be rapid. The sixteenth edition of *Cost Accounting* reflects changes occurring in the role of cost accounting in organizations.

- We have introduced sustainability strategies and the methods companies use to implement sustainability and business goals.
- We describe ideas based on academic research regarding the weights to be placed on performance measures in a balanced scorecard. We have also added a new section on methods to evaluate strategy maps such as the strength of links, differentiators, focal points, and trigger points.
- We have provided details on the transfer pricing strategies used by multinational technology firms such as Apple and Google to minimize income taxes.
- We discuss current trends in the regulation of executive compensation.
- We describe the evolution of enterprise resource planning systems and newer simplified costing systems that practice lean accounting.
- We have added new material around recent trends in big data and data analytics in predicting costs and when making demand forecasts.

Opening Vignettes

Each chapter opens with a vignette on a company situation. The vignettes engage the reader in a business situation or dilemma, illustrating why and how the concepts in the chapter are relevant in business. For example, Chapter 2 describes how surf wear company Quiksilver was driven into bankruptcy by the relatively high proportion of fixed costs in its operations. Chapter 5 explains the use of activity-based costing by General Motors to evaluate its suppliers. Chapter 9 highlights the use of lean manufacturing by Boeing to work through its backlog of orders and reduce its inventory costs. Chapter 14 shows how Delta made changes to its frequent flyer program to reward its most profitable customers, who drive a disproportionate share of Delta's revenues. Chapter 18 shows the impact on Honda of the rework costs associated with recalling millions of cars with defective airbags. Chapter 23 describes the misalignment between performance measurement and pay at Viacom, whose CEO has since been forced to step down.

Concepts in Action Boxes

Found in every chapter, these boxes cover real-world cost accounting issues across a variety of industries, including defense contracting, entertainment, manufacturing, retailing, and sports. New examples include:

- Cost–Volume–Profit Analysis Makes Subway's $5 Foot-Long Sandwiches a Success but Innovation Challenges Loom (Chapter 3)
- Can Chipotle Wrap Up Its Materials-Cost Variance Increases? (Chapter 7)
- H&M Uses Target Pricing to Bring Fast Fashion to Stores Worldwide (Chapter 13)
- Amazon Prime and Customer Profitability (Chapter 14)
- Hybrid Costing for Under Armour 3D Printed Shoes (Chapter 17)
- Netflix Works to Overcome Internet Bottlenecks (Chapter 19)

Streamlined Presentation

We continue to try to simplify and streamline our presentation of various topics to make it as easy as possible for students to learn the concepts, tools, and frameworks introduced in different chapters. We received positive feedback for the reorganization of Chapters 12 through 16 in the fifteenth edition and have maintained that order in the sixteenth edition. Chapter 13 is the first of four chapters on cost allocation. We introduce the purposes of cost allocation in Chapter 13 and discuss cost allocation for long-run product costing and pricing. Continuing the same example, Chapter 14 discusses cost allocation for customer costing. Chapter 15 builds on the Chapter 4 example to discuss cost allocation for support departments. Chapter 16 discusses joint cost allocation.

Other examples of streamlined presentations can be found in:

- Chapter 2 on the discussion of fundamental cost concepts and the managerial framework for decision making.
- Chapter 6, where the appendix ties the cash budget to the chapter example.
- Chapter 8, which has a comprehensive chart that lays out all of the variances described in Chapters 7 and 8.
- Chapter 9, which uses a single two-period example to illustrate the impact of various inventory-costing methods and denominator level choices.

Try It! Examples

Found throughout the chapter, Try It! interactive questions give students the opportunity to apply the concept they just learned. Linking in the eText will allow students to practice in Pearson MyLab Accounting© without interrupting their interaction with the eText.

Becker Multiple-Choice Questions

Sample problems, assignable in Pearson MyLab Accounting, provide an introduction to the CPA Exam format and an opportunity for early practice with CPA exam style questions.

Selected Chapter-by-Chapter Content Changes

Thank you for your continued support of Cost Accounting. In every new edition, we strive to update this text thoroughly. To ease your transition from the fifteenth edition, here are selected highlights of chapter changes for the sixteenth edition.

Chapter 1 has been rewritten to include greater discussion of sustainability and innovation and why these issues have become increasingly critical for managers. We discuss the challenges of planning and control for innovation and sustainability and how companies use these systems to manage these activities. We continue to emphasize the importance of ethics, values, and behaviors in improving the quality of financial reporting.

Chapter 2 has been updated and revised to make it easier for students to understand core cost concepts and to provide a framework for how cost accounting and cost management help managers make decisions. We have added more material on environmental costs to explain how and why these costs may be missed in costing systems even though they are a part of product costs. We discuss the challenges of accounting for R&D costs and the implications for innovation.

Chapter 3 now includes greater managerial content, using examples from real companies to illustrate the value of cost–volume–profit analysis in managerial decision making. We have rewritten the section on CVP analysis in service and not-for-profit companies using the context of a management consulting firm. Chapter 4 has been revised to discuss the creation of cost pools, the level of fixed costs in a seasonal business, and the need to adjust normal costs to actual costs using end-of-accounting-year adjustments. The chapter also develops the criteria for allocating costs and relates them to real examples to highlight why managers need allocated cost information to make decisions.

Chapter 5 adds more discussion of product undercosting and overcosting and refining a costing system. The chapter example has been changed to add new material on time-driven activity-based costing (TDABC) compared to driver-rate activity-based costing. We integrate the discussion of behavioral considerations in implementing activity-based costing with the technical material in the chapter.

Chapter 6 presents material on the mismatch between costs incurred for breakthrough innovations in the annual budget and the revenues earned in that year. The chapter describes ways to delink innovation from current year operational performance by developing measures to monitor the success of innovation efforts. The chapter discusses how stretch targets motivate greater carbon reductions. We also elaborate on tradeoffs managers must make when choosing different organization structures.

In Chapter 7, the appendix on mix and yield variances, which used a one-off example, has now been recast using the same running example that winds its way through both Chapters 7 and 8. Chapter 8 provides a revised comprehensive summary of the variances in both Chapters 7 and 8 via an innovative exhibit.

Chapter 9 retains the simplified two-period integrated example of capacity choice. There is greater emphasis now on linking the impact of the choice of capacity concept to recent changes in financial reporting and tax requirements.

Chapter 10 provides an expanded description of big data and the reasons behind the explosion in data availability and analytics today. It also incorporates several examples of how companies are gathering and using large quantities of data to make better decisions.

Chapter 11 has been revised to emphasize nonfinancial factors in decisions, particularly in environmental and innovation decisions. The chapter explicitly considers how relevant cost analysis is distinct from the absorption costing method of preparing financial statements under Generally Accepted Accounting Principles (GAAP). The focus is on identifying and understanding why relevant costs and relevant revenues are important when making decisions.

Chapter 12 introduces a completely new section around evaluating strategy maps by identifying strong and weak links, differentiators, focal points, and trigger points. There is a new exhibit to present these concepts. The chapter also ties the Chipset strategy decision to the general discussion of strategy.

The new Chapter 13 makes significant revisions to the sections on target pricing and target costing, cost-plus pricing, and life-cycle budgeting. The chapter presents new material on carbon tax, cap-and-trade auctions, and the Sustainability Accounting Standards Board (SASB). New examples have been added when discussing predatory pricing, dumping, and collusive pricing.

Chapter 14 was completely rewritten in the fifteenth edition. The current revision makes a number of changes to improve the clarity of the writing and to motivate different concepts. The section on cost-hierarchy-based operating income has been rewritten and the section on fully allocated customer profitability has been streamlined.

Chapter 15 was also heavily revised in the fifteenth edition. The current revision makes several significant changes to clarify concepts and improve exposition. The sections on single-rate and dual-rate methods, budgeted versus actual costs, and the choice of allocation bases have all been substantially rewritten. The Concepts in Action box uses updated federal cases on contract disputes centered around cost allocation.

Chapter 16 provides a discussion of the rationale for joint-cost allocation and the merits and demerits of various joint-cost allocation methods. It includes a new opening vignette and a new real-world example to highlight the controversies that can result from using inappropriate methods of joint-cost allocation.

Chapters 17 and 18 provide a managerial lens on the estimation of equivalent units and the choice between the FIFO and weighted-average costing methods, both in the chapter content and in the new vignettes and real-world examples. The exhibits have been reformatted to make clear how various components are added to get the total costs. Chapter 18 emphasizes, with illustrative examples, the theme of striving for zero waste and a sustainable environment.

Chapter 19 focuses on quality and time. The sections on control charts, weighing the costs and benefits of improving quality, and evaluating a company's quality performance have been rewritten. This revision also makes major changes to and reorganizes the section on bottlenecks and time drivers.

Chapter 20 emphasizes the importance of choosing the correct products to sell, deeply understanding customers, and pricing smartly as ways to manage inventory. It discusses the role of big data and better demand forecasts in reducing demand uncertainty and safety stocks and in implementing materials requirements planning (MRP) systems. The section on the cost of a prediction error has been revised to link to Exhibit 20-1. The section on lean accounting has been rewritten and simplified.

Chapter 21 focuses on the role of capital budgeting in supporting the choice of sustainable long-term projects. The new opening vignette looks at the financing of residential solar panels, the integrated example deals with the purchase of a new hybrid-engine bus, and various examples throughout the chapter and in the new Concepts in Action illustrate how companies incorporate sustainability in their capital budgeting decisions.

Chapter 22 has been revised to reflect the most recent developments in the controversial use of transfer prices for tax minimization by multinational corporations, with several real-world examples. The revision also highlights the changing regulatory environment across the world and provides updated information on the use of tools such as advance pricing agreements.

Chapter 23 describes the use of environmental, social, and ethical objectives by companies as part of top management's pay structures, with new examples of companies that embed sustainability targets into compensation systems. It discusses the latest SEC regulations on disclosure of executive compensation and the impact of Dodd-Frank "say on pay" rules.

Hallmark Features of *Cost Accounting*

- Exceptionally strong emphasis on managerial uses of cost information
- Clarity and understandability of the text
- Excellent balance in integrating modern topics with traditional coverage
- Emphasis on human behavior aspects
- Extensive use of real-world examples
- Ability to teach chapters in different sequences
- Excellent quantity, quality, and range of assignment material

The first thirteen chapters provide the essence of a one-term (quarter or semester) course. There is ample text and assignment material in the book's twenty-three chapters for a two-term course. This book can be used immediately after the student has had an introductory course in financial accounting. Alternatively, this book can build on an introductory course in managerial accounting.

Deciding on the sequence of chapters in a textbook is a challenge. Because every instructor has a unique way of organizing his or her course, we utilize a modular, flexible organization that permits a course to be custom tailored. *This organization facilitates diverse approaches to teaching and learning.*

As an example of the book's flexibility, consider our treatment of process costing. Process costing is described in Chapters 17 and 18. Instructors interested in filling out a student's perspective of costing systems can move directly from job-order costing described in Chapter 4 to Chapter 17 without interruption in the flow of material. Other instructors may want their students to delve into activity-based costing and budgeting and more decision-oriented topics early in the course. These instructors may prefer to postpone discussion of process costing.

Resources

In addition to this textbook and Pearson MyLab Accounting, a companion website is available for students at www.pearsonglobaleditions.com/Horngren.

The following resources are available for instructors in Pearson MyLab Accounting and on the Instructors Resource Center at www.pearsonglobaleditions.com/Horngren.

- Solutions Manual
- Test Bank in Word and TestGen, including algorithmic questions
- Instructors Manual
- PowerPoint Presentations
- Image Library

Acknowledgments

We are indebted to many people for their ideas and assistance. Our primary thanks go to the many academics and practitioners who have advanced our knowledge of cost accounting. The package of teaching materials we present is the work of skillful and valued team members developing some excellent end-of-chapter assignment material. Tommy Goodwin provided outstanding research assistance on technical issues and current developments. We would also like to thank the dedicated and hard-working supplement author team and Integra. The book is much better because of the efforts of these colleagues.

In shaping this edition and past editions we would like to thank all the reviewers and colleagues who have worked closely with us and the editorial team.

We also would like to thank our colleagues who helped us greatly by accuracy checking the text and supplements, including Molly Brown, Barbara Durham, Anna Jensen, and Sandra Cereola.

We thank the people at Pearson for their hard work and dedication, including Donna Battista, Ellen Geary, Christine Donovan, Elizabeth Geary, and Martha LaChance. We extend special thanks to Claire Hunter, the development editor on this edition, who took charge of this project and directed it across the finish line. This book would not have been possible without their dedication and skill. Sue Nodine at Integra expertly managed the production aspects of the manuscript's preparation with superb skill and tremendous dedication. We are deeply appreciative of their good spirits, loyalty, and ability to stay calm in the most hectic of times.

Appreciation also goes to the American Institute of Certified Public Accountants, the Institute of Management Accountants, the Society of Management Accountants of Canada, the Certified General Accountants Association of Canada, the Financial Executive Institute of America, and many other publishers and companies for their generous permission to quote from their publications. Problems from the Uniform CPA examinations are designated (CPA); problems from the Certified Management Accountant examination are designated (CMA); problems from the Canadian examinations administered by the Society of Management Accountants are designated (SMA); and problems from the Certified General Accountants Association are designated (CGA). Many of these problems are adapted to highlight particular points. We are grateful to the professors who contributed assignment material for this edition. Their names are indicated in parentheses at the start of their specific problems. Comments from users are welcome.

SRIKANT M. DATAR
MADHAV V. RAJAN

Global Edition Acknowledgments

Pearson would like to thank the following people for their work on the content of the Global Edition:

Contributors

Davood Askarany, The University of Auckland
Anupam De, National Institute of Technology Durgapur
Samit Paul, International Management Institute Kolkata

Reviewers

Michelle Zou Junqi, Singapore Institute of Technology
Man Lut Ko, Hong Kong Baptist University
Mabel Lam, The Open University of Hong Kong
Eric Leung, The Chinese University of Hong Kong
Patrick Leung, The Hong Kong Polytechnic University
Yukihiko Okada, University of Tsukuba
Ananda Samudhram, Monash University Malaysia
Pak Mei Sen, Monash University Malaysia
Eu-Gene Siew, Monash University Malaysia

Nancy Su, The Hong Kong Polytechnic University
Hung Woan Ting, The University of Nottingham Malaysia Campus
Loh Wei Ting, Singapore Management University
Yuichi Ubukata, doctoral student, University of Tsukuba
Angelina Seow Voon Yee, The University of Nottingham Malaysia Campus
Kevin Ow Yong, Singapore Management University
Liang Zhang, Monash University Malaysia

In memory of Charles T. Horngren 1926–2011

Chuck Horngren revolutionized cost and management accounting. He loved new ideas and introduced many new concepts. He had the unique gift of explaining these concepts in simple and creative ways. He epitomized excellence and never tired of details, whether it was finding exactly the right word or working and reworking assignment materials.

He combined his great intellect with genuine humility and warmth and a human touch that inspired others to do their best. He taught us many lessons about life through his amazing discipline, his ability to make everyone feel welcome, and his love of family.

It was a great privilege, pleasure, and honor to have known Chuck Horngren. Few individuals will have the enormous influence that Chuck had on the accounting profession. Fewer still will be able to do it with the class and style that was his hallmark. He was unique, special, and amazing in many, many ways and, at once, a role model, teacher, mentor, and friend. He will be deeply missed.

SRIKANT M. DATAR
Harvard University

MADHAV V. RAJAN
Stanford University

To Our Families

Swati, Radhika, Gayatri, Sidharth (SD)
Gayathri, Sanjana, Anupama (MVR)

The Manager and Management Accounting

1

All businesses are concerned about revenues and costs.

Managers at companies small and large must understand how revenues and costs behave or risk losing control of the performance of their firms. Managers use cost accounting information to make decisions about research and development, production planning, budgeting, pricing, and the products or services to offer customers. Sometimes these decisions involve tradeoffs. The following article shows how understanding costs and pricing helps companies like Coca-Cola increase profits even as the quantity of products sold decreases.

FOR COCA-COLA, SMALLER SIZES MEAN BIGGER PROFITS

Can selling less of something be more profitable than selling more of it? As consumers become more health conscious, they are buying less soda. "Don't want to drink too much?" Get a smaller can. "Don't want so many calories?" Buy a smaller can. "Don't want so much sugar?" Just drink a smaller can. In 2015, while overall sales of soda in the United States declined in terms of volume, industry revenue was higher. How, you ask? Soda companies are charging more for less!

Coca-Cola has been the market leader in selling smaller sizes of soda to consumers. Sales of smaller packages of Coca-Cola—including 8-packs of 12-ounce bottles and 7.5-ounce cans—rose 15% in 2015. Meanwhile, sales of larger bottles and cans fell. The price per ounce of Coke sold in smaller cans is higher than the price per ounce of Coke sold in bulk. The resulting higher profits from the sales of smaller sizes of soda made up for the decrease in total volume of soda sold. If these trends toward buying smaller cans continue, Coca-Cola will be selling less soda, but making more money, for years to come.

By studying cost accounting, you will learn how successful managers and accountants run their businesses and prepare yourself for leadership roles in the firms you work for. Many large companies, including Nike and the Pittsburgh Steelers, have senior executives with accounting backgrounds.

Sources: Mike Esterl, "Smaller Sizes Add Pop to Soda Sales," *The Wall Street Journal,* January 27, 2016 (http://www.wsj.com/articles/smaller-sizes-add-pop-to-soda-sales-1453890601); Trefis, "How Coke Is Making the Most Out of Falling Soda Volumes," January 5, 2016 (http://www.trefis.com/stock/ko/articles/327882/how-coke-is-making-the-most-out-of-falling-soda-volumes/2016-01-05).

LEARNING OBJECTIVES

1 Distinguish financial accounting from management accounting

2 Understand how management accountants help firms make strategic decisions

3 Describe the set of business functions in the value chain and identify the dimensions of performance that customers are expecting of companies

4 Explain the five-step decision-making process and its role in management accounting

5 Describe three guidelines management accountants follow in supporting managers

6 Understand how management accounting fits into an organization's structure

7 Understand what professional ethics mean to management accountants

urbanbuzz/Alamy Stock Photo

Financial Accounting, Management Accounting, and Cost Accounting

LEARNING OBJECTIVE 1

Distinguish financial accounting

...reporting on past performance to external users

from management accounting

...helping managers make decisions

As many of you have already learned in your financial accounting class, accounting systems are used to record economic events and transactions, such as sales and materials purchases, and process the data into information helpful to managers, sales representatives, production supervisors, and others. Processing any economic transaction means collecting, categorizing, summarizing, and analyzing. For example, costs are collected by category, such as materials, labor, and shipping. These costs are then summarized to determine a firm's total costs by month, quarter, or year. Accountants analyze the results and together with managers evaluate, say, how costs have changed relative to revenues from one period to the next. Accounting systems also provide the information found in a firm's income statement, balance sheet, statement of cash flow, and performance reports, such as the cost of serving customers or running an advertising campaign. Managers use this information to make decisions about the activities, businesses, or functional areas they oversee. For example, a report that shows an increase in sales of laptops and iPads at an Apple store may prompt Apple to hire more salespeople at that location. Understanding accounting information is essential for managers to do their jobs.

Individual managers often require the information in an accounting system to be presented or reported differently. Consider, for example, sales order information. A sales manager at Porsche may be interested in the total dollar amount of sales to determine the commissions paid to salespeople. A distribution manager at Porsche may be interested in the sales order quantities by geographic region and by customer-requested delivery dates to ensure vehicles get delivered to customers on time. A manufacturing manager at Porsche may be interested in the quantities of various products and their desired delivery dates so that he or she can develop an effective production schedule.

To simultaneously serve the needs of all three managers, Porsche creates a database, sometimes called a data warehouse or infobarn, consisting of small, detailed bits of information that can be used for multiple purposes. For instance, the sales order database will contain detailed information about a product, its selling price, quantity ordered, and delivery details (place and date) for each sales order. The database stores information in a way that allows different managers to access the information they need. Many companies are building their own enterprise resource planning (ERP) systems. An ERP system is a single database that collects data and feeds them into applications that support a company's business activities, such as purchasing, production, distribution, and sales.

Financial accounting and management accounting have different goals. As you know, **financial accounting** focuses on reporting financial information to external parties such as investors, government agencies, banks, and suppliers based on Generally Accepted Accounting Principles (GAAP). The most important way financial accounting information affects managers' decisions and actions is through compensation, which is often, in part, based on numbers in financial statements.

Management accounting is the process of measuring, analyzing, and reporting financial and nonfinancial information that helps managers make decisions to fulfill the goals of an organization. Managers use management accounting information to:

1. develop, communicate, and implement strategies,
2. coordinate product design, production, and marketing decisions and evaluate a company's performance.

Management accounting information and reports do not have to follow set principles or rules. The key questions are always (1) how will this information help managers do their jobs better, and (2) do the benefits of producing this information exceed the costs?

Exhibit 1-1 summarizes the major differences between management accounting and financial accounting. Note, however, that reports such as balance sheets, income statements, and statements of cash flows are common to both management accounting and financial accounting.

Cost accounting provides information for both management accounting and financial accounting professionals. **Cost accounting** is the process of measuring, analyzing, and reporting financial and nonfinancial information related to the costs of acquiring or using

EXHIBIT 1-1   Major Differences Between Management and Financial Accounting

	Management Accounting	**Financial Accounting**
Purpose of information	Help managers make decisions to fulfill an organization's goals	Communicate an organization's financial position to investors, banks, regulators, and other outside parties
Primary users	Managers of the organization	External users such as investors, banks, regulators, and suppliers
Focus and emphasis	Future-oriented (budget for 2017 prepared in 2016)	Past-oriented (reports on 2016 performance prepared in 2017)
Rules of measurement and reporting	Internal measures and reports do not have to follow GAAP but are based on cost-benefit analyses	Financial statements must be prepared in accordance with GAAP and be certified by external, independent auditors
Time span and type of reports	Varies from hourly information to 15 to 20 years, with financial and nonfinancial reports on products, departments, territories, and strategies	Annual and quarterly financial reports, primarily on the company as a whole
Behavioral implications	Designed to influence the behavior of managers and other employees	Primarily reports economic events but also influences behavior because manager's compensation is often based on reported financial results

resources in an organization. For example, calculating the cost of a product is a cost account-ing function that meets both the financial accountant's inventory-valuation needs and the management accountant's decision-making needs (such as deciding how to price products and choosing which products to promote). However, today most accounting professionals take the perspective that cost information is part of the management accounting informa-tion collected to make management decisions. Thus, the distinction between management accounting and cost accounting is not so clear-cut, and we often use these terms interchange-ably in the book.

Businesspeople frequently use the term *cost management*. Unfortunately, the term does not have an exact definition. In this book we use **cost management** to describe the activities managers undertake to use resources in a way that increases a product's value to customers and achieves an organization's goals. In other words, cost management is not only about re-ducing costs. Cost management also includes making decisions to incur additional costs—for example, to improve customer satisfaction and quality and to develop new products—with the goal of enhancing revenues and profits. Whether or not to enter new markets, implement new organizational processes, and change product designs are also cost management deci-sions. Information from accounting systems helps managers to manage costs, but the infor-mation and the accounting systems themselves are not cost management.

DECISION POINT

How is financial accounting different from management accounting?

Strategic Decisions and the Management Accountant

A company's **strategy** specifies how the organization matches its own capabilities with the opportunities in the marketplace. In other words, strategy describes how an orga-nization creates value for its customers while distinguishing itself from its competitors. Businesses follow one of two broad strategies. Some companies, such as Southwest

LEARNING OBJECTIVE 2

Understand how man-agement accountants help firms make strategic decisions

...they provide information about the sources of com-petitive advantage

Airlines and Vanguard (the mutual fund company), follow a cost leadership strategy. They profit and grow by providing quality products or services at low prices and by judiciously managing their costs. Other companies such as Apple and the pharmaceutical giant Johnson & Johnson follow a product differentiation strategy. They generate profits and growth by offering differentiated or unique products or services that appeal to their customers and are often priced higher than the less-popular products or services of their competitors.

Deciding between these strategies is a critical part of what managers do. Management accountants work closely with managers in various departments to formulate strategies by providing information about the sources of competitive advantage, such as (1) the company's cost, productivity, or efficiency advantage relative to competitors or (2) the premium prices a company can charge over its costs from distinctive product or service features. **Strategic cost management** describes cost management that specifically focuses on strategic issues.

Management accounting information helps managers formulate strategy by answering questions such as the following:

■ *Who are our most important customers, and what critical capability do we have to be competitive and deliver value to our customers?* After Amazon.com's success selling books online, management accountants at Barnes & Noble outlined the costs and benefits of several alternative approaches for enhancing the company's information technology infrastructure and developing the capability to sell books online. A similar cost–benefit analysis led Toyota to build flexible computer-integrated manufacturing plants that enable it to use the same equipment efficiently to produce a variety of cars in response to changing customer tastes.

■ *What is the bargaining power of our customers?* Kellogg Company, for example, uses the reputation of its brand to reduce the bargaining power of its customers and charge higher prices for its cereals.

■ *What is the bargaining power of our suppliers?* Management accountants at Dell Computers consider the significant bargaining power of Intel, its supplier of microprocessors, and Microsoft, its supplier of operating system software, when considering how much it must pay to acquire these products.

■ *What substitute products exist in the marketplace, and how do they differ from our product in terms of features, price, cost, and quality?* Hewlett-Packard, for example, designs, costs, and prices new printers after comparing the functionality and quality of its printers to other printers available in the marketplace.

■ *Will adequate cash be available to fund the strategy, or will additional funds need to be raised?* Procter & Gamble, for example, issued new debt and equity to fund its strategic acquisition of Gillette, a maker of shaving products.

The best-designed strategies and the best-developed capabilities are useless unless they are effectively executed. In the next section, we describe how management accountants help managers take actions that create value for their customers.

DECISION POINT

How do management accountants support strategic decisions?

LEARNING OBJECTIVE 3

Describe the set of business functions in the value chain and identify the dimensions of performance that customers are expecting of companies

…R&D, design, production, marketing, distribution, and customer service supported by administration to achieve cost and efficiency, quality, time, and innovation

Value-Chain and Supply-Chain Analysis and Key Success Factors

Customers demand much more than just a fair price; they expect quality products (goods or services) delivered in a timely way. The entire customer experience determines the value a customer derives from a product. In this section, we explore how a company goes about creating this value.

Value-Chain Analysis

The **value chain** is the sequence of business functions by which a product is made progressively more useful to customers. Exhibit 1-2 shows six primary business functions: research

EXHIBIT 1-2   Different Parts of the Value Chain

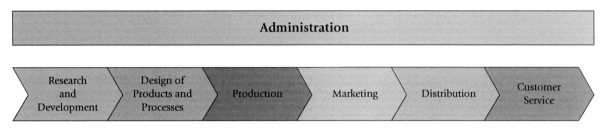

and development (R&D), design of products and processes, production, marketing, distribution, and customer service. We illustrate these business functions with Sony Corporation's television division.

1. **Research and development (R&D)**—generating and experimenting with ideas related to new products, services, or processes. At Sony, this function includes research on alternative television signal transmission and on the picture quality of different shapes and thicknesses of television screens.

2. **Design of products and processes**—detailed planning, engineering, and testing of products and processes. Design at Sony includes deciding on the component parts in a television set and determining the effect alternative product designs will have on the set's quality and manufacturing costs. Some representations of the value chain collectively refer to the first two steps as technology development.[1]

3. **Production**—procuring, transporting, and storing ("inbound logistics") and coordinating and assembling ("operations") resources to produce a product or deliver a service. The production of a Sony television set includes the procurement and assembly of the electronic parts, the screen and the packaging used for shipping.

4. **Marketing (including sales)**—promoting and selling products or services to customers or prospective customers. Sony markets its televisions at tradeshows, via advertisements in newspapers and magazines, on the Internet, and through its sales force.

5. **Distribution**—processing orders and shipping products or services to customers ("outbound logistics"). Distribution for Sony includes shipping to retail outlets, catalog vendors, direct sales via the Internet, and other channels through which customers purchase new televisions.

6. **Customer service**—providing after-sales service to customers. Sony provides customer service on its televisions in the form of customer-help telephone lines, support on the Internet, and warranty repair work.

In addition to the six primary business functions, Exhibit 1-2 shows an administration function, which includes accounting and finance, human resource management, and information technology and supports the six primary business functions. When discussing the value chain in subsequent chapters of the book, we include the administration function within the primary functions. For example, included in the marketing function is the function of analyzing, reporting, and accounting for resources spent in different marketing channels, whereas the production function includes the human resource management function of training frontline workers. Each of these business functions is essential to companies satisfying their customers and keeping them satisfied (and loyal) over time.

To implement their corporate strategies, companies such as Sony and Procter & Gamble use **customer relationship management (CRM)**, a strategy that integrates people and technology in all business functions to deepen relationships with customers, partners, and distributors. CRM initiatives use technology to coordinate all customer-facing activities (such

---

[1] M. Porter, *Competitive Advantage* (New York: Free Press, 1998).

as marketing, sales calls, distribution, and after-sales support) and the design and production activities necessary to get products to customers.

Different companies create value in different ways. Lowe's (the home-improvement retailer) does so by focusing on cost and efficiency. Toyota Motor Company does so by focusing on quality. Fast response times at eBay create quality experiences for the online auction giant's customers, whereas innovation is primarily what creates value for the customers of the biotech company Roche. The Italian apparel company Gucci creates value for its customers through the prestige of its brand. As a result, at different times and in different industries, one or more of the value-chain functions are more critical than others. For example, a company such as Roche emphasizes R&D and the design of products and processes. In contrast, a company such as Gucci focuses on marketing, distribution, and customer service to build its brand.

Exhibit 1-2 depicts the usual order in which different business-function activities physically occur. Do not, however, interpret Exhibit 1-2 to mean that managers should proceed sequentially through the value chain when planning and managing their activities. Companies gain (in terms of cost, quality, and the speed with which new products are developed) if two or more of the individual business functions of the value chain work concurrently as a team. For example, a company's production, marketing, distribution, and customer service personnel can often reduce a company's total costs by providing input for design decisions.

Managers track costs incurred in each value-chain category. Their goal is to reduce costs to improve efficiency or to spend more money to generate even greater revenues. Management accounting information helps managers make cost–benefit tradeoffs. For example, is it cheaper to buy products from a vendor or produce them in-house? How does investing resources in design and manufacturing increase revenues or reduce costs of marketing and customer service?

Supply-Chain Analysis

The parts of the value chain associated with producing and delivering a product or service—production and distribution—are referred to as the *supply chain*. The **supply chain** describes the flow of goods, services, and information from the initial sources of materials and services to the delivery of products to consumers, regardless of whether those activities occur in one organization or in multiple organizations. Consider Coke and Pepsi: Many companies play a role in bringing these products to consumers as the supply chain in Exhibit 1-3 shows. Part of cost management emphasizes integrating and coordinating activities across all companies in the supply chain to improve performance and reduce costs. For example, to reduce materials-handling costs, both the Coca-Cola Company and Pepsi Bottling Group require their suppliers (such as plastic and aluminum companies and sugar refiners) to frequently deliver small quantities of materials directly to their production floors. Similarly, to reduce inventory levels in the supply chain, Walmart requires its suppliers, such as Coca-Cola, to directly manage its inventory of products to ensure the right amount of them are in its stores at all times.

EXHIBIT 1-3   Supply Chain for a Cola Bottling Company

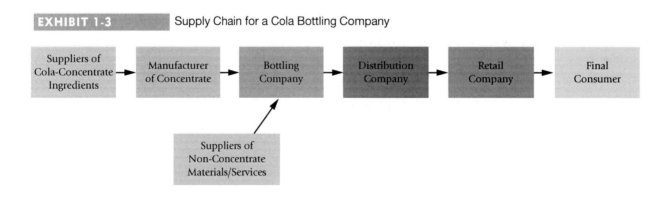

Key Success Factors

Customers want companies to use the value chain and supply chain to deliver ever-improving levels of performance when it comes to several (or even all) of the following:

- **Cost and efficiency**—Companies face continuous pressure to reduce the cost of the products they sell. To calculate and manage the cost of products, managers must first understand the activities (such as setting up machines or distributing products) that cause costs to arise as well as monitor the marketplace to determine the prices customers are willing to pay for the products. Management accounting information helps managers calculate a target cost for a product by subtracting from the "target price" the operating income per unit of product that the company wants to earn. To achieve the target cost, managers eliminate some activities (such as rework) and reduce the costs of performing other activities in all value-chain functions—from initial R&D to customer service (see Concepts in Action: Trader Joe's Recipe for Cost Leadership). Many U.S. companies have cut costs by outsourcing some of their business functions. Nike, for example, has moved its manufacturing operations to China and Mexico, and Microsoft and IBM are increasingly doing their software development in Spain, Eastern Europe, and India.

- **Quality**—Customers expect high levels of quality. **Total quality management (TQM)** is an integrative philosophy of management for continuously improving the quality of products and processes. Managers who implement TQM believe that every person in the value chain is responsible for delivering products and services that exceed customers' expectations. Using TQM, companies design products or services to meet customer needs and wants, to make these products with zero (or very few) defects and waste, and to minimize inventories. Managers use management accounting information to evaluate the costs and revenue benefits of TQM initiatives.

- **Time**—Time has many dimensions. Two of the most important dimensions are new-product development time and customer-response time. New-product development time is the time it takes for companies to create new products and bring them to market. The increasing pace of technological innovation has led to shorter product life cycles and more rapid introduction of new products. To make new-product development decisions, managers need to understand the costs and benefits of a product over its life cycle, including the time and cost of developing new products.

  Customer-response time describes the speed at which an organization responds to customer requests. To increase the satisfaction of their customers, organizations need to meet their promised delivery dates as well as reduce their delivery times. Bottlenecks are the primary cause of delays. For example, a bottleneck can occur when the work to be performed on a machine exceeds its available capacity. To deliver the product on time, managers need to increase the capacity of the machine to produce more output. Management accounting information can help managers quantify the costs and benefits of doing so.

- **Innovation**—A constant flow of innovative products or services is the basis for the ongoing success of a company. Many companies innovate in their strategies, business models, the services they provide, and the way they market, sell, and distribute their products. Managers rely on management accounting information to evaluate alternative R&D and investment decisions and the costs and benefits of implementing innovative business models, services, and marketing plans.

- **Sustainability**—Companies are increasingly applying the key success factors of cost and efficiency, quality, time, and innovation to promote **sustainability**—the development and implementation of strategies to achieve long-term financial, social, and environmental goals. The sustainability efforts of the Japanese copier company Ricoh include energy conservation, resource conservation, product recycling, and pollution prevention. By designing products that can be easily recycled, Ricoh simultaneously improves sustainability and the cost and quality of its products.

CONCEPTS IN ACTION ▶ Trader Joe's Recipe for Cost Leadership

BirchTree/Alamy Stock Photo

Trader Joe's has a special recipe for cost leadership: delivering unique products at reasonable prices. The grocery store chain stocks its shelves with low-cost, high-end staples (cage-free eggs and sustainably harvested seafood) and affordable luxuries (Speculoos cookie butter and Sriracha and roasted garlic BBQ sauce) that are distinct from what traditional supermarkets offer. Trader Joe's can offer these items at everyday low prices by judiciously managing its costs.

At Trader Joe's, customers swap selection for value. The company has relatively small stores with a carefully selected, constantly changing mix of items. While typical grocery stores carry 50,000 items, Trader Joe's sells only about 4,000 items. In recent years, it removed nonsustainable items from its shelves, including genetically modified items. About 80% of the stock bears the Trader Joe's brand, and management seeks to minimize costs of these items. The company purchases directly from manufacturers, which ship their items straight to Trader Joe's warehouses to avoid third-party distribution costs. With small stores and limited storage space, Trader Joe's trucks leave the warehouse centers daily. This encourages precise, just-in-time ordering and a relentless focus on frequent merchandise turnover.

This winning combination of quality products and low prices has turned Trader Joe's into one of the hottest retailers in the United States. Its stores sell an estimated $13 billion annually, or $1,734 in merchandise per square foot, which is nearly double Whole Foods, its top competitor.

Sources: Beth Kowitt, "Inside the Secret World of Trader Joe's," *Fortune*, August 23, 2010 (http://archive.fortune.com/2010/08/20/news/companies/inside_trader_joes_full_version.fortune/index.htm); Christopher Palmeri, "Trader Joe's Recipe for Success," *Bloomberg Businessweek*, February 21, 2008 (http://www.bloomberg.com/bw/stories/2008-02-20/trader-joes-recipe-for-success); Allessandra Ran, "Teach Us, Trader Joe: Demanding Socially Responsible Food," *The Atlantic*, August 7, 2012 (http://www.theatlantic.com/health/archive/2012/08/teach-us-trader-joe-demanding-socially-responsible-food/260786/); Aaron Ahlburn and Keisha McDonnough, "Retail ShopTopic," *Retail Research*, September 2014, Jones Lang LaSalle, Inc. (http://www.us.jll.com/united-states/en-us/Research/JLL-ShopTopic-Grocery-share.pdf); "Trader Joe's Customer Choice Award Winners," Trader Joe's Co. press release, Monrovia, CA: January 4, 2016 (http://www.traderjoes.com/digin/post/trader-joes-customer-choice-award-winners).

The interest in sustainability appears to be intensifying among companies. General Electric, Poland Springs (a bottled-water manufacturer), and Hewlett-Packard are among the many companies incorporating sustainability into their decision making. Sustainability is important to these companies for several reasons:

- More and more investors care about sustainability. These investors make investment decisions based on a company's financial, social, and environmental performance and raise questions about sustainability at shareholder meetings.

- Companies that emphasize sustainability find that sustainability goals attract and inspire employees.

- Customers prefer the products of companies with good sustainability records and boycott companies with poor sustainability records.

- Society and activist nongovernmental organizations, in particular, monitor the sustainability performance of firms and take legal action against those that violate environmental laws. Countries with fast-growing economies, such as China and India, are now either requiring or encouraging companies to develop and report on their sustainability initiatives.

DECISION POINT

How do companies add value, and what are the dimensions of performance that customers are expecting of companies?

Management accountants help managers track the key success factors of their firms as well as those of their competitors. Competitive information serves as a *benchmark* managers use to continuously improve their operations. Examples of continuous improvement include Southwest Airlines' efforts to increase the number of its flights that arrive on time, eBay's efforts to improve the access its customers have to online auctions, and Lowe's efforts to continuously reduce the cost of its home-improvement products. Sometimes, more fundamental changes and innovations in operations, such as redesigning a manufacturing process to reduce costs, may be necessary. To successfully implement their strategies, firms have to do more than analyze their value chains and supply chains and execute key success factors. They also have to have good decision-making processes.

Decision Making, Planning, and Control: The Five-Step Decision-Making Process

We illustrate a five-step decision-making process using the example of the *Daily News*, a newspaper in Boulder, Colorado. Subsequent chapters of the book describe how managers use this five-step decision-making process to make many different types of decisions.

The *Daily News* differentiates itself from its competitors by using (1) highly respected journalists who write well-researched news articles, (2) color to enhance attractiveness to readers and advertisers, and (3) a Web site that delivers up-to-the-minute news, interviews, and analyses. The newspaper has the following resources to deliver on this strategy: an automated, computer-integrated, state-of-the-art printing facility; a Web-based information technology infrastructure; and a distribution network that is one of the best in the newspaper industry.

To keep up with steadily increasing production costs, Naomi Crawford, manager of the *Daily News*, needs to increase the company's revenues in 2017. As she ponders what she should do in early 2017, Naomi works through the five-step decision-making process.

1. **Identify the problem and uncertainties.** Naomi has two main choices:

   a. increase the selling price of the newspaper or
   b. increase the rate per page charged to advertisers.

   The key uncertainty is the effect any increase in prices or rates will have on demand. A decrease in demand could offset the price or rate increases and lead to lower rather than higher revenues. These decisions would take effect in March 2017.

2. **Obtain information.** Gathering information before making a decision helps managers gain a better understanding of uncertainties. Naomi asks her marketing manager to talk to some representative readers to gauge their reaction to an increase in the newspaper's selling price. She asks her advertising sales manager to talk to current and potential advertisers to assess demand for advertising. She also reviews the effect that past increases in the price of the newspaper had on readership. Ramon Sandoval, management accountant at the *Daily News*, presents information about the effect of past increases or decreases in advertising rates on advertising revenues. He also collects and analyzes information on advertising rates competing newspapers and other media outlets charge.

3. **Make predictions about the future.** Based on this information, Naomi makes predictions about the future. She concludes that increasing prices would upset readers and decrease readership. She has a different view about advertising rates. She expects a marketwide increase in advertising rates and believes that increasing rates will have little effect on the number of advertising pages sold.

   Naomi recognizes that making predictions requires judgment. She looks for biases in her thinking. Has she correctly judged reader sentiment or is the negative publicity of a price increase overly influencing her decision making? How sure is she that competitors will increase their advertising rates? Is her thinking in this respect biased by how competitors have responded in the past? Have circumstances changed? How confident is she that her sales representatives can convince advertisers to pay higher rates? After retesting her assumptions and reviewing her thinking, Naomi feels comfortable with her predictions and judgments.

4. **Make decisions by choosing among alternatives.** When making decisions, a company's strategy serves as a vital guidepost for the many individuals in different parts of the organization making decisions at different times. Consistent strategies provide a common purpose for these disparate decisions. Only if these decisions can be aligned with its strategy will an organization achieve its goals. Without this alignment, the

LEARNING OBJECTIVE   4

Explain the five-step decision-making process

…identify the problem and uncertainties; obtain information; make predictions about the future; make decisions by choosing among alternatives; implement the decision, evaluate performance, and learn

and its role in management accounting

…planning and control of operations and activities

company's decisions will be uncoordinated, pull the organization in different directions, and produce inconsistent results.

Consistent with a product differentiation strategy, Naomi decides to increase advertising rates by 4% to $5,200 per page in March 2017, but not increase the selling price of the newspaper. She is confident that the *Daily News*'s distinctive style and Web presence will increase readership, creating value for advertisers. She communicates the new advertising rate schedule to the sales department. Ramon estimates advertising revenues of $4,160,000 ($5,200 per page × 800 pages predicted to be sold in March 2017).

Steps 1 through 4 are collectively referred to as *planning*. **Planning** consists of selecting an organization's goals and strategies, predicting results under various alternative ways of achieving those goals, deciding how to attain the desired goals, and communicating the goals and how to achieve them to the entire organization. Management accountants serve as business partners in these planning activities because they understand the key success factors and what creates value.

The most important planning tool when implementing strategy is a *budget*. A **budget** is the quantitative expression of a proposed plan of action by management and is an aid to coordinating what needs to be done to execute that plan. For March 2017, the budgeted advertising revenue of the *Daily News* equals $4,160,000. The full budget for March 2017 includes budgeted circulation revenue and the production, distribution, and customer-service costs to achieve the company's sales goals; the anticipated cash flows; and the potential financing needs. Because multiple departments help prepare the budget, personnel throughout the organization have to coordinate and communicate with one another as well as with the company's suppliers and customers.

5. **Implement the decision, evaluate performance, and learn.** Managers at the *Daily News* take action to implement and achieve the March 2017 budget. The firm's management accountants then collect information on how the company's actual performance compares to planned or budgeted performance (also referred to as scorekeeping). The information on the actual results is different from the *predecision* planning information Naomi and her staff collected in Step 2, which enabled her to better understand uncertainties, to make predictions, and to make a decision. Allowing managers to compare actual performance to budgeted performance is the *control* or *postdecision* role of information. **Control** comprises taking actions that implement the planning decisions, evaluating past performance, and providing feedback and learning to help future decision making.

Measuring actual performance informs managers how well they and their subunits are doing. Linking rewards to performance helps motivate managers. These rewards are both intrinsic (recognition for a job well done) and extrinsic (salary, bonuses, and promotions linked to performance). We discuss this in more detail in a later chapter (Chapter 23). A budget serves as much as a control tool as a planning tool. Why? Because a budget is a benchmark against which actual performance can be compared.

Consider performance evaluation at the *Daily News*. During March 2017, the newspaper sold advertising, issued invoices, and received payments. The accounting system recorded these invoices and receipts. Exhibit 1-4 shows the *Daily News*'s advertising revenues for March 2017. This performance report indicates that 760 pages of advertising (40 pages fewer than

---

EXHIBIT 1-4 Performance Report of Advertising Revenues at the *Daily News* for March 2017

	Actual Result (1)	Budgeted Amount (2)	Difference: (Actual Result − Budgeted Amount) (3) = (1) − (2)	Difference as a Percentage of Budgeted Amount (4) = (3) ÷ (2)
Advertising pages sold	760 pages	800 pages	40 pages Unfavorable	5.0% Unfavorable
Average rate per page	$5,080	$5,200	$120 Unfavorable	2.3% Unfavorable
Advertising revenues	$3,860,800	$4,160,000	$299,200 Unfavorable	7.2% Unfavorable

the budgeted 800 pages) were sold. The average rate per page was $5,080, compared with the budgeted $5,200 rate, yielding actual advertising revenues of $3,860,800. The actual advertising revenues were $299,200 less than the budgeted $4,160,000. Observe how managers use both financial and nonfinancial information, such as pages of advertising, to evaluate performance.

The performance report in Exhibit 1-4 spurs investigation and **learning**, which involves examining past performance (the control function) and systematically exploring alternative ways to make better-informed decisions and plans in the future. Learning can lead to changes in goals, strategies, the ways decision alternatives are identified, and the range of information collected when making predictions and sometimes can lead to changes in managers.

The performance report in Exhibit 1-4 would prompt the management accountant to raise several questions directing the attention of managers to problems and opportunities. Is the strategy of differentiating the *Daily News* from other newspapers attracting more readers? Did the marketing and sales department make sufficient efforts to convince advertisers that, even at the higher rate of $5,200 per page, advertising in the *Daily News* was a good buy? Why was the actual average rate per page ($5,080) less than the budgeted rate ($5,200)? Did some sales representatives offer discounted rates? Did economic conditions cause the decline in advertising revenues? Are revenues falling because editorial and production standards have declined? Are more readers getting their news online?

Answers to these questions could prompt the newspaper's publisher to take subsequent actions, including, for example, adding more sales personnel, making changes in editorial policy, putting more resources into expanding its presence online and on mobile devices, getting readers to pay for online content, and selling digital advertising. Good implementation requires the marketing, editorial, and production departments to work together and coordinate their actions.

The management accountant could go further by identifying the specific advertisers that cut back or stopped advertising after the rate increase went into effect. Managers could then decide when and how sales representatives should follow up with these advertisers.

Planning and control activities must be flexible enough so that managers can seize opportunities unforeseen at the time the plan was formulated. In no case should control mean that managers cling to a plan when unfolding events (such as a sensational news story) indicate that actions not encompassed by that plan (such as spending more money to cover the story) would offer better results for the company (from higher newspaper sales).

The left side of Exhibit 1-5 provides an overview of the decision-making processes at the *Daily News*. The right side of the exhibit highlights how the management accounting system aids in decision making.

Planning and control activities get more challenging when monitoring and managing innovation and sustainability. Consider the problem of how the *Daily News* must innovate as more of its readers migrate to the Web to get their news. Now follow the five-step process we described earlier. In Step 1, the uncertainties are much greater. Will there be demand for a newspaper? Will customers look to the *Daily News* to get their information or to other sources? In Step 2, obtaining information is more difficult because there is little history that managers can comfortably rely on. Instead, managers will have to make connections across disparate data, run experiments, engage with diverse experts, and speculate to understand how the world might evolve. In Step 3, making predictions about the future will require developing different scenarios and models. In Step 4, managers will need to make decisions knowing that conditions might change in unanticipated ways that will require them to be flexible and correct course midstream. In Step 5, the learning component is critical. How have the uncertainties evolved and what do managers need to do to respond to these changing circumstances?

Planning and control for sustainability is equally challenging. What should the *Daily News* do about energy consumption in its printing presses, recycling of newsprint, and pollution prevention? Among the uncertainties managers face is whether customers will reward the *Daily News* for these actions by being more loyal and whether investors will react favorably to managers spending resources on sustainability. Information to gauge customer and investor sentiment is not easy to obtain. Predicting how sustainability efforts might pay off in the long run is far from certain. Even as managers make decisions, the sustainability landscape will doubtlessly change with respect to environmental regulations and societal expectations, requiring managers to learn and adapt.

DECISION POINT

How do managers make decisions to implement strategy?

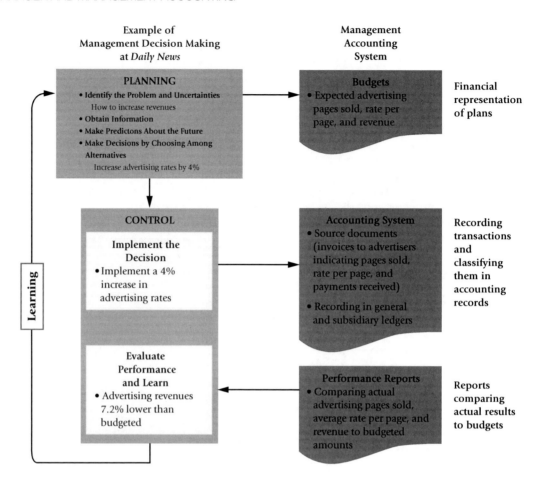

Do these challenges of implementing planning and control systems for innovation and sustainability mean that these systems should not be used for these initiatives? No. Many companies find value in using these systems to manage innovation and sustainability. But, in keeping with the challenges described earlier, companies such as Johnson & Johnson use these systems in a different way to obtain information around key strategic uncertainties, to implement plans while being mindful that circumstances might change, and to evaluate performance in order to learn. We will return to the themes of innovation and sustainability at various points in the book.

Key Management Accounting Guidelines

Three guidelines help management accountants provide the most value to the strategic and operational decision making of their companies: (1) employ a cost–benefit approach, (2) give full recognition to behavioral and technical considerations, and (3) use different costs for different purposes.

Cost–Benefit Approach

Managers continually face resource-allocation decisions, such as whether to purchase a new software package or hire a new employee. They use a **cost–benefit approach** when making these decisions. Managers should spend resources if the expected benefits to the company exceed the expected costs. Managers rely on management accounting information to quantify expected benefits and expected costs (although all benefits and costs are not easy to quantify).

Consider the installation of a consulting company's first budgeting system. Previously, the company used historical recordkeeping and little formal planning. A major benefit of installing a budgeting system is that it compels managers to plan ahead, compare actual to budgeted information, learn, and take corrective action. Although the system leads to better decisions and consequently better company performance, the exact benefits are not easy to measure. On the cost side, some costs, such as investments in software and training, are easier to quantify. Others, such as the time spent by managers on the budgeting process, are more difficult to quantify. Regardless, senior managers compare expected benefits and expected costs, exercise judgment, and reach a decision, in this case to install the budgeting system.

Behavioral and Technical Considerations

When utilizing the cost–benefit approach, managers need to keep in mind a number of technical and behavioral considerations. Technical considerations help managers make wise economic decisions by providing desired information (for example, costs in various value-chain categories) in an appropriate format (for example, actual results versus budgeted amounts) and at the preferred frequency (for example, weekly or quarterly). However, management is not confined to technical matters. Management is primarily a human activity that should focus on encouraging individuals to do their jobs better. Budgets have a behavioral effect by motivating and rewarding employees for achieving an organization's goals. So, when workers underperform, for example, behavioral considerations suggest that managers need to discuss ways to improve their performance with them rather than just sending them a report highlighting their underperformance.

Different Costs for Different Purposes

This book emphasizes that managers use alternative ways to compute costs in different decision-making situations because there are different costs for different purposes. A cost concept used for the purposes of external reporting may not be appropriate for internal, routine reporting.

Consider the advertising costs associated with Microsoft Corporation's launch of a product with a useful life of several years. For external reporting to shareholders, Generally Accepted Accounting Principles (GAAP) require television advertising costs for this product to be fully expensed in the income statement in the year they are incurred. However, for internal reporting, the television advertising costs could be capitalized and then amortized or written off as expenses over several years if Microsoft's management team believed that doing so would more accurately and fairly measure the performance of the managers that launched the new product.

We now discuss the relationships and reporting responsibilities among managers and management accountants within a company's organization structure.

> **DECISION POINT**
>
> What guidelines do management accountants use?

Organization Structure and the Management Accountant

We focus first on broad management functions and then look at how the management accounting and finance functions support managers.

> **LEARNING OBJECTIVE 6**
>
> Understand how management accounting fits into an organization's structure
>
> …for example, the responsibilities of the controller

Line and Staff Relationships

Organizations distinguish between line management and staff management. **Line management**, such as production, marketing, and distribution management, is directly responsible for achieving the goals of the organization. For example, managers of manufacturing divisions are responsible for meeting particular levels of budgeted operating income, product quality and safety, and compliance with environmental laws. Similarly, the pediatrics department in a hospital is responsible for quality of service, costs, and patient billings. **Staff management**, such as management accountants and information technology and human-resources management, provides advice, support, and assistance to line management. A plant manager (a line function) may be responsible for investing in new equipment. A management accountant (a staff function) works as a business partner of the plant manager by preparing detailed operating-cost comparisons of alternative pieces of equipment.

Increasingly, organizations such as Honda and Dell are using teams to achieve their objectives. These teams include both line and staff management so that all inputs into a decision are available simultaneously.

The Chief Financial Officer and the Controller

The **chief financial officer (CFO)**—also called the **finance director** in many countries—is the executive responsible for overseeing the financial operations of an organization. The responsibilities of the CFO vary among organizations, but they usually include the following areas:

- **Controllership**—provides financial information for reports to managers and shareholders and oversees the overall operations of the accounting system.
- **Tax**—plans income taxes, sales taxes, and international taxes.
- **Treasury**—oversees banking and short- and long-term financing, investments, and cash management.
- **Risk management**—manages the financial risk of interest-rate and exchange-rate changes and derivatives management.
- **Investor relations**—communicates with, responds to, and interacts with shareholders.
- **Strategic planning**—defines strategy and allocates resources to implement strategy.

An independent internal audit function reviews and analyzes financial and other records to attest to the integrity of the organization's financial reports and to adherence to its policies and procedures.

The **controller** (also called the *chief accounting officer*) is the financial executive primarily responsible for management accounting and financial accounting. This book focuses on the controller as the chief management accounting executive. Modern controllers have no line authority except over their own departments. Yet the controller exercises control over the entire organization in a special way. By reporting and interpreting relevant data, the controller influences the behavior of all employees and helps line managers make better decisions.

Exhibit 1-6 shows an organization chart of the CFO and the corporate controller at Nike, the leading footwear and sports apparel company. The CFO is a staff manager who reports to and supports the chief executive officer (CEO). As in most organizations, the corporate controller at Nike reports to the CFO. Nike also has regional controllers who support regional managers in the major geographic regions in which the company operates, such as the United States, Asia Pacific, Latin America, and Europe. Because they support the activities of the

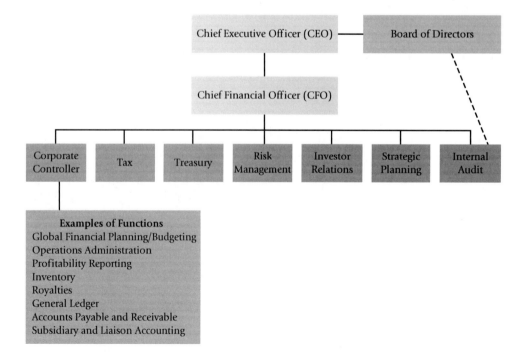

EXHIBIT 1-6

Nike: Reporting Relationship for the CFO and the Corporate Controller

regional manager, for example, by managing budgets and analyzing costs, regional controllers report to the regional manager rather than the corporate controller. At the same time, to align accounting policies and practices for the whole organization, regional controllers have a functional (often called a dotted-line) responsibility to the corporate controller. Individual countries sometimes have a country controller.

Organization charts such as the one in Exhibit 1-6 show formal reporting relationships. In most organizations, there also are informal relationships that must be understood when managers attempt to implement their decisions. Examples of informal relationships are friendships (both professional and personal) among managers and the preferences of top management about the managers they rely on when making decisions.

Think about what managers do to design and implement strategies and the organization structures within which they operate. Then think about the management accountants' and controllers' roles. It should be clear that the successful management accountant must have technical and analytical competence *as well as* behavioral and interpersonal skills.

Management Accounting Beyond the Numbers[2]

To people outside the profession, it may seem like accountants are just "numbers people." It is true that most accountants are adept financial managers, yet their skills do not stop there. The successful management accountant possesses several skills and characteristics that reach well beyond basic analytical abilities.

Management accountants must work well in cross-functional teams and as a business partner. In addition to being technically competent, the best management accountants work well in teams, learn about business issues, understand the motivations of different individuals, respect the views of their colleagues, and show empathy and trust.

Management accountants must promote fact-based analysis and make tough-minded, critical judgments without being adversarial. Management accountants must raise tough questions for managers to consider, especially when preparing budgets. They must do so thoughtfully and with the intent of improving plans and decisions. Before the investment bank JP Morgan lost more than $6 billion on "exotic" financial investments (credit-default swaps) in 2012, controllers should have raised questions about these risky investments and the fact that the firm was essentially betting that improving economic conditions abroad would earn it a large profit.

They must lead and motivate people to change and be innovative. Implementing new ideas, however good they may be, is difficult. When the United States Department of Defense (DoD) began consolidating more than 320 finance and accounting systems into a common platform, the accounting services director and his team of management accountants held meetings to make sure everyone in the agency understood the goal for such a change. Ultimately, the DoD aligned each individual's performance with the transformative change and introduced incentive pay to encourage personnel to adopt the platform and drive innovation within this new framework.

They must communicate clearly, openly, and candidly. Communicating information is a large part of a management accountant's job. When premium car companies such as Rolls Royce and Porsche design new models, management accountants work closely with engineers to ensure that each new car supports a carefully defined balance of commercial, engineering, and financial criteria. These efforts are successful because management accountants clearly communicate the information that multidisciplinary teams need to deliver new innovations profitably.

They must have high integrity. Management accountants must never succumb to pressure from managers to manipulate financial information. They must always remember that their primary commitment is to the organization and its shareholders. In 2015, Toshiba, the

DECISION POINT

Where does the management accounting function fit into an organization's structure?

[2] United States Senate Permanent Subcommittee on Investigations. *JPMorgan Chase Whale Trades: A Case History of Derivatives Risks and Abuses.* Washington, DC: Government Printing Office, March 15, 2013; Wendy Garling, "Winning the Transformation Battle at the Defense Finance and Accounting Service," Balanced Scorecard Report, May–June 2007; Bill Nixon, John Burns, and Mostafa Jazayeri, *The Role of Management Accounting in New Product Design and Development Decisions*, Volume 9, Issue 1. London: Chartered Institute of Management Accountants, November 2011; and Eric Pfanner and Magumi Fujikawa, "Toshiba Slashes Earnings for Past Seven Years," *The Wall Street Journal* (September 7, 2015).

Japanese maker of semiconductors, consumer electronics, and nuclear power plants wrote down $1.9 billion of earnings that had been overstated over the previous seven years. The problems stemmed from managers setting aggressive profit targets that subordinates could not meet without inflating divisional results by understating costs, postponing losses, and overstating revenues.

Professional Ethics

LEARNING OBJECTIVE 7

Understand what professional ethics mean to management accountants

...for example, management accountants must maintain integrity and credibility in every aspect of their job

At no time has the focus on ethical conduct been higher than it is today. Corporate scandals at Arthur Andersen, a public accounting firm; Countrywide Financial, a home mortgage company; Enron, an oil and gas company; Lehman Brothers, an investment bank; Toshiba, a Japanese conglomerate; and Bernie Madoff Investment Securities have seriously eroded the public's confidence in corporations. All employees in a company must comply with the organization's—and more broadly, society's—expectations of ethical standards.

Ethics are the foundation of a well-functioning economy. When ethics are weak, suppliers bribe executives to win supply contracts rather than invest in improving quality or lowering costs. In the absence of ethical conduct, customers have little confidence in the quality of products produced and become reluctant to buy them, causing markets to fail. Prices of products increase because of higher prices paid to suppliers and fewer products being produced and sold. Investors are unsure about the integrity of financial reports, affecting their ability to make investment decisions, resulting in a reluctance to invest and a misallocation of resources. The scandals at Ahold, an international supermarket operator, and Tyco International, a diversified global manufacturing company, and others make clear that value is quickly destroyed by unethical behavior.

Institutional Support

Accountants have special ethical obligations, given that they are responsible for the integrity of the financial information provided to internal and external parties. The Sarbanes–Oxley legislation in the United States was passed in 2002 in response to a series of corporate scandals. The act focuses on improving internal control, corporate governance, monitoring of managers, and disclosure practices of public corporations. These regulations impose tough ethical standards and criminal penalties on managers and accountants who don't meet the standards. The regulations also delineate a process for employees to report violations of illegal and unethical acts (these employees are called whistleblowers).

As part of the Sarbanes–Oxley Act, CEOs and CFOs must certify that the financial statements of their firms fairly represent the results of their operations. In order to increase the independence of auditors, the act empowers the audit committee of a company's board of directors (which is composed exclusively of independent directors) to hire, compensate, and terminate the public accounting firm to audit a company. To reduce their financial dependency on their individual clients and increase their independence, the act limits auditing firms from providing consulting, tax, and other advisory services to the companies they are auditing. The act also authorizes the Public Company Accounting Oversight Board to oversee, review, and investigate the work of the auditors.

Professional accounting organizations, which represent management accountants in many countries, offer certification programs indicating that those who have completed them have management accounting and financial management technical knowledge and expertise. These organizations also advocate high ethical standards. In the United States, the Institute of Management Accountants (IMA) has also issued ethical guidelines. Exhibit 1-7 presents the IMA's guidance on issues relating to competence, confidentiality, integrity, and credibility. To provide support to its members to act ethically at all times, the IMA runs an ethics hotline service. Members can call professional counselors at the IMA's Ethics Counseling Service to discuss their ethical dilemmas. The counselors help identify the key ethical issues and possible alternative ways of resolving them, and confidentiality is guaranteed. The IMA is just one of many institutions that help navigate management accountants through what could be turbulent ethical waters.

EXHIBIT 1-7

Standards of
Ethical Behavior
for Practitioners
of Management
Accounting and
Financial Management

STATEMENT OF ETHICAL PROFESSIONAL PRACTICE

Members of IMA shall behave ethically. A commitment to ethical professional practice includes: overarching principles that express our values, and standards that guide our conduct.

PRINCIPLES

IMA's overarching ethical principles include: Honesty, Fairness, Objectivity, and Responsibility. Members shall act in accordance with these principles and shall encourage others within their organizations to adhere to them.

STANDARDS

A member's failure to comply with the following standards may result in disciplinary action.

I. COMPETENCE

Each member has a responsibility to:

1. Maintain an appropriate level of professional expertise by continually developing knowledge and skills.
2. Perform professional duties in accordance with relevant laws, regulations, and technical standards.
3. Provide decision support information and recommendations that are accurate, clear, concise, and timely.
4. Recognize and communicate professional limitations or other constraints that would preclude responsible judgment or successful performance of an activity.

II. CONFIDENTIALITY

Each member has a responsibility to:

1. Keep information confidential except when disclosure is authorized or legally required.
2. Inform all relevant parties regarding appropriate use of confidential information. Monitor subordinates' activities to ensure compliance.
3. Refrain from using confidential information for unethical or illegal advantage.

III. INTEGRITY

Each member has a responsibility to:

1. Mitigate actual conflicts of interest, regularly communicate with business associates to avoid apparent conflicts of interest. Advise all parties of any potential conflicts.
2. Refrain from engaging in any conduct that would prejudice carrying out duties ethically.
3. Abstain from engaging in or supporting any activity that might discredit the profession.

IV. CREDIBILITY

Each member has a responsibility to:

1. Communicate information fairly and objectively.
2. Disclose all relevant information that could reasonably be expected to influence an intended user's understanding of the reports, analyses, or recommendations.
3. Disclose delays or deficiencies in information, timeliness, processing, or internal controls in conformance with organization policy and/or applicable law.

Source: IMA Statement of Ethical Professional Practice, 2016. Montvale, NJ: Institute of Management Accountants. Reprinted with permission from the Institute of Management Accountants, Montvale, NJ, www.imanet.org.

Typical Ethical Challenges

Ethical issues can confront management accountants in many ways. Here are two examples:

- **Case A:** A management accountant is concerned about the commercial potential of a software product for which development costs are currently being capitalized as an asset rather than being shown as an expense for internal reporting purposes. The firm's division manager, whose bonus is based, in part, on the division's profits, argues that showing development costs as an asset is justified because the new product will generate profits. However, he presents little evidence to support his argument. The last two products from the division have been unsuccessful. The management accountant wants to make the right decision while avoiding a difficult personal confrontation with his boss, the division manager. (This case is similar to the situation at Toshiba where senior managers set aggressive divisional targets and divisional accountants inflated divisional profits to achieve them.)

■ **Case B:** A packaging supplier, bidding for a new contract, offers a management accountant of the purchasing company an all-expenses-paid weekend to the Super Bowl. The supplier does not mention the new contract when extending the invitation. The management accountant is not a personal friend of the supplier. He knows cost issues are critical when it comes to approving the new contract and is concerned that the supplier will ask for details about the bids placed by competing packaging companies.

In each case, the management accountant is faced with an ethical dilemma. Ethical issues are not always clear-cut. Case A involves competence, credibility, and integrity. The management accountant should request that the division manager provide credible evidence that the new product is commercially viable. If the manager does not provide such evidence, expensing development costs in the current period is appropriate.

Case B involves confidentiality and integrity. The supplier in Case B may have no intention of asking questions about competitors' bids. However, the appearance of a conflict of interest in Case B is sufficient for many companies to prohibit employees from accepting "favors" from suppliers.

Exhibit 1-8 presents the IMA's guidance on "Resolution of Ethical Conflict." For example, if the divisional management accountant in Case A is not satisfied with the response of the division manager regarding the commercial viability of the product, he or she should discuss the issue with the corporate controller. The accountant in Case B should discuss the invitation with his or her immediate supervisor. If the visit is approved, the accountant should inform the supplier that the invitation has been officially approved subject to following corporate policy (which includes not disclosing confidential company information).

Most professional accounting organizations around the globe issue statements about professional ethics. These statements include many of the same issues discussed by the IMA in Exhibits 1-7 and 1-8. For example, the Chartered Institute of Management Accountants (CIMA) in the United Kingdom advocates five ethical principles similar to those shown in Exhibit 1-7: professional competence and due care, confidentiality, integrity, objectivity, and professional behavior.

DECISION POINT

What are the ethical responsibilities of management accountants?

EXHIBIT 1-8

Resolution of Ethical Conflict

RESOLUTION OF ETHICAL CONDUCT

In applying the Standards of Ethical Professional Practice, you may encounter problems identifying unethical behavior or resolving an ethical conflict. When faced with ethical issues, you should follow your organization's established policies on the resolution of such conflict. If these policies do not resolve the ethical conflict, you should consider the following courses of action:

1. Discuss the issue with your immediate supervisor except when it appears that the supervisor is involved. In that case, present the issue to the next level. If you cannot achieve a satisfactory resolution, submit the issue to the next management level. If your immediate superior is the chief executive officer or equivalent, the acceptable reviewing authority may be a group such as the audit committee, executive committee, board of directors, board of trustees, or owners. Contact with levels above the immediate superior should be initiated only with your superior's knowledge, assuming he or she is not involved. Communication of such problems to authorities or individuals not employed or engaged by the organization is not considered appropriate, unless you believe there is a clear violation of the law.

2. Clarify relevant ethical issues by initiating a confidential discussion with an IMA Ethics Counselor or other impartial advisor to obtain a better understanding of possible courses of action.

3. Consult your own attorney as to legal obligations and rights concerning the ethical conflict.

Source: IMA Statement of Ethical Professional Practice, 2016. Montvale, NJ: Institute of Management Accountants. Reprinted with permission from the Institute of Management Accountants, Montvale, NJ, www.imanet.org.

PROBLEM FOR SELF-STUDY

Campbell Soup Company incurs the following costs:

a. Purchase of tomatoes by a canning plant for Campbell's tomato soup products

b. Materials purchased for redesigning Pepperidge Farm biscuit containers to make biscuits stay fresh longer

c. Payment to Backer, Spielvogel, & Bates, the advertising agency, for advertising work on the Healthy Request line of soup products

d. Salaries of food technologists researching feasibility of a Prego pizza sauce that has minimal calories

e. Payment to Safeway for redeeming coupons on Campbell's food products

f. Cost of a toll-free telephone line used for customer inquiries about using Campbell's soup products

g. Cost of gloves used by line operators on the Swanson Fiesta breakfast-food production line

h. Cost of handheld computers used by Pepperidge Farm delivery staff serving major supermarket accounts

Classify each cost item (a–h) as one of the business functions in the value chain in Exhibit 1-2 (page 25).

Solution

a. Production

b. Design of products and processes

c. Marketing

d. Research and development

e. Marketing

f. Customer service

g. Production

h. Distribution

DECISION **POINTS**

The following question-and-answer format summarizes the chapter's learning objectives. Each decision presents a key question related to a learning objective. The guidelines are the answer to that question.

Decision	**Guidelines**
1. How is financial accounting different from management accounting?	Financial accounting is used to develop reports for external users on past financial performance using GAAP. Management accounting is used to provide future-oriented information to help managers (internal users) make decisions and achieve an organization's goals.
2. How do management accountants support strategic decisions?	Management accountants contribute to strategic decisions by providing information about the sources of competitive advantage.
3. How do companies add value, and what are the dimensions of performance that customers are expecting of companies?	Companies add value through research and development (R&D), design of products and processes, production, marketing, distribution, and customer service. Customers want companies to deliver performance through cost and efficiency, quality, timeliness, and innovation.

Decision	Guidelines
4. How do managers make decisions to implement strategy?	Managers use a five-step decision-making process to implement strategy: (1) identify the problem and uncertainties; (2) obtain information; (3) make predictions about the future; (4) make decisions by choosing among alternatives; and (5) implement the decision, evaluate performance, and learn. The first four steps are planning decisions. They include deciding on an organization's goals, predicting results under various alternative ways of achieving those goals, and deciding how to attain the desired goals. Step 5 is the control decision, which includes taking actions to implement the planning decisions, evaluating past performance, and providing feedback that will help future decision making.
5. What guidelines do management accountants use?	Three guidelines that help management accountants increase their value to managers are (a) employing a cost–benefit approach, (b) recognizing behavioral as well as technical considerations, and (c) identifying different costs for different purposes.
6. Where does the management accounting function fit into an organization's structure?	Management accounting is an integral part of the controller's function. In most organizations, the controller reports to the chief financial officer, who is a key member of the top management team.
7. What are the ethical responsibilities of management accountants?	Management accountants have ethical responsibilities that relate to competence, confidentiality, integrity, and credibility.

TERMS TO LEARN

Each chapter will include this section. Like all technical terms, accounting terms have precise meanings. Learn the definitions of new terms when you initially encounter them. The meaning of each of the following terms is given in this chapter and in the Glossary at the end of this book.

budget (**p. 30**)
chief financial officer (CFO) (**p. 34**)
control (**p. 30**)
controller (**p. 34**)
cost accounting (**p. 22**)
cost–benefit approach (**p. 32**)
cost management (**p. 23**)
customer relationship management (CRM) (**p. 25**)
customer service (**p. 25**)

design of products and processes (**p. 25**)
distribution (**p. 25**)
finance director (**p. 34**)
financial accounting (**p. 22**)
learning (**p. 31**)
line management (**p. 33**)
management accounting (**p. 22**)
marketing (**p. 25**)
planning (**p. 30**)
production (**p. 25**)

research and development (R&D) (**p. 25**)
staff management (**p. 33**)
strategic cost management (**p. 24**)
strategy (**p. 23**)
supply chain (**p. 26**)
sustainability (**p. 27**)
total quality management (TQM) (**p. 27**)
value chain (**p. 24**)

ASSIGNMENT MATERIAL

Questions

1-1 How does management accounting differ from financial accounting?
1-2 "Management accounting should not fit the straitjacket of financial accounting." Explain and give an example.
1-3 How can management accounting information help managers formulate strategies?
1-4 Define the term "value chain" and state its six primary business functions.

1-5 Explain the term *supply chain* and its importance to cost management.

1-6 "Management accounting deals only with costs." Do you agree? Explain.

1-7 How can management accountants help improve quality and achieve timely product deliveries?

1-8 Describe the five-step decision-making process.

1-9 Distinguish planning decisions from control decisions.

1-10 What three guidelines help management accountants provide the most value to managers?

1-11 "Technical and basic analytical competence are necessary but not sufficient conditions to becoming a successful management accountant." Do you agree? Why?

1-12 As the new controller, reply to the following comment made by your plant manager: "When I employ a proper accounting software, which can process all my daily accounting records and provide me with all necessary reports and analyses, I am not sure what additional value our accountants will bring to the business. I know enough about my business to understand the computer-generated reports."

1-13 Where does the management accounting function fit into an organization's structure?

1-14 What is the role of ethics in a well-functioning economy? List a few groups of stakeholders who may suffer in an economic system governed by weak ethics.

1-15 Provide one example of an ethical issue in relation to suppliers and its possible impact on customers and the market when ethics is weak.

Multiple-Choice Questions

Pearson MyLab Accounting

1-16 Which of the following is not a primary function of the management accountant?

a. Communicates financial results and position to external parties.

b. Uses information to develop and implement business strategy.

c. Aids in the decision making to help an organization meet its goals.

d. Provides input into an entity's production and marketing decisions.

©2016 DeVry/Becker Educational Development Corp. All Rights Reserved.

Exercises

1-17 Value chain and classification of costs, computer company. Compaq Computer incurs the following costs:

a. Electricity costs for the plant assembling the Presario computer line of products

b. Transportation costs for shipping the Presario line of products to a retail chain

c. Payment to David Kelley Designs for design of the Armada Notebook

d. Salary of computer scientist working on the next generation of minicomputers

e. Cost of Compaq employees' visit to a major customer to demonstrate Compaq's ability to interconnect with other computers

f. Purchase of competitors' products for testing against potential Compaq products

g. Payment to television network for running Compaq advertisements

h. Cost of cables purchased from outside supplier to be used with Compaq printers

Required

Classify each of the cost items (**a–h**) into one of the business functions of the value chain shown in Exhibit 1-2 (page 25).

1-18 Value chain and classification of costs, pharmaceutical company. Pfizer, a pharmaceutical company, incurs the following costs:

a. Payment of booth registration fee at a medical conference to promote new products to physicians

b. Cost of redesigning an insulin syringe to make it less painful

c. Cost of a toll-free telephone line used for customer inquiries about drug usage, side effects of drugs, and so on

d. Equipment purchased to conduct experiments on drugs yet to be approved by the government

e. Sponsorship of a professional golfer

f. Labor costs of workers in the packaging area of a production facility

g. Bonus paid to a salesperson for exceeding a monthly sales quota

h. Cost of FedEx courier service to deliver drugs to hospitals

Required

Classify each of the cost items (**a–h**) as one of the business functions of the value chain shown in Exhibit 1-2 (page 25).

1-19 Value chain and classification of costs, fast-food restaurant. Burger King, a hamburger fast-food restaurant, incurs the following costs:

a. Cost of oil for the deep fryer
b. Wages of the counter help who give customers the food they order
c. Cost of the costume for the King on the Burger King television commercials
d. Cost of children's toys given away free with kids' meals
e. Cost of the posters indicating the special "two cheeseburgers for $2.50"
f. Costs of frozen onion rings and French fries
g. Salaries of the food specialists who create new sandwiches for the restaurant chain
h. Cost of "to-go" bags requested by customers who could not finish their meals in the restaurant

Required

Classify each of the cost items (**a–h**) as one of the business functions of the value chain shown in Exhibit 1-2 (page 25).

1-20 Key success factors. Dominion Consulting has issued a report recommending changes for its newest manufacturing client, Gibson Engine Works. Gibson currently manufactures a single product, which is sold and distributed nationally. The report contains the following suggestions for enhancing business performance:

a. Develop a rechargeable electric engine to stay ahead of competitors.
b. Adopt a TQM philosophy to reduce waste and defects to near zero.
c. Reduce lead times (time from customer order of product to customer receipt of product) by 20% in order to increase customer retention.
d. Negotiate faster response times with direct material suppliers to allow for lower material inventory levels.
e. Benchmark the company's gross margin percentages against its major competitors.

Required

Link each of these changes to the key success factors that are important to managers.

1-21 Key success factors. Dalworth Construction Company provides construction services for major projects. Managers at the company believe that construction is a people-management business, and they list the following as factors critical to their success:

a. Hire external consultants to implement six sigma principles in the company for sustainable quality improvement.
b. Take steps to increase employee morale and motivation by applying motivational models so that overall employee productivity increases.
c. Benchmark company's total costs of projects with its major competitors so that errors and wastages are minimized.
d. Carry out a training need analysis of the existing employees and train them accordingly.
e. Use modern tools and machineries so that cost of construction goes down and overall quality improves.

Required

Match each of these factors to the key success factors that are important to managers.

1-22 Planning and control decisions. Gregor Company makes and sells brooms and mops. It takes the following actions, not necessarily in the order given. For each action (**a–e**), state whether it is a planning decision or a control decision.

a. Gregor asks its advertising team to develop fresh advertisements to market its newest product.
b. Gregor calculates customer satisfaction scores after introducing its newest product.
c. Gregor compares costs it actually incurred with costs it expected to incur for the production of the new product.
d. Gregor's design team proposes a new product to compete directly with the Swiffer.
e. Gregor estimates the costs it will incur to distribute 30,000 units of the new product in the first quarter of next fiscal year.

1-23 Planning and control decisions. Fred Harris is the president of United Maintenance Service. He takes the following actions, not necessarily in the order given. For each action (**a–e**) state whether it is a planning decision or a control decision.

a. Fred contemplates procuring a digital lathe machine advised by his chief maintenance engineer.
b. Fred estimates the job cost of providing maintenance service to a local factory.
c. Fred calculates the total cost of materials in an annual maintenance contract to a client.
d. Fred decides to expand service offerings to nearby construction companies.
e. Fred makes a comparative analysis of administrative overheads with budgeted overheads.

1-24 Five-step decision-making process, manufacturing. Real's Bees makes products for personal care and sells through retail outlets and grocery stores. Its product line includes products for facial and body skin care, lip care, baby care, and outdoor remedies. The company wishes to enter into the hair care segment to make its product line stronger. The managers at Real's Bees take the following actions before taking the final decision. The actions are not listed in the order they are performed.

a. Production managers, with the help of cost managers and research wing of the company, prepare an estimate of costs for introducing hair care products.

b. Managers expect to grab a good market quickly by selling hair care products to the existing customers.

c. The company decides to introduce a new hair care product rather than introduce a new variant of any existing product.

d. Sales managers estimate they will sell more hair care products in the middle-age group.

e. The managers feel that introduction of hair care products is necessary to cope with competitors.

f. Incremental revenues by selling the new hair care product are budgeted.

g. Sales managers conduct Internet research to find out the present sales growth in the hair care market.

Classify each of the actions (**a–g**) as a step in the five-step decision-making process (identify the problem and uncertainties; obtain information; make predictions about the future; make decisions by choosing among alternatives; implement the decision, evaluate performance, and learn).

Required

1-25 Five-step decision-making process, service firm. Brook Exteriors is a firm that provides house-painting services. Richard Brook, the owner, is trying to find new ways to increase revenues. Mr. Brook performs the following actions, not in the order listed.

a. Mr. Brook decides to buy the paint sprayers rather than hire additional painters.

b. Mr. Brook discusses with his employees the possibility of using paint sprayers instead of hand painting to increase productivity and thus profits.

c. Mr. Brook learns of a large potential job that is about to go out for bids.

d. Mr. Brook compares the expected cost of buying sprayers to the expected cost of hiring more workers who paint by hand and estimates profits from both alternatives.

e. Mr. Brook estimates that using sprayers will reduce painting time by 20%.

f. Mr. Brook researches the price of paint sprayers online.

Classify each of the actions (**a–f**) according to its step in the five-step decision-making process (identify the problem and uncertainties; obtain information; make predictions about the future; make decisions by choosing among alternatives; implement the decision, evaluate performance, and learn).

Required

1-26 Professional ethics and reporting division performance. Joshua Wilson is the controller of Apex Frame Mouldings, a division of Garman Enterprises. As the division is preparing to count year-end inventory, Wilson is approached by Doug Leonard, the division's president. A selection of inventory previously valued at $150,000 had been identified as flawed earlier that month and as a result was determined to be unfit for sale. Leonard tells Wilson that he has decided to count the selected items as regular inventory and that he will "deal with it when things settle down after the first of the year. After all," and adds, "the auditors don't know good picture frame moulding from bad. We've had a rough year, and things are looking up for next year. Our division needs all the profits we can get this year. It's just a matter of timing the write-off." Leonard is Wilson's direct supervisor.

1. Describe Wilson's ethical dilemma.

2. What should Wilson do if Leonard gives him a direct order to include the inventory?

Required

1-27 Professional ethics and reporting division performance. Hannah Gilpin is the controller of Blakemore Auto Glass, a division of Eastern Glass and Window. Her division has been under pressure to improve its divisional operating income. Currently, divisions of Eastern Glass are allocated corporate overhead based on the cost of goods sold. Jake Myers, the president of the division, has asked Gilpin to reclassify $65,000 of packaging materials, which is included in the cost of goods sold, as production cost, which is not. Doing so will save the division $30,000 in allocated corporate overhead. The packing materials in question are needed to carry the finished goods to retail outlets. Gilpin does not see a reason for the reclassification of costs, other than to avoid overhead allocation costs.

1. Describe Gilpin's ethical dilemma.

2. What should Gilpin do if Myers gives her a direct order to reclassify the costs?

Required

Problems

1-28 Planning and control decisions, Internet company. PostNews.com offers its subscribers several services, such as an annotated TV guide and local-area information on weather, restaurants, and movie theaters. Its main revenue sources are fees for banner advertisements and fees from subscribers. Recent data are as follows:

Month/Year	Advertising Revenues	Actual Number of Subscribers	Monthly Fee per Subscriber
June 2015	$ 415,972	29,745	$15.50
December 2015	867,246	55,223	20.50
June 2016	892,134	59,641	20.50
December 2016	1,517,950	87,674	20.50
June 2017	2,976,538	147,921	20.50

The following decisions were made from June through October 2017:

a. June 2017: Raised subscription fee to $25.50 per month from July 2017 onward. The budgeted number of subscribers for this monthly fee is shown in the following table.
b. June 2017: Informed existing subscribers that from July onward, monthly fee would be $25.50.
c. July 2017: Offered e-mail service to subscribers and upgraded other online services.
d. October 2017: Dismissed the vice president of marketing after significant slowdown in subscribers and subscription revenues, based on July through September 2017 data in the following table.
e. October 2017: Reduced subscription fee to $22.50 per month from November 2017 onward.

Results for July–September 2017 are as follows:

Month/Year	Budgeted Number of Subscribers	Actual Number of Subscribers	Monthly Fee per Subscriber
July 2017	145,000	129,250	$25.50
August 2017	155,000	142,726	25.50
September 2017	165,000	145,643	25.50

Required

1. Classify each of the decisions (**a–e**) as a planning or a control decision.
2. Give two examples of other planning decisions and two examples of other control decisions that may be made at PostNews.com.

1-29 Strategic decisions and management accounting. Consider the following series of independent situations in which a firm is about to make a strategic decision.

Decisions

a. Stila Cosmetics is considering introducing an anti-aging facial cream with natural ingredients.
b. Kontron Computers is deliberating to produce a special type of microprocessor with an advanced technology which will bring down the cost of production.
c. Pelican Industries wants to install biometric system in its factory to reduce idle labor time and increase productivity.
d. Coral Health Solutions decides to introduce a unique telemedicine facility for its remote patients.

Required

1. For each decision, state whether the company is following a cost leadership or a product differentiation strategy.
2. For each decision, discuss what information the managerial accountant can provide about the source of competitive advantage for these firms.

1-30 Strategic decisions and management accounting. Consider the following series of independent situations in which a firm is about to make a strategic decision.

Decisions

a. Lactalis Foods is planning to come out with a special tetrazzini made with seafood, mushrooms, cream, and cocktail sauce.
b. Vanford Soap has started producing a new bar of soap, eyeing the low-cost segment of the soap market in which the company does not have much presence.
c. Diato Inc., a manufacturer of drill machines, is considering applying to a tender by quoting a very low price to supply 1,000 pieces of drill machines with standard features.
d. Smart Pixel is considering introducing a new tablet model that features a powerful processor with ample RAM to facilitate video calling, which is one of its unique features.

Required

1. For each decision, state whether the company is following a cost leadership or a product differentiation strategy.
2. For each decision, discuss what information the management accountant can provide about the source of competitive advantage for these firms.

1-31 Management accounting guidelines. For each of the following items, identify which of the management accounting guidelines applies: cost–benefit approach, behavioral and technical considerations, or different costs for different purposes.

1. Analyzing whether to keep the billing function within an organization or outsource it.
2. Deciding to give bonuses for superior performance to the employees in a Japanese subsidiary and extra vacation time to the employees in a Swedish subsidiary.
3. Including costs of all the value-chain functions before deciding to launch a new product, but including only its manufacturing costs in determining its inventory valuation.
4. Considering the desirability of hiring an additional salesperson.
5. Giving each salesperson the compensation option of choosing either a low salary and a high-percentage sales commission or a high salary and a low-percentage sales commission.
6. Selecting the costlier computer system after considering two systems.
7. Installing a participatory budgeting system in which managers set their own performance targets, instead of top management imposing performance targets on managers.
8. Recording research costs as an expense for financial reporting purposes (as required by U.S. GAAP) but capitalizing and expensing them over a longer period for management performance-evaluation purposes.
9. Introducing a profit-sharing plan for employees.

1-32 Management accounting guidelines. For each of the following items, identify which of the management accounting guidelines applies: cost–benefit approach, behavioral and technical considerations, or different costs for different purposes.

1. Analyzing whether to avail an export order for which overtime payments are required.
2. Deciding on a short-term shutdown of a factory because of the lack of demand for products due to the seasonal factor. The short-term shutdown may save some overhead costs, but will result in incurring compensations to the retrenched workers.
3. Considering whether to charge the heavy repairs made to the factory premises as an expense for financial reporting purposes or capitalizing and expensing them over a longer period for management performance-evaluation purposes.
4. Deciding to impose supervisory control to limit the wastage of materials.
5. Considering introducing a performance bonus scheme to increase the productivity of employees.
6. Analyzing whether to increase the production capacity to meet the growing demands for products.
7. Contemplating changing the production process to save production time resulting in increased production.

1-33 Role of controller, role of chief financial officer. George Jimenez is the controller at Balkin Electronics, a manufacturer of devices for the computer industry. The company may promote him to chief financial officer.

1. In this table, indicate which executive is *primarily* responsible for each activity.

Required

Activity	Controller	CFO
Managing the company's long-term investments		
Presenting the financial statements to the board of directors		
Strategic review of different lines of businesses		
Budgeting funds for a plant upgrade		
Managing accounts receivable		
Negotiating fees with auditors		
Assessing profitability of various products		
Evaluating the costs and benefits of a new product design		

2. Based on this table and your understanding of the two roles, what types of training or experience will George find most useful for the CFO position?

1-34 Budgeting, ethics, pharmaceutical company. Chris Jackson was recently promoted to Controller of Research and Development (R&D) for BrisCor, a *Fortune* 500 pharmaceutical company that manufactures prescription drugs and nutritional supplements. The company's total R&D cost for 2017 was expected (budgeted) to be $5 billion. During the company's midyear budget review, Chris realized that current R&D expenditures were already at $3.5 billion, nearly 40% above the midyear target. At this current rate of expenditure, the R&D division was on track to exceed its total year-end budget by $2 billion!

In a meeting with CFO Ronald Meece later that day, Jackson delivered the bad news. Meece was both shocked and outraged that the R&D spending had gotten out of control. Meece wasn't any more understanding when Jackson revealed that the excess cost was entirely related to research and development of a new drug, Vyacon, which was expected to go to market next year. The new drug would result in large profits for BrisCor, if the product could be approved by year-end.

Meece had already announced his expectations of third-quarter earnings to Wall Street analysts. If the R&D expenditures weren't reduced by the end of the third quarter, Meece was certain that the targets he had announced publicly would be missed and the company's stock price would tumble. Meece instructed Jackson to make up the budget shortfall by the end of the third quarter using "whatever means necessary."

Jackson was new to the controller's position and wanted to make sure that Meece's orders were followed. Jackson came up with the following ideas for making the third-quarter budgeted targets:

a. Stop all research and development efforts on the drug Vyacon until after year-end. This change would delay the drug going to market by at least 6 months. It is possible that in the meantime a BrisCor competitor could make it to market with a similar drug.

b. Sell off rights to the drug Martek. The company had not planned on doing this because, under current market conditions, it would get less than fair value. It would, however, result in a one-time gain that could offset the budget shortfall. Of course, all future profits from Martek would be lost.

c. Capitalize some of the company's R&D expenditures, reducing R&D expense on the income statement. This transaction would not be in accordance with GAAP, but Jackson thought it was justifiable because the Vyacon drug was going to market early next year. Jackson would argue that capitalizing R&D costs this year and expensing them next year would better match revenues and expenses.

Required

1. Referring to the "Standards of Ethical Behavior for Practitioners of Management Accounting and Financial Management," Exhibit 1-7 (page 37), which of the preceding items (**a–c**) are acceptable to use? Which are unacceptable?
2. What would you recommend Jackson do?

1-35 Professional ethics and end-of-year actions. Phoenix Press produces consumer magazines. The house and home division, which sells home-improvement and home-decorating magazines, has seen a 15% reduction in operating income over the past 15 months, primarily due to an economic recession and a depressed consumer housing market. The division's Controller, Sophie Gellar, has been pressurized by the CFO to improve her division's operating results by the end of the year. Gellar is considering the following options for improving the division's performance by the end of the year:

a. Cancelling three of the division's least profitable magazines, resulting in the layoff of 30 employees.
b. Selling the new printing equipment that was purchased in February and replacing it with discarded equipment from one of the company's other divisions. The previously discarded equipment no longer meets current safety standards.
c. Recognizing unearned subscription revenue (cash received in advance for magazines that will be delivered in the future) as revenue when cash is received in the current month (just before the fiscal year-end), instead of depicting it as a liability.
d. Reducing liability and expenses related to employee pensions. This would increase the division's operating income by 5%.
e. Recognizing advertising revenues that relate to February in December.
f. Delaying maintenance on production equipment until January, although it was originally scheduled for October.

Required

1. What are the motivations for Gellar to improve the division's year-end operating earnings?
2. From the point of view of the "Standards of Ethical Behavior for Practitioners of Management Accounting and Financial Management," Exhibit 1-7 (page 37), which of the preceding items (**a–f**) are acceptable? Which of the aforementioned items are unacceptable?
3. How should Gellar handle the pressure to improve performance?

1-36 Professional ethics and end-of-year actions. Linda Butler is the new division controller of the snack-foods division of Daniel Foods. Daniel Foods has reported a minimum 15% growth in annual earnings for each of the past 5 years. The snack-foods division has reported annual earnings growth of more than 20% each year in this same period. During the current year, the economy went into a recession. The corporate controller estimates a 10% annual earnings growth rate for Daniel Foods this year. One month before the December 31 fiscal year-end of the current year, Butler estimates the snack-foods division will report an annual earnings growth of only 8%. Rex Ray, the snack-foods division president, is not happy, but he notes that the "end-of-year actions" still need to be taken.

Butler makes some inquiries and is able to compile the following list of end-of-year actions that were more or less accepted by the previous division controller:

a. Deferring December's routine monthly maintenance on packaging equipment by an independent contractor until January of next year.
b. Extending the close of the current fiscal year beyond December 31 so that some sales of next year are included in the current year.

c. Altering dates of shipping documents of next January's sales to record them as sales in December of the current year.

d. Giving salespeople a double bonus to exceed December sales targets.

e. Deferring the current period's advertising by reducing the number of television spots run in December and running more than planned in January of next year.

f. Deferring the current period's reported advertising costs by having Daniel Foods' outside advertising agency delay billing December advertisements until January of next year or by having the agency alter invoices to conceal the December date.

g. Persuading carriers to accept merchandise for shipment in December of the current year even though they normally would not have done so.

Required

1. Why might the snack-foods division president want to take these end-of-year actions?

2. Butler is deeply troubled and reads the "Standards of Ethical Behavior for Practitioners of Management Accounting and Financial Management" in Exhibit 1-7 (page 37). Classify each of the end-of-year actions (**a–g**) as acceptable or unacceptable according to that document.

3. What should Butler do if Ray suggests that these end-of-year actions are taken in every division of Daniel Foods and that she will greatly harm the snack-foods division if she does not cooperate and paint the rosiest picture possible of the division's results?

1-37 Ethical challenges, global company environmental concerns. Contemporary Interiors (CI) manufactures high-quality furniture in factories in North Carolina for sale to top American retailers. In 1995, CI purchased a lumber operation in Indonesia, and shifted from using American hardwoods to Indonesian ramin in its products. The ramin proved to be a cheaper alternative, and it was widely accepted by American consumers. CI management credits the early adoption of Indonesian wood for its ability to keep its North Carolina factories open when so many competitors closed their doors. Recently, however, consumers have become increasingly concerned about the sustainability of tropical woods, including ramin. CI has seen sales begin to fall, and the company was even singled out by an environmental group for boycott. It appears that a shift to more sustainable woods before year-end will be necessary, and more costly.

In response to the looming increase in material costs, CEO Geoff Armstrong calls a meeting of upper management. The group generates the following ideas to address customer concerns and/or salvage company profits for the current year:

a. Pay local officials in Indonesia to "certify" the ramin used by CI as sustainable. It is not certain whether the ramin would be sustainable or not. Put highly visible tags on each piece of furniture to inform consumers of the change.

b. Make deep cuts in pricing through the end of the year to generate additional revenue.

c. Record executive year-end bonus compensation accrued for the current year when it is paid in the next year after the December fiscal year-end.

d. Reject the change in materials. Counter the bad publicity with an aggressive ad campaign showing the consumer products as "made in the USA," since manufacturing takes place in North Carolina.

e. Redesign upholstered furniture to replace ramin contained inside with less expensive recycled plastic. The change in materials would not affect the appearance or durability of the furniture. The company would market the furniture as "sustainable."

f. Pressure current customers to take early delivery of goods before the end of the year so that more revenue can be reported in this year's financial statements.

g. Begin purchasing sustainable North American hardwoods and sell the Indonesian lumber subsidiary. Initiate a "plant a tree" marketing program, by which the company will plant a tree for every piece of furniture sold. Material costs would increase 25%, and prices would be passed along to customers.

h. Sell off production equipment prior to year-end. The sale would result in one-time gains that could offset the company's lagging profits. The owned equipment could be replaced with leased equipment at a lower cost in the current year.

i. Recognize sales revenues on orders received but not shipped as of the end of the year.

Required

1. As the management accountant for Contemporary Interiors, evaluate each of the preceding items (**a–i**) in the context of the "Standards of Ethical Behavior for Practitioners of Management Accounting and Financial Management," Exhibit 1-7 (page 37). Which of the items are in violation of these ethics standards and which are acceptable?

2. What should the management accountant do with regard to those items that are in violation of the ethical standards for management accountants?

2 An Introduction to Cost Terms and Purposes

What does the word *cost* mean to you?

Is it the price you pay for something of value, like a cell phone? A cash outflow, like monthly rent? Something that affects profitability, like salaries? Organizations, like individuals, deal with different types of costs. They incur costs to generate revenues. Unfortunately, when times are bad and revenues decline, companies may find that they are unable to cut costs fast enough, leading to Chapter 11 bankruptcy. This was the case with surf wear company, Quiksilver.

HIGH FIXED COSTS BANKRUPT QUIKSILVER[1]

In 2015, surf wear company, Quiksilver, announced it had filed for Chapter 11 bankruptcy. Its high fixed costs—costs that did not decrease as the number of boardshorts and hoodies sold declined—crippled the company.

    In the 1990s and early 2000s, Quiksilver rode the wave of young shoppers emulating the cool lifestyle and fashions of surfers, skateboarders, and snowboarders to financial success. During this time, the company opened hundreds of retail stores worldwide, many in expensive areas such as Times Square in New York. This expansion saddled the company with a huge amount of debt. In 2015, as sales rapidly declined, the company collapsed under the weight of its high fixed operating costs—like long-term leases and salaries—and crippling debt-servicing payments. After declaring bankruptcy, Quiksilver began rapidly selling off non-core brands and closing many retail stores.

    As the story of Quiksilver illustrates, managers must understand their firms' costs and closely manage them. Organizations as varied as the United Way, the Mayo Clinic, and Sony generate reports containing a variety of cost concepts and terms managers need to understand to effectively run their businesses. This chapter discusses cost concepts and terms that are the basis of accounting information used for internal and external reporting.

Richard Naude/Alamy Stock Photo

[1] *Sources:* Andrew Khouri, "Wipeout: Quiksilver files for Chapter 11 bankruptcy in U.S.," *Los Angeles Times*, September 9, 2015 (http://www.latimes.com/business/la-fi-quiksilver-bankruptcy-20150909-story.html); Deborah Belgum, "Oaktree Capital Working on Buying Quiksilver," *California Apparel News*, November 3, 2015 (https://www.apparelnews.net/news/2015/nov/03/oaktree-capital-working-buying-quiksilver).

Costs and Cost Terminology

A **cost** is a resource sacrificed or forgone to achieve a specific objective. A cost (such as the cost of labor or advertising) is usually measured as the monetary amount that must be paid to acquire goods or services. An **actual cost** is the cost incurred (a historical or past cost), as distinguished from a **budgeted cost**, which is a predicted, or forecasted, cost (a future cost).

When you think of a cost, you invariably think of it in the context of putting a price on a particular thing. We call this "thing" a **cost object**, which is anything for which a cost measurement is desired. Suppose you're a manager at BMW's automotive manufacturing plant in Spartanburg, South Carolina. Can you identify some of the plant's cost objects? Now look at Exhibit 2-1.

You will see that BMW managers not only want to know the cost of various products, such as the BMW X6 sports activity vehicle, but they also want to know the costs of services, projects, activities, departments, and supporting customers. Managers use their knowledge of these costs to guide decisions about, for example, product innovation, quality, and customer service.

Now think about whether a manager at BMW might want to know the *budgeted cost* or the *actual cost* of a cost object. Managers almost always need to know both types of costs when making decisions. For example, comparing budgeted costs to actual costs helps managers evaluate how well they did controlling costs and learn about how they can do better in the future.

How does a cost system determine the costs of various cost objects? Typically in two stages: accumulation followed by assignment. **Cost accumulation** is the collection of cost data in some organized way by means of an accounting system. For example, at its Spartanburg plant, BMW collects (accumulates) in various categories the costs of different types of materials, different classifications of labor, the costs incurred for supervision, and so on. The accumulated costs are then *assigned* to designated cost objects, such as the different models of cars that BMW manufactures at the plant. BMW managers use this cost information in two main ways: (1) when *making* decisions, for instance, about how to price different models of cars or how much to invest in R&D and marketing and (2) for *implementing* decisions, by influencing and motivating employees to act, for example, by providing bonuses to employees for reducing costs.

Now that we know why it is useful for management accountants to assign costs, we turn our attention to some concepts that will help us do it. Again, think of the different types of costs that we just discussed—materials, labor, and supervision. You are probably thinking that some costs, such as the costs of materials, are easier to assign to a cost object than others, such as the costs of supervision. As you will learn, this is indeed the case.

Direct Costs and Indirect Costs

Cost are classified as direct and indirect costs. Management accountants use a variety of methods to assign these costs to cost objects.

- **Direct costs of a cost object** are related to the particular cost object and can be traced to it in an economically feasible (cost-effective) way. For example, the cost of steel or tires is a direct cost of BMW X6s. The cost of the steel or tires can be easily traced to or

LEARNING OBJECTIVE 1

Define and illustrate a cost object

...examples of cost objects are products, services, activities, processes, and customers

DECISION POINT

What is a cost object?

LEARNING OBJECTIVE 2

Distinguish between direct costs

...costs that are traced to the cost object

and indirect costs

...costs that are allocated to the cost object

EXHIBIT 2-1   Examples of Cost Objects at BMW

Cost Object	Illustration
Product	A BMW X6 sports activity vehicle
Service	Telephone hotline providing information and assistance to BMW dealers
Project	R&D project on enhancing the navigation system in BMW cars
Customer	Herb Chambers Motors, the BMW dealer that purchases a broad range of BMW vehicles
Activity	Setting up machines for production or maintaining production equipment
Department	Environmental, health, and safety department

identified with the BMW X6. As workers on the BMW X6 line request materials from the warehouse, the material requisition document identifies the cost of the materials supplied to the X6. Similarly, individual workers record on their time sheets the hours and minutes they spend working on the X6. The cost of this labor can easily be traced to the X6 and is another example of a direct cost. The term **cost tracing** is used to describe the assignment of direct costs to a particular cost object.

- **Indirect costs of a cost object** are related to the particular cost object, but cannot be traced to it in an economically feasible (cost-effective) way. For example, the salaries of plant administrators (including the plant manager) who oversee production of the many different types of cars produced at the Spartanburg plant are an indirect cost of the X6s. Plant administration costs are related to the cost object (X6s) because plant administration is necessary for managing the production of these vehicles. Plant administration costs are indirect costs because plant administrators also oversee the production of other products, such as the Z4 Roadster. Unlike steel or tires, there is no specific request made by supervisors of the X6 production line for plant administration services, and it is virtually impossible to trace plant administration costs to the X6 line. The term **cost allocation** is used to describe the assignment of indirect costs to a particular cost object.

    Cost assignment is a general term that encompasses both (1) tracing direct costs to a cost object and (2) allocating indirect costs to a cost object. Exhibit 2-2 depicts direct costs and indirect costs and both forms of cost assignment—cost tracing and cost allocation—using the BMW X6 as an example.

Cost Allocation Challenges

Managers want to assign costs accurately to cost objects because inaccurate product costs will mislead managers about the profitability of different products. This could result, for example, in managers unknowingly promoting less-profitable products instead of more-profitable products.

Managers are much more confident about the accuracy of the direct costs of cost objects, such as the cost of steel and tires of the X6, because these costs can be easily traced to the cost object. Indirect costs are a different story. Some indirect costs can be assigned to cost objects reasonably accurately. Others are more difficult.

Consider the cost to lease the Spartanburg plant. This cost is an indirect cost of the X6—there is no separate lease agreement for the area of the plant where the X6 is made. Nonetheless, BMW *allocates* to the X6 a part of the lease cost of the building—for example, on the basis of an estimate of the percentage of the building's floor space occupied for the production of the X6 relative to the total floor space used to produce all models of cars. This approach measures the building resources used by each car model reasonably and accurately. The more floor space a car model occupies, the greater the lease costs assigned to it. Accurately allocating other indirect costs, such as plant administration, to the X6, however, is more difficult. For example, should these costs be allocated on the basis

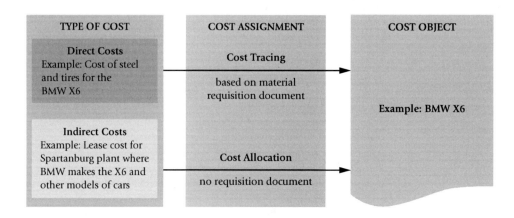

TYPE OF COST	COST ASSIGNMENT	COST OBJECT
Direct Costs Example: Cost of steel and tires for the BMW X6	**Cost Tracing** based on material requisition document	**Example: BMW X6**
Indirect Costs Example: Lease cost for Spartanburg plant where BMW makes the X6 and other models of cars	**Cost Allocation** no requisition document	

of the number of employees working on each car model or the number of cars produced of each model? Measuring the share of plant administration used by each car model is not clear-cut.

Factors Affecting Direct/Indirect Cost Classifications

Several factors affect whether a cost is classified as direct or indirect:

- **The materiality of the cost in question.** The smaller the amount of a cost—that is, the more immaterial the cost is—the less likely it is economically feasible to trace it to a particular cost object. Consider a mail-order catalog company such as Lands' End. It would be economically feasible to trace the courier charge for delivering a package to an individual customer as a direct cost. In contrast, the cost of the invoice paper included in the package would be classified as an indirect cost. Why? Although the cost of the paper can be traced to each customer, it is not cost-effective to do so. The benefits of knowing that, say, exactly 0.5¢ worth of paper is included in each package do not exceed the data processing and administrative costs of tracing the cost to each package. The time of the sales administrator, who earns a salary of $45,000 a year, is better spent organizing customer information to help with a company's marketing efforts than tracking the cost of paper.
- **Available information-gathering technology.** Improvements in information-gathering technology make it possible to consider more and more costs as direct costs. Bar codes, for example, allow manufacturing plants to treat certain low-cost materials such as clips and screws, which were previously classified as indirect costs, as direct costs of products. At Dell, component parts such as the computer chip and the DVD drive display a bar code that can be scanned at every point in the production process. Bar codes can be read into a manufacturing cost file by waving a "wand" in the same quick and efficient way supermarket checkout clerks enter the cost of each item purchased by a customer.
- **Design of operations.** Classifying a cost as direct is easier if a company's facility (or some part of it) is used exclusively for a specific cost object, such as a specific product or a particular customer. For example, General Chemicals classifies the cost of its facility dedicated to manufacturing soda ash (sodium carbonate) as a direct cost of soda ash.

Be aware that a specific cost may be both a direct cost of one cost object and an indirect cost of another cost object. *That is, the direct/indirect classification depends on the choice of the cost object.* For example, the salary of an assembly department supervisor at BMW is a direct cost if the cost object is the assembly department. However, because the assembly department assembles many different models, the supervisor's salary is an indirect cost if the cost object is a specific product such as the BMW X6 sports activity vehicle. A useful rule to remember is that the broader the cost object definition—the assembly department, rather than the X6—the higher the direct costs portion of total costs and the more confident a manager will be about the accuracy of the resulting cost amounts.

DECISION POINT

How do managers decide whether a cost is a direct or an indirect cost?

One final point. A company can incur a cost—sacrifice a resource—without the cost being recorded in the accounting system. For example, certain retirement health benefits are only recorded in the accounting system after an employee retires although the cost is incurred while the employee is actually providing the service. Environmental costs are another example. Many companies, for example General Electric, have had to incur significant costs at a later date to clean up the environmental damage that was caused by actions taken several years earlier. To force managers to consider these costs when making decisions, some companies such as Novartis, the Swiss pharmaceutical giant, are imputing a cost in their cost accounting system for every ton of greenhouse gases emitted to surrogate for future environmental costs. These costs can be a direct cost of a product if they can be traced to a specific product. More commonly, these costs are associated with operating a manufacturing facility and cannot be traced to a specific product. In this case, they are indirect costs.

Cost-Behavior Patterns: Variable Costs and Fixed Costs

Costing systems record the cost of resources acquired, such as materials, labor, and equipment, and track how those resources are used to produce and sell products or services. This allows managers to see how costs behave. Consider two basic types of cost-behavior patterns found in many accounting systems. A **variable cost** changes *in total* in proportion to changes in the related level of total activity or volume of output produced. A **fixed cost** remains unchanged *in total* for a given time period, despite wide changes in the related level of total activity or volume of output produced. Note that costs are defined as variable or fixed for *a specific activity* and for *a given time period*. Identifying a cost as variable or fixed provides valuable information for making many management decisions and is an important input when evaluating performance. To illustrate these two basic types of costs, again consider the costs at BMW's Spartanburg, South Carolina, plant.

1. **Variable costs.** If BMW buys a steering wheel at $600 for each of its BMW X6 vehicles, then the total cost of steering wheels is $600 times the number of vehicles produced, as the following table illustrates.

Number of X6s Produced (1)	Variable Cost per Steering Wheel (2)	Total Variable Cost of Steering Wheels (3) = (1) × (2)
1	$600	$ 600
1,000	600	600,000
3,000	600	1,800,000

The steering wheel cost is an example of a variable cost because *total cost* changes in proportion to changes in the number of vehicles produced. However, the *cost per unit* of a variable cost is constant. For example, the variable cost per steering wheel in column 2 is the same regardless of whether 1,000 or 3,000 X6s are produced. As a result, the total variable cost of steering wheels in column 3 changes proportionately with the number of X6s produced in column 1. So, when considering how variable costs behave, always focus on *total* costs.

Panel A in Exhibit 2-3 shows a graph of the total variable cost of steering wheels. The cost is represented by a straight line that climbs from left to right. The phrases "strictly variable" or "proportionately variable" are sometimes used to describe the variable cost behavior shown in this panel.

Now consider an example of a variable cost for a different activity—the $20 hourly wage paid each worker to set up machines at the Spartanburg plant. The setup labor cost is a variable cost for setup hours because setup cost changes in total in proportion to the number of setup hours used.

2. **Fixed costs.** Suppose BMW incurs a total cost of $2,000,000 per year for supervisors who work exclusively on the X6 line. These costs are unchanged in total over a designated range of vehicles produced during a given time span (see Exhibit 2-3, Panel B). Fixed costs become

PANEL A: Variable Cost of Steering Wheels at $600 per BMW X6 Assembled

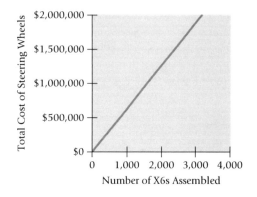

PANEL B: Supervision Costs for the BMW X6 assembly line (in millions)

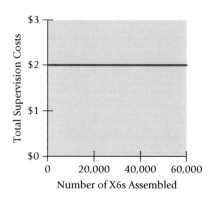

smaller and smaller on a per-unit basis as the number of vehicles assembled increases, as the following table shows.

Annual Total Fixed Supervision Costs for BMW X6 Assembly Line (1)	Number of X6s Produced (2)	Fixed Supervision Cost per X6 (3) = (1) ÷ (2)
$2,000,000	10,000	$200
$2,000,000	25,000	$ 80
$2,000,000	50,000	$ 40

It is precisely because *total* line supervision costs are fixed at $2,000,000 that the fixed supervision cost per X6 decreases as the number of X6s produced increases; the same fixed cost is spread over a larger number of X6s. Do not be misled by the change in fixed cost per unit. Just as in the case of variable costs, when considering fixed costs, always focus on *total costs*. Costs are fixed when total costs remain unchanged despite significant changes in the level of total activity or volume.

Why are some costs variable and other costs fixed? Recall that a cost is usually measured as the amount of money that must be paid to acquire goods and services. The total cost of steering wheels is a variable cost because BMW buys the steering wheels only when they are needed. As more X6s are produced, proportionately more steering wheels are acquired and proportionately more costs are incurred.

Contrast the plant's variable costs with the $2,000,000 of fixed costs per year incurred for the supervision of the X6 assembly line. This level of supervision is acquired and put in place well before BMW uses it to produce X6s and before BMW even knows how many X6s it will produce. Suppose that BMW puts in place supervisors capable of supervising the production of 60,000 X6s each year. If the demand is for only 55,000 X6s, there will be idle capacity. Supervisors on the X6 line could have supervised the production of 60,000 X6s but will supervise only 55,000 X6s because of the lower demand. However, BMW must pay for the unused line supervision capacity because the cost of supervision cannot be reduced in the short run. If demand is even lower—say only 50,000 X6s are demanded—the plant's line supervision costs will still be $2,000,000, and its idle capacity will increase.

Unlike variable costs, fixed costs of resources (such as for line supervision) cannot be quickly and easily changed to match the resources needed or used. Over time, however, managers can take action to reduce a company's fixed costs. For example, if the X6 line needs to be run for fewer hours because the demand for the vehicles falls, BMW may lay off supervisors or move them to another production line. Unlike variable costs that go away automatically if the resources are not used, reducing fixed costs requires active intervention on the part of managers.

Do not assume that individual cost items are inherently variable or fixed. Consider labor costs. Labor costs can be purely variable for units produced when workers are paid on a piece-unit basis (for each unit they make). For example, some companies pay garment workers on a per-shirt-sewed basis, so the firms' labor costs are variable. That is, total costs depend on how many shirts workers make. In contrast, other companies negotiate labor union agreements with set annual salaries that contain no-layoff clauses for workers. At a company such as this, the salaries would appropriately be classified as fixed. For decades, Japanese companies provided their workers a lifetime guarantee of employment. Although such a guarantee entails higher fixed labor costs, a firm can benefit because workers are more loyal and dedicated, which can improve productivity. However, during an economic downturn, the company risks losing money if revenues decrease while fixed costs remain unchanged. The recent global economic crisis has made companies very reluctant to lock in fixed costs. Concepts in Action: Zipcar Helps Twitter Reduce Fixed Costs describes how a car-sharing service offers companies the opportunity to convert the fixed costs of owning corporate cars into variable costs by renting cars on an as-needed basis.

A particular cost item could be variable for one level of activity and fixed for another. Consider annual registration and license costs for a fleet of planes owned by an airline company. Registration and license costs would be a variable cost that would change with the

CONCEPTS IN ACTION

Zipcar Helps Twitter Reduce Fixed Costs

Mike Kahn/Green Stock Media/Alamy Stock Photo

In many cities worldwide, car sharing is an effective way for companies to reduce spending on gas, insurance, and parking of corporate cars. Zipcar—a car sharing company that provides an "on-demand" option for urban individuals and businesses to rent a car by the week, the day, or even the hour—has rates beginning around $7 per hour and $79 per day (including gas, insurance, and about 180 miles per day).

Let's think about what Zipcar means for companies. Many businesses own company cars for getting to meetings, picking up clients, making deliveries, and running errands. Traditionally, owning these cars has involved high fixed costs, including buying the asset (car), maintenance costs, and insurance for multiple drivers.

Now, however, companies like Twitter, based in downtown San Francisco, can use Zipcar for on-demand mobility while reducing their transportation and overhead costs. From a business perspective, Zipcar allows Twitter and other companies to convert the fixed costs of owning a company car to variable costs. If business slows or a car isn't required to visit a client, Twitter is not saddled with the fixed costs of car ownership. Of course, when business is good, causing Twitter managers to use Zipcar more often, they can end up paying more overall then they would have paid if they purchased and maintained the car themselves. It is also convenient. "We ... avoid the cost of taking taxis everywhere or the time delays of mass transit," said Jack Dorsey, the online social networking service's co-founder. "Zipcar's the fastest, easiest way to get around town."

Along with cutting company spending, car sharing services like Zipcar contribute to environmental sustainability. In 2015, research found that Zipcar's business program eliminated the need for roughly 33,000 cars across North America. Kaye Ceille, the company's president said, "Businesses are increasingly conscious of their environmental footprint, and we're proud that ... Zipcar for business has many significant environmental benefits for companies, including reducing vehicles on the road."

Sources: Elizabeth Olsen, "Car Sharing Reinvents the Company Wheels," *New York Times*, May 7, 2009 (http://www.nytimes.com/2009/05/07/business/businessspecial/07CAR.html); Zipcar, Inc., "Case Studies: Twitter" (http://www.zipcar.com/business/is-it/case-studies); Zipcar, Inc., "San Francisco Bay Area Rates & Plans (http://www.zipcar.com/sf/check-rates); "New Research Finds Business Use of Zipcar Reduces Personal Car Ownership," Zipcar, Inc. press release, Boston, MA, July, 27, 2015 (http://www.zipcar.com/press/releases/z4breducescarownership).

DECISION POINT

How do managers decide whether a cost is a variable or a fixed cost?

number of planes the company owned. But the registration and license costs for a particular plane are fixed regardless of the miles flown by that plane during a year.

Some costs have both fixed and variable elements and are called *mixed* or *semivariable* costs. For example, a company's telephone costs may consist of a fixed monthly cost as well as a cost per phone-minute used. We discuss mixed costs and techniques to separate out their fixed and variable components in Chapter 10.

TRY IT! 2-1

Pepsi Corporation uses trucks to transport bottles from the warehouse to different retail outlets. Gasoline costs are $0.15 per mile driven. Insurance costs are $6,000 per year. Calculate the total costs and the cost per mile for gasoline and insurance if the truck is driven (a) 20,000 miles per year or (b) 30,000 miles per year.

Cost Drivers

A **cost driver** is a variable, such as the level of activity or volume, that causally affects costs over a given time span. An *activity* is an event, task, or unit of work with a specified purpose—for example, designing products, setting up machines, or testing products. The level of activity or volume is a cost driver if there is a cause-and-effect relationship between a change in the level of activity or volume and a change in the level of total costs. For example, if product-design costs change with the number of parts in a product, the number of parts is a cost driver of product-design costs. Similarly, the miles driven by trucks to deliver products are a cost driver of distribution costs.

The cost driver of a variable cost is the level of activity or volume whose change causes proportionate changes in the variable cost. For example, the number of vehicles assembled is the cost driver of the total cost of steering wheels. If setup workers are paid an hourly wage, the number of setup hours is the cost driver of total (variable) setup costs.

Costs that are fixed in the short run have no cost driver in the short run but may have a cost driver in the long run. Consider the costs of testing, say, 0.1% of the color printers produced at a Hewlett-Packard plant. These costs consist of equipment and staff costs of the testing department, which are difficult to change. Consequently, they are fixed in the short run regardless of changes in the volume of production. In this case, volume of production is not a cost driver of testing costs in the short run. In the long run, however, Hewlett-Packard will increase or decrease the testing department's equipment and staff to the levels needed to support future production volumes. In the long run, volume of production is a cost driver of testing costs. Costing systems that identify the cost of each activity such as testing, design, or setup are called *activity-based costing systems*.

Relevant Range

Relevant range is the band or range of normal activity level or volume in which there is a specific relationship between the level of activity or volume and the cost in question. For example, a fixed cost is fixed only in relation to a given wide range of total activity or volume (at which the company is expected to operate) and only for a given time span (usually a particular budget period). Suppose BMW contracts with Thomas Transport Company (TTC) to transport X6s to BMW dealerships. TTC rents two trucks, and each truck has an annual fixed rental cost of $40,000. The maximum annual usage of each truck is 120,000 miles. In the current year (2017), the predicted combined total hauling of the two trucks is 170,000 miles.

Exhibit 2-4 shows how annual fixed costs behave at different levels of miles of hauling. Up to 120,000 miles, TTC can operate with one truck; from 120,001 to 240,000 miles, it operates with two trucks; and from 240,001 to 360,000 miles, it operates with three trucks. This pattern will continue as TTC adds trucks to its fleet to provide more miles of hauling. Given the predicted 170,000-mile usage for 2017, the range from 120,001 to 240,000 miles hauled is the range in which TTC expects to operate, resulting in fixed rental costs of $80,000. Within this relevant range, changes in miles hauled will not affect the annual fixed costs.

Fixed costs may change from one year to the next, though. For example, if the total rental fee of the two trucks increases by $2,000 for 2018, the total level of fixed costs will increase to $82,000 (all else remaining the same). If that increase occurs, total rental costs will be fixed at this new level ($82,000) for 2018 for the miles hauled in the 120,001 to 240,000 range.

The relevant range also applies to variable costs. Outside the relevant range, variable costs, such as direct materials costs, may no longer change proportionately with changes in production volumes. For example, above a certain volume, the cost of direct materials may

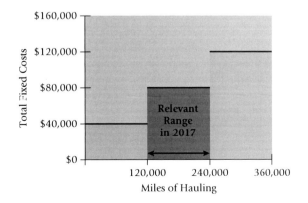

EXHIBIT 2-4

Fixed-Cost Behavior at Thomas Transport Company

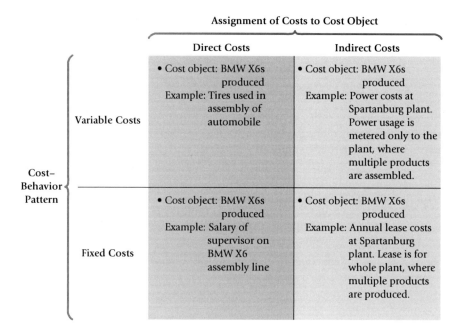

EXHIBIT 2-5

Examples of Costs in
Combinations of the
Direct/Indirect and
Variable/Fixed Cost
Classifications for a Car
Manufacturer

increase at a lower rate because a firm may be able to negotiate price discounts for purchasing
greater amounts of materials from its suppliers.

Relationships Between Types of Costs

We have introduced two major classifications of costs: direct/indirect and variable/fixed. Costs
may simultaneously be as follows:

- Direct and variable
- Direct and fixed
- Indirect and variable
- Indirect and fixed

Exhibit 2-5 shows examples of costs in each of these four cost classifications for the BMW X6.

Total Costs and Unit Costs

**LEARNING
OBJECTIVE** **4**

Interpret unit costs
cautiously

...for many decisions,
managers should use to-
tal costs, not unit costs

The preceding section concentrated on the behavior patterns of total costs in relation to activity or volume levels. But what about unit costs?

Unit Costs

A **unit cost**, also called an **average cost**, is calculated by dividing the total cost by the related
number of units produced. In many decision contexts, calculating a unit cost is essential.
Consider the booking agent who has to make the decision to book Paul McCartney to play at
Shea Stadium. She estimates the cost of the event to be $4,000,000. This knowledge is helpful
for the decision, but it is not enough.

Before reaching a decision, the booking agent also must predict the number of people
who will attend. Without knowing the number of attendees, she cannot make an informed
decision about the admission price she needs to charge to recover the cost of the event or
even on whether to have the event at all. So she computes the unit cost of the event by dividing the total cost ($4,000,000) by the expected number of people who will attend. If 50,000

people attend, the unit cost is $80 (4,000,000 ÷ 50,000) per person; if 20,000 attend, the unit cost increases to $200 ($4,000,000 ÷ 20,000). Unless the total cost is "unitized" (that is, averaged by the level of activity or volume), the $4,000,000 cost is difficult to use to make decisions. The unit cost combines the total cost and the number of people in a simple and understandable way.

Accounting systems typically report both total-cost amounts and average-cost-per-unit amounts. The units might be expressed in various ways. Examples are automobiles assembled, packages delivered, or hours worked. Consider Tennessee Products, a manufacturer of speaker systems with a plant in Memphis. Suppose that, in 2017, its first year of operations, the company incurs $40,000,000 of manufacturing costs to produce 500,000 speaker systems. Then the unit cost is $80:

$$\frac{\text{Total manufacturing costs}}{\text{Number of units manufactured}} = \frac{\$40,000,000}{500,000 \text{ units}} = \$80 \text{ per unit}$$

If 480,000 units are sold and 20,000 units remain in ending inventory, the unit-cost concept helps managers determine total costs in the income statement and balance sheet and, therefore, the financial results Tennessee Products reports to shareholders, banks, and the government.

Cost of goods sold in the income statement, 480,000 units × $80 per unit	$38,400,000
Ending inventory in the balance sheet, 20,000 units × $80 per unit	1,600,000
Total manufacturing costs of 500,000 units	$40,000,000

Unit costs are found in all areas of the value chain—for example, the unit cost of a product design, a sales visit, and a customer-service call. By summing unit costs throughout the value chain, managers calculate the unit cost of the different products or services they deliver and determine the profitability of each product or service. Managers use this information, for example, to decide the products in which they should invest more resources, such as R&D and marketing, and the prices they should charge.

Use Unit Costs Cautiously

Although unit costs are regularly used in financial reports and for making product mix and pricing decisions, *managers should think in terms of total costs rather than unit costs for many decisions.* Consider the manager of the Memphis plant of Tennessee Products. Assume the $40,000,000 in costs in 2017 consist of $10,000,000 of fixed costs and $30,000,000 of variable costs (at $60 variable cost per speaker system produced). Suppose the total fixed costs and the variable cost per speaker system in 2018 are expected to be unchanged from 2017. The budgeted costs for 2018 at different production levels, calculated on the basis of total variable costs, total fixed costs, and total costs, are:

Units Produced (1)	Variable Cost per Unit (2)	Total Variable Costs (3) = (1) × (2)	Total Fixed Costs (4)	Total Costs (5) = (3) + (4)	Unit Cost (6) = (5) ÷ (1)
100,000	$60	$ 6,000,000	$10,000,000	$16,000,000	$160.00
200,000	$60	$12,000,000	$10,000,000	$22,000,000	$110.00
500,000	$60	$30,000,000	$10,000,000	$40,000,000	$ 80.00
800,000	$60	$48,000,000	$10,000,000	$58,000,000	$ 72.50
1,000,000	$60	$60,000,000	$10,000,000	$70,000,000	$ 70.00

A plant manager who uses the 2017 unit cost of $80 per unit will underestimate actual total costs if the plant's 2018 output is below the 2017 level of 500,000 units. If the volume produced falls to 200,000 units due to, say, the presence of a new competitor and less demand, actual costs would be $22,000,000. The unit cost of $80 times 200,000 units equals $16,000,000, which underestimates the actual total costs by $6,000,000 ($22,000,000 − $16,000,000). In other words, *the unit cost of $80 applies only when the company produces 500,000 units.*

DECISION POINT

How should managers estimate and interpret cost information?

An overreliance on the unit cost in this situation could lead to insufficient cash being available to pay the company's costs if volume declines to 200,000 units. As the table indicates, for making this decision, managers should think in terms of total variable costs, total fixed costs, and total costs rather than unit cost. As a general rule, first calculate total costs, then compute the unit cost, if it is needed for a particular decision.

Business Sectors, Types of Inventory, Inventoriable Costs, and Period Costs

LEARNING OBJECTIVE 5

Distinguish inventoriable costs

...assets when incurred, then cost of goods sold

from period costs

...expenses of the period when incurred

In this section, we describe the different sectors of the economy, the different types of inventory that companies hold, and how these factors affect commonly used classifications of inventoriable and period costs.

Manufacturing-, Merchandising-, and Service-Sector Companies

We define three sectors of the economy and provide examples of companies in each sector.

1. **Manufacturing-sector companies** purchase materials and components and convert them into various finished goods. Examples are automotive companies such as Jaguar, cellular-phone producers such as Samsung, food-processing companies such as Heinz, and computer companies such as Lenovo.

2. **Merchandising-sector companies** purchase and then sell tangible products without changing their basic form. This sector includes companies engaged in retailing (for example, bookstores such as Barnes & Noble and department stores such as Target); distribution (for example, a supplier of hospital products, such as Owens and Minor); or wholesaling (for example, a supplier of electronic components such as Arrow Electronics).

3. **Service-sector companies** provide services (intangible products)—for example, legal advice or audits—to their customers. Examples are law firms such as Wachtell, Lipton, Rosen & Katz; accounting firms such as Ernst & Young; banks such as Barclays; mutual fund companies such as Fidelity; insurance companies such as Aetna; transportation companies such as Singapore Airlines; advertising agencies such as Saatchi & Saatchi; television stations such as Turner Broadcasting; Internet service providers such as Comcast; travel agencies such as American Express; and brokerage firms such as Merrill Lynch.

Types of Inventory

Manufacturing-sector companies purchase materials and components and convert them into finished goods. These companies typically have one or more of the following three types of inventory:

1. **Direct materials inventory.** Direct materials in stock that will be used in the manufacturing process (for example, computer chips and components needed to manufacture cellular phones).

2. **Work-in-process inventory.** Goods partially worked on but not yet completed (for example, cellular phones at various stages of completion in the manufacturing process). This is also called **work in progress**.

3. **Finished-goods inventory.** Goods (for example, cellular phones) completed, but not yet sold.

Merchandising-sector companies purchase tangible products and then sell them without changing their basic form. These companies hold only one type of inventory, which is products in their original purchased form, called *merchandise inventory*. Service-sector companies provide only services or intangible products and do not hold inventories of tangible products.

Commonly Used Classifications of Manufacturing Costs

Three terms commonly used when describing manufacturing costs are *direct materials costs*, *direct manufacturing labor costs*, and *indirect manufacturing costs*. These terms build on the direct versus indirect cost distinction we described earlier in the context of manufacturing costs.

1. **Direct materials costs** are the acquisition costs of all materials that eventually become part of the cost object (work in process and then finished goods) and can be traced to the cost object in an economically feasible way. The steel and tires used to make the BMW X6 and the computer chips used to make cellular phones are examples of direct material costs. Note that the costs of direct materials include not only the cost of the materials themselves, but the freight-in (inward delivery) charges, sales taxes, and customs duties that must be paid to acquire them.

2. **Direct manufacturing labor costs** include the compensation of all manufacturing labor that can be traced to the cost object (work in process and then finished goods) in an economically feasible way. Examples include wages and fringe benefits paid to machine operators and assembly-line workers who convert direct materials to finished goods.

3. **Indirect manufacturing costs** are all manufacturing costs that are related to the cost object (work in process and then finished goods), but cannot be traced to that cost object in an economically feasible way. Examples include supplies, indirect materials such as lubricants, indirect manufacturing labor such as plant maintenance and cleaning labor, plant rent, plant insurance, property taxes on the plant, plant depreciation, and the compensation of plant managers. This cost category is also referred to as **manufacturing overhead costs** or **factory overhead costs**. We use *indirect manufacturing costs* and *manufacturing overhead costs* interchangeably in this book.

We now describe the distinction between inventoriable costs and period costs.

Inventoriable Costs

Inventoriable costs are all costs of a product that are considered assets in a company's balance sheet when the costs are incurred and that are expensed as cost of goods sold only when the product is sold. For manufacturing-sector companies, all manufacturing costs are inventoriable costs. The costs first accumulate as work-in-process inventory assets (in other words, they are "inventoried") and then as finished goods inventory assets. Consider Cellular Products, a manufacturer of cellular phones. The cost of the company's direct materials, such as computer chips, direct manufacturing labor costs, and manufacturing overhead costs create new assets. They start out as work-in-process inventory and become finished-goods inventory (the cellular phones). When the cellular phones are sold, the costs move from being assets to cost of goods sold expense. This cost is matched against **revenues**, which are inflows of assets (usually cash or accounts receivable) received for products or services customers purchase.

Note that the cost of goods sold includes all manufacturing costs (direct materials, direct manufacturing labor, and manufacturing overhead costs) incurred to produce them. The cellular phones may be sold during a different accounting period than the period in which they were manufactured. Thus, inventorying manufacturing costs in the balance sheet during the accounting period when the phones are manufactured and expensing the manufacturing costs in a later income statement when the phones are sold matches revenues and expenses.

For merchandising-sector companies such as Walmart, inventoriable costs are the costs of purchasing goods that are resold in their same form. These costs are made up of the costs of the goods themselves plus any incoming freight, insurance, and handling costs for those goods. Service-sector companies provide only services or intangible products. The absence of inventories of tangible products for sale means service-sector companies have no inventoriable costs.

Period Costs

Period costs are all costs in the income statement other than cost of goods sold. Period costs, such as design costs, marketing, distribution, and customer service costs, are treated as expenses of the accounting period in which they are incurred because managers expect these

Examples of Period Costs in Combinations of the Direct/Indirect and Variable/Fixed Cost Classifications at a Bank

Assignment of Costs to Cost Object

	Direct Costs	Indirect Costs
Variable Costs	• Cost object: Number of mortgage loans Example: Fees paid to property appraisal company for each mortgage loan	• Cost object: Number of mortgage loans Example: Postage paid to deliver mortgage-loan documents to lawyers/homeowners
Fixed Costs	• Cost object: Number of mortgage loans Example: Salary paid to executives in mortgage loan department to develop new mortgage-loan products	• Cost object: Number of mortgage loans Example: Cost to the bank of sponsoring annual golf tournament

Cost-Behavior Pattern

costs to increase revenues in only that period and not in future periods. For manufacturing-sector companies, all nonmanufacturing costs in the income statement are period costs. For merchandising-sector companies, all costs in the income statement not related to the cost of goods purchased for resale are period costs. Examples of these period costs are labor costs of sales-floor personnel and advertising costs. Because there are no inventoriable costs for service-sector companies, all costs in the income statement are period costs.

An interesting question pertains to the treatment of R & D expenses as period costs.[2] As we saw in Chapter 1, for many companies in industries ranging from machine tools to consumer electronics to telecommunications to pharmaceuticals and biotechnology, innovation is increasingly becoming a key driver of success. The benefits of these innovations and R & D investments will, in most cases, only impact revenues in some future periods. So should R&D expenses still be considered period costs and be matched against revenues of the current period? Yes, because it is highly uncertain whether these innovations will be successful and result in future revenues. Even if the innovations are successful, it is very difficult to determine which future period the innovations will benefit. Some managers believe that treating R & D expenses as period costs dampens innovation because it reduces current period income.

Exhibit 2-5 showed examples of inventoriable costs in direct/indirect and variable/fixed cost classifications for a car manufacturer. Exhibit 2-6 shows examples of period costs in direct/indirect and variable/fixed cost classifications at a bank.

DECISION POINT

What are the differences in the accounting for inventoriable versus period costs?

Illustrating the Flow of Inventoriable Costs and Period Costs

LEARNING OBJECTIVE 6

Illustrate the flow of inventoriable and period costs

…in manufacturing settings, inventoriable costs flow through work-in-process and finished-goods accounts and are expensed when goods are sold; period costs are expensed as incurred

We illustrate the flow of inventoriable costs and period costs through the income statement of a manufacturing company, where the distinction between inventoriable costs and period costs is most detailed.

Manufacturing-Sector Example

Follow the flow of costs for Cellular Products in Exhibits 2-7 and 2-8. Exhibit 2-7 visually highlights the differences in the flow of inventoriable and period costs for a manufacturing-sector company. Note how, as described in the previous section, inventoriable costs go through

---

[2] Under Generally Accepted Accounting Principles (GAAP) in the U.S., all R & D costs are expensed for financial accounting. International Financial Reporting Standards (IFRS) permit the capitalization of some development costs for financial accounting.

EXHIBIT 2-7   Flow of Revenue and Costs for a Manufacturing-Sector Company, Cellular Products (in thousands)

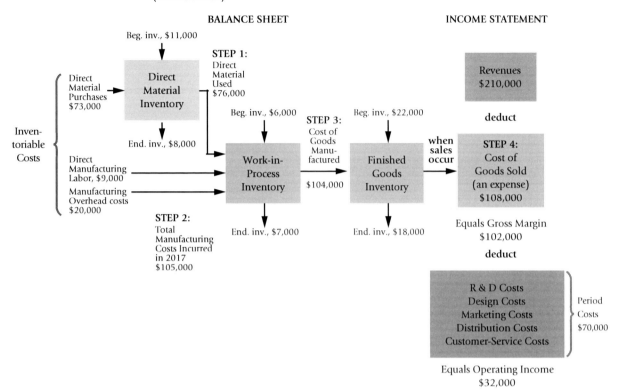

the balance sheet accounts of work-in-process inventory and finished-goods inventory before entering the cost of goods sold in the income statement. Period costs are expensed directly in the income statement. Exhibit 2-8 takes the visual presentation in Exhibit 2-7 and shows how inventoriable costs and period expenses would appear in the income statement and schedule of cost of goods manufactured of a manufacturing company.

We start by tracking the flow of direct materials shown on the left in Exhibit 2-7 and in Panel B in Exhibit 2-8. To keep things simple, all numbers are expressed in thousands, except for the per unit amounts.

Step 1: Cost of direct materials used in 2017. Note how the arrows in Exhibit 2-7 for beginning inventory, $11,000, and direct material purchases, $73,000, "fill up" the direct materials inventory box and how direct materials used, $76,000, "empties out" direct material inventory, leaving an ending inventory of direct materials of $8,000 that becomes the beginning inventory for the next year.

The cost of direct materials used is calculated in Exhibit 2-8, Panel B (light blue–shaded area), as follows:

Beginning inventory of direct materials, January 1, 2017	$11,000
+ Purchases of direct materials in 2017	73,000
− Ending inventory of direct materials, December 31, 2017	8,000
= Direct materials used in 2017	$76,000

Step 2: Total manufacturing costs incurred in 2017. Total manufacturing costs refers to all direct manufacturing costs and manufacturing overhead costs incurred during 2017 for all goods worked on during the year. Cellular Products classifies its manufacturing costs into the three categories described earlier.

(i) Direct materials used in 2017 (shaded light blue in Exhibit 2-8, Panel B)	$ 76,000
(ii) Direct manufacturing labor in 2017 (shaded blue in Exhibit 2-8, Panel B)	9,000
(iii) Manufacturing overhead costs in 2017 (shaded dark blue in Exhibit 2-8, Panel B)	20,000
Total manufacturing costs incurred in 2017	$105,000

Note how in Exhibit 2-7 these costs increase work-in-process inventory.

EXHIBIT 2-8 Income Statement and Schedule of Cost of Goods Manufactured of a Manufacturing-Sector Company, Cellular Products

	A	B	C	D
	Home Insert Page Layout Formulas Data Review View			
1	**PANEL A: INCOME STATEMENT**			
2	**Cellular Products**			
3	**Income Statement**			
4	**For the Year Ended December 31, 2017 (in thousands)**			
5	Revenues		$210,000	
6	Cost of goods sold:			
7	Beginning finished goods inventory, January 1, 2017	$ 22,000		
8	Cost of goods manufactured (see Panel B)	104,000 ◄		
9	Cost of goods available for sale	126,000		
10	Ending finished goods inventory, December 31, 2017	18,000		
11	Cost of goods sold		108,000	
12	Gross margin (or gross profit)		102,000	
13	Operating (period) costs:			
14	R&D, design, mktg., dist., and cust.-service cost	70,000		
15	Total operating costs		70,000	
16	Operating income		$ 32,000	
17				
18	**PANEL B: COST OF GOODS MANUFACTURED**			
19	**Cellular Products**			
20	**Schedule of Cost of Goods Manufactured**[a]			
21	**For the Year Ended December 31, 2017 (in thousands)**			
22	Direct materials:			
23	Beginning inventory, January 1, 2017	$ 11,000		
24	Purchases of direct materials	73,000		
25	Cost of direct materials available for use	84,000		
26	Ending inventory, December 31, 2017	8,000		
27	Direct materials used		$ 76,000	
28	Direct manufacturing labor		9,000	
29	Manufacturing overhead costs:			
30	Indirect manufacturing labor	$ 7,000		
31	Supplies	2,000		
32	Heat, light, and power	5,000		
33	Depreciation—plant building	2,000		
34	Depreciation—plant equipment	3,000		
35	Miscellaneous	1,000		
36	Total manufacturing overhead costs		20,000	
37	Manufacturing costs incurred during 2017		105,000	
38	Beginning work-in-process inventory, January 1, 2017		6,000	
39	Total manufacturing costs to account for		111,000	
40	Ending work-in-process inventory, December 31, 2017		7,000	
41	Cost of goods manufactured (to income statement)		$104,000	
42	[a]Note that this schedule can become a schedule of cost of goods manufactured and sold simply by including the beginning and ending finished goods inventory figures in the supporting schedule rather than in the body of the income statement.			

STEP 4 (rows 6–11)
STEP 1 (rows 22–26)
STEP 2 (rows 29–36)
STEP 3 (rows 37–41)

Diana Corporation provides the following information for 2017:

 2-2 **TRY IT!**

Beginning inventory of direct materials, 1/1/2017	$12,000
Purchases of direct materials in 2017	$85,000
Ending inventory of direct materials 12/31/2017	$ 7,000
Direct manufacturing labor costs in 2017	$30,000
Manufacturing overhead costs in 2017	$40,000

Calculate the total manufacturing costs incurred in 2017

Step 3: Cost of goods manufactured in 2017. Cost of goods manufactured refers to the cost of goods brought to completion, whether they were started before or during the current accounting period.

Note how the work-in-process inventory box in Exhibit 2-7 has a very similar structure to the direct materials inventory box described in Step 1. Beginning work-in-process inventory of $6,000 and total manufacturing costs incurred in 2017 of $105,000 "fill up" the work-in-process inventory box. Some of the manufacturing costs incurred during 2017 are held back as the cost of the ending work-in-process inventory. The ending work-in-process inventory of $7,000 becomes the beginning inventory for the next year, and the $104,000 cost of goods manufactured during 2017 "empties out" the work-in-process inventory while "filling up" the finished-goods inventory box.

The cost of goods manufactured in 2017 (shaded green) is calculated in Exhibit 2-8, Panel B, as follows:

Beginning work-in-process inventory, January 1, 2017	$ 6,000
+ Total manufacturing costs incurred in 2017	105,000
= Total manufacturing costs to account for	111,000
− Ending work-in-process inventory, December 31, 2017	7,000
= Cost of goods manufactured in 2017	$104,000

Step 4: Cost of goods sold in 2017. The cost of goods sold is the cost of finished-goods inventory sold to customers during the current accounting period. Looking at the finished-goods inventory box in Exhibit 2-7, we see that the beginning inventory of finished goods of $22,000 and cost of goods manufactured in 2017 of $104,000 "fill up" the finished-goods inventory box. The ending inventory of finished goods of $18,000 becomes the beginning inventory for the next year, and the $108,000 cost of goods sold during 2017 "empties out" the finished-goods inventory.

This cost of goods sold is an expense that is matched against revenues. The cost of goods sold for Cellular Products (shaded olive green) is computed in Exhibit 2-8, Panel A, as follows:

Beginning inventory of finished goods, January 1, 2017	$ 22,000
+ Cost of goods manufactured in 2017	104,000
− Ending inventory of finished goods, December 31, 2017	18,000
= Cost of goods sold in 2017	$108,000

Exhibit 2-9 shows related general ledger T-accounts for Cellular Products' manufacturing cost flow. Note how the cost of goods manufactured ($104,000) is the cost of all goods completed during the accounting period. These costs are all inventoriable costs. Goods completed during the period are transferred to finished-goods inventory. These costs become cost of goods sold in the accounting period when the goods are sold. Also note that the direct materials, direct manufacturing labor, and manufacturing overhead costs of the units in work-in-process inventory ($7,000) and finished-goods inventory ($18,000) as of December 31, 2017, will appear as an asset in the balance sheet. These costs will become expenses next year when the work-in-process inventory is converted to finished goods and the finished goods are sold.

EXHIBIT 2-9	General Ledger T-Accounts for Cellular Products' Manufacturing Cost Flow (in thousands)

Work-in-Process Inventory				Finished Goods Inventory				Cost of Goods Sold	
Bal. Jan. 1, 2017	6,000	Cost of goods		Bal. Jan. 1, 2017	22,000	Cost of		108,000	
Direct materials used	76,000	manufactured	104,000 →		→ 104,000	goods sold	108,000 ⌐		
Direct manuf. labor	9,000			Bal. Dec. 31, 2017	18,000				
Indirect manuf. costs	20,000								
Bal. Dec. 31, 2017	7,000								

TRY IT! 2-3

Diana Corporation provides the following information for 2017:

Beginning work-in-process inventory, 1/1/2017	$ 9,000
Total manufacturing costs incurred in 2017	$160,000
Ending work-in-process inventory, 12/31/2017	$ 8,000
Beginning inventory of finished goods, 1/1/2017	$ 15,000
Ending inventory of finished goods, 12/31/2017	$ 21,000

Calculate (a) Cost of goods manufactured in 2017 and (b) Cost of goods sold in 2017

We can now prepare Cellular Products' income statement for 2017. The income statement of Cellular Products is shown on the right side in Exhibit 2-7 and in Exhibit 2-8, Panel A. Revenues of Cellular Products are (in thousands) $210,000. Inventoriable costs expensed during 2017 equal cost of goods sold of $108,000.

Gross margin = Revenues − Cost of goods sold = $210,000 − $108,000 = $102,000.

The $70,000 of operating costs composed of R&D, design, marketing, distribution, and customer-service costs are period costs of Cellular Products. These period costs include, for example, salaries of salespersons, depreciation on computers and other equipment used in marketing, and the cost of leasing warehouse space for distribution. **Operating income** equals total revenues from operations minus cost of goods sold and operating (period) costs (excluding interest expense and income taxes) or, equivalently, gross margin minus period costs. The operating income of Cellular Products is $32,000 (gross margin, $102,000 − period costs, $70,000). If you are familiar with financial accounting, recall that period costs are typically called selling, general, and administrative expenses in the income statement.

Newcomers to cost accounting frequently assume that indirect costs such as rent, telephone, and depreciation are always costs of the period in which they are incurred and are not associated with inventories. When these costs are incurred in marketing or in corporate headquarters, they are period costs. However, when these costs are incurred in manufacturing, they are manufacturing overhead costs and are inventoriable.

Because costs that are inventoried are not expensed until the units associated with them are sold, a manager can produce more units than are expected to be sold in a period without reducing a firm's net income. In fact, building up inventory in this way defers the expensing of the current period's fixed manufacturing costs as manufacturing costs are inventoried and not expensed until the units are sold in a subsequent period. This in turn actually *increases* the firm's gross margin and operating income even though there is no increase in sales, causing outsiders to believe that the company is more profitable than it actually is. We will discuss this risky accounting practice in greater detail in Chapter 9.

Recap of Inventoriable Costs and Period Costs

Exhibit 2-7 highlights the differences between inventoriable costs and period costs for a manufacturing company. The manufacturing costs of finished goods include direct materials, direct manufacturing labor, and manufacturing overhead costs such as supervision, production control, and machine maintenance. All these costs are inventoriable: They are assigned to work-in-process inventory until the goods are completed and then to finished-goods inventory until the goods are sold. All nonmanufacturing costs, such as R&D, design, and distribution costs, are period costs.

Inventoriable costs and period costs flow through the income statement at a merchandising company similar to the way costs flow at a manufacturing company. At a merchandising company, however, the flow of costs is much simpler to understand and track. Exhibit 2-10 shows the inventoriable costs and period costs for a retailer or wholesaler, which buys goods for resale. The only inventoriable cost is the cost of merchandise. (This corresponds to the cost of finished goods manufactured for a manufacturing company.) Purchased goods are held as merchandise inventory, the cost of which is shown as an asset in the balance sheet. As the goods are sold, their costs are shown in the income statement as cost of goods sold. A retailer or wholesaler also has a variety of marketing, distribution, and customer-service costs, which are period costs. In the income statement, period costs are deducted from revenues without ever having been included as part of inventory.

DECISION POINT

What is the flow of inventoriable and period costs in manufacturing and merchandising settings?

Prime Costs and Conversion Costs

Two terms used to describe cost classifications in manufacturing costing systems are *prime costs* and *conversion costs*. **Prime costs** are all direct manufacturing costs. For Cellular Products,

Prime costs = Direct material costs + Direct manufacturing labor costs = $76,000 + $9,000 = $85,000

As we have already discussed, the greater the proportion of prime costs (or direct costs) to total costs, the more confident managers can be about the accuracy of the costs of products. As information-gathering technology improves, companies can add more and more direct-cost categories. For example, power costs might be metered in specific areas of a plant and identified as a direct cost of specific products. Furthermore, if a production line were dedicated to manufacturing a specific product, the depreciation on the production equipment would be a direct manufacturing cost and would be included in prime costs. Computer software companies often have a "purchased technology" direct manufacturing cost item. This item, which represents payments to suppliers who develop software algorithms for a product, is also included in prime costs. **Conversion costs** are all manufacturing costs other than direct

EXHIBIT 2-10   Flow of Revenues and Costs for a Merchandising Company (Retailer or Wholesaler)

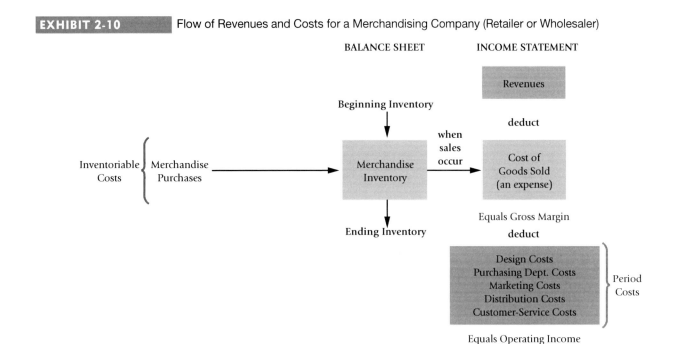

material costs. Conversion costs represent all manufacturing costs incurred to convert direct materials into finished goods. For Cellular Products,

$$\text{Conversion costs} = \frac{\text{Direct manufacturing}}{\text{labor costs}} + \frac{\text{Manufacturing}}{\text{overhead costs}} = \$9,000 + \$20,000 = \$29,000$$

Note that direct manufacturing labor costs are a part of both prime costs and conversion costs.

Some manufacturing operations, such as computer-integrated manufacturing (CIM) plants, have very few workers. The workers' roles are to monitor the manufacturing process and to maintain the equipment that produces multiple products. The costing systems in CIM plants do not have a direct manufacturing labor cost category because direct manufacturing labor cost is relatively small and because it is difficult to trace this cost to products. In a CIM plant, the only prime cost is the cost of direct materials. The conversion costs for such a plant are largely manufacturing overhead costs.

Measuring Costs Requires Judgment

Measuring costs requires judgment. That's because there are alternative ways for managers to define and classify costs. Different companies or sometimes even different subunits within the same company may define and classify costs differently. Be careful to define and understand the ways costs are measured in a company or situation. We first illustrate this point for labor costs.

Measuring Labor Costs

Consider labor costs for software programming at companies such as Apple, where programmers work on different software applications for products like the iMac, the iPad, and the iPhone. Although labor cost classifications vary among companies, many companies use multiple labor cost categories:

- Direct programming labor costs that can be traced to individual products
- Overhead costs (labor related)
  - Indirect labor compensation for
    Office staff
    Office security
    Rework labor (time spent by direct laborers correcting software errors)
    Overtime premium paid to software programmers (explained next)
    Idle time (explained next)
  - Salaries for managers, department heads, and supervisors
  - Payroll fringe costs, for example, health care premiums and pension costs (explained later)

To retain information on different categories, *indirect labor costs* are commonly divided into many subclassifications, for example, office staff and idle time costs. Note that managers' salaries usually are not classified as indirect labor costs. Instead, the compensation of supervisors, department heads, and all others who are regarded as management is placed in a separate classification of labor-related overhead.

Overtime Premium and Idle Time

Managers need to pay special attention to two classes of indirect labor—overtime premium and idle time. **Overtime premium** is the wage rate paid to workers (for both direct labor and indirect labor) in *excess* of their straight-time wage rates. Overtime premium is usually considered to be a part of indirect costs or overhead. Consider the example of George Flexner, a junior software programmer who writes software for multiple products. He is paid $40 per hour for straight-time and $60 per hour (time and a half) for overtime. His overtime premium is $20 per overtime hour. If he works 44 hours, including 4 overtime hours, in one week, his gross compensation would be classified as follows:

Direct programming labor: 44 hours × $40 per hour	$1,760
Overtime premium: 4 hours × $20 per hour	80
Total compensation for 44 hours	$1,840

In this example, why is the overtime premium of direct programming labor usually considered an overhead cost rather than a direct cost? After all, the premium can be traced to specific products that George worked on while working overtime. Overtime premium is generally not considered a direct cost because the particular job that George worked on during the overtime hours is a matter of chance. For example, assume that George worked on two products for 5 hours each on a specific workday that lasted 10 hours, including 2 overtime hours. Should the product George worked on during hours 9 and 10 be assigned the overtime premium? Or should the premium be prorated over both products? Prorating the overtime premium does not "penalize"—add to the cost of—a particular product solely because it happened to be worked on during the overtime hours. *Instead, the overtime premium is considered to be attributable to the heavy overall volume of work. Its cost is regarded as part of overhead, which is borne by both products.*

Sometimes, though, overtime can definitely be attributed to a single product. For example, the overtime needed to meet the launch deadline for a new product may clearly be the sole source of overtime. In such instances, the overtime premium is regarded as a direct cost of that product.

Another subclassification of indirect labor is the idle time of both direct and indirect labor. **Idle time** refers to the wages paid for unproductive time caused by lack of orders, machine or computer breakdowns, work delays, poor scheduling, and the like. For example, if George had no work for 3 hours during that week while waiting to receive code from another colleague, George's earnings would be classified as follows:

Direct programming labor: 41 hours × $40/hour	$1,640
Idle time (overhead): 3 hours × $40/hour	120
Overtime premium (overhead): 4 hours × $20/hour	80
Total earnings for 44 hours	$1,840

Clearly, in this case, the idle time is not related to a particular product, nor, as we have already discussed, is the overtime premium. Both the overtime premium and the costs of idle time are considered overhead costs.

Benefits of Defining Accounting Terms

Managers, accountants, suppliers, and others will avoid many problems if they thoroughly understand and agree on the classifications and meanings of the cost terms introduced in this chapter and later in this book. Consider the classification of programming labor *payroll fringe costs*, which include employer payments for employee benefits such as Social Security, life insurance, health insurance, and pensions. Consider, for example, a software programmer who is paid a wage of $40 an hour with fringe benefits totaling, say, $10 per hour. Some companies classify the $40 as a direct programming labor cost of the product for which the software is being written and the $10 as overhead cost. Other companies classify the entire $50 as direct programming labor cost. The latter approach is preferable because the stated wage and the fringe benefit costs together are a fundamental part of acquiring direct software programming labor services.

Caution: In every situation, it is important for managers and management accountants to pinpoint clearly what direct labor includes and what direct labor excludes. This clarity will help prevent disputes regarding cost-reimbursement contracts, income tax payments, and labor union matters, which often can take a substantial amount of time for managers to resolve. Consider that some countries, such as Costa Rica and Mauritius, offer substantial income tax savings to foreign companies that generate employment within their borders. In some cases, to qualify for the tax benefits, the direct labor costs must at least equal a specified percentage of a company's total costs.

When managers do not precisely define direct labor costs, disputes can arise about whether payroll fringe costs should be included as part of direct labor costs when calculating the direct labor percentage for qualifying for such tax benefits. Companies have sought to classify payroll fringe costs as part of direct labor costs to make direct labor costs a higher percentage of total costs. Tax authorities have argued that payroll fringe costs are part of overhead. In addition to payroll fringe costs, other debated items are compensation for training time, idle time, vacations, sick leave, and overtime premium. To prevent disputes, contracts and laws should be as specific as possible about accounting definitions and measurements.

Different Meanings of Product Costs

At a more general level, many cost terms used by organizations have ambiguous meanings. Consider the term *product cost*. A **product cost** is the sum of the costs assigned to a product for a specific purpose. Different purposes can result in different measures of product cost, as the brackets on the value chain in Exhibit 2-11 illustrate:

- **Pricing and product-mix decisions.** For the purposes of making decisions about pricing and promoting products that generate the most profits, managers are interested in the overall (total) profitability of different products and, consequently, assign costs incurred in all business functions of the value chain to the different products.

- **Reimbursement under government contracts.** Government contracts often reimburse contractors on the basis of the "cost of a product" plus a prespecified margin of profit. A contract such as this is referred to as a "cost-plus" agreement. Cost-plus agreements are typically used for services and development contracts when it is not easy to predict the amount of money required to design, fabricate, and test items. Because these contracts transfer the risk of cost overruns to the government, agencies such as the Department of Defense and the Department of Energy provide detailed guidelines on the cost items they will allow (and disallow) when calculating the cost of a product. For example, many government agencies explicitly exclude marketing, distribution, and customer-service costs from product costs that qualify for reimbursement, and they may only partially reimburse R&D costs. These agencies want to reimburse contractors for only those costs most closely related to delivering products under the contract. The second bracket in Exhibit 2-11 shows how the product-cost calculations for a specific contract may allow for all design and production costs but only part of R&D costs.

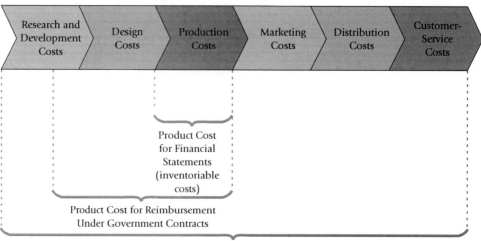

EXHIBIT 2-11

Different Product Costs for Different Purposes

1. Business function
   a. Research and development
   b. Design of products and processes
   c. Production
   d. Marketing
   e. Distribution
   f. Customer service
2. Assignment to a cost object
   a. Direct cost
   b. Indirect cost
3. Behavior pattern in relation to the level of activity or volume
   a. Variable cost
   b. Fixed cost
4. Aggregate or average
   a. Total cost
   b. Unit cost
5. Assets or expenses
   a. Inventoriable cost
   b. Period cost

- **Preparing financial statements for external reporting under Generally Accepted Accounting Principles (GAAP).** Under GAAP, only manufacturing costs can be assigned to inventories in the financial statements. For the purposes of calculating inventory costs, product costs include only inventoriable (production) costs.

As Exhibit 2-11 illustrates, product-cost measures range from a narrow set of costs for financial statements—a set that includes only production costs—to a broader set of costs for reimbursement under government contracts to a still broader set of costs for pricing and product-mix decisions.

 This section focused on how different purposes result in the inclusion of different cost items of the value chain of business functions when product costs are calculated. The same caution about the need to be clear and precise about cost concepts and their measurement applies to each cost classification introduced in this chapter. Exhibit 2-12 summarizes the key cost classifications. Using the five-step process described in Chapter 1, think about how these different classifications of costs help managers make decisions and evaluate performance.

1. **Identify the problem and uncertainties.** Consider a decision about how much to price a product. This decision often depends on how much it costs to make the product.

2. **Obtain information.** Managers identify the direct and indirect costs of a product in each business function. Managers also gather other information about customers, competitors, and the prices of competing products.

3. **Make predictions about the future.** Managers estimate what it will cost to make the product in the future. This requires managers to predict the quantity of the product they expect the company to sell as well as have an understanding of fixed and variable costs.

4. **Make decisions by choosing among alternatives.** Managers choose a price to charge based on a thorough understanding of costs and other information.

5. **Implement the decision, evaluate performance, and learn.** Managers control costs and learn by comparing the actual total and unit costs against budgeted amounts.

The next section describes how the basic concepts introduced in this chapter lead to a framework for understanding cost accounting and cost management that can then be applied to the study of many topics, such as strategy evaluation, quality, and investment decisions.

A Framework for Cost Accounting and Cost Management

The following three features of cost accounting and cost management can be used for a wide range of applications:

1. Calculating the cost of products, services, and other cost objects

2. Obtaining information for planning and control and performance evaluation

3. Analyzing the relevant information for making decisions

DECISION POINT

Why do managers assign different costs to the same cost object?

LEARNING OBJECTIVE 8

Describe a framework for cost accounting and cost management

…three features that help managers make decisions

We develop these ideas in Chapters 3 through 11. The ideas also form the foundation for the study of various topics later in the book.

Calculating the Cost of Products, Services, and Other Cost Objects

You have already learned that costing systems trace direct costs and allocate indirect costs to products. Chapters 4 and 5 describe systems such as job costing and activity-based costing, which are used to calculate total costs and unit costs of products and services. The chapters also discuss how managers use this information to formulate strategies and make pricing, product-mix, and cost-management decisions.

Obtaining Information for Planning and Control and Performance Evaluation

Budgeting is the most commonly used tool for planning and control. A budget forces managers to look ahead, to translate a company's strategy into plans, to coordinate and communicate within the organization, and to provide a benchmark for evaluating the company's performance. Managers strive to meet their budget targets, so budgeting often affects the behavior of a company's personnel and the decisions they make. Chapter 6 describes budgeting systems.

At the end of a reporting period, managers compare the company's actual results to its planned performance. The managers' tasks are to understand why differences (called variances) between actual and planned performance arise and to use the information provided by these variances as feedback to promote learning and future improvement. Managers also use variances as well as nonfinancial measures, such as defect rates and customer satisfaction ratings, to control and evaluate the performance of various departments, divisions, and managers. Chapters 7 and 8 discuss variance analysis. Chapter 9 describes planning, control, and inventory-costing issues relating to capacity. Chapters 6, 7, 8, and 9 focus on the management accountant's role in implementing strategy.

Analyzing the Relevant Information for Making Decisions

When designing strategies and implementing them, managers must understand which revenues and costs to consider and which ones to ignore. Management accountants help managers identify what information is relevant and what information is irrelevant. Consider a decision about whether to buy a product from an outside vendor or make it in-house. The costing system indicates that it costs $25 per unit to make the product in-house. A vendor offers to sell the product for $22 per unit. At first glance, it seems it will cost less for the company to buy the product rather than make it. Suppose, however, that of the $25 to make the product in-house, $5 consists of plant lease costs that the company has already paid under a lease contract. Furthermore, if the product is bought, the plant will remain idle because it is too costly to retool the plant to make another product. That is, there is no opportunity to use the plant in some other profitable way. Under these conditions, it will cost less to make the product than to buy it. That's because making the product costs only an *additional* $20 per unit ($25 − $5), compared with an *additional* $22 per unit if it is bought. The $5 per unit of lease cost is irrelevant to the decision because it is a *past* (or *sunk*) cost that has already been incurred regardless of whether the product is made or bought. Analyzing relevant information is a key aspect of making decisions.

When making strategic decisions about which products and how much to produce, managers must know how revenues and costs vary with changes in output levels. For this purpose, managers need to distinguish fixed costs from variable costs. Chapter 3 analyzes how operating income changes with changes in units sold and how managers use this information to make decisions such as how much to spend on advertising. Chapter 10 describes methods to estimate the fixed and variable components of costs. Chapter 11 applies the concept of relevance to decision making in many different situations and describes methods managers use to maximize income given the resource constraints they face.

Later chapters in the book discuss topics such as strategy evaluation, customer profitability, quality, just-in-time systems, investment decisions, transfer pricing, and performance evaluation. Each of these topics invariably has product costing, planning and control, and decision-making perspectives. A command of the first 11 chapters will help you master these topics. For example, Chapter 12 on strategy describes the balanced scorecard, a set of financial and nonfinancial measures used to implement strategy that builds on the planning and control functions. The section on strategic analysis of operating income builds on ideas of product costing and variance analysis. The section on downsizing and managing capacity builds on ideas of relevant revenues and relevant costs.

DECISION POINT

What are the three key features of cost accounting and cost management?

PROBLEM FOR SELF-STUDY

Foxwood Company is a metal- and woodcutting manufacturer, selling products to the home-construction market. Consider the following data for 2017:

Sandpaper	$ 2,000
Materials-handling costs	70,000
Lubricants and coolants	5,000
Miscellaneous indirect manufacturing labor	40,000
Direct manufacturing labor	300,000
Direct materials inventory, Jan. 1, 2017	40,000
Direct materials inventory, Dec. 31, 2017	50,000
Finished-goods inventory, Jan. 1, 2017	100,000
Finished-goods inventory, Dec. 31, 2017	150,000
Work-in-process inventory, Jan. 1, 2017	10,000
Work-in-process inventory, Dec. 31, 2017	14,000
Plant-leasing costs	54,000
Depreciation—plant equipment	36,000
Property taxes on plant equipment	4,000
Fire insurance on plant equipment	3,000
Direct materials purchased	460,000
Revenues	1,360,000
Marketing promotions	60,000
Marketing salaries	100,000
Distribution costs	70,000
Customer-service costs	100,000

Required

1. Prepare an income statement with a separate supporting schedule of cost of goods manufactured. For all manufacturing items, classify costs as direct costs or indirect costs and indicate by V or F whether each is a variable cost or a fixed cost (when the cost object is a product unit). If in doubt, decide on the basis of whether the total cost will change substantially over a wide range of units produced.
2. Suppose that both the direct material costs and the plant-leasing costs are for the production of 900,000 units. What is the direct material cost of each unit produced? What is the plant-leasing cost per unit? Assume that the plant-leasing cost is a fixed cost.
3. Suppose Foxwood Company manufactures 1,000,000 units next year. Repeat the computation in requirement 2 for direct materials and plant-leasing costs. Assume the implied cost-behavior patterns persist.
4. As a management consultant, explain concisely to the company president why the unit cost for direct materials did not change in requirements 2 and 3 but the unit cost for plant-leasing costs did change.

Solution

1.

Foxwood Company
Income Statement
For the Year Ended December 31, 2017

Revenues		$ 1,360,000
Cost of goods sold		
Beginning finished-goods inventory, January 1, 2017	$ 100,000	
Cost of goods manufactured (see the following schedule)	960,000	
Cost of goods available for sale	1,060,000	
Deduct ending finished-goods inventory, December 31, 2017	150,000	910,000
Gross margin (or gross profit)		450,000
Operating costs		
Marketing promotions	60,000	
Marketing salaries	100,000	
Distribution costs	70,000	
Customer-service costs	100,000	330,000
Operating income		$ 120,000

Foxwood Company
Schedule of Cost of Goods Manufactured
For the Year Ended December 31, 2017

Direct materials		
Beginning inventory, January 1, 2017		$ 40,000
Purchases of direct materials		460,000
Cost of direct materials available for use		500,000
Ending inventory, December 31, 2017		50,000
Direct materials used		450,000 (V)
Direct manufacturing labor		300,000 (V)
Indirect manufacturing costs		
Sandpaper	$ 2,000 (V)	
Materials-handling costs	70,000 (V)	
Lubricants and coolants	5,000 (V)	
Miscellaneous indirect manufacturing labor	40,000 (V)	
Plant-leasing costs	54,000 (F)	
Depreciation—plant equipment	36,000 (F)	
Property taxes on plant equipment	4,000 (F)	
Fire insurance on plant equipment	3,000 (F)	214,000
Manufacturing costs incurred during 2017		964,000
Beginning work-in-process inventory, January 1, 2017		10,000
Total manufacturing costs to account for		974,000
Ending work-in-process inventory, December 31, 2017		14,000
Cost of goods manufactured (to income statement)		$ 960,000

2. Direct material unit cost = Direct materials used ÷ Units produced
$$= \$450{,}000 \div 900{,}000 \text{ units} = \$0.50 \text{ per unit}$$
   Plant-leasing unit cost = Plant-leasing costs ÷ Units produced
$$= \$54{,}000 \div 900{,}000 \text{ units} = \$0.06 \text{ per unit}$$

3. The direct material costs are variable, so they would increase in total from $450,000 to $500,000 (1,000,000 units × $0.50 per unit). However, their unit cost would be unaffected: $500,000 ÷ 1,000,000 units = $0.50 per unit.

   In contrast, the plant-leasing costs of $54,000 are fixed, so they would not increase in total. However, the plant-leasing cost per unit would decline from $0.060 to $0.054: $54,000 ÷ 1,000,000 units = $0.054 per unit.

4. The explanation would begin with the answer to requirement 3. As a consultant, you should stress that the unitizing (averaging) of costs that have different behavior patterns can be misleading. A common error is to assume that a total unit cost, which is often a sum of variable unit cost and fixed unit cost, is an indicator that total costs change in proportion to changes in production levels. The next chapter demonstrates the necessity for distinguishing between cost-behavior patterns. You must be wary, especially about average fixed cost per unit. Too often, unit fixed cost is erroneously regarded as being indistinguishable from unit variable cost.

DECISION **POINTS**

The following question-and-answer format summarizes the chapter's learning objectives. Each decision presents a key question related to a learning objective. The guidelines are the answer to that question.

Decision	Guidelines
1. What is a cost object?	A cost object is anything for which a manager needs a separate measurement of cost. Examples include a product, a service, a project, a customer, a brand category, an activity, and a department.
2. How do managers decide whether a cost is a direct or an indirect cost?	A direct cost is any cost that is related to a particular cost object and can be traced to that cost object in an economically feasible way. Indirect costs are related to a particular cost object but cannot be traced to it in an economically feasible way. The same cost can be direct for one cost object and indirect for another cost object. This book uses *cost tracing* to describe the assignment of direct costs to a cost object and *cost allocation* to describe the assignment of indirect costs to a cost object.
3. How do managers decide whether a cost is a variable or a fixed cost?	A variable cost changes *in total* in proportion to changes in the related level of total activity or volume of output produced. A fixed cost remains unchanged *in total* for a given time period despite wide changes in the related level of total activity or volume of output produced.
4. How should managers estimate and interpret cost information?	In general, focus on total costs, not unit costs. When making total cost estimates think of variable costs as an amount per unit and fixed costs as a total amount. Interpret the unit cost of a cost object cautiously when it includes a fixed-cost component.
5. What are the differences in the accounting for inventoriable versus period costs?	Inventoriable costs are all costs of a product that a company regards as an asset in the accounting period in which they are incurred and which become cost of goods sold in the accounting period in which the product is sold. Period costs are expensed in the accounting period in which they are incurred and are all of the costs in an income statement other than cost of goods sold.

Decision	Guidelines
6. What is the flow of inventoriable and period costs in manufacturing and merchandising settings?	In manufacturing settings, inventoriable costs flow through work-in-process and finished-goods accounts, and are expensed as cost of goods sold. Period costs are expensed as they are incurred. In merchandising settings, only the cost of merchandise is treated as inventoriable.
7. Why do managers assign different costs to the same cost objects?	Managers can assign different costs to the same cost object depending on the purpose. For example, for the external reporting purpose in a manufacturing company, the inventoriable cost of a product includes only manufacturing costs. In contrast, costs from all business functions of the value chain often are assigned to a product for pricing and product-mix decisions.
8. What are the three key features of cost accounting and cost management?	Three features of cost accounting and cost management are (1) calculating the cost of products, services, and other cost objects; (2) obtaining information for planning and control and performance evaluation; and (3) analyzing relevant information for making decisions.

TERMS TO LEARN

This chapter contains more basic terms than any other in this book. Do not proceed before you check your understanding of the following terms. The chapter and the Glossary at the end of the book contain definitions of the following important terms:

actual cost (**p. 49**)
average cost (**p. 56**)
budgeted cost (**p. 49**)
conversion costs (**p. 65**)
cost (**p. 49**)
cost accumulation (**p. 49**)
cost allocation (**p. 50**)
cost assignment (**p. 50**)
cost driver (**p. 54**)
cost object (**p. 49**)
cost of goods manufactured (**p. 63**)
cost tracing (**p. 50**)
direct costs of a cost object (**p. 49**)

direct manufacturing labor costs (**p. 59**)
direct materials costs (**p. 59**)
direct materials inventory (**p. 58**)
factory overhead costs (**p. 59**)
finished-goods inventory (**p. 58**)
fixed cost (**p. 52**)
idle time (**p. 67**)
indirect costs of a cost object (**p. 50**)
indirect manufacturing costs (**p. 59**)
inventoriable costs (**p. 59**)
manufacturing overhead costs (**p. 59**)
manufacturing-sector companies
 (**p. 58**)

merchandising-sector companies (**p. 58**)
operating income (**p. 64**)
overtime premium (**p. 66**)
period costs (**p. 59**)
prime costs (**p. 65**)
product cost (**p. 68**)
relevant range (**p. 55**)
revenues (**p. 59**)
service-sector companies (**p. 58**)
unit cost (**p. 56**)
variable cost (**p. 52**)
work-in-process inventory (**p. 58**)
work in progress (**p. 58**)

ASSIGNMENT MATERIAL

Pearson MyLab Accounting
Questions

2-1 Define cost object and give three examples.

2-2 What is the main difference between direct costs and indirect costs?

2-3 Why do managers consider direct costs to be more accurate than indirect costs?

2-4 Name three factors that will affect the classification of a cost as direct or indirect.

2-5 Explain whether a business department can be a cost object.

2-6 What is a cost driver? Give one example.

2-7 What is the relevant range? What role does the relevant-range concept play in explaining how costs behave?

2-8 Why and when is it essential to calculate a unit cost?

2-9 Describe how manufacturing-, merchandising-, and service-sector companies differ from one another.

2-10 What are three different types of inventory that manufacturing companies hold?

2-11 Distinguish between inventoriable costs and period costs.

2-12 Define the following: direct material costs, direct manufacturing-labor costs, manufacturing overhead costs, prime costs, and conversion costs.

2-13 Why are overtime premium and idle time considered as indirect costs?

2-14 Define product cost. Describe three different purposes for computing product costs.

2-15 What are three common features of cost accounting and cost management?

Multiple-Choice Questions

In partnership with:

2-16 Applewhite Corporation, a manufacturing company, is analyzing its cost structure in a project to achieve some cost savings. Which of the following statements is/are correct?

I. The cost of the direct materials in Applewhite's products is considered a variable cost.

II. The cost of the depreciation of Applewhite's plant machinery is considered a variable cost because Applewhite uses an accelerated depreciation method for both book and income tax purposes.

III. The cost of electricity for Applewhite's manufacturing facility is considered a fixed cost, even if the cost of the electricity has both variable and fixed components.

1. I, II, and III are correct.
2. I only is correct.
3. II and III only are correct.
4. None of the listed choices is correct.

2-17 Comprehensive Care Nursing Home is required by statute and regulation to maintain a minimum 3 to 1 ratio of direct service staff to residents to maintain the licensure associated with the Nursing Home beds. The salary expense associated with direct service staff for the Comprehensive Care Nursing Home would most likely be classified as:

1. Variable cost.
2. Fixed cost.
3. Overhead costs.
4. Inventoriable costs.

2-18 Frisco Corporation is analyzing its fixed and variable costs within its current relevant range. As its cost driver activity changes within the relevant range, which of the following statements is/are correct?

I. As the cost driver level increases, total fixed cost remains unchanged.

II. As the cost driver level increases, unit fixed cost increases.

III. As the cost driver level decreases, unit variable cost decreases.

1. I, II, and III are correct.
2. I and II only are correct.
3. I only is correct.
4. II and III only are correct.

2-19 Year 1 financial data for the ABC Company is as follows:

Sales	$5,000,000
Direct materials	850,000
Direct manufacturing labor	1,700,000
Variable manufacturing overhead	400,000
Fixed manufacturing overhead	750,000
Variable SG&A	150,000
Fixed SG&A	250,000

Under the absorption method, Year 1 Cost of Goods sold will be:

a. $2,550,000   **c.** $3,100,000
b. $2,950,000   **d.** $3,700,000

2-20 The following information was extracted from the accounting records of Roosevelt Manufacturing Company:

Direct materials purchased	80,000
Direct materials used	76,000
Direct manufacturing labor costs	10,000
Indirect manufacturing labor costs	12,000
Sales salaries	14,000
Other plant expenses	22,000
Selling and administrative expenses	20,000

What was the cost of goods manufactured?

1. $124,000
2. $120,000
3. $154,000
4. $170,000

Pearson MyLab Accounting

Exercises

2-21 Computing and interpreting manufacturing unit costs. Minnesota Office Products (MOP) produces three different paper products at its Vaasa lumber plant: Supreme, Deluxe, and Regular. Each product has its own dedicated production line at the plant. It currently uses the following three-part classification for its manufacturing costs: direct materials, direct manufacturing labor, and manufacturing overhead costs. Total manufacturing overhead costs of the plant in July 2017 are $150 million ($15 million of which are fixed). This total amount is allocated to each product line on the basis of the direct manufacturing labor costs of each line. Summary data (in millions) for July 2017 are as follows:

	Supreme	Deluxe	Regular
Direct material costs	$ 89	$ 57	$ 60
Direct manufacturing labor costs	$ 16	$ 26	$ 8
Manufacturing overhead costs	$ 48	$ 78	$ 24
Units produced	125	150	140

Required

1. Compute the manufacturing cost per unit for each product produced in July 2017.
2. Suppose that, in August 2017, production was 150 million units of Supreme, 190 million units of Deluxe, and 220 million units of Regular. Why might the July 2017 information on manufacturing cost per unit be misleading when predicting total manufacturing costs in August 2017?

2-22 Direct, indirect, fixed, and variable costs. Sumitomo Cable manufactures various types of aluminum and copper cables which it sells directly to retail outlets through its distribution channels. The manufacturing process for producing cables includes a process called wire draw in which the aluminum and copper rods are pulled through a series of synthetic dies, which gradually decrease in size. The wires are then passed through an extruder, where either a single or a double coating of plastic is applied. These insulated wires are twisted into pairs by the Twisting and Stranding Department. The final shape is given to the wires by the Jacketing and Packaging department after carrying out the process of quality control.

Required

1. Costs involved in the different processes are listed below. For each cost, indicate whether it is a direct variable, direct fixed, indirect variable, or indirect fixed cost, assuming that the "units of production of each kind of wire" is the cost object.

Costs:

Aluminum and copper rods	Quality control
Insulating materials	Repairs to machines
Wages for wire draw	Normal wastages and spoilages
Depreciation on machineries	Store-keeper's salary
Depreciation on factory building	Material testing
Insurance on factory building	Materials used by jacketing and packaging department
Consumable stores and dies	Factory general utilities
Wages for machine operators	Fuel for factory generator
Power	Supervisors' salaries

2. If the cost object were the "Jacketing and Packaging department" instead, which costs from requirement 1 would now be direct instead of indirect costs?

2-23 Classification of costs, service sector. Market Focus is a marketing research firm that organizes focus groups for consumer-product companies. Each focus group has eight individuals who are paid $60 per session to provide comments on new products. These focus groups meet in hotels and are led by a trained, independent marketing specialist hired by Market Focus. Each specialist is paid a fixed retainer to conduct a minimum number of sessions and a per session fee of $2,200. A Market Focus staff member attends each session to ensure that all the logistical aspects run smoothly.

Classify each cost item **(A–H)** as follows:

Required

a. Direct or indirect (D or I) costs of each individual focus group.

b. Variable or fixed (V or F) costs of how the total costs of Market Focus change as the number of focus groups conducted changes. (If in doubt, select on the basis of whether the total costs will change substantially if there is a large change in the number of groups conducted.)

You will have two answers (D or I; V or F) for each of the following items:

Cost Item	D or I	V or F
A. Payment to individuals in each focus group to provide comments on new products		
B. Annual subscription of Market Focus to *Consumer Reports* magazine		
C. Phone calls made by Market Focus staff member to confirm individuals will attend a focus group session (Records of individual calls are not kept.)		
D. Retainer paid to focus group leader to conduct 18 focus groups per year on new medical products		
E. Recruiting cost to hire marketing specialists		
F. Lease payment by Market Focus for corporate office		
G. Cost of tapes used to record comments made by individuals in a focus group session (These tapes are sent to the company whose products are being tested.)		
H. Gasoline costs of Market Focus staff for company-owned vehicles (Staff members submit monthly bills with no mileage breakdowns.)		
I. Costs incurred to improve the design of focus groups to make them more effective		

2-24 Classification of costs, merchandising sector. Band Box Entertainment (BBE) operates a large store in Atlanta, Georgia. The store has both a movie (DVD) section and a music (CD) section. BBE reports revenues for the movie section separately from the music section.

Classify each cost item **(A–H)** as follows:

Required

a. Direct or indirect (D or I) costs of the total number of DVDs sold.

b. Variable or fixed (V or F) costs of how the total costs of the movie section change as the total number of DVDs sold changes. (If in doubt, select on the basis of whether the total costs will change substantially if there is a large change in the total number of DVDs sold.)

You will have two answers (D or I; V or F) for each of the following items:

Cost Item	D or I	V or F
A. Annual retainer paid to a video distributor		
B. Cost of store manager's salary		
C. Costs of DVDs purchased for sale to customers		
D. Subscription to *DVD Trends* magazine		
E. Leasing of computer software used for financial budgeting at the BBE store		
F. Cost of popcorn provided free to all customers of the BBE store		
G. Cost of cleaning the store every night after closing		
H. Freight-in costs of DVDs purchased by BBE		

2-25 Classification of costs, manufacturing sector. The Cooper Furniture Company of Potomac, Maryland, assembles two types of chairs (Recliners and Rockers). Separate assembly lines are used for each type of chair.

Classify each cost item **(A–I)** as follows:

Required

a. Direct or indirect (D or I) cost for the total number of Recliners assembled.

b. Variable or fixed (V or F) cost depending on how total costs change as the total number of Recliners assembled changes. (If in doubt, select on the basis of whether the total costs will change substantially if there is a large change in the total number of Recliners assembled.)

You will have two answers (D or I; V or F) for each of the following items:

Cost Item	D or I	V or F
A. Cost of fabric used on Recliners		
B. Salary of public relations manager for Cooper Furniture		
C. Annual convention for furniture manufacturers; generally Cooper Furniture attends		
D. Cost of lubricant used on the Recliner assembly line		
E. Freight costs of Recliner frames shipped from Durham to Potomac, MD		
F. Electricity costs for Recliner assembly line (single bill covers entire plant)		
G. Wages paid to temporary assembly-line workers hired in periods of high Recliner production (paid on hourly basis)		
H. Annual fire-insurance policy cost for Potomac, MD plant		
I. Wages paid to plant manager who oversees the assembly lines for both chair types		

2-26 Variable costs, fixed costs, total costs. Bridget Ashton is getting ready to open a small restaurant. She is on a tight budget and must choose between the following long-distance phone plans:

Plan A: Pay 10 cents per minute of long-distance calling.

Plan B: Pay a fixed monthly fee of $15 for up to 240 long-distance minutes and 8 cents per minute thereafter (if she uses fewer than 240 minutes in any month, she still pays $15 for the month).

Plan C: Pay a fixed monthly fee of $22 for up to 510 long-distance minutes and 5 cents per minute thereafter (if she uses fewer than 510 minutes, she still pays $22 for the month).

Required
1. Draw a graph of the total monthly costs of the three plans for different levels of monthly long-distance calling.
2. Which plan should Ashton choose if she expects to make 100 minutes of long-distance calls? 240 minutes? 540 minutes?

2-27 Variable and fixed costs. Consolidated Motors specializes in producing one specialty vehicle. It is called Surfer and is styled to easily fit multiple surfboards in its back area and top-mounted storage racks.

Consolidated has the following manufacturing costs:

Plant management costs, $1,992,000 per year

Cost of leasing equipment, $1,932,000 per year

Workers' wages, $800 per Surfer vehicle produced

Direct materials costs: Steel, $1,400 per Surfer; Tires, $150 per tire, each Surfer takes 5 tires (one spare).

City license, which is charged monthly based on the number of tires used in production:

0–500 tires	$ 40,040
501–1,000 tires	$ 65,000
more than 1,000 tires	$249,870

Consolidated currently produces 170 vehicles per month.

Required
1. What is the variable manufacturing cost per vehicle? What is the fixed manufacturing cost per month?
2. Plot a graph for the variable manufacturing costs and a second for the fixed manufacturing costs per month. How does the concept of relevant range relate to your graphs? Explain.
3. What is the total manufacturing cost of each vehicle if 80 vehicles are produced each month? 205 vehicles? How do you explain the difference in the manufacturing cost per unit?

2-28 Variable costs, fixed costs, relevant range. Dotball Candies manufactures jaw-breaker candies in a fully automated process. The machine that produces candies was purchased recently and can make 4,400 per month. The machine costs $9,500 and is depreciated using straight-line depreciation over 10 years assuming zero residual value. Rent for the factory space and warehouse and other fixed manufacturing overhead costs total $1,300 per month.

Dotball currently makes and sells 3,100 jaw-breakers per month. Dotball buys just enough materials each month to make the jaw-breakers it needs to sell. Materials cost 10 cents per jawbreaker. Next year Dotball expects demand to increase by 100%. At this volume of materials purchased, it will get a 10% discount on price. Rent and other fixed manufacturing overhead costs will remain the same.

Required
1. What is Dotball's current annual relevant range of output?
2. What is Dotball's current annual fixed manufacturing cost within the relevant range? What is the annual variable manufacturing cost?
3. What will Dotball's relevant range of output be next year? How, if at all, will total annual fixed and variable manufacturing costs change next year? Assume that if it needs to Dotball could buy an identical machine at the same cost as the one it already has.

2-29 **Cost drivers and value chain.** Torrance Technology Company (TTC) is developing a new touch-screen smartphone to compete in the cellular phone industry. The company will sell the phones at whole-sale prices to cell phone companies, which will in turn sell them in retail stores to the final customer. TTC has undertaken the following activities in its value chain to bring its product to market:

A. Perform market research on competing brands
B. Design a prototype of the TTC smartphone
C. Market the new design to cell phone companies
D. Manufacture the TTC smartphone
E. Process orders from cell phone companies
F. Deliver the TTC smartphones to the cell phone companies
G. Provide online assistance to cell phone users for use of the TTC smartphone
H. Make design changes to the smartphone based on customer feedback

During the process of product development, production, marketing, distribution, and customer service, TTC has kept track of the following cost drivers:

Number of smartphones shipped by TTC

Number of design changes

Number of deliveries made to cell phone companies

Engineering hours spent on initial product design

Hours spent researching competing market brands

Customer-service hours

Number of smartphone orders processed

Machine hours required to run the production equipment

1. Identify each value-chain activity listed at the beginning of the exercise with one of the following value-chain categories:
   a. Design of products and processes
   b. Production
   c. Marketing
   d. Distribution
   e. Customer service

2. Use the list of preceding cost drivers to find one or more reasonable cost drivers for each of the activities in TTC's value chain.

Required

2-30 **Cost drivers and functions.** The representative cost drivers in the right column of this table are randomized so they do not match the list of functions in the left column.

Function	Representative Cost Driver
1. Inspection of materials	**A.** Number of batches produced
2. Accounts receivable	**B.** Number of sales orders
3. Employee training	**C.** Number of machines repaired
4. Repairs of machines	**D.** Number of labors supervised
5. Testing of samples	**E.** Number of purchase orders
6. Dispatching	**F.** Number of bills issued to customers
7. Supervisions	**G.** Number of employees trained

1. Match each function with its representative cost driver.
2. Give a second example of a cost driver for each function.

Required

2-31 **Total costs and unit costs, service setting.** The Big Event (TBE) recently started a business organizing food and music at weddings and other large events. In order to better understand the profitability of the business, the owner has asked you for an analysis of costs—what costs are fixed, what costs are variable, and so on, for each event. You have the following cost information:

Music costs: $10,000 per event

Catering costs:

Food: $65 per guest

Setup/cleanup: $15 per guest

Fixed fee: $4,000 per event

TBE has allowed the caterer, who is also new in business, to place business cards on each table as a form of advertising. This has proved quite effective, and the caterer gives TBE a discount of $5 per guest in exchange for allowing the caterer to advertise.

Required

1. Draw a graph depicting fixed costs, variable costs, and total costs for each event versus the number of guests.
2. Suppose 150 persons attend the next event. What is TBE's total net cost and the cost per attendee?
3. Suppose instead that 200 persons attend. What is TBE's total net cost and the cost per attendee.
4. How should TBE charge customers for its services? Explain briefly.

2-32 Total and unit cost, decision making. Gayle's Glassworks makes glass flanges for scientific use. Materials cost $1 per flange, and the glass blowers are paid a wage rate of $28 per hour. A glass blower blows 10 flanges per hour. Fixed manufacturing costs for flanges are $28,000 per period. Period (nonmanufacturing) costs associated with flanges are $10,000 per period and are fixed.

Required

1. Graph the fixed, variable, and total manufacturing cost for flanges, using units (number of flanges) on the x-axis.
2. Assume Gayle's Glassworks manufactures and sells 5,000 flanges this period. Its competitor, Flora's Flasks, sells flanges for $10 each. Can Gayle sell below Flora's price and still make a profit on the flanges?
3. How would your answer to requirement 2 differ if Gayle's Glassworks made and sold 10,000 flanges this period? Why? What does this indicate about the use of unit cost in decision making?

2-33 Inventoriable costs versus period costs. Each of the following cost items pertains to one of these companies: Best Buy (a merchandising-sector company), KitchenAid (a manufacturing-sector company), and HughesNet (a service-sector company):

a. Cost of phones and computers available for sale in Best Buy's electronics department
b. Electricity used to provide lighting for assembly-line workers at a KitchenAid manufacturing plant
c. Depreciation on HughesNet satellite equipment used to provide its services
d. Electricity used to provide lighting for Best Buy's store aisles
e. Wages for personnel responsible for quality testing of the KitchenAid products during the assembly process
f. Salaries of Best Buy's marketing personnel planning local-newspaper advertising campaigns
g. Perrier mineral water purchased by HughesNet for consumption by its software engineers
h. Salaries of HughesNet area sales managers
i. Depreciation on vehicles used to transport KitchenAid products to retail stores

Required

1. Distinguish between manufacturing-, merchandising-, and service-sector companies.
2. Distinguish between inventoriable costs and period costs.
3. Classify each of the cost items (a–i) as an inventoriable cost or a period cost. Explain your answers.

Pearson MyLab Accounting

Problems

2-34 Computing cost of goods purchased and cost of goods sold. The following data are for Marvin Department Store. The account balances (in thousands) are for 2017.

Marketing, distribution, and customer-service costs	$ 37,000
Merchandise inventory, January 1, 2017	27,000
Utilities	17,000
General and administrative costs	43,000
Merchandise inventory, December 31, 2017	34,000
Purchases	155,000
Miscellaneous costs	4,000
Transportation-in	7,000
Purchase returns and allowances	4,000
Purchase discounts	6,000
Revenues	280,000

Required

1. Compute (a) the cost of goods purchased and (b) the cost of goods sold.
2. Prepare the income statement for 2017.

2-35 Cost of goods purchased, cost of goods sold, and income statement. The following data are for Huang Wong Ping Retail Outlet Stores. The account balances (in thousands) are for 2017.

Marketing and advertising costs	$ 54,300
Merchandise inventory, January 1, 2017	115,800
Shipping of merchandise to customers	5,700
Depreciation on store fixtures	10,420
Purchases	654,000
General and administrative costs	74,800
Merchandise inventory, December 31, 2017	124,200
Merchandise freight-in	25,000
Purchase returns and allowances	32,400
Purchase discounts	22,600
Revenues	798,000

1. Compute **(a)** the cost of goods purchased and **(b)** the cost of goods sold.
2. Prepare the income statement for 2017.

Required

2-36 Flow of Inventoriable Costs. Renka's Heaters selected data for October 2017 are presented here (in millions):

Direct materials inventory 10/1/2017	$ 105
Direct materials purchased	365
Direct materials used	385
Total manufacturing overhead costs	450
Variable manufacturing overhead costs	265
Total manufacturing costs incurred during October 2017	1,610
Work-in-process inventory 10/1/2017	230
Cost of goods manufactured	1,660
Finished-goods inventory 10/1/2017	130
Cost of goods sold	1,770

Calculate the following costs:

Required

1. Direct materials inventory 10/31/2017
2. Fixed manufacturing overhead costs for October 2017
3. Direct manufacturing labor costs for October 2017
4. Work-in-process inventory 10/31/2017
5. Cost of finished goods available for sale in October 2017
6. Finished goods inventory 10/31/2017

2-37 Cost of goods manufactured, income statement, manufacturing company. Consider the following account balances (in thousands) for the Peterson Company:

Peterson Company	Beginning of 2017	End of 2017
Direct materials inventory	21,000	23,000
Work-in-process inventory	26,000	25,000
Finished-goods inventory	13,000	20,000
Purchases of direct materials		74,000
Direct manufacturing labor		22,000
Indirect manufacturing labor		17,000
Plant insurance		7,000
Depreciation—plant, building, and equipment		11,000
Repairs and maintenance—plant		3,000
Marketing, distribution, and customer-service costs		91,000
General and administrative costs		24,000

1. Prepare a schedule for the cost of goods manufactured for 2017.
2. Revenues for 2017 were $310 million. Prepare the income statement for 2017.

Required

2-38 Cost of goods manufactured, income statement, manufacturing company. Consider the following account balances (in thousands) for the Carolina Corporation:

Carolina Corporation	Beginning of 2017	End of 2017
Direct materials inventory	124,000	73,000
Work-in-process inventory	173,000	145,000
Finished-goods inventory	240,000	206,000
Purchases of direct materials		262,000
Direct manufacturing labor		217,000
Indirect manufacturing labor		97,000
Plant insurance		9,000
Depreciation—plant, building, and equipment		45,000
Plant utilities		26,000
Repairs and maintenance—plant		12,000
Equipment leasing costs		65,000
Marketing, distribution, and customer-service costs		125,000
General and administrative costs		71,000

Required

1. Prepare a schedule for the cost of goods manufactured for 2017.
2. Revenues (in thousands) for 2017 were $1,300,000. Prepare the income statement for 2017.

2-39 Income statement and schedule of cost of goods manufactured. The Howell Corporation has the following account balances (in millions):

For Specific Date		For Year 2017	
Direct materials inventory, Jan. 1, 2017	$15	Purchases of direct materials	$325
Work-in-process inventory, Jan. 1, 2017	10	Direct manufacturing labor	100
Finished goods inventory, Jan. 1, 2017	70	Depreciation—plant and equipment	80
Direct materials inventory, Dec. 31, 2017	20	Plant supervisory salaries	5
Work-in-process inventory, Dec. 31, 2017	5	Miscellaneous plant overhead	35
Finished goods inventory, Dec. 31, 2017	55	Revenues	950
		Marketing, distribution, and customer-service costs	240
		Plant supplies used	10
		Plant utilities	30
		Indirect manufacturing labor	60

Required

Prepare an income statement and a supporting schedule of cost of goods manufactured for the year ended December 31, 2017. (For additional questions regarding these facts, see the next problem.)

2-40 Interpretation of statements (continuation of 2-39).

Required

1. How would the answer to Problem 2-39 be modified if you were asked for a schedule of cost of goods manufactured and sold instead of a schedule of cost of goods manufactured? Be specific.
2. Would the sales manager's salary (included in marketing, distribution, and customer-service costs) be accounted for any differently if the Howell Corporation were a merchandising-sector company instead of a manufacturing-sector company?
3. Using the flow of manufacturing costs outlined in Exhibit 2-9 (page 64), describe how the wages of an assembler in the plant would be accounted for in this manufacturing company.
4. Plant supervisory salaries are usually regarded as manufacturing overhead costs. When might some of these costs be regarded as direct manufacturing costs? Give an example.
5. Suppose that both the direct materials used and the plant and equipment depreciation are related to the manufacture of 1 million units of product. What is the unit cost for the direct materials assigned to those units? What is the unit cost for plant and equipment depreciation? Assume that yearly plant and equipment depreciation is computed on a straight-line basis.
6. Assume that the implied cost-behavior patterns in requirement 5 persist. That is, direct material costs behave as a variable cost and plant and equipment depreciation behaves as a fixed cost. Repeat the computations in requirement 5, assuming that the costs are being predicted for the manufacture of 1.2 million units of product. How would the total costs be affected?
7. As a management accountant, explain concisely to the president why the unit costs differed in requirements 5 and 6.

2-41 Income statement and schedule of cost of goods manufactured. The following items (in millions) pertain to Schaeffer Corporation:

Schaeffer's manufacturing costing system uses a three-part classification of direct materials, direct manufacturing labor, and manufacturing overhead costs.

For Specific Date		For Year 2017	
Work-in-process inventory, Jan. 1, 2017	$10	Plant utilities	$ 8
Direct materials inventory, Dec. 31, 2017	4	Indirect manufacturing labor	21
Finished-goods inventory, Dec. 31, 2017	16	Depreciation—plant and equipment	6
Accounts payable, Dec. 31, 2017	24	Revenues	359
Accounts receivable, Jan. 1, 2017	53	Miscellaneous manufacturing overhead	15
Work-in-process inventory, Dec. 31, 2017	5	Marketing, distribution, and customer-service costs	90
Finished-goods inventory, Jan 1, 2017	46	Direct materials purchased	88
Accounts receivable, Dec. 31, 2017	32	Direct manufacturing labor	40
Accounts payable, Jan. 1, 2017	45	Plant supplies used	9
Direct materials inventory, Jan. 1, 2017	34	Property taxes on plant	2

Prepare an income statement and a supporting schedule of cost of goods manufactured. (For additional questions regarding these facts, see the next problem.)

Required

2-42 Terminology, interpretation of statements (continuation of 2-41).

Required

1. Calculate total prime costs and total conversion costs.
2. Calculate total inventoriable costs and period costs.
3. Design costs and R&D costs are not considered product costs for financial statement purposes. When might some of these costs be regarded as product costs? Give an example.
4. Suppose that both the direct materials used and the depreciation on plant and equipment are related to the manufacture of 2 million units of product. Determine the unit cost for the direct materials assigned to those units and the unit cost for depreciation on plant and equipment. Assume that yearly depreciation is computed on a straight-line basis.
5. Assume that the implied cost-behavior patterns in requirement 4 persist. That is, direct material costs behave as a variable cost and depreciation on plant and equipment behaves as a fixed cost. Repeat the computations in requirement 4, assuming that the costs are being predicted for the manufacture of 3 million units of product. Determine the effect on total costs.
6. Assume that depreciation on the equipment (but not the plant) is computed based on the number of units produced because the equipment deteriorates with units produced. The depreciation rate on equipment is $1.50 per unit. Calculate the depreciation on equipment assuming (a) 2 million units of product are produced and (b) 3 million units of product are produced.

2-43 Labor cost, overtime, and idle time. Akua works in the manufacturing department of Impala Iron Works (IIW) as a machine operator. Akua, a long-time employee of IIW, is paid on an hourly basis at a rate of $25 per hour. She works five 8-hour shifts per week from Monday to Friday (40 hours). Any time Akua works beyond these 40 hours is considered overtime for which she is paid at a rate of 160% ($40 per hour). If the overtime falls on weekends, Akua is paid at a rate of double time ($50 per hour). She is also paid an additional $26 per hour for working on any holidays worked, even if it is part of her regular 40 hours. Akua is paid her regular wages even if the machines are down (not operating) due to regular machine maintenance, slow order periods, or unexpected mechanical problems. These hours are considered "idle time."

During December Akua worked the following hours:

	Hours worked including machine downtime	Machine downtime
Week 1	49	5.0
Week 2	51	6.0
Week 3	45	3.0
Week 4	47	4.0

Included in the total hours worked are two company holidays (Christmas Eve and Christmas Day) during Week 4. All overtime worked by Akua was Monday–Friday, except for the hours worked in Week 3; all of the Week 3 overtime hours were worked on a Saturday.

Required

1. Calculate (a) direct manufacturing labor, (b) idle time, (c) overtime and holiday premium, and (d) total earnings for Akua in December.
2. Is idle time and overtime premium a direct or indirect cost of the products that Akua worked on in December? Explain.

2-44 Missing records, computing inventory costs. Ron Howard recently took over as the controller of Johnson Brothers Manufacturing. Last month, the previous controller left the company with little notice and left the accounting records in disarray. Ron needs the ending inventory balances to report first-quarter numbers.

For the previous month (March 2017) Ron was able to piece together the following information:

Direct materials purchased	$120,000
Work-in-process inventory, 3/1/2017	$ 35,000
Direct materials inventory, 3/1/2017	$ 12,500
Finished-goods inventory, 3/1/2017	$160,000
Conversion costs	$330,000
Total manufacturing costs added during the period	$420,000
Cost of goods manufactured	4 times direct materials used
Gross margin as a percentage of revenues	20%
Revenues	$518,750

Calculate the cost of:

Required

1. Finished-goods inventory, 3/31/2017
2. Work-in-process inventory, 3/31/2017
3. Direct materials inventory, 3/31/2017

2-45 Comprehensive problem on unit costs, product costs. Atlanta Office Equipment manufactures and sells metal shelving. It began operations on January 1, 2017. Costs incurred for 2017 are as follows (V stands for variable; F stands for fixed):

Direct materials used	$149,500 V
Direct manufacturing labor costs	34,500 V
Plant energy costs	6,000 V
Indirect manufacturing labor costs	12,000 V
Indirect manufacturing labor costs	17,000 F
Other indirect manufacturing costs	7,000 V
Other indirect manufacturing costs	27,000 F
Marketing, distribution, and customer-service costs	126,000 V
Marketing, distribution, and customer-service costs	47,000 F
Administrative costs	58,000 F

Variable manufacturing costs are variable with respect to units produced. Variable marketing, distribution, and customer-service costs are variable with respect to units sold.

Inventory data are as follows:

	Beginning: January 1, 2017	Ending: December 31, 2017
Direct materials	0 lb	2,300 lbs
Work in process	0 units	0 units
Finished goods	0 units	? units

Production in 2017 was 115,000 units. Two pounds of direct materials are used to make one unit of finished product.

Revenues in 2017 were $540,000. The selling price per unit and the purchase price per pound of direct materials were stable throughout the year. The company's ending inventory of finished goods is carried at the average unit manufacturing cost for 2017. Finished-goods inventory at December 31, 2017, was $15,400.

Required

1. Calculate direct materials inventory, total cost, December 31, 2017.
2. Calculate finished-goods inventory, total units, December 31, 2017.
3. Calculate selling price in 2017.
4. Calculate operating income for 2017.

2-46 Different meanings of product costs. There are at least 3 different purposes for which we measure product costs. They are (1) pricing and product mix decisions, (2) determining the appropriate charge for a government contract, and (3) for preparing financial statements for external reporting following Generally Accepted Accounting Principles. On the following table, indicate whether the indicated cost would be included or excluded for the particular purpose. If your answer is not definitive (include or exclude), provide a short explanation of why.

Type of Cost	Purpose: Pricing/ Product Mix	Purpose: Government Contract	Purpose: Financial Statement (using GAAP)
Direct Material			
Direct Manufacturing Labor			
Manufacturing Overhead			
Marketing Costs			
Distribution Expense			
Customer Service			

2-47 Cost classification; ethics. Adalard Müller, the new plant manager of New Times Manufacturing Plant Number 12, has just reviewed a draft of his year-end financial statements. Müller receives a year-end bonus of 8% of the plant's operating income before tax. The year-end income statement provided by the plant's controller was disappointing to say the least. After reviewing the numbers, Müller demanded that his controller go back and "work the numbers" again. Müller insisted that if he didn't see a better operating income number the next time around he would be forced to look for a new controller.

New Times Manufacturing classifies all costs directly related to the manufacturing of its product as product costs. These costs are inventoried and later expensed as costs of goods sold when the product is sold. All other expenses, including finished goods warehousing costs of $3,570,000, are classified as period expenses. Müller had suggested that warehousing costs be included as product costs because they are "definitely related to our product." The company produced 210,000 units during the period and sold 190,000 units.

As the controller reworked the numbers, he discovered that if he included warehousing costs as product costs, he could improve operating income by $340,000. He was also sure these new numbers would make Müller happy.

1. Show numerically how operating income would improve by $340,000 just by classifying the preceding costs as product costs instead of period expenses.
2. Is Müller correct in his justification that these costs are "definitely related to our product"?
3. By how much will Müller profit personally if the controller makes the adjustments in requirement 1?
4. What should the plant controller do?

Required

2-48 Finding unknown amounts. An auditor for the Internal Revenue Service is trying to reconstruct some partially destroyed records of two taxpayers. For each case in the accompanying list, find the unknown elements designated by the letters A and B for Case 1 and C and D for Case 2.

	Case 1	Case 2
	(in thousands)	
Accounts receivable, 12/31	$ 10,250	$ 4,500
Cost of goods sold	A	33,400
Accounts payable, 1/1	5,900	2,850
Accounts payable, 12/31	2,700	2,250
Finished goods inventory, 12/31	B	6,300
Gross margin	26,000	C
Work-in-process inventory, 1/1	4,600	2,800
Work-in-process inventory, 12/31	2,300	5,500
Finished goods inventory, 1/1	6,600	5,100
Direct materials used	14,500	20,200
Direct manufacturing labor costs	5,200	7,300
Manufacturing overhead costs	10,400	D
Purchases of direct materials	13,500	10,500
Revenues	64,500	57,600
Accounts receivable, 1/1	6,400	3,200

3 ▶ Cost–Volume–Profit Analysis

LEARNING OBJECTIVES

1. Explain the features of cost–volume–profit (CVP) analysis

2. Determine the breakeven point and output level needed to achieve a target operating income

3. Understand how income taxes affect CVP analysis

4. Explain how managers use CVP analysis to make decisions

5. Explain how sensitivity analysis helps managers cope with uncertainty

6. Use CVP analysis to plan variable and fixed costs

7. Apply CVP analysis to a company producing multiple products

8. Apply CVP analysis in service and not-for-profit organizations

9. Distinguish contribution margin from gross margin

All managers want to know how profits will change as the units sold, selling price, or the cost per unit of a product or service change.

Home Depot managers, for example, might wonder how many units of a new power drill must be sold to break even or make a certain amount of profit. Procter & Gamble managers might ask themselves how expanding their business in Nigeria would affect costs, revenues, and profits. These questions have a common "what-if" theme: What if we sold more power drills? What if we started selling in Nigeria? Examining the results of these what-if possibilities and alternatives helps managers make better decisions.

The following article explains how Goldenvoice, the organizer of the Coachella music festival in California, generated additional revenues to cover its fixed costs and turn a loss into a profit.

HOW COACHELLA TUNES UP THE SWEET SOUND OF PROFITS[1]

Each year, the Coachella music festival in California features more than 150 of the biggest names in rock, hip-hop, and electronic dance music. Putting on this annual music extravaganza is a costly endeavor. Headlining acts such as Drake and Jack White command as much as $4 million to perform, and production—including stagehands, insurance, and security—costs up to $12 million before the first note is played.

To cover its high fixed costs and make a profit, Coachella needs to sell a lot of tickets. After struggling for years to turn a profit, Goldenvoice expanded Coachella to two identical editions taking place on consecutive weekends. Same venue, same lineup, and same ticket price. Goldenvoice also launched Stagecoach, a country music festival that occupies the same California venue one week after Coachella. This allowed temporary infrastructure costs such as stages and fencings to be shared across both events. With tickets prices from $375 to $889, the 2015 Coachella festival sold a staggering $84 million in tickets,

WENN Ltd/Alamy Stock Photo

¹ *Sources*: Chris Parker, "The Economics of Music Festivals: Who's Getting Rich? Who's Going Broke?" *L.A. Weekly*, April 17, 2013 (http://www.laweekly.com/music/the-economics-of-music-festivals-whos-getting-rich-whos-going-broke-4167927); Anil Patel, "Coachella: A Lesson in Strategic Growth," *Anil Patel's blog*, LinkedIn, April 17, 2015 (https://www.linkedin.com/pulse/coachella-lesson-strategic-growth-anil-patel); Ray Waddell, "Coachella Earns Over $84 Million, Breaks Attendance Records," *Billboard*, July 15, 2015 (http://www.billboard.com/articles/business/6633636/coachella-2015-earnings-84-million-breaks-attendance-records).

while the follow-on Stagecoach festival grossed more than $21 million in ticket sales. By expanding Coachella's volume, Goldenvoice was able to recover its fixed costs and tune up the sweet sound of profits.

Businesses that have high fixed costs, such as American Airlines and General Motors, have to pay particular attention to the "what-ifs" behind decisions because these companies need significant revenues just to break even. In the airline industry, for example, the profits most airlines make come from the last two to five passengers who board each flight! Consequently, when revenues at American Airlines dropped, it was forced to declare bankruptcy. In this chapter, you will see how cost–volume–profit (CVP) analysis helps managers minimize such risks.

Essentials of CVP Analysis

In Chapter 2, we discussed total revenues, total costs, and income. Managers use **cost–volume–profit (CVP) analysis** to study the behavior of and relationship among these elements as changes occur in the number of units sold, the selling price, the variable cost per unit, or the fixed costs of a product. Consider this example:

> Example: Emma Jones is a young entrepreneur who recently used *GMAT Success*, a test-prep book and software package for the business school admission test. Emma loved the book and program so much that after graduating she signed a contract with *GMAT Success*'s publisher to sell the learning materials. She recently sold them at a college fair in Boston and is now thinking of selling them at a college fair in Chicago. Emma can purchase each package (book and software) from the publisher for $120 per package, with the privilege of returning all unsold packages and receiving a full $120 refund per package. She must pay $2,000 to rent a booth at the fair. She will incur no other costs. Should she rent the booth or not?

Emma, like most managers who face such a situation, works through the series of steps introduced in Chapter 1 to make the most profitable decisions.

1. **Identify the problem and uncertainties.** Every managerial decision involves selecting a course of action. The decision to rent the booth hinges on how Emma resolves two important uncertainties: the price she can charge and the number of packages she can sell at that price. Emma must decide knowing that the outcome of the action she chooses is uncertain. The more confident she is about selling a large number of packages at a high price, the more willing she will be to rent the booth.

2. **Obtain information.** When faced with uncertainty, managers obtain information that might help them understand the uncertainties more clearly. For example, Emma gathers information about the type of individuals likely to attend the fair and other test-prep packages that might be sold at the fair. She also gathers data from her experience selling packages at the Boston fair.

3. **Make predictions about the future.** Managers make predictions using all the information available to them. Emma predicts she can charge $200 for the *GMAT Success* package. At that price, she is reasonably confident that she will be able to sell at least 30 packages and possibly as many as 60. Emma must be realistic and exercise judgment when making these predictions. If they are too optimistic, she will rent the booth when she should not. If they are too pessimistic, she will not rent the booth when she should.

   Emma's predictions rest on the belief that her experience at the Chicago fair will be similar to her experience at the Boston fair 4 months earlier. Yet Emma is uncertain about several aspects of her prediction. Are the fairs truly comparable? For example, will attendance at the two fairs be the same? Have market conditions changed over the past

4 months? Are there any biases creeping into her thinking? She is keen on selling at the Chicago fair because sales in the last couple of months have been lower than expected. Is this experience making her predictions overly optimistic? Has she ignored some of the competitive risks? Will the other test-prep vendors at the fair reduce their prices? If they do, should she? How many packages can she expect to sell if she does?

Emma rethinks her plan and retests her assumptions. She obtains data about student attendance and total sales in past years from the organizers of the fair. In the end, she feels quite confident that her predictions are reasonable, accurate, and carefully thought through.

4. **Make decisions by choosing among alternatives.** Emma uses the CVP analysis that follows and decides to rent the booth at the Chicago fair.

5. **Implement the decision, evaluate performance, and learn.** Thoughtful managers never stop learning. They compare their actual performance to predicted performance to understand why things worked out the way they did and what they might learn. At the end of the Chicago fair, for example, Emma would want to evaluate whether her predictions about price and the number of packages she could sell were correct. This will help her make better decisions about renting booths at future fairs.

How does Emma use CVP analysis in Step 4 to make her decision? She begins by identifying which costs are fixed and which costs are variable and then calculates *contribution margin*.

Contribution Margin

The booth-rental cost of $2,000 is a fixed cost because it will not change no matter how many packages Emma sells. The cost of the packages is a variable cost because it increases in proportion to the number of packages sold and she can return whatever she doesn't sell for a full refund.

To understand how her operating income will change by selling different quantities of packages, Emma calculates operating income if sales are 5 packages and if sales are 40 packages.

	5 packages sold	**40 packages sold**
Revenues	$ 1,000 ($200 per package × 5 packages)	$8,000 ($ 200 per package × 40 packages)
Variable purchase costs	600 ($120 per package × 5 packages)	4,800 ($120 per package × 40 packages)
Fixed costs	2,000	2,000
Operating income	$(1,600)	$1,200

The only numbers that change from selling different quantities of packages are *total revenues* and *total variable costs*. The difference between total revenues and total variable costs is called **contribution margin**. That is,

$$\text{Contribution margin} = \text{Total revenues} - \text{Total variable costs}$$

Contribution margin indicates why operating income changes as the number of units sold changes. The contribution margin when Emma sells 5 packages is $400 ($1,000 in total revenues minus $600 in total variable costs); the contribution margin when Emma sells 40 packages is $3,200 ($8,000 in total revenues minus $4,800 in total variable costs). When calculating the contribution margin, be sure to subtract all variable costs. For example, if Emma incurred some variable selling costs because she paid a commission to salespeople for each package they sold at the fair, variable costs would include the cost of each package plus the sales commission paid on it.

Contribution margin per unit is a useful tool for calculating contribution margin and operating income. It is defined as:

$$\text{Contribution margin per unit} = \text{Selling price} - \text{Variable cost per unit}$$

In the *GMAT Success* example, the contribution margin per package, or per unit, is $200 − $120 = $80. Contribution margin per unit recognizes the tight coupling of selling price and variable cost per unit. Unlike fixed costs, Emma will only incur the variable cost per unit of $120 when she sells a unit of *GMAT Success*.

Contribution margin per unit provides a second way to calculate contribution margin:

$$\text{Contribution margin} = \text{Contribution margin per unit} \times \text{Number of units sold}$$

For example, when Emma sells 40 packages, contribution margin = $80 per unit × 40 units = $3,200.

Even before she gets to the fair, Emma incurs $2,000 in fixed costs. Because the contribution margin per unit is $80, Emma will recover $80 for each package that she sells at the fair. Emma hopes to sell enough packages to fully recover the $2,000 she spent renting the booth and to then make a profit.

To get a feel for how operating income will change for different quantities of packages sold, Emma can prepare a contribution income statement as in Exhibit 3-1. The income statement in Exhibit 3-1 is called a **contribution income statement** because it groups costs into variable costs and fixed costs to highlight contribution margin.

$$\text{Operating income} = \text{Contribution margin} - \text{Fixed costs}$$

Each additional package sold from 0 to 1 to 5 increases contribution margin by $80 per package and helps Emma recover more and more of her fixed costs and reduce her operating loss. If Emma sells 25 packages, contribution margin equals $2,000 ($80 per package × 25 packages). This quantity exactly recovers her fixed costs and results in $0 operating income. If Emma sells 40 packages, contribution margin increases by another $1,200 ($3,200 − $2,000), all of which becomes operating income. As you look across Exhibit 3-1 from left to right, you see that the increase in contribution margin exactly equals the increase in operating income (or the decrease in operating loss).

When companies, such as Samsung and Prada, sell multiple products, calculating contribution margin per unit is cumbersome. Instead of expressing contribution margin in dollars per unit, these companies express it as a percentage called **contribution margin percentage** (or **contribution margin ratio**):

$$\text{Contribution margin percentage (or contribution margin ratio)} = \frac{\text{Contribution margin}}{\text{Revenues}}$$

Consider a sales level such as the 40 units sold in Exhibit 3-1:

$$\text{Contribution margin percentage} = \frac{\$3,200}{\$8,000} = 0.40, \text{ or } 40\%$$

Contribution margin percentage is the contribution margin per dollar of revenue. Emma earns 40% for each dollar of revenue (40 cents) she takes in. Contribution margin percentage is a handy way to calculate contribution margin for different dollar amounts of revenue. Rearranging terms in the equation defining contribution margin percentage, we get:

$$\text{Contribution margin} = \text{Contribution margin percentage} \times \text{Revenues (in dollars)}$$

	Home	Insert	Page Layout	Formulas	Data	Review	View	
	A	B	C	D	E	F	G	H
1				Number of Packages Sold				
2				0	1	5	25	40
3	Revenues	$ 200	per package	$ 0	$ 200	$ 1,000	$5,000	$8,000
4	Variable costs	$ 120	per package	0	120	600	3,000	4,800
5	Contribution margin	$ 80	per package	0	80	400	2,000	3,200
6	Fixed costs	$2,000		2,000	2,000	2,000	2,000	2,000
7	Operating income			$(2,000)	$(1,920)	$(1,600)	$ 0	$1,200

To derive the relationship between operating income and contribution margin percentage, recall that:

$$\text{Operating income} = \text{Contribution margin} - \text{Fixed costs}$$

Substituting for contribution margin in the above equation:

$$\text{Operating income} = \text{Contribution margin percentage} \times \text{Revenues} - \text{Fixed costs}$$

For example, in Exhibit 3-1, if Emma sells 40 packages:

Revenues	$8,000
Contribution margin percentage	40%
Contribution margin, 40% × $8,000	$3,200
Fixed costs	2,000
Operating income	$1,200

When there is only one product, as in our example, we can divide both the numerator and denominator of the contribution margin percentage equation by the quantity of units sold and calculate contribution margin percentage as follows:

$$\text{Contribution margin percentage} = \frac{\text{Contribution margin}/\text{Quantity of units sold}}{\text{Revenues}/\text{Quantity of units sold}}$$

$$= \frac{\text{Contribution margin per unit}}{\text{Selling price}}$$

In our example,

$$\text{Contribution margin percentage} = \frac{\$80}{\$200} = 0.40, \text{ or } 40\%$$

Contribution margin percentage is a useful tool for calculating how a change in revenues changes contribution margin. As Emma's revenues increase by $3,000 from $5,000 to $8,000, her contribution margin increases from $2,000 to $3,200 (by $1,200):

Contribution margin at revenue of $8,000, 0.40 × $8,000	$3,200
Contribution margin at revenue of $5,000, 0.40 × $5,000	2,000
Change in contribution margin when revenue increases by $3,000, 0.40 × $3,000	$1,200

$$\text{Change in contribution margin} = \text{Contribution margin percentage} \times \text{Change in revenues}$$

Contribution margin analysis is a widely used technique. For example, managers at Home Depot use contribution margin analysis to evaluate how sales fluctuations during a recession will affect the company's profitability.

Expressing CVP Relationships

How was the Excel spreadsheet in Exhibit 3-1 constructed? Underlying the exhibit are some equations that express the CVP relationships. To make good decisions using CVP analysis, we must understand these relationships and the structure of the contribution income statement in Exhibit 3-1. There are three related ways (we will call them "methods") to think more deeply about and model CVP relationships:

1. The equation method
2. The contribution margin method
3. The graph method

As you will learn later in the chapter, different methods are useful for different decisions.

The equation method and the contribution margin method are most useful when managers want to determine operating income at a few specific sales levels (for example, 5, 15, 25, and 40 units sold). The graph method helps managers visualize the relationship between units sold and operating income over a wide range of quantities.

Equation Method

Each column in Exhibit 3-1 is expressed as an equation.

$$\text{Revenues} - \text{Variable costs} - \text{Fixed costs} = \text{Operating income}$$

How are revenues in each column calculated?

$$\text{Revenues} = \text{Selling price } (SP) \times \text{Quantity of units sold } (Q)$$

How are variable costs in each column calculated?

$$\text{Variable costs} = \text{Variable cost per unit } (VCU) \times \text{Quantity of units sold} (Q)$$

So,

$$\left[\left(\begin{array}{c} \text{Selling} \\ \text{price} \end{array} \right) \times \left(\begin{array}{c} \text{Quantity of} \\ \text{units sold} \end{array} \right) - \left(\begin{array}{c} \text{Variable cost} \\ \text{per unit} \end{array} \right) \times \left(\begin{array}{c} \text{Quantity of} \\ \text{units sold} \end{array} \right) \right] - \begin{array}{c} \text{Fixed} \\ \text{costs} \end{array} = \begin{array}{c} \text{Operating} \\ \text{income} \end{array} \quad \text{(Equation 1)}$$

Equation 1 becomes the basis for calculating operating income for different quantities of units sold. For example, if you go to cell F7 in Exhibit 3-1, the calculation of operating income when Emma sells 5 packages is

$$(\$200 \times 5) - (\$120 \times 5) - \$2,000 = \$1,000 - \$600 - \$2,000 = -\$1,600$$

Contribution Margin Method

Rearranging equation 1,

$$\left[\left(\begin{array}{c} \text{Selling} \\ \text{price} \end{array} - \begin{array}{c} \text{Variable cost} \\ \text{per unit} \end{array} \right) \times \left(\begin{array}{c} \text{Quantity of} \\ \text{units sold} \end{array} \right) \right] - \begin{array}{c} \text{Fixed} \\ \text{costs} \end{array} = \begin{array}{c} \text{Operating} \\ \text{income} \end{array}$$

$$\left(\begin{array}{c} \text{Contribution margin} \\ \text{per unit} \end{array} \times \begin{array}{c} \text{Quantity of} \\ \text{units sold} \end{array} \right) - \begin{array}{c} \text{Fixed} \\ \text{costs} \end{array} = \begin{array}{c} \text{Operating} \\ \text{income} \end{array} \quad \text{(Equation 2)}$$

In our *GMAT Success* example, contribution margin per unit is $80 ($200 − $120), so when Emma sells 5 packages,

$$\text{Operating income} = (\$80 \times 5) - \$2,000 = -\$1,600$$

Equation 2 expresses the basic idea we described earlier—each unit sold helps Emma recover $80 (in contribution margin) of the $2,000 in fixed costs.

Bernard Windows is a small company that installs windows. Its cost structure is as follows:

3-1 TRY IT!

Selling price from each window installation	$ 500
Variable cost of each window installation	$ 400
Annual fixed costs	$150,000

Use (a) the equation method and (b) the contribution method to calculate operating income if Bernard installs 2,000 windows.

Graph Method

The graph method helps managers visualize the relationships between total revenues and total costs. The graph shows each relationship as a line. Exhibit 3-2 illustrates the graph method for selling *GMAT Success*. Because we have assumed that total costs and total revenues behave in a linear way, we need only two points to plot the line representing each of them.

1. **Total costs line.** The total costs line is the sum of fixed costs and variable costs. Fixed costs are $2,000 for all quantities of units sold within the relevant range. To plot the total costs line, use as one point the $2,000 fixed costs at zero units sold (point A) because variable costs are $0 when no units are sold. Select a second point by choosing any other output level (say, 40 units sold) and determine the corresponding total costs. Total variable costs at this output level are $4,800 (40 units × $120 per unit). Remember, fixed costs are $2,000 at all quantities of units sold within the relevant range, so total costs at 40 units sold equal $6,800 ($2,000 + $4,800), which is point B in Exhibit 3-2. The total costs line is the straight line from point A through point B.

2. **Total revenues line.** One convenient starting point is $0 revenues at 0 units sold, which is point C in Exhibit 3-2. Select a second point by choosing any other convenient output level and determining the corresponding total revenues. At 40 units sold, total revenues are $8,000 ($200 per unit × 40 units), which is point D in Exhibit 3-2. The total revenues line is the straight line from point C through point D.

    The profit or loss at any sales level can be determined by the vertical distance between the two lines at that level in Exhibit 3-2. For quantities fewer than 25 units sold, total costs exceed total revenues, and the purple area indicates operating losses. For quantities greater than 25 units sold, total revenues exceed total costs, and the blue-green area indicates operating incomes. At 25 units sold, total revenues equal total costs. Emma will break even by selling 25 packages.

DECISION POINT

How can CVP analysis help managers?

Like Emma, many companies, particularly small- and medium-sized companies, use the graph method to see how their revenues and costs will change as the quantity of units sold changes. The graph helps them understand their regions of profitability and unprofitability.

EXHIBIT 3-2

Cost–Volume Graph for *GMAT Success*

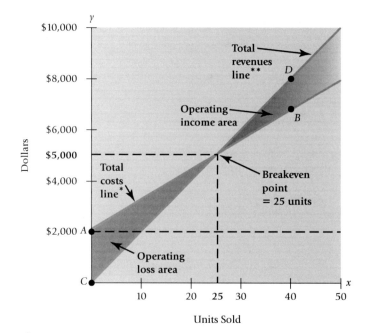

*Slope of the total costs line is the variable cost per unit = $120
**Slope of the total revenues line is the selling price = $200

Cost–Volume–Profit Assumptions

Now that you know how CVP analysis works, think about the following assumptions we made during the analysis:

1. Changes in revenues and costs arise only because of changes in the number of product (or service) units sold. The number of units sold is the only revenue driver and the only cost driver. Just as a cost driver is any factor that affects costs, a **revenue driver** is a variable, such as volume, that causally affects revenues.

2. Total costs can be separated into two components: a fixed component that does not vary with units sold (such as Emma's $2,000 booth fee) and a variable component that changes based on units sold (such as the $120 cost per *GMAT Success* package).

3. When represented graphically, the behaviors of total revenues and total costs are linear (meaning they can be represented as a straight line) in relation to units sold within a relevant range (and time period).

4. Selling price, variable cost per unit, and total fixed costs (within a relevant range and time period) are known and constant.

As you can tell from these assumptions, to conduct a CVP analysis, you need to correctly distinguish fixed from variable costs. Always keep in mind, however, that whether a cost is variable or fixed depends on the time period for a decision.

The shorter the time horizon, the higher the percentage of total costs considered fixed. For example, suppose an American Airlines plane will depart from its gate in the next hour and currently has 20 seats unsold. A potential passenger arrives with a transferable ticket from a competing airline. American's variable costs of placing one more passenger in an otherwise empty seat (such as the cost of providing the passenger with a free beverage) is negligible. With only an hour to go before the flight departs, virtually all costs (such as crew costs and baggage-handling costs) are fixed.

Alternatively, suppose American Airlines must decide whether to continue to offer this particular flight next year. If American Airlines decides to cancel this flight because very few passengers during the last year have taken it, many more of its costs, including crew costs, baggage-handling costs, and airport fees for the flight, would be considered variable: Over this longer 1-year time period, American Airlines would not have to incur these costs if the flight were no longer operating. Always consider the relevant range, the length of the time horizon, and the specific decision situation when classifying costs as variable or fixed.

Breakeven Point and Target Operating Income

In previous sections, we used the number of packages sold as an input to the contribution income statement, the equation method, the contribution margin method, and the graph method to calculate Emma's operating income for different quantities of packages sold. In this section we use the same tools to reverse the logic. We use as input the amount of operating income Emma wants to earn and then compute the number of packages Emma must sell to earn this income. A very important question is how much Emma must sell to avoid a loss.

LEARNING 2
OBJECTIVE

Determine the breakeven point and output level needed to achieve a target operating income

...compare contribution margin and fixed costs

Breakeven Point

The **breakeven point (BEP)** is that quantity of output sold at which total revenues equal total costs—that is, the quantity of output sold that results in $0 of operating income. You have already learned how to use the graph method to calculate the breakeven point. Recall from Exhibit 3-1 that operating income was $0 when Emma sold 25 units; this is the breakeven point. But by understanding the equations underlying the calculations in Exhibit 3-1, we can calculate the breakeven point directly for selling *GMAT Success* rather than trying out different quantities and checking when operating income equals $0.

Recall the equation method (equation 1):

$$\left[\left(\begin{array}{c}\text{Selling}\\ \text{price}\end{array} \times \begin{array}{c}\text{Quantity of}\\ \text{units sold}\end{array}\right) - \left(\begin{array}{c}\text{Variable cost}\\ \text{per unit}\end{array} \times \begin{array}{c}\text{Quantity of}\\ \text{units sold}\end{array}\right)\right] - \begin{array}{c}\text{Fixed}\\ \text{costs}\end{array} = \begin{array}{c}\text{Operating}\\ \text{income}\end{array}$$

Setting operating income equal to $0 and denoting quantity of output units that must be sold by Q,

$$(\$200 \times Q) - (\$120 \times Q) - \$2{,}000 = \$0$$
$$\$80 \times Q = \$2{,}000$$
$$Q = \$2{,}000 \div \$80 \text{ per unit} = 25 \text{ units}$$

If Emma sells fewer than 25 units, she will incur a loss; if she sells 25 units, she will break even; and if she sells more than 25 units, she will make a profit. Although this breakeven point is expressed in units, it can also be expressed in revenues: 25 units × $200 selling price = $5,000. Recall the contribution margin method (equation 2):

$$\left(\begin{array}{c}\text{Contribution}\\ \text{margin per unit}\end{array} \times \begin{array}{c}\text{Quantity of}\\ \text{units sold}\end{array}\right) - \text{Fixed costs} = \text{Operating income}$$

At the breakeven point, operating income is by definition $0, and so,

$$\text{Contribution margin per unit} \times \text{Breakeven quantity of units} = \text{Fixed costs} \qquad \text{(Equation 3)}$$

Rearranging equation 3 and entering the data,

$$\begin{array}{c}\text{Breakeven}\\ \text{number of units}\end{array} = \frac{\text{Fixed costs}}{\text{Contribution margin per unit}} = \frac{\$2{,}000}{\$80 \text{ per unit}} = 25 \text{ units}$$

$$\text{Breakeven revenues} = \text{Breakeven number of units} \times \text{Selling price}$$
$$= 25 \text{ units} \times \$200 \text{ per unit} = \$5{,}000$$

In practice (because companies have multiple products), management accountants usually calculate the breakeven point directly in terms of revenues using contribution margin percentages. Recall that in the *GMAT Success* example, at revenues of $8,000, contribution margin is $3,200:

$$\begin{array}{c}\text{Contribution margin}\\ \text{percentage}\end{array} = \frac{\text{Contribution margin}}{\text{Revenues}} = \frac{\$3{,}200}{\$8{,}000} = 0.40, \text{ or } 40\%$$

That is, 40% of each dollar of revenue, or 40 cents, is the contribution margin. To break even, contribution margin must equal Emma's fixed costs, which are $2,000. To earn $2,000 of contribution margin, when $1 of revenue results in a $0.40 contribution margin, revenues must equal $2,000 ÷ 0.40 = $5,000.

$$\begin{array}{c}\text{Breakeven}\\ \text{revenues}\end{array} = \frac{\text{Fixed costs}}{\text{Contribution margin \%}} = \frac{\$2{,}000}{0.40} = \$5{,}000$$

While the breakeven point tells managers how much they must sell to avoid a loss, managers are equally interested in how they will achieve the operating income targets underlying their strategies and plans. In our example, selling 25 units at a price of $200 (equal to revenue of $5,000) assures Emma that she will not lose money if she rents the booth. While this news is comforting, how does Emma determine how much she needs to sell to achieve a targeted amount of operating income?

Target Operating Income

Suppose Emma wants to earn an operating income of $1,200? How many units must she sell? One approach is to keep plugging in different quantities into Exhibit 3-1 and check when operating income equals $1,200. Exhibit 3-1 shows that operating income is $1,200 when 40 packages are sold. A more convenient approach is to use equation 1 from page 91.

$$\left[\left(\begin{array}{c} \text{Selling} \\ \text{price} \end{array} \right) \times \left(\begin{array}{c} \text{Quantity of} \\ \text{units sold} \end{array} \right) - \left(\begin{array}{c} \text{Variable cost} \\ \text{per unit} \end{array} \right) \times \left(\begin{array}{c} \text{Quantity of} \\ \text{units sold} \end{array} \right) \right] - \begin{array}{c} \text{Fixed} \\ \text{costs} \end{array} = \begin{array}{c} \text{Operating} \\ \text{income} \end{array} \quad \text{(Equation 1)}$$

We denote by Q the unknown quantity of units Emma must sell to earn an operating income of $1,200. Selling price is $200, variable cost per package is $120, fixed costs are $2,000, and target operating income is $1,200. Substituting these values into equation 1, we have

$$(\$200 \times Q) - (\$120 \times Q) - \$2,000 = \$1,200$$
$$\$80 \times Q = \$2,000 + \$1,200 = \$3,200$$
$$Q = \$3,200 \div \$80 \text{ per unit} = 40 \text{ units}$$

Alternatively, we could use equation 2,

$$\left(\begin{array}{c} \text{Contribution margin} \\ \text{per unit} \end{array} \times \begin{array}{c} \text{Quantity of} \\ \text{units sold} \end{array} \right) - \begin{array}{c} \text{Fixed} \\ \text{costs} \end{array} = \begin{array}{c} \text{Operating} \\ \text{income} \end{array} \quad \text{(Equation 2)}$$

Given a target operating income ($1,200 in this case), we can rearrange terms to get equation 4.

$$\begin{array}{c} \text{Quantity of units} \\ \text{required to be sold} \end{array} = \frac{\text{Fixed costs} + \text{Target operating income}}{\text{Contribution margin per unit}} \quad \text{(Equation 4)}$$

$$\begin{array}{c} \text{Quantity of units} \\ \text{required to be sold} \end{array} = \frac{\$2,000 + \$1,200}{\$80 \text{ per unit}} = 40 \text{ units}$$

Proof:

Revenues, $200 per unit × 40 units	$8,000
Variable costs, $120 per unit × 40 units	4,800
Contribution margin, $80 per unit × 40 units	3,200
Fixed costs	2,000
Operating income	$1,200

The revenues needed to earn an operating income of $1,200 can also be calculated directly by recognizing (1) that $3,200 of contribution margin must be earned (to cover the fixed costs of $2,000 plus earn an operating income of $1,200) and (2) that $1 of revenue earns $0.40 (40 cents) of contribution margin (the contribution margin percentage is 40%). To earn a contribution margin of $3,200, revenues must equal $3,200 ÷ 0.40 = $8,000. That is,

$$\begin{array}{c} \text{Revenues needed to earn} \\ \text{target operating income} \end{array} = \frac{\text{Fixed costs} + \text{Target operating income}}{\text{Contribution margin percentage}}$$

$$\text{Revenues needed to earn operating income of } \$1,200 = \frac{\$2,000 + \$1,200}{0.40} = \frac{\$3,200}{0.40} = \$8,000$$

3-2 TRY IT!

Bernard Windows is a small company that installs windows. Its cost structure is as follows:

Selling price from each window installation	$ 500
Variable cost of each window installation	$ 400
Annual fixed costs	$150,000

Calculate (a) the breakeven point in units and revenues and (b) the number of windows Bernard Windows must install and the revenues needed to earn a target operating income of $100,000.

EXHIBIT 3-3

Profit–Volume Graph for
GMAT Success

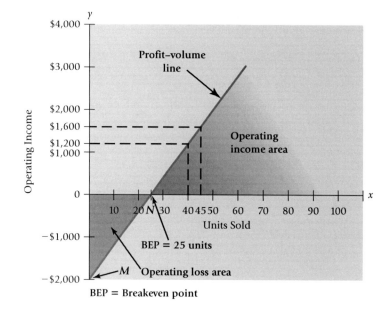

Could we use the graph method and the graph in Exhibit 3-2 to figure out how many units Emma must sell to earn an operating income of $1,200? Yes, but it is not as easy to determine the precise point at which the difference between the total revenues line and the total costs line equals $1,200. Recasting Exhibit 3-2 in the form of a profit–volume (PV) graph, however, makes it easier to answer this question.

A **PV graph** shows how changes in the quantity of units sold affect operating income. Exhibit 3-3 is the PV graph for *GMAT Success* (fixed costs, $2,000; selling price, $200; and variable cost per unit, $120). The PV line can be drawn using two points. One convenient point (M) is the operating loss at 0 units sold, which is equal to the fixed costs of $2,000 and is shown at −$2,000 on the vertical axis. A second convenient point (N) is the breakeven point, which is 25 units in our example (see page 94). The PV line is the straight line from point M through point N. To find the number of units Emma must sell to earn an operating income of $1,200, draw a horizontal line parallel to the *x*-axis corresponding to $1,200 on the vertical axis (the *y*-axis). At the point where this line intersects the PV line, draw a vertical line down to the horizontal axis (the *x*-axis). The vertical line intersects the *x*-axis at 40 units, indicating that by selling 40 units Emma will earn an operating income of $1,200.

Just like Emma, managers at larger companies such as California Pizza Kitchen use profit–volume analyses to understand how profits change with sales volumes. They use this understanding to target the sales levels they need to achieve to meet their profit plans.

Until now, we have ignored the effect of income taxes in our CVP analysis. In many companies, boards of directors want top executives and managers to consider the effect their decisions have on the company's operating income *after* income taxes because this is the measure that drives shareholders' dividends and returns. Some decisions might not result in a large operating income, but their favorable tax consequences make them attractive over other investments that have larger operating incomes but attract much higher taxes. CVP analysis can easily be adapted to consider the effect of taxes.

DECISION POINT

How can managers determine the breakeven point or the output needed to achieve a target operating income?

Income Taxes and Target Net Income

LEARNING OBJECTIVE **3**

Understand how income taxes affect CVP analysis

...focus on net income

Net income is operating income plus nonoperating revenues (such as interest revenue) minus nonoperating costs (such as interest cost) minus income taxes. For simplicity, throughout this chapter we assume nonoperating revenues and nonoperating costs are zero. So, our net income equation is:

$$\text{Net income} = \text{Operating income} - \text{Income taxes}$$

To make net income evaluations, CVP calculations for target income must be stated in terms of target net income instead of target operating income. For example, Emma may be interested in knowing the quantity of units of *GMAT Success* she must sell to earn a net income of $960, assuming an income tax rate of 40%.

$$\text{Target net income} = \left(\begin{array}{c}\text{Target}\\\text{operating income}\end{array}\right) - \left(\begin{array}{c}\text{Target}\\\text{operating income}\end{array} \times \text{Tax rate}\right)$$

$$\text{Target net income} = (\text{Target operating income}) \times (1 - \text{Tax rate})$$

$$\text{Target operating income} = \frac{\text{Target net income}}{1 - \text{Tax rate}} = \frac{\$960}{1 - 0.40} = \$1,600$$

In other words, to earn a target net income of $960, Emma's target operating income is $1,600.

Proof:

Target operating income	$1,600
Tax at 40% (0.40 × $1,600)	640
Target net income	$ 960

The key step is to take the target net income number and convert it into the corresponding target operating income number. We can then use equation 1 to determine the target operating income and substitute numbers from our *GMAT Success* example.

$$\left[\left(\begin{array}{c}\text{Selling}\\\text{price}\end{array} \times \begin{array}{c}\text{Quantity of}\\\text{units sold}\end{array}\right) - \left(\begin{array}{c}\text{Variable cost}\\\text{per unit}\end{array} \times \begin{array}{c}\text{Quantity of}\\\text{units sold}\end{array}\right)\right] - \begin{array}{c}\text{Fixed}\\\text{costs}\end{array} = \begin{array}{c}\text{Operating}\\\text{income}\end{array} \quad \text{(Equation 1)}$$

$$(\$200 \times Q) - (\$120 \times Q) - \$2,000 = \$1,600$$

$$\$80 \times Q = \$3,600$$

$$Q = \$3,600 \div \$80 \text{ per unit} = 45 \text{ units}$$

Alternatively, we can calculate the number of units Emma must sell by using the contribution margin method and equation 4:

$$\begin{array}{c}\text{Quantity of units}\\\text{required to be sold}\end{array} = \frac{\text{Fixed costs} + \text{Target operating income}}{\text{Contribution margin per unit}} \quad \text{(Equation 4)}$$

$$= \frac{\$2,000 + \$1,600}{\$80 \text{ per unit}} = 45 \text{ units}$$

Proof:

Revenues, $200 per unit × 45 units	$9,000
Variable costs, $120 per unit × 45 units	5,400
Contribution margin	3,600
Fixed costs	2,000
Operating income	1,600
Income taxes, $1,600 × 0.40	640
Net income	$ 960

Emma can also use the PV graph in Exhibit 3-3. To earn the target operating income of $1,600, Emma needs to sell 45 units.

Focusing the analysis on target net income instead of target operating income will not change the breakeven point because, by definition, operating income at the breakeven point is $0 and no income taxes are paid when there is no operating income.

DECISION POINT

How can managers incorporate income taxes into CVP analysis?

3-3 TRY IT!

Bernard Windows is a small company that installs windows. Its cost structure is as follows:

Selling price from each window installation	$ 500
Variable cost of each window installation	$ 400
Annual fixed costs	$150,000
Tax rate	30%

Calculate the number of windows Bernard Windows must install and the revenues needed to earn a target net income of $63,000.

Using CVP Analysis for Decision Making

LEARNING
OBJECTIVE 4

Explain how managers
use CVP analysis to make
decisions

…choose the alternative
that maximizes operating
income

You have learned how CVP analysis is useful for calculating the units that need to be sold to break even or to achieve a target operating income or target net income. A manager can also use CVP analysis to make other strategic decisions. Consider a decision about choosing the features for a product, such as the engine size, transmission system, or steering system for a new car model. Different choices will affect the vehicle's selling price, variable cost per unit, fixed costs, units sold, and operating income. CVP analysis helps managers make product decisions by estimating the expected profitability of these choices. We return to our *GMAT Success* example to show how Emma can use CVP analysis to make decisions about advertising and selling price.

Decision to Advertise

Suppose Emma anticipates selling 40 units of the *GMAT Success* package at the fair. Exhibit 3-3 indicates that Emma's operating income will be $1,200. Emma is considering advertising the product and its features in the fair brochure. The advertisement will be a fixed cost of $500. Emma thinks that advertising will increase sales by 10% to 44 packages. Should Emma advertise? The following table presents the CVP analysis.

	40 Packages Sold with No Advertising (1)	44 Packages Sold with Advertising (2)	Difference (3) = (2) − (1)
Revenues ($200 × 40; $200 × 44)	$8,000	$8,800	$ 800
Variable costs ($120 × 40; $120 × 44)	4,800	5,280	480
Contribution margin ($80 × 40; $80 × 44)	3,200	3,520	320
Fixed costs	2,000	2,500	500
Operating income	$1,200	$1,020	$ (180)

Operating income will decrease from $1,200 to $1,020, so Emma should not advertise. Note that Emma could focus only on the difference column and come to the same conclusion: If Emma advertises, contribution margin will increase by $320 (revenues, $800 − variable costs, $480) and fixed costs will increase by $500, resulting in a $180 decrease in operating income.

When using CVP analysis, try evaluating your decisions based on differences rather than mechanically working through the contribution income statement. What if advertising costs were $400 or $600 instead of $500? Analyzing differences allows managers to get to the heart of CVP analysis and sharpens their intuition by focusing only on the revenues and costs that will change as a result of a decision.

Decision to Reduce the Selling Price

Having decided not to advertise, Emma is contemplating whether to reduce the selling price to $175. At this price, she thinks she will sell 50 units. At this quantity, the test-prep package company that supplies *GMAT Success* will sell the packages to Emma for $115 per unit instead of $120. Should Emma reduce the selling price?

Contribution margin from lowering price to $175: ($175 − $115) per unit × 50 units	$3,000
Contribution margin from maintaining price at $200: ($200 − $120) per unit × 40 units	3,200
Change in contribution margin from lowering price	$ (200)

Decreasing the price will reduce contribution margin by $200 and, because the fixed costs of $2,000 will not change, will also reduce Emma's operating income by $200. Emma should not reduce the selling price.

Determining Target Prices

Emma could also ask, "At what price can I sell 50 units (purchased at $115 per unit) and continue to earn an operating income of $1,200?" The answer is $179, as the following calculations show:

Target operating income	$1,200
Add fixed costs	2,000
Target contribution margin	$3,200
Divided by number of units sold	÷ 50 units
Target contribution margin per unit	$ 64
Add variable cost per unit	115
Target selling price	$ 179

Proof:	Revenues, $179 per unit × 50 units	$8,950
	Variable costs, $115 per unit × 50 units	5,750
	Contribution margin	3,200
	Fixed costs	2,000
	Operating income	$1,200

Emma should also examine the effects of other decisions, such as simultaneously increasing her advertising costs and raising or lowering the price of *GMAT Success* packages. In each case, Emma will estimate the effects these actions are likely to have on the demand for *GMAT Success*. She will then compare the changes in contribution margin (through the effects on selling prices, variable costs, and quantities of units sold) to the changes in fixed costs and choose the alternative that provides the highest operating income. Concepts in Action: Cost–Volume–Profit Analysis Makes Subway's $5 Foot-Long Sandwiches a Success But Innovation

DECISION POINT

How do managers use CVP analysis to make decisions?

CONCEPTS IN ACTION ▸ Cost–Volume–Profit Analysis Makes Subway's $5 Foot-Long Sandwiches a Success But Innovation Challenges Loom

Julian Stratenschulte/dpa/picture-alliance/Newscom

Since 2008, the 44,000-location Subway restaurant chain has done big business with the success of its $5 foot-long sandwich deal. Heavily advertised, the promotion lowered the price of many sandwiches, which attracted customers in droves and helped Subway significantly boost profits. Since introducing $5 foot-longs, Subway has sold billions of the sandwiches worldwide.

How did Subway lower prices *and* boost profits, you may ask? Through higher volume and incremental sales of other items. When the price of foot-long sandwiches was lowered to $5, contribution margin per sandwich dropped but customers flocked to Subway and sales skyrocketed increasing total contribution margin.

At least two-thirds of Subway customers purchase potato chips or a soft drink with their sandwich. Subway's contribution margin on these items is very high, frequently as high as 70%. As the number of customers increased, the total contribution margin from these other items also increased. Fixed costs increased but the increases in contribution margin resulted in big increases in operating income.

But Subway faces challenges going forward. Its rapid sales growth has slowed as customer preferences have changed, and competitors from McDonalds to Firehouse Subs, Jimmy John's, and Jersey Mike's have begun offering more healthy menu options. If Subway is to continue to grow, it needs to get closer to its customers and continue to innovate its product offerings and its marketing.

Sources: Wendy Rotelli, "How Does Subway Profit From The $5 Foot-Long Deal?" *Restaurant Business* blog, Restaurants.com, April 10, 2013 (https://www.restaurants.com/blog/how-does-subway-profit-from-the-5-foot-long-deal); Drew Harwell, "The Rise and Fall of Subway, the World's Biggest Food Chain," *Washington Post*, May 30, 2015 (https://www.washingtonpost.com/business/economy/the-rise-and-fall-of-subway-the-worlds-biggest-food-chain/2015/05/29/0ca0a84a-fa7a-11e4-a13c-193b1241d51a_story.html).

Challenges Loom describes how Subway restaurant chain reduced the prices of its sandwiches to increase contribution margin and operating income but must now innovate to sustain its growth.

Strategic decisions invariably entail risk. Managers can use CVP analysis to evaluate how the operating income of their companies will be affected if the outcomes they predict are not achieved—say, if sales are 10% lower than they estimated. Evaluating this risk affects other strategic decisions a manager might make. For example, if the probability of a decline in sales seems high, a manager may take actions to change the cost structure to have more variable costs and fewer fixed costs.

Sensitivity Analysis and Margin of Safety

LEARNING OBJECTIVE 5

Explain how sensitivity analysis helps managers cope with uncertainty

...determine the effect on operating income of different assumptions

Sensitivity analysis is a "what-if" technique managers use to examine how an outcome will change if the original predicted data are not achieved or if an underlying assumption changes. The analysis answers questions such as "What will operating income be if the quantity of units sold decreases by 5% from the original prediction?" and "What will operating income be if variable cost per unit increases by 10%?" This helps visualize the possible outcomes that might occur *before* the company commits to funding a project. For example, companies such as Boeing and Airbus use CVP analysis to evaluate how many airplanes they need to sell in order to recover the multibillion-dollar costs of designing and developing new ones. The managers then do a sensitivity analysis to test how sensitive their conclusions are to different assumptions, such as the size of the market for the airplane, its selling price, and the market share they think it can capture.

Electronic spreadsheets, such as Excel, enable managers to systematically and efficiently conduct CVP-based sensitivity analyses and to examine the effect and interaction of changes in selling price, variable cost per unit, and fixed costs on target operating income. Exhibit 3-4 displays a spreadsheet for the *GMAT Success* example.

Using the spreadsheet, Emma can immediately see how many units she needs to sell to achieve particular operating-income levels, given alternative levels of fixed costs and variable cost per unit that she may face. For example, she must sell 32 units to earn an operating

EXHIBIT 3-4

Spreadsheet Analysis of CVP Relationships for *GMAT Success*

	Home	Insert	Page Layout	Formulas	Data	Review	View
	D5	▼	*fx*	=($A5+D$3)/(F1-$B5)			
	A	B	C	D	E	F
1			Number of units required to be sold at $200			
2			Selling Price to Earn Target Operating Income of			
3		Variable Costs	$0	$1,200	$1,600	$2,000
4	**Fixed Costs**	per Unit	(Breakeven point)			
5	$2,000	$100	20	32[a]	36	40
6	$2,000	$120	25	40	45	50
7	$2,000	$150	40	64	72	80
8	$2,400	$100	24	36	40	44
9	$2,400	$120	30	45	50	55
10	$2,400	$150	48	72	80	88
11	$2,800	$100	28	40	44	48
12	$2,800	$120	35	50	55	60
13	$2,800	$150	56	80	88	96
14						
15	[a]Number of units	$=\dfrac{\text{Fixed costs} + \text{Target operating income}}{\text{Contribution margin per unit}} = \dfrac{\$2,000 + \$1,200}{\$200 - \$100} = 32$				
16	required to be sold					

income of $1,200 if fixed costs are $2,000 and variable cost per unit is $100. Emma can also use cell C13 of Exhibit 3-4 to determine that she needs to sell 56 units to break even if the fixed cost of the booth rental at the Chicago fair is raised to $2,800 and if the variable cost per unit charged by the test-prep package supplier increases to $150. Emma can use this information along with sensitivity analysis and her predictions about how much she can sell to decide if she should rent the booth.

An important aspect of sensitivity analysis is **margin of safety**:

$$\text{Margin of safety} = \text{Budgeted (or actual) revenues} - \text{Breakeven revenues}$$

$$\text{Margin of safety (in units)} = \text{Budgeted (or actual) sales quantity} - \text{Breakeven quantity}$$

The margin of safety answers the "what-if" question: If budgeted revenues are above the breakeven point and drop, how far can they fall below budget before the breakeven point is reached? Sales might decrease as a result of factors such as a poorly executed marketing program or a competitor introducing a better product. Assume that Emma has fixed costs of $2,000, a selling price of $200, and variable cost per unit of $120. From Exhibit 3-1, if Emma sells 40 units, budgeted revenues are $8,000 and budgeted operating income is $1,200. The breakeven point is 25 units or $5,000 in total revenues.

$$\text{Margin of safety} = \frac{\text{Budgeted}}{\text{revenues}} - \frac{\text{Breakeven}}{\text{revenues}} = \$8,000 - \$5,000 = \$3,000$$

$$\frac{\text{Margin of}}{\text{safety (in units)}} = \frac{\text{Budgeted}}{\text{sales (units)}} - \frac{\text{Breakeven}}{\text{sales (units)}} = 40 - 25 = 15 \text{ units}$$

Sometimes margin of safety is expressed as a percentage:

$$\text{Margin of safety percentage} = \frac{\text{Margin of safety in dollars}}{\text{Budgeted (or actual) revenues}}$$

In our example, margin of safety percentage $= \dfrac{\$3,000}{\$8,000} = 37.5\%$

This result means that revenues would have to decrease substantially, by 37.5%, to reach the breakeven revenues. The high margin of safety gives Emma confidence that she is unlikely to suffer a loss.

If, however, Emma expects to sell only 30 units, budgeted revenues would be $6,000 ($200 per unit × 30 units) and the margin of safety would equal:

$$\text{Budgeted revenues} - \text{Breakeven revenues} = \$6,000 - \$5,000 = \$1,000$$

$$\frac{\text{Margin of}}{\text{safety percentage}} = \frac{\text{Margin of safety in dollars}}{\text{Budgeted (or actual) revenues}} = \frac{\$1,000}{\$6,000} = 16.67\%$$

The analysis implies that if revenues fall by more than 16.67%, Emma would suffer a loss. A low margin of safety increases the risk of a loss, which means Emma would need to look for ways to lower the breakeven point by reducing fixed costs or increasing contribution margin. For example, she would need to evaluate if her product is attractive enough to customers to allow her to charge a higher price without reducing the demand for it or if she could purchase the software at a lower cost. If Emma can neither reduce her fixed costs nor increase contribution margin and if she does not have the tolerance for this level of risk, she will prefer not to rent a booth at the fair.

Sensitivity analysis gives managers a good feel for a decision's risks. It is a simple approach to recognizing **uncertainty**, which is the possibility that an actual amount will deviate from an expected amount. A more comprehensive approach to recognizing uncertainty is to compute expected values using probability distributions. This approach is illustrated in the appendix to this chapter.

DECISION POINT

What can managers do to cope with uncertainty or changes in underlying assumptions?

TRY IT! 3-4

Bernard Windows is a small company that installs windows. Its cost structure is as follows:

Selling price from each window installation	$ 500
Variable cost of each window installation	$ 400
Annual fixed costs	$150,000

Calculate the margin of safety in units and dollars and the margin of safety percentage if Bernard Windows expects to sell 2,400 windows in the year.

Cost Planning and CVP

Managers have the ability to choose the levels of fixed and variable costs in their cost structures. This is a strategic decision that affects risk and returns. In this section, we describe how managers and management accountants think through this decision.

Alternative Fixed-Cost/Variable-Cost Structures

CVP-based sensitivity analysis highlights the risks and returns as fixed costs are substituted for variable costs in a company's cost structure. In Exhibit 3-4, compare line 6 and line 11.

	Fixed Cost	Variable Cost	Number of units required to be sold at $200 selling price to earn target operating income of	
			$0 (Breakeven point)	$2,000
Line 6	$2,000	$120	25	50
Line 11	$2,800	$100	28	48

Line 11, which has higher fixed costs and lower variable costs than line 6, has a higher break-even point but requires fewer units to be sold (48 vs. 50) to earn an operating income of $2,000. CVP analysis can help managers evaluate various fixed-cost/variable-cost structures. We next consider the effects of these choices in more detail. Suppose the Chicago fair organizers offer Emma three rental alternatives:

Option 1: $2,000 fixed fee

Option 2: $800 fixed fee plus 15% of *GMAT Success* revenues

Option 3: 25% of *GMAT Success* revenues with no fixed fee

Emma is interested in how her choice of a rental agreement will affect the income she earns and the risks she faces. Exhibit 3-5 graphically depicts the profit–volume relationship for each option.

- The line representing the relationship between units sold and operating income for Option 1 is the same as the line in the PV graph shown in Exhibit 3-3 (fixed costs of $2,000 and contribution margin per unit of $80).

- The line representing Option 2 shows fixed costs of $800 and a contribution margin per unit of $50 [selling price, $200, minus variable cost per unit, $120, minus variable rental fees per unit, $30 (0.15 × $200)].

- The line representing Option 3 shows fixed costs of $0 and a contribution margin per unit of $30 [selling price, $200, minus variable cost per unit, $120, minus variable rental fees per unit, $50 (0.25 × $200)].

Option 3 has the lowest breakeven point (0 units), and Option 1 has the highest break-even point (25 units). Option 1 is associated with the highest risk of loss if sales are low, but it also has the highest contribution margin per unit ($80) and therefore the highest operating income when sales are high (greater than 40 units).

The choice among Options 1, 2, and 3 is a strategic decision. As with most strategic decisions, what Emma decides will significantly affect her operating income (or loss), depending on the demand for the product. Faced with this uncertainty, Emma's choice will be influenced

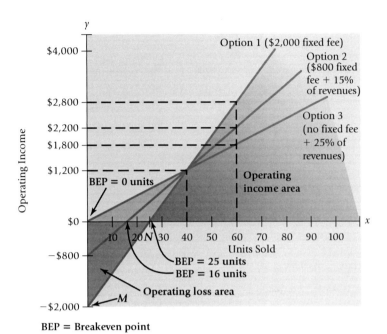

by her confidence in the level of demand for *GMAT Success* packages and her willingness to risk losses if demand is low. For example, if Emma's tolerance for risk is high, she will choose Option 1 with its high potential rewards. If, however, Emma is risk averse, she will prefer Option 3, where the rewards are smaller if sales are high but where she never suffers a loss if sales are low.

Operating Leverage

The risk-return tradeoff across alternative cost structures can be measured as *operating leverage*. **Operating leverage** describes the effects that fixed costs have on changes in operating income as changes occur in units sold and contribution margin. Organizations with a high proportion of fixed costs in their cost structures, as is the case with Option 1, have high operating leverage. The line representing Option 1 in Exhibit 3-5 is the steepest of the three lines. Small increases in sales lead to large increases in operating income. Small decreases in sales result in relatively large decreases in operating income, leading to a greater risk of operating losses. *At any given level of sales,*

$$\frac{\text{Degree of}}{\text{operating leverage}} = \frac{\text{Contribution margin}}{\text{Operating income}}$$

The following table shows the **degree of operating leverage** at sales of 40 units for the three rental options.

	Option 1	Option 2	Option 3
1. Contribution margin per unit (see page 102)	$ 80	$ 50	$ 30
2. Contribution margin (row 1 × 40 units)	$3,200	$2,000	$1,200
3. Operating income (from Exhibit 3-5)	$1,200	$1,200	$1,200
4. Degree of operating leverage (row 2 ÷ row 3)	$\frac{\$3,200}{\$1,200} = 2.67$	$\frac{\$2,000}{\$1,200} = 1.67$	$\frac{\$1,200}{\$1,200} = 1.00$

These results indicate that, when sales are 40 units, a 1% change in sales and contribution margin will result in 2.67% change in operating income for Option 1. For Option 3, a 1% change in sales and contribution margin will result in only a 1% change in operating income. Consider, for example, a sales increase of 50% from 40 to 60 units. Contribution margin will increase by 50% under each option. Operating income, however, will increase by 2.67 × 50% = 133% from $1,200 to $2,800 in Option 1, but it will increase by only

$1.00 \times 50\% = 50\%$ from \$1,200 to \$1,800 in Option 3 (see Exhibit 3-5). The degree of operating leverage at a given level of sales helps managers calculate the effect of sales fluctuations on operating income.

Keep in mind that, in the presence of fixed costs, the degree of operating leverage is different at different levels of sales. For example, at sales of 60 units, the degree of operating leverage under each of the three options is as follows:

	Option 1	Option 2	Option 3
1. Contribution margin per unit (page 102)	$ 80	$ 50	$ 30
2. Contribution margin (row 1 × 60 units)	$4,800	$3,000	$1,800
3. Operating income (from Exhibit 3-5)	$2,800	$2,200	$1,800
4. Degree of operating leverage (row 2 ÷ row 3)	$\dfrac{\$4,800}{\$2,800} = 1.71$	$\dfrac{\$3,000}{\$2,200} = 1.36$	$\dfrac{\$1,800}{\$1,800} = 1.00$

The degree of operating leverage decreases from 2.67 (at sales of 40 units) to 1.71 (at sales of 60 units) under Option 1 and from 1.67 to 1.36 under Option 2. In general, whenever there are fixed costs, the degree of operating leverage decreases as the level of sales increases beyond the breakeven point. If fixed costs are \$0 as they are in Option 3, contribution margin equals operating income and the degree of operating leverage equals 1.00 at all sales levels.

It is important for managers to monitor operating leverage carefully. Consider companies such as General Motors and American Airlines. Their high operating leverage was a major reason for their financial problems. Anticipating high demand for their services, these companies borrowed money to acquire assets, resulting in high fixed costs. As their sales declined, they suffered losses and could not generate enough cash to service their interest and debt, causing them to seek bankruptcy protection. Managers and management accountants must manage the level of fixed costs and variable costs to balance the risk-return tradeoffs in their firms.

What can managers do to reduce fixed costs? Nike, the shoe and apparel company, does no manufacturing and incurs no fixed costs of operating and maintaining manufacturing plants. Instead, it outsources production and buys its products from suppliers in countries such as China, Indonesia, and Vietnam. As a result, all of Nike's production costs are variable costs. Nike reduces its risk of loss by increasing variable costs and reducing fixed costs.

Companies that continue to do their own manufacturing are moving their facilities from the United States to lower-cost countries, such as Mexico and China, to reduce both fixed costs and variable costs. Other companies, such as General Electric and Hewlett-Packard, have shifted service functions, such as after-sales customer service, to their customer call centers in countries such as India. These decisions by companies are often controversial. Some economists argue that outsourcing or building plants in other countries helps keep costs, and therefore prices, low and enables U.S. companies to remain globally competitive. Others argue that outsourcing and setting up manufacturing in other countries reduces job opportunities in the United States and hurts working-class families.

DECISION POINT

How should managers choose among different variable-cost/fixed-cost structures?

TRY IT! 3-5

Bernard Windows is a small company that installs windows. Its cost structure is as follows:

Selling price from each window installation	$ 500
Variable cost of each window installation	$ 400
Annual fixed costs	$150,000
Number of window units sold	2,500

Bernard is considering changing its sales compensation for next year. Bernard would pay salespeople a 5% commission next year and reduce fixed selling costs by \$62,500.

Calculate the degree of operating leverage at sales of 2,500 units under the two options. Comment briefly on the result.

Effects of Sales Mix on Income

Sales mix is the quantities (or proportion) of various products (or services) that constitute a company's total unit sales. Suppose Emma is now budgeting for a subsequent college fair in New York. She plans to sell two different test-prep packages—*GMAT Success* and *GRE Guarantee*—and budgets the following:

	GMAT Success	GRE Guarantee	Total
Expected sales	60	40	100
Revenues, $200 and $100 per unit	$12,000	$4,000	$16,000
Variable costs, $120 and $70 per unit	7,200	2,800	10,000
Contribution margin, $80 and $30 per unit	$ 4,800	$1,200	6,000
Fixed costs			4,500
Operating income			$ 1,500

LEARNING OBJECTIVE 7

Apply CVP analysis to a company producing multiple products

…assume sales mix of products remains constant as total units sold changes

What is the breakeven point for Emma's business now? The total number of units that must be sold to break even in a multiproduct company depends on the sales mix. For Emma, this is the combination of the number of units of *GMAT Success* sold and the number of units of *GRE Guarantee* sold. We assume that the budgeted sales mix (60 units of *GMAT Success* sold for every 40 units of *GRE Guarantee* sold, that is, a ratio of 3:2) will not change at different levels of total unit sales. That is, we think of Emma selling a bundle of 3 units of *GMAT Success* and 2 units of *GRE Guarantee*. (Note that this does not mean that Emma physically bundles the two products together into one big package.)

Each bundle yields a contribution margin of $300, calculated as follows:

	Number of Units of GMAT Success and GRE Guarantee in Each Bundle	Contribution Margin per Unit for GMAT Success and GRE Guarantee	Contribution Margin of the Bundle
GMAT *Success*	3	$80	$240
GRE *Guarantee*	2	30	60
Total			$300

To compute the breakeven point, we calculate the number of bundles Emma needs to sell.

$$\text{Breakeven point in bundles} = \frac{\text{Fixed costs}}{\text{Contribution margin per bundle}} = \frac{\$4,500}{\$300 \text{ per bundle}} = 15 \text{ bundles}$$

The breakeven point in units of *GMAT Success* and *GRE Guarantee* is as follows:

GMAT *Success* : 15 bundles × 3 units per bundle	45 units
GRE *Guarantee* : 15 bundles × 2 units per bundle	30 units
Total number of units to break even	75 units

The breakeven point in dollars for *GMAT Success* and *GRE Guarantee* is as follows:

GMAT *Success* : 45 units × $200 per unit	$ 9,000
GRE *Guarantee* : 30 units × $100 per unit	3,000
Breakeven revenues	$12,000

When there are multiple products, it is often convenient to use the contribution margin percentage. Under this approach, Emma also calculates the revenues from selling a bundle of 3 units of *GMAT Success* and 2 units of *GRE Guarantee*:

	Number of Units of GMAT Success and GRE Guarantee in Each Bundle	Selling Price for GMAT Success and GRE Guarantee	Revenue of the Bundle
GMAT Success	3	$200	$600
GRE Guarantee	2	100	200
Total			$800

$$\begin{array}{c}\text{Contribution}\\\text{margin}\\\text{percentage for}\\\text{the bundle}\end{array} = \frac{\text{Contribution margin of the bundle}}{\text{Revenue of the bundle}} = \frac{\$300}{\$800} = 0.375, \text{ or } 37.5\%$$

$$\begin{array}{c}\text{Breakeven}\\\text{revenues}\end{array} = \frac{\text{Fixed costs}}{\text{Contribution margin \% for the bundle}} = \frac{\$4,500}{0.375} = \$12,000$$

$$\begin{array}{c}\text{Number of bundles}\\\text{required to be sold}\\\text{to break even}\end{array} = \frac{\text{Breakeven revenues}}{\text{Revenue per bundle}} = \frac{\$12,000}{\$800 \text{ per bundle}} = 15 \text{ bundles}$$

The breakeven point in units and dollars for *GMAT Success* and *GRE Guarantee* are as follows:

GMAT Success : 15 bundles × 3 units per bundle = 45 units × $200 per unit = **$9,000**

GRE Guarantee : 15 bundles × 2 units per bundle = 30 units × $100 per unit = **$3,000**

Recall that in all our calculations we have assumed that the budgeted sales mix (3 units of *GMAT Success* for every 2 units of *GRE Guarantee*) will not change at different levels of total unit sales.

Of course, there are many different sales mixes (in units) that can result in a contribution margin of $4,500 that leads to Emma breaking even, as the following table shows:

Sales Mix (Units)		Contribution Margin from		
GMAT Success (1)	**GRE Guarantee** (2)	**GMAT Success** (3) = $80 × (1)	**GRE Guarantee** (4) = $30 × (2)	**Total Contribution Margin** (5) = (3) + (4)
48	22	$3,840	$ 660	$4,500
36	54	2,880	1,620	4,500
30	70	2,400	2,100	4,500

If, for example, the sales mix changes to 3 units of *GMAT Success* for every 7 units of *GRE Guarantee*, the breakeven point increases from 75 units to 100 units, composed of 30 units of *GMAT Success* and 70 units of *GRE Guarantee*. The breakeven quantity increases because the sales mix has shifted toward the lower-contribution-margin product, *GRE Guarantee* (which is $30 per unit compared to *GMAT Success*'s $80 per unit). In general, for any given total quantity of units sold, a shift in sales mix towards units with lower contribution margins (more units of *GRE Guarantee* compared to *GMAT Success*), decreases operating income.

How do companies choose their sales mix? They adjust their mix to respond to demand changes. For example, when gasoline prices increased and customers wanted smaller cars, auto companies, such as Ford, Nissan, and Toyota, shifted their production mix to produce smaller cars. This shift to smaller cars increased the breakeven point because the sales mix had shifted toward lower-contribution-margin products. Despite this increase in the breakeven point, shifting the sales mix to smaller cars was the correct decision because the demand for larger cars had fallen. At no point should a manager focus on changing the sales mix to lower the breakeven point without taking into account customer preferences and demand. Of course, the shift in sales mix to smaller cars prompted managers at Ford, Nissan, and Toyota to increase the prices of these cars in line with demand.

The multiproduct case has two cost (and revenue) drivers, *GMAT Success* and *GRE Guarantee*. It illustrates how CVP and breakeven analyses can be adapted when there are multiple cost drivers. The key point is that many different combinations of cost drivers can result in a given contribution margin.

DECISION POINT

How can managers apply CVP analysis to a company producing multiple products?

Bernard Windows plans to sell two different brands of windows—Chad and Musk—and budgets the following:

3-6 TRY IT!

	Chad Windows	Musk Windows	Total
Expected sales	2,500	1,000	3,500
Revenues, $500 and $350 per unit	$1,250,000	$350,000	$1,600,000
Variable costs, $400 and $275 per unit	1,000,000	275,000	1,275,000
Contribution margin, $100 and $75 per unit	$ 250,000	$ 75,000	325,000
Fixed costs			195,000
Operating income			$ 130,000

Calculate the breakeven point for Bernard Windows in terms of (a) the number of units sold and (b) revenues.

CVP Analysis in Service and Not-for-Profit Organizations

So far, our CVP analysis has focused on Emma's merchandising company. Of course, managers at manufacturing companies such as BMW, service companies such as Bank of America, and not-for-profit organizations such as the United Way also use CVP analysis to make decisions. To apply CVP analysis in service and not-for-profit organizations, we need to focus on measuring their output, which is different from the tangible units sold by manufacturing and merchandising companies. Examples of output measures in various service industries (for example, airlines, hotels/motels, and hospitals) and not-for-profit organizations (for example, universities) are as follows:

LEARNING OBJECTIVE 8

Apply CVP analysis in service and not-for-profit organizations

...define appropriate output measures

Industry	Measure of Output
Airlines	Passenger miles
Hotels/motels	Room-nights occupied
Hospitals	Patient days
Universities	Student credit-hours

Variable and fixed costs are then defined with respect to the chosen output measure. The concepts of contribution margin, breakeven point, target operating income, target net income, sensitivity analysis, and operating leverage apply as we have described in the chapter.

To see the application of CVP analysis in the context of a service-sector example, consider Highbridge Consulting, a boutique management consulting firm. Highbridge measures output in terms of person-days of consulting services. It hires consultants to match the demand for consulting services. The greater the demand, the greater the number of consultants it hires.

Highbridge must hire and train new consultants before the consultants are deployed on assignments. At the start of each year, Highbridge allocates a recruiting budget for the number of employees it desires to recruit. In 2017, this budget is $1,250,000. On average, the annual cost of a consultant is $100,000. Fixed costs of recruiting including administrative salaries and expenses of the recruiting department are $250,000. How many consultants can Highbridge recruit in 2017? We can use CVP analysis to answer this question by setting the recruiting department's operating income to $0. Let Q be the number of consultants hired:

$$\text{Recruiting Budget} - \text{Variable costs} - \text{Fixed costs} = 0$$
$$\$1,250,000 - \$100,000\,Q - \$250,000 = 0$$
$$\$100,000\,Q = \$1,250,000 - \$250,000 = \$1,000,000$$
$$Q = \$1,000,000 \div \$100,000 \text{ per consultant} = 10 \text{ consultants}$$

Suppose Highbridge anticipates reduced demand for consulting services in 2018. It reduces its recruiting budget by 40% to $1,250,000 \times (1 - 0.40) = \$750,000$, expecting to hire 6 consultants (40% fewer consultants than 2017). Assuming the cost per consultant and the recruiting department's fixed costs remain the same as in 2017, is this budget correct? No, as the following calculation shows:

$$\$750,000 - \$100,000\, Q - \$250,000 = 0$$
$$\$100,000\, Q = \$750,000 - \$250,000 = \$500,000$$
$$Q = \$500,000 \div \$100,000 \text{ per consultant} = 5 \text{ consultants}$$

Highbridge will only be able to recruit 5 consultants. Note the following two characteristics of the CVP relationships in this service company situation:

1. The percentage decrease in the number of consultants hired, $(10 - 5) \div 10$, or 50%, is greater than the 40% reduction in the recruiting budget. It is greater because the $250,000 in fixed costs still must be paid, leaving a proportionately lower budget to hire consultants. In other words, the percentage drop in consultants hired exceeds the percentage drop in the recruiting budget because of the fixed costs.

2. Given the reduced recruiting budget of $750,000 in 2018, the manager can adjust recruiting activities to hire 6 consultants in one or more of the following ways: (a) by reducing the variable cost per person (the average compensation) from the current $100,000 per consultant, or (b) by reducing the recruiting department's total fixed costs from the current $250,000. For example if the recruiting department's fixed costs were reduced to $210,000 and the cost per consultant were reduced to $90,000, Highbridge would be able to hire the 6 consultants it needs, $(\$750,000 - \$210,000) \div \$90,000 = 6$ consultants.

If the fixed costs of the recruiting department remain $250,000 and Highbridge wants to hire 6 consultants at an average cost of $100,000, it would have to set the recruiting budget at $850,000 [($100,000 \times 6) + $250,000]$ instead of $750,000. Again the percentage decrease in the number of consultants hired $40\% [(10 - 6) \div 10]$ is greater than the $32\% [(\$1,250,000 - \$850,000) \div \$1,250,000]$ reduction in the recruiting budget because of the fixed costs of the recruiting department.

DECISION POINT

How do managers apply CVP analysis in service and not-for-profit organizations?

Contribution Margin Versus Gross Margin

LEARNING OBJECTIVE 9

Distinguish contribution margin

...revenues minus all variable costs

from gross margin

...revenues minus cost of goods sold

So far, we have developed two important concepts relating to profit margin—contribution margin, which was introduced in this chapter, and gross margin, which was discussed in Chapter 2. Is there a relationship between these two concepts? In the following equations, we clearly distinguish contribution margin, which provides information for CVP and risk analysis, from gross margin, a measure of competitiveness, described in Chapter 2.

$$\text{Gross margin} = \text{Revenues} - \text{Cost of goods sold}$$
$$\text{Contribution margin} = \text{Revenues} - \text{All variable costs}$$

The gross margin measures how much a company can charge for its products over and above the cost of acquiring or producing them. Companies, such as brand-name pharmaceuticals producers, have high gross margins because their products are often patented and provide unique and distinctive benefits to consumers. In contrast, manufacturers of generic medicines and basic chemicals have low gross margins because the market for these products is highly competitive. Contribution margin indicates how much of a company's revenues are available to cover fixed costs. It helps in assessing the risk of losses. For example, the risk of loss is low if the contribution margin exceeds a company's fixed costs even when sales are low. Gross margin and contribution margin are related but give different insights. For example, a company operating in a competitive market with a low gross margin will have a low risk of loss if its fixed costs are small.

Consider the distinction between gross margin and contribution margin in the manufacturing sector. The concepts differ in two ways: fixed manufacturing costs and variable nonmanufacturing costs. The following example (figures assumed) illustrates this difference:

Contribution Income Statement Emphasizing Contribution Margin (in thousands)			Financial Accounting Income Statement Emphasizing Gross Margin (in thousands)	
Revenues		$1,000	Revenues	$1,000
Variable manufacturing costs	$250		Cost of goods sold (variable manufacturing costs, $250 + fixed manufacturing costs, $160)	410
Variable nonmanufacturing costs	270	520		
Contribution margin		480	Gross margin	590
Fixed manufacturing costs	160			
Fixed nonmanufacturing costs	138	298	Nonmanufacturing costs (variable, $270 + fixed, $138)	408
Operating income		$ 182	Operating income	$ 182

Fixed manufacturing costs of $160,000 are not deducted from revenues when computing the contribution margin but are deducted when computing the gross margin. The cost of goods sold in a manufacturing company includes all variable manufacturing costs and all fixed manufacturing costs ($250,000 + $160,000). The company's variable nonmanufacturing costs (such as commissions paid to salespersons) of $270,000 are deducted from revenues when computing the contribution margin but are not deducted when computing gross margin.

Like contribution margin, gross margin can be expressed as a total, as an amount per unit, or as a percentage. For example, the **gross margin percentage** is the gross margin divided by revenues—59% ($590 ÷ $1,000) in our manufacturing-sector example.

One reason why managers sometimes confuse gross margin and contribution margin with each other is that the two are often identical in the case of merchandising companies because the cost of goods sold equals the variable cost of goods purchased (and subsequently sold).

DECISION POINT

What is the difference between contribution margin and gross margin?

PROBLEM FOR SELF-STUDY

Wembley Travel Agency specializes in flights between Los Angeles and London. It books passengers on United Airlines at $900 per round-trip ticket. Until last month, United paid Wembley a commission of 10% of the ticket price paid by each passenger. This commission was Wembley's only source of revenues. Wembley's fixed costs are $14,000 per month (for salaries, rent, and so on), and its variable costs, such as sales commissions and bonuses, are $20 per ticket purchased for a passenger.

United Airlines has just announced a revised payment schedule for all travel agents. It will now pay travel agents a 10% commission per ticket up to a maximum of $50. Any ticket costing more than $500 generates only a $50 commission, regardless of the ticket price. Wembley's managers are concerned about how United's new payment schedule will affect its breakeven point and profitability.

1. Under the old 10% commission structure, how many round-trip tickets must Wembley sell each month (a) to break even and (b) to earn an operating income of $7,000?
2. How does United's revised payment schedule affect your answers to (a) and (b) in requirement 1?

Continued

Solution

1. Wembley receives a 10% commission on each ticket: $10\% \times \$900 = \$90$. Thus,

$$\text{Selling price} = \$90 \text{ per ticket}$$
$$\text{Variable cost per unit} = \$20 \text{ per ticket}$$
$$\text{Contribution margin per unit} = \$90 - \$20 = \$70 \text{ per ticket}$$
$$\text{Fixed costs} = \$14,000 \text{ per month}$$

a.
$$\frac{\text{Breakeven number}}{\text{of tickets}} = \frac{\text{Fixed costs}}{\text{Contribution margin per unit}} = \frac{\$14,000}{\$70 \text{ per ticket}} = 200 \text{ tickets}$$

b. When target operating income = $7,000 per month,

$$\frac{\text{Quantity of tickets}}{\text{required to be sold}} = \frac{\text{Fixed costs} + \text{Target operating income}}{\text{Contribution margin per unit}}$$

$$= \frac{\$14,000 + \$7,000}{\$70 \text{ per ticket}} = \frac{\$21,000}{\$70 \text{ per ticket}} = 300 \text{ tickets}$$

2. Under the new system, Wembley would receive only $50 on the $900 ticket. Thus,

$$\text{Selling price} = \$50 \text{ per ticket}$$
$$\text{Variable cost per unit} = \$20 \text{ per ticket}$$
$$\text{Contribution margin per unit} = \$50 - \$20 = \$30 \text{ per ticket}$$
$$\text{Fixed costs} = \$14,000 \text{ per month}$$

a.
$$\frac{\text{Breakeven number}}{\text{of tickets}} = \frac{\$14,000}{\$30 \text{ per ticket}} = 467 \text{ tickets (rounded up)}$$

b.
$$\frac{\text{Quantity of tickets}}{\text{required to be sold}} = \frac{\$21,000}{\$30 \text{ per ticket}} = 700 \text{ tickets}$$

The $50 cap on the commission paid per ticket causes the breakeven point to more than double (from 200 to 467 tickets) and the tickets required to be sold to earn $7,000 per month to also more than double (from 300 to 700 tickets). As would be expected, managers at Wembley reacted very negatively to the United Airlines announcement to change commission payments. Unfortunately for Wembley, other airlines also changed their commission structure in similar ways.

DECISION POINTS

The following question-and-answer format summarizes the chapter's learning objectives. Each decision presents a key question related to a learning objective. The guidelines are the answer to that question.

Decision	Guidelines
1. How can CVP analysis help managers?	CVP analysis assists managers in understanding the behavior of a product's or service's total costs, total revenues, and operating income as changes occur in the output level, selling price, variable costs, or fixed costs.
2. How can managers determine the breakeven point or the output needed to achieve a target operating income?	The breakeven point is the quantity of output at which total revenues equal total costs. The three methods for computing the breakeven point and the quantity of output to achieve target operating income are the equation method, the contribution margin method, and the graph method. Each method is merely a restatement of the others. Managers often select the method they find easiest to use in a specific decision situation.

Decision	Guidelines
3. How can managers incorporate income taxes into CVP analysis?	Income taxes can be incorporated into CVP analysis by using the target net income to calculate the target operating income. The breakeven point is unaffected by income taxes because no income taxes are paid when operating income equals zero.
4. How do managers use CVP analysis to make decisions?	Managers compare how revenues, costs, and contribution margins change across various alternatives. They then choose the alternative that maximizes operating income.
5. What can managers do to cope with uncertainty or changes in underlying assumptions?	Sensitivity analysis is a "what-if" technique that examines how an outcome will change if the original predicted data are not achieved or if an underlying assumption changes. When making decisions, managers use CVP analysis to compare contribution margins and fixed costs under different assumptions. Managers also calculate the margin of safety equal to budgeted revenues minus breakeven revenues.
6. How should managers choose among different variable-cost/fixed-cost structures?	Choosing the variable-cost/fixed-cost structure is a strategic decision for companies. CVP analysis helps managers compare the risk of losses when revenues are low and the upside profits when revenues are high for different proportions of variable and fixed costs in a company's cost structure.
7. How can managers apply CVP analysis to a company producing multiple products?	Managers apply CVP analysis in a company producing multiple products by assuming the sales mix of products sold remains constant as the total quantity of units sold changes.
8. How do managers apply CVP analysis in service and not-for-profit organizations?	Managers define output measures such as passenger-miles in the case of airlines or patient-days in the context of hospitals and identify costs that are fixed and those that vary with these measures of output.
9. What is the difference between contribution margin and gross margin?	Contribution margin is revenues minus all variable costs whereas gross margin is revenues minus cost of goods sold. Contribution margin measures the risk of a loss, whereas gross margin measures the competitiveness of a product.

APPENDIX

Decision Models and Uncertainty[2]

This appendix explores the characteristics of uncertainty, describes an approach managers can use to make decisions in a world of uncertainty, and illustrates the insights gained when uncertainty is recognized in CVP analysis. In the face of uncertainty, managers rely on decision models to help them make the right choices.

Role of a Decision Model

Uncertainty is the possibility that an actual amount will deviate from an expected amount. In the *GMAT Success* example, Emma might forecast sales at 42 units, but actual sales might turn out to be 30 units or 60 units. A decision model helps managers deal with such uncertainty. It is a formal method for making a choice, commonly involving both quantitative and qualitative analyses. This appendix focuses on the quantitative analysis that usually includes the following steps:

Step 1: Identify a choice criterion. A **choice criterion** is an objective that can be quantified, such as maximize income or minimize costs. Managers use the choice criterion to choose the

---

[2] *Source:* Based on teaching notes prepared by R. Williamson.

best alternative action. Emma's choice criterion is to maximize expected operating income at the Chicago college fair.

Step 2: Identify the set of alternative actions that can be taken. We use the letter a with subscripts $_{1, 2,}$ and $_3$ to distinguish each of Emma's three possible actions:

$a_1 =$ Pay $2,000 fixed fee

$a_2 =$ Pay $800 fixed fee plus 15% of *GMAT Success* revenues

$a_3 =$ Pay 25% of *GMAT Success* revenues with no fixed fee

Step 3: Identify the set of events that can occur. An **event** is a possible relevant occurrence, such as the actual number of *GMAT Success* packages Emma might sell at the fair. The set of events should be mutually exclusive and collectively exhaustive. Events are mutually exclusive if they cannot occur at the same time. Events are collectively exhaustive if, taken together, they make up the entire set of possible relevant occurrences (no other event can occur). Examples of mutually exclusive and collectively exhaustive events are growth, decline, or no change in industry demand and increase, decrease, or no change in interest rates. Only one event out of the entire set of mutually exclusive and collectively exhaustive events will actually occur.

Suppose Emma's only uncertainty is the number of units of *GMAT Success* that she can sell. For simplicity, suppose Emma estimates that sales will be either 30 or 60 units. This set of events is mutually exclusive because clearly sales of 30 units and 60 units cannot both occur at the same time. It is collectively exhaustive because under our assumptions sales cannot be anything other than 30 or 60 units. We use the letter x with subscripts $_1$ and $_2$ to distinguish the set of mutually exclusive and collectively exhaustive events:

$x_1 =$ 30 units

$x_2 =$ 60 units

Step 4: Assign a probability to each event that can occur. A **probability** is the likelihood or chance that an event will occur. The decision model approach to coping with uncertainty assigns probabilities to events. A **probability distribution** describes the likelihood, or the probability, that each of the mutually exclusive and collectively exhaustive set of events will occur. In some cases, there will be much evidence to guide the assignment of probabilities. For example, the probability of obtaining heads in the toss of a coin is 1/2 and that of drawing a particular playing card from a standard, well-shuffled deck is 1/52. In business, the probability of having a specified percentage of defective units may be assigned with great confidence on the basis of production experience with thousands of units. In other cases, there will be little evidence supporting estimated probabilities—for example, expected sales of a new pharmaceutical product next year. Suppose that Emma, on the basis of past experience, assesses a 60% chance, or a 6/10 probability, that she will sell 30 units and a 40% chance, or a 4/10 probability, that she will sell 60 units. Using $P(x)$ as the notation for the probability of an event, the probabilities are as follows:

$P(x_1) = 6/10 = 0.60$

$P(x_2) = 4/10 = 0.40$

The sum of these probabilities must equal 1.00 because these events are mutually exclusive and collectively exhaustive.

Step 5: Identify the set of possible outcomes. **Outcomes** specify, in terms of the choice criterion, the predicted economic results of the various possible combinations of actions and events. In the *GMAT Success* example, the outcomes are the six possible operating incomes displayed in the decision table in Exhibit 3-6. A **decision table** is a summary of the alternative actions, events, outcomes, and probabilities of events.

Distinguish among actions, events, and outcomes. Actions are decision choices available to managers—for example, the particular rental alternatives that Emma can choose. Events are the set of all relevant occurrences that can happen—for example, the different quantities of *GMAT Success* packages that may be sold at the fair. The outcome is operating income, which depends both on the action the manager selects (rental alternative chosen) and the event that occurs (the quantity of packages sold).

EXHIBIT 3-6   Decision Table for *GMAT Success*

	A	B	C	D	E	F	G	H	I
1	Selling price = $200				**Operating Income**				
2	Package cost = $120				**Under Each Possible Event**				
3			**Percentage**						
4		**Fixed**	**of Fair**	**Event x_1: Units Sold = 30**			**Event x_2: Units Sold = 60**		
5	**Actions**	**Fee**	**Revenues**	**Probability(x_1) = 0.60**			**Probability(x_2) = 0.40**		
6	a_1: Pay $2,000 fixed fee	$2,000	0%	$400[l]			$2,800[m]		
7	a_2: Pay $800 fixed fee plus 15% of revenues	$ 800	15%	$700[n]			$2,200[p]		
8	a_3:Pay 25% of revenues with no fixed fee	$ 0	25%	$900[q]			$1,800[r]		
9									
10	[l]Operating income = ($200 – $120)(30) – $2,000	=	$ 400						
11	[m]Operating income = ($200 – $120)(60) – $2,000	=	$2,800						
12	[n]Operating income = ($200 – $120 – 15% × $200)(30) – $800	=	$ 700						
13	[p]Operating income = ($200 – $120 – 15% × $200)(60) – $800	=	$2,200						
14	[q]Operating income = ($200 – $120 – 25% × $200)(30)	=	$ 900						
15	[r]Operating income = ($200 – $120 – 25% × $200)(60)	=	$1,800						

Exhibit 3-7 presents an overview of relationships among a decision model, the implementation of a chosen action, its outcome, and subsequent performance evaluation. Thoughtful managers step back and evaluate what happened and learn from their experiences. This learning serves as feedback for adapting the decision model for future actions.

Expected Value

An **expected value** is the weighted average of the outcomes, with the probability of each outcome serving as the weight. When the outcomes are measured in monetary terms, expected value is often called **expected monetary value**. Using information in Exhibit 3-6, the expected monetary value of each booth-rental alternative denoted by $E(a_1)$, $E(a_2)$, and $E(a_3)$ is as follows:

Pay $2,000 fixed fee: $E(a_1) = (0.60 \times \$400) + (0.40 \times \$2,800) = \$1,360$
Pay $800 fixed fee plus 15% of revenues: $E(a_2) = (0.60 \times \$700) + (0.40 \times \$2,200) = \$1,300$
Pay 25% of revenues with no fixed fee: $E(a_3) = (0.60 \times \$900) + (0.40 \times \$1,800) = \$1,260$

To maximize expected operating income, Emma should select action a_1—pay the Chicago fair organizers a $2,000 fixed fee.

To interpret the expected value of selecting action a_1, imagine that Emma attends many fairs, each with the probability distribution of operating incomes given in Exhibit 3-6. For a specific fair, Emma will earn operating income of either $400, if she sells 30 units, or $2,800, if she sells 60 units. But if Emma attends 100 fairs, she will expect to earn $400 operating income 60% of the time (at 60 fairs) and $2,800 operating income 40% of the time (at 40 fairs), for a total op-

EXHIBIT 3-7   A Decision Model and Its Link to Performance Evaluation

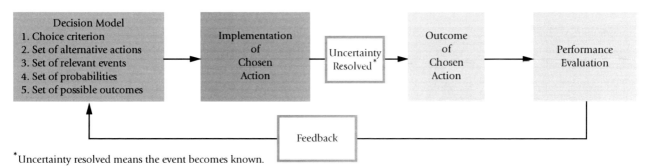

*Uncertainty resolved means the event becomes known.

erating income of $136,000 ($400 × 60 + $2,800 × 40). The expected value of $1,360 is the operating income per fair that Emma will earn when averaged across all fairs ($136,000 ÷ 100). Of course, in many real-world situations, managers must make one-time decisions under uncertainty. Even in these cases, expected value is a useful tool for choosing among alternatives.

Consider the effect of uncertainty on the preferred action choice. If Emma were certain she would sell only 30 units (that is, $P(x_1) = 1$), she would prefer alternative a_3—pay 25% of revenues with no fixed fee. To follow this reasoning, examine Exhibit 3-6. When 30 units are sold, alternative a_3 yields the maximum operating income of $900. Because fixed costs are $0, booth-rental costs are lower, equal to $1,500 (25% of revenues = 0.25 × $200 per unit × 30 units), when sales are low.

However, if Emma were certain she would sell 60 packages (that is, $P(x_2) = 1$), she would prefer alternative a_1—pay a $2,000 fixed fee. Exhibit 3-6 indicates that when 60 units are sold, alternative a_1 yields the maximum operating income of $2,800. That's because, when 60 units are sold, rental payments under a_2($800 + 0.15 × $200 per unit × 60 units = $2,600) and a_3(0.25 × $200 per unit × 60 units = $3,000) are more than the fixed $2,000 fee under a_1.

Despite the high probability of selling only 30 units, Emma still prefers to take action a_1, which is to pay a fixed fee of $2,000. That's because the high risk of low operating income (the 60% probability of selling only 30 units) is more than offset by the high return from selling 60 units, which has a 40% probability. If Emma were more averse to risk (measured in our example by the difference between operating incomes when 30 versus 60 units are sold), she might have preferred action a_2 or a_3. For example, action a_2 ensures an operating income of at least $700, greater than the operating income of $400 that she would earn under action a_1 if only 30 units were sold. Of course, choosing a_2 limits the upside potential to $2,200 relative to $2,800 under a_1, if 60 units are sold. If Emma is very concerned about downside risk, however, she may be willing to forgo some upside benefits to protect against a $400 outcome by choosing a_2.[3]

Good Decisions and Good Outcomes

Always distinguish between a good decision and a good outcome. One can exist without the other. Suppose you are offered a one-time-only gamble tossing a coin. You will win $20 if the outcome is heads, but you will lose $1 if the outcome is tails. As a decision maker, you proceed through the logical phases: gathering information, assessing outcomes, and making a choice. You accept the bet. Why? Because the expected value is $9.50 [0.5($20) + 0.5(−$1)]. The coin is tossed and the outcome is tails. You lose. From your viewpoint, this was a good decision but a bad outcome.

A decision can be made only on the basis of information that is available at the time of evaluating and making the decision. By definition, uncertainty rules out guaranteeing that the best outcome will always be obtained. As in our example, it is possible that bad luck will produce bad outcomes even when good decisions have been made. A bad outcome does not mean a bad decision was made. The best protection against a bad outcome is a good decision.

TERMS TO LEARN

This chapter and the Glossary at the end of the book contain definitions of the following important terms:

---

[3] For more formal approaches, refer to J. Moore and L. Weatherford, *Decision Modeling with Microsoft Excel*, 6th ed. (Upper Saddle River, NJ: Prentice Hall, 2001).

ASSIGNMENT MATERIAL

Note: To underscore the basic CVP relationships, the assignment material ignores income taxes unless stated otherwise.

Questions

Pearson MyLab Accounting

3-1 Define cost–volume–profit analysis.

3-2 Describe the assumptions underlying CVP analysis.

3-3 Distinguish between operating income and net income.

3-4 Define contribution margin, contribution margin per unit, and contribution margin percentage.

3-5 Describe three methods that managers can use to express CVP relationships.

3-6 Differentiate between breakeven analysis and CVP analysis.

3-7 With regard to making decisions, what do you think are the main limitations of CVP analysis? Explain.

3-8 How does an increase in the income tax rate affect the breakeven point?

3-9 Describe sensitivity analysis. How has the advent of the electronic spreadsheet affected the use of sensitivity analysis?

3-10 Is CVP analysis more focused on the short or the long term? Explain.

3-11 Is it possible to calculate the breakeven point for a company that produces and sells more than one type of product? Explain.

3-12 What is operating leverage? How is knowing the degree of operating leverage helpful to managers?

3-13 CVP analysis assumes that costs can be accurately divided into fixed and variable categories. Do you agree? Explain.

3-14 Give an example each of how a manager can decrease variable costs while increasing fixed costs and increase variable costs while decreasing fixed costs.

3-15 What is the main difference between gross margin and contribution margin? Which one is the main focus of CVP analysis? Explain briefly.

Multiple-Choice Questions

Pearson MyLab Accounting

In partnership with:

3-16 Jack's Jax has total fixed costs of $25,000. If the company's contribution margin is 60%, the income tax rate is 25% and the selling price of a box of Jax is $20, how many boxes of Jax would the company need to sell to produce a net income of $15,000?

a. 5,625
b. 4,445
c. 3,750
d. 3,333

3-17 During the current year, XYZ Company increased its variable SG&A expenses while keeping fixed SG&A expenses the same. As a result, XYZ's:

a. Contribution margin and gross margin will be lower.
b. Contribution margin will be higher, while its gross margin will remain the same.
c. Operating income will be the same under both the financial accounting income statement and contribution income statement.
d. Inventory amounts booked under the financial accounting income statement will be lower than under the contribution income statement.

3-18 Under the contribution income statement, a company's contribution margin will be:

a. Higher if fixed SG&A costs decrease.
b. Higher if variable SG&A costs increase.
c. Lower if fixed manufacturing overhead costs decrease.
d. Lower if variable manufacturing overhead costs increase.

3-19 A company needs to sell 10,000 units of its only product in order to break even. Fixed costs are $110,000, and the per unit selling price and variable costs are $20 and $9, respectively. If total sales are $220,000, the company's margin of safety will be equal to:

a. $0
b. $20,000
c. $110,000
d. $200,000

3-20 Once a company exceeds its breakeven level, operating income can be calculated by multiplying:

a. The sales price by unit sales in excess of breakeven units.

b. Unit sales by the difference between the sales price and fixed cost per unit.

c. The contribution margin ratio by the difference between unit sales and breakeven sales.

d. The contribution margin per unit by the difference between unit sales and breakeven sales.

Exercises

3-21 CVP computations. Fill in the blanks for each of the following independent cases.

Case	Revenues	Variable Costs	Fixed Costs	Total Costs	Operating Income	Contribution Margin	Operating Income %	Contribution Margin %
a.	$4,250			$3,500			30.00	60.00
b.				$6,000		$3,000	25.00	
c.	$6,600	$3,500			$2,200			
d.		$2,400	$1,800		$3,200			

3-22 CVP computations. Simplex Inc. sells its product at $80 per unit with a contribution margin of 40%. During 2016, Simplex sold 540,000 units of its product; its total fixed costs are $2,100,000.

Required

1. Calculate the (a) contribution margin, (b) variable costs, and (c) operating income.

2. The production manager of Simplex has proposed modernizing the whole production process in order to save labor costs. However, the modernization of the production process will increase the annual fixed costs by $3,800,000. The variable costs are expected to decrease by 20%. Simplex Inc. expects to maintain the same sales volume and selling price next year. How would the acceptance of the production manager's proposal affect your answers to (a) and (c) in requirement 1?

3. Should Simplex accept the production manager's proposal? Explain.

3-23 CVP analysis, changing revenues, and costs. Brilliant Travel Agency specializes in flights between Toronto and Vishakhapatnam. It books passengers on EastWest Air. Brilliant's fixed costs are $36,000 per month. EastWest Air charges passengers $1,300 per round-trip ticket.

Calculate the number of tickets Brilliant must sell each month to (a) break even and (b) make a target operating income of $12,000 per month in each of the following independent cases.

Required

1. Brilliant's variable costs are $34 per ticket. EastWest Air pays Brilliant 10% commission on ticket price.

2. Brilliant's variable costs are $30 per ticket. EastWest Air pays Brilliant 10% commission on ticket price.

3. Brilliant's variable costs are $30 per ticket. EastWest Air pays $46 fixed commission per ticket to Brilliant. Comment on the results.

4. Brilliant's variable costs are $30 per ticket. It receives $46 commission per ticket from EastWest Air. It charges its customers a delivery fee of $8 per ticket. Comment on the results.

3-24 CVP exercises. The Patisserie Hartog owns and operates 10 puff pastry outlets in and around Amsterdam. You are given the following corporate budget data for next year:

Revenues	$12,500,000
Fixed costs	$ 2,240,000
Variable costs	$ 9,750,000

Variable costs change based on the number of puff pastries sold.

Compute the budgeted operating income for each of the following deviations from the original budget data. (Consider each case independently.)

Required

1. A 15% increase in contribution margin, holding revenues constant

2. A 15% decrease in contribution margin, holding revenues constant

3. A 10% increase in fixed costs

4. A 10% decrease in fixed costs

5. A 12% increase in units sold

6. A 12% decrease in units sold

7. An 8% increase in fixed costs and an 8% increase in units sold

8. A 6% increase in fixed costs and a 6% decrease in variable costs

9. Which of these alternatives yields the highest budgeted operating income? Explain why this is the case.

3-25 CVP exercises. The Unique Toys Company manufactures and sells toys. Currently, 300,000 units are sold per year at $12.50 per unit. Fixed costs are $880,000 per year. Variable costs are $7.00 per unit. Consider each case separately:

Required

1. **a.** What is the current annual operating income?
   b. What is the present breakeven point in revenues?

Compute the new operating income for each of the following changes:

2. A 10% increase in variable costs
3. A $250,000 increase in fixed costs and a 2% increase in units sold
4. A 10% decrease in fixed costs, a 10% decrease in selling price, a 10% increase in variable cost per unit, and a 25% increase in units sold

Compute the new breakeven point in units for each of the following changes:

5. A 20% increase in fixed costs
6. A 12% increase in selling price and a $30,000 increase in fixed costs

3-26 CVP analysis, income taxes. Sonix Electronics is a dealer of industrial refrigerator. Its average selling price of an industrial refrigerator is $5,000, which it purchases from the manufacturer for $4,200. Each month, Sonix Electronics pays $52,800 in rent and other office expenditures and $75,200 for salespeople's salaries. In addition to their salaries, salespeople are paid a commission of 4% of sale price on each refrigerator they sell. Sonix Electronics also spends $18,400 each month for local advertisements. Its tax rate is 30%.

Required

1. How many refrigerators must Sonix Electronics sell each month to break even?
2. Sonix Electronics has a target monthly net income of $63,000. What is its target monthly operating income? How many refrigerators must be sold each month to reach the target monthly net income of $63,000?

3-27 CVP analysis, income taxes. The Swift Meal has two restaurants that are open 24 hours a day. Fixed costs for the two restaurants together total $456,000 per year. Service varies from a cup of coffee to full meals. The average sales check per customer is $9.50. The average cost of food and other variable costs for each customer is $3.80. The income tax rate is 30%. Target net income is $159,600.

Required

1. Compute the revenues needed to earn the target net income.
2. How many customers are needed to break even? To earn net income of $159,600?
3. Compute net income if the number of customers is 145,000.

3-28 CVP analysis, sensitivity analysis. Roughstyle Shirts Co. sells shirts wholesale to major retailers across Australia. Each shirt has a selling price of $40 with $26 in variable costs of goods sold. The company has fixed manufacturing costs of $1,600,000 and fixed marketing costs of $650,000. Sales commissions are paid to the wholesale sales reps at 10% of revenues. The company has an income tax rate of 30%.

Required

1. How many shirts must Roughstyle sell in order to break even?
2. How many shirts must it sell in order to reach:
   a. a target operating income of $600,000?
   b. a net income of $600,000?
3. How many shirts would Roughstyle have to sell to earn the net income in part 2b if: (Consider each requirement independently.)
   a. the contribution margin per unit increases by 15%.
   b. the selling price is increased to $45.00.
   c. the company outsources manufacturing to an overseas company increasing variable costs per unit by $3.00 and saving 50% of fixed manufacturing costs.

3-29 CVP analysis, margin of safety. Ariba Corporation reaches its breakeven point at $3,200,000 of revenues. At present, it is selling 105,000 units and its variable costs are $30. Fixed manufacturing costs, administrative costs, and marketing costs are $400,000, $250,000, and $150,000 respectively.

Required

1. Compute the contribution margin percentage.
2. Compute the selling price.
3. Compute the margin of safety in units and dollars.
4. What does this tell you about the risk of Ariba making a loss? What are the most likely reasons for this risk to increase?

3-30 Operating leverage. Broadpull Rugs is holding a 4-week carpet sale at Tryst's Club, a local warehouse store. Broadpull Rugs plans to sell carpets for $1,500 each. The company will purchase the carpets from a local distributor for $900 each, with the privilege of returning any unsold units for a full refund. Tryst's Club has offered Broadpull Rugs two payment alternatives for the use of space.

- Option 1: 25% of total revenues earned during the sale period
- Option 2: A fixed payment of $30,000 for the sale period

Assume Broadpull Rugs will incur no other costs.

1. Calculate the breakeven point in units for (a) option 1 and (b) option 2.
2. At what level of revenues will Broadpull Rugs earn the same operating income under either option?
   a. For what range of unit sales will Broadpull Rugs prefer option 1?
   b. For what range of unit sales will Broadpull Rugs prefer option 2?
3. Calculate the degree of operating leverage at sales of 80 units for the two rental options.
4. Briefly explain and interpret your answer to requirement 3.

3-31 CVP analysis, international cost structure differences. Plush Decor, Inc., is considering three possible countries for the sole manufacturing site of its newest area rug: Italy, Spain, and Singapore. All area rugs are to be sold to retail outlets in Australia for $200 per unit. These retail outlets add their own markup when selling to final customers. Fixed costs and variable cost per unit (area rug) differ in the three countries.

Country	Sales Price to Retail Outlets	Annual Fixed Costs	Variable Manufacturing Cost per Area Rug	Variable Marketing & Distribution Cost per Area Rug
Italy	$200.00	$ 6,386,000.00	$70.00	$27.00
Spain	200.00	5,043,000.00	61.00	16.00
Singapore	200.00	12,240,000.00	84.00	14.00

1. Compute the breakeven point for Plush Decor, Inc., in each country in (a) units sold and (b) revenues.
2. If Plush Decor, Inc., plans to produce and sell 80,000 rugs in 2014, what is the budgeted operating income for each of the three manufacturing locations? Comment on the results.

3-32 Sales mix, new and upgrade customers. Chartz 1-2-3 is a top-selling electronic spreadsheet product. Chartz is about to release version 5.0. It divides its customers into two groups: new customers and upgrade customers (those who previously purchased Chartz 1-2-3 4.0 or earlier versions). Although the same physical product is provided to each customer group, sizable differences exist in selling prices and variable marketing costs:

	New Customers		Upgrade Customers	
Selling price		$195		$115
Variable costs				
Manufacturing	$15		$15	
Marketing	50	65	20	35
Contribution margin		$130		$ 80

The fixed costs of Chartz 1-2-3 5.0 are $16,500,000. The planned sales mix in units is 60% new customers and 40% upgrade customers.

1. What is the Chartz 1-2-3 5.0 breakeven point in units, assuming that the planned 60%/40% sales mix is attained?
2. If the sales mix is attained, what is the operating income when 170,000 total units are sold?
3. Show how the breakeven point in units changes with the following customer mixes:
   a. New 40% and upgrade 60%
   b. New 80% and upgrade 20%
   c. Comment on the results.

3-33 Sales mix, three products. The Belkin Company has three product lines of coffee mugs—A, B, and C—with contribution margins of $7, $5, and $4, respectively. The president foresees sales of 240,000 units in the coming period, consisting of 40,000 units of A, 120,000 units of B, and 80,000 units of C. The company's fixed costs for the period are $552,000.

1. What is the company's breakeven point in units, assuming that the given sales mix is maintained?
2. If the sales mix is maintained, what is the total contribution margin when 220,000 units are sold? What is the operating income?
3. What would operating income be if the company sold 40,000 units of A, 100,000 units of B, and 100,000 units of C? What is the new breakeven point in units if these relationships persist in the next period?
4. Comparing the breakeven points in requirements 1 and 3, is it always better for a company to choose the sales mix that yields the lower breakeven point? Explain.

3-34 CVP, not-for-profit. Recreational Music Society is a not-for-profit organization that brings guest artists to the community's greater metropolitan area. The society just bought a small concert hall in the center of town to house its performances. The lease payments on the concert hall are expected to be $6,000 per month. The organization pays its guest performers $2,200 per concert and anticipates corresponding ticket sales to be $6,000 per concert. The society also incurs costs of approximately $1,400 per concert for marketing and advertising. The organization pays its artistic director $47,000 per year and expects to receive $23,000 in donations in addition to its ticket sales.

1. If the Recreational Music Society just breaks even, how many concerts does it hold?
2. In addition to the organization's artistic director, the society would like to hire a marketing director for $36,000 per year. What is the breakeven point? The society anticipates that the addition of a marketing director would allow the organization to increase the number of concerts to 50 per year. What is the society's operating income/loss if it hires the new marketing director?
3. The society expects to receive a grant that would provide the organization with an additional $36,000 toward the payment of the marketing director's salary. What is the breakeven point if the society hires the marketing director and receives the grant?

3-35 Contribution margin, decision making. Brandon Harris has a small bakery business called Super Bakery. Revenues and cost data of Super Bakery for the year 2016 are as follows:

Sales revenues		$475,000
Cost of goods sold (40% of sales revenues)		190,000
Gross margin		285,000
Operating costs:		
Salaries fixed	$175,000	
Sales commissions (15% of sales)	71,250	
Depreciation of equipment and fixtures	22,000	
Insurance for the year	5,000	
Store rent ($5,000 per month)	60,000	
Other operating costs	50,000	383,250
Operating income (loss)		$(98,250)

An analysis of other operating costs reveals that 80% of it varies with sales volume, and remaining 20% does not vary with sales volume rather remains same irrespective of sales volume.

1. Compute the contribution margin of Super Bakery.
2. Compute the contribution margin percentage.
3. Mr. Harris estimates that if he can spend an additional $15,000 toward sales promotion, sales revenues may increase by 30%. What should Mr. Harris' decision be?
4. What other actions can he take to improve the operating income?

3-36 Contribution margin, gross margin, and margin of safety. Roma Skincare manufactures and sells a face cream to small specialty stores in Victoria, Australia. It presents the monthly operating income statement shown here to Jacob Scott, a potential investor in the business. Help Mr. Scott understand Roma Skincare's cost structure.

	Home	Insert	Page Layout	Formulas	Data	Review	View
	A		B		C		D
1			Roma Skincare				
2			Operating Income Statement June, 2017				
3	Units sold						15,000
4	Revenues						$1,20,000
5	Cost of goods sold						
6	Variable manufacturing costs				$60,000		
7	Fixed manufacturing costs				$22,000		
8	Total cost of goods sold						$ 82,000
9	Gross margin						$ 38,000
10	Operating costs						
11	Variable marketing costs				$ 6,000		
12	Fixed marketing & admin costs				$14,000		
13	Total operating costs						$ 20,000
14	Operating income						$ 18,000

1. Recast the income statement to emphasize contribution margin.
2. Calculate the contribution margin percentage and breakeven point in units and revenues for June 2017.
3. What is the margin of safety (in units) for June 2017?
4. If sales in June were only 12,000 units and Roma Skincare's tax rate is 30%, calculate its net income.

3-37 Uncertainty and expected costs. Futuremart is an international retail store. They are considering implementing a new business-to-business (B2B) information system for processing merchandise orders. The current system costs Futuremart $2,500,000 per month and $62 per order. Futuremart has two options, a partially automated B2B and a fully automated B2B system. The partially automated B2B system will have a fixed cost of $7,200,000 per month and a variable cost of $50 per order. The fully automated B2B system has a fixed cost of $11,400,000 per month and $30 per order.

Based on data from the past two years, Futuremart has determined the following distribution on monthly orders:

Monthly Number of Orders	Probability
400,000	0.35
600,000	0.40
800,000	0.25

1. Prepare a table showing the cost of each plan for each quantity of monthly orders.
2. What is the expected cost of each plan?
3. In addition to the information systems costs, what other factors should Futuremart consider before deciding to implement a new B2B system?

Problems

3-38 CVP analysis, service firm. Appolo Healthcare Solutions provides preventive health check-up packages for men and women over 40 years of age and charges $12,000 per package on an average. The average variable costs per package are as follows:

Doctor's fees	$1,000
Pathological tests and clinical examinations	3,500
Medicines	2,800
Refreshments and health drinks	300
Costs of miscellaneous services	800
Total	$8,400

Annual fixed costs total $900,000.

1. Calculate the number of health check-up packages that must be sold to break even.
2. Calculate the revenue needed to earn a target operating income of $270,000.
3. If fixed costs increase by $25,000, what decrease in variable cost per person must be achieved to maintain the breakeven point calculated in requirement 1?
4. The managing director at Appolo proposes to increase the average price of the packages by $900 to decrease the breakeven point in units. Using information in the original problem, calculate the new breakeven point in units. What factors should the managing director consider before deciding to increase the price of the package?

3-39 CVP, target operating income, service firm. Modern Beauty Parlour provides beauty treatment for women. Its average monthly variable costs per woman are as follows:

Materials for beauty treatment	$110
Beautician's commission	50
Other supplies (soaps, napkins, etc.)	40
Total	$200

Monthly fixed costs consist of the following:

Rent	$1,250
Utilities	300
Advertisements on a local TV channel	250
Salaries	1,500
Miscellaneous	300
Total	$3,600

Modern Beauty charges $250 per woman on an average.

Required

1. Calculate the breakeven point.
2. Modern Beauty's target operating income is $4,000 per month. Compute the number of customers required to achieve the target operating income.
3. The parlor wants to move to another building for geographical advantage. Monthly rent for the new building is $2,350. With the objective of better visibility for the prospective customers, it plans to advertise on another local TV channel, incurring a monthly cost of $420. By how much should the parlor increase its average fees per customer to meet the target operating income of $4,000 per month, assuming the same number of customers as in requirement 2?

3-40 CVP analysis, margin of safety. United Project Consultants (UPC) provides project consultancy services to new business projects. For 2017, it has a total budgeted revenue of $480,000, based on an average price of $240 per business project prepared. UPC would like to achieve at least 50% as a margin of safety. The company's current fixed costs are $241,956, and variable costs average $42 per project. (Consider each of the following separately.)

Required

1. Calculate UPC's breakeven point and margin of safety in units.
2. Which of the following changes would help UPC achieve its desired margin of safety?
   a. Average revenue per business project increases to $276.
   b. Planned number of business projects prepared increases by 25%.
   c. United Project Consultants purchases new tax-software that results in a 7.5% increase in fixed costs, but makes project calculations easier. The software reduces variable costs by an average of $2 per project.

3-41 CVP analysis, income taxes. (CMA, adapted) J.T. Brooks and Company, a manufacturer of quality handmade walnut bowls, has had a steady growth in sales for the past 5 years. However, increased competition has led Mr. Brooks, the president, to believe that an aggressive marketing campaign will be necessary next year to maintain the company's present growth. To prepare for next year's marketing campaign, the company's controller has prepared and presented Mr. Brooks with the following data for the current year, 2017:

Variable cost (per bowl)	
Direct materials	$ 3.00
Direct manufacturing labor	8.00
Variable overhead (manufacturing, marketing, distribution, and customer service)	7.50
Total variable cost per bowl	$ 18.50
Fixed costs	
Manufacturing	$ 20,000
Marketing, distribution, and customer service	194,500
Total fixed costs	$214,500
Selling price	$ 35.00
Expected sales, 22,000 units	$770,000
Income tax rate	40%

Required

1. What is the projected net income for 2017?
2. What is the breakeven point in units for 2017?
3. Mr. Brooks has set the revenue target for 2018 at a level of $875,000 (or 25,000 bowls). He believes an additional marketing cost of $16,500 for advertising in 2018, with all other costs remaining constant, will be necessary to attain the revenue target. What is the net income for 2018 if the additional $16,500 is spent and the revenue target is met?
4. What is the breakeven point in revenues for 2018 if the additional $16,500 is spent for advertising?
5. If the additional $16,500 is spent, what are the required 2018 revenues for 2018 net income to equal 2017 net income?
6. At a sales level of 25,000 units, what maximum amount can be spent on advertising if a 2018 net income of $108,450 is desired?

3-42 CVP, sensitivity analysis. Mundial Nails produces a famous nail polish with a unique glossy feature and sells it for $25 per unit. The operating income for 2017 is as follows:

	Per unit ($)	Total ($)
Sales revenue	$25	$750,000
Raw materials	5	150,000
Variable manufacturing costs	4	120,000
Other variable costs	6	180,000
Contribution margin	10	300,000
Fixed cost		174,000
Operating income		$126,000

Mundial Nails would like to increase its profitability over the next year by at least 20%. To do so, the company is considering the following options:

1. Replacing a portion of its variable labor with an automated machining process. This would result in a 25% decrease in variable manufacturing costs per unit, but a 20% increase in fixed costs. Sales would remain the same.
2. Spending $30,000 on a new advertising campaign, which would increase sales by 20%.
3. Increasing both selling price by $5 per unit and raw-material costs by $3 per unit by using a higher-quality raw materials in producing its nail polish. The higher-priced nail polish would cause demand to drop by approximately 20%.
4. Adding a second manufacturing facility that would double Mundial Nails' fixed costs, but would increase sales by 60%.

Evaluate each of the alternatives considered by Mundial Nails. Do any of the options meet or exceed Mundial's targeted increase in income of 25%? What should Mundial Nails do?

3-43 CVP analysis, shoe stores. The LadyStyle sells women's shoes across the country through its chain of shoe stores. It sells 20 different styles of shoes with identical unit costs and selling prices. A unit is defined as a pair of shoes. Each store has a store manager and a store supervisor who are paid a fixed salary. Shoes are sold by sales women who receive a fixed salary and a sales commission. LadyStyle is considering opening another store that is expected to have the revenue and cost relationships shown here.

Home	Insert	Page Layout	Formulas	Data	Review	View
	A	B	C	D	E
1	Unit Variable Data (per pair of shoes)			Annual Fixed Costs	
2	Selling price	$40.00		Rent	$ 25,000
3	Cost of shoes	$29.00		Salaries	96,000
4	Sales commission	$ 2.00		Advertising	35,000
5	Variable cost per unit	$31.00		Depreciation	6,000
6				Other fixed costs	9,000
				Total fixed costs	$171,000

Consider each question independently:

1. What is the annual breakeven point in (a) units sold and (b) revenues?
2. If 15,000 units are sold, what will be the store's operating income (loss)?
3. If sales commissions are discontinued and fixed salaries are raised by a total of $19,190, what would be the annual breakeven point in (a) units sold and (b) revenues?
4. Refer to the original data. If, in addition to his fixed salary, the store supervisor and store manager are paid a commission of $0.50 per unit sold and $1.00 per unit sold, respectively, what would be the annual breakeven point in (a) units sold and (b) revenues?
5. Refer to the original data. If, in addition to his fixed salary, the store supervisor and store manager are paid a commission of $0.50 per unit and $1.00 per unit sold, respectively, in excess of the breakeven point, what would be the store's operating income if 25,000 units were sold?

3-44 CVP analysis, shoe stores (continuation of 3-43). Refer to requirement 3 of Problem 3-43. In this problem, assume the role of the owner of LadyStyle.

1. As owner, which sales compensation plan would you choose if forecasted annual sales of the new store were at least 25,000 units? What do you think of the motivational aspect of your chosen compensation plan?
2. Suppose the target operating income is $99,000. How many units must be sold to reach the target operating income under (a) the original salary-plus-commissions plan and (b) the higher-fixed-salaries-only plan? Which method would you prefer? Explain briefly.
3. You open the new store on January 1, 2017, with the original salary-plus-commission compensation plan in place. Because you expect the cost of the shoes to rise due to inflation, you place a firm bulk order for 25,000 shoes and lock in the $29 price per unit. But toward the end of the year, only 20,000 shoes are sold, and you authorize a markdown of the remaining inventory to $35 per unit. Finally, all units are sold. The salespeople get paid a commission of 5% of revenues. What is the annual operating income for the store?

3-45 Alternate cost structures, uncertainty, and sensitivity analysis. Sunshine Printing Company currently leases its only copy machine for $1,500 a month. The company is considering replacing this leasing agreement with a new contract that is entirely commission based. Under the new agreement, Sunshine would pay a commission for its printing at a rate of $10 for every 500 pages printed. The company currently charges $0.20 per page to its customers. The paper used in printing costs the company $0.08 per page and other variable costs, including hourly labor, amount to $0.07 per page.

Required

1. What is the company's breakeven point under the current leasing agreement? What is it under the new commission-based agreement?
2. For what range of sales levels will Sunshine prefer (a) the fixed lease agreement and (b) the commission agreement?
3. Do this question only if you have covered the chapter appendix in your class. Sunshine estimates that the company is equally likely to sell 30,000, 45,000, 60,000, 75,000, or 90,000 pages of print. Using information from the original problem, prepare a table that shows the expected profit at each sales level under the fixed leasing agreement and under the commission-based agreement. What is the expected value of each agreement? Which agreement should Sunshine choose?

3-46 CVP, alternative cost structures. TopHats operates a kiosk at a local mall, selling hats for $30 each. TopHats currently pays $900 a month to rent the space and pays three full-time employees to each work 160 hours a month at $12 per hour. The store shares a manager with a neighboring mall and pays 40% of the manager's annual salary of $60,000 and benefits equal to 18% of salary. The wholesale cost of the hats to the company is $10 a hat.

Required

1. How many hats does TopHats need to sell each month to break even?
2. If TopHats wants to earn an operating income of $5,000 per month, how many hats does the store need to sell?
3. If the store's hourly employees agreed to a 20% sales-commission-only pay structure, instead of their hourly pay, how many hats would TopHats need to sell to earn an operating income of $5,000?
4. Assume TopHats pays its employees hourly under the original pay structure, but is able to pay the mall 5% of its monthly revenue instead of monthly rent. At what sales levels would TopHats prefer to pay a fixed amount of monthly rent, and at what sales levels would it prefer to pay 5% of its monthly revenue as rent?

3-47 CVP analysis, income taxes, sensitivity. (CMA, adapted) Carlisle Engine Company manufactures and sells diesel engines for use in small farming equipment. For its 2014 budget, Carlisle Engine Company estimates the following:

Selling price	$ 4,000
Variable cost per engine	$ 1,000
Annual fixed costs	$4,800,000
Net income	$1,200,000
Income tax rate	20%

The first-quarter income statement, as of March 31, reported that sales were not meeting expectations. During the first quarter, only 400 units had been sold at the current price of $4,000. The income statement showed that variable and fixed costs were as planned, which meant that the 2014 annual net income projection would not be met unless management took action. A management committee was formed and presented the following mutually exclusive alternatives to the president:

Required

1. Reduce the selling price by 15%. The sales organization forecasts that at this significantly reduced price, 2,100 units can be sold during the remainder of the year. Total fixed costs and variable cost per unit will stay as budgeted.
2. Lower variable cost per unit by $300 through the use of less-expensive direct materials. The selling price will also be reduced by $400, and sales of 1,750 units are expected for the remainder of the year.
3. Reduce fixed costs by 10% and lower the selling price by 30%. Variable cost per unit will be unchanged. Sales of 2,200 units are expected for the remainder of the year.

   a. If no changes are made to the selling price or cost structure, determine the number of units that Carlisle Engine Company must sell (i) to break even and (ii) to achieve its net income objective.
   b. Determine which alternative Carlisle Engine should select to achieve its net income objective. Show your calculations.

3-48 Choosing between compensation plans, operating leverage. (CMA, adapted) AgroPharm Corporation manufactures pharmaceutical products that are sold through a network of external sales agents. The agents are paid a commission of 18% of revenues. AgroPharm is considering replacing the sales agents with its own salespeople, who would be paid a commission of 12% of revenues and total salaries of $7,950,000. The income statement for the year ending December 31, 2017, under the two scenarios is shown here.

	Home	Insert	Page Layout	Formulas	Data	Review	View
	A		B	C	D	E	
1	AgroPharm Corporation						
2	Income Statement						
3	For the Year Ended December 31, 2017						
4			Using Sales Agents		Using Own Sales Force		
5	Revenues			$45,000,000		$45,000,000	
6	Cost of goods sold						
7	Variable		$15,750,000		$15,750,000		
8	Fixed		5,425,000	21,175,000	5,425,000	21,175,000	
9	Gross margin			$23,825,000		$23,825,000	
10	Marketing costs						
11	Commissions		$ 8,100,000		$ 5,400,000		
12	Fixed costs		5,250,000	13,350,000	7,950,000	13,350,000	
13	Operating income			$10,475,000		$10,475,000	

Required

1. Calculate AgroPharm's 2017 contribution margin percentage, breakeven revenues, and degree of operating leverage under the two scenarios.
2. Describe the advantages and disadvantages of each type of sales alternative.
3. In 2018, AgroPharm uses its own salespeople, who demand a 14% commission. If all other cost-behavior patterns are unchanged, how much revenue must the salespeople generate in order to earn the same operating income as in 2017?

3-49 Sales mix, three products. The Matrix Company has three product lines of belts—A, B, and C—with contribution margins of $7, $5, and $4, respectively. The president foresees sales of 400,000 units in the coming period, consisting of 40,000 units of A, 200,000 units of B, and 160,000 units of C. The company's fixed costs for the period are $1,020,000.

Required

1. What is the company's breakeven point in units, assuming that the given sales mix is maintained?
2. If the sales mix is maintained, what is the total contribution margin when 400,000 units are sold? What is the operating income?
3. What would operating income be if 40,000 units of A, 160,000 units of B, and 200,000 units of C were sold? What is the new breakeven point in units if these relationships persist in the next period?

3-50 Multiproduct CVP and decision making. Romi Filters produces two types of water filters. One attaches to the faucet and cleans all water that passes through the faucet; the other is a pitcher-cum-filter that only purifies water meant for drinking.

The unit that attaches to the faucet is sold for $150 and has variable costs of $90.
The pitcher-cum-filter sells for $160 and has variable costs of $80.

Romi Filters sells two faucet models for every three pitchers sold. Fixed costs equal $1,260,000.

Required

1. What is the breakeven point in unit sales and dollars for each type of filter at the current sales mix?
2. Romi Filters is considering buying new production equipment. The new equipment will increase fixed cost by $240,000 per year and will decrease the variable cost of the faucet and the pitcher units by $5 and $10, respectively. Assuming the same sales mix, how many of each type of filter does Romi Filters need to sell to break even?
3. Assuming the same sales mix, at what total sales level would Romi Filters be indifferent between using the old equipment and buying the new production equipment? If total sales are expected to be 28,000 units, should Romi Filters buy the new production equipment?

3-51 Sales mix, two products. The Stackpole Company retails two products: a standard and a deluxe version of a luggage carrier. The budgeted income statement for next period is as follows:

	Standard Carrier	Deluxe Carrier	Total
Units sold	187,500	62,500	250,000
Revenues at $28 and $50 per unit	$5,250,000	$3,125,000	$8,375,000
Variable costs at $18 and $30 per unit	3,375,000	1,875,000	5,250,000
Contribution margins at $10 and $20 per unit	$1,875,000	$1,250,000	3,125,000
Fixed costs			2,250,000
Operating income			$ 875,000

Required

1. Compute the breakeven point in units, assuming that the company achieves its planned sales mix.
2. Compute the breakeven point in units (a) if only standard carriers are sold and (b) if only deluxe carriers are sold.
3. Suppose 250,000 units are sold but only 50,000 of them are deluxe. Compute the operating income. Compute the breakeven point in units. Compare your answer with the answer to requirement 1. What is the major lesson of this problem?

3-52 Gross margin and contribution margin. The Garden Club is preparing for its annual meeting in which a magic show will be shown to its contributing members only. Last year, out of 1,500 members, only 600 contributed for the magic show. Tickets for the show were $30 per attendee. The profit report for last year's show follows.

Ticket sales	$18,000
Cost of magic show	20,000
Gross margin	(2,000)
Printing, invitations, and paperwork	1,800
Profit (loss)	$ (3,800)

This year, the club committee does not want to lose money on the magic show due to poor attendance and to achieve this goal, the committee analyzed last year's costs. It found that of the $20,000 cost of the magic show, 40% was fixed costs and the remaining 60% was variable costs. Of the $1,800 cost of printing, invitations, and paperwork, 50% was fixed and 50% variable.

Required

1. Prepare last year's profit report using the contribution margin format.
2. The club committee is considering expanding this year's magic show invitation list to include volunteer members (in addition to its contributing members). If the club committee expands the magic show invitation list, it expects an 80% increase in attendance. Calculate the effect this will have on the profitability of the show assuming that fixed costs will be the same as last year.

3-53 Ethics, CVP analysis. Megaphone Corporation produces a molded plastic casing, M&M101, for many cell phones currently on the market. Summary data from its 2017 income statement are as follows:

Revenues	$5,000,000
Variable costs	3,250,000
Fixed costs	1,890,000
Operating income	$ (140,000)

Joshua Kirby, Megaphone's president, is very concerned about Megaphone Corporation's poor profitability. He asks Leroy Gibbs, production manager, and Tony DiNunzo, controller, to see if there are ways to reduce costs.

After 2 weeks, Leroy returns with a proposal to reduce variable costs to 55% of revenues by reducing the costs Megaphone currently incurs for safe disposal of wasted plastic. Tony is concerned that this would expose the company to potential environmental liabilities. He tells Leroy, "We would need to estimate some of these potential environmental costs and include them in our analysis." "You can't do that," Leroy replies. "We are not violating any laws. There is some possibility that we may have to incur environmental costs in the future, but if we bring it up now, this proposal will not go through because our senior management always assumes these costs to be larger than they turn out to be. The market is very tough, and we are in danger of shutting down the company and costing all of us our jobs. The only reason our competitors are making money is because they are doing exactly what I am proposing."

Required

1. Calculate Megaphone Corporation's breakeven revenues for 2017.
2. Calculate Megaphone Corporation's breakeven revenues if variable costs are 55% of revenues.
3. Calculate Megaphone Corporation's operating income for 2017 if variable costs had been 55% of revenues.
4. Given Leroy Gibbs's comments, what should Tony DiNunzo do?

3-54 Deciding where to produce. (CMA, adapted) Central térmica, Inc., produces the same power generator in two Spanish plants, a new plant in Los Barrios and an older plant in Ascó. The following data are available for the two plants.

	A	B	C	D	E
1		**Los Barrios**		**Ascó**	
2	Selling price		$200.00		$200.00
3	Variable manufacturing cost per unit	$80.00		$100.00	
4	Fixed manufacturing cost per unit	35.00		26.00	
5	Variable marketing cost per unit	20.00		25.00	
6	Fixed marketing cost per unit	30.00		24.00	
7	Total cost per unit		165.00		175.00
8	Operating income per unit		$ 35.00		$ 25.00
9	Production rate per day	500	units	400	units
10	Normal annual capacity usage	240	days	240	days
11	Maximum annual capacity	300	days	300	days

All fixed costs per unit are calculated based on a normal capacity usage consisting of 240 working days. When the number of working days exceeds 240, overtime charges raise the variable manufacturing costs of additional units by $5.00 per unit in Los Barrios and $10.00 per unit in Ascó.

Central térmica, Inc., is expected to produce and sell 240,000 power generators during the coming year. Wanting to take advantage of the higher operating income per unit at Ascó, the company's production manager has decided to manufacture 120,000 units at each plant, resulting in a plan in which Ascó operates at maximum capacity (400 units per day × 300 days) and Los Barrios operates at its normal volume (500 units per day × 240 days).

Required

1. Calculate the breakeven point in units for the Los Barrios plant and for the Ascó plant.
2. Calculate the operating income that would result from the production manager's plan to produce 120,000 units at each plant.
3. Determine how the production of 240,000 units should be allocated between the Los Barrios and Ascó plants to maximize operating income for Central térmica, Inc. Show your calculations.

Job Costing

4

No one likes to lose money.

Whether a company is a new startup venture providing marketing consulting services or an established manufacturer of custom-built motorcycles, knowing how to job cost—that is, knowing how much it costs to produce an individual product—is critical if a company is to generate a profit. As the following article shows, Turner Construction Company knows this all too well.

JOB COSTING AND THE WORLD'S TALLEST BUILDING[1]

Turner Construction Company was responsible for constructing, costing and pricing the world's tallest building, the 2,716-foot high, 163-story Burj Khalifa in Dubai. Completed in 2010, the $1.5 billion Burj Khalifa features 49 floors of office space, more than 1,000 apartments, a 160-room Armani Hotel with a 76th floor swimming pool, and the world's highest outdoor observation deck on the 124th floor.

To construct the Burj Khalifa, Turner managers used historical data and marketplace information to carefully estimate all costs associated with the project: direct costs, indirect costs, and general administrative costs. Direct costs included the 45,000 cubic meters of concrete, 39,000 tons of steel rebar, 26,000 exterior glass panels, and 22 million man hours required for construction. Indirect costs included the cost of supervisory labor, company-owned equipment, and safety equipment. Finally, general administrative costs allocated to the Burj Khalifa included office rent, utilities, and insurance.

Throughout the seven-year construction process, job costing was critical as on-site managers reported on the status of the mega-building. Managers identified potential problems with the project and took corrective action to ensure the luxury skyscraper was delivered on time and within the original project budget.

Knowing the costs and profitability of jobs helps managers pursue their business strategies, develop pricing plans, and manage costs.

LEARNING OBJECTIVES

1. Describe the building-block concepts of costing systems

2. Distinguish job costing from process costing

3. Describe the approaches to evaluating and implementing job-costing systems

4. Outline the seven-step approach to normal costing

5. Distinguish actual costing from normal costing

6. Track the flow of costs in a job-costing system

7. Dispose of under- or overallocated manufacturing overhead costs at the end of the fiscal year using alternative methods

8. Understand variations from normal costing

Tomas Marek/123RF

[1] *Sources*: Bill Baker and James Pawlikowski, "The Design and Construction of the World's Tallest Building: The Burj Khalifa, Dubai," *Structural Engineering International* 25 (4 2015): 389–394 (http://www.iabse.org/Images/Publications_PDF/SEI/SEI.Burj%20Dubai.pdf); Burj Khalifa, "Building a Global Icon," http://www.burjkhalifa.ae/en/the-tower/construction.aspx, accessed March 2016; Turner Construction Company, "Burj Khalifa," http://www.turnerconstruction.com/experience/project/28/burj-khalifa, accessed March 2016; SkyscraperPage.com, "World Skyscraper Construction," http://skyscraperpage.com/diagrams/?searchID=202, accessed March 2016.

Building-Block Concepts of Costing Systems

Before we begin our discussion of costing systems, let's review the cost-related terms from Chapter 2 and introduce some new terms.

1. A *cost object* is anything for which a measurement of costs is desired—for example, a product, such as an iMac computer, or a service, such as the cost of repairing an iMac computer.

2. The *direct costs of a cost object* are costs related to a particular cost object that can be traced to it in an economically feasible (cost-effective) way—for example, the cost of the main computer board and parts to make an iMac computer.

3. The *indirect costs of a cost object* are costs related to a particular cost object that cannot be traced to it in an economically feasible (cost-effective) way—for example, the salaries of supervisors who oversee multiple products, only one of which is the iMac, or the rent paid for the repair facility that repairs many different Apple computer products. Indirect costs are allocated to the cost object using a cost-allocation method. Recall that *cost assignment* is a general term for assigning costs, whether direct or indirect, to a cost object. *Cost tracing* is the process of assigning direct costs. *Cost allocation* is the process of assigning indirect costs. The relationship among these three concepts can be graphically represented as

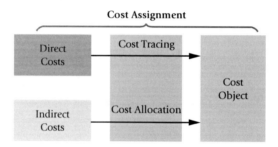

Throughout this chapter, the costs assigned to a cost object, such as a BMW Mini Cooper car, or a service, such as an audit of the MTV network, include both variable costs and costs that are fixed in the short run. Managers cost products and services to guide their long-run strategic decisions; for example: "What mix of products and services should we produce?" or "What price should we charge for each product?" In the long run, managers want revenues to exceed total (variable plus fixed) costs.

We also need to introduce and explain two more terms to understand costing systems:

4. **Cost pool.** A **cost pool** is a grouping of individual indirect cost items. Cost pools can range from broad, such as all manufacturing-plant costs, to narrow, such as the costs of operating metal-cutting machines. Cost pools simplify the allocation of indirect costs because the costing system does not have to allocate each cost individually. Instead costs that have the same cost-allocation base are grouped together and allocated to cost objects.

5. **Cost-allocation base.** How should a company allocate the costs of operating metal-cutting machines among different products? One way is to determine the number of machine-hours used to produce different products. The **cost-allocation base** (number of machine-hours) is a systematic way to link an indirect cost or group of indirect costs (operating costs of all metal-cutting machines) to cost objects (different products). For example, if the indirect costs of operating metal-cutting machines is $500,000 based on running these machines for 10,000 hours, the cost-allocation rate is $500,000 ÷ 10,000 hours = $50 per machine-hour, where machine-hours is the cost-allocation base. If a product uses 800 machine-hours, it will be allocated $40,000, or $50 per machine-hour × 800 machine-hours. The ideal cost-allocation base is the cost driver of the indirect costs because there is a cause-and-effect relationship between the cost-allocation base and the indirect costs. A cost-allocation base can be either financial (such as direct labor costs) or nonfinancial (such as the number of machine-hours). When the cost object is a job, product, service, or customer, the cost-allocation base is also called a **cost-application base**. However, when the cost object is a department or another cost pool, the cost-allocation base is *not* called a cost-application base.

Sometimes a cost may need to be allocated in a situation where the cause-and-effect relationship is not clear-cut. Consider a corporate-wide advertising program that promotes the general image of a company and its various divisions, rather than the image of an individual product. Many companies, such as PepsiCo, allocate costs like these to their individual divisions on the basis of revenues: The higher a division's revenue, the higher the business's allocated cost of the advertising program. Allocating costs this way is based on the criterion of *benefits received* rather than cause-and-effect. Divisions with higher revenues benefit from the advertising more than divisions with lower revenues and, therefore, are allocated more of the advertising costs.

Another criterion for allocating some costs is the cost object's *ability to bear* the costs allocated to it. The city government of Houston, Texas, for example, distributes the costs of the city manager's office to other city departments—including the police department, fire department, library system, and others—based on the size of their budgets. The city's rationale is that larger departments should absorb a larger share of the overhead costs. Organizations generally use the cause-and-effect criterion to allocate costs, followed by benefits received, and finally, and more rarely, by ability to bear.

The concepts represented by these five terms constitute the building blocks we will use to design the costing systems described in this chapter.

DECISION POINT

What are the building block concepts of a costing system?

Job-Costing and Process-Costing Systems

Management accountants use two basic types of costing systems to assign costs to products or services.

LEARNING OBJECTIVE 2

Distinguish job costing

…job costing is used to cost a distinct product

from process costing

…process costing is used to cost masses of identical or similar units

1. **Job-costing system**. In a job-costing system, the cost object is a unit or multiple units of a distinct product or service called a **job**. Each job generally uses different amounts of resources. The product or service is often a single unit, such as a specialized machine made at Hitachi, a construction project managed by Bechtel Corporation, a repair job done at an Audi Service Center, or an advertising campaign produced by Saatchi & Saatchi. Each special machine made by Hitachi is unique and distinct from the other machines made at the plant. An advertising campaign for one client at Saatchi & Saatchi is unique and distinct from advertising campaigns for other clients. Job costing is also used by companies such as Ethan Allen to cost multiple identical units of distinct furniture products. Because the products and services are distinct, job-costing systems are used to accumulate costs separately for each product or service.

2. **Process-costing system**. In a process-costing system, the cost object is masses of identical or similar units of a product or service. For example, Citibank provides the same service to all its customers when processing customer deposits. Intel provides the same product (say, a Core i5 chip) to each of its customers. All Minute Maid consumers receive the same frozen orange juice product. In each period, process-costing systems divide the total costs of producing an identical or similar product or service by the total number of units produced to obtain a per-unit cost. This per-unit cost is the average unit cost that applies to each of the identical or similar units produced in that period.

Exhibit 4-1 presents examples of job costing and process costing in the service, merchandising, and manufacturing sectors. These two types of costing systems lie at opposite ends of a continuum; in between, one type of system can blur into the other to some degree.

	Service Sector	Merchandising Sector	Manufacturing Sector
Job Costing Used	• Audit engagements done by PricewaterhouseCoopers • Consulting engagements done by McKinsey & Co. • Advertising-agency campaigns run by Ogilvy & Mather • Legal cases argued by Hale & Dorr • Computer-repair jobs done by CompUSA • Movies produced by Universal Studios	• L. L. Bean sending individual items by mail order • Special promotion of new products by Walmart	• Assembly of individual aircrafts at Boeing • Construction of ships at Litton Industries
Process Costing Used	• Bank-check clearing at Bank of America • Postal delivery (standard items) by U.S. Postal Service	• Grain dealing by Arthur Daniel Midlands • Lumber dealing by Weyerhauser	• Oil refining by Shell Oil • Beverage production by PepsiCo

DECISION POINT

How do you distinguish
job costing from process
costing?

Many companies have costing systems that are neither pure job-costing systems nor pure process-costing systems but—instead—have elements of both, tailored to the underlying operations. For example, Kellogg Corporation uses job costing to calculate the total cost to manufacture each of its different and distinct types of products—such as Corn Flakes, Crispix, and Froot Loops—and process costing to calculate the per-unit cost of producing each identical box of Corn Flakes, each identical box of Crispix, and so on. In this chapter, we focus on job-costing systems. Chapters 17 and 18 discuss process-costing systems.

Job Costing: Evaluation and Implementation

LEARNING OBJECTIVE **3**

Describe the approaches to
evaluating and implement-
ing job-costing systems

...to determine costs of
jobs in a timely manner

We will illustrate job costing using the example of Robinson Company, which manufactures and installs specialized machinery for the paper-making industry. In early 2017, Robinson receives a request to bid on the manufacturing and installation of a new paper-making machine for the Western Pulp and Paper Company (WPP). Robinson had never made a machine quite like this one, and its managers wonder what to bid for the job. In order to make decisions about the job, Robinson's management team works through the five-step decision-making process.

1. **Identify the problems and uncertainties.** The decision of whether and how much to bid for the WPP job depends on how management resolves two critical uncertainties: (1) what it will cost to complete the job; and (2) the prices Robinson's competitors are likely to bid.

2. **Obtain information.** Robinson's managers first evaluate whether doing the WPP job is consistent with the company's strategy. Do they want to do more of these kinds of jobs? Is this an attractive segment of the market? Will Robinson be able to develop a competitive advantage over its competitors and satisfy customers such as WPP? After completing their research, Robinson's managers conclude that the WPP job fits well with the company's strategy and capabilities.

    Robinson's managers study the drawings and engineering specifications provided by WPP and decide on the technical details of the machine. They compare the specifications of this machine to similar machines they have made in the past, identify competitors that might bid on the job, and gather information on what these bids might be.

3. **Make predictions about the future.** Robinson's managers estimate the cost of direct materials, direct manufacturing labor, and overhead for the WPP job. They also consider qualitative factors and risk factors and evaluate any biases they might have. For example, do engineers and employees working on the WPP job have the necessary skills and technical competence? Would they find the experience valuable and challenging? How accurate are the cost estimates, and what is the likelihood of cost overruns? What biases do Robinson's managers have to be careful about?

4. **Make decisions by choosing among alternatives.** Robinson's managers consider several alternative bids based on what they believe competing firms will bid, the technical expertise needed for the job, business risks, and other qualitative factors. Ultimately Robinson decides to bid $15,000. The manufacturing cost estimate is $9,800, which yields a markup of more than 50% on manufacturing cost.

5. **Implement the decision, evaluate performance, and learn.** Robinson wins the bid for the WPP job. As Robinson works on the job, management accountants carefully track all of the costs incurred (which are detailed later in this chapter). Ultimately, Robinson's managers will compare the predicted amounts against actual costs to evaluate how well the company did on the WPP job.

In its job-costing system, Robinson accumulates the costs incurred for a job in different parts of the value chain, such as manufacturing, marketing, and customer service. We focus here on Robinson's manufacturing function (which also includes the installation of the machine). To make a machine, Robinson purchases some components from outside suppliers and makes other components itself. Each of Robinson's jobs also has a service element: installing a machine at a customer's site and integrating it with the customer's other machines and processes.

One form of a job-costing system that Robinson can use is **actual costing**, which is a costing system that traces direct costs to a cost object based on the *actual direct-cost rate*s times the actual quantities of the direct-cost inputs used. Indirect costs are allocated based on the *actual indirect-cost rates* times the actual quantities of the cost-allocation bases. An actual indirect-cost rate is calculated by dividing actual annual indirect costs by the actual annual quantity of the cost-allocation base.

$$\frac{\text{Actual indirect}}{\text{cost rate}} = \frac{\text{Actual annual indirect costs}}{\text{Actual annual quantity of the cost-allocation base}}$$

As its name suggests, actual costing systems calculate the actual costs of jobs. Yet actual costing systems are not commonly found in practice because actual costs cannot be computed in a *timely* manner.[2] The problem is not with computing direct-cost rates for direct materials and direct manufacturing labor. For example, Robinson records the actual prices paid for materials. As it uses these materials, the prices paid serve as actual direct-cost rates for charging material costs to jobs. As we discuss next, calculating actual indirect-cost rates on a timely basis each week or each month is, however, a problem. Robinson can only calculate actual indirect-cost rates at the end of the fiscal year. However, the firm's managers are unwilling to wait that long to learn the costs of various jobs because they need cost information to monitor and manage the cost of jobs while they are in progress. Ongoing cost information about jobs also helps managers bid on new jobs while working on current jobs.

Time Period Used to Compute Indirect-Cost Rates

There are two reasons for using longer periods, such as a year, to calculate indirect-cost rates.

1. **The numerator reason (indirect-cost pool).** The shorter the period, the greater is the influence of seasonal patterns on the amount of costs. For example, if indirect-cost rates were calculated each month, the costs of heating (included in the numerator) would be charged to production only during the winter months. An annual period incorporates the effects of all four seasons into a single, annual indirect-cost rate.

---

[2] Actual costing is presented in more detail on pages 138–140.

Levels of total indirect costs are also affected by nonseasonal erratic costs. Nonseasonal erratic costs are the costs incurred in a particular month that benefit operations during future months, such as equipment-repair costs and the costs of vacation and holiday pay for employees. If monthly indirect-cost rates were calculated, the jobs done in a month in which there were high, nonseasonal erratic costs would be charged with these higher costs. Pooling all indirect costs together over the course of a full year and calculating a single annual indirect-cost rate helps smooth some of the erratic bumps in costs associated with shorter periods.

2. **The denominator reason (quantity of the cost-allocation base).** Another reason for longer periods is to avoid spreading monthly fixed indirect costs over fluctuating levels of monthly output and fluctuating quantities of the cost-allocation base. Consider the following example.

Reardon and Pane is a firm of tax accountants whose work follows a highly seasonal pattern. Tax season (January–April) is very busy. Other times of the year are less busy. The firm has both variable indirect costs and fixed indirect costs. Variable indirect costs (such as supplies, power, and indirect support labor) vary with the quantity of the cost-allocation base (direct professional labor-hours). Monthly fixed indirect costs (depreciation and general administrative support) do not vary with short-run fluctuations in the quantity of the cost-allocation base:

	Indirect Costs			Direct Professional Labor-Hours (4)	Variable Indirect Cost Rate per Direct Professional Labor-Hour (5) = (1) ÷ (4)	Fixed Indirect Cost Rate per Direct Professional Labor-Hour (6) = (2) ÷ (4)	Total Allocation Rate per Direct Professional Labor-Hour (7) = (3) ÷ (4)
	Variable (1)	Fixed (2)	Total (3)				
High-output month	$40,000	$60,000	$100,000	3,200	$12.50	$18.75	$31.25
Low-output month	10,000	60,000	70,000	800	$12.50	$75.00	87.50

Variable indirect costs change in proportion to changes in the number of direct professional labor-hours worked. Therefore, the variable indirect-cost rate is the same in both the high-output months and the low-output months ($12.50 in both as the table shows). Sometimes overtime payments can cause the variable indirect-cost rate to be higher in high-output months. In such cases, variable indirect costs will be allocated at a higher rate to production in high-output months relative to production in low-output months.

Now consider the fixed costs of $60,000. Reardon and Pane chooses this level of monthly fixed costs for the year recognizing that it needs to support higher professional labor-hours during some periods of the year and lower professional labor-hours during other periods. The fixed costs cause monthly total indirect-cost rates to vary considerably—from $31.25 per hour to $87.50 per hour. Few managers believe that identical jobs done in different months should be allocated such significantly different indirect-cost charges per hour ($87.50 ÷ $31.25 = 2.80, or 280%) because of fixed costs. Furthermore, if fees for preparing tax returns are based on costs, fees would be high in low-output months leading to lost business, when in fact management wants to accept more business to use the idle capacity during these months (for more details, see Chapter 9). Reardon and Pane chose a specific level of capacity based on a time horizon far beyond a mere month. An average, annualized rate based on the relationship between total annual indirect costs and the total annual level of output smoothes the effect of monthly variations in output levels. This rate is more representative of the total costs and total output the company's managers considered when choosing the level of capacity and, therefore, fixed costs.

Another denominator reason for using annual overhead rates is because the number of Monday-to-Friday workdays in a month affects the calculation of monthly indirect-cost rates. The number of workdays per month varies from 20 to 23 during a year. Because February has the fewest workdays (and consequently labor-hours), if separate rates are computed each month, jobs done in February would bear a greater share of the firm's indirect costs (such as depreciation and property taxes) than identical jobs in other months. An annual period is consistent with how managers decide on the level of fixed costs and reduces the effect that the number of working days per month has on unit costs.

DECISION POINT

What is the main challenge of implementing job-costing systems?

Normal Costing

As we indicated, because it's hard to calculate actual indirect-cost rates on a weekly or monthly basis, managers cannot calculate the actual costs of jobs as they are completed. Nonetheless, managers want a close approximation of the costs of various jobs regularly during the year, not just at the end of the fiscal year. They want to know manufacturing costs (and other costs, such as marketing costs) to price jobs, monitor and manage costs, evaluate the success of jobs, learn about what did and did not work, bid on new jobs, and prepare interim financial statements. Because companies need immediate access to job costs, few wait to allocate overhead costs until the end of the accounting year. Instead, a *predetermined* or *budgeted* indirect-cost rate is calculated for each cost pool at the beginning of a fiscal year, and overhead costs are allocated to jobs as work progresses. For the numerator and denominator reasons described previously, the **budgeted indirect-cost rate** for each cost pool is computed as:

$$\text{Budgeted indirect cost rate} = \frac{\text{Budgeted annual indirect costs}}{\text{Budgeted annual quantity of the cost-allocation base}}$$

Using budgeted indirect-cost rates gives rise to normal costing.

Normal costing is a costing system that (1) traces direct costs to a cost object by using the actual direct-cost rates times the actual quantities of the direct-cost inputs and (2) allocates indirect costs based on the *budgeted* indirect-cost rates times the actual quantities of the cost-allocation bases.

General Approach to Job Costing Using Normal Costing

We illustrate normal costing for the Robinson Company example using the following seven steps to assign costs to an individual job. This approach is commonly used by companies in the manufacturing, merchandising, and service sectors.

Step 1: Identify the Job That Is the Chosen Cost Object. The cost object in the Robinson Company example is Job WPP 298, manufacturing a paper-making machine for Western Pulp and Paper (WPP) in 2017. Robinson's managers and management accountants gather information to cost jobs through source documents. A **source document** is an original record (such as a labor time card on which an employee's work hours are recorded) that supports journal entries in an accounting system. The main source document for Job WPP 298 is a job-cost record. A **job-cost record**, also called a **job-cost sheet**, is used to record and accumulate all the costs assigned to a specific job, starting when work begins. Exhibit 4-2 shows the job-cost record for the paper-making machine ordered by WPP. Follow the various steps in costing Job WPP 298 on the job-cost record in Exhibit 4-2.

Step 2: Identify the Direct Costs of the Job. Robinson identifies two direct-manufacturing cost categories: direct materials and direct manufacturing labor.

- **Direct materials:** On the basis of the engineering specifications and drawings provided by WPP, a manufacturing engineer orders materials from the storeroom using a basic source document called a **materials-requisition record**, which contains information about the cost of direct materials used on a specific job and in a specific department. Exhibit 4-3, Panel A, shows a materials-requisition record for the Robinson Company. See how the record specifies the job for which the material is requested (WPP 298) and describes the material (Part Number MB 468-A, metal brackets), the actual quantity (8), the actual unit cost ($14), and the actual total cost ($112). The $112 actual total cost also appears on the job-cost record in Exhibit 4-2. If we add the cost of all materials requisitions, the total actual direct materials cost is $4,606, which is shown in the Direct Materials panel of the job-cost record in Exhibit 4-2.

- **Direct manufacturing labor:** Accounting for direct manufacturing labor is similar to accounting for direct materials. The source document for direct manufacturing labor is a **labor-time sheet**, which contains information about the amount of labor time used

LEARNING OBJECTIVE 4

Outline the seven-step approach to normal costing

...the seven-step approach is used to compute direct and indirect costs of a job

EXHIBIT 4-2   Source Documents at Robinson Company: Job-Cost Record

	Home	Insert	Page Layout	Formulas	Data	Review	View	
	A	B	C	D	E	F		
1			**JOB-COST RECORD**					
2	JOB NO:	WPP 298		CUSTOMER:	Western Pulp and Paper			
3	Date Started:	Feb. 6, 2017		Date Completed	Feb. 28, 2017			
4								
5								
6	DIRECT MATERIALS							
7	Date	Materials		Quantity	Unit	Total		
8	Received	Requisition No.	Part No.	Used	Cost	Costs		
9	Feb. 6, 2017	2017: 198	MB 468-A	8	$14	$ 112		
10	Feb. 6, 2017	2017: 199	TB 267-F	12	63	756		
11						•		
12						•		
13	Total					$ 4,606		
14								
15	DIRECT MANUFACTURING LABOR							
16	Period	Labor Time	Employee	Hours	Hourly	Total		
17	Covered	Record No.	No.	Used	Rate	Costs		
18	Feb. 6-12, 2017	LT 232	551-87-3076	25	$18	$ 450		
19	Feb. 6-12, 2017	LT 247	287-31-4671	5	19	95		
20	•	•	•	•	•	•		
21	•	•	•	•	•	•		
22	Total			88		$ 1,579		
23								
24	MANUFACTURING OVERHEAD*							
25		Cost Pool		Allocation Base	Allocation-	Total		
26	Date	Category	Allocation Base	Quantity Used	Base Rate	Costs		
27	Feb. 28, 2017	Manufacturing	Direct Manufacturing	88 hours	$40	$ 3,520		
28			Labor-Hours					
29								
30	Total					$ 3,520		
31	TOTAL MANUFACTURING COST OF JOB					$ 9,705		
32								
33								
34	*The Robinson Company uses a single manufacturing-overhead cost pool. The use of multiple overhead cost pools							
35	would mean multiple entries in the "Manufacturing Overhead" section of the job-cost record.							
36								

for a specific job in a specific department. Exhibit 4-3, Panel B, shows a typical weekly labor-time sheet for a particular employee (G. L. Cook). Each day Cook records the time spent on individual jobs (in this case WPP 298 and JL 256), as well as the time spent on other tasks, such as the maintenance of machines and cleaning, that are not related to a specific job.

The 25 hours that Cook spent on Job WPP 298 appears on the job-cost record in Exhibit 4-2 at a cost of $450 (25 hours × $18 per hour). Similarly, the job-cost record for Job JL 256 will show a cost of $216 (12 hours × $18 per hour). The three hours of time spent on maintenance and cleaning at $18 per hour equals $54. This cost is part of indirect manufacturing costs because it is not traceable to any particular job. This indirect cost is included as part of the manufacturing-overhead cost pool allocated to jobs. The total direct manufacturing labor costs of $1,579 for the paper-making machine that

| EXHIBIT 4-3 | Source Documents at Robinson Company: Materials-Requisition Record and Labor-Time Sheet |

PANEL A:

MATERIALS-REQUISITION RECORD				
Materials-Requisition Record No.			2017: 198	
Job No.	WPP 298	Date:	FEB. 6, 2017	
Part No.	Part Description	Quantity	Unit Cost	Total Cost
MB 468-A	Metal Brackets	8	$14	$112
Issued By: B. Clyde		Date:	Feb. 6, 2017	
Received By: L. Daley		Date:	Feb. 6, 2017	

PANEL B:

LABOR-TIME SHEET								
Labor-Time Record No:				LT 232				
Employee Name: G. L. Cook			Employee No:	551-87-3076				
Employee Classification Code:			Grade 3 Machinist					
Hourly Rate: $18								
Week Start: Feb. 6, 2017			Week End: Feb. 12, 2017					
Job. No.	M	T	W	Th	F	S	Su	Total
WPP 298	4	8	3	6	4	0	0	25
JL 256	3	0	4	2	3	0	0	12
Maintenance	1	0	1	0	1	0	0	3
Total	8	8	8	8	8	0	0	40
Supervisor: R. Stuart	Date: Feb. 12, 2017							

appears in the Direct Manufacturing Labor panel of the job-cost record in Exhibit 4-2 is the sum of all the direct manufacturing labor costs charged by different employees for producing and installing Job WPP 298.

All costs other than direct materials and direct manufacturing labor are classified as indirect costs.

Step 3: Select the Cost-Allocation Bases to Use for Allocating Indirect Costs to the Job. Recall that indirect manufacturing costs are those costs that are necessary to do a job, but that cannot be traced to a specific job. It would be impossible to complete a job without incurring indirect costs such as supervision, manufacturing engineering, utilities, and repairs. Moreover, different jobs require different quantities of indirect resources. Because these costs cannot be traced to a specific job, managers must allocate them to jobs in a systematic way.

Companies often use multiple cost-allocation bases to allocate indirect costs because different indirect costs have different cost drivers. For example, some indirect costs such as depreciation and repairs of machines are more closely related to machine-hours. Other indirect costs such as supervision and production support are more closely related to direct manufacturing labor-hours. Robinson, however, chooses direct manufacturing labor-hours as the sole allocation base for linking all indirect manufacturing costs to jobs. The managers do so because, in Robinson's labor-intensive environment, they believe the number of direct manufacturing labor-hours drives the manufacturing overhead resources required by individual jobs. (We will see in Chapter 5 that managers in many manufacturing environments often need to broaden the set of cost drivers.) In 2017, Robinson budgets 28,000 direct manufacturing labor-hours.

Step 4: Identify the Indirect Costs Associated with Each Cost-Allocation Base. Because Robinson believes that a single cost-allocation base—direct manufacturing labor-hours—can be used to allocate indirect manufacturing costs to jobs, Robinson creates a single cost pool called manufacturing overhead costs. This pool represents all indirect costs of the Manufacturing Department that are difficult to trace directly to individual jobs. In 2017, budgeted manufacturing overhead costs total $1,120,000.

As we saw in Steps 3 and 4, managers first identify cost-allocation bases and then identify the costs related to each cost-allocation base, not the other way around. They choose this order because managers must first understand their companies' cost drivers (the reasons why costs are being incurred) before they can determine the costs associated with each cost driver. Otherwise, there is nothing to guide the creation of cost pools. Of course, Steps 3 and 4 are often done almost simultaneously.

Step 5: Compute the Rate per Unit of Each Cost-Allocation Base Used to Allocate Indirect Costs to the Job. For each cost pool, the budgeted indirect-cost rate is calculated by dividing the budgeted total indirect costs in the pool (determined in Step 4) by the budgeted total quantity of the cost-allocation base (determined in Step 3). Robinson calculates the allocation rate for its single manufacturing overhead cost pool as follows:

$$\text{Budgeted manufacturing overhead rate} = \frac{\text{Budgeted manufacturing overhead costs}}{\text{Budgeted total quantity of cost-allocation base}}$$

$$= \frac{\$1,120,000}{28,000 \text{ direct manufacturing labor-hours}}$$

$$= \$40 \text{ per direct manufacturing labor-hour}$$

Step 6: Compute the Indirect Costs Allocated to the Job. The indirect costs of a job are calculated by multiplying the *actual* quantity of each different allocation base (one allocation base for each cost pool) associated with the job by the *budgeted* indirect cost rate of each allocation base (computed in Step 5). Recall that Robinson's managers selected direct manufacturing labor-hours as the only cost-allocation base. Robinson uses 88 direct manufacturing labor-hours on the WPP 298 job. Consequently, the manufacturing overhead costs allocated to WPP 298 equal $3,520 ($40 per direct manufacturing labor-hour × 88 hours) and appear in the Manufacturing Overhead panel of the WPP 298 job-cost record in Exhibit 4-2.

Step 7: Compute the Total Cost of the Job by Adding All Direct and Indirect Costs Assigned to the Job. Exhibit 4-2 shows that the total manufacturing costs of the WPP job are $9,705.

Direct manufacturing costs		
Direct materials	$4,606	
Direct manufacturing labor	1,579	$ 6,185
Manufacturing overhead costs		
($40 per direct manufacturing labor-hour × 88 hours)		3,520
Total manufacturing costs of job WPP 298		$9,705

Recall that Robinson bid a price of $15,000 for the job. At that revenue, the normal-costing system shows the job's gross margin is $5,295 ($15,000 − $9,705) and its gross-margin percentage is 35.3% ($5,295 ÷ $15,000 = 0.353).

CONCEPTS IN ACTION ▶ The Job-Costing "Game Plan" at AT&T Stadium

Tony Gutierrez/AP Images

While the Dallas Cowboys have won five Super Bowls, many football fans recognize the team for its futuristic home, AT&T Stadium in Arlington, Texas. The 80,000-seat stadium, built in 3 years, features two arches spanning a quarter-mile in length over the dome, a retractable roof, the largest retractable glass doors in the world (in each end zone), canted glass exterior walls, and a 600-ton video screen. To manage costs and make a profit, Manhattan Construction estimated and then evaluated the cost of building each feature.

The AT&T Stadium project had five stages: (1) conceptualization, (2) design and planning, (3) preconstruction, (4) construction, and (5) finalization and delivery. At each stage, the job-costing system tracked actual costs of direct materials, direct labor, and overhead costs (supervisor salaries, rent, materials handling, and so on). These costs were compared to budgeted costs to evaluate how well materials, labor and overhead resources were used. Without disciplined job costing, managing costs on this complex project would be extremely difficult. Job costing was key to Manhattan Construction turning a profit on AT&T Stadium.

Sources: Based on interview with Mark Penny, Project Manager, Manhattan Construction Co., 2010; David Dillon, "New Cowboys Stadium Has Grand Design, but Discipline Isn't Compromised," *The Dallas Morning News* (June 3, 2009); Brooke Knudson, "Profile: Dallas Cowboys Stadium," *Construction Today* (December 22, 2008); and Dallas Cowboys, "Cowboys Stadium: Architecture Fact Sheet," accessed March 2016 (http://stadium .dallascowboys.com/assets/pdf/mediaArchitectureFactSheet.pdf).

Donna Corporation manufactures custom cabinets for kitchens. It uses a normal-costing system with two direct-cost categories—direct materials and direct manu-facturing labor—and one indirect-cost pool, manufacturing overhead costs. It provides the following information for 2017.

Budgeted manufacturing overhead costs	$960,000
Budgeted direct manufacturing labor-hours	32,000 hours
Actual manufacturing overhead costs	$992,000
Actual direct manufacturing labor-hours	31,000 hours

Calculate the total manufacturing costs of the 32 Berndale Drive job using normal costing based on the following information:

Actual direct materials costs	$3,500
Actual direct manufacturing labor	160 hours
Actual direct manufacturing labor rate	$ 20 per hour

Robinson's manufacturing managers and sales managers can use the gross margin and gross-margin percentage calculations to compare the different jobs to try to understand why some jobs aren't as profitable as others. Were direct materials wasted? Was the direct manufacturing labor cost of the jobs too high? Were the jobs simply underpriced? A job-cost analysis provides the information managers needed to gauge the manufacturing and sales performance of their firms (see Concepts in Action: The Job Costing "Game Plan" at AT&T Stadium).

Exhibit 4-4 is an overview of Robinson Company's job-costing system. This exhibit represents the concepts comprising the five building blocks of job-costing systems introduced

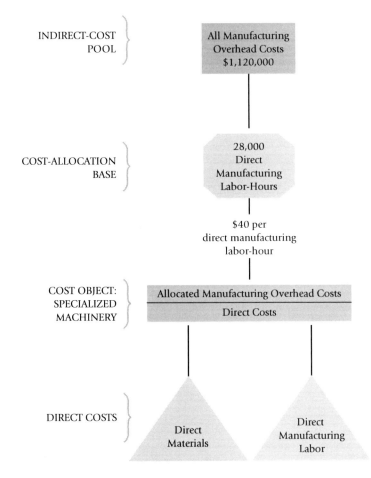

EXHIBIT 4-4

Job-Costing Overview for Determining Manufacturing Costs of Jobs at Robinson Company

INDIRECT-COST POOL — All Manufacturing Overhead Costs $1,120,000

COST-ALLOCATION BASE — 28,000 Direct Manufacturing Labor-Hours

$40 per direct manufacturing labor-hour

COST OBJECT: SPECIALIZED MACHINERY — Allocated Manufacturing Overhead Costs / Direct Costs

DIRECT COSTS — Direct Materials / Direct Manufacturing Labor

at the beginning of this chapter: (1) cost objects, (2) the direct costs of a cost object, (3) the indirect (overhead) costs of a cost object, (4) the indirect-cost pool, and (5) the cost-allocation base. (The symbols in the exhibit are used consistently in the costing-system overviews presented in this book. A triangle always identifies a direct cost, a rectangle represents the indirect-cost pool, and an octagon describes the cost-allocation base.) Costing-system overviews such as Exhibit 4-4 are important learning tools. We urge you to sketch one when you need to understand a costing system.

DECISION POINT

How do you implement a normal-costing system?

Note the similarities between Exhibit 4-4 and the cost of the WPP 298 job described in Step 7. Exhibit 4-4 shows two direct-cost categories (direct materials and direct manufacturing labor) and one indirect-cost category (manufacturing overhead) used to allocate indirect costs. The costs in Step 7 also have three dollar amounts, each corresponding respectively to the two direct-cost and one indirect-cost categories.

The Role of Technology

Information technology gives managers quick and accurate job-costing information, making it easier for them to manage and control jobs. Consider, for example, the direct materials charged to jobs. Managers control these costs as materials are purchased and used. Using Electronic Data Interchange (EDI) technology, companies like Robinson order materials from their suppliers by clicking a few keys on a computer keyboard. EDI, an electronic computer link between a company and its suppliers, ensures that the order is transmitted quickly and accurately with minimal paperwork and costs. A bar code scanner records the receipt of incoming materials, and a computer matches the receipt with the order, prints out a check to the supplier, and records the materials received. When an operator on the production floor transmits a request for materials via a computer terminal, the computer prepares a materials-requisition record, instantly recording the issue of materials in the materials and job-cost records. Each day, the computer sums the materials-requisition records charged to a particular job or manufacturing department. A performance report is then prepared monitoring the actual costs of direct materials. The use of direct materials can be reported hourly if managers believe the benefits exceed the cost of such frequent reporting.

Similarly, information about direct manufacturing labor is obtained as employees log into computer terminals and key in job numbers, their employee numbers, and the start and end times of their work on different jobs. The computer automatically prints the labor time record and, using hourly rates stored for each employee, calculates the direct manufacturing labor costs of individual jobs. Information technology can also give managers instant feedback to help them control manufacturing overhead costs, jobs in process, jobs completed, and jobs shipped and installed at customer sites.

Actual Costing

LEARNING OBJECTIVE 5

Distinguish actual costing

...actual costing uses actual indirect-cost rates

from normal costing

...normal costing uses budgeted indirect-cost rates

How would the cost of Job WPP 298 change if Robinson had used actual costing rather than normal costing? Both actual costing and normal costing trace direct costs to jobs in the same way because source documents identify the actual quantities and actual rates of direct materials and direct manufacturing labor for a job as the work is being done. The only difference between costing a job with normal costing and actual costing is that normal costing uses *budgeted* indirect-cost rates, whereas actual costing uses *actual* indirect-cost rates calculated annually at the end of the year. Exhibit 4-5 distinguishes actual costing from normal costing.

The following actual data for 2017 are for Robinson's manufacturing operations:

	Actual
Total manufacturing overhead costs	$1,215,000
Total direct manufacturing labor-hours	27,000

Steps 1 and 2 are the same in both normal and actual costing: Step 1 identifies WPP 298 as the cost object; Step 2 calculates actual direct materials costs of $4,606 and actual direct

EXHIBIT 4-5

Actual Costing and
Normal Costing
Methods

	Actual Costing	**Normal Costing**
Direct Costs	*Actual direct-cost rates* × actual quantities of direct-cost inputs	*Actual direct-cost rates* × actual quantities of direct-cost inputs
Indirect Costs	*Actual indirect-cost rates* × actual quantities of cost-allocation bases	*Budgeted indirect-cost rates* × actual quantities of cost-allocation bases

manufacturing labor costs of $1,579. Recall from Step 3 that Robinson uses a single cost-allocation base, direct manufacturing labor-hours, to allocate all manufacturing overhead costs to jobs. The actual quantity of direct manufacturing labor-hours for 2017 is 27,000 hours. In Step 4, Robinson groups all actual indirect manufacturing costs of $1,215,000 into a single manufacturing overhead cost pool. In Step 5, the **actual indirect-cost rate** is calculated by dividing actual total indirect costs in the pool (determined in Step 4) by the actual total quantity of the cost-allocation base (determined in Step 3). Robinson calculates the actual manufacturing overhead rate in 2017 for its single manufacturing overhead cost pool as follows:

$$\begin{aligned} \text{Actual manufacturing} \atop \text{overhead rate} &= \frac{\text{Actual annual manufacturing overhead costs}}{\text{Actual annual quantity of the cost-allocation base}} \\[2mm] &= \frac{\$1,215,000}{27,000 \text{ direct manufacturing labor-hours}} \\[2mm] &= \$45 \text{ per direct manufacturing labor-hour} \end{aligned}$$

In Step 6, under an actual-costing system,

$$\begin{aligned} \text{Manufacturing overhead costs} \atop \text{allocated to WPP 298} &= \frac{\text{Actual manufacturing}}{\text{overhead rate}} \times \frac{\text{Actual quantity of direct}}{\text{manufacturing labor-hours}} \\[2mm] &= \frac{\$45 \text{ per direct manuf.}}{\text{labor-hour}} \times \frac{88 \text{ direct manufacturing}}{\text{labor-hours}} \\[2mm] &= \$3,960 \end{aligned}$$

In Step 7, the cost of the job under actual costing is $10,145, calculated as follows:

Direct manufacturing costs		
Direct materials	$4,606	
Direct manufacturing labor	1,579	$ 6,185
Manufacturing overhead costs		
($45 per direct manufacturing labor-hour × 88 actual direct manufacturing labor-hours)		3,960
Total manufacturing costs of job		$10,145

The manufacturing cost of the WPP 298 job is higher by $440 under actual costing ($10,145) than it is under normal costing ($9,705) because the actual indirect-cost rate is $45 per hour, whereas the budgeted indirect-cost rate is $40 per hour. That is, ($45 − $40) × 88 actual direct manufacturing labor-hours = $440.

As we discussed previously, the manufacturing costs of a job are available much earlier in a normal-costing system. Consequently, Robinson's manufacturing and sales managers can evaluate the profitability of different jobs, the efficiency with which the jobs are done, and the pricing of different jobs as soon as they are completed, while the experience is still fresh in everyone's mind. Another advantage of normal costing is that it provides managers with information earlier—while there is still time to take corrective actions, such as improving the company's labor efficiency or reducing the company's overhead costs. At the end of the year, though, costs allocated using normal costing will not, in general, equal actual costs incurred. If the differences are significant, adjustments will need to be made so that the cost of jobs and the costs in various inventory accounts are based on actual rather than normal costing because companies need to prepare financial statements based on what actually happened rather than on what was expected to happen at the beginning of the year. We describe these adjustments later in the chapter.

The next section explains how a normal job-costing system aggregates the costs and revenues for all jobs worked on during a particular month. *Instructors and students who do not wish to explore these details can go directly to page 148 to the section "Budgeted Indirect Costs and End-of-Accounting-Year Adjustments."*

TRY IT! 4-2

Donna Corporation manufactures custom cabinets for kitchens. It uses a normal-costing system with two direct-cost categories—direct materials and direct manufacturing labor—and one indirect-cost pool, manufacturing overhead costs. It provides the following information for 2017.

Budgeted manufacturing overhead costs	$960,000
Budgeted direct manufacturing labor-hours	32,000 hours
Actual manufacturing overhead costs	$992,000
Actual direct manufacturing labor-hours	31,000 hours

Calculate the total manufacturing costs of the 32 Berndale Drive job using actual costing based on the following information:

Actual direct materials costs	$3,500
Actual direct manufacturing labor	160 hours
Actual direct manufacturing labor rate	$ 20 per hour

A Normal Job-Costing System in Manufacturing

LEARNING OBJECTIVE **6**

Track the flow of costs in a job-costing system

...from purchase of materials to sale of finished goods

The following example looks at events that occurred at Robinson Company in February 2017. Before getting into the details of normal costing, study Exhibit 4-6, which provides a broad framework for understanding the flow of costs in job costing.

The upper part of Exhibit 4-6 shows the flow of inventoriable costs from the purchase of materials and other manufacturing inputs to their conversion into work-in-process and finished goods, to the sale of finished goods.

Direct materials used and direct manufacturing labor can be easily traced to jobs. They become part of work-in-process inventory on the balance sheet because direct manufacturing labor transforms direct materials into another asset, work-in-process inventory. Robinson also incurs manufacturing overhead costs (including indirect materials and indirect manufacturing labor) to convert direct materials into work-in-process inventory. The overhead (indirect) costs, however, cannot be easily traced to individual jobs. As we described earlier in this chapter, manufacturing overhead costs are first accumulated in a manufacturing overhead account and then allocated to individual jobs. As manufacturing overhead costs are allocated, they become part of work-in-process inventory.

As we described in Chapter 2, when individual jobs are completed, work-in-process inventory becomes another balance sheet asset, finished-goods inventory. Only when finished goods are sold is the expense of cost of goods sold recognized in the income statement and matched against revenues earned.

The lower part of Exhibit 4-6 shows the period costs—marketing and customer-service costs. These costs do not create any assets on the balance sheet because they are not incurred to transform materials into a finished product. Instead, they are expensed in the income statement as they are incurred to best match revenues.

We next describe the entries made in the general ledger.

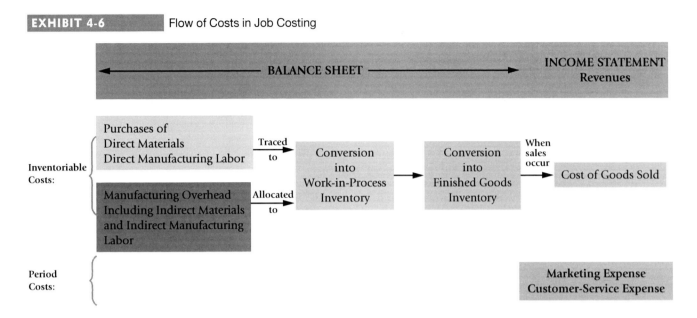

EXHIBIT 4-6 Flow of Costs in Job Costing

General Ledger

You know by this point that a job-costing system has a separate job-cost record for each job. A summary of the job-cost record is typically found in a subsidiary ledger. The general ledger account—Work-in-Process Control—presents the total of these separate job-cost records pertaining to all unfinished jobs. The job-cost records and Work-in-Process Control account track job costs from when jobs start until they are complete. When jobs are completed or sold, they are recorded in the finished-goods inventory records of jobs in the subsidiary ledger. The general ledger account Finished Goods Control records the total of these separate job-cost records for all jobs completed and subsequently for all jobs sold.

Exhibit 4-7 shows T-account relationships for Robinson Company's general ledger. The general ledger gives a "bird's-eye view" of the costing system. The amounts shown in Exhibit 4-7 are based on the monthly transactions and journal entries that follow. As you go through each journal entry, use Exhibit 4-7 to see how the various entries being made come together. General ledger accounts with "Control" in their titles (for example, Materials Control and Accounts Payable Control) have underlying subsidiary ledgers that contain additional details, such as each type of material in inventory and individual suppliers Robinson must pay.

Some companies simultaneously make entries in the general ledger and subsidiary ledger accounts. Others, such as Robinson, simplify their accounting by making entries in the subsidiary ledger when transactions occur and entries in the general ledger less frequently, often on a monthly basis, only when monthly financial statements are prepared.

A general ledger should be viewed as only one of many tools managers can use for planning and control. To control operations, managers rely on not only the source documents used to record amounts in the subsidiary ledgers, but also on nonfinancial information such as the percentage of jobs requiring rework or behind schedule.

Explanations of Transactions

We next look at a summary of Robinson Company's transactions for February 2017 and the corresponding journal entries for those transactions.

1. Purchases of materials (direct and indirect) on credit, $89,000

Materials Control	89,000	
Accounts Payable Control		89,000

EXHIBIT 4-7   Manufacturing Job-Costing System Using Normal Costing: Diagram of General Ledger Relationships for February 2017

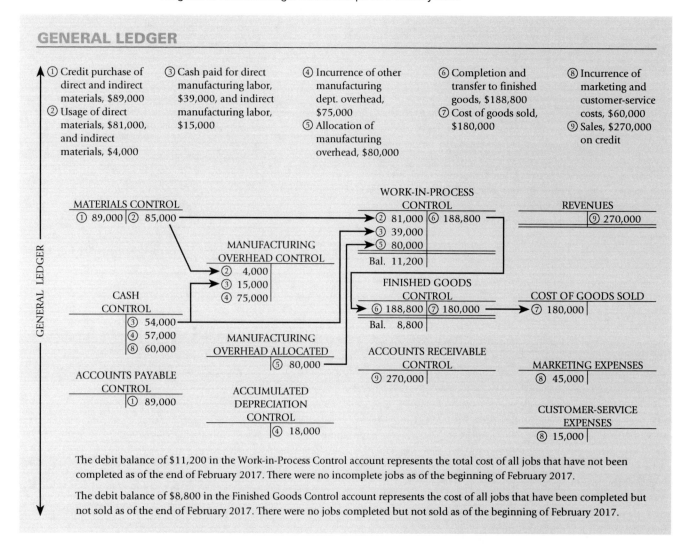

The debit balance of $11,200 in the Work-in-Process Control account represents the total cost of all jobs that have not been completed as of the end of February 2017. There were no incomplete jobs as of the beginning of February 2017.

The debit balance of $8,800 in the Finished Goods Control account represents the cost of all jobs that have been completed but not sold as of the end of February 2017. There were no jobs completed but not sold as of the beginning of February 2017.

2. Usage of direct materials, $81,000, and indirect materials, $4,000

Work-in-Process Control	81,000	
Manufacturing Overhead Control	4,000	
Materials Control		85,000

3. Manufacturing payroll for February: direct labor, $39,000, and indirect labor, $15,000, paid in cash

Work-in-Process Control	39,000	
Manufacturing Overhead Control	15,000	
Cash Control		54,000

4. Other manufacturing overhead costs incurred during February, $75,000, consisting of
   - supervision and engineering salaries, $44,000 (paid in cash);
   - plant utilities, repairs, and insurance, $13,000 (paid in cash); and
   - plant depreciation, $18,000

Manufacturing Overhead Control	75,000	
Cash Control		57,000
Accumulated Depreciation Control		18,000

5. Allocation of manufacturing overhead to jobs, $80,000

Work-in-Process Control	80,000	
Manufacturing Overhead Allocated		80,000

Under normal costing, **manufacturing overhead allocated**—or **manufacturing overhead applied**—is the amount of manufacturing overhead costs allocated to individual jobs based on the budgeted rate ($40 per direct manufacturing labor-hour) multiplied by the actual quantity of the allocation base used for each job. (The total actual direct manufacturing labor-hours across all jobs in February 2017 total 2,000.) Manufacturing overhead allocated contains all manufacturing overhead costs assigned to jobs using a cost-allocation base because overhead costs cannot be traced specifically to jobs in an economically feasible way.

Keep in mind the distinct difference between transactions 4 and 5. In transaction 4, actual overhead costs incurred throughout the month are added (debited) to the Manufacturing Overhead Control account. These costs are not debited to Work-in-Process Control because, unlike direct costs, they cannot be traced to individual jobs. Manufacturing overhead costs are added (debited) to individual jobs and to Work-in-Process Control *only when* manufacturing overhead costs are allocated in transaction 5. At the time these costs are allocated, Manufacturing Overhead Control is, *in effect*, decreased (credited) via its contra account, Manufacturing Overhead Allocated. Manufacturing Overhead Allocated is referred to as a *contra account* because the amounts debited to it represent the amounts credited to the Manufacturing Overhead Control account. Having Manufacturing Overhead Allocated as a contra account allows the job-costing system to separately retain information about the manufacturing overhead costs the company has *incurred* (in the Manufacturing Overhead Control account) as well as the amount of manufacturing overhead costs it has *allocated* (in the Manufacturing Overhead Allocated account). If the allocated manufacturing overhead had been credited to manufacturing overhead control, the company would lose information about the actual manufacturing overhead costs it is incurring.

Under the normal-costing system described in our Robinson Company example, at the beginning of the year, the company calculated the budgeted manufacturing overhead rate of $40 per direct manufacturing labor-hour by predicting the company's annual manufacturing overhead costs and annual quantity of the cost-allocation base. Almost certainly, the actual amounts allocated will differ from the predictions. We discuss what to do with this difference later in the chapter.

6. The sum of all individual jobs completed and transferred to finished goods in February 2017 is $188,800

Finished Goods Control	188,800	
Work-in-Process Control		188,800

7. Cost of goods sold, $180,000

Cost of Goods Sold	180,000	
Finished Goods Control		180,000

8. Marketing costs for February 2017, $45,000, and customer-service costs for February 2017, $15,000, paid in cash

Marketing Expenses	45,000	
Customer-Service Expenses	15,000	
Cash Control		60,000

9. Sales revenues from all jobs sold and delivered in February 2017, all on credit, $270,000

Accounts Receivable Control	270,000	
Revenues		270,000

TRY IT! 4-3

Donna Corporation manufactures custom cabinets for kitchens. It uses a normal-costing system with two direct-cost categories—direct materials and direct manufacturing labor—and one indirect-cost pool, manufacturing overhead costs. It provides the following information about manufacturing overhead costs for April 2017.

Actual direct materials used	$60,000
Actual direct manufacturing labor costs paid in cash	54,000
Indirect materials used	$3,000
Supervision and engineering salaries paid in cash	$50,000
Plant utilities and repairs paid in cash	10,000
Plant depreciation	$16,000
Actual direct manufacturing labor-hours	2,700
Cost of individual jobs completed and transferred to finished goods	$180,000
Cost of goods sold	$175,000

The following information is also available for 2017:

Budgeted manufacturing overhead costs for 2017	$960,000
Direct manufacturing labor-hours for 2017	32,000 hours

Present journal entries for (a) usage of direct and indirect materials, (b) manufacturing labor incurred, (c) manufacturing overhead costs incurred, (d) allocation of manufacturing overhead costs to jobs, (e) cost of jobs completed and transferred to finished goods, and (f) cost of goods sold.

Subsidiary Ledgers

Exhibits 4-8 and 4-9 present subsidiary ledgers that contain the underlying details—the "worm's-eye view"—that help Robinson's managers keep track of the WPP 298 job, as opposed to the "bird's-eye view" of the general ledger. The sum of all entries in underlying subsidiary ledgers equals the total amount in the corresponding general ledger control accounts.

Materials Records by Type of Material

The subsidiary ledger for materials at Robinson Company—called *Materials Records*—is used to continuously record the quantity of materials received, issued to jobs, and the inventory balances for each type of material. Panel A of Exhibit 4-8 shows the Materials Record for Metal Brackets (Part No. MB 468-A). In many companies, the source documents supporting the receipt and issue of materials [the material requisition record in Exhibit 4-3, Panel A, (page 135)] are scanned into a computer. Software programs then automatically update the Materials Records and make all the necessary accounting entries in the subsidiary and general ledgers. The cost of materials received across all types of direct and indirect material records for February 2017 is $89,000 (Exhibit 4-8, Panel A). The cost of materials issued across all types of direct and indirect material records for February 2017 is $85,000 (Exhibit 4-8, Panel A).

As direct materials are used, they are recorded as issued in the Materials Records (see Exhibit 4-8, Panel A, for a record of the Metal Brackets issued for the WPP machine job). Direct materials are also charged to Work-in-Process Inventory Records for Jobs, which are the subsidiary ledger accounts for the Work-in-Process Control account in the general ledger. For example, the metal brackets used in the WPP machine job appear as direct material costs of $112 in the subsidiary ledger under the work-in-process inventory record for WPP 298 [Exhibit 4-9, Panel A, which is based on the job-cost record source document in Exhibit 4-2, (page 134)]. The cost of direct materials used across all job-cost records for February 2017 is $81,000 (Exhibit 4-9, Panel A).

As indirect materials (for example, lubricants) are used, they are charged to the Manufacturing Department overhead records (Exhibit 4-8, Panel C), which comprise the

| **EXHIBIT 4-8** | Subsidiary Ledgers for Materials, Labor, and Manufacturing Department Overhead[1] |

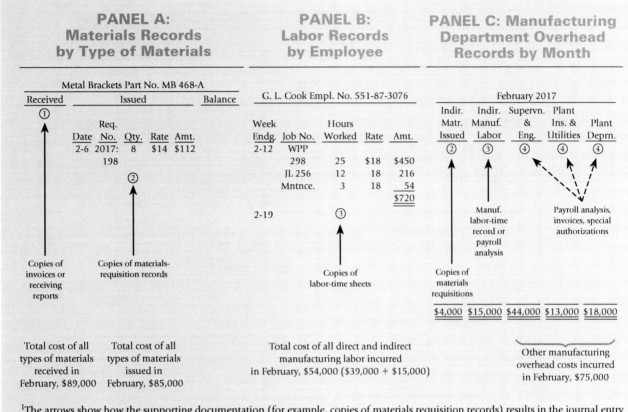

[1]The arrows show how the supporting documentation (for example, copies of materials requisition records) results in the journal entry number shown in circles (for example, journal entry number 2) that corresponds to the entries in Exhibit 4-7.

subsidiary ledger for the Manufacturing Overhead Control account. The Manufacturing Department overhead records are used to accumulate actual costs in individual overhead categories by each indirect-cost-pool account in the general ledger. Recall that Robinson has only one indirect-cost pool: Manufacturing Overhead. The cost of indirect materials used is not added directly to individual job records. Instead, this cost is allocated to individual job records as a part of manufacturing overhead.

Labor Records by Employee

Labor records by employee (see Exhibit 4-8, Panel B, for G. L. Cook) are used to trace the costs of direct manufacturing labor to individual jobs and to accumulate the costs of indirect manufacturing labor in the Manufacturing Department overhead records (Exhibit 4-8, Panel C). The labor records are based on the labor-time sheet source documents [see Exhibit 4-3, Panel B, (page 135)]. The subsidiary ledger for employee labor records (Exhibit 4-8, Panel B) shows the different jobs that G. L. Cook, Employee No. 551-87-3076, worked on and the $720 of wages owed to Cook, for the week ending February 12. The sum of total wages owed to all employees for February 2017 is $54,000. The job-cost record for WPP 298 shows direct manufacturing labor costs of $450 for the time Cook spent on the WPP machine job during that week (Exhibit 4-9, Panel A). Total direct manufacturing labor costs recorded in all job-cost records (the subsidiary ledger for Work-in-Process Control) for February 2017 is $39,000.

G. L. Cook's employee record shows $54 for maintenance, which is an indirect manufacturing labor cost. The total indirect manufacturing labor costs of $15,000 for February 2017 appear in the Manufacturing Department overhead records in the subsidiary ledger (Exhibit 4-8, Panel C). These costs, by definition, cannot be traced to an individual job. Instead, they are allocated to individual jobs as a part of manufacturing overhead.

EXHIBIT 4-9   Subsidiary Ledgers for Individual Jobs[1]

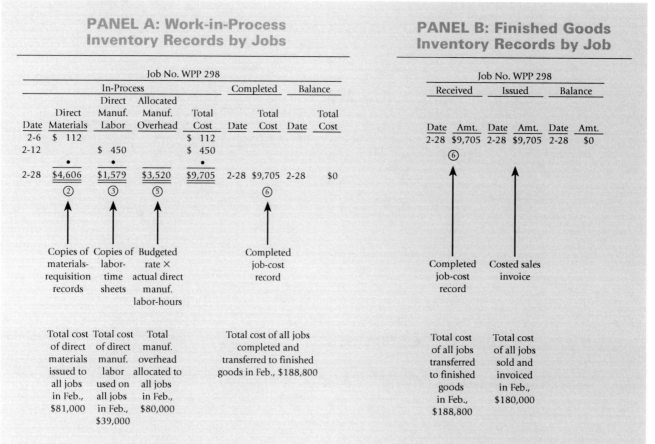

[1]The arrows show how the supporting documentation (for example, copies of materials requisition records) results in the journal entry number shown in circles (for example, journal entry number 2) that corresponds to the entries in Exhibit 4-7.

Manufacturing Department Overhead Records by Month

The Manufacturing Department overhead records (see Exhibit 4-8, Panel C) that make up the subsidiary ledger for the Manufacturing Overhead Control account show details of different categories of overhead costs such as indirect materials, indirect manufacturing labor, supervision and engineering, plant insurance and utilities, and plant depreciation. The source documents for these entries include invoices (for example, a utility bill) and special schedules (for example, a depreciation schedule) from the responsible accounting officer. Manufacturing department overhead for February 2017 is indirect materials, $4,000; indirect manufacturing labor, $15,000; and other manufacturing overhead, $75,000 (Exhibit 4-8, Panel C).

Work-in-Process Inventory Records by Jobs

As we have already discussed, the job-cost record for each individual job in the subsidiary ledger is debited by the actual cost of direct materials and direct manufacturing labor used by individual jobs. In Robinson's normal-costing system, the job-cost record for each individual job in the subsidiary ledger is also debited for manufacturing overhead allocated based on the budgeted manufacturing overhead rate times the actual direct manufacturing labor-hours used in that job. For example, the job-cost record for Job WPP 298 (Exhibit 4-9, Panel A) shows Manufacturing Overhead Allocated of $3,520 (the budgeted rate of $40 per labor-hour × 88 actual direct manufacturing labor-hours used). For the

2,000 actual direct manufacturing labor-hours used for all jobs in February 2017, the total manufacturing overhead allocated equals $40 per labor-hour × 2,000 direct manufacturing labor-hours = $80,000.

Finished Goods Inventory Records by Jobs

Exhibit 4-9, Panel A, shows that Job WPP 298 was completed at a cost of $9,705. Job WPP 298 also simultaneously appears in the finished-goods records of the subsidiary ledger. The total cost of all jobs completed and transferred to finished goods in February 2017 is $188,800 (Exhibit 4-9, Panels A and B). Exhibit 4-9, Panel B, indicates that Job WPP 298 was sold and delivered to the customer on February 28, 2017, at which time $9,705 was transferred from finished goods to cost of goods sold. The total cost of all jobs sold and invoiced in February 2017 is $180,000 (Exhibit 4-9, Panel B).

Other Subsidiary Records

Just as it does for manufacturing payroll, Robinson maintains employee labor records in subsidiary ledgers for marketing and customer-service payroll as well as records for different types of advertising costs (print, television, and radio). An accounts receivable subsidiary ledger is also used to record the February 2017 amounts due from each customer, including the $15,000 due from the sale of Job WPP 298.

At this point, pause and review the nine entries in this example. Exhibit 4-7 is a handy summary of all nine general-ledger entries presented in the form of T-accounts. Be sure to trace each journal entry, step by step, to T-accounts in the general ledger presented in Exhibit 4-7. Robinson's managers will use this information to evaluate how Robinson has performed on the WPP job.

Exhibit 4-10 provides Robinson's income statement for February 2017 using information from entries 7, 8, and 9. Managers could further subdivide the cost of goods sold calculations and present them in the format of Exhibit 2-8 [(page 62)]. The benefit of using the subdivided format is that it allows managers to discern detailed performance trends that can help them improve the efficiency on future jobs.

Nonmanufacturing Costs and Job Costing

In Chapter 2 (pages 68–69), you learned that companies use product costs for different purposes. The product costs reported as inventoriable costs to shareholders may differ from the product costs reported to managers to guide their pricing and product-mix decisions. Managers must keep in mind that even though marketing and customer-service costs are expensed when incurred for financial accounting purposes, companies often trace or allocate these costs to individual jobs for pricing, product-mix, and cost-management decisions.

Revenues		$270,000
Cost of goods sold ($180,000 + $14,000[1])		194,000
Gross margin		76,000
Operating costs		
Marketing costs	$45,000	
Customer-service costs	15,000	
Total operating costs		60,000
Operating income		$ 16,000

Robinson Company
Income Statement
for the Month Ending
February 2017

[1]Cost of goods sold has been increased by $14,000, the difference between the Manufacturing overhead control account ($94,000) and the Manufacturing overhead allocated ($80,000). In a later section of this chapter, we discuss this adjustment, which represents the amount by which actual manufacturing overhead cost exceeds the manufacturing overhead allocated to jobs during February 2017.

Robinson can trace direct marketing costs and customer-service costs to jobs the same way in which it traces direct manufacturing costs to jobs. What about indirect marketing and customer-service costs? Assume these costs have the same cost-allocation base, revenues, and are included in a single cost pool. Robinson can then calculate a budgeted indirect-cost rate by dividing budgeted indirect marketing costs plus budgeted indirect customer-service costs by budgeted revenues. Robinson can use this rate to allocate these indirect costs to jobs. For example, if this rate were 15% of revenues, Robinson would allocate $2,250 to Job WPP 298 (0.15 $\times$ $15,000, the revenue from the job). By assigning both manufacturing costs and nonmanufacturing costs to jobs, Robinson can compare all costs against the revenues of different jobs.

DECISION POINT

How are transactions recorded in a manufacturing job-costing system?

Budgeted Indirect Costs and End-of-Accounting-Year Adjustments

LEARNING OBJECTIVE 7

Dispose of under- or overallocated manufacturing overhead costs at the end of the fiscal year using alternative methods

...for example, writing off this amount to the Cost of Goods Sold account

Managers try to closely approximate actual manufacturing overhead costs and actual direct manufacturing labor-hours when calculating the budgeted indirect cost rate. However, for the numerator and denominator reasons explained earlier in the chapter, under normal costing, a company's actual overhead costs incurred each month are not likely to equal its overhead costs allocated each month. Even at the end of the year, allocated costs are unlikely to equal actual costs because they are based on estimates made up to 12 months before actual costs are incurred. For financial statement purposes, companies are required under Generally Accepted Accounting Principles to report results based on actual costs. We now describe adjustments that management accountants need to make when, at the end of the fiscal year, indirect costs allocated differ from actual indirect costs incurred.

Underallocated and Overallocated Indirect Costs

Underallocated indirect costs occur when the allocated amount of indirect costs in an accounting period is less than the actual (incurred) amount. **Overallocated indirect costs** occur when the allocated amount of indirect costs in an accounting period is greater than the actual (incurred) amount.

Underallocated (overallocated) indirect costs = Actual indirect costs incurred − Indirect costs allocated

Underallocated (overallocated) indirect costs are also called **underapplied (overapplied) indirect costs** and **underabsorbed (overabsorbed) indirect costs**.

Consider the manufacturing overhead cost pool at Robinson Company. There are two indirect-cost accounts in the general ledger related to manufacturing overhead:

1. Manufacturing Overhead Control, the record of the actual costs in all the individual overhead categories (such as indirect materials, indirect manufacturing labor, supervision, engineering, utilities, and plant depreciation)

2. Manufacturing Overhead Allocated, the record of the manufacturing overhead allocated to individual jobs on the basis of the budgeted rate multiplied by actual direct manufacturing labor-hours

At the end of the year, the overhead accounts show the following amounts.

Manufacturing Overhead Control		Manufacturing Overhead Allocated	
Bal. Dec. 31, 2017	1,215,000	Bal. Dec. 31, 2017	1,080,000

The $1,080,000 credit balance in Manufacturing Overhead Allocated results from multiplying the 27,000 actual direct manufacturing labor-hours worked on all jobs in 2017 by the budgeted rate of $40 per direct manufacturing labor-hour.

The $135,000 ($1,215,000 − $1,080,000) difference (a net debit) is an underallocated amount because actual manufacturing overhead costs are greater than the allocated amount. This difference arises for two reasons related to the computation of the $40 budgeted hourly rate:

1. **Numerator reason (indirect-cost pool).** Actual manufacturing overhead costs of $1,215,000 are greater than the budgeted amount of $1,120,000.
2. **Denominator reason (quantity of allocation base).** Actual direct manufacturing labor-hours of 27,000 are fewer than the budgeted 28,000 hours.

There are three main approaches to accounting for the $135,000 underallocated manufacturing overhead caused by Robinson underestimating manufacturing overhead costs and overestimating the quantity of the cost-allocation base: (1) adjusted allocation-rate approach, (2) proration approach, and (3) write-off to cost of goods sold approach.

Adjusted Allocation-Rate Approach

The **adjusted allocation-rate approach** restates all overhead entries in the general ledger and subsidiary ledgers using actual cost rates rather than budgeted cost rates. First, the actual manufacturing overhead rate is computed at the end of the fiscal year. Then the manufacturing overhead costs allocated to every job during the year are recomputed using the actual manufacturing overhead rate (rather than the budgeted manufacturing overhead rate). Finally, end-of-year closing entries are made. The result is that at year-end, every job-cost record and finished-goods record—as well as the ending Work-in-Process Control, Finished Goods Control, and Cost of Goods Sold accounts—represent actual manufacturing overhead costs incurred.

The widespread adoption of computerized accounting systems has greatly reduced the cost of using the adjusted allocation-rate approach. In our Robinson example, the actual manufacturing overhead ($1,215,000) exceeds the manufacturing overhead allocated ($1,080,000) by 12.5% [($1,215,000 − $1,080,000) ÷ $1,080,000]. At year-end, Robinson could increase the manufacturing overhead allocated to each job in 2017 by 12.5% using a single software command. The command would adjust both the subsidiary ledgers and the general ledger.

Consider the Western Pulp and Paper machine job, WPP 298. Under normal costing, the manufacturing overhead allocated to the job is $3,520 (the budgeted rate of $40 per direct manufacturing labor-hour × 88 hours). Increasing the manufacturing overhead allocated by 12.5%, or $440 ($3,520 × 0.125), means the adjusted amount of manufacturing overhead allocated to Job WPP 298 equals $3,960 ($3,520+$440). Note from page 139 that using actual costing, manufacturing overhead allocated to this job is $3,960 (the actual rate of $45 per direct manufacturing labor-hour × 88 hours). Making this adjustment under normal costing for each job in the subsidiary ledgers ensures that actual manufacturing overhead costs of $1,215,000 are allocated to jobs.

The adjusted allocation-rate approach yields the benefits of both the *timeliness and convenience of normal costing during the year and the allocation of actual manufacturing overhead costs at year-end*. Each individual job-cost record and the end-of-year account balances for inventories and cost of goods sold are adjusted to actual costs. These adjustments, in turn, will affect the income Robinson reports. Knowing the actual profitability of individual jobs after they are completed provides managers with accurate and useful insights for future decisions about which jobs to undertake, how to price them, and how to manage their costs.

Proration Approach

The **proration** approach spreads underallocated overhead or overallocated overhead among ending work-in-process inventory, finished-goods inventory, and cost of goods sold. Materials inventory is not included in this proration because no manufacturing overhead costs have been allocated to it. We illustrate end-of-year proration in the Robinson Company example. Assume the following actual results for Robinson Company in 2017:

	Home	Insert	Page Layout	Formulas	Data
	A		B	C	
1	**Account**		**Account Balance (Before Proration)**	**Manufacturing Overhead in Each Account Balance Allocated in the Current Year (Before Proration)**	
2	Work-in-process control		$ 50,000	$ 16,200	
3	Finished goods control		75,000	31,320	
4	Cost of goods sold		2,375,000	1,032,480	
5			$2,500,000	$1,080,000	

How should Robinson prorate the underallocated $135,000 of manufacturing overhead at the end of 2017?

On the basis of the total amount of manufacturing overhead allocated in 2017 (before proration) in the ending balances of Work-in-Process Control, Finished Goods Control, and Cost of Goods Sold accounts. The $135,000 underallocated overhead is prorated over the three accounts in proportion to the total amount of manufacturing overhead allocated (before proration) in column 2 of the following table, resulting in the ending balances (after proration) in column 5 at actual costs.

	Home	Insert	Page Layout	Formulas	Data	Review	View		
	A	B	C	D	E		F	G	
10		**Account Balance (Before Proration)**	**Manufacturing Overhead in Each Account Balance Allocated in the Current Year (Before Proration)**	**Manufacturing Overhead in Each Account Balance Allocated in the Current Year as a Percent of Total**	**Proration of $135,000 of Underallocated Manufacturing Overhead**			**Account Balance (After Proration)**	
11	**Account**	**(1)**	**(2)**	**(3) = (2) / $1,080,000**	**(4) = (3) × $135,000**			**(5) = (1) + (4)**	
12	Work-in-process control	$ 50,000	$ 16,200	1.5%	0.015 × $135,000 =	$ 2,025		$ 52,025	
13	Finished goods control	75,000	31,320	2.9%	0.029 × 135,000 =	3,915		78,915	
14	Cost of goods sold	2,375,000	1,032,480	95.6%	0.956 × 135,000 =	129,060		2,504,060	
15	Total	$2,500,000	$1,080,000	100.0%		$135,000		$2,635,000	

Prorating on the basis of the manufacturing overhead allocated (before proration) results in Robinson allocating manufacturing overhead based on actual manufacturing overhead costs. Recall that Robinson's actual manufacturing overhead ($1,215,000) in 2017 exceeds its manufacturing overhead allocated ($1,080,000) in 2017 by 12.5%. The proration amounts in column 4 can also be derived by multiplying the balances in column 2 by 0.125. For example, the $3,915 proration to Finished Goods is 0.125 × $31,320. Adding these amounts effectively means allocating manufacturing overhead at 112.5% of what had been allocated before. The journal entry to record this proration is:

Work-in-Process Control	2,025	
Finished Goods Control	3,915	
Cost of Goods Sold	129,060	
Manufacturing Overhead Allocated	1,080,000	
Manufacturing Overhead Control		1,215,000

If manufacturing overhead had been overallocated, the Work-in-Process Control, Finished Goods Control, and Cost of Goods Sold accounts would be decreased (credited) instead of increased (debited).

This journal entry closes (brings to zero) the manufacturing overhead-related accounts and restates the 2017 ending balances for Work-in-Process Control, Finished Goods Control, and Cost of Goods Sold to what they would have been if actual manufacturing overhead rates had been used rather than budgeted manufacturing overhead rates. This method reports the same 2017 ending balances in the general ledger as the adjusted allocation-rate approach. However, unlike the adjusted allocation-rate approach, the sum of the amounts shown in the subsidiary ledgers will not match the amounts shown in the general ledger after proration because no adjustments from budgeted to actual manufacturing overhead rates are made in the individual job-cost records. The objective of the proration approach is to only adjust the general ledger to actual manufacturing overhead rates for purposes of financial reporting. The increase in cost of goods sold expense by $129,060 as a result of the proration causes Robinson's reported operating income to decrease by the same amount.

Some companies use the proration approach, but base it on the ending balances of Work-in-Process Control, Finished Goods Control, and Cost of Goods Sold accounts prior to proration (see column 1 of the preceding table). The following table shows that prorations based on ending account balances are not the same as the more accurate prorations calculated earlier based on the amount of manufacturing overhead allocated to the accounts because the proportions of manufacturing overhead costs to total costs in these accounts are not the same.

Home	Insert	Page Layout	Formulas	Data	Review	View	
	A	B	C	D	E	F
1		**Account Balance (Before Proration)**	**Account Balance as a Percent of Total**	**Proration of $135,000 of Underallocated Manufacturing Overhead**		**Account Balance (After Proration)**
2	**Account**	**(1)**	**(2) = (1) / $2,500,000**	**(3) = (2) × $135,000**		**(4) = (1) + (3)**
3	Work-in-process control	$ 50,000	2.0%	0.02 × $135,000 =	$ 2,700	$ 52,700
4	Finished goods control	75,000	3.0%	0.03 × 135,000 =	4,050	79,050
5	Cost of goods sold	2,375,000	95.0%	0.95 × 135,000 =	128,250	2,503,250
6	Total	$2,500,000	100.0%		$135,000	$2,635,000

However, proration based on ending balances is frequently justified as being an expedient way of approximating the more accurate results from using manufacturing overhead costs allocated.

Write-off to Cost of Goods Sold Approach

Under the write-off approach, the total under- or overallocated manufacturing overhead is included in this year's Cost of Goods Sold. For Robinson, the journal entry would be as follows:

Cost of Goods Sold	135,000	
Manufacturing Overhead Allocated	1,080,000	
Manufacturing Overhead Control		1,215,000

Robinson's two Manufacturing Overhead accounts—Manufacturing Overhead Control and Manufacturing Overhead Allocated—are closed with the difference between them included in Cost of Goods Sold. The Cost of Goods Sold account after the write-off equals $2,510,000, the balance before the write-off of $2,375,000 *plus the underallocated* manufacturing overhead amount of $135,000. This results in operating income decreasing by $135,000.

TRY IT! 4-4

Donna Corporation manufactures custom cabinets for kitchens. It uses a normal-costing system with two direct-cost categories—direct materials and direct manufacturing labor—and one indirect-cost pool, manufacturing overhead costs. It provides the following information about manufacturing overhead costs for 2017.

Budgeted manufacturing overhead costs	$960,000
Budgeted direct manufacturing labor-hours	32,000 hours
Actual manufacturing overhead costs	$992,000
Actual direct manufacturing labor-hours	31,000 hours

The following information is available as of December 31, 2017.

Account	Account Balance (Before Proration)	Manufacturing Overhead in Each Account Balance Allocated in the Current Year (Before Proration)
Work-in-Process Control	$ 40,000	$ 14,400
Finished Goods Control	60,000	24,000
Cost of Goods Sold	1,900,000	921,600
	$2,000,000	$960,000

Calculate the underallocated or overallocated manufacturing overhead at the end of 2017 and prorate it to Work-in-Process Control, Finished Goods Control, and Cost of Goods Sold accounts based on the allocated manufacturing overhead in each account balance using normal costing.

Choosing Among Approaches

Which of the three approaches of dealing with underallocated overhead and overallocated overhead is the best one to use? When making this decision, managers should consider the amount of underallocated or overallocated overhead and the purpose of the adjustment, as the following table indicates.

If the purpose of the adjustment is to...	and the total amount of underallocation or overallocation is...	then managers prefer to use the...
state the balance sheet and income statements based on actual rather than budgeted manufacturing overhead rates	big, relative to total operating income, and inventory levels are high	proration method because it is the most accurate method of allocating actual manufacturing overhead costs to the general ledger accounts.
state the balance sheet and income statements based on actual rather than budgeted manufacturing overhead rates	small, relative to total operating income, or inventory levels are low	write-off to cost of goods sold approach because it is a good approximation of the more accurate proration method.
provide an accurate record of actual individual job costs in order to conduct a profitability analysis, learn how to better manage the costs of jobs, and bid on future jobs	big, relative to total operating income,	adjusted allocation-rate method because it makes adjustments in individual job records in addition to the general ledger accounts.

Many management accountants and managers argue that to the extent that the underallocated overhead cost measures inefficiency during the period, it should be written off to the Cost of Goods Sold account instead of being prorated to the Work-in-Process or Finished-Goods inventory accounts. This line of reasoning favors applying a combination of the write-off and proration methods. For example, the portion of the underallocated overhead cost that is due to inefficiency (say, because of excessive spending or idle capacity) and that could have been avoided should be written off to the Cost of Goods Sold account, whereas the portion that is unavoidable should be prorated. Unlike full proration, this approach avoids making the costs of inefficiency part of inventory assets.

As our discussion suggests, choosing which method to use and determining the amount to be written off is often a matter of judgment. The method managers choose affects the operating income a company reports. In the case of underallocated overhead, the method of writing off to cost of goods sold results in lower operating income compared to proration. In the case of overallocated overhead, proration results in lower operating income compared to writing the overhead off to cost of goods sold.

Do managers prefer to report lower or higher operating income? Reporting lower operating income lowers the company's taxes, saving the company cash and increasing company value. But managers are often compensated based on operating income and so favor reporting higher operating incomes even if it results in higher taxes. Managers of companies in financial difficulty also tend to report higher incomes to avoid violating financial covenants. Shareholders and boards of directors seek to motivate managerial actions that increase company value. For this reason, many compensation plans include metrics such as after-tax cash flow, in addition to operating income. At no time should managers make choices that are illegal or unethical. We discuss these issues in more detail in Chapter 23.

Robinson's managers believed that a single manufacturing overhead cost pool with direct manufacturing labor-hours as the cost-allocation base was appropriate for allocating all manufacturing overhead costs to jobs. Had Robinson's managers felt that different manufacturing departments (for example, machining and assembly) used overhead resources differently, they would have assigned overhead costs to each department and calculated a separate overhead allocation rate for each department based on the cost driver of the overhead costs in each department. The general ledger would contain Manufacturing Overhead Control and Manufacturing Overhead Allocated accounts for each department, resulting in end-of-year adjustments for underallocated or overallocated overhead costs for each department.

Instructors and students interested in exploring these more detailed allocations can go to Chapter 15, where we continue the Robinson Company example.

DECISION POINT

How should managers dispose of under- or overallocated manufacturing overhead costs at the end of the accounting year?

Variations from Normal Costing: A Service-Sector Example

Job costing is also very useful in service organizations such as accounting and consulting firms, advertising agencies, auto repair shops, and hospitals. In an accounting firm, each audit is a job. The costs of each audit are accumulated in a job-cost record, much like the document used by Robinson Company, based on the seven-step approach described earlier. On the basis of labor-time sheets, direct labor costs of the professional staff—audit partners, audit managers, and audit staff—are traced to individual jobs. Other direct costs, such as travel, out-of-town meals and lodging, phone, fax, and copying, are also traced to jobs. The costs of secretarial support, office staff, rent, and depreciation of furniture and equipment are indirect costs because these costs cannot be traced to jobs in an economically feasible way. Indirect costs are allocated to jobs, for example, using a cost-allocation base such as number of professional labor-hours.

In some service organizations, a variation from normal costing is helpful because actual direct-labor costs, the largest component of total costs, can be difficult to trace to jobs as they are completed. For example, the actual direct-labor costs of an audit may include bonuses that become known only at the end of the year (a numerator reason). Also, the hours worked each period might vary significantly depending on the number of working days each

LEARNING OBJECTIVE   8

Understand variations from normal costing

...some variations from normal costing use budgeted direct-cost rates

month and the demand for services (a denominator reason) while the direct-labor costs remain largely fixed. It would be inappropriate to charge a job with higher actual direct labor costs simply because a month had fewer working days or demand for services was low in that month. Using budgeted rates gives a better picture of the direct labor cost per hour that the company had planned when it hired the workers. In situations like these, a company needing timely information during the progress of an audit will use budgeted rates for some direct costs and budgeted rates for other indirect costs. All budgeted rates are calculated at the start of the fiscal year. In contrast, normal costing uses actual cost rates for all direct costs and budgeted cost rates only for indirect costs.

The mechanics of using budgeted rates for direct costs are similar to the methods employed when using budgeted rates for indirect costs in normal costing. We illustrate this for Donahue and Associates, a public accounting firm. For 2017, Donahue budgets total direct-labor costs of $14,400,000, total indirect costs of $12,960,000, and total direct (professional) labor-hours of 288,000. In this case,

$$\text{Budgeted direct-labor cost rate} = \frac{\text{Budgeted total direct-labor costs}}{\text{Budgeted total direct-labor hours}}$$

$$= \frac{\$14,400,000}{288,000 \text{ direct labor-hours}} = \$50 \text{ per direct labor-hour}$$

Assuming only one indirect-cost pool and total direct-labor costs as the cost-allocation base,

$$\text{Budgeted indirect cost rate} = \frac{\text{Budgeted total costs in indirect cost pool}}{\text{Budgeted total quantity of cost-allocation base (direct-labor costs)}}$$

$$= \frac{\$12,960,000}{\$14,400,000} = 0.90, \text{ or } 90\% \text{ of direct-labor costs}$$

Suppose that in March 2017, an audit of Hanley Transport, a client of Donahue, uses 800 direct labor-hours. Donahue calculates the direct-labor costs of the audit by multiplying the budgeted direct-labor cost rate, $50 per direct labor-hour, by 800, the actual quantity of direct labor-hours. The indirect costs allocated to the Hanley Transport audit are determined by multiplying the budgeted indirect-cost rate (90%) by the direct-labor costs assigned to the job ($40,000). Assuming no other direct costs for travel and the like, the cost of the Hanley Transport audit is:

Direct-labor costs, $50 × 800	$40,000
Indirect costs allocated, 90% × $40,000	36,000
Total	$76,000

At the end of the fiscal year, the direct costs traced to jobs using budgeted rates will generally not equal actual direct costs because the actual rate and the budgeted rate are developed at different times using different information. End-of-year adjustments for underallocated or overallocated direct costs would need to be made in the same way that adjustments are made for underallocated or overallocated indirect costs.

The Donahue and Associates example illustrates that all costing systems do not exactly match either the actual-costing system or the normal-costing system described earlier in the chapter. As another example, engineering consulting firms, such as Tata Consulting Engineers in India and Terracon Consulting Engineers in the United States, often use budgeted rates to allocate indirect costs (such as engineering and office-support costs) as well as some direct costs (such as professional labor-hours) and trace some actual direct costs (such as the cost of making blueprints and fees paid to outside experts). Users of costing systems should be aware of the different systems that they may encounter.

DECISION POINT

What are some variations of normal costing?

PROBLEM FOR SELF-STUDY

Your manager asks you to bring the following incomplete accounts of Endeavor Printing, Inc., up to date through January 31, 2017. Consider the data that appear in the T-accounts as well as the following information in items (a) through (j).

Endeavor's normal-costing system has two direct-cost categories (direct material costs and direct manufacturing labor costs) and one indirect-cost pool (manufacturing overhead costs, which are allocated using direct manufacturing labor costs).

Materials Control	Wages Payable Control
12-31-2016 Bal. 30,000	1-31-2017 Bal. 6,000

Work-in-Process Control	Manufacturing Overhead Control
	1-31-2017 Bal. 114,000

Finished Goods Control	Costs of Goods Sold
12-31-2016 Bal. 40,000	

Additional information follows:

a. Manufacturing overhead is allocated using a budgeted rate that is set every December. You forecast next year's manufacturing overhead costs and next year's direct manufacturing labor costs. The budget for 2017 is $1,200,000 for manufacturing overhead costs and $800,000 for direct manufacturing labor costs.
b. The only job unfinished on January 31, 2017, is No. 419, on which direct manufacturing labor costs are $4,000 (250 direct manufacturing labor-hours) and direct material costs are $16,000.
c. Total direct materials issued to production during January 2017 are $180,000.
d. Cost of goods completed during January is $360,000.
e. Materials inventory as of January 31, 2017, is $40,000.
f. Finished-goods inventory as of January 31, 2017, is $30,000.
g. All plant workers earn the same wage rate. Direct manufacturing labor-hours used for January total 5,000 hours. Other labor costs total $20,000.
h. The gross plant payroll paid in January equals $104,000. Ignore withholdings.
i. All "actual" manufacturing overhead cost incurred during January has already been posted.
j. All materials are direct materials.

Calculate the following:

1. Materials purchased during January
2. Cost of Goods Sold during January
3. Direct manufacturing labor costs incurred during January
4. Manufacturing Overhead Allocated during January
5. Balance, Wages Payable Control, December 31, 2016
6. Balance, Work-in-Process Control, January 31, 2017
7. Balance, Work-in-Process Control, December 31, 2016
8. Manufacturing Overhead Underallocated or Overallocated for January 2017

Solution

Amounts from the T-accounts are labeled "(T)."
1. From Materials Control T-account, Materials purchased: $180,000 (c) + $40,000 (e) − $30,000 (T) = $190,000
2. From Finished Goods Control T-account, Cost of Goods Sold: $40,000 (T) + $360,000 (d) − $30,000 (f) = $370,000

3. Direct manufacturing wage rate: $4,000 (b) ÷ 250 direct manufacturing labor-hours (b) = $16 per direct manufacturing labor-hour
   Direct manufacturing labor costs: 5,000 direct manufacturing labor-hours (g) × $16 per direct manufacturing labor-hour = $80,000

4. Manufacturing overhead rate: $1,200,000 (a) ÷ $800,000 (a) = 150%
   Manufacturing Overhead Allocated: 150% of $80,000 (see 3) = 1.50 × $80,000 = $120,000

5. From Wages Payable Control T-account, Wages Payable Control, December 31, 2016: $104,000 (h) + $6,000 (T) − $80,000 (see 3) − $20,000 (g) = $10,000

6. Work-in-Process Control, January 31, 2017: $16,000 (b) + $4,000 (b) + 150% of $4,000 (b) = $26,000 (This answer is used in item 7.)

7. From Work-in-Process Control T-account, Work-in-Process Control, December 31, 2016: $360,000 (d) + $26,000 (see 6) − $180,000 (c) − $80,000 (see 3) − $120,000 (see 4) = $6,000

8. Manufacturing overhead overallocated: $120,000 (see 4) − $114,000 (T) = $6,000.

Letters alongside entries in T-accounts correspond to letters in the preceding additional information. Numbers alongside entries in T-accounts correspond to numbers in the preceding requirements.

Materials Control

December 31, 2016, Bal.	(given)	30,000			
	(1)	190,000*		(c)	180,000
January 31, 2017, Bal.	(e)	40,000			

Work-in-Process Control

December 31, 2016, Bal.	(7)	6,000		(d)	360,000
Direct materials	(c)	180,000			
Direct manufacturing labor	(b) (g) (3)	80,000			
Manufacturing overhead allocated	(3) (a) (4)	120,000			
January 31, 2017, Bal.	(b) (6)	26,000			

Finished Goods Control

December 31, 2016, Bal.	(given)	40,000		(2)	370,000
	(d)	360,000			
January 31, 2017, Bal.	(f)	30,000			

Wages Payable Control

	(h)	104,000	December 31, 2016, Bal.	(5)	10,000
				(g) (3)	80,000
				(g)	20,000
			January 31, 2017	(given)	6,000

Manufacturing Overhead Control

Total January charges	(given)	114,000	

Manufacturing Overhead Allocated

			(3) (a) (4)	120,000

Cost of Goods Sold

	(d) (f) (2)	370,000	

---

*Can be computed only after all other postings in the account have been made.

DECISION **POINTS**

The following question-and-answer format summarizes the chapter's learning objectives. Each decision presents a key question related to a learning objective. The guidelines are the answer to that question.

Decision	**Guidelines**
1. What are the building-block concepts of a costing system?	The building-block concepts of a costing system are a cost object, direct costs of a cost object, indirect costs of a cost object, cost pool, and cost-allocation base. Costing-system overview diagrams represent these concepts in a systematic way. Costing systems aim to report cost numbers that reflect the way cost objects (such as products or services) use the resources of an organization.
2. How do you distinguish job costing from process costing?	Job-costing systems assign costs to distinct units of a product or service. Process-costing systems assign costs to masses of identical or similar units and compute unit costs on an average basis. These two costing systems represent opposite ends of a continuum. The costing systems of many companies combine some elements of both job costing and process costing.
3. What is the main challenge of implementing job-costing systems?	The main challenge of implementing job-costing systems is estimating actual costs of jobs in a timely manner.
4. How do you implement a normal-costing system?	A general seven-step approach to normal costing requires identifying (1) the job, (2) the actual direct costs, (3) the budgeted cost-allocation bases, (4) the budgeted indirect-cost pools, (5) the budgeted cost-allocation rates, (6) the allocated indirect costs (budgeted rates times actual quantities of the cost-allocation bases), and (7) the total direct and indirect costs of a job.
5. How do you distinguish actual costing from normal costing?	Actual costing and normal costing differ in the type of indirect-cost rates used:

	Actual Costing	**Normal Costing**
Direct-cost rates	Actual rates	Actual rates
Indirect-cost rates	Actual rates	Budgeted rates

Both systems use actual quantities of inputs for tracing direct costs and actual quantities of the cost-allocation bases for allocating indirect costs.

| 6. How are transactions recorded in a manufacturing job-costing system? | A job-costing system in manufacturing records the flow of inventoriable costs in the general and subsidiary ledgers for (a) acquisition of materials and other manufacturing inputs, (b) their conversion into work in process, (c) their conversion into finished goods, and (d) the sale of finished goods. The job-costing system expenses period costs, such as marketing costs, as they are incurred. |

Decision	Guidelines
7. How should managers dispose of under- or overallocated manufacturing overhead costs at the end of the accounting year?	The two standard approaches to disposing of under- or overallocated manufacturing overhead costs at the end of the accounting year for the purposes of stating balance sheet and income statement amounts at actual costs are: (1) to adjust the allocation rate and (2) to prorate on the basis of the total amount of the allocated manufacturing overhead cost in the ending balances of Work-in-Process Control, Finished Goods Control, and Cost of Goods Sold accounts. Many companies write off amounts of under- or overallocated manufacturing overhead to Cost of Goods Sold when amounts are immaterial or underallocated overhead costs are the result of inefficiencies.
8. What are some variations of normal costing?	In some variations from normal costing, organizations use budgeted rates to assign direct costs, as well as indirect costs, to jobs.

TERMS TO LEARN

This chapter and the Glossary at the end of the book contain definitions of the following important terms:

actual costing (**p. 131**)

actual indirect-cost rate (**p. 139**)

adjusted allocation-rate approach (**p. 149**)

budgeted indirect-cost rate (**p. 133**)

cost-allocation base (**p. 128**)

cost-application base (**p. 128**)

cost pool (**p. 128**)

job (**p. 129**)

job-cost record (**p. 133**)

job-cost sheet (**p. 133**)

job-costing system (**p. 129**)

labor-time sheet (**p. 133**)

manufacturing overhead allocated (**p. 143**)

manufacturing overhead applied (**p. 143**)

materials-requisition record (**p. 133**)

normal costing (**p. 133**)

overabsorbed indirect costs (**p. 148**)

overallocated indirect costs (**p. 148**)

overapplied indirect costs (**p. 148**)

process-costing system (**p. 129**)

proration (**p. 149**)

source document (**p. 133**)

underabsorbed indirect costs (**p. 148**)

underallocated indirect costs (**p. 148**)

underapplied indirect costs (**p. 148**)

ASSIGNMENT MATERIAL

Pearson MyLab Accounting

Questions

4-1 Define cost pool, cost tracing, cost allocation, and cost-allocation base.

4-2 What is the main difference between job costing and process costing? Provide one example for each costing method.

4-3 Why might an advertising agency use job costing for an advertising campaign by PepsiCo, whereas a bank might use process costing to determine the cost of checking account deposits?

4-4 Explain how you can determine the cost of a cost object/job under job-costing system.

4-5 Give examples of two cost objects in companies using job costing.

4-6 Describe three major source documents used in job-costing systems.

4-7 What is the role of information technology in job costing?

4-8 Seasonal patterns and fluctuating levels of monthly outputs are the two main factors for most organizations to use an annual period rather than a weekly or a monthly period to compute budgeted indirect-cost rates. Explain how annual indirect rates alleviate the impacts of these two factors.

4-9 Distinguish between actual costing and normal costing.

4-10 Explain how job-costing information may be used for decision making.

4-11 Comment on the following statement: There is no difference between "actual costing" and "normal costing" systems as both use the product of actual direct-cost rates and actual quantities of direct-cost inputs.

4-12 Describe the flow of costs in a normal job-costing system.

4-13 Describe three alternative ways to dispose of under- or overallocated overhead costs.

4-14 When might a company use budgeted costs rather than actual costs to compute direct-labor rates?

4-15 Describe briefly why Electronic Data Interchange (EDI) is helpful to managers.

Multiple-Choice Questions

In partnership with:

4-16 Which of the following does not accurately describe the application of job-order costing?
a. Finished goods that are purchased by customers will directly impact cost of goods sold.
b. Indirect manufacturing labor and indirect materials are part of the actual manufacturing costs incurred.
c. Direct materials and direct manufacturing labor are included in total manufacturing costs.
d. Manufacturing overhead costs incurred is used to determine total manufacturing costs.

4-17 Sturdy Manufacturing Co. assembled the following cost data for job order #23:

Direct manufacturing labor	$80,000
Indirect manufacturing labor	12,000
Equipment depreciation	1,000
Other indirect manufacturing costs	1,500
Direct materials	95,000
Indirect materials	4,000
Manufacturing overhead overapplied	2,000

What are the total manufacturing costs for job order #23 if the company uses normal job-order costing?
a. $191,500   **b.** $193,500
c. $194,500   **d.** $195,500

4-18 For which of the following industries would job-order costing most likely not be appropriate?
a. Small business printing.   **b.** Cereal production.
c. Home construction.   **d.** Aircraft assembly.

4-19 ABC Company uses job-order costing and has assembled the following cost data for the production and assembly of item X:

Direct manufacturing labor wages	$35,000
Direct material used	70,000
Indirect manufacturing labor	4,000
Utilities	400
Fire insurance	500
Manufacturing overhead applied	11,000
Indirect materials	6,000
Depreciation on equipment	600

Based on the above cost data, the manufacturing overhead for item X is:
a. $500 overallocated.
b. $600 underallocated.
c. $500 underallocated
d. $600 overallocated.

4-20 Under Stanford Corporation's job costing system, manufacturing overhead is applied to work in process using a predetermined annual overhead rate. During November, Year 1, Stanford's transactions included the following:

Direct materials issued to production	$180,000
Indirect materials issued to production	16,000
Manufacturing overhead incurred	250,000
Manufacturing overhead applied	226,000
Direct manufacturing labor costs	214,000

Stanford had neither beginning nor ending work-in-process inventory. What was the cost of jobs completed and transferred to finished goods in November 20X1?

1. $604,000   2. $644,000
3. $620,000   4. $660,000

Pearson MyLab Accounting

Exercises

4-21 Job order costing, process costing. In each of the following situations, determine whether job costing or process costing would be more appropriate.

a. A hospital
b. A car manufacturer
c. A computer manufacturer
d. A road construction firm
e. A soap manufacturer
f. A solicitor firm
g. A glassware manufacturer
h. A land development company
i. An event management company
j. An oil mill
k. A wine manufacturer

l. An advertisement film producer
m. A travel agent company
n. A health drink manufacturer
o. A cost audit firm
p. A boiler manufacturer
q. A electric lamp manufacturer
r. A courier service agency
s. A pharmaceutical company
t. A cosmetic products manufacturer
u. A cell phone manufacturer

4-22 Actual costing, normal costing, accounting for manufacturing overhead. Carolin Chemicals produces a range of chemical products for industries on getting bulk orders. It uses a job-costing system to calculate the cost of a particular job. Materials and labors used in the manufacturing process are direct in nature, but manufacturing overhead is allocated to different jobs using direct manufacturing labor costs. Carolin provides the following information:

	Budget for 2017	Actual Results for 2017
Direct material costs	$2,750,000	$3,000,000
Direct manufacturing labor costs	1,830,000	2,250,000
Manufacturing overhead costs	3,294,000	3,780,000

Required

1. Compute the actual and budgeted manufacturing overhead rates for 2017.
2. During March, the job-cost records for Job 635 contained the following information:

Direct materials used	$73,500
Direct manufacturing labor costs	$51,000

Compute the cost of Job 635 using (a) actual costing and (b) normal costing.
3. At the end of 2017, compute the under- or overallocated manufacturing overhead under normal costing. Why is there no under- or overallocated overhead under actual costing?
4. Why might managers at Carolin Chemicals prefer to use normal costing?

4-23 Job costing, normal and actual costing. Caldwell Toys produces toys mainly for the domestic market. The company uses a job-costing system under which materials and labors used in the manufacturing process are directly allocated to different jobs. Whereas costs incurred in the manufacturing support department are indirect in nature and allocated to different jobs on the basis of direct labor-hours. Caldwell budgets 2017 manufacturing-support costs to be $5,100,000 and 2017 direct labor-hours to be 150,000.

At the end of 2017, Caldwell collects the cost-related data of different jobs that were started and completed in 2017 for comparison. They are as follows:

	Steel Wheels	Magic Wheels
Production period	Jan–May 2017	May–Sept 2017
Direct material costs	$78,290	$94,650
Direct labor costs	$25,445	$32,752
Direct labor-hours	840	960

Direct materials and direct labor are paid for on a contractual basis. The costs of each are known when direct materials are used or when direct labor-hours are worked. The 2017 actual manufacturing-support costs were $5,355,000 and the actual direct labor-hours were 153,000.

Required

1. Compute the (a) budgeted indirect-cost rate and (b) actual indirect-cost rate. Why do they differ?
2. What are the job costs of the Steel Wheels and the Magic Wheels using (a) normal costing and (b) actual costing?
3. Why might Caldwell Toys prefer normal costing over actual costing?

4-24 Budgeted manufacturing overhead rate, allocated manufacturing overhead. Gammaro Company uses normal costing. It allocates manufacturing overhead costs using a budgeted rate per machine-hour. The following data are available for 2017:

Budgeted manufacturing overhead costs	$4,600,000
Budgeted machine-hours	184,000
Actual manufacturing overhead costs	$4,830,000
Actual machine-hours	180,000

Required

1. Calculate the budgeted manufacturing overhead rate.
2. Calculate the manufacturing overhead allocated during 2017.
3. Calculate the amount of under- or overallocated manufacturing overhead. Why do Gammaro's managers need to calculate this amount?

4-25 Job costing, accounting for manufacturing overhead, budgeted rates. The Lynn Company uses a normal job-costing system at its Minneapolis plant. The plant has a machining department and an assembly department. Its job-costing system has two direct-cost categories (direct materials and direct manufacturing labor) and two manufacturing overhead cost pools (the machining department overhead, allocated to jobs based on actual machine-hours, and the assembly department overhead, allocated to jobs based on actual direct manufacturing labor costs). The 2014 budget for the plant is as follows:

	Machining Department	Assembly Department
Manufacturing overhead	$1,800,000	$3,600,000
Direct manufacturing labor costs	$1,400,000	$2,000,000
Direct manufacturing labor-hours	100,000	200,000
Machine-hours	50,000	200,000

Required

1. Present an overview diagram of Lynn's job-costing system. Compute the budgeted manufacturing overhead rate for each department.
2. During February, the job-cost record for Job 494 contained the following:

	Machining Department	Assembly Department
Direct materials used	$45,000	$70,000
Direct manufacturing labor costs	$14,000	$15,000
Direct manufacturing labor-hours	1,000	1,500
Machine-hours	2,000	1,000

Compute the total manufacturing overhead costs allocated to Job 494.
3. At the end of 2014, the actual manufacturing overhead costs were $2,100,000 in machining and $3,700,000 in assembly. Assume that 55,000 actual machine-hours were used in machining and that actual direct manufacturing labor costs in assembly were $2,200,000. Compute the over- or underallocated manufacturing overhead for each department.

4-26 Job costing, consulting firm. Global Enterprize, a management consulting firm, has the following condensed budget for 2017:

Revenues		$42,000,000
Total costs:		
Direct costs		
Professional Labor	$15,000,000	
Indirect costs		
Client support	22,170,000	37,170,000
Operating income		$ 4,830,000

Global Enterprize has a single direct-cost category (professional labor) and a single indirect-cost pool (client support). Indirect costs are allocated to jobs on the basis of professional labor costs.

1. Prepare an overview diagram of the job-costing system. Calculate the 2017 budgeted indirect-cost rate for Global Enterprize.
2. The markup rate for pricing jobs is intended to produce operating income equal to 11.50% of revenues. Calculate the markup rate as a percentage of professional labor costs.
3. Global Enterprize is bidding on a consulting job for Horizon Telecommunications, a wireless communications company. The budgeted breakdown of professional labor on the job is as follows:

Professional Labor Category	Budgeted Rate per Hour	Budgeted Hours
Director	$175	8
Partner	80	20
Associate	40	75
Assistant	25	180

Calculate the budgeted cost of the Horizon Telecommunications job. How much will Global Enterprize bid for the job if it is to earn its target operating income of 11.50% of revenues?

4-27 Time period used to compute indirect cost rates. Plunge Manufacturing produces outdoor wading and slide pools. The company uses a normal-costing system and allocates manufacturing overhead on the basis of direct manufacturing labor-hours. Most of the company's production and sales occur in the first and second quarters of the year. The company is in danger of losing one of its larger customers, Socha Wholesale, due to large fluctuations in price. The owner of Plunge has requested an analysis of the manufacturing cost per unit in the second and third quarters. You have been provided the following budgeted information for the coming year:

	Quarter			
	1	2	3	4
Pools manufactured and sold	565	490	245	100

It takes 1 direct manufacturing labor-hour to make each pool. The actual direct material cost is $14.00 per pool. The actual direct manufacturing labor rate is $20 per hour. The budgeted variable manufacturing overhead rate is $15 per direct manufacturing labor-hour. Budgeted fixed manufacturing overhead costs are $12,250 each quarter.

1. Calculate the total manufacturing cost per unit for the second and third quarter assuming the company allocates manufacturing overhead costs based on the budgeted manufacturing overhead rate determined for each quarter.
2. Calculate the total manufacturing cost per unit for the second and third quarter assuming the company allocates manufacturing overhead costs based on an annual budgeted manufacturing overhead rate.
3. Plunge Manufacturing prices its pools at manufacturing cost plus 30%. Why might Socha Wholesale be seeing large fluctuations in the prices of pools? Which of the methods described in requirements 1 and 2 would you recommend Plunge use? Explain.

4-28 Accounting for manufacturing overhead. Holland Woodworking uses normal costing and allocates manufacturing overhead to jobs based on a budgeted labor-hour rate and actual direct labor-hours. Under- or over-allocated overhead, if immaterial, is written off to cost of goods sold. During 2014, Holland recorded the following:

Budgeted manufacturing overhead costs	$4,400,000
Budgeted direct labor-hours	200,000
Actual manufacturing overhead costs	$4,650,000
Actual direct labor-hours	212,000

1. Compute the budgeted manufacturing overhead rate.
2. Prepare the summary journal entry to record the allocation of manufacturing overhead.
3. Compute the amount of under- or overallocated manufacturing overhead. Is the amount significant enough to warrant proration of overhead costs, or would it be permissible to write it off to cost of goods sold? Prepare the journal entry to dispose of the under- or overallocated overhead.

4-29 Job costing, journal entries. The University of Chicago Press is wholly owned by the university. It performs the bulk of its work for other university departments, which pay as though the press were an outside business enterprise. The press also publishes and maintains a stock of books for general sale. The press uses normal costing to cost each job. Its job-costing system has two direct-cost categories (direct materials and direct manufacturing labor) and one indirect-cost pool (manufacturing overhead, allocated on the basis of direct manufacturing labor costs).

The following data (in thousands) pertain to 2017:

Direct materials and supplies purchased on credit	$ 800
Direct materials used	710
Indirect materials issued to various production departments	100
Direct manufacturing labor	1,300
Indirect manufacturing labor incurred by various production departments	900
Depreciation on building and manufacturing equipment	400
Miscellaneous manufacturing overhead* incurred by various production departments (ordinarily would be detailed as repairs, photocopying, utilities, etc.)	550
Manufacturing overhead allocated at 160% of direct manufacturing labor costs	?
Cost of goods manufactured	4,120
Revenues	8,000
Cost of goods sold (before adjustment for under- or overallocated manufacturing overhead)	4,020
Inventories, December 31, 2016 (not 2017):	
Materials Control	100
Work-in-Process Control	60
Finished Goods Control	500

Required

1. Prepare an overview diagram of the job-costing system at the University of Chicago Press.
2. Prepare journal entries to summarize the 2017 transactions. As your final entry, dispose of the year-end under- or overallocated manufacturing overhead as a write-off to Cost of Goods Sold. Number your entries. Explanations for each entry may be omitted.
3. Show posted T-accounts for all inventories, Cost of Goods Sold, Manufacturing Overhead Control, and Manufacturing Overhead Allocated.
4. How did the University of Chicago Press perform in 2017?

4-30 Journal entries, T-accounts, and source documents. Visual Company produces gadgets for the coveted small appliance market. The following data reflect activity for the year 2017:

Costs incurred:	
Purchases of direct materials (net) on credit	$121,000
Direct manufacturing labor cost	87,000
Indirect labor	54,400
Depreciation, factory equipment	53,000
Depreciation, office equipment	7,700
Maintenance, factory equipment	46,000
Miscellaneous factory overhead	9,100
Rent, factory building	99,000
Advertising expense	97,000
Sales commissions	39,000

Inventories:

	January 1, 2017	December 31, 2017
Direct materials	$ 9,400	$18,000
Work in process	6,500	26,000
Finished goods	60,000	31,000

Visual Co. uses a normal-costing system and allocates overhead to work in process at a rate of $3.10 per direct manufacturing labor dollar. Indirect materials are insignificant so there is no inventory account for indirect materials.

Required

1. Prepare journal entries to record the transactions for 2017 including an entry to close out over- or underallocated overhead to cost of goods sold. For each journal entry indicate the source document that

---

* The term *manufacturing overhead* is not used uniformly. Other terms that are often encountered in printing companies include *job overhead* and *shop overhead*.

would be used to authorize each entry. Also note which subsidiary ledger, if any, should be referenced as backup for the entry.

2. Post the journal entries to T-accounts for all of the inventories, Cost of Goods Sold, the Manufacturing Overhead Control Account, and the Manufacturing Overhead Allocated Account.

4-31 Job costing, journal entries. Donald Transport assembles prestige manufactured homes. Its job-costing system has two direct-cost categories (direct materials and direct manufacturing labor) and one indirect-cost pool (manufacturing overhead allocated at a budgeted $31 per machine-hour in 2017). The following data (in millions) show operation costs for 2017:

Materials Control, beginning balance, January 1, 2017	$ 18
Work-in-Process Control, beginning balance, January 1, 2017	9
Finished Goods Control, beginning balance, January 1, 2017	10
Materials and supplies purchased on credit	154
Direct materials used	152
Indirect materials (supplies) issued to various production departments	19
Direct manufacturing labor	96
Indirect manufacturing labor incurred by various production departments	34
Depreciation on plant and manufacturing equipment	28
Miscellaneous manufacturing overhead incurred (ordinarily would be detailed as repairs, utilities, etc., with a corresponding credit to various liability accounts)	13
Manufacturing overhead allocated, 3,000,000 actual machine-hours	?
Cost of goods manufactured	298
Revenues	410
Cost of goods sold	294

Required

1. Prepare an overview diagram of Donald Transport's job-costing system.
2. Prepare journal entries. Number your entries. Explanations for each entry may be omitted. Post to T-accounts. What is the ending balance of Work-in-Process Control?
3. Show the journal entry for disposing of under- or overallocated manufacturing overhead directly as a year-end writeoff to Cost of Goods Sold. Post the entry to T-accounts.
4. How did Donald Transport perform in 2017?

4-32 Job costing, unit cost, ending work in process. Rafael Company produces pipes for concert-quality organs. Each job is unique. In April 2013, it completed all outstanding orders, and then, in May 2013, it worked on only two jobs, M1 and M2:

	Home Insert Page Layout Formulas Data		
	A	B	C
1	**Rafael Company, May 2013**	**Job M1**	**Job M2**
2	Direct materials	$ 78,000	$ 51,000
3	Direct manufacturing labor	273,000	208,000

Direct manufacturing labor is paid at the rate of $26 per hour. Manufacturing overhead costs are allocated at a budgeted rate of $20 per direct manufacturing labor-hour. Only Job M1 was completed in May.

Required

1. Calculate the total cost for Job M1.
2. 1,100 pipes were produced for Job M1. Calculate the cost per pipe.
3. Prepare the journal entry transferring Job M1 to finished goods.
4. What is the ending balance in the work-in-process control account?

4-33 Job costing; actual, normal, and variation from normal costing. Cheney & Partners, a Quebecbased public accounting partnership, specializes in audit services. Its job-costing system has a single direct-cost category (professional labor) and a single indirect-cost pool (audit support, which contains all costs of the Audit Support Department). Audit support costs are allocated to individual jobs using actual professional labor-hours. Cheney & Partners employs 10 professionals to perform audit services

Budgeted and actual amounts for 2017 are as follows:

	Home	Insert	Page Layout	Formulas	Data
	A			B	C
1	**Cheney & Partners**				
2	**Budget for 2017**				
3	Professional labor compensation			$960,000	
4	Audit support department costs			720,000	
5	Professional labor-hours billed to clients			16,000	hours
6					
7	**Actual results for 2017**				
8	Audit support department costs			$744,000	
9	Professional labor-hours billed to clients			15,500	hours
10	Actual professional labor cost rate			$ 53	per hour

Required

1. Compute the direct-cost rate and the indirect-cost rate per professional labor-hour for 2017 under (a) actual costing, (b) normal costing, and (c) the variation from normal costing that uses budgeted rates for direct costs.
2. Which job-costing system would you recommend Cheney & Partners use? Explain.
3. Cheney's 2017 audit of Pierre & Co. was budgeted to take 170 hours of professional labor time. The actual professional labor time spent on the audit was 185 hours. Compute the cost of the Pierre & Co. audit using (a) actual costing, (b) normal costing, and (c) the variation from normal costing that uses budgeted rates for direct costs. Explain any differences in the job cost.

4-34 Job costing; variation on actual, normal, and variation from normal costing. Creative Solutions designs Web pages for clients in the education sector. The company's job-costing system has a single direct cost category (Web-designing labor) and a single indirect cost pool composed of all overhead costs. Overhead costs are allocated to individual jobs based on direct labor-hours. The company employs six Web designers. Budgeted and actual information regarding Creative Solutions follows:

Budget for 2017:

Direct labor costs	$273,000
Direct labor-hours	10,500
Overhead costs	$157,500

Actual results for 2017:

Direct labor costs	$285,000
Direct labor-hours	11,400
Overhead costs	$159,600

Required

1. Compute the direct-cost rate and the indirect-cost rate per Web-designing labor-hour for 2017 under (a) actual costing, (b) normal costing, and (c) the variation from normal costing that uses budgeted rates for direct costs.
2. Which method would you suggest Creative Solutions use? Explain.
3. Creative Solutions' Web design for Greenville Day School was budgeted to take 86 direct labor-hours. The actual time spent on the project was 79 hours. Compute the cost of the Greenville Day School job using (a) actual costing, (b) normal costing, and (c) the variation from normal costing that uses budgeted rates for direct costs.

4-35 Proration of overhead. The Ride-On-Wave Company (ROW) produces a line of non-motorized boats. ROW uses a normal-costing system and allocates manufacturing overhead using direct manufacturing labor cost. The following data are for 2017:

Budgeted manufacturing overhead cost	$125,000
Budgeted direct manufacturing labor cost	$250,000
Actual manufacturing overhead cost	$117,000
Actual direct manufacturing labor cost	$228,000

Inventory balances on December 31, 2017, were as follows:

Account	Ending balance	2017 direct manufacturing labor cost in ending balance
Work in process	$50,700	$20,520
Finished goods	245,050	59,280
Cost of goods sold	549,250	148,200

Required

1. Calculate the manufacturing overhead allocation rate.
2. Compute the amount of under- or overallocated manufacturing overhead.
3. Calculate the ending balances in work in process, finished goods, and cost of goods sold if under- or overallocated manufacturing overhead is as follows:
   a. Written off to cost of goods sold
   b. Prorated based on ending balances (before proration) in each of the three accounts
   c. Prorated based on the overhead allocated in 2017 in the ending balances (before proration) in each of the three accounts
4. Which method would you choose? Justify your answer.

Problems

4-36 Job costing, accounting for manufacturing overhead, budgeted rates. The Pisano Company uses a job-costing system at its Dover, Delaware, plant. The plant has a machining department and a finishing department. Pisano uses normal costing with two direct-cost categories (direct materials and direct manufacturing labor) and two manufacturing overhead cost pools (the machining department with machine-hours as the allocation base and the finishing department with direct manufacturing labor costs as the allocation base). The 2014 budget for the plant is as follows:

	Machining Department	Finishing Department
Manufacturing overhead costs	$9,065,000	$8,181,000
Direct manufacturing labor costs	$ 970,000	$4,050,000
Direct manufacturing labor-hours	36,000	155,000
Machine-hours	185,000	37,000

Required

1. Prepare an overview diagram of Pisano's job-costing system.
2. What is the budgeted manufacturing overhead rate in the machining department? In the finishing department?
3. During the month of January, the job-cost record for Job 431 shows the following:

	Machining Department	Finishing Department
Direct materials used	$13,000	$5,000
Direct manufacturing labor costs	$ 900	$1,250
Direct manufacturing labor-hours	20	70
Machine-hours	140	20

Compute the total manufacturing overhead cost allocated to Job 431.
4. Assuming that Job 431 consisted of 300 units of product, what is the cost per unit?
5. Amounts at the end of 2014 are as follows:

	Machining Department	Finishing Department
Manufacturing overhead incurred	$10,000,000	$7,982,000
Direct manufacturing labor costs	$ 1,030,000	$4,100,000
Machine-hours	200,000	34,000

Compute the under- or overallocated manufacturing overhead for each department and for the Dover plant as a whole.
6. Why might Pisano use two different manufacturing overhead cost pools in its job-costing system?

4-37 Service industry, job costing, law firm. Kidman & Associates is a law firm specializing in labor relations and employee-related work. It employs 30 professionals (5 partners and 25 associates) who work directly with its clients. The average budgeted total compensation per professional for 2017 is $97,500. Each professional is budgeted to have 1,500 billable hours to clients in 2017. All professionals work for clients to their maximum 1,500 billable hours available. All professional labor costs are included in a single direct-cost category and are traced to jobs on a per-hour basis. All costs of Kidman & Associates other than professional labor costs are included in a single indirect-cost pool (legal support) and are allocated to jobs using professional labor-hours as the allocation base. The budgeted level of indirect costs in 2017 is $2,475,000.

Required

1. Prepare an overview diagram of Kidman's job-costing system.
2. Compute the 2017 budgeted direct-cost rate per hour of professional labor.
3. Compute the 2017 budgeted indirect-cost rate per hour of professional labor.
4. Kidman & Associates is considering bidding on two jobs:
   a. Litigation work for Richardson, Inc., which requires 120 budgeted hours of professional labor
   b. Labor contract work for Punch, Inc., which requires 160 budgeted hours of professional labor. Prepare a cost estimate for each job.

4-38 Service industry, job costing, two direct- and two indirect-cost categories, law firm (continuation of 4-37). Kidman has just completed a review of its job-costing system. This review included a detailed analysis of how past jobs used the firm's resources and interviews with personnel about what factors drive the level of indirect costs. Management concluded that a system with two direct-cost categories (professional partner labor and professional associate labor) and two indirect-cost categories (general support and secretarial support) would yield more accurate job costs. Budgeted information for 2017 related to the two direct-cost categories is as follows:

	Professional Partner Labor	Professional Associate Labor
Number of professionals	5	25
Hours of billable time per professional	1,500 per year	1,500 per year
Total compensation (average per professional)	$210,000	$75,000

Budgeted information for 2017 relating to the two indirect-cost categories is as follows:

	General Support	Secretarial Support
Total costs	$2,025,000	$450,000
Cost-allocation base	Professional labor-hours	Partner labor-hours

Required

1. Compute the 2017 budgeted direct-cost rates for (a) professional partners and (b) professional associates.
2. Compute the 2017 budgeted indirect-cost rates for (a) general support and (b) secretarial support.
3. Compute the budgeted costs for the Richardson and Punch jobs, given the following information:

	Richardson, Inc.	Punch, Inc.
Professional partners	48 hours	32 hours
Professional associates	72 hours	128 hours

4. Comment on the results in requirement 3. Why are the job costs different from those computed in Problem 4-37?
5. Would you recommend Kidman & Associates use the job-costing system in Problem 4-37 or the job-costing system in this problem? Explain.

4-39 Proration of overhead. (Z. Iqbal, adapted) The Zaf Radiator Company uses a normal-costing system with a single manufacturing overhead cost pool and machine-hours as the cost-allocation base. The following data are for 2017:

Budgeted manufacturing overhead costs	$4,800,000
Overhead allocation base	Machine-hours
Budgeted machine-hours	80,000
Manufacturing overhead costs incurred	$4,900,000
Actual machine-hours	75,000

Machine-hours data and the ending balances (before proration of under- or overallocated overhead) are as follows:

	Actual Machine-Hours	2017 End-of-Year Balance
Cost of Goods Sold	60,000	$8,000,000
Finished Goods Control	11,000	1,250,000
Work-in-Process Control	4,000	750,000

Required

1. Compute the budgeted manufacturing overhead rate for 2017.
2. Compute the under- or overallocated manufacturing overhead of Zaf Radiator in 2017. Dispose of this amount using the following:
   a. Write-off to Cost of Goods Sold
   b. Proration based on ending balances (before proration) in Work-in-Process Control, Finished Goods Control, and Cost of Goods Sold
   c. Proration based on the overhead allocated in 2017 (before proration) in the ending balances of Work-in-Process Control, Finished Goods Control, and Cost of Goods Sold
3. Which method do you prefer in requirement 2? Explain.

4-40 Normal costing, overhead allocation, working backward. Gardi Manufacturing uses normal costing for its job-costing system, which has two direct-cost categories (direct materials and direct manufacturing labor) and one indirect-cost category (manufacturing overhead). The following information is obtained for 2017:

- Total manufacturing costs, $8,300,000
- Manufacturing overhead allocated, $4,100,000 (allocated at a rate of 250% of direct manufacturing labor costs)
- Work-in-process inventory on January 1, 2017, $420,000
- Cost of finished goods manufactured, $8,100,000

Required

1. Use information in the first two bullet points to calculate (a) direct manufacturing labor costs in 2017 and (b) cost of direct materials used in 2017.
2. Calculate the ending work-in-process inventory on December 31, 2017.

4-41 Proration of overhead with two indirect cost pools. Premier Golf Carts makes custom golf carts that it sells to dealers across the Southeast. The carts are produced in two departments, fabrication (a mostly automated department) and custom finishing (a mostly manual department). The company uses a normal-costing system in which overhead in the fabrication department is allocated to jobs on the basis of machine-hours and overhead in the finishing department is allocated to jobs based on direct labor-hours. During May, Premier Golf Carts reported actual overhead of $49,500 in the fabrication department and $22,200 in the finishing department. Additional information follows:

Manufacturing overhead rate (fabrication department)	$20 per machine-hour
Manufacturing overhead rate (finishing department)	$16 per direct labor-hour
Machine-hours (fabrication department) for May	2,000 machine-hours
Direct labor-hours (finishing department) for May	1,200 labor-hours
Work in process inventory, May 31	$50,000
Finished goods inventory, May 31	$150,000
Cost of goods sold, May 31	$300,000

Premier Golf Carts prorates under- and overallocated overhead monthly to work in process, finished goods, and cost of goods sold based on the ending balance in each account.

Required

1. Calculate the amount of overhead allocated in the fabrication department and the finishing department in May.
2. Calculate the amount of under- or overallocated overhead in each department and in total.
3. How much of the under- or overallocated overhead will be prorated to (a) work in process inventory, (b) finished goods inventory, and (c) cost of goods sold based on the ending balance (before proration) in each of the three accounts? What will be the balance in work in process, finished goods, and cost of goods sold after proration?
4. What would be the effect of writing off under- and overallocated overhead to cost of goods sold? Would it be reasonable for Premier Golf Carts to change to this simpler method?

4-42 General ledger relationships, under- and overallocation. (S. Sridhar, adapted) Keezel Company uses normal costing in its job-costing system. Partially completed T-accounts and additional information for Keezel for 2017 are as follows:

Direct Materials Control			Work-in-Process Control			Finished Goods Control		
1-1-2017	42,000	148,000	1-1-2017	82,000		1-1-2017	105,000	700,000
	135,000		Dir. manuf.				705,000	
			labor	285,000				

Manufacturing Overhead Control		Manufacturing Overhead Allocated		Cost of Goods Sold	
425,000					

Additional information follows:

a. Direct manufacturing labor wage rate was $15 per hour.
b. Manufacturing overhead was allocated at $20 per direct manufacturing labor-hour.
c. During the year, sales revenues were $1,550,000, and marketing and distribution costs were $810,000.

Required

1. What was the amount of direct materials issued to production during 2017?
2. What was the amount of manufacturing overhead allocated to jobs during 2017?
3. What was the total cost of jobs completed during 2017?
4. What was the balance of work-in-process inventory on December 31, 2017?
5. What was the cost of goods sold before proration of under- or overallocated overhead?
6. What was the under- or overallocated manufacturing overhead in 2017?
7. Dispose of the under- or overallocated manufacturing overhead using the following:
   a. Write-off to Cost of Goods Sold
   b. Proration based on ending balances (before proration) in Work-in-Process Control, Finished Goods Control, and Cost of Goods Sold
8. Using each of the approaches in requirement 7, calculate Keezel's operating income for 2017.
9. Which approach in requirement 7 do you recommend Keezel use? Explain your answer briefly.

4-43 Overview of general ledger relationships. Brandon Company uses normal costing in its job-costing system. The company produces custom bikes for toddlers. The beginning balances (December 1) and ending balances (as of December 30) in their inventory accounts are as follows:

	Beginning Balance 12/1	Ending Balance 12/31
Materials control	$2,100	$ 8,500
Work-in-process control	6,700	9,000
Manufacturing department overhead control	_____	94,000
Finished goods control	4,400	19,400

Additional information follows:

a. Direct materials purchased during December were $66,300.
b. Cost of goods manufactured for December was $234,000.
c. No direct materials were returned to suppliers.
d. No units were started or completed on December 31 and no direct materials were requisitioned on December 31.
e. The manufacturing labor costs for the December 31 working day: direct manufacturing labor, $4,300, and indirect manufacturing labor, $1,400.
f. Manufacturing overhead has been allocated at 110% of direct manufacturing labor costs through December 31.

Required

1. Prepare journal entries for the December 31 payroll.
2. Use T-accounts to compute the following:
   a. The total amount of materials requisitioned into work in process during December
   b. The total amount of direct manufacturing labor recorded in work in process during December (Hint: You have to solve requirements **2b** and **2c** simultaneously)
   c. The total amount of manufacturing overhead recorded in work in process during December
   d. Ending balance in work in process, December 31
   e. Cost of goods sold for December before adjustments for under- or overallocated manufacturing overhead
3. Prepare closing journal entries related to manufacturing overhead. Assume that all under- or overallocated manufacturing overhead is closed directly to cost of goods sold.

4-44 Allocation and proration of overhead. InStep Company prints custom training material for corporations. The business was started January 1, 2017. The company uses a normal-costing system. It has two direct cost pools, materials and labor, and one indirect cost pool, overhead. Overhead is charged to printing jobs on the basis of direct labor cost. The following information is available for 2017.

Budgeted direct labor costs	$225,000
Budgeted overhead costs	$315,000
Costs of actual material used	$148,500
Actual direct labor costs	$213,500
Actual overhead costs	$302,100

There were two jobs in process on December 31, 2017: Job 11 and Job 12. Costs added to each job as of December 31 are as follows:

	Direct materials	Direct labor
Job 11	$4,870	$5,100
Job 12	$5,910	$6,800

InStep Company has no finished goods inventories because all printing jobs are transferred to cost of goods sold when completed.

Required

1. Compute the overhead allocation rate.
2. Calculate the balance in ending work in process and cost of goods sold before any adjustments for under- or overallocated overhead.
3. Calculate under- or overallocated overhead.
4. Calculate the ending balances in work in process and cost of goods sold if the under- or overallocated overhead amount is as follows:
   a. Written off to cost of goods sold
   b. Prorated using the overhead allocated in 2017 (before proration) in the ending balances of cost of goods sold and work-in-process control accounts
5. Which of the methods in requirement 4 would you choose? Explain.

4-45 (25–30 min.) **Job costing, ethics.** Joseph Underwood joined Anderson Enterprises as controller in October 2016. Anderson Enterprises manufactures and installs home greenhouses. The company uses a normal-costing system with two direct-cost pools, direct materials and direct manufacturing labor, and one indirect-cost pool, manufacturing overhead. In 2016, manufacturing overhead was allocated to jobs at 150% of direct manufacturing labor cost. At the end of 2016, an immaterial amount of underallocated overhead was closed out to cost of goods sold, and the company showed a small loss.

Underwood is eager to impress his new employer, and he knows that in 2017, Anderson's upper management is under pressure to show a profit in a challenging competitive environment because they are hoping to be acquired by a large private equity firm sometime in 2018. At the end of 2016, Underwood decides to adjust the manufacturing overhead rate to 160% of direct labor cost. He explains to the company president that, because overhead was underallocated in 2016, this adjustment is necessary. Cost information for 2017 follows:

Direct materials control, 1/1/2017	25,000
Direct materials purchased, 2017	650,000
Direct materials added to production, 2017	630,000
Work in process control, 1/1/2017	280,000
Direct manufacturing labor, 2017	880,000
Cost of goods manufactured, 2017	2,900,000
Finished goods control, 1/1/2017	320,000
Finished goods control, 12/31/2017	290,000
Manufacturing overhead costs, 2017	1,300,000

Anderson's revenue for 2017 was $5,550,000, and the company's selling and administrative expenses were $2,720,000.

Required

1. Insert the given information in the T-accounts below. Calculate the following amounts to complete the T-accounts:
   a. Direct materials control, 12/31/2017
   b. Manufacturing overhead allocated, 2017
   c. Cost of goods sold, 2017

Direct Materials Control	Work-in-Process Control	Finished Goods Control

Manufacturing OH Control	Manufacturing OH Allocated	Cost of Goods Sold

2. Calculate the amount of under- or overallocated manufacturing overhead.

3. Calculate Anderson's net operating income under the following:
   a. Under- or overallocated manufacturing overhead is written off to cost of goods sold.
   b. Under- or overallocated manufacturing overhead is prorated based on the ending balances in work in process, finished goods, and cost of goods sold.

4. Underwood chooses option 3a above, stating that the amount is immaterial. Comment on the ethical implications of his choice. Do you think that there were any ethical issues when he established the manufacturing overhead rate for 2017 back in late 2016? Refer to the IMA Statement of Ethical Professional Practice.

4-46 Job costing—service industry. Market Pulse performs market research for consumer product companies across the country. The company conducts telephone surveys and gathers consumers together in focus groups to review foods, cleaning products, and toiletries. Market Pulse uses a normal-costing system with one direct-cost pool, labor, and one indirect-cost pool, general overhead. General overhead is allocated to each job based on 150% of direct labor cost. Actual overhead equaled allocated overhead as of April 30, 2017. Actual overhead in May was $122,000. All costs incurred during the planning stage for a market research job and during the job are gathered in a balance sheet account called "Jobs in Progress (JIP)." When a job is completed, the costs are transferred to an income statement account called "Cost of Completed Jobs (CCJ)." Following is cost information for May 2017:

| | From Beginning JIP | | Incurred in May |
Band	Labor	General Overhead Allocated	Labor
Cococrunch Candy Bars	$18,000	$27,000	$16,000
Brite Toothpaste	4,000	6,000	34,000
Verde Organic Salsa	—	—	22,400
Sparkle Dish Liquid	—	—	5,600

As of May 1, there were two jobs in progress: *Cococrunch Candy Bars,* and *Brite Toothpaste.* The jobs for *Verde Organic Salsa* and *Sparkle Dish Liquid* were started during May. The jobs for *Cococrunch Candy Bars* and *Sparkle Dish Liquid* were completed during May.

1. Calculate JIP at the end of May.
2. Calculate CCJ for May.
3. Calculate under- or overallocated overhead at the end of May.
4. Calculate the ending balances in JIP and CCJ if the under- or overallocated overhead amount is as follows:
   a. Written off to CCJ
   b. Prorated based on the ending balances (before proration) in JIP and CCJ
   c. Prorated based on the overhead allocated in May in the ending balances of JIP and CCJ (before proration)
5. Which method would you choose? Explain. Would your choice depend on whether overhead cost is underallocated or overallocated? Explain.

Required

5 Activity-Based Costing and Activity-Based Management

LEARNING OBJECTIVES

1 Explain how broad averaging undercosts and overcosts products or services

2 Present three guidelines for refining a costing system

3 Distinguish between simple and activity-based costing systems

4 Describe a four-part cost hierarchy

5 Cost products or services using activity-based costing

6 Evaluate the benefits and costs of implementing activity-based costing systems

7 Explain how managers use activity-based costing systems in activity-based management

8 Compare activity-based costing systems and department costing systems

A good mystery never fails to capture the imagination.

Business and organizations are like a good mystery. Their costing systems are often filled with unresolved questions: Why are we bleeding red ink? Are we pricing our products accurately? Activity-based costing can help unravel the mystery and result in improved operations. General Motors uses activity-based costing to evaluate the cost of its suppliers' products.

GENERAL MOTORS AND ACTIVITY-BASED COSTING[1]

In 2015, General Motors (GM) launched an automotive parts-buying program that forgoes conventional supplier bidding. Under the new program, any automotive parts supplier that wants GM's business agrees to let a team of GM engineers and purchasing managers evaluate the supplier's factories and cost data using activity-based costing. This evaluation assesses material costs, labor, scrap, production cycle times, and other factors that, in turn, help GM attach activity costs to each of the tens of thousands of parts needed to build its lineup of cars, trucks, and SUVs.

This new program allows GM, which spent approximately $85 billion in 2005 on parts and supplies, to develop more realistic cost estimates for its vehicles. Each year, GM can update its activity-based costing analyses to see whether suppliers can cut costs by more efficient production. Suppliers in the program benefit by receiving long-term contracts from GM, who agrees not to seek competing bids from other vendors.

In this chapter, we show how ABC systems help managers make cost-management decisions by improving product designs, processes, and efficiency.

Drive Images/Alamy Stock Photo

[1] Sources: David Sedgwick, "GM to Suppliers: Let's See Books, Not Bids," *Automotive News*, May 11, 2015 (http://www.autonews.com/article/20150511/OEM10/305119952/gm-to-suppliers:-lets-see-books-not-bids); General Motors Company, 2015 Annual Report.

Broad Averaging and Its Consequences

Historically, companies (such as television and automobile manufacturers) produced a limited variety of products. These companies used few overhead resources to support these simple operations, so indirect (or overhead) costs were a relatively small percentage of total costs. Managers used simple costing systems to allocate overhead costs broadly in an easy, inexpensive, and reasonably accurate way. But as product diversity and indirect costs increased, broad averaging led to inaccurate product costs. That's because simple *peanut-butter costing* (yes, that's what it's called) broadly averages or spreads the cost of resources uniformly to cost objects (such as products or services) when, in fact, the individual products or services use those resources in nonuniform ways.

LEARNING OBJECTIVE 1

Explain how broad averaging undercosts and overcosts products or services

…it does not measure the different resources consumed by different products and services

Undercosting and Overcosting

The following example illustrates how averaging can result in inaccurate and misleading cost data. Consider the cost of a restaurant bill for four colleagues who meet monthly to discuss business developments. Each diner orders separate entrees, desserts, and drinks. The restaurant bill for the most recent meeting is as follows.

	Emma	James	Jessica	Matthew	Total	Average
Entree	$11	$20	$15	$14	$ 60	$15
Dessert	0	8	4	4	16	4
Drinks	4	14	8	6	32	8
Total	$15	$42	$27	$24	$108	$27

If the $108 total restaurant bill is divided evenly, $27 is the average cost per diner. This cost-averaging approach treats each diner the same. When costs are averaged across all four diners, both Emma and Matthew are overcosted (the cost allocated to them is higher than their individual cost), James is undercosted (the cost allocated to him is lower than his individual cost), and Jessica is (by coincidence) accurately costed. Emma, especially, may object to paying the average bill of $27 because her individual bill is only $15.

Broad averaging often leads to undercosting or overcosting of products or services:

- **Product undercosting**—a product is reported to have a low cost per unit but consumes a higher level of resources per unit (James's dinner).

- **Product overcosting**—a product is reported to have a high cost per unit but consumes a lower level of resources per unit (Emma's dinner).

What are the strategic consequences of product undercosting and overcosting? Suppose a manager uses cost information about products to guide pricing decisions. Undercosted products will be underpriced and may even lead to sales that actually result in losses because the sales may bring in less revenue than the cost of resources they use. Overcosted products will lead to overpricing, causing those products to lose market share to competitors producing similar products. But what if prices of products, such as refrigerators, are determined by the market based on consumer demand and competition among companies? Consider a company manufacturing refrigerators with different features and complexities (such as different types of internal compartments, cooling systems, and vents). Suppose the complex refrigerator is undercosted and the simple refrigerator is overcosted. In this case, the complex refrigerator will appear to be more profitable than it actually is while the simple refrigerator will appear to be less profitable than it actually is. Managers may strategically promote the complex undercosted refrigerators thinking they are highly profitable, when in fact these refrigerators consume large amounts of resources and are far less profitable than they appear. They may underinvest in the simple overcosted refrigerator, which shows low profits when in fact the profits from this refrigerator may be considerably better. Alternatively, they may focus on trying to reduce the cost of the simple refrigerator to make it more profitable when, in fact, this refrigerator is reasonably profitable and the opportunities to reduce its costs may be quite limited.

Product-Cost Cross-Subsidization

Product-cost cross-subsidization means that if a company undercosts one of its products, it will overcost at least one of its other products. Similarly, if a company overcosts one of its products, it will undercost at least one of its other products. Product-cost cross-subsidization is very common when a cost is uniformly spread—meaning it is broadly averaged—across multiple products without managers recognizing the amount of resources each product consumes.

In the restaurant-bill example, the amount of cost cross-subsidization of each diner can be readily computed *because all cost items can be traced as direct costs to each diner.* If all diners pay $27, Emma is paying $12 more than her actual cost of $15. She is cross-subsidizing James who is paying $15 less than his actual cost of $42. Calculating the amount of cost cross-subsidization takes more work when there are indirect costs to be considered. Why? Because when two or more diners use the resources represented by indirect costs, we need to find a way to allocate costs to each diner. Consider, for example, a $40 bottle of wine whose cost is shared equally. Each diner would pay $10 ($40 ÷ 4). Suppose Matthew drinks two glasses of wine, while Emma, James, and Jessica drink one glass each for a total of five glasses. Allocating the cost of the bottle of wine on the basis of the glasses of wine that each diner drinks would result in Matthew paying $16 ($40 × 2/5) and each of the others paying $8 ($40 × 1/5). In this case, by sharing the cost equally, Emma, James, and Jessica are each paying $2($10 − $8) more and are cross-subsidizing Matthew who is paying $6($16 − $10) less for his wine for the night.

To see the effects of broad averaging on direct and indirect costs, we next consider Plastim Corporation's costing system.

DECISION POINT

When does product undercosting or overcosting occur?

Simple Costing System at Plastim Corporation

Plastim Corporation manufactures lenses for the rear taillights of automobiles. A lens, made from black, red, orange, or white plastic, is the part of the taillight visible on the automobile's exterior. Lenses are made by injecting molten plastic into a mold, which gives the lens its desired shape. The mold is cooled to allow the molten plastic to solidify, and the lens is removed.

Plastim sells all its lenses to Giovanni Motors, a major automobile manufacturer. Under the contract, Plastim manufactures two types of lenses for Giovanni: a simple lens called S3 and a complex lens called C5. The complex lens is large and has special features, such as multicolor molding (when more than one color is injected into the mold) and a complex shape that wraps around the corner of the car. Manufacturing C5 lenses is complicated because various parts in the mold must align and fit precisely. The S3 lens is simpler to make because it has a single color and few special features.

Design, Manufacturing, and Distribution Processes

Whether lenses are simple or complex, Plastim follows this sequence of steps to design, produce, and distribute them:

- **Design products and processes.** Each year Giovanni Motors specifies details of the simple and complex lenses it needs for its new models of cars. Plastim's design department designs the new molds and specifies the manufacturing process to make the lenses.
- **Manufacture lenses.** The lenses are molded, finished, cleaned, and inspected.
- **Distribute lenses.** Finished lenses are packed and sent to Giovanni Motors' plants.

Plastim is operating at capacity and incurs very low marketing costs. Because of its high-quality products, Plastim has minimal customer-service costs. Plastim competes with several other companies who also manufacture simple lenses. At a recent meeting, Giovanni's purchasing manager informed Plastim's sales manager that Bandix, which makes only simple lenses, is offering to supply the S3 lens to Giovanni at a price of $53, well below the $63 price that Plastim is currently projecting and budgeting for 2017. Unless Plastim can lower its selling price, it will lose the Giovanni business for the simple lens for the upcoming model year. Fortunately, the same competitive pressures do not exist for the complex lens, which Plastim currently sells to Giovanni at $137 per lens.

Plastim's managers have two primary options:

- Give up the Giovanni business in simple lenses if selling them is unprofitable. Bandix makes only simple lenses and perhaps, therefore, uses simpler technology and processes than Plastim. The simpler operations may give Bandix a cost advantage that Plastim cannot match. If so, it is better for Plastim to not supply the S3 lens to Giovanni.

- Reduce the price of the simple lens and either accept a lower margin or aggressively seek to reduce costs.

To make these long-run strategic decisions, managers first need to understand the costs to design, make, and distribute the S3 and C5 lenses.

Bandix makes only simple lenses and can fairly accurately calculate the cost of a lens by dividing total costs by the number of simple lenses produced. Plastim's costing environment is more challenging because the manufacturing overhead costs support the production of both simple and complex lenses. Plastim's managers and management accountants need to find a way to allocate overhead costs to each type of lens.

In computing costs, Plastim assigns both variable costs and costs that are fixed in the short run to the S3 and C5 lenses. Managers cost products and services to guide long-run strategic decisions, such as what mix of products and services to produce and sell and what prices to charge for them. In the long run, managers have the ability to influence all costs. The firm will only survive in the long run if revenues exceed total costs, regardless of whether these costs are variable or fixed in the short run.

To guide pricing and cost-management decisions, Plastim's managers need to consider all costs and therefore assign both manufacturing and nonmanufacturing costs to the S3 and C5 lenses. If managers had wanted to calculate the cost of inventory, Plastim's management accountants would have assigned only manufacturing costs to the lenses, as required by Generally Accepted Accounting Principles. Surveys of company practice across the globe indicate that the vast majority of companies use costing systems not just for inventory costing but also for strategic purposes, such as pricing and product-mix decisions and decisions about cost reduction, process improvement, design, and planning and budgeting. Managers of these companies assign all costs to products and services. Even merchandising-sector companies (for whom inventory costing is straightforward) and service-sector companies (who have no inventory) expend considerable resources in designing and operating their costing systems to allocate costs for strategic purposes.

Simple Costing System Using a Single Indirect-Cost Pool

Plastim currently has a simple costing system that allocates indirect costs using a single indirect-cost rate, the type of system described in Chapter 4. The only difference between these two chapters is that Chapter 4 focuses on jobs while here the cost objects are products. Exhibit 5-1 shows an overview of Plastim's simple costing system. Use this exhibit as a guide as you study the following steps, each of which is marked in Exhibit 5-1.

Step 1: Identify the Products That Are the Chosen Cost Objects. The cost objects are the 60,000 simple S3 lenses and the 15,000 complex C5 lenses that Plastim will produce in 2017. Plastim's management accountants first calculate the total costs and then the unit cost of designing, manufacturing, and distributing lenses.

Step 2: Identify the Direct Costs of the Products. The direct costs are direct materials and direct manufacturing labor. Exhibit 5-2 shows the direct and indirect costs for the S3 and the C5 lenses using the simple costing system. The direct-cost calculations appear on lines 5, 6, and 7 in Exhibit 5-2. Plastim's simple costing system classifies all costs other than direct materials and direct manufacturing labor as indirect costs.

Step 3: Select the Cost-Allocation Bases to Use for Allocating Indirect (or Overhead) Costs to the Products. A majority of the indirect costs consists of salaries paid to supervisors, engineers, manufacturing support, and maintenance staff that support direct manufacturing labor. Plastim's managers use direct manufacturing labor-hours as the only

EXHIBIT 5-1

Overview of Plastim's
Simple Costing System

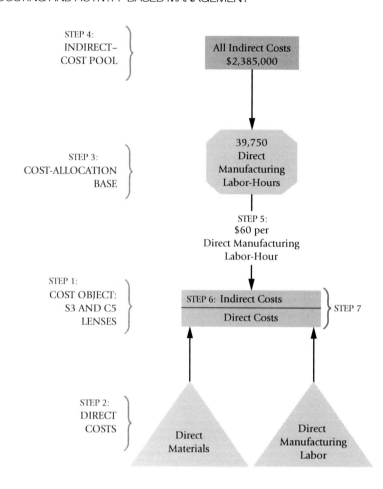

allocation base to allocate all manufacturing and nonmanufacturing indirect costs to S3 and C5. Historically, many companies used such simple costing systems because overhead costs were only a small component of costs and because a single cost driver accurately reflected how overhead resources were used. In 2017, Plastim's managers budget 39,750 direct manufacturing labor-hours.

Step 4: Identify the Indirect Costs Associated with Each Cost-Allocation Base. Because Plastim uses only a single cost-allocation base, Plastim's management accountants group all budgeted indirect costs of $2,385,000 for 2017 into a single overhead cost pool.

EXHIBIT 5-2   Plastim's Product Costs Using the Simple Costing System

	A	B	C	D	E	F	G
1		60,000			15,000		
2		Simple Lenses (S3)			Complex Lenses (C5)		
3		Total	per Unit		Total	per Unit	Total
4		(1)	(2) = (1) ÷ 60,000		(3)	(4) = (3) ÷ 15,000	(5) = (1) + (3)
5	Direct materials	$1,125,000	$18.75		$ 675,000	$45.00	$1,800,000
6	Direct manufacturing labor	600,000	10.00		195,000	13.00	795,000
7	Total direct costs (Step 2)	1,725,000	28.75		870,000	58.00	2,595,000
8	Indirect costs allocated (Step 6)	1,800,000	30.00		585,000	39.00	2,385,000
9	Total costs (Step 7)	$3,525,000	$58.75		$1,455,000	$97.00	$4,980,000
10							

Step 5: Compute the Rate per Unit of Each Cost-Allocation Base.

$$\text{Budgeted indirect-cost rate} = \frac{\text{Budgeted total costs in indirect-cost pool}}{\text{Budgeted total quantity of cost-allocation base}}$$

$$= \frac{\$2,385,000}{39,750 \text{ direct manufacturing labor-hours}}$$

$$= \$60 \text{ per direct manufacturing labor-hour}$$

Step 6: Compute the Indirect Costs Allocated to the Products. Plastim's managers budget 30,000 total direct manufacturing labor-hours to make the 60,000 S3 lenses and 9,750 total direct manufacturing labor-hours to make the 15,000 C5 lenses. Exhibit 5-2 shows indirect costs of $1,800,000 ($60 per direct manufacturing labor-hour × 30,000 direct manufacturing labor-hours) allocated to the simple lens and $585,000 ($60 per direct manufacturing labor-hour × 9,750 direct manufacturing labor-hours) allocated to the complex lens.

Step 7: Compute the Total Cost of the Products by Adding All Direct and Indirect Costs Assigned to the Products. Exhibit 5-2 presents the product costs for the simple and complex lenses. The direct costs are calculated in Step 2 and the indirect costs in Step 6. Be sure you see the parallel between the simple costing system overview diagram (Exhibit 5-1) and the costs calculated in Step 7. Exhibit 5-1 shows two direct-cost categories and one indirect-cost category. Therefore, the budgeted cost of each type of lens in Step 7 (Exhibit 5-2) has three line items: two for direct costs and one for allocated indirect costs. It is very helpful to draw overview diagrams to see the big picture of costing systems before getting into the detailed costing of products and services. The budgeted cost per S3 lens is $58.75, well above the $53 selling price quoted by Bandix. The budgeted cost per C5 lens is $97.

Amherst Metal Works produces two types of metal lamps. Amherst manufactures 20,000 basic lamps and 5,000 designer lamps. Its simple costing system uses a single indirect-cost pool and allocates costs to the two lamps on the basis of direct manufacturing labor-hours. It provides the following budgeted cost information:

5-1 TRY IT!

	Basic Lamps	Designer Lamps	Total
Direct materials per lamp	$ 9	$15	
Direct manufacturing labor per lamp	0.5 hours	0.6 hours	
Direct manufacturing labor rate per hour	$20	$20	
Indirect manufacturing costs			$234,000

Calculate the total budgeted costs of the basic and designer lamps using Amherst's simple costing system.

Applying the Five-Step Decision-Making Process at Plastim

To decide how it should respond to the threat that Bandix poses to its S3 lens business, Plastim's managers work through the five-step decision-making process introduced in Chapter 1.

Step 1: Identify the Problem and Uncertainties. The problem is clear: If Plastim wants to retain the Giovanni business for S3 lenses and make a profit, it must find a way to reduce the price and costs of the S3 lens. The two major uncertainties Plastim faces are (1) whether its technology and processes for the S3 lens are competitive with Bandix's and (2) whether Plastim's S3 lens is overcosted by the simple costing system.

Step 2: Obtain Information. Senior management asks a team of design and process engineers to analyze and evaluate the design, manufacturing, and distribution operations for the S3 lens. The team is very confident that the technology and processes for the S3 lens are not inferior to those of Bandix and other competitors because Plastim has many years of experience in manufacturing and distributing the S3 lens with a history and culture of continuous process improvements. The team is less certain about Plastim's capabilities in manufacturing and distributing complex lenses because it only recently started making this type of lens. Given these doubts, senior management is happy that Giovanni Motors considers the price of the C5 lens to be competitive. Plastim's managers are puzzled, though, by how, at the currently budgeted prices, Plastim is expected to earn a very large profit margin percentage (operating income ÷ revenues) on the C5 lenses and a small profit margin on the S3 lenses:

	60,000 Simple Lenses (S3)		15,000 Complex Lenses (C5)		
	Total (1)	per Unit (2) = (1) ÷ 60,000	Total (3)	per Unit (4) = (3) ÷ 15,000	Total (5) = (1)+(3)
Revenues	$3,780,000	$63.00	$2,055,000	$137.00	$5,835,000
Total costs	3,525,000	58.75	1,455,000	97.00	4,980,000
Operating income	$ 255,000	$ 4.25	$ 600,000	$ 40.00	$ 855,000
Profit margin percentage		6.75%		29.20%	

As they continue to gather information, Plastim's managers begin to ponder why the profit margins are under so much pressure for the S3 lens, where the company has strong capabilities, but not on the newer, less-established C5 lens. Plastim is not deliberately charging a low price for S3, so managers begin to evaluate the costing system. Plastim's simple costing system may be overcosting the simple S3 lens (assigning too much cost to it) and undercosting the complex C5 lens (assigning too little cost to it).

Step 3: Make Predictions About the Future. Plastim's key challenge is to get a better estimate of what it will cost to design, make, and distribute the S3 and C5 lenses. Managers are fairly confident about the direct material and direct manufacturing labor cost of each lens because these costs are easily traced to the lenses. Of greater concern is how accurately the simple costing system measures the indirect resources used by each type of lens. The managers believe the costing system can be substantially improved.

Even as they come to this conclusion, managers want to avoid biased thinking. In particular, they want to be careful that the desire to be competitive on the S3 lens does not lead to assumptions that bias them in favor of lowering costs of the S3 lens.

Step 4: Make Decisions by Choosing Among Alternatives. On the basis of predicted costs and taking into account how Bandix might respond, Plastim's managers must decide whether they should bid for Giovanni Motors' S3 lens business and, if they do bid, what price they should offer.

Step 5: Implement the Decision, Evaluate Performance, and Learn. If Plastim bids and wins Giovanni's S3 lens business, it must compare actual costs as it makes and ships the S3 lenses to predicted costs and learn why actual costs deviate from predicted costs. Such evaluation and learning form the basis for future improvements.

The next few sections focus on Steps 3, 4, and 5: (3) how Plastim improves the allocation of indirect costs to the S3 and C5 lenses, (4) how it uses these predictions to bid for the S3 lens business, and (5) how it evaluates performance, makes product design and process improvements, and learns using the new system.

LEARNING OBJECTIVE 2

Present three guidelines for refining a costing system

…classify more costs as direct costs, expand the number of indirect-cost pools, and identify cost drivers

Refining a Costing System

A **refined costing system** reduces the use of broad averages for assigning the cost of resources to cost objects (such as jobs, products, and services) and provides better measurement of the costs of indirect resources used by different cost objects, no matter how differently various cost objects use indirect resources. Refining a costing system helps managers make better decisions about how to allocate resources and which products to produce.

Reasons for Refining a Costing System

Three principal reasons have accelerated the demand for refinements to the costing system.

1. **Increase in product diversity.** The growing demand for customized products has led managers to increase the variety of products and services their companies offer. Kanthal, a Swedish manufacturer of heating elements, for example, produces more than 10,000 different types of electrical heating wires and thermostats. Banks, such as Barclays Bank in the United Kingdom, offer many different types of accounts and services: special passbook accounts, ATMs, credit cards, and electronic banking products. Producing these products places different demands on resources because of differences in volume, process, technology, and complexity. For example, the computer and network resources needed to support electronic banking products are much greater than the computer and network resources needed to support a passbook savings account. The use of broad averages fails to capture these differences in demand and leads to distorted and inaccurate cost information.

2. **Increase in indirect costs with different cost drivers.** The use of product and process technology such as computer-integrated manufacturing (CIM) and flexible manufacturing systems (FMS) has led to an increase in indirect costs and a decrease in direct costs, particularly direct manufacturing labor costs. In CIM and FMS, computers on the manufacturing floor instruct equipment to set up and run quickly and automatically. The computers accurately measure hundreds of production parameters and directly control the manufacturing processes to achieve high-quality output. Managing complex technology and producing diverse products also require additional support function resources for activities such as production scheduling, product and process design, and engineering. Because direct manufacturing labor is not a cost driver of these costs, allocating indirect costs on the basis of direct manufacturing labor (as in Plastim's simple costing system) does not accurately measure how resources are being used by different products.

3. **Competition in product markets.** As markets have become more competitive, managers have felt the need to obtain more accurate cost information to help them make important strategic decisions, such as how to price products and which products to sell. Making correct decisions about pricing and product mix is critical in competitive markets because competitors quickly capitalize on a manager's mistakes. For example, if Plastim overcosts the S3 lens and charges a higher price, a competitor aware of the true costs of making the lens could charge a lower price and gain the S3 business as Bandix is attempting to do.

The preceding factors explain why managers want to refine cost systems. Refining costing systems requires gathering, validating, analyzing, and storing vast quantities of data. Advances in information technology have drastically reduced the costs of performing these activities.

Guidelines for Refining a Costing System

There are three main guidelines for refining a costing system:

1. **Direct-cost tracing.** Identify as many direct costs as is economically feasible. This guideline aims to reduce the amount of costs classified as indirect, thereby minimizing the extent to which costs have to be allocated rather than traced.

2. **Indirect-cost pools.** Expand the number of indirect-cost pools until each pool is more homogeneous. All costs in a *homogeneous cost pool* have the same or a similar cause-and-effect (or benefits-received) relationship with a single cost driver that is used as the cost-allocation base. Consider, for example, a single indirect-cost pool containing both indirect machining costs and indirect distribution costs that are allocated to products using machine-hours. This pool is not homogeneous because machine-hours are a cost driver of machining costs but not of distribution costs, which has a different cost driver, cubic feet of product delivered. If, instead, machining costs and distribution costs are separated into two indirect-cost pools, with machine-hours as the cost-allocation base for the machining cost pool and cubic feet of product delivered as the cost-allocation base for the distribution cost pool, each indirect-cost pool would become homogeneous.

DECISION POINT

How do managers refine a costing system?

3. **Cost-allocation bases.** As we describe later in the chapter, whenever possible, managers should use the cost driver (the cause of indirect costs) as the cost-allocation base for each homogeneous indirect-cost pool (the effect).

Activity-Based Costing Systems

LEARNING OBJECTIVE **3**

Distinguish between simple and activity-based costing systems

...unlike simple systems, activity-based costing systems calculate costs of individual activities to cost products

One of the best tools for refining a costing system is *activity-based costing*. **Activity-based costing (ABC)** refines a costing system by identifying individual activities as the fundamental cost objects. An **activity** is an event, task, or unit of work with a specified purpose—for example, designing products, setting up machines, operating machines, or distributing products. More informally, activities are verbs; they are things that a firm does. To help make strategic decisions, ABC systems identify activities in all functions of the value chain, calculate costs of individual activities, and assign costs to cost objects such as products and services on the basis of the mix of activities needed to produce each product or service.[2]

Plastim's ABC System

After reviewing its simple costing system and the potential miscosting of product costs, Plastim's managers decide to implement an ABC system. Direct material costs and direct manufacturing labor costs can be traced to products easily, so the ABC system focuses on refining the assignment of indirect costs to departments, processes, products, or other cost objects. To identify activities, Plastim organizes a team of managers from design, manufacturing, distribution, accounting, and administration. Plastim's ABC system then uses activities to break down its current single indirect-cost pool into finer pools of costs related to the various activities.

Defining activities is difficult. The team evaluates hundreds of tasks performed at Plastim. It must decide which tasks should be classified as separate activities and which should be combined. For example, should maintenance of molding machines, operations of molding machines, and process control be regarded as separate activities or combined into a single activity? An activity-based costing system with many activities becomes overly detailed and unwieldy to operate. An activity-based costing system with too few activities may not be refined enough to measure cause-and-effect relationships between cost drivers and various indirect costs. To achieve an effective balance, Plastim's team focuses on activities that account for a sizable fraction of indirect costs and combines activities that have the same cost driver into a single activity. For example, the team decides to combine maintenance of molding machines, operations of molding machines, and process control into a single activity—molding machine operations—because all these activities have the same cost driver: molding machine-hours.

The team identifies the following seven activities based on the steps and processes needed to design, manufacture, and distribute S3 and C5 lenses.

a. Design products and processes
b. Set up molding machines to ensure that the molds are properly held in place and parts are properly aligned before manufacturing starts

---

[2] For more details on ABC systems, see R. Cooper and R. S. Kaplan, *The Design of Cost Management Systems* (Upper Saddle River, NJ: Prentice Hall, 1999); G. Cokins, *Activity-Based Cost Management: An Executive's Guide* (Hoboken, NJ: John Wiley & Sons, 2001); and R. S. Kaplan and S. Anderson, *Time-Driven Activity-Based Costing: A Simpler and More Powerful Path to Higher Profits* (Boston: Harvard Business School Press, 2007).

c. Operate molding machines to manufacture lenses
d. Clean and maintain the molds after lenses are manufactured
e. Prepare batches of finished lenses for shipment
f. Distribute lenses to customers
g. Administer and manage all processes at Plastim

These activity descriptions (or *activity list* or *activity dictionary*) form the basis of the activity-based costing system. Compiling the list of tasks, however, is only the first step in implementing activity-based costing systems. Plastim must also identify the cost of each activity and the related cost driver by using the three guidelines for refining a costing system described on pages 179–180.

1. **Direct-cost tracing.** Plastim's ABC system subdivides the single indirect-cost pool into seven smaller cost pools related to the different activities. The costs in the cleaning and maintenance activity cost pool (item d) consist of salaries and wages paid to workers who clean the mold. These costs are direct costs because they can be economically traced to a specific mold and lens.

2. **Indirect-cost pools.** The remaining six activity cost pools are indirect-cost pools. Unlike the single indirect-cost pool of Plastim's simple costing system, each of the activity-related cost pools is homogeneous. That is, each activity cost pool includes only those narrow and focused sets of costs that have the same cost driver. Consider, for example, distribution costs. Managers identify cubic feet of packages delivered as the only cost driver of distribution costs because all distribution costs (such as wages of truck drivers) vary with the cubic feet of packages delivered. In the simple costing system, Plastim pooled all indirect costs together and used a single cost-allocation base, direct manufacturing labor-hours, which was not a cost driver of all indirect costs. Managers were therefore unable to measure how different cost objects (the S3 and C5 lenses) used resources.

    To determine the costs of activity pools, managers assign costs accumulated in various account classifications (such as salaries, wages, maintenance, and electricity) to each of the activity cost pools. This process is commonly called *first-stage allocation*. For example, as we will see later in the chapter, of the $2,385,000 in the total indirect-cost pool, Plastim identifies setup costs of $300,000. Setup costs include depreciation and maintenance costs of setup equipment, wages of setup workers, and allocated salaries of design engineers, process engineers, and supervisors. We discuss *first-stage allocation* in more detail in Chapters 14 and 15. We focus here on the *second-stage allocation*, the allocation of costs of activity cost pools to products.

3. **Cost-allocation bases.** For each activity cost pool, Plastim uses the cost driver (whenever possible) as the cost-allocation base. To identify cost drivers, Plastim's managers consider various alternatives and use their knowledge of operations to choose among them. For example, Plastim's managers choose setup-hours rather than the number of setups as the cost driver of setup costs because Plastim's managers believe that the more complex setups of C5 lenses take more time and are more costly. Over time, Plastim's managers can use data to test their beliefs. (Chapter 10 discusses several methods to estimate the relationship between a cost driver and costs.)

The logic of ABC systems is twofold. First, when managers structure activity cost pools more finely, using cost drivers for each activity cost pool as the cost-allocation base, it leads to more accurate costing of activities. Second, allocating these costs to products by measuring the cost-allocation bases of different activities used by different products leads to more accurate product costs. We illustrate this logic by focusing on the setup activity at Plastim.

Setting up molding machines frequently entails trial runs, fine-tuning, and adjustments. Improper setups cause quality problems such as scratches on the surface of the lens. The resources needed for each setup depend on the complexity of the manufacturing operation. Complex lenses require more setup resources (setup-hours) per setup than simple lenses. Furthermore, complex lenses can be produced only in small batches because the molds for complex lenses need to be cleaned more often than molds for simple lenses. Relative to simple lenses, complex lenses therefore not only use more setup-hours per setup, but also require more frequent setups.

Setup data for the simple S3 lens and the complex C5 lens are as follows.

		Simple S3 Lens	Complex C5 Lens	Total
1	Quantity of lenses produced	60,000	15,000	
2	Number of lenses produced per batch	240	50	
3 = (1) ÷ (2)	Number of batches	250	300	
4	Setup time per batch	2 hours	5 hours	
5 = (3) × (4)	Total setup-hours	500 hours	1,500 hours	2,000 hours

Recall that in its simple costing system, Plastim uses direct manufacturing labor-hours to allocate all $2,385,000 of indirect costs (which includes $300,000 of indirect setup costs) to products. The following table compares how setup costs allocated to simple and complex lenses will be different if Plastim allocates setup costs to lenses based on setup-hours rather than direct manufacturing labor-hours. Of the $60 total rate per direct manufacturing labor-hour (page 177), the setup cost per direct manufacturing labor-hour amounts to $7.54717 ($300,000 ÷ 39,750 total direct manufacturing labor-hours). The setup cost per setup-hour equals $150 ($300,000 ÷ 2,000 total setup-hours).

	Simple S3 Lens	Complex C5 Lens	Total
Setup cost allocated using direct manufacturing labor-hours:			
$7.54717 × 30,000; $7.54717 × 9,750	$226,415	$ 73,585	$300,000
Setup cost allocated using setup-hours:			
$150 × 500; $150 × 1,500	$ 75,000	$225,000	$300,000

ABC systems that use available time (setup-hours in our example) to calculate the cost of a resource and to allocate costs to cost objects are sometimes called *time-driven activity-based costing (TDABC) systems*. Following guidelines 2 and 3, Plastim should use setup hours, the cost driver of set up costs, and not direct manufacturing labor hours, to allocate setup costs to products. The C5 lens uses substantially more setup-hours than the S3 lens (1,500 hours ÷ 2,000 hours = 75% of the total setup-hours) because the C5 requires a greater number of setups (batches) and each setup is more challenging and requires more setup-hours.

The ABC system therefore allocates significantly more setup costs to C5 than to S3. When direct manufacturing labor-hours rather than setup-hours are used to allocate setup costs in the simple costing system, the S3 lens is allocated a very large share of the setup costs because the S3 lens uses a larger proportion of direct manufacturing labor-hours (30,000 ÷ 39,750 = 75.47%). As a result, the simple costing system overcosts the S3 lens with regard to setup costs.

As we will see later in the chapter, ABC systems provide valuable information to managers beyond more accurate product costs. For example, identifying setup-hours as the cost driver correctly orients managers' cost reduction efforts on reducing setup-hours and cost per setup-hour. Note that setup-hours are related to batches (or groups) of lenses made, not the number of individual lenses. Activity-based costing attempts to identify the most relevant cause-and-effect relationship for each activity pool without restricting the cost driver to be units of output or variables related to units of output (such as direct manufacturing labor-hours). As our discussion of setups illustrates, limiting cost-allocation bases to only units of output weakens the cause-and-effect relationship between the cost-allocation base and the costs in a cost pool. Broadening cost drivers to batches (or groups) of lenses, not just individual lenses, leads us to *cost hierarchies*.

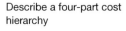

DECISION POINT

What is the difference between the design of a simple costing system and an activity-based costing (ABC) system?

LEARNING OBJECTIVE 4

Describe a four-part cost hierarchy

…a four-part cost hierarchy is used to categorize costs based on different types of cost drivers— for example, costs that vary with each unit of a product versus costs that vary with each batch of products

Cost Hierarchies

A **cost hierarchy** categorizes various activity cost pools on the basis of the different types of cost drivers, cost-allocation bases, or different degrees of difficulty in determining cause-and-effect (or benefits-received) relationships. ABC systems commonly use a cost hierarchy with four levels to identify cost-allocation bases that are cost drivers of the activity cost pools: (1) output unit–level costs, (2) batch-level costs, (3) product-sustaining costs, and (4) facility-sustaining costs.

Output unit–level costs are the costs of activities performed on each individual unit of a product or service. Machine operations costs (such as the cost of energy, machine depreciation, and repair) related to the activity of running the automated molding machines are output unit–level costs because, over time, the cost of this activity increases with additional units of output produced (or machine-hours used). Plastim's ABC system uses molding machine-hours, an output unit–level cost-allocation base, to allocate machine operations costs to products.

Batch-level costs are the costs of activities related to a group of units of a product or service rather than each individual unit of product or service. In the Plastim example, setup costs are batch-level costs because, over time, the cost of this setup activity varies with the setup-hours needed to produce batches (groups) of lenses regardless of the total number of lenses produced. For example, if Plastim produces 20% fewer lenses using the same number of setup hours, would setup costs change? No, because setup hours not the number of lenses produced drive setup costs.

As described in the table on page 182, the S3 lens requires 500 setup-hours (2 setup-hours per batch × 250 batches). The C5 lens requires 1,500 setup-hours (5 setup-hours per batch × 300 batches). The total setup costs allocated to S3 and C5 depend on the total setup-hours required by each type of lens, not on the number of lenses of S3 and C5 produced. Plastim's ABC system uses setup-hours, a batch-level cost-allocation base, to allocate setup costs to products. Other examples of batch-level costs are material-handling and quality-inspection costs associated with batches (not the quantities) of products produced and costs of placing purchase orders, receiving materials, and paying invoices related to the number of purchase orders placed rather than the quantity or value of materials purchased.

Product-sustaining costs (service-sustaining costs) are the costs of activities undertaken to support individual products or services regardless of the number of units or batches in which the units are produced or services provided. In the Plastim example, design costs are product-sustaining costs. Over time, design costs depend largely on the time designers spend on designing and modifying the product, mold, and process, not on the number of lenses subsequently produced or the number of batches in which the lenses are produced using the mold. These design costs are a function of the complexity of the mold, measured by the number of parts in the mold multiplied by the area (in square feet) over which the molten plastic must flow (12 parts × 2.5 square feet, or 30 parts-square feet for the S3 lens; and 14 parts × 5 square feet, or 70 parts-square feet for the C5 lens). Plastim's ABC system uses parts-square feet, a product-sustaining cost-allocation base, to allocate design costs to products. Other examples of product-sustaining costs are product research and development costs, costs of making engineering changes, and marketing costs to launch new products.

Facility-sustaining costs are the costs of activities that managers cannot trace to individual products or services but that support the organization as a whole. In the Plastim example and at companies such as Volvo, Samsung, and General Electric, the general administration costs (including top management compensation, rent, and building security) are facility-sustaining costs. It is usually difficult to find a good cause-and-effect relationship between these costs and the cost-allocation base, so some companies deduct facility-sustaining costs as a separate lump-sum amount from operating income rather than allocate these costs to products. Managers who follow this approach need to keep in mind that when making decisions based on costs (such as pricing), some lump-sum costs have not been allocated. They must set prices that are much greater than the allocated costs to recover some of the unallocated facility-sustaining costs. Other companies, such as Plastim, allocate facility-sustaining costs to products on some basis—for example, direct manufacturing labor-hours—because management believes all costs should be allocated to products even if it's done in a somewhat arbitrary way. Allocating all costs to products or services ensures that managers take into account all costs when making decisions based on costs. So long as managers are aware of the nature of facility-sustaining costs and the pros and cons of allocating them, which method a manager chooses is a matter of personal preference.

DECISION POINT

What is a cost hierarchy?

Implementing Activity-Based Costing

Now that you understand the basic concepts of ABC, let's see how Plastim's managers refine the simple costing system, evaluate the two systems, and identify the factors to consider when deciding whether to develop the ABC system.

Implementing ABC at Plastim

To implement ABC, Plastim's managers follow the seven-step approach to costing and the three guidelines for refining costing systems (increase direct-cost tracing, create homogeneous indirect-cost pools, and identify cost-allocation bases that have cause-and-effect relationships with costs in the cost pool). Exhibit 5-3 shows an overview of Plastim's ABC system. Use this exhibit as a guide as you study the following steps, each of which is marked in Exhibit 5-3.

Step 1: Identify the Products That Are the Chosen Cost Objects. The cost objects are the 60,000 S3 and the 15,000 C5 lenses that Plastim will produce in 2017. Plastim's managers want to determine the total costs and then the per-unit cost of designing, manufacturing, and distributing these lenses.

Step 2: Identify the Direct Costs of the Products. The managers identify the following direct costs of the lenses because these costs can be economically traced to a specific mold and lens: direct material costs, direct manufacturing labor costs, and mold cleaning and maintenance costs.

Exhibit 5-5 shows the direct and indirect costs for the S3 and C5 lenses using the ABC system. The direct costs calculations appear on lines 6, 7, 8, and 9 in Exhibit 5-5. Plastim's managers classify all other costs as indirect costs, as we will see in Exhibit 5-4.

Step 3: Select the Activities and Cost-Allocation Bases to Use for Allocating Indirect Costs to the Products. Following guideline 2 (subdivide into homogeneous cost pools) and guideline

EXHIBIT 5-3   Overview of Plastim's Activity-Based Costing System

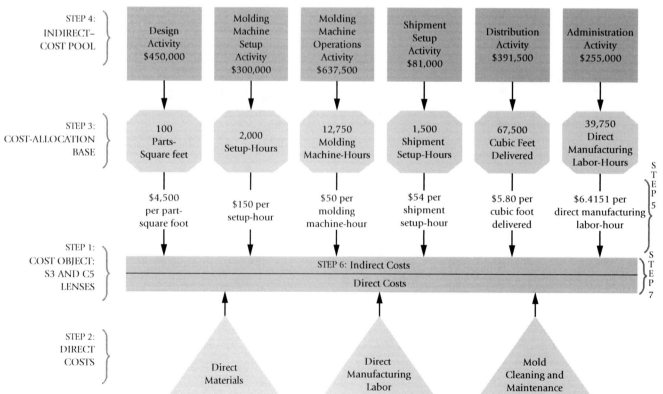

EXHIBIT 5-4   Activity-Cost Rates for Indirect-Cost Pools

	Home	Insert	Page Layout	Formulas	Data	Review	View	
	A	B	C	D	E	F	G	H
1			**(Step 4)**	**(Step 3)**		**(Step 5)**		
2	**Activity**	**Cost Hierarchy Category**	**Total Budgeted Indirect Costs**	**Budgeted Quantity of Cost-Allocation Base**		**Budgeted Indirect Cost Rate**		**Cause-and-Effect Relationship Between Allocation Base and Activity Cost**
3	(1)	(2)	(3)	(4)		(5) = (3) ÷ (4)		(6)
4	Design	Product-sustaining	$450,000	100	parts-square feet	$ 4,500	per part-square foot	Design Department indirect costs increase with more complex molds (more parts, larger surface area).
5	Molding machine setup	Batch-level	$300,000	2,000	setup-hours	$ 150	per setup-hour	Indirect setup costs increase with setup-hours.
6	Machine operations	Output unit-level	$637,500	12,750	molding machine-hours	$ 50	per molding machine-hour	Indirect costs of operating molding machines increases with molding machine-hours.
7	Shipment setup	Batch-level	$ 81,000	1,500	shipment setup-hours	$ 54	per shipment setup-hour	Shipping costs incurred to prepare batches for shipment increase with the number of shipment setup-hours.
8	Distribution	Output-unit-level	$391,500	67,500	cubic feet delivered	$ 5.80	per cubic foot delivered	Distribution costs increase with the cubic feet of packages delivered.
9	Administration	Facility sustaining	$255,000	39,750	direct manuf. labor-hours	$6.4151	per direct manuf. labor-hour	The demand for administrative resources increases with direct manufacturing labor-hours.

3 (identify relevant cost-allocation bases) for refining a costing system (pages 179–180), Plastim's managers identify six activities for allocating indirect costs to products: (a) design, (b) molding machine setup, (c) machine operations, (d) shipment setup, (e) distribution, and (f) administration. Exhibit 5-4, column 2, shows the cost hierarchy category, and column 4 shows the cost-allocation base and the budgeted quantity of the cost-allocation base for each activity described in column 1.

Identifying the cost-allocation bases defines the number of activity pools into which costs must be grouped in an ABC system. For example, rather than define the design activities of product design, process design, and prototyping as separate activities, Plastim's managers define these three activities together as a combined "design" activity and form a homogeneous design cost pool. Why? Because the same cost driver—the complexity of the mold—drives the costs of each design activity. A second consideration for choosing a cost-allocation base is the availability of reliable data and measures. For example, in its ABC system, Plastim's managers measure mold complexity in terms of the number of parts in the mold and the surface area of the mold (parts-square feet). If these data are difficult to obtain or measure, Plastim's managers may be forced to use some other measure of complexity, such as the amount of material flowing through the mold that may only be weakly related to the cost of the design activity.

Step 4: Identify the Indirect Costs Associated with Each Cost-Allocation Base. In this step, Plastim's managers try to assign budgeted indirect costs for 2017 to activities (see Exhibit 5-4, column 3) on the basis of a cause-and-effect relationship between the cost-allocation base for an activity and the cost. For example, all costs that have a cause-and-effect relationship to cubic feet of packages moved are assigned to the distribution cost pool. Of course, the strength of the cause-and-effect relationship between the cost-allocation base and the cost of an activity varies across cost pools. For example, the cause-and-effect relationship between direct manufacturing labor-hours and administration activity costs, which as we discussed earlier is somewhat arbitrary, is not as strong as the relationship between setup-hours and setup activity costs, where setup-hours is the cost driver of setup costs.

Some costs can be directly identified with a particular activity. For example, salaries paid to design engineers and depreciation of equipment used in the design department are directly identified with the design activity. Other costs need to be allocated across activities. For example, on the basis of interviews or time records, manufacturing engineers and supervisors estimate the time they will spend on design, molding machine setup, and molding machine operations. If a manufacturing engineer spends 15% of her time on design, 45% of her time managing molding machine setups, and 40% of her time on molding operations, the company will allocate the manufacturing engineer's salary to each of these activities in proportion to the time spent. Still other costs are allocated to activity-cost pools using allocation bases that measure how these costs support different activities. For example, rent costs are allocated to activity-cost pools on the basis of square-feet area used by different activities.

As you can see, most costs do not fit neatly into activity categories. Often, costs may first need to be allocated to activities (Stage 1 of the two-stage cost-allocation model) before the costs of the activities can be allocated to products (Stage 2).

The following table shows the assignment of costs to the seven activities identified earlier. Recall that Plastim's management accountants reclassify mold cleaning costs as a direct cost because these costs can be easily traced to a specific mold and lens.

	Design	Molding Machine Setups	Molding Operations	Mold Cleaning	Shipment Setup	Distribution	Administration	Total
Salaries (supervisors, design engineers, process engineers)	$320,000	$105,000	$137,500	$ 0	$21,000	$ 61,500	$165,000	$ 810,000
Wages of support staff	65,000	115,000	70,000	234,000	34,000	125,000	40,000	683,000
Depreciation	24,000	30,000	290,000	18,000	11,000	140,000	15,000	528,000
Maintenance	13,000	16,000	45,000	12,000	6,000	25,000	5,000	122,000
Power and fuel	18,000	20,000	35,000	6,000	5,000	30,000	10,000	124,000
Rent	10,000	14,000	60,000	0	4,000	10,000	20,000	118,000
Total	$450,000	$300,000	$637,500	$270,000	$81,000	$391,500	$255,000	$2,385,000

Step 5: Compute the Rate per Unit of Each Cost-Allocation Base. Exhibit 5-4, column 5, summarizes the calculation of the budgeted indirect-cost rates using the budgeted quantity of the cost-allocation base from Step 3 and the total budgeted indirect costs of each activity from Step 4.

Step 6: Compute the Indirect Costs Allocated to the Products. Exhibit 5-5 shows total budgeted indirect costs of $1,153,953 allocated to the simple lens and $961,047 allocated to the complex lens. Follow the budgeted indirect-cost calculations for each lens in Exhibit 5-5. For each activity, Plastim's operations personnel indicate the total quantity of the cost-allocation base that will be used by each type of lens (recall that Plastim operates at capacity). For example, lines 15 and 16 in Exhibit 5-5 show that of the 2,000 total setup-hours, the S3 lens is budgeted to use 500 hours and the C5 lens 1,500 hours. The budgeted indirect-cost rate is $150 per setup-hour (Exhibit 5-4, column 5, line 5). Therefore, the total budgeted cost of the setup activity allocated to the S3 lens is $75,000 (500 setup-hours × $150 per setup-hour) and to the C5 lens is $225,000 (1,500 setup-hours × $150 per setup-hour). Budgeted setup cost per unit equals $1.25 ($75,000 ÷ 60,000 units) for the S3 lens and $15 ($225,000 ÷ 15,000 units) for the C5 lens.

Next consider shipment setup costs. Plastim supplies its S3 and C5 lenses to two different Giovanni plants. One of these is an international plant in Mexico. Preparing for these

EXHIBIT 5-5   Plastim's Product Costs Using Activity-Based Costing System

	A	B	C	D	E	F	G
		60,000			**15,000**		
1							
2		Simple Lenses (S3)			Complex Lenses (C5)		
3		Total	per Unit		Total	per Unit	Total
4	**Cost Description**	(1)	(2)＝(1)÷60,000		(3)	(4)＝(3)÷15,000	(5)＝(1)+(3)
5	Direct costs						
6	Direct materials	$1,125,000	$18.75		$ 675,000	$ 45.00	$1,800,000
7	Direct manufacturing labor	600,000	10.00		195,000	13.00	795,000
8	Direct mold cleaning and maintenance costs	120,000	2.00		150,000	10.00	270,000
9	Total direct costs (Step 2)	1,845,000	30.75		1,020,000	68.00	2,865,000
10	Indirect Costs of Activities						
11	Design						
12	S3, 30 parts-sq.ft. × $4,500	135,000	2.25				} 450,000
13	C5, 70 parts-sq.ft. × $4,500				315,000	21.00	
14	Setup of molding machines						
15	S3, 500 setup-hours × $150	75,000	1.25				} 300,000
16	C5, 1,500 setup-hours × $150				225,000	15.00	
17	Machine operations						
18	S3, 9,000 molding machine-hours × $50	450,000	7.50				} 637,500
19	C5, 3,750 molding machine-hours × $50				187,500	12.50	
20	Shipment setup						
21	S3, 750 shipment setup hours × $54	40,500	0.67				} 81,000
22	C5, 750 shipment setup hours × $54				40,500	2.70	
23	Distribution						
24	S3, 45,000 cubic feet delivered × $5.80	261,000	4.35				} 391,500
25	C5, 22,500 cubic feet delivered × $5.80				130,500	8.70	
26	Administration						
27	S3, 30,000 dir. manuf. labor-hours × $6.4151	192,453	3.21				} 255,000
28	C5, 9,750 dir. manuf. labor-hours × $6.4151				62,547	4.17	
29	Total indirect costs allocated (Step 6)	1,153,953	19.23		961,047	64.07	2,115,000
30	Total Costs (Step 7)	$2,998,953	$49.98		$1,981,047	$132.07	$4,980,000
31							

shipments is more time consuming than preparing shipments to the local plant in Indiana because of additional documents related to customs, taxes, and insurance. The following table shows the budgeted number of shipments of S3 and C5 lenses to each plant.

	Mexico Plant Shipments	Indiana Plant Shipments	Total Shipments
Simple S3 lens shipments	10	100	110
Complex C5 lens shipments	30	60	90
			200

Each shipment to the Mexico plant requires 12.5 hours of the shipment department personnel's time while each shipment to the Indiana plant requires half that time, 6.25 hours. The following table indicates the budgeted shipping setup-hours for the S3 and C5 lenses.

	Shipment Setup-Hours for Mexico Plant	Shipment Setup-Hours for Indiana Plant	Total Shipment Setup-Hours
Simple S3 lens shipment setup-hours (12.5 hours × 10; 6.25 hours × 100)	125	625	750
Complex C5 lens shipment setup-hours (12.5 hours × 30; 6.25 hours × 60)	375	375	750
			1,500

The budgeted indirect-cost rate is $54 per shipment setup-hour (Exhibit 5-4, column 5, line 7). Therefore, lines 21 and 22 in Exhibit 5-5 show that the total budgeted cost of the shipment setup activity allocated to the S3 lens is $40,500 (750 shipment setup-hours × $54 per shipment setup-hour) and to the C5 lens is $40,500 (750 shipment setup-hours × $54 per shipment setup-hour). Budgeted setup cost per unit equals $0.67 ($40,500 ÷ 60,000 units) for the S3 lens and $2.70 ($40,500 ÷ 15,000 units) for the C5 lens.

Costing for shipment setups using shipment setup-hours as the cost driver is another example of time-driven activity-based costing (TDABC) because it leverages the time taken for different activities within a cost pool. TDABC allows Plastim's managers to account for different complexities of shipments of S3 and C5 lenses. Notice that if Plastim had ignored the complexity of different shipments and allocated costs to lenses based only on the number of shipments, it would have calculated a budgeted indirect-cost rate of $405 per shipment in Exhibit 5-4 ($81,000 ÷ 200 shipments). Using this rate the total budgeted cost of the shipment setup activity allocated to the S3 lens is $44,550 (110 shipments × $405 per shipment) and to the C5 lens is $36,450 (90 shipments × $54 per shipment). The budgeted setup cost per unit equals $0.74 ($44,550 ÷ 60,000 units) for the S3 lens and $2.43 ($36,450 ÷ 15,000 units) for the C5 lens. Using the number of shipments, rather than shipment setup-hours, as the cost driver would overcost the simple S3 lens and undercost the complex C5 lens.

Step 7: Compute the Total Cost of the Products by Adding All Direct and Indirect Costs Assigned to the Products. Exhibit 5-5 presents the product costs for the simple and complex lenses. The direct costs are calculated in Step 2, and the indirect costs are calculated in Step 6. The ABC system overview in Exhibit 5-3 shows three direct-cost categories and six indirect-cost categories. The budgeted cost of each lens type in Exhibit 5-5 has nine line items, three for direct costs and six for indirect costs. The differences between the ABC product costs of S3 and C5 calculated in Exhibit 5-5 highlight how each of these products uses different amounts of direct and indirect costs in each activity area.

TRY IT! **5-2**

Amherst Metal Works produces two types of metal lamps. Amherst manufactures 20,000 basic lamps and 5,000 designer lamps. Its activity-based costing system uses two indirect-cost pools. One cost pool is for setup costs and the other for general manufacturing overhead. Amherst allocates setup costs to the two lamps based on setup labor-hours and general manufacturing overhead costs on the basis of direct manufacturing labor-hours. It provides the following budgeted cost information:

	Basic Lamps	Designer Lamps	Total
Direct materials per lamp	$9	$15	
Direct manufacturing labor-hours per lamp	0.5 hours	0.6 hours	
Direct manufacturing labor rate per hour	$20	$20	
Setup costs			$114,000
Lamps produced per batch	250	50	
Setup-hours per batch	1 hour	3 hours	
General manufacturing overhead costs			$120,000

Calculate the total budgeted costs of the basic and designer lamps using Amherst's activity-based costing system.

We emphasize two features of ABC systems. First, these systems identify all costs used by products, whether the costs are variable or fixed in the short run. When making long-run strategic decisions using ABC information, managers want revenues to exceed total costs. Otherwise, a company will make losses and will be unable to continue in business. Second, recognizing the hierarchy of costs is critical when allocating costs to products. Management accountants use the cost hierarchy to first calculate the total costs of each product. They then derive per-unit costs by dividing total costs by the number of units produced.

DECISION POINT

How do managers cost products or services using ABC systems?

Comparing Alternative Costing Systems

Exhibit 5-6 compares the simple costing system using a single indirect-cost pool (Exhibits 5-1 and 5-2) that Plastim had been using and the ABC system (Exhibits 5-3 and 5-5). Note three points in Exhibit 5-6, consistent with the guidelines for refining a costing system: (1) ABC systems trace more costs as direct costs; (2) ABC systems create homogeneous cost pools linked to different activities; and (3) for each activity-cost pool, ABC systems seek a cost-allocation base that has a cause-and-effect relationship with costs in the cost pool.

The homogeneous cost pools and the choice of cost-allocation bases, tied to the cost hierarchy, give Plastim's managers greater confidence in the activity and product cost numbers from the ABC system. The bottom part of Exhibit 5-6 shows that allocating costs to lenses

| **EXHIBIT 5-6** | Comparing Alternative Costing Systems |

	Simple Costing System Using a Single Indirect-Cost Pool (1)	ABC System (2)	Difference (3) = (2) − (1)
Direct-cost categories	2	3	1
	Direct materials	Direct materials	
	Direct manufacturing labor	Direct manufacturing labor	
		Direct mold cleaning and maintenance labor	
Total direct costs	$2,595,000	$2,865,000	$270,000
Indirect-cost pools	1	6	5
	Single indirect-cost pool allocated using direct manufacturing labor-hours	Design (parts-square feet)[1]	
		Molding machine setup (setup-hours)	
		Machine operations (molding machine-hours)	
		Shipment setup (shipment setup-hours)	
		Distribution (cubic feet delivered)	
		Administration (direct manufacturing labor-hours)	
Total indirect costs	$2,385,000	$2,115,000	($270,000)
Total costs assigned to simple (S3) lens	$3,525,000	$2,998,953	($526,047)
Cost per unit of simple (S3) lens	$58.75	$49.98	($8.77)
Total costs assigned to complex (C5) lens	$1,455,000	$1,981,047	$526,047
Cost per unit of complex (C5) lens	$97.00	$132.07	$35.07

[1]Cost drivers for the various indirect-cost pools are shown in parentheses.

using only an output unit–level allocation base—direct manufacturing labor-hours, as in the single indirect-cost pool system used prior to ABC—overcosts the simple S3 lens by $8.77 per unit and undercosts the complex C5 lens by $35.07 per unit. The C5 lens uses a disproportionately larger amount of output unit–level, batch-level, and product-sustaining costs than is represented by the direct manufacturing labor-hour cost-allocation base. The S3 lens uses a disproportionately smaller amount of these costs.

The benefit of an ABC system is that it provides information to make better decisions. But managers must weigh this benefit against the measurement and implementation costs of an ABC system.

Considerations in Implementing Activity-Based Costing Systems

Managers choose the level of detail to use in a costing system by evaluating the expected costs of the system against the expected benefits that result from better decisions.

Benefits and Costs of Activity-Based Costing Systems

Here are some of the telltale signs when an ABC system is likely to provide the most benefits:

- Significant amounts of indirect costs are allocated using only one or two cost pools.
- All or most indirect costs are identified as output unit–level costs (few indirect costs are described as batch-level costs, product-sustaining costs, or facility-sustaining costs).
- Products make diverse demands on resources because of differences in volume, process steps, batch size, or complexity.
- Products that a company is well suited to make and sell show small profits; whereas products that a company is less suited to make and sell show large profits.
- Operations staff has substantial disagreement with the reported costs of manufacturing and marketing products and services.

When managers decide to implement ABC, they must make important choices about the level of detail to use. Should managers choose many finely specified activities, cost drivers, and cost pools, or would a few suffice? For example, Plastim's managers could identify a different molding machine-hour rate for each different type of molding machine. In making such choices, managers weigh the benefits against the costs and limitations of implementing a more detailed costing system.

The main costs and limitations of an ABC system are the measurements necessary to implement it. ABC systems require managers to estimate costs of activity pools and to identify and measure cost drivers for these pools to serve as cost-allocation bases. Even basic ABC systems require many calculations to determine costs of products and services. These measurements are costly. Activity-cost rates also need to be updated regularly.

As ABC systems get very detailed and more cost pools are created, more allocations are necessary to calculate activity costs for each cost pool, which increases the chances of misidentifying the costs of different activity cost pools. For example, supervisors are more prone to incorrectly identify the time they spend on different activities if they have to allocate their time over five activities rather than only two activities.

Occasionally, managers are also forced to use allocation bases for which data are readily available rather than allocation bases they would have liked to use. For example, a manager might be forced to use the number of loads moved, instead of the degree of difficulty and distance of different loads moved, as the allocation base for material-handling costs because data on degree of difficulty and distance of moves are difficult to obtain. When incorrect cost-allocation bases are used, activity-cost information can be misleading. For example, if the cost per load moved decreases, a company may conclude that it has become more efficient in its materials-handling operations. In fact, the lower cost per load moved may have resulted solely from moving many lighter loads over shorter distances.

Many companies, such as Kanthal, a Swedish heating elements manufacturer, have found the strategic and operational benefits of a less-detailed ABC system to be good enough to not warrant incurring the costs and challenges of operating a more detailed system. Other organizations, such as Hewlett-Packard, have implemented ABC in only certain divisions (such as the Roseville Networks Division, which manufactures printed circuit boards) or functions (such as procurement and production). As improvements in information technology and accompanying declines in measurement costs continue, more detailed ABC systems have become a practical alternative in many companies. As these advancements become more widespread, more detailed ABC systems will be better able to pass the cost–benefit test.

Global surveys of company practice suggest that ABC implementation varies among companies. Nevertheless, its framework and ideas provide a standard for judging whether any simple costing system is good enough for a particular management's purposes. ABC thinking can help managers improve any simple costing system.

Behavioral Issues in Implementing Activity-Based Costing Systems

Successfully implementing ABC systems requires more than an understanding of the technical details. ABC implementation often represents a significant change in the costing system and, as the chapter indicates, requires a manager to choose how to define activities and the level of detail. What then are some of the behavioral issues to which managers and management accountants must be sensitive?

1. **Gaining support of top management and creating a sense of urgency for the ABC effort.** This requires managers and management accountants to clearly communicate the strategic benefits of ABC, such as improvements in product and process design. For example, at USAA Federal Savings Bank, managers calculated the cost of individual activities such as opening and closing accounts and demonstrated how the information gained from ABC provided insights into ways of improving the efficiency of bank operations that were previously unavailable.

2. **Creating a guiding coalition of managers throughout the value chain for the ABC effort.** ABC systems measure how the resources of an organization are used. Managers responsible for these resources have the best knowledge about activities and cost drivers. Getting managers to cooperate and take the initiative for implementing ABC is essential for gaining the required expertise, the proper credibility, greater commitment, valuable coordination, and the necessary leadership.

3. **Educating and training employees in ABC as a basis for employee empowerment.** Management accountants must disseminate information about ABC throughout the organization to enable employees in all areas of a business to use their knowledge of ABC to make improvements. For example, WS Industries, an Indian manufacturer of insulators, not only shared ABC information with its workers but also established an incentive plan that gave them a percentage of the cost savings. The results were dramatic because employees were empowered and motivated to implement numerous cost-saving projects.

4. **Seeking small short-run successes as proof that the ABC implementation is yielding results.** Too often, managers and management accountants seek big results and major changes far too quickly. In many situations, achieving a significant change overnight is difficult. However, showing how ABC information has helped improve a process and save costs, even if only in small ways, motivates the team to stay on course and build momentum. The credibility gained from small victories leads to additional and bigger improvements involving larger numbers of people and different parts of the organization. Eventually ABC becomes rooted in the culture of the organization. Sharing short-term successes also helps motivate employees to be innovative. At USAA Federal Savings Bank, managers created a "process improvement" mailbox in Microsoft Outlook to facilitate the sharing of process improvement ideas.

DECISION
POINT

What should managers
consider when deciding to
implement ABC systems?

5. **Recognizing that ABC information is not perfect because it balances the need for better information against the costs of creating a complex system that few managers and employees can understand.** The management accountant must help managers recognize both the value and the limitations of ABC and not oversell it. Open and honest communication about ABC ensures that managers use ABC thoughtfully to make good decisions. Managers can then make critical judgments without being adversarial and can ask tough questions to help drive better decisions about the system.

Activity-Based Management

LEARNING
OBJECTIVE 7

Explain how managers
use activity-based costing
systems in activity-based
management

...such as pricing deci-
sions, product-mix deci-
sions, and cost reduction

The emphasis of this chapter so far has been on the role of ABC systems in obtaining better product costs. However, Plastim's managers must now use this information to make decisions (Step 4 of the five-step decision process, page 178) and to implement the decision, evaluate performance, and learn (Step 5, page 178). **Activity-based management (ABM)** is a method of management decision making that uses activity-based costing information to improve customer satisfaction and profitability. We define ABM broadly to include decisions about pricing and product mix, cost reduction, process improvement, and product and process design.

Pricing and Product-Mix Decisions

An ABC system gives managers information about the costs of making and selling diverse products. With this information, managers can make pricing and product-mix decisions. For example, the ABC system indicates that Plastim can match its competitor's price of $53 for the S3 lens and still make a profit because the ABC cost of S3 is $49.98 (see Exhibit 5-5).

Plastim's managers offer Giovanni Motors a price of $52 for the S3 lens. Plastim's managers are confident that they can use the deeper understanding of costs that the ABC system provides to improve efficiency and further reduce the cost of the S3 lens. Without information from the ABC system, Plastim managers might have erroneously concluded that they would incur an operating loss on the S3 lens at a price of $53. This incorrect conclusion would have probably caused Plastim to reduce or exit its business in simple lenses and focus instead on complex lenses, where its single indirect-cost-pool system indicated it is very profitable.

Focusing on complex lenses would have been a mistake. The ABC system indicates that the cost of making the complex lens is much higher—$132.07 versus $97 indicated by the direct manufacturing labor-hour-based costing system Plastim had been using. As Plastim's operations staff had thought all along, Plastim has no competitive advantage in making C5 lenses. At a price of $137 per lens for C5, the profit margin is very small ($137.00 − $132.07 = $4.93). As Plastim reduces its prices on simple lenses, it would need to negotiate a higher price for complex lenses while also reducing costs.

Cost Reduction and Process Improvement Decisions

Managers use ABC systems to focus on how and where to reduce costs. They set cost reduction targets for the cost per unit of the cost-allocation base in different activity areas. For example, the supervisor of the distribution activity area at Plastim could have a performance target of decreasing distribution cost per cubic foot of products delivered from $5.80 to $5.40 by reducing distribution labor and warehouse rental costs. The goal is to reduce these costs by improving the way work is done without compromising customer service or the actual or perceived value (usefulness) customers obtain from the product or service. That is, the supervisor will attempt to take out only those costs that are *nonvalue added*.

Controlling cost drivers, such as setup-hours or cubic feet delivered, is another fundamental way that operating personnel manage costs. For example, the distribution department can decrease distribution costs by packing the lenses in a way that reduces the bulkiness of the packages delivered.

The following table shows the reduction in distribution costs of the S3 and C5 lenses as a result of actions that lower cost per cubic foot delivered (from $5.80 to $5.40) and total cubic feet of deliveries (from 45,000 to 40,000 for S3 and 22,500 to 20,000 for C5).

	60,000 (S3) Lenses		15,000 (C5) Lenses	
	Total (1)	per Unit (2) = (1) ÷ 60,000	Total (3)	per Unit (4) = (3) ÷ 15,000
Distribution costs (from Exhibit 5-5)				
S3: 45,000 cubic feet × $5.80/cubic feet	$261,000	$4.35		
C5: 22,500 cubic feet × $5.80/cubic feet			$130,500	$8.70
Distribution costs as a result of process improvements				
S3: 40,000 cubic feet × $5.40/cubic feet	216,000	3.60		
C5: 20,000 cubic feet × $5.40/cubic feet			108,000	7.20
Savings in distribution costs from process improvements	$ 45,000	$0.75	$ 22,500	$1.50

In the long run, total distribution costs will decrease from $391,500 ($261,000 + $130,500) to $324,000 ($216,000 + $108,000). In the short run, however, distribution costs may be fixed and may not decrease. Suppose all $391,500 of distribution costs are fixed costs in the short run. The efficiency improvements (using less distribution labor and space) mean that the same $391,500 of distribution costs can now be used to distribute $72,500 \left(= \dfrac{\$391,500}{\$5.40 \text{ per cubic feet}} \right)$ cubic feet of lenses compared to the 67,500 cubic feet of lenses it currently distributes (see Exhibit 5-4). In this case, how should costs be allocated to the S3 and C5 lenses?

ABC systems distinguish costs incurred from resources used to design, manufacture, and deliver products and services. For the distribution activity, after process improvements,

Costs incurred = $391,500

Resources used = $216,000 (for S3 lens) + $108,000 (for C5 lens) = $324,000

On the basis of the resources used by each product, Plastim's ABC system allocates $216,000 to S3 and $108,000 to C5 for a total of $324,000. The difference of $67,500 ($391,500 − $324,000) is shown as costs of unused but available distribution capacity. Plastim's ABC system does not allocate the costs of unused capacity to products so as not to burden the product costs of S3 and C5 with the cost of resources not used by these products. Instead, the system highlights the amount of unused capacity as a separate line item to alert managers to reduce these costs, such as by redeploying labor to other uses or laying off workers. Chapter 9 discusses issues related to unused capacity in more detail.

Design Decisions

ABC systems help managers to evaluate the effect of current product and process designs on activities and costs and to identify new designs to reduce costs. For example, design decisions that decrease the complexity of the mold reduce costs of design, but also materials, labor, machine setups, machine operations, and mold cleaning and maintenance because a less-complex design reduces scrap and the time for setups and operations of the molding machine. Plastim's customers may be willing to give up some features of the lens in exchange for a lower price. Note that Plastim's previous costing system, which used direct manufacturing labor-hours as the cost-allocation base for all indirect costs, would have mistakenly signaled that Plastim choose designs that most reduce direct manufacturing labor-hours. In fact, there is a weak cause-and-effect relationship between direct manufacturing labor-hours and indirect costs.

Planning and Managing Activities

Most managers implementing ABC systems for the first time start by analyzing actual costs to identify activity-cost pools and activity-cost rates. Managers then calculate a budgeted rate (as in the Plastim example) that they use for planning, making decisions, and managing activities. At year-end, managers compare budgeted costs and actual costs to evaluate how well activities were managed. Management accountants make adjustments for underallocated or overallocated indirect costs for each activity using methods described in Chapter 4. As activities and processes change, managers calculate new activity-cost rates.

We return to activity-based management in later chapters. Management decisions that use activity-based costing information are described in Chapter 6, where we discuss activity-based budgeting; in Chapter 11, where we discuss outsourcing and adding or dropping business segments; in Chapter 12, where we present reengineering and downsizing; in Chapter 13, where we evaluate alternative design choices to improve efficiency and reduce nonvalue-added costs; in Chapter 14, where we explore managing customer profitability; in Chapter 19, where we explain quality improvements; and in Chapter 20, where we describe how to evaluate suppliers.

DECISION POINT

How can ABC systems be used to manage better?

Activity-Based Costing and Department Costing Systems

LEARNING OBJECTIVE 8

Compare activity-based costing systems and department costing systems

...activity-based costing systems refine department costing systems into more-focused and homogenous cost pools

Companies often use costing systems that have features of ABC systems—such as multiple cost pools and multiple cost-allocation bases—but that do not emphasize individual activities. Many companies have evolved their costing systems from using a single indirect cost rate system to using separate indirect cost rates for each department (such as design, manufacturing, and distribution) or each subdepartment (such as machining and assembly departments within manufacturing) that often represent broad tasks. ABC systems, with their focus on specific activities, are a further refinement of department costing systems. In this section, we compare ABC systems and department costing systems.

Plastim uses the design department indirect cost rate to cost its design activity. To do so Plastim calculates the design activity rate by dividing total design department costs by total parts-square feet, a measure of the complexity of the mold and the driver of design department costs. Plastim does not find it worthwhile to calculate separate activity rates within the design department for the different design activities, such as designing products, making temporary molds, and designing processes. The complexity of a mold is an appropriate cost-allocation base for costs incurred in each design activity because design department costs are homogeneous with respect to this cost-allocation base.

In contrast, the manufacturing department identifies two activity cost pools—a setup cost pool and a machine operations cost pool—instead of a single manufacturing department overhead cost pool. It identifies these activity-cost pools for two reasons. First, each of these activities within manufacturing incurs significant costs and has a different cost driver, setup-hours for the setup cost pool and machine-hours for the machine operations cost pool. Second, the S3 and C5 lenses do not use resources from these two activity areas in the same proportion. For example, C5 uses 75% (1,500 ÷ 2,000) of the setup-hours but only 29.4% (3,750 ÷ 12,750) of the machine-hours. Using only machine-hours, say, to allocate all manufacturing department costs at Plastim would result in C5 being undercosted because it would not be charged for the significant amounts of setup resources it actually uses.

For the reasons we just explained, using department indirect-cost rates to allocate costs to products results in similar information as activity cost rates if (1) a single activity accounts for a sizable proportion of the department's costs; or (2) significant costs are incurred on different activities within a department, but each activity has the same cost driver and therefore cost-allocation base (as was the case in Plastim's design department). From a purely product costing standpoint, department and activity indirect-cost rates will also result in the same product costs if (1) significant costs are incurred for different activities with different cost-allocation bases within a department but (2) different products use resources from the different activity areas in the same proportions (for example, if C5 had used 65%, say, of the setup-hours and 65% of the machine-hours). In this case, though, not identifying activities and cost drivers within departments conceals activity cost information that would help managers manage costs and improve design and processes.

We close this section with a note of caution: Do not assume that because department costing systems require the creation of multiple indirect-cost pools that they properly recognize the drivers of costs within departments as well as how resources are used by products. As we have indicated, in many situations, department costing systems can be refined using ABC. Emphasizing activities leads to more-focused and homogeneous cost pools, aids in identifying cost-allocation bases for activities that have a better cause-and-effect relationship with the costs in activity-cost pools, and leads to better design and process decisions. But these benefits of an ABC system would need to be balanced against its costs and limitations.

DECISION POINT
When can department costing systems be used instead of ABC systems?

ABC in Service and Merchandising Companies

Although many early examples of ABC originated in manufacturing, managers also use ABC in service and merchandising companies. For instance, the Plastim example includes the application of ABC to a service activity—design—and to a merchandising activity—distribution. Companies such as USAA Federal Savings Bank, Braintree Hospital, BCTel in the telecommunications industry, and Union Pacific in the railroad industry have implemented some form of ABC system to identify profitable product mixes, improve efficiency, and satisfy customers. Similarly, many retail and wholesale companies—for example, Supervalu, a retailer and distributor of grocery store products, and Owens and Minor, a medical supplies distributor—have used ABC systems. As we describe in Chapter 14, a large number of financial services companies (as well as other companies) employ variations of ABC systems to analyze and improve the profitability of their customer interactions.

The widespread use of ABC systems in service and merchandising companies reinforces the idea that ABC systems are used by managers for strategic decisions rather than for inventory valuation. (Inventory valuation is fairly straightforward in merchandising companies and not needed in service companies.) Service companies, in particular, find great value from ABC because a vast majority of their cost structure is composed of indirect costs. After all, there are few direct costs when a bank makes a loan or when a representative answers a phone call at a call center. As we have seen, a major benefit of ABC is its ability to assign indirect costs to cost objects by identifying activities and cost drivers. As a result, ABC systems provide greater insight than traditional systems into the management of these indirect costs. The general approach to ABC in service and merchandising companies is similar to the ABC approach in manufacturing.

USAA Federal Savings Bank followed the approach described in this chapter when it implemented ABC in its banking operations. Managers calculated the cost rates of various activities, such as performing ATM transactions, opening and closing accounts, administering mortgages, and processing Visa transactions by dividing the cost of these activities by the time available to do them. Managers used these time-based rates to cost individual products, such as checking accounts, mortgages, and Visa cards, and to calculate the costs of supporting different types of customers. Information from this time-driven activity-based costing system helped USAA Federal Savings Bank to improve its processes and to identify profitable products and customer segments. Concepts in Action: Mayo Clinic Uses Time-Driven Activity-Based Costing to Reduce Costs and Improve Care describes how the Mayo Clinic has similarly benefited from ABC analysis.

Activity-based costing raises some interesting issues when it is applied to a public service institution, such as the U.S. Postal Service. The costs of delivering mail to remote locations are far greater than the costs of delivering mail within urban areas. However, for fairness and community-building reasons, the Postal Service does not charge higher prices to customers in remote areas. In this case, activity-based costing is valuable for understanding, managing, and reducing costs but not for pricing decisions.

CONCEPTS IN ACTION ▶ Mayo Clinic Uses Time-Driven Activity-Based Costing to Reduce Costs and Improve Care

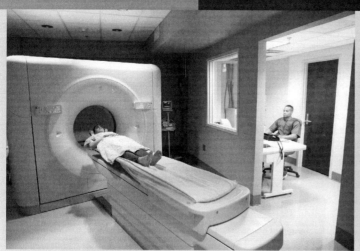

Fuse/Corbis/Getty Images

By 2024, $1 of every $5 spent in the United States will be on health care. Several medical centers, such as the Mayo Clinic in Rochester, Minnesota, are using time-driven activity-based costing (TDABC) to help bring accurate cost and value measurement practices into the health care delivery system.

TDABC assigns all of the organization's resource costs to cost objects using a framework that requires two sets of estimates. TDABC first calculates the cost of supplying resource capacity, such as a doctor's time. The total cost of resources—including personnel, supervision, insurance, space occupancy, technology, and supplies—is divided by the available capacity—the time available for doctors to do their work—to obtain the capacity cost rate. Next, TDABC uses the capacity cost rate to drive resource costs to cost objects, such as the number of patients seen, by estimating the demand for resource capacity (time) that the cost object requires.

Medical centers implementing TDABC have succeeded in reducing costs. For orthopedic procedures at the Mayo Clinic, the TDABC-modified process resulted in shorter stays for patients, a 24% decrease in patients discharged to expensive skilled nursing facilities, and a 15% decrease in cost. Follow-on improvements have included obtaining patient-reported outcomes from tablets and smartphones and eliminating major variations in the cost of prostheses and other supplies.

More broadly, health care providers implementing TDABC have found that better outcomes for patients often go hand in hand with lower total costs. For example, spending more on early detection and better diagnosis of disease reduces patient suffering and often leads to less-complex and less-expensive care. With the insights from TDABC, health care providers can utilize medical staff, equipment, facilities, and administrative resources far more efficiently; streamline the path of patients through the system; and select treatment approaches that improve outcomes while eliminating services that do not.

Sources: Derek A. Haas, Richard A. Helmers, March Rucci, Meredith Brady, and Robert S. Kaplan, "The Mayo Clinic Model for Running a Value-Improvement Program," HBR.org, October 22, 2015 (https://hbr.org/2015/10/the-mayo-clinic-model-for-running-a-value-improvement-program); Dan Mangan, "$1 of Every $5 Spent in US Will Be on Health Care," CNBC, July 28, 2015 (http://www.cnbc.com/2015/07/28/1-of-every-5-spent-in-us-will-be-on-health-care.html); Robert S. Kaplan and Michael E. Porter, "How to Solve the Cost Crisis in Health Care," *Harvard Business Review*, September 2011 (https://hbr.org/2011/09/how-to-solve-the-cost-crisis-in-health-care); Robert S. Kaplan and Steven R. Anderson, "The Innovation of Time-Driven Activity-Based Costing," *Journal of Cost Management*, 21, no. 2 (March-April 2007): 5–15.

PROBLEM FOR SELF-STUDY

Family Supermarkets (FS) has decided to increase the size of its Memphis store. It wants information about the profitability of individual product lines: soft drinks, fresh produce, and packaged food. FS provides the following data for 2017 for each product line:

	Soft Drinks	Fresh Produce	Packaged Food
Revenues	$317,400	$840,240	$483,960
Cost of goods sold	$240,000	$600,000	$360,000
Cost of bottles returned	$ 4,800	$ 0	$ 0
Number of purchase orders placed	144	336	144
Number of deliveries received	120	876	264
Hours of shelf-stocking time	216	2,160	1,080
Items sold	50,400	441,600	122,400

FS also provides the following information for 2017:

Activity (1)	Description of Activity (2)	Total Support Costs (3)	Cost-Allocation Base (4)
1. Bottle returns	Returning of empty bottles to store	$ 4,800	Direct tracing to soft-drink line
2. Ordering	Placing of orders for purchases	$ 62,400	624 purchase orders
3. Delivery	Physical delivery and receipt of merchandise	$100,800	1,260 deliveries
4. Shelf-stocking	Stocking of merchandise on store shelves and ongoing restocking	$ 69,120	3,456 hours of shelf-stocking time
5. Customer support	Assistance provided to customers, including checkout and bagging	$122,880	614,400 items sold
Total		$360,000	

Required

1. Family Supermarkets currently allocates store support costs (all costs other than cost of goods sold) to product lines on the basis of cost of goods sold of each product line. Calculate the operating income and operating income as a percentage of revenues for each product line.
2. If Family Supermarkets allocates store support costs (all costs other than cost of goods sold) to product lines using an ABC system, calculate the operating income and operating income as a percentage of revenues for each product line.
3. Comment on your answers in requirements 1 and 2.

Solution

1. The following table shows the operating income and operating income as a percentage of revenues for each product line. All store support costs (all costs other than cost of goods sold) are allocated to product lines using cost of goods sold of each product line as the cost-allocation base. Total store support costs equal $360,000 (cost of bottles returned, $4,800 + cost of purchase orders, $62,400 + cost of deliveries, $100,800 + cost of shelf-stocking, $69,120 + cost of customer support, $122,880). The allocation rate for store support costs = $360,000 ÷ $1,200,000 (soft drinks $240,000 + fresh produce $600,000 + packaged food, $360,000) = 30% of cost of goods sold. To allocate support costs to each product line, FS multiplies the cost of goods sold of each product line by 0.30.

	Soft Drinks	Fresh Produce	Packaged Food	Total
Revenues	$317,400	$840,240	$483,960	$1,641,600
Cost of goods sold	240,000	600,000	360,000	1,200,000
Store support cost ($240,000; $600,000; $360,000) × 0.30	72,000	180,000	108,000	360,000
Total costs	312,000	780,000	468,000	1,560,000
Operating income	$ 5,400	$ 60,240	$ 15,960	$ 81,600
Operating income ÷ Revenues	1.70%	7.17%	3.30%	4.97%

2. The ABC system identifies bottle-return costs as a direct cost because these costs can be traced to the soft-drink product line. FS then calculates cost-allocation rates for each activity area (as in Step 5 of the seven-step costing system, described earlier on page 186). The activity rates are as follows.

Activity (1)	Cost Hierarchy (2)	Total Costs (3)	Quantity of Cost-Allocation Base (4)	Overhead Allocation Rate (5) = (3) ÷ (4)
Ordering	Batch-level	$ 62,400	624 purchase orders	$100 per purchase order
Delivery	Batch-level	$100,800	1,260 deliveries	$80 per delivery
Shelf-stocking	Output unit-level	$ 69,120	3,456 shelf-stocking hours	$20 per stocking-hour
Customer support	Output unit-level	$122,880	614,400 items sold	$0.20 per item sold

Store support costs for each product line by activity are obtained by multiplying the total quantity of the cost-allocation base for each product line by the activity-cost rate. Operating income and operating income as a percentage of revenues for each product line are as follows:

	Soft Drinks	Fresh Produce	Packaged Food	Total
Revenues	$317,400	$840,240	$483,960	$1,641,600
Cost of goods sold	240,000	600,000	360,000	1,200,000
Bottle-return costs	4,800	0	0	4,800
Ordering costs	14,400	33,600	14,400	62,400
(144; 336; 144) purchase orders × $100				
Delivery costs				
(120; 876; 264) deliveries × $80	9,600	70,080	21,120	100,800
Shelf-stocking costs	4,320	43,200	21,600	69,120
(216; 2,160; 1,080) stocking-hours × $20				
Customer-support costs				
(50,400; 441,600; 122,400) items sold × $0.20	10,080	88,320	24,480	122,880
Total costs	283,200	835,200	441,600	1,560,000
Operating income	$ 34,200	$ 5,040	$ 42,360	$ 81,600
Operating income ÷ Revenues	10.78%	0.60%	8.75%	4.97%

3. Managers believe the ABC system is more credible than the simple costing system. The ABC system distinguishes the different types of activities at FS more precisely. It also tracks more accurately how individual product lines use resources. Rankings of relative profitability—operating income as a percentage of revenues—of the three product lines under the simple costing system and under the ABC system are as follows.

Simple Costing System		ABC System	
1. Fresh produce	7.17%	1. Soft drinks	10.78%
2. Packaged food	3.30%	2. Packaged food	8.75%
3. Soft drinks	1.70%	3. Fresh produce	0.60%

The percentage of revenues, cost of goods sold, and activity costs for each product line are as follows.

	Soft Drinks	Fresh Produce	Packaged Food
Revenues	19.34%	51.18%	29.48%
Cost of goods sold	20.00	50.00	30.00
Bottle returns	100.00	0	0
Activity areas:			
Ordering	23.08	53.84	23.08
Delivery	9.53	69.52	20.95
Shelf-stocking	6.25	62.50	31.25
Customer support	8.20	71.88	19.92

Soft drinks have fewer deliveries and require less shelf-stocking time and customer support than either fresh produce or packaged food. Most major soft-drink suppliers deliver merchandise to the store shelves and stock the shelves themselves. In contrast, the fresh produce area has the most deliveries and consumes a large percentage of shelf-stocking time. It also has the highest number of individual sales items and so requires the most customer support. The simple costing system assumed that each product line used the resources in each activity area in the same ratio as their respective individual cost of goods sold to total cost of goods sold. Clearly, this assumption is incorrect. Relative to cost of goods sold, soft drinks and packaged food use fewer resources while fresh produce uses more resources. As a result, the ABC system reduces the costs assigned to soft drinks and packaged food and increases the costs assigned to fresh produce. The simple costing system is an example of averaging that is too broad.

FS managers can use the ABC information to guide decisions such as how to allocate a planned increase in floor space. An increase in the percentage of space allocated to soft drinks is warranted. Note, however, that ABC information is only one input into decisions about shelf-space allocation. In many situations, companies cannot make product decisions in isolation but must consider the effect that dropping or de-emphasizing a product might have on customer demand for other products. For example, FS will have a minimum limit on the shelf space allocated to fresh produce because reducing the choice of fresh produce will lead to customers not shopping at FS, resulting in loss of sales of other, more profitable products.

Pricing decisions can also be made in a more informed way with ABC information. For example, suppose a competitor announces a 5% reduction in soft-drink prices. Given the 10.78% margin FS currently earns on its soft-drink product line, it has flexibility to reduce prices and still make a profit on this product line. In contrast, the simple costing system erroneously implied that soft drinks only had a 1.70% margin, leaving little room to counter a competitor's pricing initiatives.

DECISION **POINTS**

The following question-and-answer format summarizes the chapter's learning objectives. Each decision presents a key question related to a learning objective. The guidelines are the answer to that question.

Decision	Guidelines
1. When does product undercosting or overcosting occur?	Product undercosting (overcosting) occurs when a product or service is reported to have a low (high) cost but consumes a high (low) level of resources. Broad averaging, or peanut-butter costing, a common cause of undercosting or overcosting, is the result of using broad averages that uniformly assign, or spread, the cost of resources to products when the individual products use those resources in a nonuniform way. Product-cost cross-subsidization exists when one undercosted (overcosted) product results in at least one other product being overcosted (undercosted).
2. How do managers refine a costing system?	Refining a costing system means making changes that result in cost numbers better measuring the way different cost objects, such as products, use different amounts of resources of the company. These changes can require additional direct-cost tracing, the choice of more-homogeneous indirect-cost pools, or the use of cost drivers as cost-allocation bases.
3. What is the difference between the design of a simple costing system and an activity-based costing (ABC) system?	The ABC system differs from the simple system by its fundamental focus on activities. The ABC system typically has more homogeneous indirect-cost pools than the simple system, and more cost drivers are used as cost-allocation bases.
4. What is a cost hierarchy?	A cost hierarchy categorizes costs into different cost pools on the basis of the different types of cost-allocation bases or different degrees of difficulty in determining cause-and-effect (or benefits-received) relationships. A four-part hierarchy to cost products consists of output unit–level costs, batch-level costs, product-sustaining or service-sustaining costs, and facility-sustaining costs.
5. How do managers cost products or services using ABC systems?	In ABC, costs of activities are used to assign costs to other cost objects such as products or services based on the activities the products or services consume.

Decision	Guidelines
6. What should managers consider when deciding to implement ABC systems?	ABC systems are likely to yield the most decision-making benefits when indirect costs are a high percentage of total costs or when products and services make diverse demands on indirect resources. The main costs of ABC systems are the difficulties of the measurements necessary to implement and update the systems.
7. How can ABC systems be used to manage better?	Activity-based management (ABM) is a management method of decision making that uses ABC information to satisfy customers and improve profits. ABC systems are used for such management decisions as pricing, product-mix, cost reduction, process improvement, product and process redesign, and planning and managing activities.
8. When can department costing systems be used instead of ABC systems?	Activity-based costing systems are a refinement of department costing systems into more-focused and homogeneous cost pools. Cost information in department costing systems approximates cost information in ABC systems only when each department has a single activity (or a single activity accounts for a significant proportion of department costs) or a single cost driver for different activities or when different products use the different activities of the department in the same proportions.

TERMS TO LEARN

This chapter and the Glossary at the end of this book contain definitions of the following important terms:

activity (**p. 180**)
activity-based costing (ABC) (**p. 180**)
activity-based management (ABM) (**p. 192**)
batch-level costs (**p. 183**)

cost hierarchy (**p. 182**)
facility-sustaining costs (**p. 183**)
output unit–level costs (**p. 183**)
product-cost cross-subsidization (**p. 174**)

product overcosting (**p. 173**)
product-sustaining costs (**p. 183**)
product undercosting (**p. 173**)
refined costing system (**p. 178**)
service-sustaining costs (**p. 183**)

ASSIGNMENT MATERIAL

Questions

5-1 What is broad averaging, and what consequences can it have on costs?

5-2 Inaccurate costing can result in two deviations. Name the two deviations and explain how they can impact a business.

5-3 What is costing system refinement? Describe three guidelines for refinement.

5-4 What are the fundamental cost objects in activity-based costing? How does activity-based costing work?

5-5 How can a cost hierarchy lead to a more accurate costing system?

5-6 Which levels of cost hierarchy (under activity-based costing) are not used in simple costing systems and why are they important?

5-7 Differentiate between simple costing systems and ABC systems.

5-8 How can ABC help with cost reduction and process improvement decisions?

5-9 "The cost of cost objects under simple costing systems and under activity-based costing are never the same." Do you agree? Explain.

5-10 Describe the main barriers for adopting an ABC system.

5-11 What are the main behavioral issues in implementing ABC systems?

5-12 Explain why ABC is equally important for both manufacturing and service companies.

5-13 "Activity-based costing is providing more accurate and detailed information and should replace simple costing." Do you agree? Explain.

5-14 What are the main factors determining the number of indirect-cost pools in a costing system, to increase the accuracy of product or service costs? Explain.

5-15 The total annual production cost of a manufacturing company that produces three different USB devices is $10,000,000. The manager of the company states that the contribution margins of all three products guarantee and justify their productions and, therefore, there is no need to adopt ABC as the total manufacturing costs of the company would remain the same if the company did adopt ABC. How can you convince the manager to change his mind?

Multiple-Choice Questions

Pearson MyLab Accounting

In partnership with:

BECKER
PROFESSIONAL EDUCATION®

5-16 Conroe Company is reviewing the data provided by its management accounting system. Which of the following statements is/are correct?

I.   A cost driver is a causal factor that increases the total cost of a cost object.
II. Cost drivers may be volume based or activity based.
III. Cost drivers are normally the largest cost in the manufacturing process.

1. I, II, and III are correct.
2. I and II only are correct.
3. I only is correct.
4. II and III only are correct.

5-17 Nobis Company uses an ABC system. Which of the following statements is/are correct with respect to ABC?

I.   Departmental costing systems are a refinement of ABC systems.
II. ABC systems are useful in manufacturing, but not in merchandising or service industries.
III. ABC systems can eliminate cost distortions because ABC develops cost drivers that have a cause-and-effect relationship with the activities performed.

1. I, II, and III are correct.
2. II and III only are correct.
3. III only is correct.
4. None of the listed choices is correct.

Exercises

5-18 Cost hierarchy. SharpPitch, Inc., manufactures karaoke machines for several well-known companies. The machines differ significantly in their complexity and their manufacturing batch sizes. The following costs were incurred in 2014:

a. Indirect manufacturing labor costs such as supervision that supports direct manufacturing labor, $950,000.
b. Procurement costs of placing purchase orders, receiving materials, and paying suppliers related to the number of purchase orders placed, $675,000.
c. Cost of indirect materials, $180,000.
d. Costs incurred to set up machines each time a different product needs to be manufactured, $450,000.
e. Designing processes, drawing process charts, and making engineering process changes for products, $315,000.
f. Machine-related overhead costs such as depreciation, maintenance, and production engineering, $975,500. (These resources relate to the activity of running the machines.)
g. Plant management, plant rent, and plant insurance, $578,000.

Required

1. Classify each of the preceding costs as output unit-level, batch-level, product-sustaining, or facility-sustaining. Explain each answer.
2. Consider two types of karaoke machines made by SharpPitch, Inc. One machine, designed for professional use, is complex to make and is produced in many batches. The other machine, designed for home use, is simple to make and is produced in few batches. Suppose that SharpPitch needs the same number of machine-hours to make each type of karaoke machine and that SharpPitch allocates all overhead costs using machine-hours as the only allocation base. How, if at all, would the machines be miscosted? Briefly explain why.
3. How is the cost hierarchy helpful to SharpPitch in managing its business?

5-19 ABC, cost hierarchy, service. (CMA, adapted) CoreTech Laboratories does heat testing (HT) and stress testing (ST) on materials and operates at capacity. Under its current simple costing system, CoreTech aggregates all operating costs of $1,800,000 into a single overhead cost pool. CoreTech calculates a rate per test-hour of $20 ($1,800,000 ÷ 90,000 total test-hours). HT uses 50,000 test-hours, and ST uses 40,000 test-hours. Gary Celeste, CoreTech's controller, believes that there is enough variation in test procedures and cost structures to establish separate costing and billing rates for HT and ST. The market for test services is becoming competitive. Without this information, any miscosting and mispricing of its services could cause CoreTech to lose business. Celeste divides CoreTech's costs into four activity-cost categories.

a. Direct-labor costs, $276,000. These costs can be directly traced to HT, $204,000, and ST, $72,000.
b. Equipment-related costs (rent, maintenance, energy, and so on), $495,000. These costs are allocated to HT and ST on the basis of test-hours.
c. Setup costs, $630,000. These costs are allocated to HT and ST on the basis of the number of setup-hours required. HT requires 15,000 setup-hours, and ST requires 6,000 setup-hours.
d. Costs of designing tests, $399,000. These costs are allocated to HT and ST on the basis of the time required for designing the tests. HT requires 4,000 hours, and ST requires 2,000 hours.

Required

1. Classify each activity cost as output unit-level, batch-level, product- or service-sustaining, or facility-sustaining. Explain each answer.
2. Calculate the cost per test-hour for HT and ST. Explain briefly the reasons why these numbers differ from the $20 per test-hour that CoreTech calculated using its simple costing system.
3. Explain the accuracy of the product costs calculated using the simple costing system and the ABC system. How might CoreTech's management use the cost hierarchy and ABC information to better manage its business?

5-20 Alternative allocation bases for a professional services firm. The Walliston Group (WG) provides tax advice to multinational firms. WG charges clients for (a) direct professional time (at an hourly rate) and (b) support services (at 30% of the direct professional costs billed). The three professionals in WG and their rates per professional hour are as follows:

Professional	Billing Rate per Hour
Max Walliston	$640
Alexa Boutin	220
Jacob Abbington	100

WG has just prepared the May 2017 bills for two clients. The hours of professional time spent on each client are as follows:

	Hours per Client	
Professional	San Antonio Dominion	Amsterdam Enterprises
Walliston	26	4
Boutin	5	14
Abbington	39	52
Total	70	70

Required

1. What amounts did WG bill to San Antonio Dominion and Amsterdam Enterprises for May 2017?
2. Suppose support services were billed at $75 per professional labor-hour (instead of 30% of professional labor costs). How would this change affect the amounts WG billed to the two clients for May 2017? Comment on the differences between the amounts billed in requirements 1 and 2.
3. How would you determine whether professional labor costs or professional labor-hours is the more appropriate allocation base for WG's support services?

5-21 Plant-wide, department, and ABC indirect-cost rates. Automotive Products (AP) designs and produces automotive parts. In 2017, actual variable manufacturing overhead is $308,600. AP's simple costing system allocates variable manufacturing overhead to its three customers based on machine-hours and prices its contracts based on full costs. One of its customers has regularly complained of being charged noncompetitive prices, so AP's controller Devon Smith realizes that it is time to examine the consumption of overhead resources more closely. He knows that there are three main departments that consume overhead resources: design, production, and engineering. Interviews with the department personnel and examination of time records yield the following detailed information:

			Usage of Cost Drivers by Customer Contract		
			United	Holden	Leland
Department	**Cost Driver**	**Manufacturing Overhead in 2017**	**Motors**	**Motors**	**Auto**
Design	CAD–design–hours	$ 39,000	110	200	80
Production	Engineering–hours	29,600	70	60	240
Engineering	Machine–hours	240,000	120	2,800	1,080
Total		$308,600			

Required

1. Compute the manufacturing overhead allocated to each customer in 2017 using the simple costing system that uses machine-hours as the allocation base.
2. Compute the manufacturing overhead allocated to each customer in 2017 using department-based manufacturing overhead rates.
3. Comment on your answers in requirements 1 and 2. Which customer do you think was complaining about being overcharged in the simple system? If the new department-based rates are used to price contracts, which customer(s) will be unhappy? How would you respond to these concerns?
4. How else might AP use the information available from its department-by-department analysis of manufacturing overhead costs?
5. AP's managers are wondering if they should further refine the department-by-department costing system into an ABC system by identifying different activities within each department. Under what conditions would it not be worthwhile to further refine the department costing system into an ABC system?

5-22 Plant-wide, department, and activity-cost rates. Triumph Trophies makes trophies and plaques and operates at capacity. Triumph does large custom orders, such as the participant trophies for the Minnetonka Little League. The controller has asked you to compare plant-wide, department, and activity-based cost allocation.

Triumph Trophies Budgeted Information for the Year Ended November 30, 2014

Forming Department	Trophies	Plaques	Total
Direct materials	$26,000	$22,500	$48,500
Direct manufacturing labor	31,200	18,000	49,200
Overhead costs			
Setup			24,000
General overhead			20,772
Assembly Department	**Trophies**	**Plaques**	**Total**
Direct materials	$ 5,200	$18,750	$23,950
Direct manufacturing labor	15,600	21,000	36,600
Overhead costs			
Set up			46,000
Supervision			21,920

Other information follows:
Setup costs in each department vary with the number of batches processed in each department. The budgeted number of batches for each product line in each department is as follows:

	Trophies	Plaques
Forming department	40	116
Assembly department	43	103

Required

Supervision costs in each department vary with direct manufacturing labor costs in each department

1. Calculate the budgeted cost of trophies and plaques based on a single plant-wide overhead rate, if total overhead is allocated based on total direct costs
2. Calculate the budgeted cost of trophies and plaques based on departmental overhead rates, where forming department overhead costs are allocated based on direct manufacturing labor costs of the forming department and assembly department overhead costs are allocated based on total direct costs of the assembly department.

3. Calculate the budgeted cost of trophies and plaques if Triumph allocates overhead costs in each department using activity-based costing.
4. Explain how the disaggregation of information could improve or reduce decision quality.

5-23 ABC, process costing. Parker Company produces mathematical and financial calculators and operates at capacity. Data related to the two products are presented here:

	Mathematical	**Financial**
Annual production in units	60,000	120,000
Direct material costs	$240,000	$480,000
Direct manufacturing labor costs	$ 75,000	$150,000
Direct manufacturing labor-hours	5,000	10,000
Machine-hours	40,000	80,000
Number of production runs	60	60
Inspection hours	1,500	750

Total manufacturing overhead costs are as follows:

	Total
Machining costs	$720,000
Setup costs	150,000
Inspection costs	135,000

Required

1. Choose a cost driver for each overhead cost pool and calculate the manufacturing overhead cost per unit for each product.
2. Compute the manufacturing cost per unit for each product.
3. How might Parker's managers use the new cost information from its activity-based costing system to better manage its business?

5-24 Department costing, service company. CKM is an architectural firm that designs and builds buildings. It prices each job on a cost plus 20% basis. Overhead costs in 2017 are $4,011,780. CKM's simple costing system allocates overhead costs to its jobs based on number of jobs. There were three jobs in 2017. One customer, Sanders, has complained that the cost of its building in Chicago was not competitive. As a result, the controller has initiated a detailed review of the overhead allocation to determine if overhead costs are charged to jobs in proportion to consumption of overhead resources by jobs. She gathers the following information:

			Quantity of Cost Drivers Used by Each Project		
Department	**Cost Driver**	**Overhead Costs in 2017**	**Sanders**	**Hanley**	**Stanley**
Design	Design department hours	$1,500,000	1,000	5,000	4,000
Engineering	Number of engineering hours	$ 500,030	2,000	2,000	2,200
Construction	Labor-hours	$2,011,750	20,800	21,500	19,600
		$4,011,780			

Required

1. Compute the overhead allocated to each project in 2017 using the simple costing system.
2. Compute the overhead allocated to each project in 2017 using department overhead cost rates.
3. Do you think Sanders had a valid reason for dissatisfaction with the cost? How does the allocation, based on department rates, change costs for each project?
4. What value, if any, would CKM get by allocating costs of each department based on the activities done in that department?

5-25 Activity-based costing, service company. Speediprint Corporation owns a small printing press that prints leaflets, brochures, and advertising materials. Speediprint classifies its various printing jobs as standard jobs or special jobs. Speediprint's simple job-costing system has two direct-cost categories (direct materials and direct labor) and a single indirect-cost pool. Speediprint operates at capacity and allocates all indirect costs using printing machine-hours as the allocation base.

Speediprint is concerned about the accuracy of the costs assigned to standard and special jobs and therefore is planning to implement an activity-based costing system. Speediprint's ABC system would have the same direct-cost categories as its simple costing system. However, instead of a single indirect-cost pool there would now be six categories for assigning indirect costs: design, purchasing, setup, printing machine operations, marketing, and administration. To see how activity-based costing would affect the costs of standard and special jobs, Speediprint collects the following information for the fiscal year 2017 that just ended.

	A	B	C	D	E	F	G	H
	Home Insert Page Layout Formulas Data Review View							
1		Standard Job	Special Job	Total	Cause-and-Effect Relationship Between Allocation Base and Activity Cost			
2	Number of printing jobs	400	200					
3	Price per job	$ 600	$ 750					
4	Cost of supplies per job	$ 100	$ 125					
5	Direct labor costs per job	$ 90	$ 100					
6	Printing machine-hours per job	10	10					
7	Cost of printing machine operations			$ 75,000	Indirect costs of operating printing machines			
8					increase with printing machine-hours			
9	Setup-hours per job	4	7					
10	Setup costs			$ 45,000	Indirect setup costs increase with setup-hours			
11	Total number of purchase orders	400	500					
12	Purchase order costs			$ 18,000	Indirect purchase order costs increase with			
13					number of purchase orders			
14	Design costs	$4,000	$16,000	$ 20,000	Design costs are allocated to standard and special			
15					jobs based on a special study of the design department			
16	Marketing costs as a percentage of revenues	5%	5%	$ 19,500				
17	Administration costs			$ 24,000	Demand for administrative resources increases with direct labor costs			

Required

1. Calculate the cost of a standard job and a special job under the simple costing system.
2. Calculate the cost of a standard job and a special job under the activity-based costing system.
3. Compare the costs of a standard job and a special job in requirements 1 and 2. Why do the simple and activity-based costing systems differ in the cost of a standard job and a special job?
4. How might Speediprint use the new cost information from its activity-based costing system to better manage its business?

5-26 Activity-based costing, manufacturing. Decorative Doors, Inc., produces two types of doors, interior and exterior. The company's simple costing system has two direct-cost categories (materials and labor) and one indirect-cost pool. The simple costing system allocates indirect costs on the basis of machine-hours. Recently, the owners of Decorative Doors have been concerned about a decline in the market share for their interior doors, usually their biggest seller. Information related to Decorative Doors production for the most recent year follows:

	Interior	Exterior
Units sold	3,200	1,800
Selling price	$ 125	$ 200
Direct material cost per unit	$ 30	$ 45
Direct manufacturing labor cost per hour	$ 16	$ 16
Direct manufacturing labor-hours per unit	1.50	2.25
Production runs	40	85
Material moves	72	168
Machine setups	45	155
Machine-hours	5,500	4,500
Number of inspections	250	150

The owners have heard of other companies in the industry that are now using an activity-based costing system and are curious how an ABC system would affect their product costing decisions. After analyzing the indirect-cost pool for Decorative Doors, the owners identify six activities as generating indirect costs: production scheduling, material handling, machine setup, assembly, inspection, and marketing. Decorative Doors collected the following data related to the indirect-cost activities:

Activity	Activity Cost	Activity Cost Driver
Production scheduling	$95,000	Production runs
Material handling	$45,000	Material moves
Machine setup	$25,000	Machine setups
Assembly	$60,000	Machine-hours
Inspection	$ 8,000	Number of inspections

Marketing costs were determined to be 3% of the sales revenue for each type of door.

Required

1. Calculate the cost of an interior door and an exterior door under the existing simple costing system.
2. Calculate the cost of an interior door and an exterior door under an activity-based costing system.
3. Compare the costs of the doors in requirements 1 and 2. Why do the simple and activity-based costing systems differ in the cost of an interior door and an exterior door?
4. How might Decorative Doors, Inc., use the new cost information from its activity-based costing system to address the declining market share for interior doors?

5-27 ABC, retail product-line profitability. Henderson Supermarkets (HS) operates at capacity and decides to apply ABC analysis to three product lines: baked goods, milk and fruit juice, and frozen foods. It identifies four activities and their activity cost rates as follows:

Ordering	$ 104	per purchase order
Delivery and receipt of merchandise	$ 80	per delivery
Shelf-stocking	$ 22	per hour
Customer support and assistance	$0.25	per item sold

The revenues, cost of goods sold, store support costs, activities that account for the store support costs, and activity-area usage of the three product lines are as follows:

	Baked Goods	Milk and Fruit Juice	Frozen Products
Financial data			
Revenues	$63,000	$68,500	$54,000
Cost of goods sold	$39,000	$52,000	$36,000
Store support	$11,700	$15,600	$10,800
Activity-area usage (cost-allocation base)			
Ordering (purchase orders)	21	18	13
Delivery (deliveries)	88	32	26
Shelf-stocking (hours)	185	176	38
Customer support (items sold)	12,200	16,400	7,600

Under its simple costing system, HS allocated support costs to products at the rate of 30% of cost of goods sold.

Required

1. Use the simple costing system to prepare a product-line profitability report for HS.
2. Use the ABC system to prepare a product-line profitability report for HS.
3. What new insights does the ABC system in requirement 2 provide to HS managers?

5-28 ABC, wholesale, customer profitability. Ramirez Wholesalers operates at capacity and sells furniture items to four department-store chains (customers). Mr. Ramirez commented, "We apply ABC to determine product-line profitability. The same ideas apply to customer profitability, and we should find out our customer profitability as well." Ramirez Wholesalers sends catalogs to corporate purchasing departments on a monthly basis. The customers are entitled to return unsold merchandise within a six-month period from the purchase date and receive a full purchase price refund. The following data were collected from last year's operations:

	Chain			
	1	2	3	4
Gross sales	$50,000	$30,000	$100,000	$70,000
Sales returns:				
Number of items	100	26	60	40
Amount	$10,000	$ 5,000	$ 7,000	$ 6,000
Number of orders:				
Regular	40	150	50	70
Rush	10	50	10	30

Ramirez has calculated the following activity rates:

Activity	Cost-Driver Rate
Regular order processing	$20 per regular order
Rush order processing	$100 per rush order
Returned items processing	$10 per item
Catalogs and customer support	$1,000 per customer

1. Customers pay the transportation costs. The cost of goods sold averages 80% of sales.
2. Determine the contribution to profit from each chain last year. Comment on your solution.

5-29 Activity-based costing. The job costing system at Sheri's Custom Framing has five indirect-cost pools (purchasing, material handling, machine maintenance, product inspection, and packaging). The company is in the process of bidding on two jobs: Job 215, an order of 15 intricate personalized frames, and Job 325, an order of 6 standard personalized frames. The controller wants you to compare overhead allocated under the current simple job-costing system and a newly designed activity-based job-costing system. Total budgeted costs in each indirect-cost pool and the budgeted quantity of activity driver are as follows:

	Budgeted Overhead	Activity Driver	Budgeted Quantity of Activity Driver
Purchasing	$ 35,000	Purchase orders processed	2,000
Material handling	43,750	Material moves	5,000
Machine maintenance	118,650	Machine-hours	10,500
Product inspection	9,450	Inspections	1,200
Packaging	19,950	Units produced	3,800
	$226,800		

Information related to Job 215 and Job 325 follows. Job 215 incurs more batch-level costs because it uses more types of materials that need to be purchased, moved, and inspected relative to Job 325.

	Job 215	Job 325
Number of purchase orders	25	8
Number of material moves	10	4
Machine-hours	40	60
Number of inspections	9	3
Units produced	15	6

1. Compute the total overhead allocated to each job under a simple costing system, where overhead is allocated based on machine-hours.
2. Compute the total overhead allocated to each job under an activity-based costing system using the appropriate activity drivers.
3. Explain why Sheri's Custom Framing might favor the ABC job-costing system over the simple job-costing system, especially in its bidding process.

5-30 ABC, product costing at banks, cross-subsidization. Legion Bank (LB) is examining the profitability of its Star Account, a combined savings and checking account. Depositors receive a 6% annual interest rate on their average deposit. LB earns an interest rate spread of 3% (the difference between the rate at which it lends money and the rate it pays depositors) by lending money for home-loan purposes at 9%. Thus, LB would gain $150 on the interest spread if a depositor had an average Star Account balance of $5,000 in 2017 ($5,000 $\times$ 3% = $150).

The Star Account allows depositors unlimited use of services such as deposits, withdrawals, checking accounts, and foreign currency drafts. Depositors with Star Account balances of $1,000 or more receive unlimited free use of services. Depositors with minimum balances of less than $1,000 pay a $25-a-month service fee for their Star Account.

LB recently conducted an activity-based costing study of its services. It assessed the following costs for six individual services. The use of these services in 2017 by three customers is as follows:

	Activity-Based Cost per "Transaction"	Lindell	Welker	Colston
Deposit/withdrawal with teller	$2.75	46	53	5
Deposit/withdrawal with automatic teller machine (ATM)	0.75	14	25	12
Deposit/withdrawal on prearranged monthly basis	0.6	0	16	55
Bank checks written	8.5	10	3	4
Foreign currency drafts	12.25	7	2	7
Inquiries about account balance	1.8	8	14	5
Average Star Account balance for 2017		$1,500	$800	$26,600

Assume Lindell and Colston always maintain a balance above $1,000, whereas Welker always has a balance below $1,000.

Required

1. Compute the 2017 profitability of the Lindell, Welker, and Colston Star Accounts at LB.
2. Why might LB worry about the profitability of individual customers if the Star Account product offering is profitable as a whole?
3. What changes would you recommend for LB's Star Account?

Problems

5-31 Job costing with single direct-cost category, single indirect-cost pool, law firm. Bradley Associates is a recently formed law partnership. Emmit Harrington, the managing partner of Bradley Associates, has just finished a tense phone call with Martin Omar, president of Campa Coal. Omar strongly complained about the price Bradley charged for some legal work done for Campa Coal.

Harrington also received a phone call from its only other client (St. Edith's Glass), which was very pleased with both the quality of the work and the price charged on its most recent job.

Bradley Associates operates at capacity and uses a cost-based approach to pricing (billing) each job. Currently it uses a simple costing system with a single direct-cost category (professional labor-hours) and a single indirect-cost pool (general support). Indirect costs are allocated to cases on the basis of professional labor-hours per case. The job files show the following:

	Campa Coal	St. Edith's Glass
Professional labor	150 hours	100 hours

Professional labor costs at Bradley Associates are $80 an hour. Indirect costs are allocated to cases at $100 an hour. Total indirect costs in the most recent period were $25,000.

Required

1. Why is it important for Bradley Associates to understand the costs associated with individual jobs?
2. Compute the costs of the Campa Coal and St. Edith's Glass jobs using Bradley's simple costing system.

5-32 Job costing with multiple direct-cost categories, single indirect-cost pool, law firm (continuation of 5-31). Harrington asks his assistant to collect details on those costs included in the $25,000 indirect-cost pool that can be traced to each individual job. After analysis, Bradley is able to reclassify $15,000 of the $25,000 as direct costs:

Other Direct Costs	Campa Coal	St. Edith's Glass
Research support labor	$1,800	$ 3,850
Computer time	400	1,600
Travel and allowances	700	4,200
Telephones/faxes	250	1,200
Photocopying	300	700
Total	$3,450	$11,550

Harrington decides to calculate the costs of each job as if Bradley had used six direct-cost pools and a single indirect-cost pool. The single indirect-cost pool would have $10,000 of costs and would be allocated to each case using the professional labor-hours base.

Required

1. Calculate the revised indirect-cost allocation rate per professional labor-hour for Bradley Associates when total indirect costs are $10,000.
2. Compute the costs of the Campa and St. Edith's jobs if Bradley Associates had used its refined costing system with multiple direct-cost categories and one indirect-cost pool.
3. Compare the costs of Campa and St. Edith's jobs in requirement 2 with those in requirement 2 of Problem 5-31. Comment on the results.

5-33 Job costing with multiple direct-cost categories, multiple indirect-cost pools, law firm (continuation of 5-31 and 5-32). Bradley has two classifications of professional staff: partners and associates. Harrington asks his assistant to examine the relative use of partners and associates on the recent Campa Coal and St. Edith's jobs. The Campa job used 50 partner-hours and 100 associate-hours. The St. Edith's job used 75 partner-hours and 25 associate-hours. Therefore, totals of the two jobs together were 125 partner-hours and 125 associate-hours. Harrington decides to examine how using separate direct-cost rates for partners and associates and using separate indirect-cost pools for partners and associates would have affected the costs of the Campa and St. Edith's jobs. Indirect costs in each indirect-cost pool would be allocated on the basis of total hours of that category of professional labor. From the total indirect-cost pool of $10,000, $6,000 is attributable to the activities of partners and $4,000 is attributable to the activities of associates. The rates per category of professional labor are as follows:

Category of Professional Labor	Direct Cost per Hour	Indirect Cost per Hour
Partner	$100	$6,000 ÷ 125 hours = $48
Associate	$ 60	$4,000 ÷ 125 hours = $32

Required

1. Compute the costs of the Campa and St. Edith's cases using Bradley's further refined system, with multiple direct-cost categories and multiple indirect-cost pools.
2. For what decisions might Bradley Associates find it more useful to use this job-costing approach rather than the approaches in Problem 5-31 or 5-32?

5-34 First stage allocation, activity-based costing, manufacturing sector. Marshall's Devices uses activity-based costing to allocate overhead costs to customer orders for pricing purposes. Many customer orders are won through competitive bidding. Direct material and direct manufacturing labor costs are traced directly to each order. Marshall's Devices direct manufacturing labor rate is $25 per hour. The company reports the following yearly overhead costs:

Wages and salaries	$ 600,000
Depreciation	72,000
Rent	128,000
Other overhead	280,000
Total overhead costs	$1,080,000

Marshall's Devices has established four activity cost pools:

Activity Cost Pool	Activity Measure	Budgeted Total Activity for the Year
Direct manufacturing labor support	Number of direct manufacturing labor-hours	32,000 direct manufacturing labor-hours
Order processing	Number of customer orders	440 orders
Design support	Number of custom design-hours	2,500 custom design-hours
Other	Facility-sustaining costs allocated to orders based on direct manufacturing labor-hours	32,000 direct manufacturing labor-hours

Some customer orders require more complex designs, while others need simple designs. Marshall estimates that it will do 100 complex designs during a year, which will each take 13 hours for a total of 1,300 design-hours. It estimates it will do 150 simple designs, which will each take 8 hours for a total of 1,200 design-hours.

Paul Napoli, Marshall's Devices' controller, has prepared the following estimates for distribution of the over head costs across the four activity cost pools:

	Direct Manufacturing Labor Support	Order Processing	Design Support	Other	Total
Wages	35%	30%	25%	10%	100%
Depreciation	20%	15%	15%	50%	100%
Rent	25%	30%	15%	30%	100%
Other	25%	25%	40%	10%	100%

Order 277100 consists of six different metal products. Four products require a complex design and two require a simple design. Order 277100 requires $5,500 of direct materials and 100 direct manufacturing labor-hours.

Required

1. Allocate the overhead costs to each activity cost pool. Calculate the activity rate for each pool.
2. Determine the cost of Order 277100.
3. How does activity-based costing enhance Marshall's Devices' ability to price its orders? Suppose Marshall's Devices used a traditional costing system to allocate all overhead costs to orders on the basis of direct manufacturing labor-hours. How might this have affected Marshall's Devices' pricing decisions?
4. When designing its activity-based costing system, Marshall uses time-driven activity-based costing (TDABC) system for its design department. What does this approach allow Marshall to do? How would the cost of Order 277100 have been different if Marshall has used the number of customer designs rather than the number of custom design-hours to allocate costs to different customer orders? Which cost driver do you prefer for design support? Why?

5-35 First-stage allocation, time-driven activity-based costing, service sector. LawnCare USA provides lawn care and landscaping services to commercial clients. LawnCare USA uses activity-based costing to bid on jobs and to evaluate their profitability. LawnCare USA reports the following budgeted annual costs:

Wages and salaries	$360,000
Depreciation	72,000
Supplies	120,000
Other overhead	288,000
Total overhead costs	$840,000

John Gilroy, controller of LawnCare USA, has established four activity cost pools and the following budgeted activity for each cost pool:

Activity Cost Pool	Activity Measure	Total Activity for the Year
Estimating jobs	Number of job estimates	250 estimates
Lawn care	Number of direct labor-hours	10,000 direct labor-hours
Landscape design	Number of design hours	500 design hours
Other	Facility-sustaining costs that are not allocated to jobs	Not applicable

Gilroy estimates that LawnCare USA's costs are distributed to the activity-cost pools as follows:

	Estimating Jobs	Lawn Care	Landscape Design	Other	Total
Wages and salaries	5%	70%	15%	10%	100%
Depreciation	10%	65%	10%	15%	100%
Supplies	0%	100%	0%	0%	100%
Other overhead	15%	50%	20%	15%	100%

Sunset Office Park, a new development in a nearby community, has contacted LawnCare USA to provide an estimate on landscape design and annual lawn maintenance. The job is estimated to require a single landscape design requiring 40 design hours in total and 250 direct labor-hours annually. LawnCare USA has a policy of pricing estimates at 150% of cost.

Required

1. Allocate LawnCare USA's costs to the activity-cost pools and determine the activity rate for each pool.
2. Estimate total cost for the Sunset Office Park job. How much would LawnCare USA bid to perform the job?
3. LawnCare USA does 30 landscape designs for its customers each year. Estimate the total cost for the Sunset Office park job if LawnCare USA allocated costs of the Landscape Design activity based on the number of landscape designs rather than the number of landscape design-hours. How much would LawnCare USA bid to perform the job? Which cost driver do you prefer for the Landscape Design activity? Why?
4. Sunset Office Park asks LawnCare USA to give an estimate for providing its services for a 2-year period. What are the advantages and disadvantages for LawnCare USA to provide a 2-year estimate?

5-36 Department and activity-cost rates, service sector. Vital Dimension's Radiology Center (VDRC) performs X-rays, ultrasounds, computer tomography (CT) scans, and magnetic resonance imaging (MRI). VDRC has developed a reputation as a top radiology center in the state. VDRC has achieved this status because it constantly reexamines its processes and procedures. VDRC has been using a single, facility-wide overhead allocation rate. The vice president of finance believes that VDRC can make better process improvements if it uses more disaggregated cost information. She says, "We have state-of-the-art medical imaging technology. Can't we have state-of-the-art accounting technology?"

	X-rays	Ultrasound	CT Scan	MRI	Total
Technician labor	$ 74,000	$122,000	$178,000	$ 118,000	$ 492,000
Depreciation	45,230	264,320	432,550	895,900	1,638,000
Materials	24,500	21,400	26,300	36,800	109,000
Administration					24,000
Maintenance					275,500
Sanitation					276,200
Utilities					162,300
	$143,730	$407,720	$636,850	$1,050,700	$2,977,000
Number of procedures	4,254	4,024	3,344	2,698	
Minutes to clean after each procedure	10	15	20	30	
Minutes for each procedure	15	20	30	35	

VDRC operates at capacity. The proposed allocation bases for overhead are as follows:

Administration	Number of procedures
Maintenance (including parts)	Capital cost of the equipment (use depreciation)
Sanitation	Total cleaning minutes
Utilities	Total procedure minutes

Required

1. Calculate the budgeted cost per service for X-rays, ultrasounds, CT scans, and MRI using direct technician labor costs as the allocation basis.
2. Calculate the budgeted cost per service of X-rays, ultrasounds, CT scans, and MRI if VDRC allocated overhead costs using activity-based costing.
3. Explain how the disaggregation of information could be helpful to VDRC's intention to continuously improve its services.

5-37 Activity-based costing, merchandising. Pharmahelp, Inc., a distributor of special pharmaceutical products, operates at capacity and has three main market segments:

a. General supermarket chains
b. Drugstore chains
c. Mom-and-pop single-store pharmacies

Rick Flair, the new controller of Pharmahelp, reported the following data for 2017.

	Home	Insert	Page Layout	Formulas	Data	Review	View
	A			B	C	D	E
1							
2	Pharmahelp, 2017			General			
3				Supermarket	Drugstore	Mom-and-Pop	Total For
4				Chains	Chains	Single Stores	Pharmahelp
5	Revenues			$3,708,000	$3,150,000	$1,980,000	$8,838,000
6	Cost of goods sold			3,600,000	3,000,000	1,800,000	8,400,000
7	Gross margin			$ 108,000	$ 150,000	$ 180,000	438,000
8	Other operating costs						301,080
9	Operating income						$ 136,920

For many years, Pharmahelp has used gross margin percentage [(Revenue − Cost of goods sold) ÷ Revenue] to evaluate the relative profitability of its market segments. But Flair recently attended a seminar on activity-based costing and is considering using it at Pharmahelp to analyze and allocate "other operating costs." He meets with all the key managers and several of his operations and sales staff, and they agree that there are five key activities that drive other operating costs at Pharmahelp:

Activity Area	Cost Driver
Order processing	Number of customer purchase orders
Line-item processing	Number of line items ordered by customers
Delivering to stores	Number of store deliveries
Cartons shipped to store	Number of cartons shipped
Stocking of customer store shelves	Hours of shelf-stocking

Each customer order consists of one or more line items. A line item represents a single product (such as Extra-Strength Tylenol Tablets). Each product line item is delivered in one or more separate cartons. Each store delivery entails the delivery of one or more cartons of products to a customer. Pharmahelp's staff stacks cartons directly onto display shelves in customers' stores. Currently, there is no additional charge to the customer for shelf-stocking and not all customers use Pharmahelp for this activity. The level of each activity in the three market segments and the total cost incurred for each activity in 2017 is as follows:

	Home	Insert	Page Layout	Formulas	Data	Review	View	
	A		B	C		D	E	
13								
14	Activity-based Cost Data			Activity Level				
15	Pharmahelp 2017		General				Total Cost	
16			Supermarket	Drugstore		Mom-and-Pop	of Activity	
17	Activity		Chains	Chains		Single Stores	in 2017	
18	Orders processed (number)		140	360		1,500	$ 80,000	
19	Line-items ordered (number)		1,960	4,320		15,000	63,840	
20	Store deliveries made (number)		120	360		1,000	71,000	
21	Cartons shipped to stores (number)		36,000	24,000		16,000	76,000	
22	Shelf stocking (hours)		360	180		100	10,240	
23							$301,080	

Required

1. Compute the 2017 gross-margin percentage for each of Pharmahelp's three market segments.
2. Compute the cost driver rates for each of the five activity areas.
3. Use the activity-based costing information to allocate the $301,080 of "other operating costs" to each of the market segments. Compute the operating income for each market segment.
4. Comment on the results. What new insights are available with the activity-based costing information?

5-38 Choosing cost drivers, activity-based costing, activity-based management. Shades & Hues (S&H) is a designer of high-quality curtains and bedsheets. Each design is made in small batches. Each spring, S&H comes out with new designs for the curtains and for the bedsheets. The company uses these designs for a year and then moves on to the next trend. The products are all made on the same fabrication equipment that is expected to operate at capacity. The equipment must be switched over to a new design and set up to prepare for the production of each new batch of products. When completed, each batch of products is immediately shipped to a wholesaler. Shipping costs vary with the number of shipments. Budgeted information for the year is as follows:

Shades & Hues
Budget for Costs and Activities
For the Year Ended February 28, 2017

Direct materials—bedsheets	$ 3,82,260
Direct materials—curtains	5,10,425
Direct manufacturing labor—bedsheets	1,12,500
Direct manufacturing labor—curtains	1,26,000
Setup	78,250
Shipping	84,500
Design	1,93,200
Plant utilities and administration	2,55,775
Total	$17,42,910

Other budget information follows:

	Curtains	Bedsheets	Total
Number of products	6,240	3,075	9,315
Hours of production	1,755	2,655	4,410
Number of batches	150	100	250
Number of designs	4	6	10

1. Identify the cost hierarchy level for each cost category.
2. Identify the most appropriate cost driver for each cost category. Explain briefly your choice of cost driver.
3. Calculate the budgeted cost per unit of cost driver for each cost category.
4. Calculate the budgeted total costs and cost per unit for each product line.
5. Explain how you could use the information in requirement 4 to reduce costs.

5-39 ABC, health care. Crosstown Health Center runs two programs: drug addict rehabilitation and after-care (counseling and support of patients after release from a mental hospital). The center's budget for 2017 follows.

Professional salaries:		
4 physicians × $150,000	$600,000	
12 psychologists × $75,000	900,000	
16 nurses × $30,000	480,000	$1,980,000
Medical supplies		242,000
Rent and clinic maintenance		138,600
Administrative costs to manage patient charts, food, laundry		484,000
Laboratory services		92,400
Total		$2,937,000

Kim Yu, the director of the center, is keen on determining the cost of each program. Yu compiles the following data describing employee allocations to individual programs:

	Drug	Aftercare	Total Employees
Physicians	4		4
Psychologists	4	8	12
Nurses	6	10	16

Yu has recently become aware of activity-based costing as a method to refine costing systems. She asks her accountant, Gus Gates, how she should apply this technique. Gates obtains the following budgeted information for 2017:

	Drug	Aftercare	Total
Square feet of space occupied by each program	9,000	12,000	21,000
Patient-years of service	50	60	110
Number of laboratory tests	1,400	700	2,100

1. a. Selecting cost-allocation bases that you believe are the most appropriate for allocating indirect costs to programs, calculate the budgeted indirect cost rates for medical supplies; rent and clinic maintenance; administrative costs for patient charts, food, and laundry; and laboratory services.
   b. Using an activity-based costing approach to cost analysis, calculate the budgeted cost of each program and the budgeted cost per patient-year of the drug program.
   c. What benefits can Crosstown Health Center obtain by implementing the ABC system?
2. What factors, other than cost, do you think Crosstown Health Center should consider in allocating resources to its programs?

5-40 Unused capacity, activity-based costing, activity-based management. Zarson's Netballs is a manufacturer of high-quality basketballs and volleyballs. Setup costs are driven by the number of setups. Equipment and maintenance costs increase with the number of machine-hours, and lease rent is paid per square foot. Capacity of the facility is 14,000 square feet, and Zarson is using only 80% of this capacity.

Zarson records the cost of unused capacity as a separate line item and not as a product cost. The following is the budgeted information for Zarson:

Zarson's Netballs
Budgeted Costs and Activities
For the Year Ended December 31, 2017

Direct materials—basketballs	$ 168,100
Direct materials—volleyballs	303,280
Direct manufacturing labor—basketballs	111,800
Direct manufacturing labor—volleyballs	100,820
Setup	157,500
Equipment and maintenance costs	115,200
Lease rent	210,000
Total	$1,166,700

Other budget information follows:

	Basketballs	Volleyballs
Number of balls	58,000	85,000
Machine-hours	13,500	10,500
Number of setups	450	300
Square footage of production space used	3,200	8,000

1. Calculate the budgeted cost per unit of cost driver for each indirect cost pool.
2. What is the budgeted cost of unused capacity?
3. What is the budgeted total cost and the cost per unit of resources used to produce (a) basketballs and (b) volleyballs?
4. Why might excess capacity be beneficial for Zarson? What are some of the issues Zarson should consider before increasing production to use the space?

5-41 Unused capacity, activity-based costing, activity-based management. Whitewater Adventures manufactures two models of kayaks, Basic and Deluxe, using a combination of machining and hand finishing. Machine setup costs are driven by the number of setups. Indirect manufacturing labor costs increase with direct manufacturing labor costs. Equipment and maintenance costs increase with the number of machine-hours, and facility rent is paid per square foot. Capacity of the facility is 6,250 square feet, and Whitewater is using only 80% of this capacity. Whitewater records the cost of unused capacity as a separate line item and not as a product cost. For the current year, Whitewater has budgeted the following:

Whitewater Adventures
Budgeted Costs and Activities
For the Year Ended December 31, 2017

Direct materials—Basic kayaks	$ 325,000
Direct materials—Deluxe kayaks	240,000
Direct manufacturing labor—Basic kayaks	110,000
Direct manufacturing labor—Deluxe kayaks	130,000
Indirect manufacturing labor costs	72,000
Machine setup costs	40,500
Equipment and maintenance costs	235,000
Facility rent	200,000
Total	$1,352,500

Other budget information follows:

	Basic	Deluxe
Number of kayaks	5,000	3,000
Machine-hours	11,000	12,500
Number of setups	300	200
Square footage of production space used	2,860	2,140

1. Calculate the cost per unit of each cost-allocation base.
2. What is the budgeted cost of unused capacity?

3. Calculate the budgeted total cost and the cost per unit for each model.
4. Why might excess capacity be beneficial for Whitewater? What are some of the issues Whitewater should consider before increasing production to use the space?

5-42 ABC, implementation, ethics. (CMA, adapted) Plum Electronics, a division of Berry Corporation, manufactures two large-screen television models: the Mammoth, which has been produced since 2013 and sells for $990, and the Maximum, a newer model introduced in early 2015 that sells for $1,254. Based on the following income statement for the year ended November 30, 2017, senior management at Berry have decided to concentrate Plum's marketing resources on the Maximum model and to begin to phase out the Mammoth model because Maximum generates a much bigger operating income per unit.

Plum Electronics
Income Statement for the
Fiscal Year Ended November 30, 2017

	Mammoth	Maximum	Total
Revenues	$21,780,000	$5,016,000	$26,796,000
Cost of goods sold	13,794,000	3,511,200	17,305,200
Gross margin	7,986,000	1,504,800	9,490,800
Selling and administrative expense	6,413,000	1,075,800	7,488,800
Operating income	$ 1,573,000	$ 429,000	$ 2,002,000
Units produced and sold	22,000	4,000	
Operating income per unit sold	$ 71.50	$ 107.25	

Details for cost of goods sold for Mammoth and Maximum are as follows:

	Mammoth		Maximum	
	Total	Per Unit	Total	Per Unit
Direct materials	$ 5,033,600	$ 228.80	$2,569,600	$642.40
Direct manufacturing labor[a]	435,600	19.80	184,800	46.20
Machine costs[b]	3,484,800	158.40	316,800	79.20
Total direct costs	$ 8,954,000	$ 407.00	$3,071,200	$767.80
Manufacturing overhead costs[c]	$ 4,840,000	$ 220.00	$ 440,000	$110.00
Total cost of goods sold	$13,794,000	$ 627.00	$3,511,200	$877.80

[a] Mammoth requires 1.5 hours per unit and Maximum requires 3.5 hours per unit. The direct manufacturing labor cost is $13.20 per hour.

[b] Machine costs include lease costs of the machine, repairs, and maintenance. Mammoth requires 8 machine-hours per unit and Maximum requires 4 machine-hours per unit. The machine-hour rate is $19.80 per hour.

[c] Manufacturing overhead costs are allocated to products based on machine-hours at the rate of $27.50 per hour.

Plum's controller, Steve Jacobs, is advocating the use of activity-based costing and activity-based management and has gathered the following information about the company's manufacturing overhead costs for the year ended November 30, 2017.

		Units of the Cost-Allocation Base		
Activity Center (Cost-Allocation Base)	Total Activity Costs	Mammoth	Maximum	Total
Soldering (number of solder points)	$1,036,200	1,185,000	385,000	1,570,000
Shipments (number of shipments)	946,000	16,200	3,800	20,000
Quality control (number of inspections)	1,364,000	56,200	21,300	77,500
Purchase orders (number of orders)	1,045,440	80,100	109,980	190,080
Machine power (machine-hours)	63,360	176,000	16,000	192,000
Machine setups (number of setups)	825,000	16,000	14,000	30,000
Total manufacturing overhead	$5,280,000			

After completing his analysis, Jacobs shows the results to Charles Clark, the Plum division president. Clark does not like what he sees. "If you show headquarters this analysis, they are going to ask us to phase out the Maximum line, which we have just introduced. This whole costing stuff has been a major problem for us. First Mammoth was not profitable and now Maximum.

"Looking at the ABC analysis, I see two problems. First, we do many more activities than the ones you have listed. If you had included all activities, maybe your conclusions would be different. Second, you used number of setups and number of inspections as allocation bases. The numbers would be different had you used setup-hours and inspection-hours instead. I know that measurement problems precluded you from using these other cost-allocation bases, but I believe you ought to make some adjustments to our current numbers to compensate for these issues. I know you can do better. We can't afford to phase out either product."

Jacobs knows that his numbers are fairly accurate. As a quick check, he calculates the profitability of Maximum and Mammoth using more and different allocation bases. The set of activities and activity rates he had used results in numbers that closely approximate those based on more detailed analyses. He is confident that headquarters, knowing that Maximum was introduced only recently, will not ask Plum to phase it out. He is also aware that a sizable portion of Clark's bonus is based on division revenues. Phasing out either product would adversely affect his bonus. Still, he feels some pressure from Clark to do something.

1. Using activity-based costing, calculate the gross margin per unit of the Maximum and Mammoth models.
2. Explain briefly why these numbers differ from the gross margin per unit of the Maximum and Mammoth models calculated using Plum's existing simple costing system.
3. Comment on Clark's concerns about the accuracy and limitations of ABC.
4. How might Plum find the ABC information helpful in managing its business?
5. What should Steve Jacobs do in response to Clark's comments?

5-43 Activity-based costing, activity-based management, merchandising. Main Street Books and Café (MSBC) is a large city bookstore that sells books and music CDs and has a café. MSBC operates at capacity and allocates selling, general, and administration (S, G, & A) costs to each product line using the cost of merchandise of each product line. MSBC wants to optimize the pricing and cost management of each product line. MSBC is wondering if its accounting system is providing it with the best information for making such decisions.

Main Street Books and Café
Product Line Information
For the Year Ended December 31, 2017

	Books	CDs	Café
Revenues	$3,720,480	$2,315,360	$736,216
Cost of merchandise	$2,656,727	$1,722,311	$556,685
Cost of café cleaning			$ 18,250
Number of purchase orders placed	2,800	2,500	2,000
Number of deliveries received	1,400	1,700	1,600
Hours of shelf stocking time	15,000	10,000	10,000
Items sold	124,016	115,768	368,108

Main Street Books and Café incurs the following selling, general, and administration costs:

Main Street Books and Café
Selling, General, and Administration (S, G, & A) Costs
For the Year Ended December 31, 2017

Purchasing department exercise	$ 474,500
Receiving department expense	432,400
Shelf stocking labor expense	487,500
Customer support expense (cashiers and floor employees)	91,184
	$1,485,584

1. Suppose MSBC uses cost of merchandise to allocate all S, G, & A costs. Prepare product line and total company income statements.
2. Identify an improved method for allocating costs to the three product lines. Explain. Use the method for allocating S, G, & A costs that you propose to prepare new product line and total company income statements. Compare your results to the results in requirement 1.
3. Write a memo to MSBC management describing how the improved system might be useful for managing the store.

Master Budget and Responsibility Accounting

No one likes to run out of cash.

To manage their spending, businesses, like individuals, need budgets. Budgets help managers and their employees know whether they're on target for their growth and spending goals. Budgets are important for all types of companies: large financial institutions, such as Citigroup, which suffered big financial losses after the housing bubble burst in the mid-2000s; large retailers, such as Home Depot, whose profit margins are thin; profitable computer companies, such as Apple, which sell high dollar-value goods; and luxury hotels, such as the Ritz-Carlton, which sell high dollar-value services.

"SCRIMPING" AT THE RITZ: MASTER BUDGETS

"Ladies and gentlemen serving ladies and gentlemen." That's the motto of the Ritz-Carlton. However, the aura of the chain's old-world elegance stands in contrast to its emphasis— behind the scenes, of course—on cost control and budgets. A Ritz hotel's performance is the responsibility of its general manager and controller at each location. Local forecasts and budgets are prepared annually and are the basis of subsequent performance evaluations for the hotel and people who work there. The budget comprises revenue forecasts and standard costs for hotel rooms, conventions, weddings, meeting facilities, merchandise, and food and beverages. Managers monitor the revenue budget daily, review occupancy rates and adjust prices if necessary. Corporate headquarters monitors actual performance each month against the approved budget and other Ritz hotels. Any ideas for boosting revenues and reducing costs are regularly shared among hotels.

Why do successful companies budget? Because, as the Ritz-Carlton example illustrates, budgeting is a critical function in an organization's decision-making process. Southwest Airlines, for example, uses budgets to monitor and manage fluctuating fuel costs. Walmart depends on its budget to maintain razor-thin margins as it competes with Target. Gillette uses budgets to plan marketing campaigns for its razors and blades.

Even though budgeting is essential for businesses, many managers are often frustrated by the budgeting process. They find it difficult to predict the future and dislike superiors challenging them to improve the performance of their departments. They also dislike being personally evaluated on targets that are challenging and prefer to develop budgets that they can beat. We discuss these issues and the ways thoughtful managers deal with them later in this chapter. For now, we highlight some of the benefits managers get from budgeting.

Suzanne Porter/Rough Guides/Dorling Kindersley, Ltd.

LEARNING OBJECTIVES

1. Describe the master budget and explain its benefits

2. Describe the advantages of budgets

3. Prepare the operating budget and its supporting schedules

4. Use computer-based financial planning models for sensitivity analysis

5. Describe responsibility centers and responsibility accounting

6. Recognize the human aspects of budgeting

7. Appreciate the special challenges of budgeting in multinational companies

Budgets help managers:

1. Communicate directions and goals to different departments of a company to help them coordinate the actions they must pursue to satisfy customers and succeed in the marketplace.

2. Judge performance by measuring financial results against planned objectives, activities, and timelines and learn about potential problems.

3. Motivate employees to achieve their goals.

Interestingly, even when it comes to entrepreneurial activities, research shows that business planning increases a new venture's probability of survival, as well as its product development and venture-organizing activities.[1] As the old adage goes: "If you fail to plan, you plan to fail."

In this chapter, you will see that a budget is based on an organization's strategy and expresses its operating and financial plans. Most importantly, you will see that budgeting is a human activity that requires judgment and wise interpretation.

Budgets and the Budgeting Cycle

LEARNING OBJECTIVE 1

Describe the master budget

…the master budget is the initial budget prepared before the start of a period

and explain its benefits

…benefits include planning, coordination, and control

A *budget* is (a) the quantitative expression of a proposed plan of action by management for a specified period and (b) an aid to coordinate what needs to be done to implement that plan. The budget generally includes both the plan's financial and nonfinancial aspects and serves as a road map for the company to follow in an upcoming period. A financial budget quantifies managers' expectations regarding a company's income, cash flows, and financial position. Just as financial statements are prepared for past periods, financial statements can be prepared for future periods—for example, a budgeted income statement, a budgeted statement of cash flows, or a budgeted balance sheet. Managers develop financial budgets using supporting information from nonfinancial budgets for, say, units manufactured or sold, number of employees, and number of new products being introduced to the marketplace.

Strategic Plans and Operating Plans

Budgeting is most useful when it is integrated with a company's strategy. *Strategy* specifies how an organization matches its capabilities with the opportunities in the marketplace to accomplish its objectives. To develop successful strategies, managers must consider questions such as the following:

- What are our objectives?
- How do we create value for our customers while distinguishing ourselves from our competitors?
- Are the markets for our products local, regional, national, or global? What trends affect our markets? How do the economy, our industry, and our competitors affect us?
- What organizational and financial structures serve us best?
- What are the risks and opportunities of alternative strategies, and what are our contingency plans if our preferred plan fails?

A company, such as Home Depot, can have a strategy of providing quality products or services at a low price. Another company, such as Porsche or the Ritz-Carlton, can have a strategy of providing a unique product or service that is priced higher than the products or services of competitors. Exhibit 6-1 shows that strategic plans are expressed through long-run budgets and operating plans are expressed via short-run budgets. But there is more to the story! The exhibit shows arrows pointing backward as well as forward. The backward arrows show that budgets can lead to changes in plans and strategies. Budgets help managers assess strategic risks and opportunities by providing them with feedback about the likely effects of their strategies and plans. Sometimes that feedback prompts managers to revise their plans and possibly their strategies.

---

[1] For more details, see Frederic Delmar and Scott Shane, "Does Business Planning Facilitate the Development of New Ventures?" *Strategic Management Journal* (December 2003).

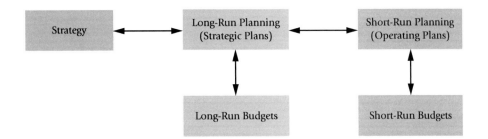

EXHIBIT 6-1

Strategy, Planning, and Budgets

Boeing's experience with the 747-8 program illustrates how budgets can help managers rework their operating plans. Boeing believed that utilizing some of the design concepts it was implementing in its 787 Dreamliner program would be a relatively inexpensive way to reconfigure its 747-8 jet. However, continued cost overruns and delays undermined that strategy: In early 2012, the 747-8 program was already $2 billion over budget and a year behind schedule. As a result, the company expected to earn no profit on any of the more than 100 orders for 747-8 planes it had on its books. And with the budget revealing higher-than-expected costs in design, rework, and production, Boeing postponed production plans for the 747-8 program. The problems with the 747-8 continue. Boeing plans to manufacture less than ten 747-8 aircraft each year.

Budgeting Cycle and Master Budget

Well-managed companies usually cycle through the following steps during the course of the fiscal year:

1. Before the start of the fiscal year, managers at all levels take into account the company's past performance, market feedback, and anticipated future changes to initiate plans for the next period. For example, an anticipated economic recovery from a recession may cause managers to plan for sales increases, higher production, and greater promotion expenses. Managers and management accountants work together to develop plans for the company as a whole and the performance of its subunits, such as departments or divisions.

2. At the beginning of the fiscal year, senior managers give subordinate managers a frame of reference, a set of specific financial or nonfinancial expectations against which they will compare actual results.

3. During the course of the year, management accountants help managers investigate any deviations from the plans, such as an unexpected decline in sales. If necessary, corrective action follows—changes in a product's features, a reduction in prices to boost sales, or cutting of costs to maintain profitability.

The preceding three steps describe the ongoing budget-related processes. The working document at the core of this process is called the *master budget*. The **master budget** expresses management's operating and financial plans for a specified period, usually a fiscal year, and it includes a set of budgeted financial statements. The master budget is the initial plan of what the company intends to accomplish in the period and evolves from both the operating and financing decisions managers make as they prepare the budget.

- Operating decisions deal with how to best use the limited resources of an organization.
- Financing decisions deal with how to obtain the funds to acquire those resources.

The terminology used to describe budgets varies among companies. For example, budgeted financial statements are sometimes called **pro forma statements**. Some companies, such as Hewlett-Packard, refer to budgeting as *targeting*. And many companies, such as Nissan Motor Company and Owens Corning, refer to the budget as a *profit plan*. Microsoft refers to goals as *commitments* and distributes firm-level goals across the company, connecting them to organizational, team, and—ultimately—individual commitments.

This book focuses on how management accounting helps managers make operating decisions, which is why operating budgets are emphasized here. Managers spend a significant part of their time preparing and analyzing budgets because budgeting yields many advantages.

DECISION POINT

What is the master budget and why is it useful?

Advantages and Challenges of Implementing Budgets

LEARNING OBJECTIVE 2

Describe the advantages of budgets

...advantages include coordination, communication, perfor-mance evaluation, and managerial motivation

Budgets are an integral part of management control systems. As we have discussed at the start of this chapter, when administered thoughtfully by managers, budgets do the following:

- Promote coordination and communication among subunits within the company
- Provide a framework for judging performance and facilitating learning
- Motivate managers and other employees

Promoting Coordination and Communication

Coordination is meshing and balancing all aspects of production or service and all depart-ments in a company in the best way for the company to meet its goals. *Communication* is making sure all employees understand those goals. Coordination forces executives to think about the relationships among individual departments within the company, as well as between the company and its supply-chain partners.

Consider budgeting at Pace, a United Kingdom–based manufacturer of electronic prod-ucts. A key product is Pace's digital set-top box for decoding satellite broadcasts. The produc-tion manager can achieve more timely production by coordinating and communicating with the company's marketing team to understand when set-top boxes need to be shipped to cus-tomers. In turn, the marketing team can make better predictions of future demand for set-top boxes by coordinating and communicating with Pace's customers.

Suppose BSkyB, one of Pace's largest customers, is planning to launch a new high-definition personal video recorder service. If Pace's marketing group is able to obtain in-formation about the launch date for the service, it can share this information with Pace's manufacturing group. The manufacturing group must then coordinate and communicate with Pace's materials-procurement group, and so on. The point to understand is that Pace is more likely to have personal video recorders in the quantities customers demand if Pace coordinates and communicates both within its business functions and with its customers and suppliers during the budgeting and production processes.

Providing a Framework for Judging Performance and Facilitating Learning

Budgets enable a company's managers to measure actual performance against predicted per-formance. Budgets can overcome two limitations of using past performance as a basis for judging actual results. One limitation is that past results often incorporate past miscues and substandard performance. Suppose the cellular telephone company Mobile Communications is examining the current-year (2017) performance of its sales force. The sales force's 2016 per-formance incorporated the efforts of an unusually high number of salespeople who have since left the company because they did not have a good understanding of the marketplace. The president of Mobile said of those salespeople, "They could not sell ice cream in a heat wave." Using the sales record of those departed employees would set the performance bar for 2017 much too low.

The other limitation of using past performance is that future conditions can be expected to differ from the past. Suppose, in 2017, Mobile had a 20% revenue increase, compared with a 10% revenue increase in 2016. Does this increase indicate outstanding sales perfor-mance? Not if the forecasted and actual 2017 industry growth rate was 40%. In this case, Mobile's 20% actual revenue gain in 2017 doesn't look so good, even though it exceeded the 2016 actual growth rate of 10%. Using the 40% budgeted growth rate for the industry pro-vides Mobile Communications with a better benchmark against which to evaluate its 2017 sales performance than using the 2016 actual growth rate of 10%. This is why many compa-nies also evaluate their performance relative to their peers. Using only the budget to evaluate performance creates an incentive for subordinates to set targets that are relatively easy to achieve.[2] Of course, managers at all levels recognize this incentive and therefore work to make the budget more challenging to achieve for the individuals who report to them. Still, the budget is the end product of negotiations among senior and subordinate managers. At the end of the year, senior managers gain information about the performance of competitors and external market conditions. This is valuable information that they can use to judge the performance of subordinate managers.

One of the most valuable benefits of budgeting is that it helps managers gather information for improving future performance. When actual outcomes fall short of budgeted or planned results, it prompts thoughtful senior managers to ask questions about what happened and why and how this knowledge can be used to ensure that such shortfalls do not occur again. This probing and learning is one of the most important reasons why budgeting helps improve performance.

Motivating Managers and Other Employees

Research shows that the performance of employees improves when they receive a challenging budget. Why? Because they view not meeting it as a failure. Most employees are motivated to work more intensely to avoid failure than to achieve success (they are loss-averse). As employees get closer to a goal, they work harder to achieve it. Creating a little anxiety improves performance. However, overly ambitious and unachievable budgets can actually de-motivate employees because they see little chance of avoiding failure. As a result, many executives like to set demanding, but achievable, goals for their subordinate managers and employees.[3] General Electric's former CEO Jack Welch describes challenging, yet achievable, budgets as energizing, motivating, and satisfying for managers and other employees and capable of unleashing out-of-the-box and creative thinking. We will return to the topic of setting difficult-to-achieve targets and how it affects employees later in the chapter.

Challenges in Administering Budgets

The budgeting process involves all levels of management. Top managers want lower-level managers to participate in the budgeting process because they have more specialized knowledge and firsthand experience with the day-to-day aspects of running the business. Participation also creates greater commitment and accountability toward the budget among lower-level managers. This is the bottom-up aspect of the budgeting process. This is counterbalanced by the top-down feature of budgeting where senior managers probe and debate the budgets submitted by subordinates with the goal of setting demanding, but achievable, budget targets.

The budgeting process, however, is time-consuming. Estimates suggest that senior managers spend about 10–20% of their time on budgeting, and financial planning departments spend as much as 50% of their time on it.[4] For most organizations, the annual budget process is a months-long exercise that consumes a tremendous amount of resources.

The widespread use of budgets in companies ranging from major multinational corporations to small local businesses indicates that the advantages of budgeting systems outweigh the costs. To gain the benefits of budgeting, however, management at all levels of a company, particularly senior managers, should understand and support the budget and all aspects of the management control system. Lower-level managers who feel that top managers do not "believe" in budgets are unlikely to be active participants in the formulation and successful administration of budgets.

Budgets should not be administered rigidly. Attaining the budget is not an end in itself, especially when conditions change dramatically. A manager may commit to a budget, but if a situation arises in which some unplanned repairs or an unplanned advertising program would serve the long-run interests of the company, the manager should undertake the additional spending. For example, Chipotle, devastated by food-safety issues that sickened about 500 diners in the

---

[2] For several examples, see Jeremy Hope and Robin Fraser, *Beyond Budgeting* (Boston: Harvard Business School Press, 2003). The authors also criticize the tendency for managers to administer budgets rigidly even when changing market conditions have rendered the budgets obsolete.

[3] For a detailed discussion and several examples of the merits of setting specific hard goals, see Gary P. Latham, "The Motivational Benefits of Goal-Setting," *Academy of Management Executive* 18, no. 4 (2004).

[4] See Peter Horvath and Ralf Sauter, "Why Budgeting Fails: One Management System Is Not Enough," *Balanced Scorecard Report* (September 2004).

DECISION POINT

When should a company prepare budgets? What are the advantages of preparing budgets?

second half of 2015 and resulted in a halving of its stock price, has responded with a new marketing campaign and the largest media buy in its history in an effort to woo customers back. On the flip side, the dramatic decline in consumer demand during the 2007–2009 recession led designers such as Gucci to slash their ad budgets and put on hold planned new boutiques. Macy's and other retailers, stuck with shelves of merchandise ordered before the financial crisis, had no recourse but to slash prices and cut their workforces. J. C. Penney eventually missed its sales projections for 2009 by $2 billion. However, its aggressive actions during the year enabled it to survive the recession. Unfortunately, in 2012, J. C. Penney suffered steep declines in sales as a result of changing its strategy away from offering discounts and deals to everyday low pricing.

Developing an Operating Budget

LEARNING OBJECTIVE 3

Prepare the operating budget

…the budgeted income statement

and its supporting schedules

…such as cost of goods sold and nonmanufacturing costs

Budgets are typically developed for a set period, such as a month, quarter, or year, which can be then broken into subperiods. For example, a 12-month cash budget may be broken into 12 monthly periods so that cash inflows and outflows can be better coordinated.

Time Coverage of Budgets

The motive for creating a budget should guide a manager in choosing the period for the budget. For example, consider budgeting for a new Harley-Davidson 500-cc motorcycle. If the purpose is to budget for the total profitability of this new model, a 5-year period (or more) may be suitable and long enough to cover the product from design to manufacturing, sales, and after-sales support. In contrast, consider budgeting for a seasonal theater production, which is expected to run for a few months. If the purpose is to estimate all cash outlays, a 6-month period from the planning stage to the final performance should suffice.

The most frequently used budget period is 1 year, which is often subdivided into quarters and months. The budgeted data for a year are frequently revised as the year goes on. At the end of the second quarter, management may change the budget for the next two quarters in light of new information obtained during the first 6 months. For example, with the decline in the value of the pound against the euro following Britain's vote to exit the European Union, sales of Opel's Corsa and Insignia models have been sluggish in Britain. In order to reduce its cost of operations by around $400 million to deal with the sudden turn of events, General Motors recently decided to reduce work hours and production in its Opel plants in Germany.

Businesses are increasingly using *rolling budgets*. A **rolling budget**, also called a **continuous budget** or **rolling forecast**, is a budget that is always available for a specified future period. It is created by continually adding a month, quarter, or year to the period that just ended. Consider Electrolux, a global appliance company, which has a 3- to 5-year strategic plan and a 4-quarter rolling budget. A 4-quarter rolling budget for the April 2016 to March 2017 period is superseded in the next quarter—that is, in June 2016—by a 4-quarter rolling budget for July 2016 to June 2017, and so on. There is always a 12-month budget (for the next year) in place. Rolling budgets constantly force Electrolux's management to think about the forthcoming 12 months, regardless of the quarter at hand. Some companies, such as Borealis, Europe's leading polyolefin plastics manufacturer; Millipore, a life sciences research and manufacturing firm headquartered in Massachusetts; and Nordea, the largest financial services group in the Nordic and Baltic Sea region, prepare rolling financial forecasts that look ahead five quarters. Other companies, such as EMC Corporation, the information infrastructure giant, employ a 6-quarter rolling-forecast process so that budget allocations can be constantly adjusted to meet changing market conditions.

Steps in Preparing an Operating Budget

The best way to learn how to prepare an operating budget is by walking through the steps a company would take to develop it. Consider Stylistic Furniture, a company that makes two types of granite-top coffee tables: Casual and Deluxe. It is late 2016 and Stylistic's CEO, Rex Jordan, is very concerned about how to respond to the board of directors' mandate to increase profits by 10% in the coming year. Jordan goes through the five-step decision-making process introduced in Chapter 1.

1. **Identify the Problem and Uncertainties.** The problem is to identify a strategy and to build a budget to achieve 10% profit growth. There are several uncertainties. Can Stylistic dramatically increase the sales of its more profitable Deluxe tables? What price pressures are Stylistic likely to face? Will the cost of materials increase? Can Stylistic reduce costs through efficiency improvements?

2. **Obtain Information.** Stylistic's managers gather information about sales of tables in the current year. They are delighted to learn that sales of Deluxe tables have been stronger than expected. Moreover, one of the key competitors in Stylistic's Casual tables' line has had quality problems that are unlikely to be resolved until 2017. Unfortunately, Stylistic's managers also discover that the prices of direct materials have increased slightly during 2016 when compared to 2015.

3. **Make Predictions About the Future.** Stylistic's managers feel confident that with a little more marketing, they will be able to grow the Deluxe tables' business in 2017 and even increase prices moderately relative to 2016. They also do not expect significant price pressures on Casual tables during the year because of the quality problems faced by a key competitor.

   The purchasing manager anticipates that prices of direct materials will be about the same in 2017 as it was in 2016. The manufacturing manager believes that efficiency improvements would allow the costs of manufacturing the tables to be maintained at 2016 costs despite an increase in the prices of other inputs. Achieving these efficiency improvements is important if Stylistic is to maintain its 12% operating margin (that is, operating income $\div$ sales = 12%) and to grow sales and operating income.

4. **Make Decisions by Choosing Among Alternatives.** Jordan and his managers feel confident about their strategy to increase the sales of Deluxe tables. This decision has some risks, but is the best option available for Stylistic to increase its profits by 10%.

5. **Implement the Decision, Evaluate Performance, and Learn.** As we will discuss in Chapters 7 and 8, managers compare a company's actual performance to its predicted performance to learn why things turned out the way they did and how to do better. Stylistic's managers would want to know whether their predictions about the prices of Casual and Deluxe tables were correct. Did the prices of inputs increase more or less than anticipated? Did efficiency improvements occur? Such learning would be helpful in building budgets in subsequent years.

Stylistic's managers begin their work on the 2017 budget. Exhibit 6-2 shows the various parts of the master budget, which is composed of the financial projections for Stylistic's operating and financial budgets for 2017. The light, medium, and dark green boxes in Exhibit 6-2 show the budgeted income statement and its supporting budget schedules, which together are called the **operating budget**.

We show the revenues budget box in light green to indicate that it is often the starting point of the operating budget. The supporting schedules—shown in medium green—quantify the budgets for various business functions of the value chain, from research and development to distribution costs. These schedules build up to the budgeted income statement—the key summary statement in the operating budget—shown in dark green.

The orange and purple boxes in the exhibit are the **financial budget**, which is that part of the master budget made up of the capital expenditures budget, the cash budget, the budgeted balance sheet, and the budgeted statement of cash flows. A financial budget focuses on how operations and planned capital outlays affect cash—shown in orange. Management accountants use the cash budget and the budgeted income statement to prepare two other summary financial statements—the budgeted balance sheet and the budgeted statement of cash flows, which are shown in purple.

Top managers and line managers responsible for various business functions in the value chain finalize the master budget after several rounds of discussions. We next present the steps in preparing an operating budget for Stylistic Furniture for 2017 using Exhibit 6-2 as a guide. The appendix to this chapter presents Stylistic's cash budget, which is another key component of the master budget. The following details are needed to prepare the budget:

- Stylistic sells two models of granite-top coffee tables: Casual and Deluxe. Revenue unrelated to sales, such as interest income, is zero.

- Work-in-process inventory is negligible and is ignored.

EXHIBIT 6-2

Overview of the Master
Budget for Stylistic
Furniture

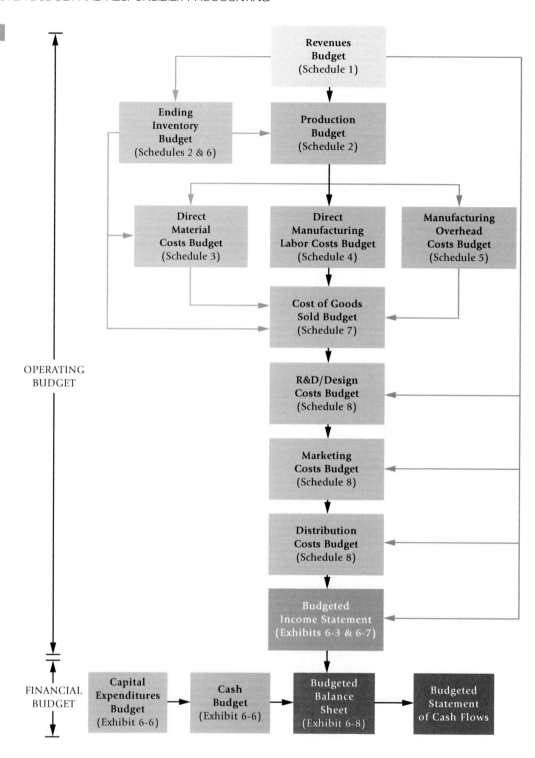

- Direct materials inventory and finished-goods inventory are costed using the first-in, first-out (FIFO) method. The unit costs of direct materials purchased and unit costs of finished-goods sold remain unchanged throughout each budget year, but can change from year to year.

- There are two types of direct materials: red oak (RO) and granite slabs (GS). The direct material costs are variable with respect to units of output—coffee tables.

- Direct manufacturing labor workers are hired on an hourly basis; no overtime is worked.

- There are two cost drivers for manufacturing overhead costs—direct manufacturing labor-hours and setup labor-hours, and two manufacturing overhead cost pools—manufacturing operations overhead and machine setup overhead.

- Direct manufacturing labor-hours is the cost driver for the variable portion of manufacturing operations overhead. The fixed component of manufacturing operations overhead is tied to the manufacturing capacity of 300,000 direct manufacturing labor-hours Stylistic has planned for 2017.

- Setup labor-hours are the cost driver for the variable portion of machine setup overhead. The fixed component of machine setup overhead is tied to the setup capacity of 15,000 setup labor-hours Stylistic has planned for 2017.

- For computing inventoriable costs, Stylistic allocates all (variable and fixed) manufacturing operations overhead costs using direct manufacturing labor-hours and machine setup overhead costs using setup labor-hours.

- Nonmanufacturing costs consist of product design, marketing, and distribution costs. All product design costs are fixed costs for 2017. The variable component of marketing costs is the 6.5% sales commission on revenues paid to salespeople. The variable portion of distribution costs varies with cubic feet of tables sold and shipped.

The following data are available for the 2017 budget:

Direct materials
Red oak	$ 7 per board foot (b.f.) (same as in 2016)
Granite	$10 per square foot (sq. ft.) (same as in 2016)
Direct manufacturing labor	$20 per hour

	Content of Each Product Unit	
	Casual Granite Table	Deluxe Granite Table
Red oak	12 board feet	12 board feet
Granite	6 square feet	8 square feet
Direct manufacturing labor	4 hours	6 hours

	Product	
	Casual Granite Table	Deluxe Granite Table
Expected sales in units	50,000	10,000
Selling price	$ 600	$ 800
Target ending inventory in units	11,000	500
Beginning inventory in units	1,000	500
Beginning inventory in dollars	$384,000	$262,000

	Direct Materials	
	Red oak	Granite
Beginning inventory	70,000 b.f.	60,000 sq. ft.
Target ending inventory	80,000 b.f.	20,000 sq. ft.

Stylistic bases its budgeted cost information on the costs predicted to support its revenues budget, taking into account the efficiency improvements it expects to make in 2017. Recall from Step 3 of the decision-making process (page 223) that efficiency improvements are critical to offset the anticipated increases in the cost of inputs and to maintain Stylistic's 12% operating margin.

Most companies have a budget manual that contains a company's particular instructions and information for preparing its budgets. Although the details differ among companies, the following basic steps are common for developing the operating budget for a manufacturing company. Beginning with the revenues budget, each of the other budgets follows step by step in logical fashion. As you go through the details for preparing a budget, think about two things: (1) the information needed to prepare each budget and (2) the actions managers can plan to take to improve the company's performance.

Step 1: Prepare the Revenues Budget. Stylistic's managers plan to continue to sell two models of granite-top coffee tables: Casual and Deluxe. The revenues budget accounts for the quantities and prices of Casual and Deluxe tables that Stylistic expects to sell in 2017.

A revenues budget is the usual starting point for the operating budget. Why? Because the forecasted level of unit sales or revenues has a major impact on the production capacity and the inventory levels planned for 2017—and therefore, manufacturing and nonmanufacturing costs. Many factors affect the sales forecast, including the sales volume in recent periods, general economic and industry conditions, market research studies, pricing policies, advertising and sales promotions, competition, and regulatory policies. The key to Stylistic achieving its goal of growing its profits by 10% is to grow its sales of Deluxe tables from 8,000 tables in 2016 to 10,000 tables in 2017.

Managers use customer relationship management (CRM) or sales management systems to gather information. Statistical approaches such as regression and trend analysis based on indicators of economic activity and past sales data help in forecasting future sales. Sales managers and sales representatives debate how best to position, price, and promote Casual and Deluxe tables relative to competitors' products. Together with top management, they consider various actions, such as adding product features, digital advertising, and changing sales incentives, to increase revenues. The costs of these actions are included in the various cost budgets. In the final analysis, the sales forecast represents the collective experience and judgment of managers.

Top managers decide on the budgeted sales quantities and prices shown in the revenues budget in Schedule 1. These are difficult targets designed to motivate the organization to achieve higher levels of performance.

Schedule 1: Revenues Budget
for the Year Ending December 31, 2017

	Units	Selling Price	Total Revenues
Casual	50,000	$600	$30,000,000
Deluxe	10,000	800	8,000,000
Total			$38,000,000

The $38,000,000 is the amount of revenues in the budgeted income statement.

Revenues budgets are usually based on market conditions and expected demand because demand for a company's products is invariably the limiting factor for achieving profit goals. Occasionally, other factors, such as available production capacity (being less than demand) or a manufacturing input in short supply, limit budgeted revenues. In these cases, managers base the revenues budget on the maximum units that can be produced because sales will be limited by the available production.

Step 2: Prepare the Production Budget (in Units). The next step in the budgeting process is to plan the production quantities of Casual and Deluxe tables. The only new information managers need to prepare the production budget is the desired level of finished goods inventory. High inventory levels increase the cost of carrying inventory, the costs of quality, and shrinkage costs. On the flip side, low inventory levels increase setup costs and result in lost sales because of product unavailability. Stylistic's management decides to maintain the inventory level of Deluxe tables and increase the inventory of Casual tables to avoid the effects of supply shortages that the company encountered in 2016.

The manufacturing manager prepares the production budget, shown in Schedule 2. The units of finished goods to be produced depend on budgeted unit sales (calculated in Step 1), the target ending finished-goods inventory, and the beginning finished-goods inventory:

$$\begin{matrix} \text{Budget} \\ \text{production} \\ \text{(units)} \end{matrix} = \begin{matrix} \text{Budget} \\ \text{sales} \\ \text{(units)} \end{matrix} + \begin{matrix} \text{Target ending} \\ \text{finished goods} \\ \text{inventory} \\ \text{(units)} \end{matrix} - \begin{matrix} \text{Beginning} \\ \text{finished goods} \\ \text{inventory} \\ \text{(units)} \end{matrix}$$

Schedule 2: Production Budget (in Units)
for the Year Ending December 31, 2017

	Product	
	Casual	Deluxe
Budgeted sales in units (Schedule 1)	50,000	10,000
Add target ending finished-goods inventory	11,000	500
Total required units	61,000	10,500
Deduct beginning finished-goods inventory	1,000	500
Units of finished goods to be produced	60,000	10,000

The production budget determines budgeted production costs (for example, direct materials, direct manufacturing labor, and manufacturing overhead) after considering efficiency improvements planned for 2017. Costs are also influenced by actions such as product redesign needed to support the revenues budget.

Managers are always looking for opportunities to reduce costs, for example, by improving processes, streamlining manufacturing, and reducing the time it takes to complete various activities, such as setting up machines or transporting materials. Making these changes improves a company's competitiveness, but it also requires investment. The budgeting exercise is an ideal time for managers to evaluate plans and request the needed financial resources.

Jimenez Corporation manufactures and sells two types of decorative lamps, Knox and Ayer. The following data are available for the year 2017.

◄ 6-1 TRY IT!

	Product	
	Knox	Ayer
Expected sales in units	21,000	10,000
Selling price	$ 25	$ 40
Target ending inventory in units	2,000	1,000
Beginning inventory in units	3,000	1,000

Calculate the revenues budget (label it Schedule 1) and the production budget in units (label it Schedule 2) for year ending December 31, 2017.

Step 3: Prepare the Direct Materials Usage Budget and Direct Materials Purchases Budget. The budgeted production, calculated in Schedule 2, determines the quantities and dollars of direct materials used. The direct material quantities used depends on the efficiency with which workers use materials to produce a table. In determining budgets, managers are constantly anticipating ways to make process improvements that increase quality and reduce waste, thereby reducing direct material usage and costs. Senior managers set budgets that motivate production managers to reduce direct material costs and keep negligible work-in-process inventory. We ignore work-in-process inventory when preparing Stylistic's budgets for 2017.

Like many companies, Stylistic has a *bill of materials* stored in its computer systems that it constantly updates for efficiency improvements. This document identifies how each product is manufactured, specifying all materials (and components), the sequence in which the materials are used, the quantity of materials in each finished unit, and the work centers where the operations are performed. For example, the bill of materials would indicate that 12 board feet of red oak and 6 square feet of granite are needed to produce each Casual coffee table and 12 board feet of red oak and 8 square feet of granite are needed to produce each Deluxe coffee table. Direct materials inventories are costed using the first-in, first-out (FIFO) method. The management accountant uses this information to calculate the direct materials usage budget in Schedule 3A.

Schedule 3A: Direct Materials Usage Budget in Quantity and Dollars
for the Year Ending December 31, 2017

	Material		
	Red oak	**Granite**	**Total**
Physical Units Budget			
Direct materials required for Casual tables (60,000 units × 12 b.f. and 6 sq. ft.)	720,000 b.f.	360,000 sq. ft.	
Direct materials required for Deluxe tables (10,000 units × 12 b.f. and 8 sq. ft.)	120,000 b.f.	80,000 sq. ft.	
Total quantity of direct materials to be used	840,000 b.f.	440,000 sq. ft.	
Cost Budget			
Available from beginning direct materials inventory (under a FIFO cost-flow assumption) (Given)			
Red oak: 70,000 b.f. × $7 per b.f.	$ 490,000		
Granite: 60,000 sq. ft. × $10 per sq. ft.		$ 600,000	
To be purchased and used this period			
Red oak: (840,000 − 70,000) b.f. × $7 per b.f.	5,390,000		
Granite: (440,000 − 60,000) sq. ft. × $10 per sq. ft.		3,800,000	
Direct materials to be used this period	$5,880,000	$4,400,000	$10,280,000

The only new information needed to prepare the direct materials purchases budget is the desired levels of direct materials inventory. During 2017, Stylistic's managers plan to increase the inventory of red oak, but reduce the inventory of granite to the levels of ending inventory described on page 225. The purchasing manager then prepares the budget for direct material purchases, shown in Schedule 3B:

Schedule 3B: Direct Materials Purchases Budget
for the Year Ending December 31, 2017

	Material		
	Red oak	**Granite**	**Total**
Physical Units Budget			
To be used in production (from Schedule 3A)	840,000 b.f.	440,000 sq. ft.	
Add target ending inventory	80,000 b.f.	20,000 sq. ft.	
Total requirements	920,000 b.f.	460,000 sq. ft.	
Deduct beginning inventory	70,000 b.f.	60,000 sq. ft.	
Purchases to be made	850,000 b.f.	400,000 sq. ft.	
Cost Budget			
Red oak: 850,000 b.f. × $7 per b.f.	$5,950,000		
Granite: 400,000 sq. ft. × $10 per sq. ft.		$4,000,000	
Direct materials to be purchased this period	$5,950,000	$4,000,000	$9,950,000

Step 4: Prepare the Direct Manufacturing Labor Costs Budget. To create the budget for direct manufacturing labor costs, Stylistic's managers estimate wage rates, production methods, process and efficiency improvements, and hiring plans. The company hires direct manufacturing labor workers on an hourly basis. These workers do not work overtime. Manufacturing managers use *labor standards*, the time allowed per unit of output, to calculate the direct manufacturing labor costs budget in Schedule 4 based on the information on pages 225–227.

Schedule 4: Direct Manufacturing Labor Costs Budget
for the Year Ending December 31, 2017

	Output Units Produced (Schedule 2)	Direct Manufacturing Labor-Hours per Unit	Total Hours	Hourly Wage Rate	Total
Casual	60,000	4	240,000	$20	$4,800,000
Deluxe	10,000	6	60,000	20	1,200,000
Total			300,000		$6,000,000

Jimenez Corporation manufactures and sells two types of decorative lamps, Knox and Ayer. It expects to manufacture 20,000 Knox lamps and 10,000 Ayer lamps in 2017. The following data are available for the year 2017.

6-2 TRY IT!

Direct materials
    Metal $ 3 per pound (same as in 2016)
    Fabric $ 4 per yard (same as in 2016)
    Direct manufacturing labor $20 per hour

Content of Each Product Unit

	Product	
	Knox	Ayer
Metal	2 pounds	3 pounds
Fabric	1 yard	1.5 yards
Direct manufacturing labor	0.15 hours	0.2 hours

	Direct Materials	
	Metal	Fabric
Beginning inventory	12,000 pounds	7,000 yards
Target ending inventory	10,000 pounds	5,000 yards

Calculate (a) the direct materials usage budget in quantity and dollars (label it Schedule 3A); (b) the direct materials purchase budget in quantity and dollars (label it Schedule 3B); and (c) the direct manufacturing labor costs budget (label it Schedule 4) for the year ending December 31, 2017.

Step 5: Prepare the Manufacturing Overhead Costs Budget. Stylistic's managers next budget for manufacturing overhead costs such as supervision, depreciation, maintenance, supplies, and power. Managing overhead costs is important but also challenging because it requires managers to understand the various activities needed to manufacture products and the cost drivers of those activities. As we described earlier (page 225), Stylistic's managers identify two activities for manufacturing overhead costs in its activity-based costing system: manufacturing operations and machine setups. The following table presents the activities and their cost drivers.

Manufacturing Overhead Costs	Cost Driver of Variable Component of Overhead Costs	Cost Driver of Fixed Component of Overhead Costs	Manufacturing and Setup Capacity in 2017
Manufacturing Operations Overhead Costs	Direct manufacturing labor-hours	Manufacturing capacity	300,000 direct manufacturing labor-hours
Machine Setup Overhead Costs	Setup labor-hours	Setup capacity	15,000 setup labor-hours

The use of activity-based cost drivers gives rise to **activity-based budgeting (ABB)**, a budgeting method that focuses on the budgeted cost of the activities necessary to produce and sell products and services.

In its activity-based costing system, Stylistic's manufacturing managers estimate various line items of overhead costs that comprise manufacturing operations overhead (that is, all costs for which direct manufacturing labor-hours is the cost driver). Managers identify opportunities for process and efficiency improvements, such as reducing defect rates and the time to manufacture a table, and then calculate budgeted manufacturing operations overhead costs in the operating department. They also determine the resources that they will need from the two support departments—kilowatt-hours of energy from the power department and hours of maintenance service from the maintenance department. The support department managers, in turn, plan the costs of personnel and supplies that they will need in order to provide the operating department with the support services it requires. The costs of the support departments are then allocated (first-stage cost allocation) as part of manufacturing operations overhead. Chapter 15 describes the allocation of support department costs to operating departments when support departments provide services to each other and to operating departments. The first half of Schedule 5 (page 231) shows the various line items of costs that constitute manufacturing operations overhead costs—that is, all variable and fixed overhead costs (in the operating and support departments) that are caused by the 300,000 direct manufacturing labor-hours (the cost driver).

Stylistic budgets costs differently for variable and fixed overhead costs. Consider variable overhead costs of supplies: Stylistic's managers use past historical data and their knowledge of operations to estimate the cost of supplies per direct manufacturing labor-hour of $5. The total budgeted cost of supplies for 2017 is, therefore, $5 multiplied by the 300,000 budgeted direct manufacturing labor-hours, for a total of $1,500,000. The total variable manufacturing operations overhead cost equals $21.60 per direct manufacturing labor-hour multiplied by the 300,000 budgeted direct manufacturing labor-hours, for a total of $6,480,000.

Stylistic measures manufacturing operations capacity in terms of the direct manufacturing labor-hours that the facility is configured to support. It currently has a capacity of 300,000 direct manufacturing labor-hours. To support this level of capacity, and taking into account potential cost improvements, managers estimate total fixed manufacturing operations overhead costs of $2,520,000. (Note that, unlike 2017, Stylistic may not operate at full capacity each year, but its fixed manufacturing operations costs will still be $2,520,000.) Its fixed manufacturing overhead cost is $2,520,000 ÷ 300,000 = $8.40 per direct manufacturing labor-hour (regardless of the budgeted direct manufacturing labor-hours, which may be less than 300,000 in a particular year). That is, each direct manufacturing labor-hour will absorb $21.60 of variable manufacturing operations overhead plus $8.40 of fixed manufacturing operations overhead for a total of $30 of manufacturing operations overhead cost per direct manufacturing labor-hour.

Next, Stylistic's managers determine how setups will be done for the Casual and Deluxe line of tables, taking into account past experiences and potential improvements in setup efficiency.

For example, managers consider the following:

- Increasing the number of tables produced per batch so fewer batches (and therefore fewer setups) are needed for the budgeted production of tables
- Decreasing the setup time per batch
- Reducing the supervisory time needed, for example by increasing the skill base of workers

Stylistic's managers forecast the following setup information for the Casual and Deluxe tables:

	Casual Tables	Deluxe Tables	Total
1. Quantity of tables to be produced	60,000 tables	10,000 tables	
2. Number of tables to be produced per batch	50 tables/batch	40 tables/batch	
3. Number of batches (1) ÷ (2)	1,200 batches	250 batches	
5. Setup time per batch	10 hours/batch	12 hours/batch	
6. Total setup-hours (3) × (4)	12,000 hours	3,000 hours	15,000 hours
8. Setup-hours per table (5) ÷ (1)	0.2 hour	0.3 hour	

Using an approach similar to the one described for manufacturing operations overhead costs, Stylistic's managers estimate various line items of costs that comprise variable machine setup overhead costs (supplies, indirect manufacturing labor, power, depreciation, and supervision)—that is, all costs caused by the 15,000 setup labor-hours (the cost driver): The second half of Schedule 5 summarizes (1) total variable machine setup overhead costs per setup labor-hour = \$88(\$26 + \$56 + \$6) × the budgeted 15,000 setup labor-hours = \$1,320,000 and (2) fixed machine setup overhead costs of \$1,680,000 needed to support the 15,000 setup labor-hours of capacity that Stylistic's managers have planned. (Again, Stylistic may not operate at full capacity each year. However, the fixed machine setup costs will still be \$1,680,000.) The fixed machine setup cost is \$1,680,000 ÷ 15,000 = \$112 per setup labor-hour (regardless of the budgeted setup labor-hours, which may be less than 15,000 in a particular year). That is, each setup labor-hour will absorb \$88 of variable machine setup overhead cost plus \$112 of fixed machine setup overhead cost for a total of \$200 of machine setup overhead cost per setup labor-hour.

Schedule 5: Manufacturing Overhead Costs Budget
for the Year Ending December 31, 2017

Manufacturing Operations Overhead Costs

Variable costs (for 300,000 direct manufacturing labor-hours)		
Supplies (\$5 per direct manufacturing labor-hour)	\$1,500,000	
Indirect manufacturing labor (\$5.60 per direct manufacturing labor-hour)	1,680,000	
Power (support department costs) (\$7 per direct manufacturing labor-hour)	2,100,000	
Maintenance (support department costs) (\$4 per direct manufacturing labor-hour)	1,200,000	\$6,480,000
Fixed costs (to support capacity of 300,000 direct manufacturing labor-hours)		
Depreciation	1,020,000	
Supervision	390,000	
Power (support department costs)	630,000	
Maintenance (support department costs)	480,000	2,520,000
Total manufacturing operations overhead costs		\$9,000,000

Machine Setup Overhead Costs

Variable costs (for 15,000 setup labor-hours)		
Supplies (\$26 per setup labor-hour)	\$ 390,000	
Indirect manufacturing labor (\$56 per setup labor-hour)	840,000	
Power (support department costs) (\$6 per setup labor-hour)	90,000	\$ 1,320,000
Fixed costs (to support capacity of 15,000 setup labor-hours)		
Depreciation	603,000	
Supervision	1,050,000	
Power (support department costs)	27,000	1,680,000
Total machine setup overhead costs		\$ 3,000,000
Total manufacturing overhead costs		\$12,000,000

Note how using activity-based cost drivers provide additional and detailed information that improves decision making compared with budgeting based solely on output-based cost drivers. Of course, managers must always evaluate whether the expected benefit of adding more cost drivers exceeds the expected cost.[5]

Note that Stylistic is scheduled to operate at capacity. Therefore, the budgeted quantity of the cost allocation base/cost driver is the same for variable overhead costs and fixed overhead costs—300,000 direct manufacturing labor-hours for manufacturing operations overhead costs and 15,000 setup labor-hours for machine setup overhead costs. In this case, the budgeted rate for the manufacturing operations overhead cost does not have to be calculated separately for variable costs and for fixed costs as we did earlier. Instead, it can be calculated directly by estimating total budgeted manufacturing operations overhead: \$9,000,000 ÷ 300,000 direct

---

[5] The Stylistic example illustrates ABB using manufacturing operations and setup costs included in Stylistic's manufacturing overhead costs budget. ABB implementations in practice include costs in many parts of the value chain. For an example, see Sofia Borjesson, "A Case Study on Activity-Based Budgeting," *Journal of Cost Management* 10, no. 4 (Winter 1997): 7–18.

manufacturing labor-hours = $30 per direct manufacturing labor-hour. Similarly, the budgeted rate for machine setup overhead cost can be calculated as total budgeted machine setup overhead: $3,000,000 ÷ 15,000 budgeted setup hours = $200 per setup-hour.

TRY IT! 6-3 ▶

Jimenez Corporation manufactures and sells two types of decorative lamps, Knox and Ayer. The following data are available for the year 2017. Machine setup-hours is the only driver of manufacturing overhead costs. Jimenez has a setup capacity of 1,100 hours

		Knox	Ayer
1.	Quantity of lamps to be produced	20,000 lamps	10,000 lamps
2.	Number of lamps to be produced per batch	100 lamps/batch	80 lamps/batch
3.	Setup time per batch	3 hours/batch	4 hours/batch

Variable cost = $60 per setup-hour
Fixed cost = $77,000
Calculate the manufacturing overhead costs budget (label it Schedule 5).

Step 6: Prepare the Ending Inventories Budget. Schedule 6A shows the computation of the unit cost of coffee tables started and completed in 2017. These calculations are needed to calculate the ending inventories budget and the budgeted cost of goods sold. In accordance with Generally Accepted Accounting Principles, Stylistic treats both variable and fixed manufacturing overhead as inventoriable (product) costs. Manufacturing operations overhead costs are allocated to finished-goods inventory at the budgeted rate of $30 per direct manufacturing labor-hour. Machine setup overhead costs are allocated to finished-goods inventory at the budgeted rate of $200 per setup-hour.

**Schedule 6A: Budgeted Unit Costs of Ending
Finished-Goods Inventory December 31, 2017**

		Product			
		Casual Tables		Deluxe Tables	
	Cost per Unit of Input	Input per Unit of Output	Total	Input per Unit of Output	Total
Red oak	$ 7	12 b.f.	$ 84	12 b.f.	$ 84
Granite	10	6 sq. ft.	60	8 sq. ft.	80
Direct manufacturing labor	20	4 hrs.	80	6 hrs.	120
Manufacturing operations overhead	30	4 hrs.	120	6 hrs.	180
Machine setup overhead	200	0.2 hrs.	40	0.3 hrs.	60
Total			$384		$524

Under the FIFO method, managers use this unit cost to calculate the cost of target ending inventories of finished goods in Schedule 6B.

Schedule 6B: Ending Inventories Budget December 31, 2017

	Quantity	Cost per Unit		Total
Direct materials				
Red oak	80,000*	$7	$ 560,000	
Granite	20,000*	10	200,000	$ 760,000
Finished goods				
Casual	11,000**	$384***	$4,224,000	
Deluxe	500**	524***	262,000	4,486,000
Total ending inventory				$5,246,000

*Data are from page 225. **Data are from page 225. ***From Schedule 6A, this is based on 2017 costs of manufacturing finished goods because under the FIFO costing method, the units in finished-goods ending inventory consists of units that are produced during 2017.

Jimenez Corporation manufactures and sells two types of decorative lamps, Knox and Ayer. The following data are available for the year 2017.

6-4 TRY IT!

	Product	
	Knox	Ayer
Target ending inventory in units	2,000	1,000

Direct materials

Metal	$ 3 per pound (same as in 2016)
Fabric	$ 4 per yard (same as in 2016)
Direct manufacturing labor	$ 20 per hour
Machine setup overhead	$130 per hour

	Content of Each Product Unit	
	Knox	Ayer
Metal	2 pounds	3 pounds
Fabric	1 yard	1.5 yards
Direct manufacturing labor	0.15 hours	0.2 hours
Machine setup overhead	0.03 hours	0.05 hours

	Direct Materials	
	Metal	Fabric
Target ending inventory	10,000 pounds	5,000 yards

Calculate (1) the budgeted unit costs of ending finished-goods inventory on December 31, 2017 (label it Schedule 6A) and (2) the ending inventories budget on December 31, 2017 (label it Schedule 6B).

Step 7: Prepare the Cost of Goods Sold Budget. The manufacturing and purchase managers, together with the management accountant, use information from Schedules 3–6 to prepare Schedule 7—the cost of goods sold expense budget that will be matched against revenues to calculate Stylistic's budgeted gross margin for 2017.

Schedule 7: Cost of Goods Sold Budget
for the Year Ending December 31, 2017

	From Schedule		Total
Beginning finished-goods inventory, January 1, 2017	Given*		$ 646,000
Direct materials used	3A	$10,280,000	
Direct manufacturing labor	4	6,000,000	
Manufacturing overhead	5	12,000,000	
Cost of goods manufactured			28,280,000
Cost of goods available for sale			28,926,000
Deduct ending finished-goods inventory, December 31, 2017	6B		4,486,000
Cost of goods sold			$24,440,000

*Based on beginning inventory values in 2017 for Casual tables, $384,000, and Deluxe tables, $262,000 (page 225).

Step 8: Prepare the Nonmanufacturing Costs Budget. Schedules 2–7 represent budgets for Stylistic's manufacturing costs. Stylistic also incurs nonmanufacturing costs in other parts of the value chain—product design, marketing, and distribution. Just as in the case of manufacturing costs, the key to managing nonmanufacturing overhead costs is to understand the various activities that will be needed to support the design, marketing, and distribution of Deluxe and Casual tables in 2017 and the cost drivers of those activities. Managers in these functions of the value chain build in process and efficiency improvements and prepare nonmanufacturing cost budgets on the basis of the quantities of cost drivers planned for 2017.

The number of design changes is the cost driver for product design costs. Product design costs of $1,024,000 are fixed costs for 2017 and adjusted at the start of the year based on the number of design changes planned for 2017.

Total revenue is the cost driver for the variable portion of marketing (and sales) costs. The commission paid to salespeople equals 6.5 cents per dollar (or 6.5%) of revenues. Managers budget the fixed component of marketing costs, $1,330,000, at the start of the year based on budgeted revenues for 2017.

Cubic feet of tables sold and shipped (Casual: 18 cubic feet × 50,000 tables + Deluxe: 24 cubic feet × 10,000 tables = 1,140,000 cubic feet) is the cost driver of the variable component of budgeted distribution costs. Variable distribution costs equal $2 per cubic foot. The fixed component of budgeted distribution costs equal to $1,596,000 varies with the company's distribution capacity, which in 2017 is 1,140,000 cubic feet (to support the distribution of 50,000 Casual tables and 10,000 Deluxe tables). For brevity, Schedule 8 shows the product design, marketing, and distribution costs budget for 2017 in a single schedule.

Schedule 8: Nonmanufacturing Costs Budget
for the Year Ending December 31, 2017

Business Function	Variable Costs	Fixed Costs	Total Costs
Product design	—	$1,024,000	$1,024,000
Marketing (Variable cost: $38,000,000 × 0.065)	$2,470,000	1,330,000	3,800,000
Distribution (Variable cost: $2 × 1,140,000 cu. ft.)	2,280,000	1,596,000	3,876,000
	$4,750,000	$3,950,000	$8,700,000

The nonmanufacturing costs in our example focused on activities Stylistic needs to undertake to achieve its revenue goals for the year. The innovations in product design were incremental innovations necessary to generate higher revenues in 2017. Sometimes companies need to invest in research and development (R&D) in a particular year that, if successful, will only result in revenues in a subsequent year. When companies engage in radical rather than incremental innovation, R&D costs may have to be incurred for several years before the company sees the benefits of the R&D in the form of revenues. Many critics argue that the short-term costs of engaging in innovation for uncertain long-term benefits result in companies underinvesting in radical or breakthrough innovations.

Companies that engage in breakthrough innovation budget separately for these resources in their annual budgets. In this way, they separate the operational performance for the year from investments in innovation for subsequent years. They ensure that the innovations pursued are closely linked to their intended strategies and develop project milestones, such as expert evaluations, intellectual property creation, patents received, and customer engagement, to monitor progress and value creation of the innovation projects.

Step 9: Prepare the Budgeted Income Statement. The CEO and managers of various business functions, with help from the management accountant, use information in Schedules 1, 7, and 8 to finalize the budgeted income statement, shown in Exhibit 6-3. The style used in Exhibit 6-3 is typical, but managers and accountants could include more details in the income statement. As more details are put in the income statement, fewer supporting schedules are needed.

Budgeting is a cross-functional activity. The strategies developed by top managers for achieving a company's revenue and operating income goals affect the costs planned for the different business functions of the value chain. For example, the budgeted increase in sales at Stylistic is based on spending more for marketing and must be matched with higher production costs to ensure there is an adequate supply of tables and with higher distribution costs to ensure the timely delivery of tables to customers. Rex Jordan, the CEO of Stylistic Furniture, is very pleased with the 2017 budget. It calls for a 10% increase in operating income compared with 2016. The keys to achieving a higher operating income are a significant increase in sales

EXHIBIT 6-3

Budgeted Income Statement for Stylistic Furniture

	Home	Insert	Page Layout	Formulas	Data	Review	View
	A	**B**		**C**		**D**	
1	Budgeted Income Statement for Stylistic Furniture						
2	For the Year Ending December 31, 2017						
3	Revenues	Schedule 1				$38,000,000	
4	Cost of goods sold	Schedule 7				24,440,000	
5	Gross margin					13,560,000	
6	Operating costs						
7	Product design costs	Schedule 8		$1,024,000			
8	Marketing costs	Schedule 8		3,800,000			
9	Distribution costs	Schedule 8		3,876,000		8,700,000	
10	Operating income					$ 4,860,000	

of Deluxe tables and process improvements and efficiency gains throughout the value chain. As Rex studies the budget more carefully, however, he is struck by two comments appended to the budget: First, to achieve the budgeted number of tables sold, Stylistic may need to reduce its selling prices by 3% to $582 for Casual tables and to $776 for Deluxe tables. Second, a supply shortage in direct materials may result in a 5% increase in the prices of direct materials (red oak and granite) above the material prices anticipated in the 2017 budget. Even if direct materials prices increase, selling prices are anticipated to remain unchanged. He asks Tina Larsen, a management accountant, to use Stylistic's financial planning model to evaluate how these outcomes will affect budgeted operating income.

DECISION POINT

What is the operating budget and what are its components?

Jimenez Corporation manufactures and sells two types of decorative lamps, Knox and Ayer. The following data are available for the year 2017. The numbers below represent the calculations from the previous Try It! examples (6-1 through 6-4) together with the relevant schedule numbers from those examples.

6-5 TRY IT!

Revenues (Schedule 1)	$925,000
Beginning inventory of finished goods (1-1-2017)	76,200
Ending inventory of finished goods, 12-31-2017 (Schedule 6B)	59,300
Direct materials used (Schedule 3A)	350,000
Direct manufacturing labor (Schedule 4)	100,000
Manufacturing overhead (Schedule 5)	143,000
Variable marketing costs (4% of revenues)	
Fixed marketing costs	43,000
Variable distribution costs ($1.50 per cu. ft. for 30,000 cu. ft.)	
Fixed distribution costs	40,000
Fixed administration costs	75,000

Calculate (1) the cost of goods sold budget (label it Schedule 7); (2) the nonmanufacturing costs budget (label it Schedule 8); and (3) the operating income budget for the year ending December 31, 2017.

LEARNING OBJECTIVE 4

Use computer-based financial planning models for sensitivity analysis

…for example, understand the effects of changes in selling prices and direct material prices on budgeted income

Financial Planning Models and Sensitivity Analysis

Financial planning models are mathematical representations of the relationships among operating activities, financing activities, and other factors that affect the master budget. Managers use computer-based systems, such as enterprise resource planning (ERP) systems, to manage their businesses and to perform calculations for these planning models. Budgeting tools within ERP systems simplify budgeting, reduce the need to re-input data, and reduce the time required to prepare budgets. ERP systems store vast quantities of information about the materials, machines and equipment, labor, power, maintenance, and setups needed to produce different products. Once managers identify sales quantities for different products, the software can quickly compute the budgeted costs for manufacturing these products. ERP systems also help managers budget for nonmanufacturing costs. Many service companies, such as banks, hospitals, and airlines, also use ERP systems to manage their operations. The Concepts in Action: 24 Hour Fitness and Internet-Based Budgeting is an example of a service company using a software platform to coordinate and manage its budgets across multiple locations.

As they prepare operating budgets, managers do not focus only on what they can achieve. They also identify the risks they face such as a potential decline in demand for the company's products, the entry of a new competitor, or an increase in the prices of different inputs. Sensitivity analysis is a useful tool that helps managers evaluate these risks. *Sensitivity analysis* is a "what-if" technique that examines how a result will change if the original predicted data are not achieved or if an underlying assumption changes. Software packages typically have a sensitivity analysis module that managers can use in their planning and budgeting activities.

To see how sensitivity analysis works, we consider two scenarios identified as possibly affecting Stylistic Furniture's budget model for 2017. Either of the two scenarios could happen, but not both together.

Scenario 1: A 3% decrease in the selling price of the Casual table and a 3% decrease in the selling price of the Deluxe table.

Scenario 2: A 5% increase in the price per board foot of red oak and a 5% increase in the price per square foot of granite.

Exhibit 6-4 presents the budgeted operating income for the two scenarios.

In the case of Scenario 1, note that a change in the selling price per table affects revenues (Schedule 1) as well as variable marketing costs (sales commissions, Schedule 8). The Problem for Self-Study at the end of the chapter shows the revised schedules for Scenario 1. Similarly, a change in the price of direct materials affects the direct material usage budget (Schedule 3A), the unit cost of ending finished-goods inventory (Schedule 6A), the ending finished-goods inventories budget (Schedule 6B), and the cost of goods sold budget (Schedule 7). Sensitivity analysis is especially useful to managers incorporating these interrelationships into their budgeting decisions.

Exhibit 6-4 shows that operating income decreases substantially if selling prices decrease by 3%, but declines much less if direct materials prices increase by 5%. The sensitivity analysis prompts Stylistic's managers to put in place contingency plans. For example, if selling prices decline in 2017, Stylistic may need to reduce costs even more than planned. More generally, when the success or viability of a venture is highly dependent on attaining a certain income target, managers should frequently update their budgets as uncertainty is resolved. These updated budgets can help managers adjust expenditure levels as circumstances change.

DECISION POINT

How can managers plan for changes in the assumptions underlying the budget and manage risk?

EXHIBIT 6-4 Effect of Changes in Budget Assumptions on Budgeted Operating Income for Stylistic Furniture

What-If Scenario	Units Sold Casual	Deluxe	Selling Price Casual	Deluxe	Direct Material Cost Red Oak	Granite	Budgeted Operating Income Dollars	Change from Master Budget
Master budget	50,000	10,000	$600	$800	$7.00	$10.00	$4,860,000	
Scenario 1	50,000	10,000	582	776	$7.00	$10.00	3,794,100	22% decrease
Scenario 2	50,000	10,000	600	800	$7.35	$10.50	4,418,000	9% decrease

CONCEPTS IN ACTION

24 Hour Fitness and Internet-Based Budgeting

B Christopher/Alamy Stock Photo

24 Hour Fitness is one of the largest fitness-club chains in the United States, with nearly 4 million members, more than 450 clubs in 16 states and $1.5 billion in annual revenues. The company uses Longview, an Internet-based software platform, to manage its planning and budgeting process.

Using detailed operational statistics including number of members, number of workouts, and hours worked by each category of staff, accounting and finance managers sign on to the platform and develop budgets for each club. Advertising costs are allocated to each club based on the size, age, and traffic of each club. Using Longview at 24 Hour Fitness has resulted in more accurate budgets and forecasts being developed in less time. Managers can also conduct "what if" budget scenario analysis.

The platform also allows each club manager to track very-detailed revenue and expense data covering individual aspects of club activity, including juice bars, personal training sessions, product sales, and credit card membership dues and to take corrective action. It also enables staff to better support senior management decision making by responding more quickly to information requests. Mike Patano, Senior Director of Financial Planning & Analysis, summarized, "Day to day, it's about being able to thoroughly understand our business, benchmark the performance of our clubs, and understand our business drivers much better and quicker."

Sources: Longview Solutions, "Longview Case Study: 24 Hour Fitness," 2014 (http://info.longview.com/CaseStudy-24HourFitness.html); 24 Hour Fitness, "About Us," http://www.24hourfitness.com/company/about_us/, accessed March 2016.

Earlier in this chapter we described a rolling budget as a budget that is always available for a specified future period. Rolling budgets are constantly updated to reflect the latest cost and revenue information and make managers responsive to changing conditions and market needs.

Instructors and students who, at this point, want to explore the cash budget and the budgeted balance sheet for the Stylistic Furniture example can skip ahead to the appendix on page 246.

Budgeting and Responsibility Accounting

To attain the goals described in the master budget, top managers must coordinate the efforts of all of the firm's employees—from senior executives through middle levels of management to every supervised worker. To coordinate the company's efforts, top managers assign a certain amount of responsibility to lower-level managers and then hold them accountable for how they perform. Consequently, how each company structures its organization significantly shapes how it coordinates its actions.

Organization Structure and Responsibility

Organization structure is an arrangement of lines of responsibility within an organization. A company such as Exxon Mobil is organized by business function—refining, marketing, and so on—with the president of each business function having decision-making authority over his or her function. Functional organizations develop strong competencies within each function but are generally less focused on particular markets or customers. To respond to this concern, other companies, such as Procter & Gamble, the household-products giant, are organized primarily by product line or brand. The managers of the individual divisions (toothpaste, soap, and so on) have decision-making authority concerning all the business functions (manufacturing, marketing, and so on) within that division. This results in some inefficiencies as support functions get duplicated in different divisions without sufficient scale or competence. Some companies combine functional and divisional

LEARNING OBJECTIVE 5

Describe responsibility centers

...a part of an organization that a manager is accountable for

and responsibility accounting

...measurement of plans and actual results that a manager is accountable for

structures, for example leaving marketing within divisions but having manufacturing organized as a business function to supply products to different divisions. There is no perfect organization structure. Companies choose the structure that best meets their needs at that time making the tradeoff between efficiency and end-to-end business authority.

Each manager, regardless of level, is in charge of a responsibility center. A **responsibility center** is a part, segment, or subunit of an organization whose manager is accountable for a specified set of activities. Higher-level managers supervise centers with broader responsibility and larger numbers of subordinates. **Responsibility accounting** is a system that measures the plans, budgets, actions, and actual results of each responsibility center. There are four types of responsibility centers:

1. **Cost center**—the manager is accountable for costs only.
2. **Revenue center**—the manager is accountable for revenues only.
3. **Profit center**—the manager is accountable for revenues and costs.
4. **Investment center**—the manager is accountable for investments, revenues, and costs.

The maintenance department of a Marriott hotel is a cost center because the maintenance manager is responsible only for costs and the budget is based only on costs. The sales department is a revenue center because the sales manager is responsible primarily for revenues, and the department's budget is primarily based on revenues. The hotel manager is in charge of a profit center because the manager is accountable for both revenues and costs, and the hotel's budget is based on revenues and costs. The regional manager responsible for determining the amount to be invested in new hotel projects and for revenues and costs generated from these investments is in charge of an investment center. So, this center's budget is based on revenues, costs, and the investment base.

A responsibility center can be structured to promote better alignment of individual and company goals. For example, until recently, OPD, an office products distributor, operated its sales department solely as a revenue center. Each salesperson received a commission of 3% of the revenues per order, regardless of its size, the cost of processing it, or the cost of delivering the office products. Upon analyzing customer profitability, OPD found that many customers were unprofitable. The main reason was the high ordering and delivery costs of small orders. OPD's managers decided to make the sales department a profit center, accountable for revenues and costs, and to change the incentive system for salespeople to 15% of the monthly profits of their customers. The costs for each customer included the ordering and delivery costs. The effect of this change was immediate. The sales department began charging customers for ordering and delivery, and salespeople at OPD actively encouraged customers to consolidate their purchases into fewer orders. As a result, each order began producing larger revenues. The profitability of customers increased because of a 40% reduction in ordering and delivery costs in 1 year.

Feedback

Budgets coupled with responsibility accounting provide feedback to top managers about the performance relative to the budget of different responsibility center managers.

Differences between actual results and budgeted amounts—called *variances*—can help managers implement strategies and evaluate them in three ways:

1. **Early warning.** Variances alert managers early to events not easily or immediately evident. Managers can then take corrective actions or exploit the available opportunities. For example, after observing a small decline in sales during a period, managers may want to investigate if this is an indication of an even steeper decline to come later in the year.
2. **Performance evaluation.** Variances prompt managers to probe how well the company has implemented its strategies. Were materials and labor used efficiently? Was R&D spending increased as planned? Did product warranty costs decrease as planned?
3. **Evaluating strategy.** Variances sometimes signal to managers that their strategies are ineffective. For example, a company seeking to compete by reducing costs and improving quality may find that it is achieving these goals but that it is having little effect on sales and profits. Top management may then want to reevaluate the strategy.

Responsibility and Controllability

Controllability is the degree of influence a specific manager has over costs, revenues, or related items for which he or she is responsible. A **controllable cost** is any cost primarily subject to the influence of a given *responsibility center manager* for a given *period*. A responsibility accounting system could either exclude all uncontrollable costs from a manager's performance report or segregate such costs from the controllable costs. For example, a machining supervisor's performance report might be confined to direct materials, direct manufacturing labor, power, and machine maintenance costs and might exclude costs such as rent and taxes paid on the plant.

In practice, controllability is difficult to pinpoint for two main reasons:

1. Few costs are clearly under the sole influence of one manager. For example, purchasing managers are able to affect the prices their firms pay for direct materials, but these prices also depend on market conditions beyond the managers' control. Similarly, the decisions production managers make can affect the quantities of direct materials used but also depend on the quality of materials purchased. Moreover, managers often work in teams. Think about how difficult it is to evaluate individual responsibility in a team situation.

2. With a long enough time span, all costs will come under somebody's control. However, most performance reports focus on periods of a year or less. A current manager may benefit from a predecessor's accomplishments or may inherit a predecessor's problems and inefficiencies. For example, managers may have to work with undesirable contracts with suppliers or labor unions negotiated by their predecessors. How can we separate what the current manager actually controls from the results of decisions other managers made? Exactly what is the current manager accountable for? The answers may not be clear-cut.

Executives differ in how they embrace the controllability notion when evaluating people reporting to them. Some CEOs regard the budget as a firm commitment subordinates must meet and that "numbers always tell the story." Failing to meet the budget is viewed unfavorably. An executive once noted, "You can miss your plan once, but you wouldn't want to miss it twice." Such an approach forces managers to learn to perform under adverse circumstances and to deliver consistent results year after year. It removes the need to discuss which costs are controllable and which are uncontrollable because it does not matter whether the performance was due to controllable or uncontrollable factors. The disadvantage of this approach is that it subjects a manager's compensation to greater risk. It also de-motivates managers when uncontrollable factors adversely affect their performance evaluations even though they have performed well in terms of factors they could control.

Other CEOs believe that focusing on making the numbers in a budget puts excessive pressure on managers. These CEOs adjust for uncontrollable factors and evaluate managers only on what they can control, such as their performance relative to competitors. Using relative performance measures takes out the effects of favorable or unfavorable business conditions that are outside the manager's control and affect all competing managers in the same way. The challenge is in finding the correct benchmarks. Relative performance measures, however, reduce the pressure on managers to perform when circumstances are difficult.

Managers should avoid thinking about controllability only in the context of performance evaluation. Responsibility accounting is more far-reaching. It focuses on gaining *information and knowledge*, not only on control. *Responsibility accounting helps managers to first focus on whom they should ask to obtain information and not on whom they should blame.* Comparing the shortfall of actual revenues to budgeted revenues is certainly relevant when evaluating the performance of the sales managers of Ritz-Carlton hotels. But the more fundamental purpose of responsibility accounting is to gather information from the sales managers to enable future improvement. Holding them accountable for sales motivates them to learn about market conditions and dynamics outside of their personal control but which are relevant for deciding the actions the hotels might take to increase future sales. Similarly, purchasing managers may be held accountable for total purchase costs, not because of their ability to control market prices, but because of their ability to predict and respond to uncontrollable prices and understand their causes.

Performance reports for responsibility centers are sometimes designed to change managers' behavior in the direction top managers desire even if the reports decrease controllability.

DECISION POINT

How do companies use responsibility centers? Should performance reports of responsibility center managers include only costs the manager can control?

Consider a manufacturing department. If the department is designated as a cost center, the manufacturing manager may emphasize efficiency and de-emphasize the pleas of sales personnel for faster service and rush orders that reduce efficiency and increase costs. Evaluating the department as a profit center decreases the manufacturing manager's controllability (because the manufacturing manager has limited influence on sales) but it motivates the manager to look more favorably at rush orders that benefit sales. She will weigh the impact of decisions on costs and revenues rather than on costs alone.

Call centers provide another example. If designated as a cost center, the call-center manager will focus on controlling operating costs, for example, by decreasing the time customer representatives spend on each call. If designed as a profit center, the call-center manager will cause customer-service representatives to balance efficiency against better customer service and lead to efforts to upsell and cross-sell other products. Hewlett-Packard, Microsoft, Oracle, and others offer software platforms designed to prompt and help call-center personnel turn their cost centers into profit centers. The new adage is, "Every service call is a sales call."

Human Aspects of Budgeting

LEARNING OBJECTIVE 6

Recognize the human aspects of budgeting

...to engage subordinate managers in the budgeting process

Why did we discuss the master budget and responsibility accounting in the same chapter? Primarily to emphasize that human factors are crucial in budgeting. Too often, budgeting is thought of as a mechanical tool because the budgeting techniques themselves are free of emotion. However, the administration of budgeting requires education, persuasion, and intelligent interpretation.

Budgetary Slack

As we discussed earlier in this chapter, budgeting is most effective when lower-level managers actively participate and meaningfully engage in the budgeting process. Participation adds credibility to the budgeting process and makes employees more committed and accountable for meeting the budget. But participation requires "honest" communication about the business from subordinates and lower-level managers to their bosses.

At times, subordinates may try to "play games" and build in *budgetary slack*. **Budgetary slack** is the practice of underestimating budgeted revenues or overestimating budgeted costs to make budgeted targets easier to achieve. This practice frequently occurs when budget variances (the differences between actual results and budgeted amounts) are used to evaluate the performance of line managers and their subordinates. Line managers are also unlikely to be fully honest in their budget communications if top managers mechanically institute across-the-board cost reductions (say, a 10% reduction in all areas) in the face of projected revenue reductions.

Budgetary slack provides managers with a hedge against unexpected adverse circumstances. But budgetary slack also misleads top managers about the true profit potential of the company, which leads to inefficient resource planning and allocation and poor coordination of activities across different parts of the company.

To avoid the problems of budgetary slack, some companies use budgets primarily for planning and to a lesser extent for performance evaluation. They evaluate the performance of managers using multiple indicators that take into account various factors that become known during the course of the year, such as the prevailing business environment and the performance of their industry or their competitors. Evaluating performance in this way takes time and requires careful judgment.

One approach to dealing with budgetary slack is to obtain good benchmark data when setting the budget. Consider the plant manager of a beverage bottler. Suppose top managers could purchase a consulting firm's study of productivity levels—such as the number of bottles filled per hour—at a number of comparable plants owned by other bottling companies. The managers could then share this independent information with the plant manager and use it to set the operations budget. Using external benchmark performance measures reduces a manager's ability to set budget levels that are easy to achieve.

Rolling budgets are another approach to reducing budgetary slack. As we discussed earlier in the chapter, companies that use rolling budgets always have a budget for a defined period, say 12 months, by adding, at the end of each quarter, a budget for one more quarter to replace the quarter just ended. The continuous updating of budget information and the richer information it provides reduce the opportunity to create budgetary slack relative to when budgeting is done only annually.

Some companies, such as IBM, have designed innovative performance evaluation measures that reward managers based on the subsequent accuracy of the forecasts used in preparing budgets. For example, the *higher and more accurate* the budgeted profit forecasts of division managers, the higher their incentive bonuses.[6] Another approach to reducing budgetary slack is for managers to involve themselves regularly in understanding what their subordinates are doing. Such involvement should not result in managers dictating the decisions and actions of subordinates. Rather, a manager's involvement should take the form of providing support, challenging in a motivational way the assumptions subordinates make, and enhancing mutual learning about the operations. Regular interaction with their subordinates allows managers to become knowledgeable about the operations and diminishes the ability of subordinates to create slack in their budgets. Instead, the subordinates and their superiors have in-depth dialogues about the budgets and performance goals. Managers then evaluate the performance of subordinates using both subjective and objective measures. Of course, using subjective measures requires that subordinates trust their managers to evaluate them fairly.

In addition to developing their organization's strategies, top managers are responsible for defining a company's core values and norms and building employee commitment toward adhering to them. These values and norms describe what constitutes acceptable and unacceptable behavior. For example, Johnson & Johnson (J&J) has a credo that describes its responsibilities to doctors, patients, employees, communities, and shareholders. Employees are trained in the credo to help them understand the behavior that is expected of them. J&J managers are often promoted from within and are therefore very familiar with the work of the employees reporting to them. J&J also has a strong culture of mentoring subordinates. J&J's values and employee practices create an environment where managers know their subordinates well, which helps to reduce budgetary slack.

Stretch Targets

Many of the best performing companies, such as General Electric, Microsoft, and Novartis, set "stretch" targets. Stretch targets are challenging but achievable levels of expected performance, intended to create a little discomfort. Creating some performance anxiety motivates employees to exert extra effort and attain better performance, but setting targets that are very difficult or impossible to achieve hurts performance because employees give up on achieving them. Organizations such as Goldman Sachs also use "horizontal" stretch goal initiatives. The aim is to enhance professional development of employees by asking them to take on significantly different responsibilities or roles outside their comfort zone.

A major rationale for stretch targets is their psychological motivation. Consider the following two compensation arrangements offered to a salesperson:

- In the first arrangement, the salesperson is paid $80,000 for achieving a sales target of $1,000,000 and 8 cents for every dollar of sales above $1,000,000 up to $1,100,000.

- In the second arrangement, the salesperson is paid $88,000 for achieving a sales target of $1,100,000 (a stretch target) with a reduction in compensation of 8 cents for every dollar of sales less than $1,100,000 up to $1,000,000.

For simplicity we assume that sales will be between $1,000,000 and $1,100,000.

The salesperson receives the same level of compensation under the two arrangements for all levels of sales between $1,000,000 and $1,100,000. The question is whether the psychological motivation is the same in the two compensation arrangements. Many executives who favor stretch targets point to the asymmetric way in which salespeople psychologically perceive the two compensation arrangements. In the first arrangement, achieving the sales target of $1,000,000 is seen as good and everything above it as a bonus. In the second arrangement, not reaching the stretch

---

[6] For an excellent discussion of these issues, see Chapter 14 ("Formal Models in Budgeting and Incentive Contracts") in Robert S. Kaplan and Anthony A. Atkinson, *Advanced Management Accounting*, 3rd ed. (Upper Saddle River, NJ: Prentice Hall, 1998).

sales target of $1,100,000 is seen as a failure. If salespeople are loss averse, that is, they feel the pain of loss more than the joy of success, they will work harder under the second arrangement to achieve sales of $1,100,000 and not fail.

Ethics

At no point should the pressure for performance embedded in stretch targets push employees to engage in illegal or unethical practices. The more a company tries to push performance, the greater the emphasis it must place on training employees to follow its code of conduct to prohibit behavior that is out of bounds (for example, no bribery, side payments, or dishonest dealings) and its norms and values (for example, putting customers first and not compromising on quality).

Some ethical questions are subtle and not clear-cut. Consider, for example, a division manager, faced with the choice of doing maintenance on a machine at the end of 2016 or early in 2017. It is preferable to do the maintenance in 2016 because delaying maintenance increases the probability of the machine breaking down. But doing so would mean that the manager will not reach his 2016 stretch target for operating income and lose some of his bonus. If the risks of a breakdown and loss are substantial, many observers would view delaying maintenance as unethical. If the risk is minimal, there may be more debate as to whether delaying maintenance is unethical.

Kaizen Budgeting

Chapter 1 noted the importance of continuous improvement, or *kaizen* in Japanese. **Kaizen budgeting** explicitly incorporates continuous improvement anticipated during the budget period into the budget numbers. A number of companies that focus on cost reduction, including General Electric in the United States and Toyota in Japan, use Kaizen budgeting to continuously reduce costs. Much of the cost reduction associated with Kaizen budgeting arises from many small improvements rather than "quantum leaps." The improvements tend to come from employee suggestions as a result of managers creating a culture that values, recognizes, and rewards these suggestions. Employees who actually do the job, whether in manufacturing, sales, or distribution, have the best information and knowledge of how the job can be done better.

As an example, throughout our nine budgeting steps for Stylistic Furniture, we assumed 4 hours of direct labor time were required to manufacture each Casual coffee table. A Kaizen budgeting approach would incorporate continuous improvement based on 4.00 direct manufacturing labor-hours per table for the first quarter of 2017, 3.95 hours for the second quarter, 3.90 hours for the third quarter, and so on. The implications of these reductions would be lower direct manufacturing labor costs as well as lower variable manufacturing operations overhead costs because direct manufacturing labor is the driver of these costs. If Stylistic Furniture doesn't meet continuous improvement goals, its managers will explore the reasons behind the failure to meet the goals and either adjust the targets or seek input from employees to implement process improvements. Of course, top managers should also encourage managers and employees at all levels to try to find a way to achieve bigger (if periodic) cost reductions by changing operating processes and supply-chain relationships.

Managers can also apply Kaizen budgeting to activities such as setups with the goal of reducing setup time and setup costs or distribution with the goal of reducing the cost per cubic foot of shipping tables. Kaizen budgeting for specific activities is a key building block of the master budget for companies that use the Kaizen approach.

A growing number of cash-strapped states and agencies in the United States are using Kaizen techniques to bring together government workers, regulators, and end users of government processes to identify ways to reduce inefficiencies and eliminate bureaucratic procedures. Several state environmental agencies, for example, have conducted a Kaizen session or are planning one.[7] The U.S. Postal Service has identified many different programs to reduce its costs. The success of these efforts will depend heavily on human factors such as the commitment and engagement of managers and other employees to make these changes.

DECISION POINT

Why are human factors crucial in budgeting?

---

[7] For details, see "State Governments, Including Ohio's, Embrace Kaizen to Seek Efficiency via Japanese Methods," http://www.cleveland.com (December 12, 2008).

Budgeting for Reducing Carbon Emissions

In response to pressures from consumers, investors, governments, and NGOs, many companies proactively manage and report on environmental performance. Budgeting is a very effective tool to motivate managers to lessen carbon emissions. Several companies, such as British Telecom, Novartis, and Unilever, set science-based carbon reduction goals based on climate models whose goal is to limit increases in average temperatures to no more than 2°C. The methodology allocates the annual global emissions budget to individual sectors of the economy and then calculates each company's share of that total sector activity.

These science-based targets are stretched to spur innovation, prompt the development of new technologies and business models, and prepare companies for future regulatory and policy changes. What is the effect of stretched targets on actual emission reduction? Some recent research shows that companies that set more difficult targets (to be achieved over several years) complete a higher percentage of such targets. This is particularly true for carbon reduction projects in high-polluting industries that require more innovation.[8]

Many managers regard budgets negatively. To them, the word *budget* is about as popular as, say, *downsizing, layoff,* or *strike*. Top managers must convince their subordinates that the budget is a tool designed to help them set and reach goals. As with all tools of management, it has its benefits and challenges. Budgets must be used thoughtfully and wisely, but whatever the manager's perspective on budgets—pro or con—they are not remedies for weak management talent, faulty organization, or a poor accounting system.

Budgeting in Multinational Companies

Multinational companies, such as FedEx, Kraft, and Pfizer, have operations in many countries. An international presence has benefits—access to new markets and resources—and drawbacks—operating in less-familiar business environments and exposure to currency fluctuations. Multinational companies earn revenues and incur expenses in many different currencies and must translate their operating performance into a single currency (say, U.S. dollars) for reporting results to their shareholders each quarter. This translation is based on the average exchange rates that prevail during the quarter. As a result, managers of multinational companies budget in different currencies and also budget for foreign exchange rates. This requires managers and management accountants to anticipate potential changes in exchange rates that might occur during the year. To reduce the possible negative impact a company could experience as a result of unfavorable exchange rate movements, finance managers frequently use sophisticated techniques such as forward, future, and option contracts to minimize exposure to foreign currency fluctuations (see Chapter 11). Besides currency issues, managers at multinational companies need to understand the political, legal, and, in particular, economic environments of the different countries in which they operate when preparing budgets. For example, in countries such as Turkey, Zimbabwe, and Guinea, annual inflation rates are very high, resulting in sharp declines in the value of the local currency. Managers also need to consider differences in tax regimes, especially when the company transfers goods or services across the many countries in which it operates (see Chapter 22).

When there is considerable business and exchange rate uncertainty related to global operations, a natural question to ask is: "Do the managers of multinational companies find budgeting to be a helpful tool?" The answer is yes. However, in these circumstances the budgeting is not done to evaluate the firm's performance relative to its budgets—which can be meaningless when conditions are so volatile—but to help managers adapt their plans and coordinate their actions as circumstances change. Senior managers evaluate performance more subjectively, based on how well subordinate managers have managed in these constantly shifting and volatile environments.

LEARNING OBJECTIVE **7**

Appreciate the special challenges of budgeting in multinational companies

…exposure to currency fluctuations and to different legal, political, and economic environments

DECISION POINT

What are the special challenges involved in budgeting at multinational companies?

---

8 See Ioannis Ioannou, Shelley Xin Li, and George Serafeim, "The Effect of Target Difficulty on Target Completion: The Case of Reducing Carbon Emissions," *The Accounting Review* (2016).

PROBLEM FOR SELF-STUDY

Consider the Stylistic Furniture example described earlier. Suppose that to maintain its sales quantities, Stylistic needs to decrease selling prices to $582 per Casual table and $776 per Deluxe table, a 3% decrease in the selling prices used in the chapter illustration. All other data are unchanged.

Required

Prepare a budgeted income statement, including all necessary detailed supporting budget schedules that are different from the schedules presented in the chapter. Indicate those schedules that will remain unchanged.

Solution

Schedules 1 and 8 will change. Schedule 1 changes because a change in selling price affects revenues. Schedule 8 changes because revenues are a cost driver of marketing costs (sales commissions). The remaining Schedules 2–7 will not change because a change in selling price has no effect on manufacturing costs. The revised schedules and the new budgeted income statement follow.

Schedule 1: Revenues Budget
for the Year Ending December 31, 2017

	Selling Price	Units	Total Revenues
Casual tables	$582	50,000	$29,100,000
Deluxe tables	776	10,000	7,760,000
Total			$36,860,000

Schedule 8: Nonmanufacturing Costs Budget
for the Year Ending December 31, 2017

Business Function	Variable Costs	Fixed Costs (as in Schedule 8, page 234)	Total Costs
Product design		$1,024,000	$1,024,000
Marketing (Variable cost: $36,860,000 × 0.065)	$2,395,900	1,330,000	3,725,900
Distribution (Variable cost: $2 × 1,140,000 cu. ft.)	2,280,000	1,596,000	3,876,000
	$4,675,900	$3,950,000	$8,625,900

Stylistic Furniture Budgeted Income Statement
for the Year Ending December 31, 2017

Revenues	Schedule 1		$36,860,000
Cost of goods sold	Schedule 7		24,440,000
Gross margin			12,420,000
Operating costs			
Product design	Schedule 8	$1,024,000	
Marketing costs	Schedule 8	3,725,900	
Distribution costs	Schedule 8	3,876,000	8,625,900
Operating income			$ 3,794,100

DECISION **POINTS**

The following question-and-answer format summarizes the chapter's learning objectives. Each decision presents a key question related to a learning objective. The guidelines are the answer to that question.

Decision	**Guidelines**
1. What is the master budget, and why is it useful?	The master budget summarizes the financial projections of all the company's budgets. It expresses management's operating and financing plans—the formalized outline of the company's financial objectives and how they will be attained. Budgets are tools that, by themselves, are neither good nor bad. Budgets are useful when administered skillfully.
2. When should a company prepare budgets? What are the advantages of preparing budgets?	Budgets should be prepared when their expected benefits exceed their expected costs. There are four key advantages of budgets: (a) they compel strategic analysis and planning, (b) they promote coordination and communication among subunits of the company, (c) they provide a framework for judging performance and facilitating learning, and (d) they motivate managers and other employees.
3. What is the operating budget and what are its components?	The operating budget is the budgeted income statement and its supporting budget schedules. The starting point for the operating budget is generally the revenues budget. The following supporting schedules are derived from the revenues budget and the activities needed to support the revenues budget: production budget, direct materials usage budget, direct materials purchases budget, direct manufacturing labor cost budget, manufacturing overhead costs budget, ending inventories budget, cost of goods sold budget, R&D/product design cost budget, marketing cost budget, distribution cost budget, and customer-service cost budget.
4. How can managers plan for changes in the assumptions underlying the budget and manage risk?	Managers can use financial planning models—mathematical statements of the relationships among operating activities, financing activities, and other factors that affect the budget. These models make it possible for managers to conduct a what-if (sensitivity) analysis of the risks that changes in the original predicted data or changes in underlying assumptions would have on the master budget and to develop plans to respond to changed conditions.
5. How do companies use responsibility centers? Should performance reports of responsibility center managers include only costs the manager can control?	A responsibility center is a part, segment, or subunit of an organization whose manager is accountable for a specified set of activities. Four types of responsibility centers are cost centers, revenue centers, profit centers, and investment centers. Responsibility accounting systems are useful because they measure the plans, budgets, actions, and actual results of each responsibility center. Controllable costs are costs primarily subject to the influence of a given responsibility center manager for a given time period. Performance reports of responsibility center managers often include costs, revenues, and investments that the managers cannot control. Responsibility accounting associates financial items with managers on the basis of which manager has the most knowledge and information about specific items, regardless of the manager's ability to exercise full control.

Decision	Guidelines
6. Why are human factors crucial in budgeting?	The administration of budgets requires education, participation, persuasion, and intelligent interpretation. When wisely administered, budgets create commitment, accountability, and honest communication among employees and can be used as the basis for continuous improvement efforts. When badly managed, budgeting can lead to game-playing and budgetary slack—the practice of making budget targets more easily achievable.
7. What are the special challenges involved in budgeting at multinational companies?	Budgeting is a valuable tool for multinational companies but is challenging because of the uncertainties posed by operating in multiple countries. In addition to budgeting in different currencies, managers in multinational companies also need to budget for foreign exchange rates and consider the political, legal, and economic environments of the different countries in which they operate. In times of high uncertainty, managers use budgets to help the organization learn and adapt to its circumstances rather than to evaluate performance.

APPENDIX

The Cash Budget

The chapter illustrated the operating budget, which is one part of the master budget. The other part is the financial budget, which is composed of the capital expenditures budget, the cash budget, the budgeted balance sheet, and the budgeted statement of cash flows. This appendix focuses on the cash budget and the budgeted balance sheet. We discuss capital budgeting in Chapter 21. The budgeted statement of cash flows is beyond the scope of this book and generally is covered in financial accounting and corporate finance courses.

Why should Stylistic's managers want a cash budget in addition to the operating income budget presented in the chapter? Recall that Stylistic's management accountants prepared the operating budget on an accrual accounting basis consistent with how the company reports its actual operating income. But Stylistic's managers also need to plan cash flows to ensure that the company has adequate cash to pay vendors, meet payroll, and pay operating expenses as these payments come due. Stylistic could be very profitable, but the pattern of cash receipts from revenues might be delayed and result in insufficient cash being available to make scheduled payments. Stylistic's managers may then need to initiate a plan to borrow money to finance any shortfall. Building a profitable operating plan does not guarantee that adequate cash will be available, so Stylistic's managers need to prepare a cash budget in addition to an operating income budget.

Exhibit 6-5 shows Stylistic Furniture's balance sheet for the year ended December 31, 2016. The budgeted cash flows for 2017 are:

	Quarters			
	1	**2**	**3**	**4**
Collections from customers	$9,136,600	$10,122,000	$10,263,200	$8,561,200
Disbursements				
Direct materials	3,031,400	2,636,967	2,167,900	2,242,033
Direct manufacturing labor payroll	1,888,000	1,432,000	1,272,000	1,408,000
Manufacturing overhead costs	3,265,296	2,476,644	2,199,924	2,435,136
Nonmanufacturing costs	2,147,750	2,279,000	2,268,250	2,005,000
Machinery purchase	—	—	758,000	—
Income taxes	725,000	400,000	400,000	400,000

EXHIBIT 6-5

Balance Sheet for
Stylistic Furniture,
December 31, 2016

	A	B	C	D
	Home　Insert　Page Layout　Formulas　Data　Review　View			
1	Stylistic Furniture Balance Sheet			
2	December 31, 2016			
3	Assets			
4	Current assets			
5	Cash		$　300,000	
6	Accounts receivable		1,711,000	
7	Direct materials inventory		1,090,000	
8	Finished goods inventory		646,000	$ 3,747,000
9	Property, Plant, and equipment			
10	Land		2,000,000	
11	Building and equipment	$ 22,000,000		
12	Accumulated depreciation	(6,900,000)	15,100,000	17,100,000
13	Total			$20,847,000
14	Liabilities and Stockholders' Equity			
15	Current liabilities			
16	Accounts payable		$　904,000	
17	Income taxes payable		325,000	$ 1,229,000
18	Stockholders' equity			
19	Common stock, no-par 25,000 shares outstanding		3,500,000	
20	Retained earnings		16,118,000	19,618,000
21	Total			$20,847,000

The quarterly data are based on the budgeted cash effects of the operations formulated in Schedules 1–8 in the chapter, but the details of that formulation are not shown here to keep this illustration as brief and as focused as possible.

Stylistic wants to maintain a $320,000 minimum cash balance at the end of each quarter. The company can borrow or repay money at an interest rate of 12% per year. Management does not want to borrow any more short-term cash than is necessary. By special arrangement with the bank, Stylistic pays interest when repaying the principal. Assume, for simplicity, that borrowing takes place at the beginning and repayment at the end of the quarter under consideration (in multiples of $1,000). Interest is computed to the nearest dollar.

Suppose a management accountant at Stylistic receives the preceding data and the other data contained in the budgets in the chapter (pages 224–235). Her manager asks her to:

1. Prepare a cash budget for 2017 by quarter. That is, prepare a statement of cash receipts and disbursements by quarter, including details of borrowing, repayment, and interest.

2. Prepare a budgeted income statement for the year ending December 31, 2017. This statement should include interest expense and income taxes (at a rate of 40% of operating income).

3. Prepare a budgeted balance sheet on December 31, 2017.

Preparation of Budgets

1. The **cash budget** is a schedule of expected cash receipts and cash disbursements. It predicts the effects on the cash position at the given level of operations. Exhibit 6-6 presents the cash budget by quarters to show the impact of cash flow timing on bank loans and their repayment. In practice, monthly—and sometimes weekly or even daily—cash budgets are critical for cash planning and control. Cash budgets help avoid unnecessary idle

EXHIBIT 6-6 Cash Budget for Stylistic Furniture for the Year Ending December 31, 2017

	A	B	C	D	E	F
1	Stylistic Furniture					
2	Cash Budget					
3	For Year Ending December 31, 2017					
4		Quarter 1	Quarter 2	Quarter 3	Quarter 4	Year as a Whole
5	Cash balance, beginning	$ 300,000	$ 320,154	$ 320,783	$ 324,359	$ 300,000
6	Add receipts					
7	Collections from customers	9,136,600	10,122,000	10,263,200	8,561,200	38,083,000
8	Total cash available for needs (x)	9,436,600	10,442,154	10,583,983	8,885,559	38,383,000
9	Cash disbursements					
10	Direct materials	3,031,400	2,636,967	2,167,900	2,242,033	10,078,300
11	Direct maufacturing labor payroll	1,888,000	1,432,000	1,272,000	1,408,000	6,000,000
12	Manufacturing overhead costs	3,265,296	2,476,644	2,199,924	2,435,136	10,377,000
13	Nonmanufacturing costs	2,147,750	2,279,000	2,268,250	2,005,000	8,700,000
14	Machinery purchase			758,000		758,000
15	Income taxes	725,000	400,000	400,000	400,000	1,925,000
16	Total cash disbursements (y)	11,057,446	9,224,611	9,066,074	8,490,169	37,838,300
17	Minimum cash balance desired	320,000	320,000	320,000	320,000	320,000
18	Total cash needed	11,377,446	9,544,611	9,386,074	8,810,169	38,158,300
19	Cash excess (deficiency)*	$ (1,940,846)	$ 897,543	$ 1,197,909	$ 75,390	$ 224,700
20	Financing					
21	Borrowing (at beginning)	$ 1,941,000	$ 0	$ 0	$ 0	$ 1,941,000
22	Repayment (at end)	0	(846,000)	(1,095,000)	0	(1,941,000)
23	Interest (at 12% per year)**	0	(50,760)	(98,550)	0	(149,310)
24	Total effects of financing (z)	1,941,000	(896,760)	(1,193,550)	0	(149,310)
25	Cash balance, ending***	$ 320,154	$ 320,783	$ 324,359	$ 395,390	$ 395,390
26	*Excess of total cash available − Total cash needed before financing					
27	**Note that the short-term interest payments pertain only to the amount of principal being repaid at the end of a quarter. The specific computations regarding interest are $846,000 × 0.12 × 0.5 = $50,760; $1,095,000 × 0.12 × 0.75 = $98,550. Also note that *depreciation does not require a cash outlay.*					
28	***Ending cash balance = Total cash available for needs (x) − Total disbursements (y) + Total effects of financing (z)					

cash and unexpected cash deficiencies. They thus keep cash balances in line with needs. Ordinarily, the cash budget has these main sections:

a. **Cash available for needs (before any financing).** The beginning cash balance plus cash receipts equals the total cash available for needs before any financing. Cash receipts depend on collections of accounts receivable, cash sales, and miscellaneous recurring sources, such as rental or royalty receipts. Information on the expected collectability of accounts receivable is needed for accurate predictions. Key factors include bad-debt (uncollectible accounts) experience (not an issue in the Stylistic case because Stylistic sells to only a few large wholesalers) and average time lag between sales and collections.

b. **Cash disbursements.** Cash disbursements by Stylistic Furniture include:

i. *Direct materials purchases.* Suppliers are paid in full in the month after the goods are delivered.

ii. *Direct manufacturing labor and other wage and salary outlays.* All payroll-related costs are paid in the month in which the labor effort occurs.

iii. *Other costs.* These depend on timing and credit terms. (In the Stylistic case, all other costs are paid in the month in which the cost is incurred.) *Note that depreciation does not require a cash outlay.*

iv. *Other cash disbursements.* These include outlays for property, plant, equipment, and other long-term investments.

v. Income tax payments as shown each quarter.

c. **Financing effects.** Short-term financing requirements depend on how the total cash available for needs [keyed as (x) in Exhibit 6-6] compares with the total cash disbursements [keyed as (y)], plus the minimum ending cash balance desired. The financing plans will depend on the relationship between total cash available for needs and total cash needed. If there is a deficiency of cash, Stylistic obtains loans. If there is excess cash, Stylistic repays any outstanding loans.

d. **Ending cash balance.** The cash budget in Exhibit 6-6 shows the pattern of short-term "self-liquidating" cash loans. In quarter 1, Stylistic budgets a $1,940,846 cash deficiency. The company therefore undertakes short-term borrowing of $1,941,000 that it pays off over the course of the year. Seasonal peaks of production or sales often result in heavy cash disbursements for purchases, payroll, and other operating outlays as the company produces and sells products. Cash receipts from customers typically lag behind sales. The loan is *self-liquidating* in the sense that the company uses the borrowed money to acquire resources that it uses to produce and sell finished goods and uses the proceeds from sales to repay the loan. This self-liquidating cycle is the movement from cash to inventories to receivables and back to cash.

2. The budgeted income statement is presented in Exhibit 6-7. It is merely the budgeted operating income statement in Exhibit 6-3 (page 235) expanded to include interest expense and income taxes.

3. The budgeted balance sheet is presented in Exhibit 6-8. Each item is projected in light of the details of the business plan as expressed in all the previous budget schedules. For example, the ending balance of accounts receivable of $1,628,000 is computed by adding the budgeted revenues of $38,000,000 (from Schedule 1 on page 226) to the beginning balance of accounts receivable of $1,711,000 (from Exhibit 6-5) and subtracting cash receipts of $38,083,000 (from Exhibit 6-6).

For simplicity, this example explicitly gave the cash receipts and disbursements. Usually, the receipts and disbursements are calculated based on the lags between the items reported on the accrual basis of accounting in an income statement and balance sheet and their related cash receipts and disbursements. Consider accounts receivable.

EXHIBIT 6-7

Budgeted Income Statement for Stylistic Furniture for the Year Ending December 31, 2017

	Home	Insert	Page Layout	Formulas	Data	Review	View
	A		B		C		D
1	Stylistic Furniture						
2	Budgeted Income Statement						
3	For the Year Ending December 31, 2017						
4	Revenues		Schedule 1				$38,000,000
5	COGS		Schedule 7				24,440,000
6	Gross margin						13,560,000
7	Operating costs						
8	Product design costs		Schedule 8		$1,024,000		
9	Marketing costs		Schedule 8		3,800,000		
10	Distribution costs		Schedule 8		3,876,000		8,700,000
11	Operating income						4,860,000
12	Interest expense		Exhibit 6-6				149,310
13	Income before income taxes						4,710,690
14	Income taxes (at 40%)						1,884,276
15	Net income						$ 2,826,414

EXHIBIT 6-8 Budgeted Balance Sheet for Stylistic Furniture, December 31, 2017

	Home Insert Page Layout Formulas Data Review View			
	A	B	C	D
1	Stylistic Furniture			
2	Budgeted Balance Sheet			
3	December 31, 2017			
4	Assets			
5	Current assets			
6	Cash (from Exhibit 6-6)		$ 395,390	
7	Accounts receivable (1)		1,628,000	
8	Direct materials inventory (2)		760,000	
9	Finished goods inventory (2)		4,486,000	$ 7,269,390
10	Property, Plant, and equipment			
11	Land (3)		2,000,000	
12	Building and equipment (4)	$22,758,000		
13	Accumulated depreciation (5)	(8,523,000)	14,235,000	16,235,000
14	Total			$23,504,390
15	Liabilities and Stockholders' Equity			
16	Current liabilities			
17	Accounts payable (6)		$ 775,700	
18	Income taxes payable (7)		284,276	$ 1,059,976
19	Stockholders' equity			
20	Common stock, no-par, 25,000 shares outstanding (8)		3,500,000	
21	Retained earnings (9)		18,944,414	22,444,414
22	Total			$23,504,390
23				
24	Notes:			
25	Beginning balances are used as the starting point for most of the following computations			
26	(1) $1,711,000 + $38,000,000 revenues − $38,083,000 receipts (Exhibit 6-6) = $1,628,000			
27	(2) From Schedule 6B, p. 232			
28	(3) From opening balance sheet (Exhibit 6-5)			
29	(4) $22,000,000 (Exhibit 6-5) + $758,000 purchases (Exhibit 6-6) = $22,758,000			
30	(5) $6,900,000 (Exhibit 6-5) + $1,020,000 + $603,000 depreciation from Schedule 5, p. 231			
31	(6) $904,000 (Exhibit 6-5) + $9,950,000 (Schedule 3B) − $10,078,300 (Exhibit 6-6) = $775,300			
32	There are no other current liabilities. From Exhibit 6-6: Cash flows for direct manufacturing labor = $6,000,000 from Schedule 4 Cash flows for manufacturing overhead costs = $10,377,000 ($12,000,000 − depreciation $1,623,000) from Schedule 5 Cash flows for nonmanufacturing costs = $8,700,000 from Schedule 8.			
33	(7) $325,000 (Exhibit 6-5) + $1,884,276 (from Exhibit 6-7) − $1,925,000 payment (Exhibit 6-6) = $284,276			
34	(8) From opening balance sheet (Exhibit 6-5)			
35	(9) $16,118,000 (Exhibit 6-5) + net income $2,826,414 (Exhibit 6-7) = $18,944,414			

The budgeted sales for the year are broken down into sales budgets for each month and quarter. For example, Stylistic Furniture budgets sales by quarter of $9,282,000, $10,332,000, $10,246,000, and $8,140,000, which equal 2017 budgeted sales of $38,000,000.

	Quarter 1		Quarter 2		Quarter 3		Quarter 4	
	Casual	Deluxe	Casual	Deluxe	Casual	Deluxe	Casual	Deluxe
Budgeted sales in units	12,270	2,400	13,620	2,700	13,610	2,600	10,500	2,300
Selling price	$ 600	$ 800	$ 600	$ 800	$ 600	$ 800	$ 600	$ 800
Budgeted revenues	$7,362,000	$1,920,000	$8,172,000	$2,160,000	$8,166,000	$2,080,000	$6,300,000	$1,840,000
	$9,282,000		$10,332,000		$10,246,000		$8,140,000	

Notice that sales are expected to be higher in the second and third quarters relative to the first and fourth quarters when weather conditions limit the number of customers shopping for furniture.

Once Stylistic's managers determine the sales budget, a management accountant prepares a schedule of cash collections that serves as an input for the preparation of the cash budget. Stylistic estimates that 80% of all sales made in a quarter are collected in the same quarter and 20% are collected in the following quarter. Estimated collections from customers each quarter are calculated in the following table:

Schedule of Cash Collections

	Quarters			
	1	2	3	4
Accounts receivable balance on 1-1-2017 (Fourth-quarter sales from prior year collected in first quarter of 2017)	$1,711,000			
From first-quarter 2017 sales ($9,282,000 × 0.80; $9,282,000 × 0.20)	7,425,600	$ 1,856,400		
From second-quarter 2017 sales ($10,332,000 × 0.80; $10,332,000 × 0.20)		8,265,600	$ 2,066,400	
From third-quarter 2017 sales ($10,246,000 × 0.80; $10,246,000 × 0.20)			8,196,800	$2,049,200
From fourth-quarter 2017 sales ($8,140,000 × 0.80)				6,512,000
Total collections	$9,136,600	$10,122,000	$10,263,200	$8,561,200

Uncollected fourth-quarter 2017 sales of $1,628,000 ($ 8,140,000 × 0.20) appear as accounts receivable in the budgeted balance sheet of December 31, 2017 (see Exhibit 6-8). Note that the quarterly cash collections from customers calculated in this schedule equal the cash collections by quarter shown on page 246.

Jimenez Corporation manufactures and sells two types of decorative lamps, Knox and Ayer. The following data are available for the year 2017.

◀ 6-6 TRY IT!

Accounts receivable (January 1, 2017)	$ 46,000
Budgeted sales in Quarter 1 (January 1 to March 31, 2017)	230,000
Budgeted sales in Quarter 2 (April 1 to June 30, 2017)	245,000
Budgeted sales in Quarter 3 (July 1 to September 30, 2017)	210,000
Budgeted sales in Quarter 4 (October 1 to December 31, 2017)	240,000

All sales are made on account with 80% of sales made in a quarter collected in the same quarter and 20% collected in the following quarter.
Calculate the cash collected from receivables in each of the 4 quarters of 2017.

Sensitivity Analysis and Cash Flows

Exhibit 6-4 (page 236) shows how differing assumptions about selling prices of coffee tables and direct material prices led to differing amounts for budgeted operating income for Stylistic Furniture. A key use of sensitivity analysis is to budget cash flow. Exhibit 6-9 outlines the short-term borrowing implications of the two combinations examined in Exhibit 6-4. Scenario 1, with the lower selling prices per table ($582 for the Casual table and $776 for the Deluxe table), requires $2,146,000 of short-term borrowing in quarter 1 that cannot be fully repaid as of December 31, 2017. Scenario 2, with the 5% higher direct material costs, requires $2,048,000 borrowing by Stylistic Furniture that also cannot be repaid by December 31, 2017. Sensitivity analysis helps managers anticipate such outcomes and take steps to minimize the effects of expected reductions in cash flows from operations.

EXHIBIT 6-9   Sensitivity Analysis: Effects of Key Budget Assumptions in Exhibit 6-4 on 2017 Short-Term Borrowing for Stylistic Furniture

	Home	Insert	Page Layout	Formulas	Data	Review	View				
	A	B	C	D	E	F	G	H	I	J
1				Direct Material			Short-Term Borrowing and Repayment by Quarter			
2		Selling Price		Purchase Costs		Budgeted		Quarters		
3	Scenario	Casual	Deluxe	Red Oak	Granite	Operating Income	1	2	3	4
4	1	$582	$776	$7.00	$10.00	$3,794,100	$2,146,000	$(579,000)	$(834,000)	$170,000
5	2	$600	$800	7.35	10.50	4,483,800	2,048,000	$(722,000)	$(999,000)	$41,000

TERMS TO LEARN

This chapter and the Glossary at the end of the book contain definitions of the following important terms:

activity-based budgeting (ABB) (**p. 229**)
budgetary slack (**p. 240**)
cash budget (**p. 247**)
continuous budget (**p. 222**)
controllability (**p. 239**)
controllable cost (**p. 239**)
cost center (**p. 238**)

financial budget (**p. 223**)
financial planning models (**p. 235**)
investment center (**p. 238**)
Kaizen budgeting (**p. 242**)
master budget (**p. 219**)
operating budget (**p. 223**)
organization structure (**p. 237**)

pro forma statements (**p. 219**)
profit center (**p. 238**)
responsibility accounting (**p. 238**)
responsibility center (**p. 238**)
revenue center (**p. 238**)
rolling budget (**p. 222**)
rolling forecast (**p. 222**)

ASSIGNMENT MATERIAL

Questions

6-1   What are the four elements of the budgeting cycle?

6-2   Define master budget.

6-3   List the five key questions that must be considered by managers for developing successful strategies.

6-4   "Budgets provide a framework for evaluating performance and improving learning." Do you agree? Explain.

6-5   "Budgets can promote coordination and communication among subunits within the company." Do you agree? Explain.

6-6   "Budgets motivate managers and other employees to the company's goals." Do you agree? Explain.

6-7   Define rolling budget. Give an example.

6-8   Outline the steps in preparing an operating budget.

6-9   What is the usual starting point for an operating budget?

6-10   How can sensitivity analysis be used to increase the benefits of budgeting?

6-11   What is the key emphasis in Kaizen budgeting?

6-12   Describe how nonoutput-based cost drivers can be incorporated into budgeting.

6-13   Explain how the choice of the type of responsibility center (cost, revenue, profit, or investment) affects behavior.

6-14   What are some additional considerations that arise when budgeting in multinational companies?

6-15   Explain why cash budgets are important.

Multiple-Choice Questions

In partnership with:
BECKER
PROFESSIONAL EDUCATION*

6-16 Master budget. Which of the following statements is correct regarding the components of the master budget?
   a. The cash budget is used to create the capital budget.
   b. Operating budgets are used to create cash budgets.
   c. The manufacturing overhead budget is used to create the production budget.
   d. The cost of goods sold budget is used to create the selling and administrative expense budget.

6-17 Operating and financial budgets. Which of the following statements is correct regarding the drivers of operating and financial budgets?
   a. The sales budget will drive the cost of goods sold budget.
   b. The cost of goods sold budget will drive the units of production budget.
   c. The production budget will drive the selling and administrative expense budget.
   d. The cash budget will drive the production and selling and administrative expense budgets.

6-18 Production budget. Superior Industries sales budget shows quarterly sales for the next year as follows: Quarter 1–10,000; Quarter 2–8,000; Quarter 3–12,000; Quarter 4–14,000. Company policy is to have a target finished-goods inventory at the end of each quarter equal to 20% of the next quarter's sales. Budgeted production for the second quarter of next year would be:
   1. 7,200 units; 2. 8,800 units; 3. 12,000 units; 4. 10,400 units

6-19 Responsibility centers. Elmhurst Corporation is considering changes to its responsibility accounting system. Which of the following statements is/are correct for a responsibility accounting system.
   i. In a cost center, managers are responsible for controlling costs but not revenue.
   ii. The idea behind responsibility accounting is that a manager should be held responsible for those items that the manager can control to a significant extent.
   iii. To be effective, a good responsibility accounting system must help managers to plan and to control.
   iv. Costs that are allocated to a responsibility center are normally controllable by the responsibility center manager.
   1. I and II only are correct.
   2. II and III only are correct.
   3. I, II, and III are correct.
   4. I, II and IV are correct.

6-20 Cash budget. Mary Jacobs, the controller of the Jenks Company is working on Jenks' cash budget for year 2. She has information on each of the following items:
   i. Wages due to workers accrued as of December 31, year 1.
   ii. Limits on a line of credit that may be used to fund Jenks' operations in year 2.
   iii. The balance in accounts payable as of December 31, year 1, from credit purchases made in year 1.

Which of the items above should Jacobs take into account when building the cash budget for year 2?
   a. I, II   **b.** I, III
   c. II, III   **d.** I, II, III

Exercises

6-21 Sales budget, service setting. In 2017, Rouse & Sons, a small environmental-testing firm, performed 12,200 radon tests for $290 each and 16,400 lead tests for $240 each. Because newer homes are being built with lead-free pipes, lead-testing volume is expected to decrease by 10% next year. However, awareness of radon-related health hazards is expected to result in a 6% increase in radon-test volume each year in the near future. Jim Rouse feels that if he lowers his price for lead testing to $230 per test, he will have to face only a 7% decline in lead-test sales in 2018.

   1. Prepare a 2018 sales budget for Rouse & Sons assuming that Rouse holds prices at 2017 levels.
   2. Prepare a 2018 sales budget for Rouse & Sons assuming that Rouse lowers the price of a lead test to $230. Should Rouse lower the price of a lead test in 2018 if the company's goal is to maximize sales revenue?

Required

6-22 Sales and production budget. The Albright Company manufactures ball pens and expects sales of 452,000 units in 2018. Albright estimates that its ending inventory for 2018 will be 65,400 pens. The beginning inventory is 46,500 pens. Compute the number of pens budgeted for production in 2018.

6-23 Direct material budget. Polyhidron Corporation produces 5-gallon plastic buckets. The company expects to produce 430,000 buckets in 2018. Polyhidron purchases high-quality plastic granules for the production of buckets. Each pound of plastic granules produces two 5-gallon buckets. Target ending inventory of the company is 35,200 pounds of plastic granules; its beginning inventory is 22,500. Compute how many pounds of plastic granules need to be purchased in 2018.

6-24 Material purchases budget. The Ceremicon Company produces teapots from stoneware clay. The company has prepared a sales budget of 150,000 units of teapots for a 3-month period. It has an inventory of 34,000 units of teapots on hand at December 31 and has estimated an inventory of 38,000 units of teapots at the end of the succeeding quarter.

One unit of teapot needs 2 pounds of stoneware clay. The company has an inventory of 82,000 pounds of stoneware clay at December 31 and has a target ending inventory of 95,000 pounds of stoneware clay at the end of the succeeding quarter. How many pounds of direct materials (stoneware clay) should Ceremicon purchase during the 3 months ending March 31?

6-25 Revenues, production, and purchases budgets. The Deluxe Motorcar in northern California manufactures motor cars of all categories. Its budgeted sales for the most popular sedan model XE8 in 2018 is 4,000 units. Deluxe Motorcar has a beginning finished inventory of 600 units. Its ending inventory is 450 units. The present selling price of model XE8 to the distributors and dealers is $35,200. The company does not want to increase its selling price in 2018.

Deluxe Motorcar does not produce tires. It buys the tires from an outside supplier. One complete car requires five tires including the tire for the extra wheel. The company's target ending inventory is 400 tires, and its beginning inventory is 350 tires. The budgeted purchase price is $45 per tire.

Required

1. Compute the budgeted revenues in dollars.
2. Compute the number of cars that Deluxe Motorcar should produce.
3. Compute the budgeted purchases of tires in units and in dollars.
4. What actions can Deluxe Motorcar's managers take to reduce budgeted purchasing costs of tires assuming the same budgeted sales for Model XE8?

6-26 Revenues and production budget. Price, Inc., bottles and distributes mineral water from the company's natural springs in northern Oregon. Price markets two products: 12-ounce disposable plastic bottles and 1-gallon reusable plastic containers.

Required

1. For 2015, Price marketing managers project monthly sales of 420,000 12-ounce bottles and 170,000 1-gallon containers. Average selling prices are estimated at $0.20 per 12-ounce bottle and $1.50 per 1-gallon container. Prepare a revenues budget for Price, Inc., for the year ending December 31, 2015.
2. Price begins 2015 with 890,000 12-ounce bottles in inventory. The vice president of operations requests that 12-ounce bottles ending inventory on December 31, 2015, be no less than 680,000 bottles. Based on sales projections as budgeted previously, what is the minimum number of 12-ounce bottles Price must produce during 2015?
3. The VP of operations requests that ending inventory of 1-gallon containers on December 31, 2015, be 240,000 units. If the production budget calls for Price to produce 1,900,000 1-gallon containers during 2015, what is the beginning inventory of 1-gallon containers on January 1, 2015?

6-27 Budgeting; direct material usage, manufacturing cost, and gross margin. Xander Manufacturing Company manufactures blue rugs, using wool and dye as direct materials. One rug is budgeted to use 36 skeins of wool at a cost of $2 per skein and 0.8 gallons of dye at a cost of $6 per gallon. All other materials are indirect. At the beginning of the year Xander has an inventory of 458,000 skeins of wool at a cost of $961,800 and 4,000 gallons of dye at a cost of $23,680. Target ending inventory of wool and dye is zero. Xander uses the FIFO inventory cost-flow method.

Xander blue rugs are very popular and demand is high, but because of capacity constraints the firm will produce only 200,000 blue rugs per year. The budgeted selling price is $2,000 each. There are no rugs in beginning inventory. Target ending inventory of rugs is also zero.

Xander makes rugs by hand, but uses a machine to dye the wool. Thus, overhead costs are accumulated in two cost pools—one for weaving and the other for dyeing. Weaving overhead is allocated to products based on direct manufacturing labor-hours (DMLH). Dyeing overhead is allocated to products based on machine-hours (MH).

There is no direct manufacturing labor cost for dyeing. Xander budgets 62 direct manufacturing labor-hours to weave a rug at a budgeted rate of $13 per hour. It budgets 0.2 machine-hours to dye each skein in the dyeing process.

The following table presents the budgeted overhead costs for the dyeing and weaving cost pools:

	Dyeing (based on 1,440,000 MH)	Weaving (based on 12,400,000 DMLH)
Variable costs		
Indirect materials	$ 0	$15,400,000
Maintenance	6,560,000	5,540,000
Utilities	7,550,000	2,890,000
Fixed costs		
Indirect labor	347,000	1,700,000
Depreciation	2,100,000	274,000
Other	723,000	5,816,000
Total budgeted costs	$17,280,000	$31,620,000

Required

1. Prepare a direct materials usage budget in both units and dollars.
2. Calculate the budgeted overhead allocation rates for weaving and dyeing.
3. Calculate the budgeted unit cost of a blue rug for the year.
4. Prepare a revenues budget for blue rugs for the year, assuming Xander sells (a) 200,000 or (b) 185,000 blue rugs (that is, at two different sales levels).
5. Calculate the budgeted cost of goods sold for blue rugs under each sales assumption.
6. Find the budgeted gross margin for blue rugs under each sales assumption.
7. What actions might you take as a manager to improve profitability if sales drop to 185,000 blue rugs?
8. How might top management at Xander use the budget developed in requirements 1–6 to better manage the company?

6-28 Budgeting, service company. Ever Clean Company provides gutter cleaning services to residential clients. The company has enjoyed considerable growth in recent years due to a successful marketing campaign and favorable reviews on service-rating Web sites. Ever Clean owner Joanne Clark makes sales calls herself and quotes on jobs based on length of gutter surface. Ever Clean hires college students to drive the company vans to jobs and clean the gutters. A part-time bookkeeper takes care of billing customers and other office tasks. Overhead is allocated based on direct labor-hours (DLH).

Joanne Clark estimates that her gutter cleaners will work a total of 1,000 jobs during the year. Each job averages 600 feet of gutter surface and requires 12 direct labor-hours. Clark pays her gutter cleaners $15 per hour, inclusive of taxes and benefits. The following table presents the budgeted overhead costs for 2018:

Variable costs	
Supplies ($6.50 per DLH)	$ 78,000
Fixed costs (to support capacity of 12,000 DLH)	
Indirect labor	25,000
Depreciation	17,000
Other	24,000
Total budgeted costs	$144,000

Required

1. Prepare a direct labor budget in both hours and dollars.
2. Calculate the budgeted overhead allocation rate based on the budgeted quantity of the cost drivers.
3. Calculate the budgeted total cost of all jobs for the year and the budgeted cost of an average 600-foot gutter-cleaning job.
4. Prepare a revenues budget for the year, assuming that Ever Clean charges customers $0.60 per square foot.
5. Calculate the budgeted operating income.
6. What actions can Clark take if sales should decline to 900 jobs annually?

6-29 Budgets for production and direct manufacturing labor. (CMA, adapted) Roletter Company makes and sells artistic frames for pictures of weddings, graduations, and other special events. Bob Anderson, the controller, is responsible for preparing Roletter's master budget and has accumulated the following information for 2018:

	2018				
	January	February	March	April	May
Estimated sales in units	10,000	14,000	7,000	8,000	8,000
Selling price	$54.00	$50.50	$50.50	$50.50	$50.50
Direct manufacturing labor-hours per unit	2.0	2.0	1.5	1.5	1.5
Wage per direct manufacturing labor-hour	$12.00	$12.00	$12.00	$13.00	$13.00

In addition to wages, direct manufacturing labor-related costs include pension contributions of $0.50 per hour, worker's compensation insurance of $0.20 per hour, employee medical insurance of $0.30 per hour, and Social Security taxes. Assume that as of January 1, 2018, the Social Security tax rates are 7.5% for employers and 7.5% for employees. The cost of employee benefits paid by Roletter on its employees is treated as a direct manufacturing labor cost.

Roletter has a labor contract that calls for a wage increase to $13 per hour on April 1, 2018. New labor-saving machinery has been installed and will be fully operational by March 1, 2018. Roletter expects to have 17,500 frames on hand at December 31, 2017, and it has a policy of carrying an end-of-month inventory of 100% of the following month's sales plus 50% of the second following month's sales.

Required

1. Prepare a production budget and a direct manufacturing labor budget for Roletter Company by month and for the first quarter of 2018. You may combine both budgets in one schedule. The direct manufacturing labor budget should include labor-hours and show the details for each labor cost category.
2. What actions has the budget process prompted Roletter's management to take?
3. How might Roletter's managers use the budget developed in requirement 1 to better manage the company?

6-30 Activity-based budgeting. The Jerico store of Jiffy Mart, a chain of small neighborhood convenience stores, is preparing its activity-based budget for January 2018. Jiffy Mart has three product categories: soft drinks (35% of cost of goods sold [COGS]), fresh produce (25% of COGS), and packaged food (40% of COGS). The following table shows the four activities that consume indirect resources at the Jerico store, the cost drivers and their rates, and the cost-driver amount budgeted to be consumed by each activity in January 2018.

Activity	Cost Driver	January 2018 Budgeted Cost-Driver Rate	January 2018 Budgeted Amount of Cost Driver Used		
			Soft Drinks	Fresh Snacks	Packaged Food
Ordering	Number of purchase orders	$ 45	14	24	14
Delivery	Number of deliveries	$ 41	12	62	19
Shelf stocking	Hours of stocking time	$10.50	16	172	94
Customer support	Number of items sold	$ 0.09	4,600	34,200	10,750

Required

1. What is the total budgeted indirect cost at the Jerico store in January 2018? What is the total budgeted cost of each activity at the Jerico store for January 2018? What is the budgeted indirect cost of each product category for January 2018?
2. Which product category has the largest fraction of total budgeted indirect costs?
3. Given your answer in requirement 2, what advantage does Jiffy Mart gain by using an activity-based approach to budgeting over, say, allocating indirect costs to products based on cost of goods sold?

6-31 Kaizen approach to activity-based budgeting (continuation of 6-30). Jiffy Mart has a Kaizen (continuous improvement) approach to budgeting monthly activity costs for each month of 2018. Each successive month, the budgeted cost-driver rate decreases by 0.4% relative to the preceding month. So, for example, February's budgeted cost-driver rate is 0.996 times January's budgeted cost-driver rate, and March's budgeted cost-driver rate is 0.996 times the budgeted February rate. Jiffy Mart assumes that the budgeted amount of cost-driver usage remains the same each month.

Required

1. What are the total budgeted cost for each activity and the total budgeted indirect cost for March 2018?
2. What are the benefits of using a Kaizen approach to budgeting? What are the limitations of this approach, and how might Jiffy Mart management overcome them?

6-32 Responsibility and controllability. Consider each of the following independent situations for Prestige Fountains. Prestige manufactures and sells decorative fountains for commercial properties. The company also contracts to service both its own and other brands of fountains. Prestige has a manufacturing plant, a supply warehouse that supplies both the manufacturing plant and the service technicians (who often need parts to repair fountains), and 12 service vans. The service technicians drive to customer sites to service the fountains. Prestige owns the vans, pays for the gas, and supplies fountain parts, but the technicians own their own tools.

1. In the manufacturing plant, the production manager is not happy with the motors that the purchasing manager has been purchasing. In May, the production manager stops requesting motors from the supply warehouse and starts purchasing them directly from a different motor manufacturer. Actual materials costs in May are higher than budgeted.
2. Overhead costs in the manufacturing plant for June are much higher than budgeted. Investigation reveals a utility rate hike in effect that was not figured into the budget.

3. Gasoline costs for each van are budgeted based on the service area of the van and the amount of driving expected for the month. The driver of van 3 routinely has monthly gasoline costs exceeding the budget for van 3. After investigating, the service manager finds that the driver has been driving the van for personal use.

4. Regency Mall, one of Prestige's fountain service customers, calls the service people only for emergencies and not for routine maintenance. Thus, the materials and labor costs for these service calls exceeds the monthly budgeted costs for a contract customer.

5. Prestige's service technicians are paid an hourly wage of $22, regardless of experience or time with the company. As a result of an analysis performed last month, the service manager determined that service technicians in their first year of employment worked on average 20% more slowly than other employees. Prestige bills customers per service call, not per hour.

6. The cost of health insurance for service technicians has increased by 40% this year, which caused the actual health insurance costs to greatly exceed the budgeted health insurance costs for the service technicians.

For each situation described, determine where (that is, with whom) (a) responsibility and (b) controllability lie. Suggest ways to solve the problem or to improve the situation.

Required

6-33 Responsibility, controllability, and stretch targets. Consider each of the following independent situations for Sunrise Tours, a company owned by David Bartlett that sells motor coach tours to schools and other groups. Sunshine Tours owns a fleet of 10 motor coaches and employs 12 drivers, 1 maintenance technician, 3 sales representatives, and an office manager. Sunshine Tours pays for all fuel and maintenance on the coaches. Drivers are paid $0.50 per mile while in transit, plus $15 per hour while idle (time spent waiting while tour groups are visiting their destinations). The maintenance technician and office manager are both full-time salaried employees. The sales representatives work on straight commission.

1. When the office manager receives calls from potential customers, she is instructed to handle the contracts herself. Recently, however, the number of contracts written up by the office manager has declined. At the same time, one of the sales representatives has experienced a significant increase in contracts. The other two representatives believe that the office manager has been colluding with the third representative to send him the prospective customers.

2. One of the motor coach drivers seems to be reaching his destinations more quickly than any of the other drivers and is reporting longer idle time.

3. Regular preventive maintenance of the motor coaches has been proven to improve fuel efficiency and reduce overall operating costs by averting costly repairs. During busy months, however, it is difficult for the maintenance technician to complete all of the maintenance tasks within his 40-hour workweek.

4. David Bartlett has read about stretch targets, and he believes that a change in the compensation structure of the sales representatives may improve sales. Rather than a straight commission of 10% of sales, he is considering a system where each representative is given a monthly goal of 50 contracts. If the goal is met, the representative is paid a 12% commission. If the goal is not met, the commission falls to 8%. Currently, each sales representative averages 45 contracts per month.

5. Fuel consumption has increased significantly in recent months. David Bartlett is considering ways to promote improved fuel efficiency and reduce harmful emissions using stretch environmental targets, where drivers and the maintenance mechanic would receive a bonus if fuel consumption falls below 90% of budgeted fuel usage per mile driven.

For situations 1–3, discuss which employee has responsibility for the related costs and the extent to which costs are controllable and by whom. What are the risks or costs to the company? What can be done to solve the problem or improve the situation? For situations 4 and 5, describe the potential benefits and costs of establishing stretch targets.

Required

6-34 Cash flow analysis, sensitivity analysis. HealthMart is a retail store selling home medical supplies. HealthMart also services home oxygen equipment, for which the company bills customers monthly. HealthMart has budgeted for increases in service revenue of $500 each month due to a recent advertising campaign. The forecast of sales and service revenue for the March–June 2018 is as follows:

Sales and Service Revenues Budget March–June 2018

Month	Expected Sales Revenue	Expected Service Revenue	Total Revenue
March	$7,200	$5,000	$12,200
April	8,400	5,500	13,900
May	9,100	6,000	15,100
June	10,500	6,500	17,000

Almost all of the retail sales are credit card sales; cash sales are negligible. The credit card company deposits 92% of the revenue recorded each day into HealthMart's account overnight. 70% of oxygen service billed each month is collected in the month of the service, and 30% is collected in the month after the service.

Required

1. Calculate the cash that HealthMart expects to collect in April, May, and June 2018. Show calculations for each month.
2. HealthMart has budgeted expenditures for May of $14,100.
   a. Given your answer to requirement 1, and assuming a beginning cash balance for May of $650, will HealthMart be able to cover its payments for May?
   b. Assume (independently for each situation) that May revenues might also be 10% lower or that costs might be 5% higher. Under each of those two scenarios, show the total net cash for May and the amount HealthMart would have to borrow if cash receipts are less than cash payments. The company requires a minimum cash balance of $600. (Again, assume a balance of $650 on May 1.)
3. Why do HealthMart's managers prepare a cash budget in addition to the revenue, expenses, and operating income budget? Has preparing the cash budget been helpful? Explain briefly.

Pearson MyLab Accounting

Problems

6-35 Budget schedules for a manufacturer. Lame Specialties manufactures, among other things, woolen blankets for the athletic teams of the two local high schools. The company sews the blankets from fabric and sews on a logo patch purchased from the licensed logo store site. The teams are as follows:

- Knights, with red blankets and the Knights logo
- Raiders, with black blankets and the Raider logo

Also, the black blankets are slightly larger than the red blankets.

The budgeted direct-cost inputs for each product in 2017 are as follows:

	Knights Blanket	Raiders Blanket
Red wool fabric	4 yards	0 yards
Black wool fabric	0	5
Knight logo patches	1	0
Raider logo patches	0	1
Direct manufacturing labor	3 hours	4 hours

Unit data pertaining to the direct materials for March 2017 are as follows:

Actual Beginning Direct Materials Inventory (3/1/2017)

	Knights Blanket	Raiders Blanket
Red wool fabric	35 yards	0 yards
Black wool fabric	0	15
Knight logo patches	45	0
Raider logo patches	0	60

Target Ending Direct Materials Inventory (3/31/2017)

	Knights Blanket	Raiders Blanket
Red wool fabric	25 yards	0 yards
Black wool fabric	0	25
Knight logo patches	25	0
Raider logo patches	0	25

Unit cost data for direct-cost inputs pertaining to February 2017 and March 2017 are as follows:

	February 2017 (actual)	March 2017 (budgeted)
Red wool fabric (per yard)	$9	$10
Black wool fabric (per yard)	12	11
Knight logo patches (per patch)	7	7
Raider logo patches (per patch)	6	8
Manufacturing labor cost per hour	26	27

Manufacturing overhead (both variable and fixed) is allocated to each blanket on the basis of budgeted direct manufacturing labor-hours per blanket. The budgeted variable manufacturing overhead rate for March 2017 is $16 per direct manufacturing labor-hour. The budgeted fixed manufacturing overhead for March 2017 is $14,640. Both variable and fixed manufacturing overhead costs are allocated to each unit of finished goods.

Data relating to finished goods inventory for March 2017 are as follows:

	Knights Blanket	Raiders Blanket
Beginning inventory in units	12	17
Beginning inventory in dollars (cost)	$1,440	$2,550
Target ending inventory in units	22	27

Budgeted sales for March 2017 are 130 units of the Knights blankets and 190 units of the Raiders blankets. The budgeted selling prices per unit in March 2014 are $229 for the Knights blankets and $296 for the Raiders blankets. Assume the following in your answer:

- Work-in-process inventories are negligible and ignored.
- Direct materials inventory and finished goods inventory are costed using the FIFO method.
- Unit costs of direct materials purchased and finished goods are constant in March 2017.

Required

1. Prepare the following budgets for March 2017:
   a. Revenues budget
   b. Production budget in units
   c. Direct material usage budget and direct material purchases budget
   d. Direct manufacturing labor budget
   e. Manufacturing overhead budget
   f. Ending inventories budget (direct materials and finished goods)
   g. Cost of goods sold budget
2. Suppose Lame Specialties decides to incorporate continuous improvement into its budgeting process. Describe two areas where it could incorporate continuous improvement into the budget schedules in requirement 1.

6-36 Budgeted costs, Kaizen improvements environmental costs. Tom's Apparels (Ghana) manufactures plain white and solid-colored T-shirts. Budgeted inputs include the following:

	Price	Quantity	Cost per unit of output
Fabric	$ 12 per yard	0.75 yard per unit	$9 per unit
Labor	$20 per DMLH	0.25 DMLH per unit	$5 per unit
Dye*	$0.75 per ounce	4 ounces per unit	$3 per unit

*For colored T-shirts only

Budgeted sales and selling price per unit are as follows:

	Budgeted Sales	Selling Price per Unit
White T-shirts	15,000 units	$15 per T-shirt
Colored T-shirts	60,000 units	$18 per T-shirt

Tom's Apparels has the opportunity to switch from using the dye it currently uses to using an environmentally friendly dye that costs $1.50 per ounce. The company would still need 4 ounces of dye per shirt. Tom's is reluctant to change because of the increase in costs (and decrease in profit), but the Environmental Protection Agency has threatened to fine the company $140,000 if it continues to use the harmful but less expensive dye.

Required

1. Given the preceding information, would Tom's be better off financially by switching to the environmentally friendly dye? (Assume all other costs would remain the same.)
2. Assume Tom's chooses to be environmentally responsible regardless of cost, and it switches to the new dye. The production manager suggests trying Kaizen costing. If Tom's can reduce fabric and labor costs each by 1% per month on all the shirts it manufactures, how close will it be at the end of 12 months to the profit it would have earned before switching to the more expensive dye? (Round to the nearest dollar for calculating cost reductions.)
3. Refer to requirement 2. How could the reduction in material and labor costs be accomplished? Are there any problems with this plan?

6-37 Revenue and production budgets. (CPA, adapted) The Sabat Corporation manufactures and sells two products: Thingone and Thingtwo. In July 2016, Sabat's budget department gathered the following data to prepare budgets for 2017:

2017 Projected Sales

Product	Units	Price
Thingone	62,000	$172
Thingtwo	46,000	$264

2017 Inventories in Units

	Expected Target	
Product	January 1, 2017	December 31, 2017
Thingone	21,000	26,000
Thingtwo	13,000	14,000

The following direct materials are used in the two products:

		Amount Used per Unit	
Direct Material	Unit	Thingone	Thingtwo
A	pound	5	6
B	pound	3	4
C	each	0	2

Projected data for 2017 for direct materials are as follows:

Direct Material	Anticipated Purchase Price	Expected Inventories January 1, 2017	Target Inventories December 31, 2017
A	$11	37,000 lb.	40,000 lb.
B	6	32,000 lb.	35,000 lb.
C	5	10,000 units	12,000 units

Projected direct manufacturing labor requirements and rates for 2017 are as follows:

Product	Hours per Unit	Rate per Hour
Thingone	3	$11
Thingtwo	4	$14

Manufacturing overhead is allocated at the rate of $19 per direct manufacturing labor-hour.

Required

Based on the preceding projections and budget requirements for Thingone and Thingtwo, prepare the following budgets for 2017:

1. Revenues budget (in dollars)
2. What questions might the CEO ask the marketing manager when reviewing the revenues budget? Explain briefly.
3. Production budget (in units)
4. Direct material purchases budget (in quantities)
5. Direct material purchases budget (in dollars)
6. Direct manufacturing labor budget (in dollars)
7. Budgeted finished-goods inventory at December 31, 2017 (in dollars)
8. What questions might the CEO ask the production manager when reviewing the production, direct materials, and direct manufacturing labor budgets?
9. How does preparing a budget help Sabat Corporation's top management better manage the company?

6-38 Budgeted income statement. (CMA, adapted) Smart Video Company is a manufacturer of video-conferencing products. Maintaining the videoconferencing equipment is an important area of customer satisfaction. A recent downturn in the computer industry has caused the videoconferencing equipment segment to suffer, leading to a decline in Smart Video's financial performance. The following income statement shows results for 2017:

Smart Video Company Income Statement for the Year Ended December 31, 2017 (in thousands)

Revenues		
Equipment	$8,000	
Maintenance contracts	1,900	
Total revenues		$9,900
Cost of goods sold		4,000
Gross margin		5,900
Operating costs		
Marketing	630	
Distribution	100	
Customer maintenance	1,100	
Administration	920	
Total operating costs		2,750
Operating income		$3,150

Smart Video's management team is preparing the 2018 budget and is studying the following information:

1. Selling prices of equipment are expected to increase by 10% as the economic recovery begins. The selling price of each maintenance contract is expected to remain unchanged from 2017.
2. Equipment sales in units are expected to increase by 6%, with a corresponding 6% growth in units of maintenance contracts.
3. Cost of each unit sold is expected to increase by 5% to pay for the necessary technology and quality improvements.
4. Marketing costs are expected to increase by $290,000, but administration costs are expected to remain at 2017 levels.
5. Distribution costs vary in proportion to the number of units of equipment sold.
6. Two maintenance technicians are to be hired at a total cost of $160,000, which covers wages and related travel costs. The objective is to improve customer service and shorten response time.
7. There is no beginning or ending inventory of equipment.

Required

1. Prepare a budgeted income statement for the year ending December 31, 2018.
2. How well does the budget align with Smart Video's strategy?
3. How does preparing the budget help Smart Video's management team better manage the company?

6-39 Responsibility in a restaurant. Christa Schuller owns an outlet of a popular chain of restaurants in the southern part of Germany. One of the chain's popular lunch items is the cheeseburger. It is a hamburger topped with cheese. On demand, purchasing agents from each outlet orders the cheese and meat patties from the Central Warehouse. In January 2018, one of the freezers in Central Warehouse broke down and the production of meat patty and storing of cheese were reduced by 20-30% for 4 days. During these 4 days, Christa's franchise runs out of meat patties and cheese slices while facing a high demand for cheeseburgers. Christa's chef, Kelly Lyn, decides to prepare cheeseburgers using ingredients from a local market, sending one of the kitchen helpers to the market to buy the ingredients. Although the customers' are satisfied, Christa's restaurant has to pay twice the cost of the Central Warehouse's products to procure meat and cheese from the local market, and the restaurant loses money on this item for those 4 days. Christa is angry with the purchasing agent for not ordering enough meat patty and cheese to avoid running out of stock, and with Kelly for spending too much money on the procurement of meat and cheese.

Required

Who is responsible for the cost of the meat patty and cheese as ingredients of a cheeseburger? At what level is the cost controllable? Do you agree that Christa should be angry with the purchasing agent? With Kelly? Why or why not?

6-40 Comprehensive problem with ABC costing. Animal Gear Company makes two pet carriers, the Cat-allac and the Dog-eriffic. They are both made of plastic with metal doors, but the Cat-allac is smaller. Information for the two products for the month of April is given in the following tables:

Input Prices

Direct materials	
Plastic	$ 5 per pound
Metal	$ 4 per pound
Direct manufacturing labor	$10 per direct manufacturing labor-hour

Input Quantities per Unit of Output

	Cat-allac	Dog-eriffic
Direct materials		
Plastic	4 pounds	6 pounds
Metal	0.5 pounds	1 pound
Direct manufacturing labor-hours	3 hours	5 hours
Machine-hours (MH)	11 MH	19 MH

Inventory Information, Direct Materials

	Plastic	Metal
Beginning inventory	290 pounds	70 pounds
Target ending inventory	410 pounds	65 pounds
Cost of beginning inventory	$1,102	$217

Animal Gear accounts for direct materials using a FIFO cost-flow assumption.

Sales and Inventory Information, Finished Goods

	Cat-allac	Dog-eriffic
Expected sales in units	530	225
Selling price	$ 205	$ 310
Target ending inventory in units	30	10
Beginning inventory in units	10	19
Beginning inventory in dollars	$1,000	$4,650

Animal Gear uses a FIFO cost-flow assumption for finished-goods inventory.

Animal Gear uses an activity-based costing system and classifies overhead into three activity pools: Setup, Processing, and Inspection. Activity rates for these activities are $105 per setup-hour, $10 per machine-hour, and $15 per inspection-hour, respectively. Other information follows:

Cost-Driver Information

	Cat-allac	Dog-eriffic
Number of units per batch	25	9
Setup time per batch	1.50 hours	1.75 hours
Inspection time per batch	0.5 hour	0.7 hour

If necessary, round up to calculate number of batches.

Nonmanufacturing fixed costs for March equal $32,000, half of which are salaries. Salaries are expected to increase 5% in April. Other nonmanufacturing fixed costs will remain the same. The only variable nonmanufacturing cost is sales commission, equal to 1% of sales revenue.

Required

Prepare the following for April:

1. Revenues budget
2. Production budget in units
3. Direct material usage budget and direct material purchases budget
4. Direct manufacturing labor cost budget
5. Manufacturing overhead cost budgets for each of the three activities
6. Budgeted unit cost of ending finished-goods inventory and ending inventories budget
7. Cost of goods sold budget
8. Nonmanufacturing costs budget
9. Budgeted income statement (ignore income taxes)
10. How does preparing the budget help Animal Gear's management team better manage the company?

6-41   Cash budget (continuation of 6-40). Refer to the information in Problem 6-40.

Assume the following: Animal Gear (AG) does not make any sales on credit. AG sells only to the public and accepts cash and credit cards; 90% of its sales are to customers using credit cards, for which AG gets the cash right away, less a 2% transaction fee.

Purchases of materials are on account. AG pays for half the purchases in the period of the purchase and the other half in the following period. At the end of March, AG owes suppliers $8,000.

AG plans to replace a machine in April at a net cash cost of $13,000.

Labor, other manufacturing costs, and nonmanufacturing costs are paid in cash in the month incurred except of course depreciation, which is not a cash flow. Depreciation is $25,000 of the manufacturing cost and $10,000 of the nonmanufacturing cost for April.

AG currently has a $2,000 loan at an annual interest rate of 12%. The interest is paid at the end of each month. If AG has more than $7,000 cash at the end of April it will pay back the loan. AG owes $5,000 in income taxes that need to be remitted in April. AG has cash of $5,900 on hand at the end of March.

Required

1. Prepare a cash budget for April for Animal Gear.
2. Why do Animal Gear's managers prepare a cash budget in addition to the revenue, expenses, and operating income budget?

6-42 Comprehensive operating budget. Skulas, Inc., manufactures and sells snowboards. Skulas manufactures a single model, the Pipex. In late 2017, Skulas's management accountant gathered the following data to prepare budgets for January 2018:

Materials and Labor Requirements

Direct materials	
Wood	9 board feet (b.f.) per snowboard
Fiberglass	10 yards per snowboard
Direct manufacturing labor	5 hours per snowboard

Skulas's CEO expects to sell 2,900 snowboards during January 2018 at an estimated retail price of $650 per board. Further, the CEO expects 2018 beginning inventory of 500 snowboards and would like to end January 2018 with 200 snowboards in stock.

Direct Materials Inventories

	Beginning Inventory 1/1/2018	Ending Inventory 1/31/2018
Wood	2,040 b.f.	1,540 b.f.
Fiberglass	1,040 yards	2,040 yards

Variable manufacturing overhead is $7 per direct manufacturing labor-hour. There are also $81,000 in fixed manufacturing overhead costs budgeted for January 2018. Skulas combines both variable and fixed manufacturing overhead into a single rate based on direct manufacturing labor-hours. Variable marketing costs are allocated at the rate of $250 per sales visit. The marketing plan calls for 38 sales visits during January 2018. Finally, there are $35,000 in fixed nonmanufacturing costs budgeted for January 2018.

Other data include:

	2017 Unit Price	2018 Unit Price
Wood	$32.00 per b.f.	$34.00 per b.f.
Fiberglass	$ 8.00 per yard	$ 9.00 per yard
Direct manufacturing labor	$28.00 per hour	$29.00 per hour

The inventoriable unit cost for ending finished-goods inventory on December 31, 2017, is $374.80. Assume Skulas uses a FIFO inventory method for both direct materials and finished goods. Ignore work in process in your calculations.

Required

1. Prepare the January 2018 revenues budget (in dollars).
2. Prepare the January 2018 production budget (in units).
3. Prepare the direct material usage and purchases budgets for January 2018.
4. Prepare a direct manufacturing labor costs budget for January 2018.
5. Prepare a manufacturing overhead costs budget for January 2018.
6. What is the budgeted manufacturing overhead rate for January 2018?
7. What is the budgeted manufacturing overhead cost per output unit in January 2018?
8. Calculate the cost of a snowboard manufactured in January 2018.
9. Prepare an ending inventory budget for both direct materials and finished goods for January 2018.
10. Prepare a cost of goods sold budget for January 2018.
11. Prepare the budgeted income statement for Skulas, Inc., for January 2018.
12. What questions might the CEO ask the management team when reviewing the budget? Should the CEO set stretch targets? Explain briefly.
13. How does preparing the budget help Skulas's management team better manage the company?

6-43 Cash budgeting, budgeted balance sheet. (Continuation of 6-42) (Appendix)
Refer to the information in Problem 6-42.
Budgeted balances at January 31, 2018 are as follows:

Cash	?
Accounts receivable	?
Inventory	?
Property, plant and equipment (net)	$1,175,600
Accounts payable	?
Long-term liabilities	182,000
Stockholders' equity	?

Selected budget information for December 2017 follows:

Cash balance, December 31, 2017	$ 124,000
Budgeted sales	1,650,000
Budgeted materials purchases	820,000

Customer invoices are payable within 30 days. From past experience, Skulas's accountant projects 40% of invoices will be collected in the month invoiced, and 60% will be collected in the following month.

Accounts payable relates only to the purchase of direct materials. Direct materials are purchased on credit with 50% of direct materials purchases paid during the month of the purchase, and 50% paid in the month following purchase.

Fixed manufacturing overhead costs include $64,000 of depreciation costs and fixed nonmanufacturing overhead costs include $10,000 of depreciation costs. Direct manufacturing labor and the remaining manufacturing and nonmanufacturing overhead costs are paid monthly.

All property, plant, and equipment acquired during January 2018 were purchased on credit and did not entail any outflow of cash.

There were no borrowings or repayments with respect to long-term liabilities in January 2018.

On December 15, 2017, Skulas's board of directors voted to pay a $160,000 dividend to stockholders on January 31, 2018.

Required

1. Prepare a cash budget for January 2018. Show supporting schedules for the calculation of collection of receivables and payments of accounts payable, and for disbursements for fixed manufacturing and nonmanufacturing overhead.
2. Skulas is interested in maintaining a minimum cash balance of $120,000 at the end of each month. Will Skulas be in a position to pay the $160,000 dividend on January 31?
3. Why do Skulas's managers prepare a cash budget in addition to the revenue, expenses, and operating income budget?
4. Prepare a budgeted balance sheet for January 31, 2018 by calculating the January 31, 2018 balances in (a) cash (b) accounts receivable (c) inventory (d) accounts payable and (e) plugging in the balance for stockholders' equity.

6-44 Comprehensive problem; ABC manufacturing, two products. Hazlett, Inc., operates at capacity and makes plastic combs and hairbrushes. Although the combs and brushes are a matching set, they are sold individually and so the sales mix is not 1:1. Hazlett's management is planning its annual budget for fiscal year 2018. Here is information for 2018:

Input Prices

Direct materials
    Plastic $ 0.30 per ounce
    Bristles $ 0.75 per bunch
Direct manufacturing labor $ 18 per direct manufacturing labor-hour

Input Quantities per Unit of Output

	Combs	Brushes
Direct materials		
Plastic	5 ounces	8 ounces
Bristles	—	16 bunches
Direct manufacturing labor	0.05 hours	0.2 hours
Machine-hours (MH)	0.025 MH	0.1 MH

Inventory Information, Direct Materials

	Plastic	Bristles
Beginning inventory	1,600 ounces	1,820 bunches
Target ending inventory	1,766 ounces	2,272 bunches
Cost of beginning inventory	$456	$1,419

Hazlett accounts for direct materials using a FIFO cost flow.

Sales and Inventory Information, Finished Goods

	Combs	Brushes
Expected sales in units	12,000	14,000
Selling price	$ 9	$ 30
Target ending inventory in units	1,200	1,400
Beginning inventory in units	600	1,200
Beginning inventory in dollars	$ 2,700	$27,180

Hazlett uses a FIFO cost-flow assumption for finished-goods inventory.

Combs are manufactured in batches of 200, and brushes are manufactured in batches of 100. It takes 20 minutes to set up for a batch of combs and 1 hour to set up for a batch of brushes.

Hazlett uses activity-based costing and has classified all overhead costs as shown in the following table. Budgeted fixed overhead costs vary with capacity. Hazlett operates at capacity so budgeted fixed overhead cost per unit equals the budgeted fixed overhead costs divided by the budgeted quantities of the cost allocation base.

Cost Type	Budgeted Variable	Budgeted Fixed	Cost Driver/Allocation Base
Manufacturing			
Materials handling	$17,235	$22,500	Number of ounces of plastic used
Setup	10,245	16,650	Setup-hours
Processing	11,640	30,000	Machine-hours
Inspection	10,500	1,560	Number of units produced
Nonmanufacturing			
Marketing	$21,150	$90,000	Sales revenue
Distribution	0	1,170	Number of deliveries

Delivery trucks transport units sold in delivery sizes of 1,000 combs or 1,000 brushes.

Do the following for the year 2018:

Required

1. Prepare the revenues budget.
2. Use the revenues budget to:
   a. Find the budgeted allocation rate for marketing costs.
   b. Find the budgeted number of deliveries and allocation rate for distribution costs.
3. Prepare the production budget in units.
4. Use the production budget to:
   a. Find the budgeted number of setups and setup-hours and the allocation rate for setup costs.
   b. Find the budgeted total machine-hours and the allocation rate for processing costs.
   c. Find the budgeted total units produced and the allocation rate for inspection costs.
5. Prepare the direct material usage budget and the direct material purchases budget in both units and dollars; round to whole dollars.
6. Use the direct material usage budget to find the budgeted allocation rate for materials-handling costs.
7. Prepare the direct manufacturing labor cost budget.
8. Prepare the manufacturing overhead cost budget for materials handling, setup, processing, and inspection costs.
9. Prepare the budgeted unit cost of ending finished-goods inventory and ending inventories budget.
10. Prepare the cost of goods sold budget.
11. Prepare the nonmanufacturing overhead costs budget for marketing and distribution.
12. Prepare a budgeted income statement (ignore income taxes).
13. How does preparing the budget help Hazlett's management team better manage the company?

6-45 Cash budget. (Continuation of 6-44) (Appendix)

Refer to the information in Problem 6-44.

All purchases made in a given month are paid for in the following month, and direct material purchases make up all of the accounts payable balance and are reflected in the accounts payable balances at the beginning and the end of the year.

Sales are made to customers with terms net 45 days. Fifty percent of a month's sales are collected in the month of the sale, 25% are collected in the month following the sale, and 25% are collected two months after the sale and are reflected in the accounts receivables balances at the beginning and the end of the year.

Direct manufacturing labor, variable manufacturing overhead and variable marketing costs are paid as they are incurred. Fifty percent of fixed manufacturing overhead costs, 60% of fixed marketing costs, and 100% of fixed distribution costs are depreciation expenses. The remaining fixed manufacturing overhead and marketing costs are paid as they are incurred.

Selected balances for December 31, 2017, follow:

Cash	$29,200
Accounts payable	21,450
Accounts receivable	40,000

Selected budget information for December 2018 follows:

Accounts payable	$27,770
Accounts receivable	48,500

Hazlett has budgeted to purchase equipment costing $145,000 for cash during 2018. Hazlett desires a minimum cash balance of $25,000. The company has a line of credit from which it may borrow in increments of $1,000 at an interest rate of 12% per year. By special arrangement, with the bank, Hazlett pays interest when repaying the principal, which only needs to be repaid in 2019.

Required

1. Prepare a cash budget for 2018. If Hazlett must borrow cash to meet its desired ending cash balance, show the amount that must be borrowed.
2. Does the cash budget for 2018 give Hazlett's managers all of the information necessary to manage cash in 2018? How might that be improved?
3. What insight does the cash budget give to Hazlett's managers that the budgeted income statement does not?

6-46 Budgeting and ethics. Jayzee Company manufactures a variety of products in a variety of departments and evaluates departments and departmental managers by comparing actual cost and output relative to the budget. Departmental managers help create the budgets and usually provide information about input quantities for materials, labor, and overhead costs.

Kurt Jackson is the manager of the department that produces product Z. Kurt has estimated these inputs for product Z:

Input	Budget Quantity per Unit of Output
Direct material	8 pounds
Direct manufacturing labor	30 minutes
Machine time	24 minutes

The department produces about 100 units of product Z each day. Kurt's department always gets excellent evaluations, sometimes exceeding budgeted production quantities. For each 100 units of product Z produced, the company uses, on average, about 48 hours of direct manufacturing labor (eight people working 6 hours each), 790 pounds of material, and 39.5 machine-hours.

Top management of Jayzee Company has decided to implement budget standards that will challenge the workers in each department, and it has asked Kurt to design more challenging input standards for product Z. Kurt provides top management with the following input quantities:

Input	Budget Quantity per Unit of Output
Direct material	7.9 pounds
Direct manufacturing labor	29 minutes
Machine time	23.6 minutes

Required

Discuss the following:

1. Are these budget standards challenging for the department that produces product Z?
2. Why do you suppose Kurt picked these particular standards?
3. What steps can Jayzee Company's top management take to make sure Kurt's standards really meet the goals of the firm?

6-47 Kaizen budgeting for carbon emissions. Apex Chemical Company currently operates three manufacturing plants in Colorado, Utah, and Arizona. Annual carbon emissions for these plants in the first quarter of 2018 are 125,000 metric tons per quarter (or 500,000 metric tons in 2018). Apex management is investigating improved manufacturing techniques that will reduce annual carbon emissions to below 475,000 metric tons so that the company can meet Environmental Protection Agency guidelines by 2019. Costs and benefits are as follows:

Total cost to reduce carbon emissions	$10 per metric ton reduced in 2019 below 500,000 metric tons
Fine in 2019 if EPA guidelines are not met	$300,000

Apex Management has chosen to use Kaizen budgeting to achieve its goal for carbon emissions.

Required

1. If Apex reduces emissions by 1% each quarter, beginning with the second quarter of 2018, will the company reach its goal of 475,000 metric tons by the end of 2019?
2. What would be the net financial cost or benefit of their plan? Ignore the time value of money.
3. What factors other than cost might weigh into Apex's decision to carry out this plan?

6-48 Comprehensive budgeting problem; activity-based costing, operating and financial budgets. Tyva makes a very popular undyed cloth sandal in one style, but in Regular and Deluxe. The Regular sandals have cloth soles and the Deluxe sandals have cloth-covered wooden soles. Tyva is preparing its budget for June 2018 and has estimated sales based on past experience.

Other information for the month of June follows:

Input Prices

Direct materials
Cloth	$5.25 per yard
Wood	$7.50 per board foot
Direct manufacturing labor	$15 per direct manufacturing labor-hour

Input Quantities per Unit of Output (per pair of sandals)

	Regular	Deluxe
Direct materials		
Cloth	1.3 yards	1.5 yards
Wood	0	2 b.f.
Direct manufacturing labor-hours (DMLH)	5 hours	7 hours
Setup-hours per batch	2 hours	3 hours

Inventory Information, Direct Materials

	Cloth	Wood
Beginning inventory	610 yards	800 b.f.
Target ending inventory	386 yards	295 b.f.
Cost of beginning inventory	$3,219	$6,060

Tyva accounts for direct materials using a FIFO cost-flow assumption.

Sales and Inventory Information, Finished Goods

	Regular	Deluxe
Expected sales in units (pairs of sandals)	2,000	3,000
Selling price	$ 120	$ 195
Target ending inventory in units	400	600
Beginning inventory in units	250	650
Beginning inventory in dollars	$23,250	$92,625

Tyva uses a FIFO cost-flow assumption for finished-goods inventory.

All the sandals are made in batches of 50 pairs of sandals. Tyva incurs manufacturing overhead costs, marketing and general administration, and shipping costs. Besides materials and labor, manufacturing costs include setup, processing, and inspection costs. Tyva ships 40 pairs of sandals per shipment. Tyva uses activity-based costing and has classified all overhead costs for the month of June as shown in the following chart:

Cost Type	Denominator Activity	Rate
Manufacturing		
Setup	Setup-hours	$ 18 per setup-hour
Processing	Direct manufacturing labor-hours (DMLH)	$1.80 per DMLH
Inspection	Number of pairs of sandals	$1.35 per pair
Nonmanufacturing		
Marketing and general administration	Sales revenue	8%
Shipping	Number of shipments	$ 15 per shipment

Required

1. Prepare each of the following for June:
   a. Revenues budget
   b. Production budget in units
   c. Direct material usage budget and direct material purchases budget in both units and dollars; round to dollars
   d. Direct manufacturing labor cost budget
   e. Manufacturing overhead cost budgets for setup, processing, and inspection activities
   f. Budgeted unit cost of ending finished-goods inventory and ending inventories budget
   g. Cost of goods sold budget
   h. Marketing and general administration and shipping costs budget

2. Tyva's balance sheet for May 31 follows.

Tyva Balance Sheet as of May 31

Assets		
Cash		$ 9,435
Accounts receivable	$324,000	
Less: Allowance for bad debts	16,200	307,800
Inventories		
Direct materials		9,279
Finished goods		115,875
Fixed assets	$870,000	
Less: Accumulated depreciation	136,335	733,665
Total assets		$1,176,054

Liabilities and Equity	
Accounts payable	$ 15,600
Taxes payable	10,800
Interest payable	750
Long-term debt	150,000
Common stock	300,000
Retained earnings	698,904
Total liabilities and equity	$1,176,054

Use the balance sheet and the following information to prepare a cash budget for Tyva for June. Round to dollars.

- All sales are on account; 60% are collected in the month of the sale, 38% are collected the following month, and 2% are never collected and written off as bad debts.
- All purchases of materials are on account. Tyva pays for 80% of purchases in the month of purchase and 20% in the following month.
- All other costs are paid in the month incurred, including the declaration and payment of a $15,000 cash dividend in June.
- Tyva is making monthly interest payments of 0.5% (6% per year) on a $150,000 long-term loan.
- Tyva plans to pay the $10,800 of taxes owed as of May 31 in the month of June. Income tax expense for June is zero.
- 30% of processing, setup, and inspection costs and 10% of marketing and general administration and shipping costs are depreciation.

3. Prepare a budgeted income statement for June and a budgeted balance sheet for Tyva as of June 30, 2018.

Flexible Budgets, Direct-Cost Variances, and Management Control

7

Every organization, regardless of its profitability or growth, has to maintain control over its expenses.

And when customers are cautious in their spending choices, the need for managers to use budgeting and variance analysis tools for cost control becomes especially critical. By studying variances, managers can focus on where specific performances have fallen short and make corrective adjustments and achieve significant savings for their companies. The drive to achieve cost reductions might seem at odds with the growing push for organizations to pursue environmentally sound business practices. To the contrary, managers looking to be more efficient with their plants and operations have found that cornerstones of the sustainability movement, such as reducing waste and power usage, offer fresh ways to help them manage risk and control costs, as the following article shows.

SINGADELI BAKERY AND INCENTIVE CONTROLS

SingaDeli is a bakery company in Singapore. The company produces pastries and festive items such as moon cakes and Christmas puddings. Moon cake is a delicacy traditionally eaten during the Mid-Autumn Festival that falls on the fifteenth day of the eighth lunar month. Typical moon cakes are round pastries with a filling usually made from lotus seed paste.

During the last festival, SingaDeli hired two chefs solely for the baking of moon cakes. The chefs were empowered to order raw materials and to source from the best suppliers. They were paid $1.20 per moon cake produced, plus 50% of favorable material price variance. SingaDeli estimated that its moon cake requires 50 grams of materials at the cost of $11.80 per kilogram. One month before the festival, the chefs ordered 600 kilograms of raw materials from a supplier at the price of $9.80 per kilogram.

During the festival, a total of 11,000 moon cakes were produced, of which 2,000 were sold at a discount of 70% due to poor quality.

SingaDeli's management was disappointed with the high percentage of poor quality cakes, amounting to about 20% of total production. The problem arose because the chefs were paid by product quantity, without accountability for quality or saleability. The incentive payment based on favorable price variance would induce the

LEARNING OBJECTIVES

1 Understand static budgets and static-budget variances
2 Examine the concept of a flexible budget and learn how to develop it
3 Calculate flexible-budget variances and sales-volume variances
4 Explain why standard costs are often used in variance analysis
5 Compute price variances and efficiency variances for direct-cost categories
6 Understand how managers use variances
7 Describe benchmarking and explain its role in cost management

269

purchase of the cheapest material, regardless of quality. Excessive quantities were also bought to increase the total favorable variance because the chefs were not responsible for the inventory.

SingaDeli's experience shows that if standard cost variances are to be used for performance evaluation and incentive payment, employees' empowerment has to be commensurate with their accountability. The design of the measurement system has to be comprehensive with due consideration of all of the key factors relating to resource consumption, such as material quantity, quality, and price. Otherwise, only what gets measured gets done, while other dimensions of business performance that may be impacted negatively are ignored. The wrong measurement and reward will motivate suboptimal behavior, which will be detrimental to the company as a whole. Therefore, the management must utilize comprehensive, holistic measurement and appraisal systems that discourage the promotion of one set of metrics that may have an adverse impact on other key dimensions of business performance.

In Chapter 6, you saw how budgets help managers with their planning function. We now explain how budgets, specifically flexible budgets, are used to compute variances, which assist managers in their control function. Variance analysis supports the critical final function in the five-step decision-making process by enabling managers to *evaluate performance and learn* after decisions are implemented. In this chapter and the next, we explain how.

Static Budgets and Variances

LEARNING OBJECTIVE 1

Understand static budgets

…the master budget based on output planned at start of period

and static-budget variances

…the difference between the actual result and the corresponding budgeted amount in the static budget

A **variance** is the difference between actual results and expected performance. The expected performance is also called **budgeted performance**, which is a point of reference for making comparisons.

The Use of Variances

Variances bring together the planning and control functions of management and facilitate management by exception. **Management by exception** is a practice whereby managers focus more closely on areas that are not operating as expected and less closely on areas that are. Consider the scrap and rework costs at a Maytag appliances plant. If the plant's actual costs are much higher than originally budgeted, the variances will prompt managers to find out why and correct the problem so future operations result in less scrap and rework. Sometimes a large positive variance may occur, such as a significant decrease in the manufacturing costs of a product. Managers will try to understand the reasons for the decrease (better operator training or changes in manufacturing methods, for example) so these practices can be continued and implemented by other divisions within the organization.

Variances are also used for evaluating performance and to motivate managers. Production-line managers at Maytag may have quarterly efficiency incentives linked to achieving a budgeted amount of operating costs.

Sometimes variances suggest that the company should consider a change in strategy. For example, large negative variances caused by excessive defect rates for a new product may suggest a flawed product design. Managers may then want to investigate the product design and potentially change the mix of products being offered. Variances also help managers make more informed predictions about the future and thereby improve the quality of the five-step decision-making process.

The benefits of variance analysis are not restricted to companies. In today's difficult economic environment, public officials have realized that the ability to make timely tactical changes based on variance information can result in their having to make fewer draconian adjustments later. For example, the city of Scottsdale, Arizona, monitors its tax and fee performance against expenditures monthly. Why? One of the city's goals is to keep its water usage rates stable. By monitoring the extent to which the city's water revenues are matching its current expenses, Scottsdale can avoid sudden spikes in the rate it charges residents for water as well as finance water-related infrastructure projects.[1]

---

[1] For an excellent discussion and other related examples from governmental settings, see S. Kavanagh and C. Swanson, "Tactical Financial Management: Cash Flow and Budgetary Variance Analysis," *Government Finance Review* (October 1, 2009).

How important of a decision-making tool is variance analysis? Very! A survey by the United Kingdom's Chartered Institute of Management Accountants found that it was easily the most popular costing tool used by organizations of all sizes.

Static Budgets and Static-Budget Variances

We will take a closer look at variances by examining one company's accounting system. As you study the exhibits in this chapter, note that "level" followed by a number denotes the amount of detail shown by a variance analysis. Level 1 reports the least detail; level 2 offers more information; and so on.

Consider Webb Company, a firm that manufactures and sells jackets. The jackets require tailoring and many other hand operations. Webb sells exclusively to distributors, who in turn sell to independent clothing stores and retail chains. For simplicity, we assume the following:

1. Webb's only costs are in the manufacturing function; Webb incurs no costs in other value-chain functions, such as marketing and distribution.
2. All units manufactured in April 2017 are sold in April 2017.
3. There is no direct materials inventory at either the beginning or the end of the period. No work-in-process or finished-goods inventories exist at either the beginning or the end of the period.

Webb has three variable-cost categories. The budgeted variable cost per jacket for each category is as follows:

Cost Category	Variable Cost per Jacket
Direct materials costs	$60
Direct manufacturing labor costs	16
Variable manufacturing overhead costs	12
Total variable costs	$88

The *number of units manufactured* is the cost driver for direct materials, direct manufacturing labor, and variable manufacturing overhead. The relevant range for the cost driver is from 0 to 12,000 jackets. Budgeted and actual data for April 2017 are:

Budgeted fixed costs for production between 0 and 12,000 jackets	$276,000
Budgeted selling price	$ 120 per jacket
Budgeted production and sales	12,000 jackets
Actual production and sales	10,000 jackets

The **static budget**, or master budget, is based on the level of output planned at the start of the budget period. The master budget is called a static budget because the budget for the period is developed around a single (static) planned output level. Exhibit 7-1, column 3, presents the static budget for Webb Company for April 2017 that was prepared at the end of 2016. For each line item in the income statement, Exhibit 7-1, column 1, displays data for the actual April results. For example, actual revenues are $1,250,000, and the actual selling price is $1,250,000 ÷ 10,000 jackets = $125 per jacket—compared with the budgeted selling price of $120 per jacket. Similarly, actual direct materials costs are $621,600, and the direct material cost per jacket is $621,600 ÷ 10,000 = $62.16 per jacket—compared with the budgeted direct material cost per jacket of $60. We describe potential reasons and explanations for these differences as we discuss different variances throughout the chapter.

The **static-budget variance** (see Exhibit 7-1, column 2) is the difference between the actual result and the corresponding budgeted amount in the static budget.

A **favorable variance**—denoted F in this book —has the effect, when considered in isolation, of increasing operating income relative to the budgeted amount. For revenue items, F means actual revenues exceed budgeted revenues. For cost items, F means actual costs are less than budgeted costs. An **unfavorable variance**—denoted U in this book —has the effect, when viewed in isolation, of decreasing operating income relative to the budgeted amount. Unfavorable variances are also called *adverse variances* in some countries, such as the United Kingdom.

EXHIBIT 7-1

Static-Budget-Based
Variance Analysis for
Webb Company for
April 2017[a]

Level 1 Analysis

	Actual Results (1)	Static-Budget Variances (2) = (1) – (3)	Static Budget (3)
Units sold	10,000	2,000 U	12,000
Revenues	$ 1,250,000	$190,000 U	$1,440,000
Variable costs			
Direct materials	621,600	98,400 F	720,000
Direct manufacturing labor	198,000	6,000 U	192,000
Variable manufacturing overhead	130,500	13,500 F	144,000
Total variable costs	950,100	105,900 F	1,056,000
Contribution margin	299,900	84,100 U	384,000
Fixed costs	285,000	9,000 U	276,000
Operating income	$ 14,900	$ 93,100 U	$ 108,000
		$ 93,100 U	
		Static-budget variance	

[a]F = favorable effect on operating income; U = unfavorable effect on operating income.

The unfavorable static-budget variance for operating income of $93,100 in Exhibit 7-1 is calculated by subtracting static-budget operating income of $108,000 from actual operating income of $14,900:

$$\text{Static-budget variance for operating income} = \text{Actual result} - \text{Static-budget amount}$$

$$= \$14,900 - \$108,000$$
$$= \$93,100 \text{ U.}$$

The analysis in Exhibit 7-1 provides managers with additional information on the static-budget variance for operating income of $93,100 U. The more detailed breakdown indicates how the line items that comprise operating income—revenues, individual variable costs, and fixed costs—add up to the static-budget variance of $93,100.

Recall that Webb produced and sold only 10,000 jackets, although managers anticipated an output of 12,000 jackets in the static budget. *Managers want to know how much of the static-budget variance is due to Webb inaccurately forecasting what it expected to produce and sell and how much is due to how it actually performed manufacturing and selling 10,000 jackets.* Managers, therefore, create a flexible budget, which enables a more in-depth understanding of deviations from the static budget.

DECISION POINT

What are static budgets and static-budget variances?

TRY IT! 7-1

Zenefit Corporation sold laser pointers for $11 each in 2017. Its budgeted selling price was $12 per unit. Other information related to its performance is given below:

	Actual	Budgeted
Units made and sold	28,000	27,500
Variable costs	$90,000	$ 3 per unit
Fixed costs	$55,000	$58,000

Calculate Zenefit's static-budget variance for (a) revenues, (b) variable costs, (c) fixed costs, and (d) operating income.

Flexible Budgets

A **flexible budget** calculates budgeted revenues and budgeted costs based on *the actual output in the budget period*. The flexible budget is prepared at the end of the period (April 2017 for Webb), after managers know the actual output of 10,000 jackets. The flexible budget is the *hypothetical* budget that Webb would have prepared at the start of the budget period if it had correctly forecast the actual output of 10,000 jackets. In other words, the flexible budget is not the plan Webb initially had in mind for April 2017 (remember Webb planned for an output of 12,000 jackets). Rather, it is the budget Webb *would have* put together for April if it knew in advance that the output for the month would be 10,000 jackets. In preparing the flexible budget, note that:

- The budgeted selling price is the same $120 per jacket used in the static budget.
- The budgeted unit variable cost is the same $88 per jacket used in the static budget.
- The budgeted *total* fixed costs are the same static-budget amount of $276,000. Why? Because the 10,000 jackets produced falls within the relevant range of 0 to 12,000 jackets. Therefore, Webb would have budgeted the same amount of fixed costs, $276,000, whether it anticipated making 10,000 or 12,000 jackets.

The *only* difference between the static budget and the flexible budget is that the static budget is prepared for the planned output of 12,000 jackets, whereas the flexible budget is prepared retroactively based on the actual output of 10,000 jackets. In other words, the static budget is being "flexed," or adjusted, from 12,000 jackets to 10,000 jackets.[2] The flexible budget for 10,000 jackets assumes all costs are either completely variable or completely fixed with respect to the number of jackets produced.

Webb develops its flexible budget in three steps.

Step 1: Identify the Actual Quantity of Output. In April 2017, Webb produced and sold 10,000 jackets.

Step 2: Calculate the Flexible Budget for Revenues Based on the Budgeted Selling Price and Actual Quantity of Output.

$$\text{Flexible-budget revenues} = \$120 \text{ per jacket} \times 10,000 \text{ jackets}$$
$$= \$1,200,000$$

Step 3: Calculate the Flexible Budget for Costs Based on the Budgeted Variable Cost per Output Unit, Actual Quantity of Output, and Budgeted Fixed Costs.

Flexible-budget variable costs	
Direct materials, $60 per jacket × 10,000 jackets	$ 600,000
Direct manufacturing labor, $16 per jacket × 10,000 jackets	160,000
Variable manufacturing overhead, $12 per jacket × 10,000 jackets	120,000
Total flexible-budget variable costs	880,000
Flexible-budget fixed costs	276,000
Flexible-budget total costs	$1,156,000

These three steps enable Webb to prepare a flexible budget, as shown in Exhibit 7-2, column 3. The flexible budget allows for a more detailed analysis of the $93,100 unfavorable static-budget variance for operating income.

LEARNING OBJECTIVE **2**

Examine the concept of a flexible budget

…the budget that is adjusted (flexed) to recognize the actual output level

and learn how to develop it

…proportionately increase variable costs; keep fixed costs the same

DECISION POINT

How can managers develop a flexible budget and why is it useful to do so?

Consider Zenefit Corporation. With the same information for 2017 as provided in Try It 7-1, calculate Zenefit's flexible budget for (a) revenues, (b) variable costs, (c) fixed costs, and (d) operating income.

7-2 TRY IT!

---

[2] Suppose Webb, when preparing its annual budget for 2017 at the end of 2016, had perfectly anticipated that its output in April 2017 would equal 10,000 jackets. Then the flexible budget for April 2017 would be identical to the static budget.

| EXHIBIT 7-2 | Level 2 Flexible-Budget-Based Variance Analysis for Webb Company for April 2017[a] |

Level 2 Analysis

	Actual Results (1)	Flexible-Budget Variances (2) = (1) − (3)	Flexible Budget (3)	Sales-Volume Variances (4) = (3) − (5)	Static Budget (5)
Units sold	10,000	0	10,000	2,000 U	12,000
Revenues	$1,250,000	$50,000 F	$1,200,000	$240,000 U	$1,440,000
Variable costs					
Direct materials	621,600	21,600 U	600,000	120,000 F	720,000
Direct manufacturing labor	198,000	38,000 U	160,000	32,000 F	192,000
Variable manufacturing overhead	130,500	10,500 U	120,000	24,000 F	144,000
Total variable costs	950,100	70,100 U	880,000	176,000 F	1,056,000
Contribution margin	299,900	20,100 U	320,000	64,000 U	384,000
Fixed manufacturing costs	285,000	9,000 U	276,000	0	276,000
Operating income	$ 14,900	$29,100 U	$ 44,000	$ 64,000 U	$ 108,000
Level 2		$29,100 U		$ 64,000 U	
		Flexible-budget variance		Sales-volume variance	
Level 1			$93,100 U		
			Static-budget variance		

[a]F = favorable effect on operating income; U = unfavorable effect on operating income.

Flexible-Budget Variances and Sales-Volume Variances

LEARNING
OBJECTIVE **3**

Calculate flexible-budget variances

...each flexible-budget variance is the difference between an actual result and a flexible-budget amount

and sales-volume variances

...each sales-volume variance is the difference between a flexible-budget amount and a static-budget amount

Exhibit 7-2 shows the flexible-budget-based variance analysis for Webb, which subdivides the $93,100 unfavorable static-budget variance for operating income into two parts: a flexible-budget variance of $29,100 U and a sales-volume variance of $64,000 U. The **sales-volume variance** is the difference between a flexible-budget amount and the corresponding static-budget amount. The **flexible-budget variance** is the difference between an actual result and the corresponding flexible-budget amount.

Sales-Volume Variances

Keep in mind that the flexible-budget amounts in column 3 of Exhibit 7-2 and the static-budget amounts in column 5 are both computed using budgeted selling prices, budgeted variable cost per jacket, and budgeted fixed costs. The difference between the static-budget and the flexible-budget amounts is called the sales-volume variance because it arises *solely* from the difference between the 10,000 actual quantity (or volume) of jackets sold and the 12,000 quantity of jackets expected to be sold in the static budget.

$$\text{Sales-volume variance for operating income} = \text{Flexible-budget amount} - \text{Static-budget amount}$$

$$= \$44,000 - \$108,000$$

$$= \$64,000 \text{ U}$$

The sales-volume variance in operating income for Webb measures the change in the budgeted contribution margin because Webb sold only 10,000 jackets rather than the budgeted 12,000.

$$\begin{aligned}
\text{Sales-volume variance for operating income} &= \left(\begin{array}{c}\text{Budgeted contribution}\\\text{margin per unit}\end{array}\right) \times \left(\begin{array}{c}\text{Actual units}\\\text{sold}\end{array} - \begin{array}{c}\text{Static-budget}\\\text{units sold}\end{array}\right)\\[2mm]
&= \left(\begin{array}{c}\text{Budgeted selling}\\\text{price}\end{array} - \begin{array}{c}\text{Budgeted variable}\\\text{cost per unit}\end{array}\right) \times \left(\begin{array}{c}\text{Actual units}\\\text{sold}\end{array} - \begin{array}{c}\text{Static-budget}\\\text{units sold}\end{array}\right)\\[2mm]
&= (\$120 \text{ per jacket} - \$88 \text{ per jacket}) \times (10{,}000 \text{ jackets} - 12{,}000 \text{ jackets})\\[2mm]
&= \$32 \text{ per jacket} \times (-2{,}000 \text{ jackets})\\[2mm]
&= \$64{,}000 \text{ U}
\end{aligned}$$

Exhibit 7-2, column 4, shows the components of this overall variance by identifying the sales-volume variance for each of the line items in the income statement. The unfavorable sales-volume variance in operating income arises because of one or more of the following reasons:

1. Failure of Webb's managers to execute the sales plans
2. Weaker than anticipated overall demand for jackets
3. Competitors taking away market share from Webb
4. Unexpected changes in customer tastes and preferences away from Webb's designs
5. Quality problems leading to customer dissatisfaction with Webb's jackets

How Webb responds to the unfavorable sales-volume variance will depend on what its managers believe caused the variance. For example, if Webb's managers believe the unfavorable sales-volume variance was caused by market-related reasons (reasons 1, 2, 3, or 4), the sales manager would be in the best position to explain what happened and suggest corrective actions that may be needed, such as sales promotions, market studies, or changes to advertising plans. If, however, managers believe the unfavorable sales-volume variance was caused by unanticipated quality problems (reason 5), the production manager would be in the best position to analyze the causes and suggest strategies for improvement, such as changes in the manufacturing process or investments in new machines.

The static-budget variances compared actual revenues and costs for 10,000 jackets against budgeted revenues and costs for 12,000 jackets. A portion of this difference, the sales-volume variance, reflects the effects of selling fewer units or inaccurate forecasting of sales. By removing this component from the static-budget variance, managers can compare their firm's revenues earned and costs incurred for April 2017 against the flexible budget—the revenues and costs Webb would have budgeted for the 10,000 jackets actually produced and sold. *Flexible-budget variances are a better measure of sales price and cost performance than static-budget variances because they compare actual revenues to budgeted revenues and actual costs to budgeted costs for the same 10,000 jackets of output.*

Flexible-Budget Variances

The first three columns of Exhibit 7-2 compare Webb's actual results with its flexible-budget amounts. The flexible-budget variances for each line item in the income statement are shown in column 2:

$$\frac{\text{Flexible-budget}}{\text{variance}} = \frac{\text{Actual}}{\text{result}} - \frac{\text{Flexible-budget}}{\text{amount}}$$

The operating income line in Exhibit 7-2 shows the flexible-budget variance is $29,100 U ($14,900 $44,000). The $29,100 U arises because the actual selling price, actual variable cost per unit, and actual fixed costs differ from their budgeted amounts. The actual results and budgeted amounts for the selling price and variable cost per unit are as follows:

	Actual Result	**Budgeted Amount**
Selling price	$125.00 ($1,250,000 ÷ 10,000 jackets)	$120.00 ($1,200,000 ÷ 10,000 jackets)
Variable cost per jacket	$ 95.01 ($ 950,100 ÷ 10,000 jackets)	$ 88.00 ($ 880,000 ÷ 10,000 jackets)

The flexible-budget variance for revenues is called the **selling-price variance** because it arises solely from the difference between the actual selling price and the budgeted selling price:

$$\begin{aligned}\text{Selling-price variance} &= \left(\begin{array}{c}\text{Actual}\\\text{selling price}\end{array} - \begin{array}{c}\text{Budgeted}\\\text{selling price}\end{array}\right) \times \begin{array}{c}\text{Actual}\\\text{units sold}\end{array}\\&= (\$125 \text{ per jacket} - \$120 \text{ per jacket}) \times 10,000 \text{ jackets}\\&= \$50,000 \text{ F}\end{aligned}$$

Webb has a favorable selling-price variance because the $125 actual selling price exceeds the $120 budgeted amount, which increases operating income. Marketing managers are generally in the best position to understand and explain the reason for a selling price difference. For example, was the difference due to better quality? Or was it due to an overall increase in market prices? Webb's managers concluded it was due to a general increase in prices.

The flexible-budget variance for total variable costs is unfavorable ($70,100 U) for the actual output of 10,000 jackets. It's unfavorable because of one or both of the following:

- Webb used greater quantities of inputs (such as direct manufacturing labor-hours) compared to the budgeted quantities of inputs.
- Webb incurred higher prices per unit for the inputs (such as the wage rate per direct manufacturing labor-hour) compared to the budgeted prices per unit of the inputs.

Higher input quantities and/or higher input prices relative to the budgeted amounts could be the result of Webb deciding to produce a better product than what was planned or the result of inefficiencies related to Webb's manufacturing and purchasing operations or both. *You should always think of variance analysis as providing suggestions for further investigation rather than as establishing conclusive evidence of good or bad performance.*

The actual fixed costs of $285,000 are $9,000 more than the budgeted amount of $276,000. This unfavorable flexible-budget variance reflects unexpected increases in the cost of fixed indirect resources, such as the factory's rent or supervisors' salaries.

In the rest of this chapter, we will focus on variable direct-cost input variances. Chapter 8 emphasizes indirect (overhead) cost variances.

DECISION POINT

How are flexible-budget and sales-volume variances calculated?

TRY IT! 7-3 Consider Zenefit Corporation again. With the same information for 2017 as provided in Try It 7-1, calculate Zenefit's flexible-budget and sales-volume variances for (a) revenues, (b) variable costs, (c) fixed costs, and (d) operating income.

Standard Costs for Variance Analysis

LEARNING OBJECTIVE 4

Explain why standard costs are often used in variance analysis

...standard costs exclude past inefficiencies and take into account expected future changes

To gain further insight, a company will subdivide the flexible-budget variance for its direct-cost inputs into two more-detailed variances:

1. A price variance that reflects the difference between an actual input price and a budgeted input price
2. An efficiency variance that reflects the difference between an actual input quantity and a budgeted input quantity

We will call these level 3 variances. Managers generally have more control over efficiency variances than price variances because the quantity of inputs used is primarily affected by factors inside the company (such as the efficiency with which operations are performed), whereas changes in the price of materials or in wage rates may be largely dictated by market forces outside the company.

Obtaining Budgeted Input Prices and Budgeted Input Quantities

To calculate price and efficiency variances, Webb needs to obtain budgeted input prices and budgeted input quantities. Webb's three main sources for this information are: (1) past data, (2) data from similar companies, and (3) standards. Each source has its advantages and disadvantages.

1. **Actual input data from past periods.** Most companies have past data on actual input prices and actual input quantities. These historical data could be analyzed for trends or patterns using some of the techniques we will discuss in another chapter (Chapter 10) to obtain estimates of budgeted prices and quantities.

    Advantages: Past data represent quantities and prices that are real rather than hypothetical, so they can be very useful benchmarks for measuring improvements in performance. Moreover, past data are typically easy to collect at a low cost.

    Disadvantages: A firm's inefficiencies, such as the wastage of direct materials, are incorporated in past data. Consequently, the data do not represent the performance the firm could have ideally attained, only the performance it achieved in the past. Past data also do not incorporate any changes expected for the budget period, such as improvements resulting from new investments in technology.

2. **Data from other companies that have similar processes.** Another source of information is data from peer companies or companies that have similar processes, which can serve as a benchmark. For example, Baptist Healthcare System in Louisville, Kentucky, benchmarks its labor performance data against those of similar top-ranked hospitals. (We will discuss benchmarking in more detail later in the chapter.)

    Advantages: Data from other companies can provide a firm useful information about how it's performing relative to its competitors.

    Disadvantages: Input-price and input-quantity data from other companies are often not available or may not be comparable to a particular company's situation. Consider Costco, which pays hourly workers an average of more than $20 per hour, well above the national average of $11.39 for a retail sales worker. Also unusually, Costco provides the vast majority of its workforce with company-sponsored health care. The reason is Costco's focus on employee satisfaction, with the idea that a more pleasant workplace will lead to lower employee turnover and higher productivity.

3. **Standards developed by the firm itself.** A **standard** is a carefully determined price, cost, or quantity that is used as a benchmark for judging performance. Standards are usually expressed on a per-unit basis. Consider how Webb determines its direct manufacturing labor standards. Webb conducts engineering studies to obtain a detailed breakdown of the steps required to make a jacket. Each step is assigned a standard time based on work performed by a *skilled* worker using equipment operating in an *efficient* manner. Similarly, Webb determines the standard quantity of square yards of cloth based on what is required by a skilled operator to make a jacket.

    Advantages: Standard times (1) aim to exclude past inefficiencies and (2) take into account changes expected to occur in the budget period. An example of the latter would be a decision by Webb's managers to lease new, faster, and more accurate sewing machines. Webb would incorporate the resulting higher level of efficiency into the new standards it sets.

    Disdvantages: Because they are not based on realized benchmarks, the standards might not be achievable, and workers could get discouraged trying to meet them.

The term *standard* refers to many different things:

- A **standard input** is a carefully determined quantity of input, such as square yards of cloth or direct manufacturing labor-hours, required for one unit of output, such as a jacket.

- A **standard price** is a carefully determined price a company expects to pay for a unit of input. In the Webb example, the standard wage rate the firm expects to pay its operators is an example of a standard price of a direct manufacturing labor-hour.

- A **standard cost** is a carefully determined cost of a unit of output, such as the standard direct manufacturing labor cost of a jacket at Webb.

$$\begin{array}{c}\text{Standard cost per output unit for} \\ \text{each variable direct-cost input}\end{array} = \begin{array}{c}\text{Standard input allowed} \\ \text{for one output unit}\end{array} \times \begin{array}{c}\text{Standard price} \\ \text{per input unit}\end{array}$$

Standard direct material cost per jacket: 2 square yards of cloth input allowed per output unit (jacket) manufactured, at $30 standard price per square yard

$$\text{Standard direct material cost per jacket} = \text{2 square yards} \times \text{\$30 per square yard} = \text{\$60}$$

Standard direct manufacturing labor cost per jacket: 0.8 manufacturing labor-hour of input allowed per output unit manufactured, at $20 standard price per hour

$$\text{Standard direct manufacturing labor cost per jacket} = \text{0.8 labor-hour} \times \text{\$20 per labor-hour} = \text{\$16}$$

How are the words *budget* and *standard* related? Budget is the broader term. To clarify, budgeted input prices, input quantities, and costs need *not* be based on standards. As we saw previously, they could be based on past data or competitive benchmarks. However, when standards *are* used to obtain budgeted input quantities and prices, the terms *standard* and *budget* are used interchangeably. The standard cost of each input required for one unit of output is determined by the standard quantity of the input required for one unit of output and the standard price per input unit. Notice how the standard-cost computations shown previously for direct materials and direct manufacturing labor result in the budgeted direct material cost per jacket of $60 and the budgeted direct manufacturing labor cost of $16 referred to earlier.

In its standard costing system, Webb uses standards that are attainable by operating efficiently but that allow for normal disruptions. A normal disruption could include, for example, a short delay in the receipt of materials needed to produce the jackets or a production hold-up because a piece of equipment needed a minor repair. An alternative is to set more-challenging standards that are more difficult to attain. As we discussed in Chapter 6, setting challenging standards can increase the motivation of employees and a firm's performance. However, if workers believe the standards are unachievable, they can become frustrated and the firm's performance could suffer.

DECISION POINT

What is a standard cost and what are its purposes?

Price Variances and Efficiency Variances for Direct-Cost Inputs

LEARNING OBJECTIVE 5

Compute price variances

...each price variance is the difference between an actual input price and a budgeted input price

and efficiency variances

...each efficiency variance is the difference between an actual input quantity and a budgeted input quantity for actual output

for direct-cost categories

Consider Webb's two direct-cost categories. The actual cost for each of these categories for the 10,000 jackets manufactured and sold in April 2017 is as follows:

Direct Materials Purchased and Used[3]

1. Square yards of cloth purchased and used	22,200
2. Actual price incurred per square yard	$ 28
3. Direct material costs (22,200 × $28) [shown in Exhibit 7-2, column 1]	$621,600

Direct Manufacturing Labor Used

1. Direct manufacturing labor-hours used	9,000
2. Actual price incurred per direct manufacturing labor-hour	$ 22
3. Direct manufacturing labor costs (9,000 × $22) [shown in Exhibit 7-2, column 1]	$198,000

Let's use the Webb Company data to illustrate the price variance and the efficiency variance for direct-cost inputs.

A **price variance** is the difference between actual price and budgeted price, multiplied by the actual input quantity, such as direct materials purchased. A price variance is sometimes called a **rate variance**, especially when it's used to describe the price variance for direct

---

[3] The Problem for Self-Study (pages 269–270) relaxes the assumption that the quantity of direct materials used equals the quantity of direct materials purchased.

manufacturing labor. An **efficiency variance** is the difference between the actual input quantity used (such as square yards of cloth) and the budgeted input quantity allowed for actual output, multiplied by budgeted price. An efficiency variance is sometimes called a **usage variance**. Let's explore price and efficiency variances in greater detail so we can see how managers use them.

Price Variances

The formula for computing the price variance is as follows:

$$\begin{matrix} \text{Price} \\ \text{variance} \end{matrix} = \left(\begin{matrix} \text{Actual price} \\ \text{of input} \end{matrix} - \begin{matrix} \text{Budgeted price} \\ \text{of input} \end{matrix} \right) \times \begin{matrix} \text{Actual quantity} \\ \text{of input} \end{matrix}$$

The price variances for Webb's two direct-cost categories are as follows:

Direct-Cost Category	$\left(\begin{matrix} \textbf{Actual price} \\ \textbf{of input} \end{matrix} - \begin{matrix} \textbf{Budgeted price} \\ \textbf{of input} \end{matrix} \right) \times$	**Actual quantity of input**	$=$	**Price Variance**
Direct materials	($28 per sq. yard) − $30 per sq. yard) ×	22,200 square yards	=	$44,400 F
Direct manufacturing labor	($22 per hour − $20 per hour) ×	9,000 hours	=	$18,000 U

The direct materials price variance is favorable because the actual price of cloth is less than the budgeted price, resulting in an increase in operating income. The direct manufacturing labor price variance is unfavorable because the actual wage rate paid to labor is more than the budgeted rate, resulting in a decrease in operating income.

Managers should always consider a broad range of possible causes for a price variance. For example, Webb's favorable direct materials price variance could be due to one or more of the following:

- Webb's purchasing manager negotiated the direct materials prices more skillfully than was planned for in the budget.
- The purchasing manager switched to a lower-price supplier.
- The purchasing manager ordered larger quantities than the quantities budgeted, thereby obtaining quantity discounts.
- Direct materials prices decreased unexpectedly due to an oversupply of materials in the industry.
- The budgeted purchase prices of direct materials were set too high because managers did not carefully analyze market conditions.
- The purchasing manager negotiated favorable prices because he was willing to accept unfavorable terms on factors other than prices (such as agree to lower-quality material).

How Webb's managers respond to the direct materials price variance depends on what they believe caused it. For example, if they believe the purchasing manager received quantity discounts by ordering a larger amount of materials than budgeted, Webb could investigate whether the larger quantities resulted in higher storage costs for the firm. If the increase in storage and inventory holding costs exceeds the quantity discounts, purchasing in larger quantities is not beneficial. Some companies have reduced their materials storage areas to prevent their purchasing managers from ordering in larger quantities.

Efficiency Variance

For any actual level of output, the efficiency variance is the difference between the actual quantity of input used and the budgeted quantity of input allowed for that output level, multiplied by the budgeted input price:

$$\begin{matrix} \text{Efficiency} \\ \text{variance} \end{matrix} = \left(\begin{matrix} \text{Actual} \\ \text{quantity of} \\ \text{input used} \end{matrix} - \begin{matrix} \text{Budgeted quantity} \\ \text{of input allowed} \\ \text{for actual output} \end{matrix} \right) \times \begin{matrix} \text{Budgeted price} \\ \text{of input} \end{matrix}$$

The idea here is that, given a certain output level, a company is inefficient if it uses a larger quantity of input than budgeted. Conversely, a company is efficient if it uses a smaller input quantity than was budgeted for that output level.

The efficiency variances for each of Webb's direct-cost categories are as follows:

Direct-Cost Category	$\begin{pmatrix} \text{Actual} & \text{Budgeted quantity} \\ \text{quantity of} - \text{of input allowed} \\ \text{input used} & \text{for actual output} \end{pmatrix} \times \begin{matrix} \text{Budgeted price} \\ \text{of input} \end{matrix} = \begin{matrix} \text{Efficiency} \\ \text{variance} \end{matrix}$		
Direct materials	[22,200 sq. yds. − (10,000 units × 2 sq. yds./unit)]	× $30 per sq. yard	
	= (22,200 sq. yds. − 20,000 sq. yds.)	× $30 per sq. yard	= $66,000 U
Direct manufacturing labor	[9,000 hours − (10,000 units × 0.8 hour/unit)]	× $20 per hour	
	= (9,000 hours − 8,000 hours)	× $20 per hour	= $20,000 U

The two manufacturing efficiency variances—the direct materials efficiency variance and the direct manufacturing labor efficiency variance—are each unfavorable. Why? Because given the firm's actual output, more of these inputs were used than were budgeted for. This lowered Webb's operating income.

As with price variances, there is a broad range of possible causes for these efficiency variances. For example, Webb's unfavorable efficiency variance for direct manufacturing labor could be because of one or more of the following:

- Webb's workers took longer to make each jacket because they worked more slowly or made poor-quality jackets that required reworking.
- Webb's personnel manager hired underskilled workers.
- Webb's production scheduler inefficiently scheduled work, resulting in more manufacturing labor time than budgeted being used per jacket.
- Webb's maintenance department did not properly maintain machines, resulting in more manufacturing labor time than budgeted being used per jacket.
- Webb's budgeted time standards were too tight because the skill levels of employees and the environment in which they operated weren't accurately evaluated.

Suppose Webb's managers determine that the unfavorable variance is due to poor machine maintenance. Webb could then establish a team consisting of plant engineers and machine operators to develop a maintenance schedule to reduce future breakdowns and prevent adverse effects on labor time and product quality.[4]

Exhibit 7-3 provides an alternative way to calculate price and efficiency variances. It shows how the price variance and the efficiency variance subdivide the flexible-budget variance. Consider direct materials. The direct materials flexible-budget variance of $21,600 U is the difference between the actual costs incurred (actual input quantity × actual price) of $621,600 shown in column 1 and the flexible budget (budgeted input quantity allowed for actual output × budgeted price) of $600,000 shown in column 3. Column 2 (actual input quantity × budgeted price) is inserted between column 1 and column 3. Then:

- The difference between columns 1 and 2 is the price variance of $44,400 F. This price variance occurs because the same actual input quantity (22,200 sq. yds.) is multiplied by the *actual price* ($28) in column 1 and the *budgeted price* ($30) in column 2.
- The difference between columns 2 and 3 is the efficiency variance of $66,000 U. This efficieny variance occurs because the same budgeted price ($30) is multiplied by the *actual input quantity* (22,200 sq. yds.) in column 2 and the *budgeted input quantity allowed for actual output* (20,000 sq. yds.) in column 3.
- The sum of the direct materials price variance, $44,400 F, and the direct materials efficiency variance, $66,000 U, equals the direct materials flexible budget variance, $21,600 U.

---

[4] When there are multiple inputs, such as different types of materials, that can be substituted for one another, the efficiency variance can be further decomposed into mix and yield variances. The appendix to this chapter describes how these variances are calculated.

EXHIBIT 7-3   Columnar Presentation of Variance Analysis: Direct Costs for Webb Company for April 2017[a]

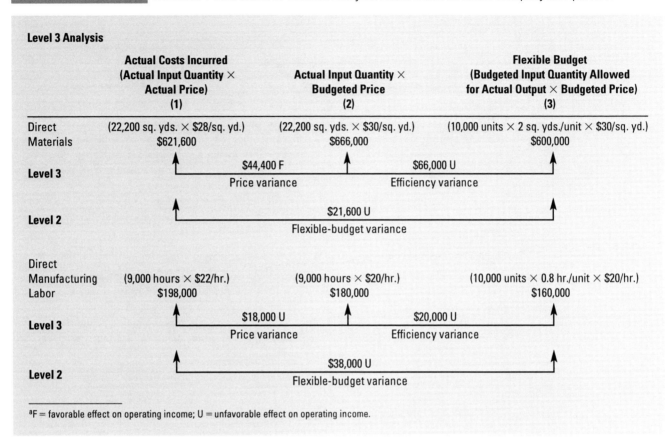

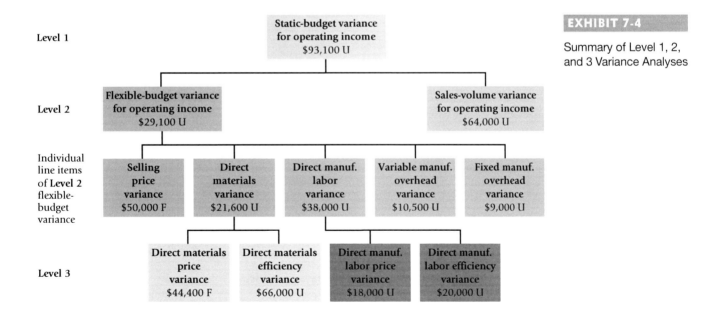

Exhibit 7-4 provides a summary of the different variances. Note how the variances at each higher level provide disaggregated and more detailed information for evaluating performance.

We now present Webb's journal entries under its standard costing system.

TRY IT! 7-4

Jamie Draperies manufactures curtains. To complete a curtain, Jamie requires the following inputs:

Direct materials standard:	10 square yards at $5 per yard
Direct manufacturing labor standard:	5 hours at $10 per hour

During the second quarter, Jamie Draperies made 1,500 curtains and used 14,000 square yards of fabric costing $68,600. Direct manufacturing labor totaled 7,600 hours for $79,800.

a. Compute the direct materials price and efficiency variances for the quarter.
b. Compute the direct manufacturing labor price and efficiency variances for the quarter.

Journal Entries Using Standard Costs

Chapter 4 illustrated journal entries when normal costing is used. We will now illustrate journal entries for Webb Company using standard costing. Our focus is on direct materials and direct manufacturing labor. All the numbers included in the following journal entries are found in Exhibit 7-3.

Note: In each of the following entries, unfavorable variances are always debits (they decrease operating income), and favorable variances are always credits (they increase operating income).

Journal Entry 1A

Isolate the direct materials price variance at the time the materials were purchased. This is done by increasing (debiting) the Direct Materials Control account by the standard price Webb established for purchasing the materials. This is the earliest time possible to isolate this variance.

1a.	Direct Materials Control		
	(22,200 square yards × $30 per square yard)	666,000	
	Direct Materials Price Variance		
	(22,200 square yards × $2 per square yard)		44,400
	Accounts Payable Control		
	(22,200 square yards × $28 per square yard)		621,600
	This records the direct materials purchased.		

Journal Entry 1B

Isolate the direct materials efficiency variance at the time the direct materials are used by increasing (debiting) the Work-in-Process Control account. Use the standard quantities allowed for the actual output units manufactured times their standard purchase prices.

1b.	Work-in-Process Control		
	(10,000 jackets × 2 yards per jacket × $30 per square yard)	600,000	
	Direct Materials Efficiency Variance		
	(2,200 square yards × $30 per square yard)	66,000	
	Direct Materials Control		
	(22,200 square yards × $30 per square yard)		666,000
	This records the direct materials used.		

Journal Entry 2

Isolate the direct manufacturing labor price variance and efficiency variance at the time the labor is used by increasing (debiting) the Work-in-Process Control by the standard hours and standard wage rates allowed for the actual units manufactured. Note that the Wages Payable Control account measures the actual amounts payable to workers based on the actual hours they worked and their actual wage rate.

2. Work-in-Process Control

(10,000 jackets × 0.80 hour per jacket × $20 per hour)	160,000	
Direct Manufacturing Labor Price Variance		
(9,000 hours × $2 per hour)	18,000	
Direct Manufacturing Labor Efficiency Variance		
(1,000 hours × $20 per hour)	20,000	
Wages Payable Control		
(9,000 hours × $22 per hour)		198,000

This records the liability for Webb's direct manufacturing labor costs.

You have learned how standard costing and variance analysis help managers focus on areas not operating as expected. The journal entries here point to another advantage of standard costing systems: Standard costs simplify product costing. As each unit is manufactured, costs are assigned to it using the standard cost of direct materials, the standard cost of direct manufacturing labor, and, as you will see in a later chapter (Chapter 8), the standard manufacturing overhead cost.

From the perspective of control, variances should be isolated at the earliest possible time. For example, the direct materials price variance should be calculated at the time materials are purchased. By doing so, managers can take corrective actions—such as trying to obtain cost reductions from the firm's current suppliers or obtaining price quotes from other potential suppliers—immediately when a large unfavorable variance is known rather than waiting until after the materials are used in production.

If the variance accounts are immaterial in amount at the end of the fiscal year, they are written off to the cost of goods sold. For simplicity, we assume that the balances in the different direct-cost variance accounts as of April 2017 are also the balances at the end of 2017 and are immaterial in total. Webb would record the following journal entry to write off the direct-cost variance accounts to the Cost of Goods Sold account.

Cost of Goods Sold	59,600	
Direct Materials Price Variance	44,400	
Direct Materials Efficiency Variance		66,000
Direct Manufacturing Labor Price Variance		18,000
Direct Manufacturing Labor Efficiency Variance		20,000

Alternatively, assuming Webb has inventories at the end of the fiscal year and the variances are material in their amounts, the variance accounts will be prorated among the cost of goods sold and various inventory accounts using the methods described in Chapter 4 (pages 148–151). For example, the Direct Materials Price Variance will be prorated among Materials Control, Work-in-Process Control, Finished Goods Control, and Cost of Goods Sold on the basis of the standard costs of direct materials in each account's ending balance. Direct Materials Efficiency Variance is prorated among Work-in-Process Control, Finished Goods Control, and Cost of Goods Sold on the basis of the direct material costs in each account's ending balance (after proration of the direct materials price variance).

As discussed in Chapter 4, many accountants, industrial engineers, and managers argue that to the extent variances measure inefficiency during the year, they should be written off against income for that period instead of being prorated among inventories and the cost of goods sold. These people believe it's better to apply a combination of the write-off and proration methods for each individual variance. That way, unlike full proration, the firm doesn't end up carrying the costs of inefficiency as part of its inventoriable costs. Consider the efficiency variance: The portion of the variance due to avoidable inefficiencies should be written off to cost of goods sold. In contrast, the portion that is unavoidable should be prorated. Likewise, if a portion of the direct materials price variance is unavoidable because it is entirely caused by general market conditions, it too should be prorated.

Implementing Standard Costing

Standard costing provides valuable information that is used for the management and control of materials, labor, and other activities related to production.

Standard Costing and Information Technology

Both large and small firms are increasingly using computerized standard costing systems. For example, companies such as Sandoz, a maker of generic drugs, and Dell store standard prices and standard quantities in their computer systems. A bar code scanner records the receipt of materials, immediately costing each material using its stored standard price. The receipt of materials is then matched with the firm's purchase orders and recorded in accounts payable, and the direct material price variance is isolated.

The direct materials efficiency variance is calculated as output is completed by comparing the standard quantity of direct materials that should have been used with the computerized request for direct materials submitted by an operator on the production floor. Labor variances are calculated as employees log into production-floor terminals and punch in their employee numbers, start and end times, and the quantity of product they helped produce. Managers use this instantaneous feedback from variances to immediately detect and correct any cost-related problem.

Wide Applicability of Standard Costing

Manufacturing firms as well as firms in the service sector find standard costing to be a useful tool. Companies implementing total quality management programs use standard costing to control materials costs. Service-sector companies such as McDonald's are labor intensive and use standard costs to control labor costs. Companies that have implemented computer-integrated manufacturing (CIM), such as Toyota, use flexible budgeting and standard costing to manage activities such as materials handling and setups. The increased use of enterprise resource planning (ERP) systems, as described in Chapter 6, has made it easy for firms to keep track of the standard, average, and actual costs of items in inventory and to make real-time assessments of variances. Managers use variance information to identify areas of the firm's manufacturing or purchasing process that most need attention.

DECISION POINT

Why should a company calculate price and efficiency variances?

LEARNING OBJECTIVE 6

Understand how managers use variances

...managers use variances to improve future performance

Management's Use of Variances

Managers and management accountants use variances to evaluate performance after decisions are implemented, to trigger organization learning, and to make continuous improvements. Variances serve as an early warning system to alert managers to existing problems or to prospective opportunities. When done well, variance analysis enables managers to evaluate the effectiveness of the actions and performance of personnel in the current period, as well as to fine-tune strategies for achieving improved performance in the future. Concepts in Action: Can Chipotle Wrap Up Its Materials-Cost Variance Increases? shows the importance to the fast casual dining giant of paying careful attention to variance analysis with respect to its direct costs.

Multiple Causes of Variances

To interpret variances correctly and make appropriate decisions based on them, managers need to recognize that variances can have multiple causes. Managers must not interpret variances in isolation of each other. The causes of variances in one part of the value chain can be

CONCEPTS IN ACTION ▶ Can Chipotle Wrap Up Its Materials-Cost Variance Increases?

Patrick T. Fallon/Bloomberg/Getty Images

Along with burritos, Chipotle has cooked up profitable growth for many years. The company's build-your-own meal model and focus on organic and naturally raised ingredients successfully attracted millions of customers in the United States and beyond. As it continues to grow, Chipotle's success depends on the company's ability to wrap up keep its materials-cost variance increases.

For Chipotle, profitability depends on making each burrito at the lowest possible cost. In each Chipotle store, the two key direct costs are labor and materials costs. Labor costs include wages for restaurant managers and staff, along with benefits such as health insurance. Materials costs include the "critical seven" expensive food ingredients—steak, carnitas, barbacoa, chicken, cheese, guacamole, and sour cream—and items such as foil, paper bags, and plastic silverware.

To reduce labor costs, Chipotle often makes subtle recipe shifts to find the right balance between taste and cost. For example, it uses pre-chopped tomatoes shipped in plastic bags to make salsa because chopping tomatoes by hand takes too much labor. From 2010–2014, tweaks like that lowered Chipotle's labor costs from 24.7% of revenue to 22.0%. At the same time, however, materials costs rose from 30.5% of revenue to 34.6% due to the company's focus on naturally raised ingredients. Responsibly raised meat and fresh local produce cost Chipotle more than conventional ingredients, which reduces profitability. As a result, each Chipotle store aggressively manages portion control. While employees gladly oblige customers asking for extra rice, beans, or salsa, they are trained to be stingy with the "critical seven" food ingredients.

After E. coli and norovirus outbreaks in 2015, Chipotle made changes to its operations to improve food safety and reduce materials-cost variances. Cheese and some vegetables now arrive in stores pre-cut and shredded, while pork and barbacoa beef are now pre-cooked and delivered in sealed bags. With future profitability dependent on lowering its materials-cost variance, Chipotle's "food with integrity" will need to be managed very closely going forward.

Sources: Sarah Nassauer, "Inside Chipotle's Kitchen: What's Really Handmade," *The Wall Street Journal* (February 24, 2015); Candice Choi, "Chipotle Makes Food Prep Changes after E. Coli Scare," *Claims Journal* (December 28, 2015).

the result of decisions made in another part of the value chain. Consider an unfavorable direct materials efficiency variance on Webb's production line. Possible operational causes of this variance across the value chain of the company are:

1. Poor design of products or processes

2. Poor work on the production line because of underskilled workers or faulty machines

3. Inappropriate assignment of labor or machines to specific jobs

4. Congestion due to scheduling a large number of rush orders placed by Webb's sales representatives

5. Webb's cloth suppliers not manufacturing materials of uniformly high quality

Item 5 offers an even broader reason for the cause of the unfavorable direct materials efficiency variance by considering inefficiencies in the supply chain of companies—in this case, by the cloth suppliers for Webb's jackets. Whenever possible, managers must attempt to understand the root causes of the variances.

When to Investigate Variances

Because a standard is not a single measure but rather a range of acceptable input quantities, costs, output quantities, or prices, managers should expect small variances to arise. A variance within an acceptable range is considered to be an "in-control occurrence" and calls for no investigation or action by managers. So when do managers need to investigate variances?

Frequently, managers investigate variances based on subjective judgments or rules of thumb. For critical items, such as product defects, even a small variance can prompt an investigation. For other items, such as direct material costs, labor costs, and repair costs, companies generally have rules such as "investigate all variances exceeding $5,000 or 20% of the budgeted cost, whichever is lower." The idea is that a 4% variance in direct material costs of $1 million—a $40,000 variance—deserves more attention than a 15% variance in repair costs of $10,000—a $1,500 variance. In other words, variance analysis is subject to the same cost–benefit test as all other phases of a management control system.

Using Variances for Performance Measurement

Managers often use variance analysis when evaluating the performance of their employees or business units. Two attributes of performance are commonly evaluated:

1. **Effectiveness**: the degree to which a predetermined objective or target is met, such as the sales, market share, and customer satisfaction ratings of Starbucks' VIA® Ready Brew line of instant coffees.

2. **Efficiency**: the relative amount of inputs used to achieve a given output level. For example, the smaller the quantity of Arabica beans used to make a given number of VIA packets or the greater the number of VIA packets made from a given quantity of beans, the greater the efficiency.

As we discussed earlier, it is important to understand the causes of a variance before using it for performance evaluation. Suppose a purchasing manager for Starbucks has just negotiated a deal that results in a favorable price variance for direct materials. The deal could have achieved a favorable variance for any or all of the following reasons:

1. The purchasing manager bargained effectively with suppliers.

2. The purchasing manager secured a discount for buying in bulk with fewer purchase orders. (However, buying larger quantities than necessary for the short run resulted in excessive inventory.)

3. The purchasing manager accepted a bid from the lowest-priced supplier without fully checking the supplier's quality-monitoring procedures.

If the purchasing manager's performance is evaluated solely on price variances, then the evaluation will be positive. Reason 1 would support this conclusion: The purchasing manager bargained effectively. Reasons 2 and 3, buying in bulk or buying without checking the supplier's quality-monitoring procedures, will lead to short-run gains. But should these lead to a positive evaluation for the purchasing manager? Not necessarily. These short-run gains could be offset by higher inventory storage costs or higher inspection costs and defect rates. Starbucks may ultimately lose more money because of reasons 2 and 3 than it gains from the favorable price variance.

Bottom line: Managers should not automatically interpret a favorable variance as "good news" or assume it means their subordinates performed well.

Firms benefit from variance analysis because it highlights individual aspects of performance. However, if any single performance measure (for example, achieving a certain labor efficiency variance or a certain consumer rating) is overemphasized, managers will tend to make decisions that will cause the particular performance measure to look good. These actions may conflict with the company's overall goals, inhibiting the goals from being achieved. This faulty perspective on performance usually arises when top management designs a performance evaluation and reward system that does not emphasize total company objectives.

Organization Learning

The goal of variance analysis is for managers to understand why variances arise, to learn, and to improve their firm's future performance. For instance, to reduce the unfavorable direct materials efficiency variance, Webb's managers may attempt to improve the design of its jackets, the commitment of its workers to do the job right the first time, and the quality of the materials. Sometimes an unfavorable direct materials efficiency variance may signal a need to change the strategy related to a product, perhaps because it cannot be made at a low enough cost. Variance analysis should not be used to "play the blame game" (find someone to blame for every unfavorable variance) but to help managers learn about what happened and how to perform better in the future.

Companies need to strike a delicate balance between using variances to evaluate the performance of managers and employees and improve learning within the organization. If the performance evaluation aspect is overemphasized, managers will focus on setting and meeting targets that are easy to attain rather than targets that are challenging, require creativity and resourcefulness, and result in continuous improvement. For example, Webb's manufacturing manager will prefer an easy standard that allows workers ample time to manufacture a jacket. But that will provide the manufacturing department little incentive to improve processes and identify methods to reduce production times and costs. Alternatively, the manufacturing manager might urge workers to produce jackets within the time allowed, even if this leads to poorer quality jackets being produced, which would later hurt revenues. If variance analysis is seen as a way to promote learning within the organization, negative effects such as these can be minimized.

Continuous Improvement

Managers can also use variance analysis to create a virtuous cycle of continuous improvement. How? By repeatedly identifying the causes of variances, taking corrective actions, and evaluating the results. Improvement opportunities are often easier to identify when the company first produces a product. Once managers identify easy improvements, much more ingenuity may be required to identify successive ones. Some companies use Kaizen budgeting (Chapter 6, p. 242) to specifically target reductions in budgeted costs over successive periods. The advantage of Kaizen budgeting is that it makes continuous improvement goals explicit.

It is important to make sure though that continuous improvement goals are implemented thoughtfully. In a research or design setting, injecting too much discipline and focusing on incremental improvement may well dissuade creativity and truly innovative approaches. An overt reliance on gaining efficiencies should not deter employees from a willingness to take risky approaches or from challenging the basic assumptions of how business is carried out.

Financial and Nonfinancial Performance Measures

Almost all companies use a combination of financial and nonfinancial performance measures for planning and control rather than relying exclusively on either type of measure. To control a production process, supervisors cannot wait for an accounting report with variances reported in dollars. Instead, timely nonfinancial performance measures are frequently used for control purposes. For example, Nissan and many other manufacturers display real-time defect rates and production levels on large screens throughout their plants for workers and managers to see.

In Webb's cutting room, cloth is laid out and cut into pieces, which are then matched and assembled. Managers exercise control in the cutting room by observing workers and by focusing on *nonfinancial measures*, such as number of square yards of cloth used to produce 1,000 jackets or the percentage of jackets started and completed without requiring any rework. Webb's production workers find these nonfinancial measures easy to understand. Webb's managers also use *financial measures* to evaluate the overall cost efficiency with which operations are being run and to help guide decisions about, say, changing the mix of inputs used in manufacturing jackets. Financial measures are critical in a company because they indicate the economic impact of diverse physical activities. This knowledge allows managers to make trade-offs, such as increasing the costs of one physical activity (say, cutting) to reduce the costs of another physical measure (say, defects).

DECISION POINT

How do managers use variances?

LEARNING OBJECTIVE 7

Describe benchmarking and explain its role in cost management

...benchmarking compares actual performance against the best levels of performance

Benchmarking and Variance Analysis

Webb Company based its budgeted amounts on analysis of its own operations. We now turn to the situation in which companies develop standards based on the operations of other companies. **Benchmarking** is the continuous process of comparing your firm's performance levels against the best levels of performance in competing companies or in companies having similar processes. When benchmarks are used as standards, managers and management accountants know that the company will be competitive in the marketplace if it can meet or beat those standards.

Companies develop benchmarks and calculate variances on items that are the most important to their businesses. A common unit of measurement used to compare the efficiency of airlines is cost per available seat mile. Available seat mile (ASM) is a measure of airline size and equals the total seats in a plane multiplied by the distance the plane traveled. Consider the cost per available seat mile for United. Assume United uses data from each of six competing U.S. airlines in its benchmark cost comparisons. Summary data are in Exhibit 7-5. The benchmark companies are in alphabetical order in column A. Also reported in Exhibit 7-5 are operating cost per ASM, operating revenue per ASM, operating income per ASM, fuel cost per ASM, labor cost per ASM, and total available seat miles for each airline. The recovery of the travel industry from the recession induced by the financial crisis as well as the benefits of lower fuel costs and greater industry consolidation are evident in the fact that all of the airlines have positive levels of operating income.

How well did United manage its costs? The answer depends on which specific benchmark is being used for comparison. United's actual operating cost of 13.65 cents per ASM is above the average operating cost of 12.78 cents per ASM of the six other airlines. Moreover, United's operating cost per ASM is 23.3% higher than Alaska Airways, the lowest-cost competitor at 11.07 cents per ASM $[(13.65 - 11.07) \div 11.07 = 0.233]$. So why is United's operating cost per ASM so high? Columns E and F suggest that both fuel cost and labor cost are possible reasons. These benchmarking data alert management at United that it needs to become more efficient in its use of both material and labor inputs to become cost competitive.

It can be difficult for firms to find appropriate benchmarks such as those in Exhibit 7-5. Many companies purchase benchmark data from consulting firms. Another problem is ensuring the benchmark numbers are comparable. In other words, there needs to be an "apples to apples" comparison. Differences can exist across companies in their strategies, inventory costing methods, depreciation methods, and so on. For example, JetBlue serves fewer cities and

EXHIBIT 7-5   Available Seat Mile (ASM) Benchmark Comparison of United Airlines with Six Other Airlines

	A	B	C	D	E	F	G
1		**Operating Cost**	**Operating Revenue**	**Operating Income**	**Fuel Cost**	**Labor Cost**	**Total ASMs**
2		**(cents per ASM)**	**(cents per ASM)**	**(cents per ASM)**	**(cents per ASM)**	**(cents per ASM)**	**(Millions)**
3	Airline	(1)	(2)	(3) = (2) – (1)	(4)	(5)	(6)
4							
5	United Airlines	13.65	13.66	0.01	4.30	4.27	214,061
6	Airlines used as benchmarks:						
7	Alaska Airlines	11.07	13.13	2.06	3.60	3.45	32,434
8	American Airlines	13.76	14.13	0.37	4.40	3.80	157,598
9	Delta Airlines	14.98	15.45	0.47	5.50	4.41	212,235
10	JetBlue Airways	11.69	12.47	0.78	4.10	3.04	45,200
11	Southwest Airlines	12.42	14.13	1.71	3.90	4.35	131,259
12	U.S. Airways	12.75	14.42	1.67	4.10	3.75	79,913
13	Average of airlines						
14	used as benchmarks	12.78	13.96	1.18	4.27	3.80	109,773
15							
16	Source: 2014 *data from the MIT Global Airline Industry Program*						

flies mostly long-haul routes compared with United, which serves almost all major U.S. cities and several international cities and flies both long-haul and short-haul routes. Southwest Airlines differs from United because it specializes in short-haul direct flights and offers fewer services on board its planes. Because United's strategy is different from the strategies of JetBlue and Southwest, one might expect its cost per ASM to be different, too. United's strategy is more comparable to the strategies of American and Delta. Note that its costs per ASM are relatively more competitive with these airlines. But United competes head to head with Alaska, JetBlue, and Southwest in several cities and markets, so it needs to benchmark against these carriers as well.

United's management accountants can use benchmarking data to address several questions. How do factors such as plane size and type or the duration of flights affect the cost per ASM? Do airlines differ in their fixed cost/variable cost structures? To what extent can United's performance be improved by rerouting flights, using different types of aircraft on different routes, or changing the frequency or timing of specific flights? What explains revenue differences per ASM across airlines? Is it differences in the service quality passengers perceive or differences in an airline's competitive power at specific airports? Management accountants are more valuable to managers when they use benchmarking data to provide insight into *why* costs or revenues differ across companies or within plants of the same company, as distinguished from simply reporting the magnitude of the differences.

DECISION POINT

What is benchmarking and why is it useful?

PROBLEM FOR SELF-STUDY

O'Shea Company manufactures ceramic vases. It uses its standard costing system when developing its flexible-budget amounts. In September 2017, O'Shea produced 2,000 finished units. The following information relates to its two direct manufacturing cost categories: direct materials and direct manufacturing labor.

Direct materials used were 4,400 kilograms (kg). The standard direct materials input allowed for one output unit is 2 kilograms at $15 per kilogram. O'Shea purchased 5,000 kilograms of materials at $16.50 per kilogram, a total of $82,500. (This Problem for Self-Study illustrates how to calculate direct materials variances when the quantity of materials purchased in a period differs from the quantity of materials used in that period.)

Actual direct manufacturing labor-hours were 3,250, at a total cost of $66,300. Standard manufacturing labor time allowed is 1.5 hours per output unit, and the standard direct manufacturing labor cost is $20 per hour.

Required

1. Calculate the direct materials price variance and efficiency variance and the direct manufacturing labor price variance and efficiency variance. Base the direct materials price variance on a flexible budget for *actual quantity purchased*, but base the direct materials efficiency variance on a flexible budget for *actual quantity used*.
2. Prepare journal entries for a standard costing system that isolates variances at the earliest possible time.

Solution

1. Exhibit 7-6 shows how the columnar presentation of variances introduced in Exhibit 7-3 can be adjusted for the difference in timing between purchase and use of materials. Note, in particular, the two sets of computations in column 2 for direct materials—the $75,000 for direct materials purchased and the $66,000 for direct materials used. The direct materials price variance is calculated on purchases so that managers responsible for the purchase can immediately identify and isolate reasons for the variance and initiate any desired corrective action. The efficiency variance is the responsibility of the production manager, so this variance is identified only at the time materials are used.

EXHIBIT 7-6 Columnar Presentation of Variance Analysis for O'Shea Company: Direct Materials and Direct Manufacturing Labor for September 2017[a]

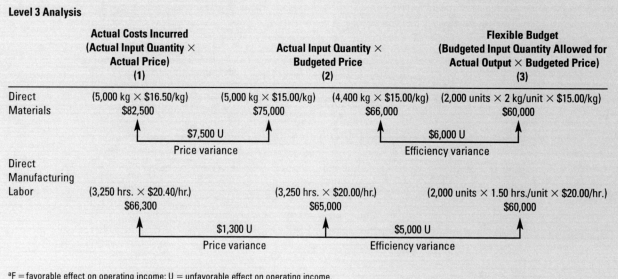

Level 3 Analysis

	Actual Costs Incurred (Actual Input Quantity × Actual Price) (1)	Actual Input Quantity × Budgeted Price (2)	Flexible Budget (Budgeted Input Quantity Allowed for Actual Output × Budgeted Price) (3)
Direct Materials	(5,000 kg × $16.50/kg) $82,500	(5,000 kg × $15.00/kg) $75,000 \qquad (4,400 kg × $15.00/kg) $66,000	(2,000 units × 2 kg/unit × $15.00/kg) $60,000
		$7,500 U — Price variance	$6,000 U — Efficiency variance
Direct Manufacturing Labor	(3,250 hrs. × $20.40/hr.) $66,300	(3,250 hrs. × $20.00/hr.) $65,000	(2,000 units × 1.50 hrs./unit × $20.00/hr.) $60,000
		$1,300 U — Price variance	$5,000 U — Efficiency variance

[a]F = favorable effect on operating income; U = unfavorable effect on operating income.

2. Materials Control (5,000 kg × $15 per kg)	75,000	
Direct Materials Price Variance (5,000 kg × $1.50 per kg)	7,500	
Accounts Payable Control (5,000 kg × $16.50 per kg)		82,500
Work-in-Process Control (2,000 units × 2 kg per unit × $15 per kg)	60,000	
Direct Materials Efficiency Variance (400 kg × $15 per kg)	6,000	
Materials Control (4,400 kg × $15 per kg)		66,000
Work-in-Process Control (2,000 units × 1.5 hours per unit × $20 per hour)	60,000	
Direct Manufacturing Labor Price Variance (3,250 hours × $0.40 per hour)	1,300	
Direct Manufacturing Labor Efficiency Variance (250 hours × $20 per hour)	5,000	
Wages Payable Control (3,250 hours × $20.40 per hour)		66,300

Note: All the variances are debits because they are unfavorable and therefore reduce operating income.

DECISION POINTS

The following question-and-answer format summarizes the chapter's learning objectives. Each decision presents a key question related to a learning objective. The guidelines are the answer to that question.

Decision	Guidelines
1. What are static budgets and static-budget variances?	A static budget is based on the level of output planned at the start of the budget period. The static-budget variance is the difference between the actual result and the corresponding budgeted amount in the static budget.
2. How can managers develop a flexible budget, and why is it useful to do so?	A flexible budget is adjusted (flexed) to recognize the actual output level of the budget period. Managers use a three-step procedure to develop a flexible budget. When all costs are either variable or fixed with respect to output, these three steps require only information about the budgeted selling price, budgeted variable cost per output unit, budgeted fixed costs, and actual quantity of output units. Flexible budgets help managers gain more insight into the causes of variances than is available from static budgets.

Decision	Guidelines
3. How are flexible-budget and sales-volume variances calculated?	The static-budget variance can be subdivided into a flexible-budget variance (the difference between the actual result and the corresponding flexible-budget amount) and a sales-volume variance (the difference between the flexible-budget amount and the corresponding static-budget amount).
4. What is a standard cost and what are its purposes?	A standard cost is a carefully determined cost used as a benchmark for judging performance. The purposes of a standard cost are to exclude past inefficiencies and to take into account changes expected to occur in the budget period.
5. Why should a company calculate price and efficiency variables?	The computation of price and efficiency variances helps managers gain insight into two different—but not independent—aspects of performance. The price variance focuses on the difference between the actual input price and the budgeted input price. The efficiency variance focuses on the difference between the actual quantity of input and the budgeted quantity of input allowed for actual output.
6. How do managers use variances?	Managers use variances for control, decision making, performance evaluation, organization learning, and continuous improvement. When using variances for these purposes, managers should consider several variances together rather than focusing only on an individual variance.
7. What is benchmarking and why is it useful?	Benchmarking is the continuous process of comparing your firm's performance against the best levels of performance in competing companies or companies with similar processes. Benchmarking measures how well a company and its managers are doing in comparison to other organizations.

APPENDIX

Mix and Yield Variances for Substitutable Inputs

The Webb Company example illustrates how to calculate price and efficiency variances for production inputs when there is a single form of each input. Webb used a single material (cloth) and a single type of direct labor. But what if managers have leeway in combining and substituting inputs? For example, Del Monte Foods can combine material inputs (such as pineapples, cherries, and grapes) in varying proportions for its cans of fruit cocktail. Within limits, these individual fruits are *substitutable inputs* in making the fruit cocktail.

We illustrate how the efficiency variance discussed in this chapter (pages 279–280) can be subdivided into variances that highlight the financial impact of input mix and input yield when inputs are substitutable. We consider a variation of the Webb Company example. For simplicity, we focus on direct manufacturing labor inputs and substitution among three of these inputs. The same approach can also be used to examine substitutable direct materials inputs.

Mode Company also manufactures jackets but, unlike Webb, employs workers of different skill (or experience) levels. Workers are of Low, Medium, or High skill. Workers with greater skill levels focus on the more complicated aspects of the jacket, such as adding darts and fancy seam lines. They are compensated accordingly. Mode's production standards require 0.80 labor-hours to produce 1 jacket; 50% of the hours are budgeted to be Low skill,

30% Medium, and 20% High. The direct manufacturing labor inputs budgeted to produce 1 jacket are as follows:

0.40 (50% of 0.80) hours of Low at $12 per hour	$ 4.80
0.24 (30% of 0.80) hours of Medium at $20 per hour	4.80
0.16 (20% of 0.80) hours of High at $40 per hour	6.40
Total budgeted direct manufacturing labor cost of 1 jacket	$16.00

With an expected $16 in labor cost for a jacket that requires 0.80 labor hours, note that the production standards imply a weighted average labor rate of $20 per hour ($16 ÷ 0.80 hours).

In April 2017, Mode produced 10,000 jackets using a total of 9,000 labor-hours. The breakdown for this input usage is as follows:

4,500	hours of Low at actual cost of $12 per hour	$ 54,000
3,150	hours of Medium at actual cost of $26 per hour	81,900
1,350	hours of High at actual cost of $46 per hour	62,100
9,000	hours of direct manufacturing labor	198,000
	Budgeted cost of 8,000 direct manufacturing labor-hours at $20 per hour	160,000
	Flexible-budget variance for direct manufacturing labor	$ 38,000 U

Direct Manufacturing Labor Price and Efficiency Variances

Mode's flexible budget and actual costs for direct manufacturing labor are identical to those in the Webb Company example. As a result, Mode has the same flexible-budget variance for direct manufacturing labor ($38,000). The breakdown of this amount into price and efficiency variances is different, however, because Mode employs three categories of substitutable direct manufacturing labor inputs.

Exhibit 7-7 presents in columnar format the analysis of Mode's flexible-budget variance for direct manufacturing labor. The labor price and efficiency variances are calculated separately for each category of direct manufacturing labor and then added together. The variance analysis prompts Webb to investigate the unfavorable price and efficiency variances in each category. Why did it pay more for certain types of labor and use more hours than it had budgeted? Were actual wage rates higher, in general, or could the personnel department have negotiated lower rates? Did the additional labor costs result from inefficiencies in processing?

EXHIBIT 7-7   Direct Manufacturing Labor Price and Efficiency Variances for Mode Company for April 2017[a]

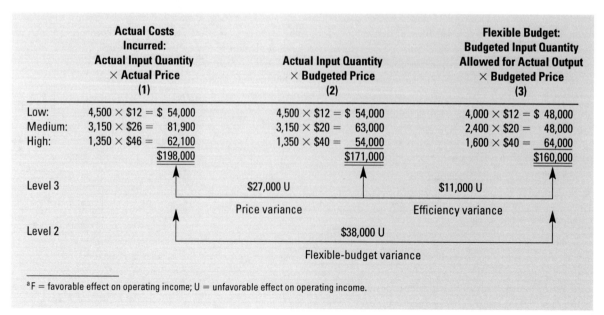

	Actual Costs Incurred: Actual Input Quantity × Actual Price (1)	Actual Input Quantity × Budgeted Price (2)	Flexible Budget: Budgeted Input Quantity Allowed for Actual Output × Budgeted Price (3)
Low:	4,500 × $12 = $ 54,000	4,500 × $12 = $ 54,000	4,000 × $12 = $ 48,000
Medium:	3,150 × $26 = 81,900	3,150 × $20 = 63,000	2,400 × $20 = 48,000
High:	1,350 × $46 = 62,100	1,350 × $40 = 54,000	1,600 × $40 = 64,000
	$198,000	$171,000	$160,000

Level 3 $27,000 U $11,000 U

Price variance   Efficiency variance

Level 2 $38,000 U

Flexible-budget variance

[a] F = favorable effect on operating income; U = unfavorable effect on operating income.

Direct Manufacturing Labor Mix and Yield Variances

Managers sometimes have discretion to substitute one input for another. The manager of Mode's operations has some leeway in combining Low, Medium, and High skill workers without affecting the quality of the jackets. We will assume that to maintain quality, mix percentages of each type of labor can only vary up to 5% from standard mix. For example, the percentage of Low skill labor in the mix can vary between 45% and 55% (50% ± 5%). When inputs are substitutable, direct manufacturing labor efficiency improvement relative to budgeted costs can come from two sources: (1) using a cheaper mix to produce a given quantity of output, measured by the mix variance, and (2) using less input to achieve a given quantity of output, measured by the yield variance.

Holding actual total quantity of all direct manufacturing labor inputs used constant, the total **direct manufacturing labor mix variance** is the difference between:

1. budgeted cost for actual mix of actual total quantity of direct manufacturing labor used and
2. budgeted cost of budgeted mix of actual total quantity of direct manufacturing labor used.

Holding budgeted input mix constant, the **direct manufacturing labor yield variance** is the difference between:

1. budgeted cost of direct manufacturing labor based on actual total quantity of direct manufacturing labor used and
2. flexible-budget cost of direct manufacturing labor based on budgeted total quantity of direct manufacturing labor allowed for actual output produced.

Exhibit 7-8 presents the direct manufacturing labor mix and yield variances for Mode Company. Note that column (1) in this exhibit is identical to column (2) in Exhibit 7-7, and column (3) is the same in both exhibits.

Direct Manufacturing Labor Mix Variance

The total direct manufacturing labor mix variance is the sum of the direct manufacturing labor mix variances for each input:

$$
\begin{pmatrix} \text{Direct} \\ \text{labor} \\ \text{mix variance} \\ \text{for each input} \end{pmatrix} = \begin{pmatrix} \text{Actual total} \\ \text{quantity of all} \\ \text{direct labor} \\ \text{inputs used} \end{pmatrix} \times \begin{pmatrix} \text{Actual} \\ \text{direct labor} \\ \text{input mix} \\ \text{percentage} \end{pmatrix} - \begin{pmatrix} \text{Budgeted} \\ \text{direct labor} \\ \text{input mix} \\ \text{percentage} \end{pmatrix} \times \begin{pmatrix} \text{Budegeted} \\ \text{price of} \\ \text{direct labor} \\ \text{input} \end{pmatrix}
$$

EXHIBIT 7-8   Direct Manufacturing Labor Yield and Mix Variances for Mode Company for April 2017[a]

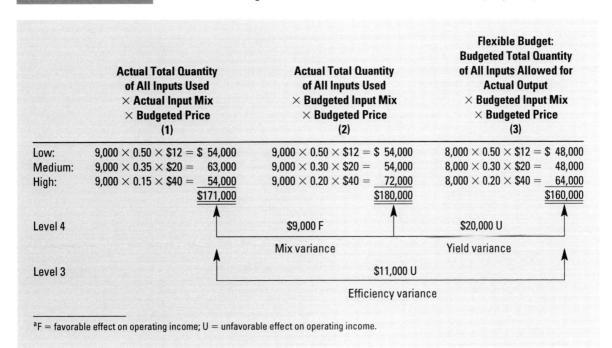

	Actual Total Quantity of All Inputs Used × Actual Input Mix × Budgeted Price (1)	Actual Total Quantity of All Inputs Used × Budgeted Input Mix × Budgeted Price (2)	Flexible Budget: Budgeted Total Quantity of All Inputs Allowed for Actual Output × Budgeted Input Mix × Budgeted Price (3)
Low:	9,000 × 0.50 × $12 = $ 54,000	9,000 × 0.50 × $12 = $ 54,000	8,000 × 0.50 × $12 = $ 48,000
Medium:	9,000 × 0.35 × $20 = 63,000	9,000 × 0.30 × $20 = 54,000	8,000 × 0.30 × $20 = 48,000
High:	9,000 × 0.15 × $40 = 54,000	9,000 × 0.20 × $40 = 72,000	8,000 × 0.20 × $40 = 64,000
	$171,000	$180,000	$160,000

Level 4 $9,000 F $20,000 U
                     Mix variance   Yield variance

Level 3 $11,000 U
                              Efficiency variance

[a]F = favorable effect on operating income; U = unfavorable effect on operating income.

The direct manufacturing labor mix variances are as follows:

Low:	9,000 hours × (0.50 − 0.50) × $12 per hour = 9,000 × 0.00 × $12 =	$ 0
Medium:	9,000 hours × (0.35 − 0.30) × $20 per hour = 9,000 × 0.05 × $20 =	9,000 U
High:	9,000 hours × (0.15 − 0.20) × $40 per hour = 9,000 × −0.05 × $40 =	18,000 F
Total direct manufacturing labor mix variance		$ 9,000 F

The total direct manufacturing labor mix variance is favorable because, relative to the budgeted mix, Mode substitutes 5% of the cheaper Medium skill labor for 5% of the more-expensive High skill.

Direct Manufacturing Labor Yield Variance

The yield variance is the sum of the direct manufacturing labor yield variances for each input:

$$
\begin{pmatrix} \text{Direct} \\ \text{labor} \\ \text{yield variance} \\ \text{for each input} \end{pmatrix} = \begin{pmatrix} \text{Actual total} \\ \text{quantity of} \\ \text{all direct} \\ \text{labor} \\ \text{inputs used} \end{pmatrix} - \begin{pmatrix} \text{Budgeted total} \\ \text{quantity of all} \\ \text{direct labor} \\ \text{input allowed} \\ \text{for actual output} \end{pmatrix} \times \begin{pmatrix} \text{Budgeted} \\ \text{direct labor} \\ \text{input mix} \\ \text{percentage} \end{pmatrix} \times \begin{pmatrix} \text{Budegeted} \\ \text{price of} \\ \text{direct labor} \\ \text{input} \end{pmatrix}
$$

The direct manufacturing labor yield variances are as follows:

Low:	(9,000 − 8,000) hours × 0.50 × $12 per hour = 1,000 × 0.50 × $12 =	$ 6,000 U
Medium:	(9,000 − 8,000) hours × 0.30 × $20 per hour = 1,000 × 0.30 × $20 =	6,000 U
High:	(9,000 − 8,000) hours × 0.20 × $40 per hour = 1,000 × 0.20 × $40 =	8,000 U
Total direct manufacturing labor yield variance		$20,000 U

The total direct manufacturing labor yield variance is unfavorable because Mode used 9,000 hours of labor rather than the 8,000 hours that it should have used to produce 10,000 jackets. The budgeted cost per hour of labor in the budgeted mix is $20 per hour. The unfavorable yield variance represents the budgeted cost of using 1,000 more hours of direct manufacturing labor, (9,000 − 8,000) hours × $20 per hour = $20,000 U. Mode would want to investigate reasons for this unfavorable yield variance. For example, did the substitution of the cheaper Medium skill for High skill labor, which resulted in the favorable mix variance, also cause the unfavorable yield variance?

The direct manufacturing labor variances computed in Exhibits 7-7 and 7-8 can be summarized as follows:

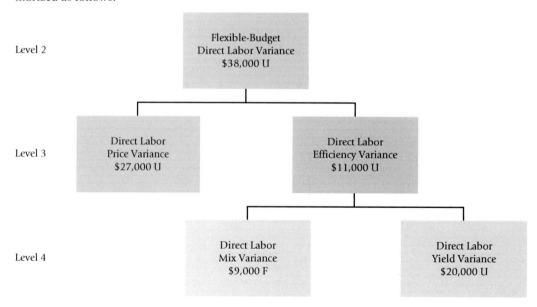

TERMS TO LEARN

This chapter and the Glossary at the end of the book contain definitions of the following important terms:

benchmarking (**p. 287**)
budgeted performance (**p. 270**)
direct manufacturing labor mix
  variance (**p. 293**)
direct manufacturing labor yield
  variance (**p. 293**)
effectiveness (**p. 286**)
efficiency (**p. 286**)
efficiency variance (**p. 279**)

favorable variance (**p. 271**)
flexible budget (**p. 273**)
flexible-budget variance (**p. 274**)
management by exception (**p. 270**)
price variance (**p. 278**)
rate variance (**p. 278**)
sales-volume variance (**p. 274**)
selling-price variance (**p. 276**)
standard (**p. 277**)

standard cost (**p. 278**)
standard input (**p. 277**)
standard price (**p. 277**)
static budget (**p. 271**)
static-budget variance (**p. 271**)
unfavorable variance (**p. 271**)
usage variance (**p. 279**)
variance (**p. 270**)

ASSIGNMENT MATERIAL

Questions

7-1 What are the main uses of variance analysis in an organization?

7-2 When using standard costing, what are the two main components of variances for materials in a flexible budget?

7-3 What are the impacts of variances on an operating income?

7-4 Why should the performance of variance analyses be based on flexible budgets rather than static budgets?

7-5 What is the main component of sales variance if a flexible-sales budget is used?

7-6 When is a flexible budget similar to a static budget? Why?

7-7 What is the main advantage of standard costs versus past costs?

7-8 How are the main components of materials variances interrelated in a flexible budget?

7-9 List three causes of a favorable direct materials price variance.

7-10 Describe three reasons for an unfavorable direct manufacturing labor efficiency variance.

7-11 How does variance analysis help in continuous improvement?

7-12 Why might an analyst examining variances in the production area look beyond that business function for explanations of those variances?

7-13 Comment on the following statement made by a management accountant: "The plant manager has little knowledge of the individual impacts of the purchase department, the sales department, and the production department on the total unfavorable variance in our operating income."

7-14 When inputs are substitutable, how can the direct materials efficiency variance be decomposed further to obtain useful information?

7-15 "Benchmarking is about comparing your firm's performance against the best levels of performance in the market and has nothing to do with variance analyses." Do you agree?

Multiple-Choice Questions

In partnership with:

BECKER
PROFESSIONAL EDUCATION®

7-16 Metal Shelf Company's standard cost for raw materials is $4.00 per pound and it is expected that each metal shelf uses two pounds of material. During October Year 2, 25,000 pounds of materials are purchased from a new supplier for $97,000 and 13,000 shelves are produced using 27,000 pounds of materials. Which statement is a possible explanation concerning the direct materials variances?

a. The production department had to use more materials since the quality of the materials was inferior.
b. The purchasing manager paid more than expected for materials.
c. Production workers were more efficient than anticipated.
d. The overall materials variance is positive; no further analysis is necessary.

7-17 All of the following statements regarding standards are accurate except:

a. Standards allow management to budget at a per-unit level.
b. Ideal standards account for a minimal amount of normal spoilage.
c. Participative standards usually take longer to implement than authoritative standards.
d. Currently attainable standards take into account the level of training available to employees.

7-18 Amalgamated Manipulation Manufacturing's (AMM) standards anticipate that there will be 3 pounds of raw material used for every unit of finished goods produced. AMM began the month of May with 5,000 pounds of raw material, purchased 15,000 pounds for $19,500 and ended the month with 4,000 pounds on hand. The company produced 5,000 units of finished goods. The company estimates standard costs at $1.50 per pound. The materials price and efficiency variances for the month of May were:

	Price Variance	Efficiency Variance
1.	$3,000 U	$1,500 F
2.	$3,000 F	$ 0
3.	$3,000 F	$1,500 U
4.	$3,200 F	$1,500 U

7-19 Atlantic Company has a manufacturing facility in Brooklyn that manufactures robotic equipment for the auto industry. For Year 1, Atlantic collected the following information from its main production line:

Actual quantity purchased	200 units
Actual quantity used	110 units
Units standard quantity	100 units
Actual price paid	$ 8 per unit
Standard price	$ 10 per unit

Atlantic isolates price variances at the time of purchase. What is the materials price variance for Year 1?

1. $400 favorable.
2. $400 unfavorable.
3. $220 favorable.
4. $220 unfavorable.

7-20 Basix Inc. calculates direct manufacturing labor variances and has the following information:

Actual hours worked: 200
Standard hours: 250
Actual rate per hour: $12
Standard rate per hour: $10

Given the information above, which of the following is correct regarding direct manufacturing labor variances?

a. The price and efficiency variances are favorable.
b. The price and efficiency variances are unfavorable.
c. The price variance is favorable, while the efficiency variance is unfavorable.
d. The price variance is unfavorable, while the efficiency variance is favorable.

Exercises

7-21 Flexible budget. Brabham Enterprises manufactures tires for the Formula I motor racing circuit. For August 2017, it budgeted to manufacture and sell 3,000 tires at a variable cost of $74 per tire and total fixed costs of $54,000. The budgeted selling price was $110 per tire. Actual results in August 2017 were 2,800 tires manufactured and sold at a selling price of $112 per tire. The actual total variable costs were $229,600, and the actual total fixed costs were $50,000.

Required

1. Prepare a performance report (akin to Exhibit 7-2, page 274) that uses a flexible budget and a static budget.
2. Comment on the results in requirement 1.

7-22 Flexible budget. Beta Company's budgeted prices for direct materials, direct manufacturing labor, and direct marketing (distribution) labor per luxury wallet are $41, $5, and $11, respectively. The president is pleased with the following performance report:

	Actual Costs	Static Budget	Variance
Direct materials	$373,500	$410,000	$36,500 F
Direct manufacturing labor	48,600	50,000	1,400 F
Direct marketing (distribution) labor	103,500	110,000	6,500 F

Actual output was 9,000 luxury wallets. Assume all three direct-cost items shown are variable costs. Is the president's pleasure justified? Prepare a revised performance report that uses a flexible budget and a static budget.

Required

7-23 Flexible-budget preparation and analysis. XYZ Printers, Inc., produces luxury checkbooks with three checks and stubs per page. Each checkbook is designed for an individual customer and is ordered through the customer's bank. The company's operating budget for September 2017 included these data:

Number of checkbooks	20,000
Selling price per book	$ 22
Variable cost per book	$ 9
Fixed costs for the month	$150,000

The actual results for September 2017 were as follows:

Number of checkbooks produced and sold	15,000
Average selling price per book	$ 23
Variable cost per book	$ 8
Fixed costs for the month	$155,000

The executive vice president of the company observed that the operating income for September was much lower than anticipated, despite a higher-than-budgeted selling price and a lower-than-budgeted variable cost per unit. As the company's management accountant, you have been asked to provide explanations for the disappointing September results.

XYZ develops its flexible budget on the basis of budgeted per-output-unit revenue and per-output-unit variable costs without detailed analysis of budgeted inputs.

1. Prepare a static-budget-based variance analysis of the September performance.
2. Prepare a flexible-budget-based variance analysis of the September performance.
3. Why might XYZ printers find the flexible-budget-based variance analysis more informative than the static-budget-based variance analysis? Explain your answer.

Required

7-24 Flexible budget, working backward. The Alpha Company manufactures designer jewelry for jewelry stores. A new accountant intern at Alpha Company has accidentally deleted the calculations on the company's variance analysis calculations for the year ended December 31, 2017. The following table is what remains of the data.

	Home	Insert	Page Layout	Formulas	Data	Review	View	
	A	B	C	D	E	F		
1	Performance Report, Year Ended December 31, 2017							
2								
3		Actual Results	Flexible-Budget Variances	Flexible Budget	Sales-Volume Variances	Static Budget		
4	Units sold	150,000				140,000		
5	Revenues (sales)	$975,000				$630,000		
6	Variable costs	675,000				350,000		
7	Contribution margin	300,000				280,000		
8	Fixed costs	150,000				130,000		
9	Operating income	$150,000				$150,000		

Required

1. Calculate all the required variances. (If your work is accurate, you will find that the total static-budget variance is $0.)
2. What are the actual and budgeted selling prices? What are the actual and budgeted variable costs per unit?
3. Review the variances you have calculated and discuss possible causes and potential problems. What is the important lesson learned here?

7-25 Flexible-budget and sales volume variances. Luster, Inc., produces the basic fillings used in many popular frozen desserts and treats—vanilla and chocolate ice creams, puddings, meringues, and fudge. Luster uses standard costing and carries over no inventory from one month to the next. The ice-cream product group's results for June 2017 were as follows:

	A	B	C
	Home	Insert	Page Layout	Formulas	Data
		A	B	C
1	Performance Report, June 2017		
2		Actual Results	Static Budget
3	Units (pounds)	350,000	335,000
4	Revenues	$2,012,500	$1,976,500
5	Variable manufacturing costs	1,137,500	1,038,500
6	Contribution margin	$ 875,000	$ 938,000

Sam Adler, the business manager for ice-cream products, is pleased that more pounds of ice cream were sold than budgeted and that revenues were up. Unfortunately, variable manufacturing costs went up, too. The bottom line is that contribution margin declined by $63,000, which is less than 3% of the budgeted revenues of $1,976,500. Overall, Adler feels that the business is running fine.

Required

1. Calculate the static-budget variance in units, revenues, variable manufacturing costs, and contribution margin. What percentage is each static-budget variance relative to its static-budget amount?
2. Break down each static-budget variance into a flexible-budget variance and a sales-volume variance.
3. Calculate the selling-price variance.
4. Assume the role of management accountant at Luster. How would you present the results to Sam Adler? Should he be more concerned? If so, why?

7-26 Price and efficiency variances. Modern Tiles Ltd. manufactures ceramic tiles. For January 2017, it budgeted to purchase and use 10,000 pounds of clay at $0.70 a pound. Actual purchases and usage for January 2017 were 11,000 pounds at $0.65 a pound. Modern Tiles Ltd. budgeted for 40,000 ceramic tiles. Actual output was 43,000 ceramic tiles.

Required

1. Compute the flexible-budget variance.
2. Compute the price and efficiency variances.
3. Comment on the results for requirements 1 and 2 and provide a possible explanation for them.

7-27 Materials and manufacturing labor variances. Consider the following data collected for Theta Homes, Inc.:

	Direct Materials	Direct Manufacturing Labor
Cost incurred: Actual inputs × actual prices	$150,000	$100,000
Actual inputs × standard prices	162,000	95,000
Standard inputs allowed for actual output × standard prices	168,000	90,000

Required

Compute the price, efficiency, and flexible-budget variances for direct materials and direct manufacturing labor.

7-28 Direct materials and direct manufacturing labor variances. SallyMay, Inc., designs and manufactures T-shirts. It sells its T-shirts to brand-name clothes retailers in lots of one dozen. SallyMay's May 2016 static budget and actual results for direct inputs are as follows:

Static Budget

Number of T-shirt lots (1 lot = 1 dozen)	400

Per Lot of Jackets:

Direct materials	14 meters at $1.70 per meter = $23.80
Direct manufacturing labor	1.6 hours at $8.10 per hour = $12.96

Actual Results

Number of T-shirt lots sold	450

Total Direct Inputs:

Direct materials	6,840 meters at $1.95 per meter = $13,338
Direct manufacturing labor	675 hours at $8.20 per hour = $5,535

SallyMay has a policy of analyzing all input variances when they add up to more than 10% of the total cost of materials and labor in the flexible budget, and this is true in May 2016. The production manager discusses the sources of the variances: "A new type of material was purchased in May. This led to faster cutting and sewing, but the workers used more material than usual as they learned to work with it. For now, the standards are fine."

Required

1. Calculate the direct materials and direct manufacturing labor price and efficiency variances in May 2016. What is the total flexible-budget variance for both inputs (direct materials and direct manufacturing labor) combined? What percentage is this variance of the total cost of direct materials and direct manufacturing labor in the flexible budget?
2. Comment on the May 2016 results. Would you continue the "experiment" of using the new material?

7-29 Price and efficiency variances, journal entries. The Schuyler Corporation manufactures lamps. It has set up the following standards per finished unit for direct materials and direct manufacturing labor:

Direct materials: 10 lb. at $4.50 per lb.	$45.00
Direct manufacturing labor: 0.5 hour at $30 per hour	15.00

The number of finished units budgeted for January 2017 was 10,000; 9,850 units were actually produced. Actual results in January 2017 were as follows:

Direct materials: 98,055 lb. used	
Direct manufacturing labor: 4,900 hours	$154,350

Assume that there was no beginning inventory of either direct materials or finished units.

During the month, materials purchased amounted to 100,000 lb., at a total cost of $465,000. Input price variances are isolated upon purchase. Input-efficiency variances are isolated at the time of usage.

Required

1. Compute the January 2017 price and efficiency variances of direct materials and direct manufacturing labor.
2. Prepare journal entries to record the variances in requirement 1.
3. Comment on the January 2017 price and efficiency variances of Schuyler Corporation.
4. Why might Schuyler calculate direct materials price variances and direct materials efficiency variances with reference to different points in time?

7-30 Materials and manufacturing labor variances, standard costs. Dunn, Inc., is a privately held furniture manufacturer. For August 2017, Dunn had the following standards for one of its products, a wicker chair:

Standards per Chair	
Direct materials	2 square yards of input at $5 per square yard
Direct manufacturing labor	0.5 hour of input at $10 per hour

The following data were compiled regarding actual performance: actual output units (chairs) produced, 2,000; square yards of input purchased and used, 3,700; price per square yard, $5.10; direct manufacturing labor costs, $8,820; actual hours of input, 900; labor price per hour, $9.80.

1. Show computations of price and efficiency variances for direct materials and direct manufacturing labor. Give a plausible explanation of why each variance occurred.
2. Suppose 6,000 square yards of materials were purchased (at $5.10 per square yard), even though only 3,700 square yards were used. Suppose further that variances are identified at their most timely control point; accordingly, direct materials price variances are isolated and traced at the time of purchase to the purchasing department rather than to the production department. Compute the price and efficiency variances under this approach.

7-31 Journal entries and T-accounts (continuation of 7-30). Prepare journal entries and post them to T-accounts for all transactions in Exercise 7-30, including requirement 2. Summarize how these journal entries differ from the normal-costing entries described in Chapter 4, pages 140–143.

7-32 Price and efficiency variances, benchmarking. Topiary Co. produces molded plastic garden pots and other plastic containers. In June 2017, Topiary produces 1,000 lots (each lot is 12 dozen pots) of its most popular line of pots, the 14-inch "Grecian urns," at each of its two plants, which are located in Mineola and Bayside. The production manager, Janice Roberts, asks her assistant, Alastair Ramy, to find out the precise per-unit budgeted variable costs at the two plants and the variable costs of a competitor, Land Art, who offers similar-quality pots at cheaper prices. Ramy pulls together the following information for each lot:

Per Lot	Mineola Plant	Bayside Plant	Land Art
Direct materials	13.50 lbs. @ $9.20 per lb.	14.00 lbs. @ $9.00 per lb.	13.00 lbs. @ $8.80 per lb.
Direct labor	3 hours @ $10.15 per hour	2.7 hours @ $10.20 per hour	2.5 hours @ $10.00 per hour
Variable overhead	$12 per lot	$11 per lot	$11 per lot

1. What is the budgeted variable cost per lot at the Mineola Plant, the Bayside Plant, and at Land Art?
2. Using the Land Art data as the standard, calculate the direct materials and direct labor price and efficiency variances for the Mineola and Bayside plants.
3. What advantage does Topiary get by using Land Art's benchmark data as standards in calculating its variances? Identify two issues that Roberts should keep in mind in using the Land Art data as the standards.

7-33 Static and flexible budgets, service sector. Student Finance (StuFi) is a start-up that aims to use the power of social communities to transform the student loan market. It connects participants through a dedicated lending pool, enabling current students to borrow from a school's alumni community. StuFi's revenue model is to take an upfront fee of 40 basis points (0.40%) *each* from the alumni investor and the student borrower for every loan originated on its platform.

StuFi hopes to go public in the near future and is keen to ensure that its financial results are in line with that ambition. StuFi's budgeted and actual results for the third quarter of 2017 are presented below.

	Home	Insert	Page Layout	Formulas	Data	Review	View	
	A		B	C		D		E
1			Static Budget			Actual Results		
2	New loans originated		8,200			10,250		
3	Average amount of loan		$145,000			$162,000		
4	Variable costs per loan:							
5	Professional labor		$360	(8 hrs at $45 per hour)		$475	(9.5 hrs at $50 per hour)	
6	Credit verification		$100			$100		
7	Federal documentation fees		$120			$125		
8	Courier services		$50			$54		
9	Administrative costs (fixed)		$800,000			$945,000		
10	Technology costs (fixed)		$1,300,000			$1,415,000		

1. Prepare StuFi's static budget of operating income for the third quarter of 2017.
2. Prepare an analysis of variances for the third quarter of 2017 along the lines of Exhibit 7-2; identify the sales volume and flexible budget variances for operating income.
3. Compute the professional labor price and efficiency variances for the third quarter of 2017.
4. What factors would you consider in evaluating the effectiveness of professional labor in the third quarter of 2017?

Problems

7-34 Flexible budget, direct materials, and direct manufacturing labor variances. Milan Statuary manufactures bust statues of famous historical figures. All statues are the same size. Each unit requires the same amount of resources. The following information is from the static budget for 2017:

Expected production and sales	6,100 units
Expected selling price per unit	$ 700
Total fixed costs	$1,350,000

Standard quantities, standard prices, and standard unit costs follow for direct materials and direct manufacturing labor:

	Standard Quantity	Standard Price	Standard Unit Cost
Direct materials	16 pounds	$14 per pound	$224
Direct manufacturing labor	3.8 hours	$30 per hour	$114

During 2017, actual number of units produced and sold was 5,100, at an average selling price of $730. Actual cost of direct materials used was $1,149,400, based on 70,000 pounds purchased at $16.42 per pound. Direct manufacturing labor-hours actually used were 17,000, at the rate of $33.70 per hour. As a result, actual direct manufacturing labor costs were $572,900. Actual fixed costs were $1,200,000. There were no beginning or ending inventories.

1. Calculate the sales-volume variance and flexible-budget variance for operating income.
2. Compute price and efficiency variances for direct materials and direct manufacturing labor.

7-35 Variance analysis, nonmanufacturing setting. Marcus McQueen has run In-A-Flash Car Detailing for the past 10 years. His static budget and actual results for June 2017 are provided next. Marcus has one employee who has been with him for all 10 years that he has been in business. In addition, at any given time he also employs two other less experienced workers. It usually takes each employee 2 hours to detail a vehicle, regardless of his or her experience. Marcus pays his experienced employee $30 per vehicle and the other two employees $15 per vehicle. There were no wage increases in June.

In-A-Flash Car Detailing
Actual and Budgeted Income Statements
For the Month Ended June 30, 2017

	Budget	Actual
Offices cleaned	280	320
Revenue	$53,200	$72,000
Variable costs:		
Costs of supplies	1,260	1,360
Labor	6,720	8,400
Total variable costs	7,980	9,760
Contribution margin	45,220	62,240
Fixed costs	9,800	9,800
Operating income	$35,420	$52,440

1. How many cars, on average, did Marcus budget for each employee? How many cars did each employee actually detail?
2. Prepare a flexible budget for June 2017.
3. Compute the sales price variance and the labor efficiency variance for each labor type.
4. What information, in addition to that provided in the income statements, would you want Marcus to gather, if you wanted to improve operational efficiency?

7-36 Comprehensive variance analysis review. Omega Animal Health, Inc. produces a generic medication used to treat cats with feline diabetes. The liquid medication is sold in 100 ml vials. Omega employs a team of sales representatives who are paid varying amounts of commission.

Given the narrow margins in the generic veterinary drugs industry, Omega relies on tight standards and cost controls to manage its operations. Omega has the following budgeted standards for the month of April 2017:

Average selling price per vial	$ 9.40
Total direct materials cost per vial	$ 3.90
Direct manufacturing labor cost per hour	$ 17.00
Average labor productivity rate (vials per hour)	100
Sales commission cost per unit	$ 0.76
Fixed administrative and manufacturing overhead	$800,000

Omega budgeted sales of 800,000 vials for April. At the end of the month, the controller revealed that actual results for April had deviated from the budget in several ways:

- Unit sales and production were 80% of plan.
- Actual average selling price increased to $9.50.
- Productivity dropped to 80 vials per hour.
- Actual direct manufacturing labor cost was $17.30 per hour.
- Actual total direct material cost per unit increased to $4.20.
- Actual sales commissions were $0.74 per unit.
- Fixed overhead costs were $30,000 above budget.

Calculate the following amounts for Omega for April 2017:

1. Static-budget and actual operating income
2. Static-budget variance for operating income
3. Flexible-budget operating income
4. Flexible-budget variance for operating income
5. Sales-volume variance for operating income
6. Price and efficiency variances for direct manufacturing labor
7. Flexible-budget variance for direct manufacturing labor

7-37 Possible causes for price and efficiency variances. You have been invited to interview for an internship with an international food manufacturing company. When you arrive for the interview, you are given the following information related to a fictitious Belgian chocolatier for the month of June. The chocolatier manufactures truffles in 12-piece boxes. The production is labor intensive, and the delicate nature of the chocolate requires a high degree of skill.

Actual	
Boxes produced	12,000
Direct materials used in production	2,640,000 g
Actual direct material cost	72,500 euro
Actual direct manufacturing labor-hours	1,300
Actual direct manufacturing labor cost	15,360 euro

Standards	
Purchase price of direct materials	0.029 euro/g
Materials per box	200 g
Wage rate	13 euro/hour
Boxes per hour	10

Please respond to the following questions as if you were in an interview situation:

Required

1. Calculate the materials efficiency and price variance and the wage and labor efficiency variances for the month of June.
2. Discuss some possible causes of the variances you have calculated. Can you make any possible connection between the material and labor variances? What recommendations do you have for future improvement?

7-38 Material-cost variances, use of variances for performance evaluation. Katharine Johnson is the owner of Best Bikes, a company that produces high-quality cross-country bicycles. Best Bikes participates in a supply chain that consists of suppliers, manufacturers, distributors, and elite bicycle shops. For several years Best Bikes has purchased titanium from suppliers in the supply chain. Best Bikes uses titanium for the bicycle frames because it is stronger and lighter than other metals and therefore increases the quality of the bicycle. Earlier this year, Best Bikes hired Michael Bentfield, a recent graduate from State University, as purchasing manager. Michael believed that he could reduce costs if he purchased titanium from an online marketplace at a lower price.

Best Bikes established the following standards based upon the company's experience with previous suppliers. The standards are as follows:

Cost of titanium	$18 per pound
Titanium used per bicycle	8 lbs.

Actual results for the first month using the online supplier of titanium are as follows:

Bicycles produced	400
Titanium purchased	5,200 lb. for $88,400
Titanium used in production	4,700 lb.

Required

1. Compute the direct materials price and efficiency variances.
2. What factors can explain the variances identified in requirement 1? Could any other variances be affected?
3. Was switching suppliers a good idea for Best Bikes? Explain why or why not.
4. Should Michael Bentfield's performance evaluation be based solely on price variances? Should the production manager's evaluation be based solely on efficiency variances? Why is it important for Katharine Johnson to understand the causes of a variance before she evaluates performance?
5. Other than performance evaluation, what reasons are there for calculating variances?
6. What future problems could result from Best Bikes' decision to buy a lower quality of titanium from the online marketplace?

7-39 Direct manufacturing labor and direct materials variances, missing data. (CMA, heavily adapted) Young Bay Surfboards manufactures fiberglass surfboards. The standard cost of direct materials and direct manufacturing labor is $223 per board. This includes 40 pounds of direct materials, at the budgeted price of $2 per pound, and 10 hours of direct manufacturing labor, at the budgeted rate of $14.30 per hour. Following are additional data for the month of July:

Units completed	5,500 units
Direct material purchases	160,000 pounds
Cost of direct material purchases	$432,000
Actual direct manufacturing labor-hours	41,000 hours
Actual direct labor cost	$594,500
Direct materials efficiency variance	$ 1,700 F

There were no beginning inventories.

1. Compute direct manufacturing labor variances for July.
2. Compute the actual pounds of direct materials used in production in July.
3. Calculate the actual price per pound of direct materials purchased.
4. Calculate the direct materials price variance.

7-40 Direct materials efficiency, mix, and yield variances. Gamma's Snacks produces snack mixes for the gourmet and natural foods market. Its most popular product is Tempting Trail Mix, a mixture of peanuts, dried cranberries, and chocolate pieces. For each batch, the budgeted quantities, budgeted prices, and budgeted mix of direct materials are as follows:

	Quantity per Batch	Price per Cup	Budgeted Mix
Peanuts	50 cups	$ 1	50%
Dried cranberries	30 cups	$ 2	30%
Chocolate pieces	20 cups	$ 3	20%

Changing the standard mix of direct material quantities slightly does not significantly affect the overall end product. In addition, not all ingredients added to production end up in the finished product, as some are rejected during inspection.

In the current period, Gamma's Snacks made 100 batches of Tempting Trail Mix with the following actual quantity, cost, and mix of inputs:

	Actual Quantity	Actual Cost	Actual Mix
Peanuts	6,050 cups	$ 5,445	55%
Dried cranberries	3,080 cups	$ 6,930	28%
Chocolate pieces	1,870 cups	$ 5,423	17%
Total	**11,000 cups**	**$17,798**	**100%**

1. What is the budgeted cost of direct materials for the 100 batches?
2. Calculate the total direct materials efficiency variance..
3. Calculate the total direct materials mix and yield variances.
4. Illustrate the relationship between the variances calculated in requirement 2 and 3. What are the variances calculated in requirement 3 telling you about the 100 batches produced this period? Are the variances large enough to investigate?

7-41 Direct materials and manufacturing labor variances, solving unknowns. (CPA, adapted) On May 1, 2017, Lowell Company began the manufacture of a new paging machine known as Dandy. The company installed a standard costing system to account for manufacturing costs. The standard costs for a unit of Dandy follow:

Direct materials (2 lb. at $3 per lb.)	$6.00
Direct manufacturing labor (1/2 hour at $16 per hour)	8.00
Manufacturing overhead (80% of direct manufacturing labor costs)	6.40
	$20.40

The following data were obtained from Lowell's records for the month of May:

	Debit	Credit
Revenues		$150,000
Accounts payable control (for May's purchases of direct materials)		36,300
Direct materials price variance	$4,500	
Direct materials efficiency variance	2,900	
Direct manufacturing labor price variance	1,700	
Direct manufacturing labor efficiency variance		2,000

Actual production in May was 4,700 units of Dandy, and actual sales in May were 3,000 units.

The amount shown for direct materials price variance applies to materials purchased during May. There was no beginning inventory of materials on May 1, 2017. Compute each of the following items for Lowell for the month of May. Show your computations.

1. Standard direct manufacturing labor-hours allowed for actual output produced
2. Actual direct manufacturing labor-hours worked

3. Actual direct manufacturing labor wage rate
4. Standard quantity of direct materials allowed (in pounds)
5. Actual quantity of direct materials used (in pounds)
6. Actual quantity of direct materials purchased (in pounds)
7. Actual direct materials price per pound

7-42 Direct materials and manufacturing labor variances, journal entries. Zanella's Smart Shawls, Inc., is a small business that Zanella developed while in college. She began hand-knitting shawls for her dorm friends to wear while studying. As demand grew, she hired some workers and began to manage the operation. Zanella's shawls require wool and labor. She experiments with the type of wool that she uses, and she has great variety in the shawls she produces. Zanella has bimodal turnover in her labor. She has some employees who have been with her for a very long time and others who are new and inexperienced.

Zanella uses standard costing for her shawls. She expects that a typical shawl should take 3 hours to produce, and the standard wage rate is $9.00 per hour. An average shawl uses 13 skeins of wool. Zanella shops around for good deals and expects to pay $3.40 per skein.

Zanella uses a just-in-time inventory system, as she has clients tell her what type and color of wool they would like her to use.

For the month of April, Zanella's workers produced 200 shawls using 580 hours and 3,500 skeins of wool. Zanella bought wool for $9,000 (and used the entire quantity) and incurred labor costs of $5,520.

Required

1. Calculate the price and efficiency variances for the wool and the price and efficiency variances for direct manufacturing labor.
2. Record the journal entries for the variances incurred.
3. Discuss logical explanations for the combination of variances that Zanella experienced.

7-43 Use of materials and manufacturing labor variances for benchmarking. You are a new junior accountant at In Focus Corporation, maker of lenses for eyeglasses. Your company sells generic-quality lenses for a moderate price. Your boss, the controller, has given you the latest month's report for the lens trade association. This report includes information related to operations for your firm and three of your competitors within the trade association. The report also includes information related to the industry benchmark for each line item in the report. You do not know which firm is which, except that you know you are Firm A.

**Unit Variable Costs Member Firms
for the Month Ended September 30, 2017**

	Firm A	Firm B	Firm C	Firm D	Industry Benchmark	
Materials input	2.15	2.00	2.20	2.60	2.15	oz. of glass
Materials price	$ 5.00	$ 5.25	$5.10	$ 4.50	$ 5.10	per oz.
Labor-hours used	0.75	1.00	0.65	0.70	0.70	hours
Wage rate	$14.50	$14.00	$14.25	$15.25	$12.50	per DLH
Variable overhead rate	$ 9.25	$14.00	$ 7.75	$11.75	$12.25	per DLH

Required

1. Calculate the total variable cost per unit for each firm in the trade association. Compute the percent of total for the material, labor, and variable overhead components.
2. Using the trade association's industry benchmark, calculate direct materials and direct manufacturing labor price and efficiency variances for the four firms. Calculate the percent over standard for each firm and each variance.
3. Write a brief memo to your boss outlining the advantages and disadvantages of belonging to this trade association for benchmarking purposes. Include a few ideas to improve productivity that you want your boss to take to the department heads' meeting.

7-44 Direct manufacturing labor variances: price, efficiency, mix, and yield. Trevor Joseph employs two workers in his guitar-making business. The first worker, George, has been making guitars for 20 years and is paid $30 per hour. The second worker, Earl, is less experienced and is paid $20 per hour. One guitar requires, on average, 10 hours of labor. The budgeted direct labor quantities and prices for one guitar are as follows:

	Quantity	Price per Hour of Labor	Cost for One Guitar
George	6 hours	$30 per hour	$180
Earl	4 hours	$20 per hour	80

That is, each guitar is budgeted to require 10 hours of direct labor, composed of 60% of George's labor and 40% of Earl's, although sometimes Earl works more hours on a particular guitar and George less, or vice versa, with no obvious change in the quality or function of the guitar.

During the month of August, Joseph manufactures 25 guitars. Actual direct labor costs are as follows:

George (145 hours)	$ 4,350
Earl (108 hours)	2,160
Total actual direct labor cost	$ 6,510

Required

1. What is the budgeted cost of direct labor for 25 guitars?
2. Calculate the total direct labor price and efficiency variances.
3. For the 25 guitars, what is the total actual amount of direct labor used? What is the actual direct labor input mix percentage? What is the budgeted amount of George's and Earl's labor that should have been used for the 25 guitars?
4. Calculate the total direct labor mix and yield variances. How do these numbers relate to the total direct labor efficiency variance? What do these variances tell you?

7-45 Direct-cost and selling price variances. MicroDisk is the market leader in the Secure Digital (SD) card industry and sells memory cards for use in portable devices such as mobile phones, tablets, and digital cameras. Its most popular card is the Mini SD, which it sells through outlets such as Target and Walmart for an average selling price of $8. MicroDisk has a standard monthly production level of 420,000 Mini SDs in its Taiwan facility. The standard input quantities and prices for direct-cost inputs are as follows:

	Home	Insert	Page Layout	Formulas	Data	Review	View

	A	B	C	D	E
1		Quantity per		Standard	
2	Cost Item	Mini SD card		Unit Costs	
3	Direct materials:				
4	Specialty polymer	17	mm	$0.05	/mm
5	Connector pins	10	units	0.10	/unit
6	Wi-Fi transreceiver	1	unit	0.50	/unit
7					
8	Direct manufacturing labor:				
9	Setup	1	min.	24.00	/hr.
10	Fabrication	2	min.	30.00	/hr.

Phoebe King, the CEO, is disappointed with the results for June 2017, especially in comparison to her expectations based on the standard cost data.

	Home	Insert	Page Layout	Formulas	Data	Review	View

	Performance Report, June 2017				
13					
14		Actual	Budget	Variance	
15	Output units	462,000	420,000	42,000	F
16	Revenues	$3,626,700	$3,360,000	$266,700	F
17	Direct materials	1,200,000	987,000	213,000	U
18	Direct manufacturing labor	628,400	588,000	40,400	U

King observes that despite the significant increase in the output of Mini SDs in June, the product's contribution to the company's profitability has been lower than expected. She gathers the following information to help analyze the situation:

	Home	Insert	Page Layout	Formulas	Data	Review	View
21			**Input Usage Report, June 2017**				
22		**Cost Item**		**Quantity**		**Actual Cost**	
23	Direct materials:						
24	Specialty polymer		8,300,000	mm		$415,000	
25	Connector pins		5,000,000	units		550,000	
26	Wi-Fi transreceiver		470,000	units		235,000	
27							
28	Direct manufacturing labor:						
29	Setup		455,000	min.		182,000	
30	Fabrication		864,000	min.		446,400	

Calculate the following variances. Comment on the variances and provide potential reasons why they might have arisen, with particular attention to the variances that may be related to one another:

Required

1. Selling-price variance
2. Direct materials price variance, for each category of materials
3. Direct materials efficiency variance, for each category of materials
4. Direct manufacturing labor price variance, for setup and fabrication
5. Direct manufacturing labor efficiency variance, for setup and fabrication

7-46 Variances in the service sector. Derek Wilson operates Clean Ride Enterprises, an auto detailing company with 20 employees. Jamal Jackson has recently been hired by Wilson as a controller. Clean Ride's previous accountant had done very little in the area of variance analysis, but Jackson believes that the company could benefit from a greater understanding of his business processes. Because of the labor-intensive nature of the business, he decides to focus on calculating labor variances.

Jackson examines past accounting records, and establishes some standards for the price and quantity of labor. While Clean Ride's employees earn a range of hourly wages, they fall into two general categories: skilled labor, with an average wage of $20 per hour, and unskilled labor, with an average wage of $10 per hour. One standard 5-hour detailing job typically requires a combination of 3 skilled hours and 2 unskilled hours.

Actual data from last month, when 600 detailing jobs were completed, are as follows:

Skilled (2,006 hours)	$ 39,117
Unskilled (944 hours)	9,292
Total actual direct labor cost	$ 48,409

Looking over last month's data, Jackson determines that Clean Ride's labor price variance was $1,151 favorable, but the labor efficiency variance was $1,560 unfavorable. When Jackson presents his findings to Wilson, the latter is furious. "Do you mean to tell me that my employees wasted $1,560 worth of time last month? I've had enough. They had better shape up, or else!" Jackson tries to calm him down, saying that in this case the efficiency variance doesn't necessarily mean that employees were wasting time. Jackson tells him that he is going to perform a more detailed analysis, and will get back to him with more information soon.

Required

1. What is the budgeted cost of direct labor for 600 detailing jobs?
2. How were the $1,151 favorable price variance and the $1,560 unfavorable labor efficiency variance calculated? What was the company's flexible-budget variance?
3. What do you think Jackson meant when said that "in this case the efficiency variance doesn't necessarily mean that employees were wasting time"?
4. For the 600 detailing jobs performed last month, what is the actual direct labor input mix percentage? What was the standard mix for labor?
5. Calculate the total direct labor mix and yield variances.
6. How could these variances be interpreted? Did the employees waste time? Upon further investigation, you discover that there were some unfilled vacancies last month in the unskilled labor positions that have recently been filled. How will this new information likely impact the variances going forward?

7-47 Price and efficiency variances, benchmarking and ethics. Sunto Scientific manufactures GPS devices for a chain of retail stores. Its most popular model, the Magellan XS, is assembled in a dedicated facility in Savannah, Georgia. Sunto is keenly aware of the competitive threat from smartphones that use Google Maps and has put in a standard cost system to manage production of the Magellan XS. It has also implemented a just-in-time system so the Savannah facility operates with no inventory of any kind.

Producing the Magellan XS involves combining a navigation system (imported from Sunto's plant in Dresden at a fixed price), an LCD screen made of polarized glass, and a casing developed from specialty plastic. The budgeted and actual amounts for Magellan XS for July 2017 were as follows:

	Budgeted Amounts	Actual Amounts
Magellan XS units produced	4,000	4,400
Navigation systems cost	$81,600	$89,000
Navigation systems	4,080	4,450
Polarized glass cost	$40,000	$40,300
Sheets of polarized glass used	800	816
Plastic casing cost	$12,000	$12,500
Ounces of specialty plastic used	4,000	4,250
Direct manufacturing labor costs	$36,000	$37,200
Direct manufacturing labor-hours	2,000	2,040

The controller of the Savannah plant, Jim Williams, is disappointed with the standard costing system in place. The standards were developed on the basis of a study done by an outside consultant at the start of the year. Williams points out that he has rarely seen a significant unfavorable variance under this system. He observes that even at the present level of output, workers seem to have a substantial amount of idle time. Moreover, he is concerned that the production supervisor, John Kelso, is aware of the issue but is unwilling to tighten the standards because the current lenient benchmarks make his performance look good.

Required

1. Compute the price and efficiency variances for the three categories of direct materials and for direct manufacturing labor in July 2017.
2. Describe the types of actions the employees at the Savannah plant may have taken to reduce the accuracy of the standards set by the outside consultant. Why would employees take those actions? Is this behavior ethical?
3. If Williams does nothing about the standard costs, will his behavior violate any of the standards of ethical conduct for practitioners described in the IMA Statement of Ethical Professional Practice (see Exhibit 1-7 on page 37)?
4. What actions should Williams take?
5. Williams can obtain benchmarking information about the estimated costs of Sunto's competitors such as Garmin and TomTom from the Competitive Intelligence Institute (CII). Discuss the pros and cons of using the CII information to compute the variances in requirement 1.

Flexible Budgets, Overhead Cost Variances, and Management Control

8

What do this week's weather forecast and an organization's performance have in common?

Much of the time, reality doesn't match what people expect. Rain that results in a little league game being canceled may suddenly give way to sunshine. Business owners expecting to "whistle their way to the bank" may change their tune after tallying their monthly bills and discovering that skyrocketing operational costs have significantly reduced their profits. Differences, or variances, are all around us.

Analyzing variances is a valuable activity for firms because the process highlights the areas where performance most lags expectations. By using this information to make corrective adjustments, companies can achieve significant savings. Furthermore, the process of setting up standards requires firms to have a thorough understanding of their fixed and variable overhead costs, which brings its own benefits, as the following article shows.

TESLA MOTORS GIGAFACTORY[1]

Tesla Motors is a Silicon Valley-based electric car manufacturer. To meet its planned production of 500,000 cars per year by 2018, Tesla is building the Gigafactory, a 5.8 million square foot state-of-the-art facility in Nevada that will produce the lithium ion batteries the company needs to power its electric vehicles. In building the $5 billion Gigafactory, Tesla Motors required an in-depth understanding of its fixed and variable overhead costs for planning and control purposes.

The Gigafactory has significant fixed overhead costs. Roughly the size of 100 football fields, the Gigafactory required Tesla to make up-front fixed-cost investments designed to benefit the company for many years. These include depreciation and taxes, construction costs, insurance, and environmentally friendly investments such as covering the Gigafactory in solar panels to ensure no fossil fuels are used in production. Variable costs at the Gigafactory will ultimately include production employee salaries, utilities, and office supplies, among others.

Understanding its fixed and variable overhead costs will allow Tesla's management accountants to develop the company's budgeted fixed and variable overhead cost rates for each battery produced. Once the Gigafactory is complete, battery production for Tesla cars—all the way down to the cell level—will happen in one facility. As a result, the cost to produce batteries should decrease by at least 30% compared to 2016 costs.

In Chapter 7, you learned how managers use flexible budgets and variance analysis to help plan and control the direct-cost categories of direct materials and direct manufacturing labor. In this chapter, you will learn how managers plan for and control the indirect-cost categories of variable manufacturing overhead and fixed manufacturing overhead.

MShieldsPhotos/Alamy Stock Photo

---

[1] *Sources:* Dana Hull, "Inside the Gigafactory That Will Decide Tesla's Fate," *Bloomberg.com*, May 6, 2016; Max Chafkin, "Elon Musk Powers Up: Inside Tesla's $5 billion Gigafactory," *Fast Company*, November 17, 2015; Colin Lecher, "Inside Nevada's $1.3 Billion Gamble on Tesla," *The Verge*, February 8, 2016.

Planning of Variable and Fixed Overhead Costs

We'll use the Webb Company example again to illustrate the planning and control of variable and fixed overhead costs. Recall that Webb manufactures jackets it sells to distributors, who in turn sell them to independent clothing stores and retail chains. Because we assume Webb's only costs are manufacturing costs, for simplicity we use the term "overhead costs" instead of "manufacturing overhead costs" in this chapter. Webb's variable overhead costs include energy, machine maintenance, engineering support, and indirect materials. Webb's fixed overhead costs include plant leasing costs, depreciation on plant equipment, and the salaries of the plant managers.

LEARNING OBJECTIVE 1

Explain the similarities and differences in planning variable overhead costs and fixed overhead costs

...for both, plan only essential activities and be efficient; fixed overhead costs are usually determined well before the budget period begins

Planning Variable Overhead Costs

To effectively plan variable overhead costs for a product or service, managers must focus on the activities that create a superior product or service for their customers and eliminate activities that do not add value. For example, customers expect Webb's jackets to last, so Webb's managers consider sewing to be an essential activity. Therefore, maintenance activities for sewing machines, which are included in Webb's variable overhead costs, are also essential activities for which management must plan. Such maintenance should be done in a cost-effective way, such as by scheduling periodic equipment maintenance rather than waiting for sewing machines to break down. For many companies today, it is critical to plan for ways to reduce the consumption of energy, a rapidly growing component of variable overhead costs. Webb installs smart meters in order to monitor energy use in real time and steer production operations away from peak consumption periods.

Planning Fixed Overhead Costs

Planning fixed overhead costs is similar to planning variable overhead costs—undertake only essential activities and then plan to be efficient in that undertaking. But there is an additional strategic issue when it comes to planning fixed overhead costs: choosing the appropriate level of capacity or investment that will benefit the company in the long run. Consider Webb's leasing of sewing machines, each of which has a fixed cost per year. Leasing too many machines will result in overcapacity and unnecessary fixed leasing costs. Leasing too few machines will result in an inability to meet demand, lost sales of jackets, and unhappy customers. Consider AT&T, which did not initially foresee the iPhone's appeal or the proliferation of "apps" and consequently did not upgrade its network sufficiently to handle the resulting data traffic. AT&T subsequently had to impose limits on how customers could use the iPhone (such as by curtailing tethering and the streaming of Webcasts). This explains why, at one point following the iPhone's release, AT&T had the lowest customer satisfaction ratings among all major carriers.

The planning of fixed overhead costs differs from the planning of variable overhead costs in another regard as well: timing. At the start of a budget period, management will have made most of the decisions determining the level of fixed overhead costs to be incurred. But it's the day-to-day, ongoing operating decisions that mainly determine the level of variable overhead costs incurred in that period. For example, the variable overhead costs of hospitals, which include the costs of disposable supplies, doses of medication, suture packets, and medical waste disposal, are a function of the number and nature of procedures carried out, as well as the practice patterns of the physicians. However, most of the costs of providing hospital service are fixed overhead costs—those related to buildings, equipment, and salaried labor. These costs are unrelated to a hospital's volume of activity.[2]

DECISION POINT

How do managers plan variable overhead costs and fixed overhead costs?

---

[2] Free-standing surgery centers have thrived because they have lower fixed overhead costs compared to traditional hospitals. For an enlightening summary of costing issues in health care, see A. Macario, "What Does One Minute of Operating Room Time Cost?" *Journal of Clinical Anesthesia*, June 2010.

Standard Costing at Webb Company

Webb uses standard costing. Chapter 7 explained how the standards for Webb's direct manufacturing costs were developed. This chapter explains how the standards for Webb's manufacturing overhead costs are developed. **Standard costing** is a costing system that (1) traces direct costs to output produced by multiplying the standard prices or rates by the standard quantities of inputs allowed for actual outputs produced, and (2) allocates overhead costs on the basis of the standard overhead cost rates times the standard quantities of the allocation bases allowed for the actual outputs produced.

The standard cost of Webb's jackets can be computed at the start of the budget period. This feature of standard costing simplifies recordkeeping because no record is needed of the actual overhead costs or of the actual quantities of the cost-allocation bases used for making the jackets. What managers *do* need are the standard overhead cost rates for Webb's variable and fixed overhead. Management accountants calculate these cost rates based on the planned amounts of variable and fixed overhead and the standard quantities of the allocation bases. We describe these computations next. Note that once managers set these standards, the costs of using standard costing are low relative to the costs of using actual costing or normal costing.

Developing Budgeted Variable Overhead Rates

Budgeted variable overhead cost-allocation rates can be developed in four steps. Throughout the chapter, we use the broader term *budgeted rate* rather than *standard rate* to be consistent with the term used to describe normal costing in earlier chapters. When standard costing is used, as is the case with Webb, the budgeted rates are standard rates.

Step 1: Choose the Period to Be Used for the Budget. Webb uses a 12-month budget period. Chapter 4 (pages 131–132) provided two reasons for using annual overhead rates rather than, say, monthly rates. The first relates to the numerator, such as reducing the influence of seasonality on the firm's cost structure. The second relates to the denominator, such as reducing the effect of varying output and number of days in a month. In addition, setting overhead rates once a year rather than 12 times a year saves managers time.

Step 2: Select the Cost-Allocation Bases to Use in Allocating the Variable Overhead Costs to the Output Produced. Webb's operating managers select machine-hours as the cost-allocation base because they believe that the number of machine-hours is the sole cost driver of variable overhead. Based on an engineering study, Webb estimates it will take 0.40 of a machine-hour per actual output unit. For its budgeted output of 144,000 jackets in 2017, Webb budgets 57,600 (0.40 × 144,000) machine-hours.

Step 3: Identify the Variable Overhead Costs Associated with Each Cost-Allocation Base. Webb groups all of its variable overhead costs, including the costs of energy, machine maintenance, engineering support, indirect materials, and indirect manufacturing labor, in a single cost pool. Webb's total budgeted variable overhead costs for 2017 are $1,728,000.

Step 4: Compute the Rate per Unit of Each Cost-Allocation Base Used to Allocate the Variable Overhead Costs to the Output Produced. Dividing the amount in Step 3 ($1,728,000) by the amount in Step 2 (57,600 machine-hours), Webb estimates a rate of $30 per standard machine-hour for allocating its variable overhead costs.

When standard costing is used, the variable overhead rate per unit of the cost-allocation base ($30 per machine-hour for Webb) is generally expressed as a standard rate per output unit. Webb calculates the budgeted variable overhead cost rate per output unit as follows:

$$\begin{array}{c}\text{Budgeted variable} \\ \text{overhead cost rate} \\ \text{per output unit}\end{array} = \begin{array}{c}\text{Budgeted input} \\ \text{allowed per} \\ \text{output unit}\end{array} \times \begin{array}{c}\text{Budgeted variable} \\ \text{overhead cost rate} \\ \text{per input unit}\end{array}$$

$$= \text{0.40 hour per jacket} \times \text{\$30 per hour}$$

$$= \text{\$12 per jacket}$$

The $12-per-jacket rate is the budgeted variable overhead cost rate in Webb's static budget for 2017 as well as in the monthly performance reports the firm prepares during 2017.

The $12-per-jacket rate represents the amount by which managers expect Webb's variable overhead costs to change when the amount of output changes. As the number of jackets manufactured increases, the variable overhead costs allocated to output (for inventory costing) increase at the rate of $12 per jacket. The $12 per jacket constitutes the firm's total variable overhead costs per unit of output, including the costs of energy, repairs, indirect labor, and so on. Managers control variable overhead costs by setting a budget for each of these line items and then investigating the possible causes of any significant variances.

Developing Budgeted Fixed Overhead Rates

Fixed overhead costs are, by definition, a lump sum of costs that remains unchanged for a given period, despite wide changes in a firm's level of activity or output. Fixed costs are included in flexible budgets, but they remain the same within the relevant range of activity regardless of the output level chosen to "flex" the variable costs and revenues. Recall from Exhibit 7-2 and the steps in developing a flexible budget that Webb's monthly fixed overhead costs of $276,000 are the same in the static budget as they are in the flexible budget. Do not assume, however, that these costs can never be changed. Managers can reduce them by selling equipment or laying off employees, for example. But the costs are fixed in the sense that, unlike variable costs such as direct material costs, fixed costs do not *automatically* increase or decrease with the level of activity within the relevant range.

The process of developing the budgeted fixed overhead rate is the same as the one for calculating the budgeted variable overhead rate. The steps are as follows:

Step 1: Choose the Period to Use for the Budget. As with variable overhead costs, the budget period for fixed overhead costs is typically one year, to help smooth out seasonal effects.

Step 2: Select the Cost-Allocation Bases to Use in Allocating the Fixed Overhead Costs to the Output Produced. Webb uses machine-hours as the only cost-allocation base for the firm's fixed overhead costs. Why? Because Webb's managers believe that, in the long run, the company's fixed overhead costs will increase or decrease to the levels needed to support the amount of machine-hours. Therefore, in the long run, the amount of machine-hours used is the only cost driver of fixed overhead costs. The number of machine-hours is the denominator in the budgeted fixed overhead rate computation and is called the **denominator level**. For simplicity, we assume Webb expects to operate at capacity in fiscal year 2017, with a budgeted usage of 57,600 machine-hours for a budgeted output of 144,000 jackets.[3]

Step 3: Identify the Fixed Overhead Costs Associated with Each Cost-Allocation Base. Because Webb identifies a single cost-allocation base—machine-hours—to allocate fixed overhead costs, it groups all such costs into a single cost pool. Costs in this pool include depreciation on plant and equipment, plant and equipment leasing costs, and the plant manager's salary. Webb's fixed overhead budget for 2017 is $3,312,000.

Step 4: Compute the Rate per Unit of Each Cost-Allocation Base Used to Allocate Fixed Overhead Costs to the Output Produced. By dividing the $3,312,000 from Step 3 by the 57,600 machine-hours from Step 2, Webb estimates a fixed overhead cost rate of $57.50 per machine-hour:

$$\begin{array}{c}\text{Budgeted fixed}\\\text{overhead cost per}\\\text{unit of cost-allocation}\\\text{base}\end{array} = \begin{array}{c}\text{Budgeted total costs}\\\text{in fixed overhead cost pool}\\\hline\text{Budgeted total quantity of}\\\text{cost-allocation base}\end{array} = \frac{\$3{,}312{,}000}{57{,}600} = \$57.50 \text{ per machine-hour}$$

---

[3] Because Webb plans its capacity over multiple periods, anticipated demand in 2017 could be such that budgeted output for 2017 is less than Webb's capacity. Companies vary in the denominator levels they choose. Some choose budgeted output and others choose capacity. In either case, the approach and analysis presented in this chapter is unchanged. Chapter 9 discusses in more detail the implications of choosing a denominator level.

Under standard costing, the $57.50 fixed overhead cost per machine-hour is usually expressed as a standard cost per output unit. Recall that Webb's engineering study estimates that it will take 0.40 machine-hour per output unit. Webb can now calculate the budgeted fixed overhead cost per output unit as follows:

$$\begin{array}{c}\text{Budgeted fixed}\\\text{overhead cost per}\\\text{output unit}\end{array} = \begin{array}{c}\text{Budgeted quantity}\\\text{of cost-allocation}\\\text{base allowed per}\\\text{output unit}\end{array} \times \begin{array}{c}\text{Budgeted fixed}\\\text{overhead cost}\\\text{per unit of}\\\text{cost-allocation base}\end{array}$$

$$= 0.40 \text{ of a machine-hour per jacket} \times \$57.50 \text{ per machine-hour}$$

$$= \$23.00 \text{ per jacket}$$

When preparing monthly budgets for 2017, Webb divides the $3,312,000 annual total fixed costs into 12 equal monthly amounts of $276,000.

Variable Overhead Cost Variances

We now illustrate how the budgeted variable overhead rate is used to compute Webb's variable overhead cost variances. The following data are for April 2017, when Webb produced and sold 10,000 jackets:

	Actual Result	**Flexible-Budget Amount**
1. Output units (jackets)	10,000	10,000
2. Machine-hours per output unit	0.45	0.40
3. Machine-hours (1 × 2)	4,500	4,000
4. Variable overhead costs	$130,500	$120,000
5. Variable overhead costs per machine-hour (4 ÷ 3)	$ 29.00	$ 30.00
6. Variable overhead costs per output unit (4 ÷ 1)	$ 13.05	$ 12.00

As we saw in Chapter 7, the flexible budget enables Webb to highlight the differences between actual costs and actual quantities versus budgeted costs and budgeted quantities for the actual output level of 10,000 jackets.

Flexible-Budget Analysis

The **variable overhead flexible-budget variance** measures the difference between actual variable overhead costs incurred and flexible-budget variable overhead amounts.

$$\begin{array}{c}\text{Variable overhead}\\\text{flexible-budget variance}\end{array} = \begin{array}{c}\text{Actual costs}\\\text{incurred}\end{array} - \begin{array}{c}\text{Flexible-budget}\\\text{amount}\end{array}$$

$$= \$130,500 - \$120,000$$

$$= \$10,500 \text{ U}$$

This $10,500 unfavorable flexible-budget variance means Webb's actual variable overhead exceeded the flexible-budget amount by $10,500 for the 10,000 jackets actually produced and sold. Webb's managers would want to know why. Did Webb use more machine-hours than planned to produce the 10,000 jackets? If so, was it because workers were less skilled than expected in using machines? Or did Webb spend more on variable overhead costs, such as maintenance?

Just as we illustrated in Chapter 7 with the flexible-budget variance for direct-cost items, Webb's managers can get further insight into the reason for the $10,500 unfavorable variance by subdividing it into the efficiency variance and spending variance.

Variable Overhead Efficiency Variance

The **variable overhead efficiency variance** is the difference between the actual quantity of the cost-allocation base used and budgeted quantity of the cost-allocation base that should have been used to produce the actual output, multiplied by the budgeted variable overhead cost per unit of the cost-allocation base.

$$\begin{pmatrix} \text{Variable} \\ \text{overhead} \\ \text{efficiency} \\ \text{variance} \end{pmatrix} = \begin{pmatrix} \text{Actual quantity of} & \text{Budgeted quantity of} \\ \text{variable overhead} & \text{variable overhead} \\ \text{cost-allocation base} - \text{cost-allocation base} \\ \text{used for actual} & \text{allowed for} \\ \text{output} & \text{actual output} \end{pmatrix} \times \begin{pmatrix} \text{Budgeted variable} \\ \text{overhead cost per unit} \\ \text{of cost-allocation base} \end{pmatrix}$$

$$= (4{,}500 \text{ hours} - 0.40 \text{ hr./unit} \times 10{,}000 \text{ units}) \times \$30 \text{ per hour}$$

$$= (4{,}500 \text{ hours} - 4{,}000 \text{ hours}) \times \$30 \text{ per hour}$$

$$= \$15{,}000 \text{ U}$$

Columns 2 and 3 of Exhibit 8-1 depict the variable overhead efficiency variance. The variance arises solely because of the difference between the actual quantity (4,500 hours) and budgeted quantity (4,000 hours) of the cost-allocation base. The variable overhead efficiency variance is computed the same way the efficiency variance for direct-cost items is (Chapter 7, pages 279–280). However, the interpretation of the variance is different. The efficiency variances for direct-cost items are based on the differences between the actual inputs used and the budgeted inputs allowed for the actual output produced. For example, a forensic laboratory (the kind popularized by television shows such as *CSI* and *Dexter*) would calculate a direct labor efficiency variance based on whether the lab used more or fewer hours than the standard hours allowed for the actual number of DNA tests. In contrast, the efficiency variance for variable overhead is based on the efficiency with which *the cost-allocation base is used*. Webb's unfavorable variable overhead efficiency variance of $15,000 means that the actual machine-hours (the cost-allocation base) of 4,500 hours was higher than the budgeted machine-hours of 4,000 hours allowed to manufacture 10,000 jackets and this, to the extent machine-hours are a cost driver for variable overhead, pushed up the potential spending on variable overhead.

EXHIBIT 8-1   Columnar Presentation of Variable Overhead Variance Analysis: Webb Company for April 2017[a]

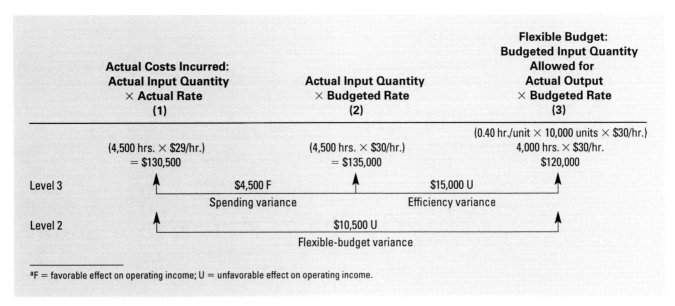

[a]F = favorable effect on operating income; U = unfavorable effect on operating income.

The following table shows possible causes for Webb's actual machine-hours exceeding the budgeted machine-hours and Webb's potential responses to each of these causes.

Possible Causes for Exceeding Budget	Potential Management Responses
1. Workers were less efficient than expected in using machines.	1. Encourage the human resources department to implement better employee-hiring practices and training procedures.
2. The production scheduler inefficiently scheduled jobs, resulting in more machine-hours used than budgeted.	2. Improve plant operations by installing production-scheduling software.
3. Machines were not maintained in good operating condition.	3. Ensure preventive maintenance is done on all machines.
4. Webb's sales staff promised a distributor a rush delivery, which resulted in more machine-hours used than budgeted.	4. Coordinate production schedules with sales staff and distributors and share information with them.
5. Budgeted machine time standards were set too tight.	5. Commit more resources to develop appropriate standards.

Note how, depending on the cause(s) of the $15,000 U variance, corrective actions may need to be taken not just in manufacturing but also in other business functions of the value chain, such as sales and distribution.

Webb's managers discovered that one reason for the unfavorable variance was that workers were underskilled. As a result, Webb is improving its hiring and training practices. Insufficient maintenance performed in the two months prior to April 2017 was another reason. A former plant manager had delayed the maintenance in an attempt to meet Webb's monthly cost targets. As we discussed in Chapter 6, managers should not focus on meeting short-run cost targets if they are likely to result in harmful long-run consequences. For example, if Webb's employees were to hurt themselves while operating poorly maintained machinery, the consequences would not only be harmful, they could be deadly. Webb is now strengthening its internal maintenance procedures so that failure to do monthly maintenance as needed will raise a "red flag" that must be immediately explained to management. Webb is also taking a hard look at its evaluation practices to determine if they inadvertently pressure managers to fixate on short-term targets to the long-run detriment of the firm.

Variable Overhead Spending Variance

The **variable overhead spending variance** is the difference between the actual variable overhead cost per unit of the cost-allocation base and the budgeted variable overhead cost per unit of the cost-allocation base, multiplied by the actual quantity of variable overhead cost-allocation base used.

$$\begin{pmatrix} \text{Variable} \\ \text{overhead} \\ \text{spending} \\ \text{variance} \end{pmatrix} = \begin{pmatrix} \text{Actual variable} & & \text{Budgeted variable} \\ \text{overhead cost per unit} & - & \text{overhead cost per unit} \\ \text{of cost-allocation base} & & \text{of cost-allocation base} \end{pmatrix} \times \begin{pmatrix} \text{Actual quantity of} \\ \text{variable overhead} \\ \text{cost-allocation base} \\ \text{used} \end{pmatrix}$$

$$= (\$29 \text{ per machine-hour} - \$30 \text{ per machine-hour}) \times 4,500 \text{ machine-hours}$$

$$= (-\$1 \text{ per machine-hour}) \times 4,500 \text{ machine-hours}$$

$$= \$4,500 \text{ F}$$

Webb operated in April 2017 with a lower-than-budgeted variable overhead cost per machine-hour, so there is a favorable variable overhead spending variance. Columns 1 and 2 in Exhibit 8-1 depict this variance.

To understand why the favorable variable overhead spending variance occurred, Webb's managers need to recognize why *actual* variable overhead cost per unit of the cost-allocation base ($29 per machine-hour) is *lower* than the *budgeted* variable overhead cost per unit of the cost-allocation base ($30 per machine-hour).

Overall, Webb used 4,500 machine-hours, which is 12.5% greater than the flexible-budget amount of 4,000 machine-hours. However, actual variable overhead costs of $130,500 are only 8.75% greater than the flexible-budget amount of $120,000. Thus, relative to the flexible budget, the percentage increase in actual variable overhead costs is *less* than the percentage increase in machine-hours. Consequently, the actual variable overhead cost per machine-hour is lower than the budgeted amount, resulting in a favorable variable overhead spending variance.

Why might the percentage increase in actual variable overhead costs come in lower than the percentage increase in machine-hours? Here are two possible reasons:

1. The actual prices of the individual inputs included in variable overhead costs, such as the price of energy, indirect materials, or indirect labor, are lower than budgeted prices of these inputs. For example, the actual price of electricity may only be $0.09 per kilowatt-hour, compared with a price of $0.10 per kilowatt-hour in the flexible budget.

2. Relative to the flexible budget, the percentage increase in the actual use of individual items in the variable overhead-cost pool is less than the percentage increase in machine-hours. Compared with the flexible-budget amount of 30,000 kilowatt-hours, suppose the actual energy use was 32,400 kilowatt-hours, or 8% higher. The fact that this is a smaller percentage increase than the 12.5% increase in machine-hours (4,500 actual machine-hours versus a flexible budget of 4,000 machine-hours) will lead to a favorable variable overhead spending variance, which can be partially or completely traced to the efficient use of energy and other variable overhead items.

As part of the last stage of the five-step decision-making process, Webb's managers will need to examine the signals provided by the variable overhead variances to *evaluate the firm's performance and learn.* By understanding the reasons for these variances, Webb can take appropriate actions and make more precise predictions in order to achieve improved results in future periods.

For example, Webb's managers must examine why the actual prices of variable overhead cost items are different from the budgeted prices. The differences could be the result of skillful negotiation on the part of the purchasing manager, oversupply in the market, or lower quality of inputs such as indirect materials. Webb's response depends on what is believed to be the cause of the variance. If the concerns are about quality, for instance, Webb may want to put in place new quality management systems.

Similarly, Webb's managers should understand the possible causes for the efficiency with which variable overhead resources are used. These causes include the skill levels of workers, maintenance of machines, and the efficiency of the manufacturing process. Webb's managers discovered that Webb used fewer indirect labor resources per machine-hour because of manufacturing process improvements. As a result, the firm began organizing cross-functional teams to see if more process improvements could be achieved.

We emphasize that a manager should not always view a favorable variable overhead spending variance as desirable. For example, the variable overhead spending variance would be favorable if Webb's managers purchased lower-priced, poor-quality indirect materials, hired less-talented supervisors, or performed less machine maintenance. These decisions, however, are likely to hurt product quality and harm the long-run prospects of the business.

To clarify the concepts of variable overhead efficiency variance and variable overhead spending variance, consider the following example. Suppose that (a) energy is the only item of variable overhead cost and machine-hours is the cost-allocation base; (b) actual machine-hours used equals the number of machine-hours under the flexible budget; and (c) the actual price of energy equals the budgeted price. From (a) and (b), it follows that there is no efficiency variance—the company has been efficient with respect to the number of machine-hours (the cost-allocation base) used to produce the actual output. However, and despite (c), there could still be a spending variance. Why? Because even though the company used the correct number of machine-hours, the energy consumed *per machine-hour* could be higher than budgeted (for example, because the machines have not been maintained correctly). The cost of this higher energy usage would be reflected in an unfavorable spending variance.

TRY IT! 8-1

Duvet Company manufactures pillows. The 2017 operating budget was based on production of 25,000 pillows, with 0.75 machine-hours allowed per pillow. Budgeted variable overhead per hour was $25.

Actual production for 2017 was 27,000 pillows using 19,050 machine-hours. Actual variable costs were $23 per machine-hour.

Calculate the following:

a. the budgeted variable overhead for 2017;

b. the variable overhead spending variance; and

c. the variable overhead efficiency variance.

Journal Entries for Variable Overhead Costs and Variances

We now prepare journal entries for the Variable Overhead Control account and the contra account Variable Overhead Allocated.

Entries for variable overhead for April 2017 (data from Exhibit 8-1) are as follows:

1. Variable Overhead Control	130,500	
Accounts Payable and various other accounts		130,500
To record actual variable overhead costs incurred.		
2. Work-in-Process Control	120,000	
Variable Overhead Allocated		120,000
To record variable overhead cost allocated		
(0.40 machine-hour/unit × 10,000 units × $30/machine-hour). (The costs accumulated in Work-in-Process Control are transferred to Finished-Goods Control when production is completed and to Cost of Goods Sold when the products are sold.)		
3. Variable Overhead Allocated	120,000	
Variable Overhead Efficiency Variance	15,000	
Variable Overhead Control		130,500
Variable Overhead Spending Variance		4,500
This records the variances for the accounting period.		

These variances are the underallocated or overallocated variable overhead costs. At the end of the fiscal year, the variance accounts are written off to cost of goods sold if immaterial in amount. If the variances are material in amount, they are prorated among the Work-in-Process Control, Finished-Goods Control, and Cost of Goods Sold accounts on the basis of the variable overhead allocated to these accounts, as described in Chapter 4, pages 149–151. As we discussed in Chapter 7, only unavoidable costs are prorated. Any part of the variances attributable to avoidable inefficiency is written off in the period. Assume that the balances in the variable overhead variance accounts as of April 2017 are also the balances at the end of the 2017 fiscal year and are immaterial in amount. The following journal entry records the write-off of the variance accounts to the Cost of Goods Sold:

DECISION POINT

What variances can be calculated for variable overhead costs?

Cost of Goods Sold	10,500	
Variable Overhead Spending Variance	4,500	
Variable Overhead Efficiency Variance		15,000

Next we demonstrate how to calculate fixed overhead cost variances.

Fixed Overhead Cost Variances

The flexible-budget amount for a fixed-cost item is also the amount included in the static budget prepared at the start of the period. No adjustment is required for differences between actual output and budgeted output for fixed costs because fixed costs are unaffected by changes in the output level within the relevant range. At the start of 2017, Webb budgeted its fixed overhead costs to be $276,000 per month. The actual amount for April 2017 turned out to be $285,000. The **fixed overhead flexible-budget variance** is the difference between actual fixed overhead costs and fixed overhead costs in the flexible budget:

LEARNING OBJECTIVE 4

Compute the fixed overhead flexible-budget variance,

...difference between actual fixed overhead costs and flexible-budget fixed overhead amounts

the fixed overhead spending variance,

...same as the preceding explanation

and the fixed overhead production-volume variance

...difference between budgeted fixed overhead and fixed overhead allocated on the basis of actual output produced

$$\text{Fixed overhead} \atop \text{flexible-budget variance} = \text{Actual costs} \atop \text{incurred} - \text{Flexible-budget} \atop \text{amount}$$

$$= \$285,000 - \$276,000$$

$$= \$9,000 \text{ U}$$

The variance is unfavorable because the $285,000 actual fixed overhead costs exceed the $276,000 budgeted for April 2017, which decreases that month's operating income by $9,000.

The variable overhead flexible-budget variance described earlier in this chapter was subdivided into a spending variance and an efficiency variance. There is no efficiency variance for fixed overhead costs. That's because a given lump sum of fixed overhead costs will be unaffected by how efficiently machine-hours are used to produce output in a given budget period. As Exhibit 8-2 shows, because there is no efficiency variance, the **fixed overhead spending variance** is the same amount as the fixed overhead flexible-budget variance:

$$\text{Fixed overhead} \atop \text{spending variance} = \text{Actual costs} \atop \text{incurred} - \text{Flexible-budget} \atop \text{amount}$$

$$= \$285,000 - \$276,000$$

$$= \$9,000 \text{ U}$$

Reasons for the unfavorable spending variance could be higher plant-leasing costs, higher depreciation on plant and equipment, or higher administrative costs, such as a higher-than-budgeted salary paid to the plant manager. Webb investigated this variance and found that there was a $9,000 per month unexpected increase in its equipment-leasing costs. However,

---

EXHIBIT 8-2   Columnar Presentation of Fixed Overhead Variance Analysis: Webb Company for April 2017[a]

Actual Costs Incurred (1)	Flexible Budget: Same Budgeted Lump Sum (as in Static Budget) Regardless of Output Level (2)	Allocated: Budgeted Input Quantity Allowed for Actual Output × Budgeted Rate (3)
		(0.40 hr./unit × 10,000 units × $57.50/hr.)
		(4,000 hrs. × $57.50/hr.)
$285,000	$276,000	$230,000

Level 3   ↑——— $9,000 U ———↑ ——— $46,000 U ———↑
         Spending variance   Production-volume variance

Level 2 ↑——— $9,000 U ———↑
         Flexible-budget variance

[a]F = favorable effect on operating income; U = unfavorable effect on operating income.

managers concluded that the new lease rates were competitive with lease rates available else-where. If this were not the case, Webb would look to lease equipment from other suppliers.

Production-Volume Variance

The **production-volume variance** arises only for fixed costs. It is the difference between the budgeted fixed overhead and the fixed overhead allocated on the basis of actual output produced. Recall that at the start of the year, Webb calculated a budgeted fixed overhead rate of $57.50 per machine-hour based on monthly budgeted fixed overhead costs of $276,000. Under standard costing, Webb's fixed overhead costs are allocated to the actual output produced during each period at the rate of $57.50 per standard machine-hour, which is equivalent to a rate of $23 per jacket (0.40 machine-hour per jacket × $57.50 per machine-hour). If Webb produces 1,000 jackets, $23,000 ($23 per jacket × 1,000 jackets) out of April's budgeted fixed overhead costs of $276,000 will be allocated to the jackets. If Webb produces 10,000 jackets, $230,000 ($23 per jacket × 10,000 jackets) will be allocated. Only if Webb produces 12,000 jackets (that is, operates, as budgeted, at capacity) will all $276,000 ($23 per jacket × 12,000 jackets) of the budgeted fixed overhead costs be allocated to the jacket output. The key point here is that even though Webb budgeted its fixed overhead costs to be $276,000, it does not necessarily allocate all these costs to output. The reason is that Webb budgets $276,000 of fixed costs to support its planned production of 12,000 jackets. If Webb produces fewer than 12,000 jackets, it only allocates the budgeted cost of capacity actually needed and used to produce the jackets.

The production-volume variance, also referred to as the **denominator-level variance**, is the difference between the budgeted and allocated fixed overhead amounts. Note that the allocated overhead can be expressed in terms of allocation-base units (machine-hours for Webb) or in terms of the budgeted fixed cost per unit:

$$\begin{aligned}\frac{\text{Production}}{\text{volume variance}} &= \frac{\text{Budgeted}}{\text{fixed overhead}} - \frac{\text{Fixed overhead allocated}}{\text{for actual output units produced}}\\[4pt]
&= \$276{,}000 - (0.40 \text{ hour per jacket} \times \$57.50 \text{ per hour} \times 10{,}000 \text{ jackets})\\[4pt]
&= \$276{,}000 - (\$23 \text{ per jacket} \times 10{,}000 \text{ jackets})\\[4pt]
&= \$276{,}000 - \$230{,}000\\[4pt]
&= \$46{,}000 \text{ U}\end{aligned}$$

As shown in Exhibit 8-2, the budgeted fixed overhead ($276,000) will be the lump sum shown in the static budget and also in any flexible budget within the relevant range. The fixed overhead allocated ($230,000) is calculated by multiplying the number of output units produced during the budget period (10,000 units) by the budgeted cost per output unit ($23). The $46,000 U production-volume variance can also be thought of as $23 per jacket × 2,000 jackets that were *not* produced. We will explore possible causes for the unfavorable production-volume variance and its management implications in the following section.

Exhibit 8-3 shows Webb's production-volume variance. For planning and control purposes, Webb's fixed (manufacturing) overhead costs do not change in the 0- to 12,000-unit relevant range. Contrast this behavior of fixed costs with how these costs are depicted for the purpose of inventory costing in Exhibit 8-3. Under Generally Accepted Accounting Principles (GAAP), fixed (manufacturing) overhead costs are allocated as an inventoriable cost to the output units produced. Every output unit that Webb manufactures will increase the fixed overhead allocated to products by $23. That is, for purposes of allocating fixed overhead costs to jackets, these costs are viewed *as if* they had a variable-cost behavior pattern. As the graph in Exhibit 8-3 shows, the difference between the $276,000 in fixed overhead costs budgeted and the $230,000 of costs allocated is the $46,000 unfavorable production-volume variance.

Managers should be careful to distinguish the true behavior of fixed costs from the manner in which fixed costs are assigned to products. In particular, although fixed costs are unitized (i.e., converted into per-unit amounts) and allocated for inventory-costing purposes, managers should be wary of using the same per-unit fixed overhead costs for planning and control purposes. When forecasting fixed costs, managers should concentrate on total

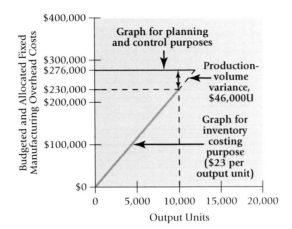

EXHIBIT 8-3

Behavior of Fixed
Manufacturing Overhead
Costs: Budgeted for
Planning and Control
Purposes and Allocated
for Inventory Costing
Purposes for Webb
Company for April 2017

lump-sum costs instead of unitized costs. Similarly, when managers are looking to assign costs for control purposes or identify the best way to use capacity resources fixed in the short run, we will see in Chapters 9 and 11 that the use of unitized fixed costs often leads to incorrect decisions.

Interpreting the Production-Volume Variance

Lump-sum fixed costs represent the costs of acquiring capacity. These costs do not decrease automatically if the capacity needed turns out to be less than the capacity acquired. Sometimes costs are fixed for a specific time period for contractual reasons, such as an annual lease contract for a plant. At other times, costs are fixed because capacity has to be acquired or disposed of in fixed increments, or lumps. For example, suppose that acquiring a sewing machine gives Webb the ability to produce 1,000 jackets. If it is not possible to buy or lease a fraction of a machine, Webb can add capacity only in increments of 1,000 jackets. That is, Webb may choose capacity levels of 10,000, 11,000, or 12,000 jackets, but nothing in between.

Webb's management would want to analyze the $46,000 unfavorable production-volume variance. Why did this overcapacity occur? Why were 10,000 jackets produced instead of 12,000? Is demand weak? Should Webb reevaluate its product and marketing strategies? Is there a quality problem? Or did Webb make a strategic mistake by acquiring too much capacity? The causes of the $46,000 unfavorable production-volume variance will determine the actions Webb's managers take in response to the variance.

In contrast, a favorable production-volume variance indicates an overallocation of fixed overhead costs. That is, the overhead costs allocated to the actual output produced exceed the budgeted fixed overhead costs of $276,000. The favorable production-volume variance is composed of the fixed costs recorded in excess of $276,000.

Be careful when drawing conclusions about a company's capacity planning on the basis of the production-volume variance. To correctly interpret Webb's $46,000 unfavorable production-volume variance, its managers should consider why it sold only 10,000 jackets in April. Suppose a new competitor gained market share by pricing its jackets lower than Webb's. To sell the budgeted 12,000 jackets, Webb might have had to reduce its own selling price on all 12,000 jackets. Suppose it decided that selling 10,000 jackets at a higher price yielded higher operating income than selling 12,000 jackets at a lower price. The production-volume variance does not take into account such information. The failure of the production-volume variance to consider such information is why Webb should not interpret the $46,000 U amount as the total economic cost of selling 2,000 jackets fewer than the 12,000 jackets budgeted. If, however, Webb's managers anticipate they will not need capacity beyond 10,000 jackets, they may reduce the excess capacity, for example, by canceling the lease on some of the machines.

Companies plan their plant capacity strategically on the basis of market information about how much capacity will be needed over some future time horizon. For 2017, Webb's budgeted quantity of output is equal to the maximum capacity of the plant for that budget period. Actual demand (and quantity produced) turned out to be below the budgeted quantity of output, so Webb reports an unfavorable production-volume variance for April 2017.

However, it would be incorrect to conclude that Webb's management made a poor planning decision regarding its plant capacity. The demand for Webb's jackets might be highly uncertain. Given this uncertainty and the cost of not having sufficient capacity to meet sudden demand surges (including lost contribution margins as well as reduced repeat business), Webb's management may have made a wise capacity choice for 2017.

So what should Webb's managers ultimately do about the unfavorable variance in April? Should they try to reduce capacity, increase sales, or do nothing? Based on their analysis of the situation, Webb's managers decided to reduce some capacity, but continued to maintain some excess capacity to accommodate unexpected surges in demand. Chapters 9 and 12 examine these issues in more detail. Concepts in Action: Variance Analysis and Standard Costing Help Sandoz Manage Its Overhead Costs highlights another example of managers using variances to help guide their decisions.

Next we describe the journal entries Webb would make to record fixed overhead costs using standard costing.

TRY IT! 8-2

Sanjana Company makes watches. For 2017, the company expected fixed overhead costs of $648,000. Sanjana uses direct labor-hours to allocate fixed overhead and anticipates 21,600 hours during the year for an expected output of 540,000 units. An equal number of units are budgeted for each month.

During October, 48,000 watches were produced and $52,000 was spent on fixed overhead.

Calculate the following:

a. the fixed overhead rate for 2017;

b. the fixed overhead spending variance for October; and

c. the production-volume variance for October.

Journal Entries for Fixed Overhead Costs and Variances

We illustrate journal entries for fixed overhead costs for April 2017 using the Fixed Overhead Control account and the contra account Fixed Overhead Allocated (data from Exhibit 8-2).

1. Fixed Overhead Control	285,000	
Salaries Payable, Accumulated Depreciation, and various other accounts		285,000
To record actual fixed overhead costs incurred.		
2. Work-in-Process Control	230,000	
Fixed Overhead Allocated		230,000
To record fixed overhead costs allocated.		
(0.40 machine-hour/unit × 10,000 units × $57.50/machine-hour). (The costs accumulated in Work-in-Process Control are transferred to Finished-Goods Control when production is completed and to the Cost of Goods Sold when the products are sold.)		
3. Fixed Overhead Allocated	230,000	
Fixed Overhead Spending Variance	9,000	
Fixed Overhead Production-Volume Variance	46,000	
Fixed Overhead Control		285,000
To record variances for the accounting period.		

Overall, $285,000 of fixed overhead costs were incurred during April, but only $230,000 were allocated to jackets. The difference of $55,000 is precisely the underallocated fixed overhead costs we introduced when studying normal costing in Chapter 4. The third entry illustrates how the fixed overhead spending variance of $9,000 and the fixed overhead production-volume variance of $46,000 together record this amount in a standard costing system.

CONCEPTS IN ACTION

Variance Analysis and Standard Costing Help Sandoz Manage Its Overhead Costs

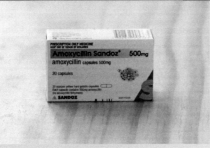

Fir Mamat/Alamy Stock Photo

Sandoz, the $10.1 billion generics division of Swiss-based Novartis AG, is the world's second largest generic drug manufacturer. Generic pharmaceuticals help reduce the cost of health care around the world. In the United States, for example, 88% of all prescription drugs dispensed were generics, but they accounted for only 28% of total drug costs. Market pricing pressure means that Sandoz operates on razor-thin margins. As a result, the company must ensure that managers have a full and accurate understanding of its costs, including of accounting for overhead costs. Sandoz uses standard costing and variance analysis to manage its overhead costs.

Each year, Sandoz prepares an overhead budget based on a detailed production plan, planned overhead spending, and other factors. Sandoz then uses activity-based costing to assign budgeted overhead costs to different work centers (for example, mixing, blending, tableting, testing, and packaging). Finally, overhead costs are assigned to products based on the activity levels required by each product at each work center. The resulting standard product cost is used in product profitability analysis and as a basis for making pricing decisions. The two main focal points in Sandoz's performance analyses are overhead absorption analysis and manufacturing overhead variance analysis.

Each month, Sandoz uses absorption analysis to compare actual production and actual costs to the standard costs of processed inventory. The monthly analysis evaluates two key trends:

1. Are costs in line with the budget? If not, the reasons are examined and the accountable managers are notified.

2. Are production volume and product mix conforming to plan? If not, Sandoz reviews and adjusts machine capacities and the absorption trend is deemed to be permanent.

Manufacturing overhead variances are examined at the work center level. These variances help determine when equipment is not running as expected so it can be repaired or replaced. Variances also help in identifying inefficiencies in processing and setup and cleaning times, which leads to more efficient ways to use equipment. Sometimes, the manufacturing overhead variance analysis leads to the review and improvement of the standards themselves—a critical element in planning the level of plant capacity. Management also reviews current and future capacity on a monthly basis to identify constraints and future capital needs.

Sources: Novartis AG, 2015 Form 20-F (Basel, Switzerland: Novartis AG, 2016); IMS Institute for Healthcare Informatics/Generic *Pharmaceutical Association, Generic Drug Savings in the United States*, November 2015; Conversations with, and documents prepared by, Eric Evans and Erich Erchr of Sandoz, 2004; Conversations with, and documents prepared by, Tobias Hestler and Chris Lewis of Sandoz, 2016.

At the end of the fiscal year, the fixed overhead spending variance is written off to the Cost of Goods Sold if it is immaterial in amount or prorated among Work-in-Process Control, Finished-Goods Control, and Cost of Goods Sold on the basis of the fixed overhead allocated to these accounts as described in Chapter 4, pages 149–151. Some companies combine the write-off and proration methods—that is, they write off the portion of the variance that is due to inefficiency and could have been avoided and prorate the portion of the variance that is unavoidable. Assume that the balance in the Fixed Overhead Spending Variance account as of April 2017 is also the balance at the end of 2017 and is immaterial in amount. The following journal entry records the write-off to Cost of Goods Sold.

Cost of Goods Sold	9,000	
Fixed Overhead Spending Variance		9,000

We now consider the production-volume variance. Assume that the balance in the Fixed Overhead Production-Volume Variance account as of April 2017 is also the balance at the end of 2017. Also assume that some of the jackets manufactured during 2017 are in work-in-process and finished-goods inventory at the end of the year. Many management accountants make a strong argument for writing off to Cost of Goods Sold and not prorating an unfavorable production-volume variance. Proponents of this argument contend that the unfavorable production-volume variance of $46,000 measures the cost of resources expended for 2,000 jackets that were not produced ($23 per jacket $\times$ 2,000 jackets = $46,000). Prorating these costs would inappropriately allocate the fixed overhead costs incurred for the 2,000 jackets not produced to the jackets that were produced. The jackets produced already bear their representative share of fixed overhead costs of $23 per jacket. Therefore, this argument favors charging the unfavorable production-volume variance against the year's revenues so that fixed costs of unused capacity are not carried in work-in-process inventory and finished-goods inventory.

There is, however, an alternative view. This view regards the denominator level as a "soft" rather than a "hard" measure of the fixed resources required and needed to produce each jacket. Suppose that, either because of the design of the jacket or the functioning of the machines, it took more machine-hours than previously thought to manufacture each jacket. Consequently, Webb could make only 10,000 jackets rather than the planned 12,000 in April. In this case, the $276,000 of budgeted fixed overhead costs support the production of the 10,000 jackets manufactured. Under this reasoning, prorating the fixed overhead production-volume variance would appropriately spread the fixed overhead costs among the Work-in-Process Control, Finished-Goods Control, and Cost of Goods Sold accounts.

What about a favorable production-volume variance? Suppose Webb manufactured 13,800 jackets in April 2017.

$$\text{Production-volume variance} = \begin{matrix} \text{Budgeted} \\ \text{fixed} \\ \text{overhead} \end{matrix} - \begin{matrix} \text{Fixed overhead allocated using} \\ \text{budgeted cost per output unit overhead} \\ \text{allowed for actual output produced} \end{matrix}$$

$$= \$276,000 - (\$23 \text{ per jacket} \times 13,800 \text{ jackets})$$

$$= \$276,000 - \$317,400 = \$41,400 \text{ F}$$

Because actual production exceeded the planned capacity level, clearly the fixed overhead costs of $276,000 supported the production of all 13,800 jackets and should therefore be allocated to them. Prorating the favorable production-volume variance achieves this outcome and reduces the amounts in the Work-in-Process Control, Finished-Goods Control, and Cost of Goods Sold accounts. Proration is also the more conservative approach in the sense that it results in a lower operating income than if the entire favorable production-volume variance were credited to Cost of Goods Sold.

Another point relevant to this discussion is that if variances are always written off to Cost of Goods Sold, a company could set its standards to either increase (for financial reporting purposes) or decrease (for tax purposes) its operating income. In other words, always writing off variances invites gaming behavior. For example, Webb could generate a favorable production-volume variance by setting the denominator level used to allocate the firm's fixed overhead costs low and thereby increase its operating income. Or the firm could do just the opposite if it wanted to decrease its operating income to lower its taxes. The proration method has the effect of approximating the allocation of fixed costs based on actual costs and actual output, so it is not susceptible to this type of manipulation.

There is no clear-cut or preferred approach for closing out the production-volume variance. The appropriate accounting procedure is a matter of judgment and depends on the circumstances of each case. Variations of the proration method may be desirable. For example, a company may choose to write off a portion of the production-volume variance and prorate the rest. The goal is to write off that part of the production-volume variance that represents the cost of capacity not used to support the production of output during the period. The rest of the production-volume variance is prorated to Work-in-Process Control, Finished-Goods Control, and Cost of Goods Sold.

If Webb were to write off the production-volume variance to Cost of Goods Sold, it would make the following journal entry.

DECISION POINT

What variances can be calculated for fixed overhead costs?

Cost of Goods Sold	46,000	
Fixed Overhead Production-Volume Variance		46,000

Integrated Analysis of Overhead Cost Variances

As our discussion indicates, the variance calculations for variable overhead and fixed overhead differ:

- Variable overhead has no production-volume variance.
- Fixed overhead has no efficiency variance.

Exhibit 8-4 presents an integrated summary of the variable overhead variances and the fixed overhead variances computed using standard costs for April 2017. Panel A shows the variances for variable overhead, whereas Panel B contains the fixed overhead variances. As you study Exhibit 8-4, note how the columns in Panels A and B are aligned to measure the different variances. In both Panels A and B,

- the difference between columns 1 and 2 measures the spending variance.
- the difference between columns 2 and 3 measures the efficiency variance (if applicable).
- the difference between columns 3 and 4 measures the production-volume variance (if applicable).

Panel A contains an efficiency variance; Panel B has no efficiency variance for fixed overhead. As we discussed, a lump-sum amount of fixed costs will be unaffected by the degree of operating efficiency in a given budget period.

Panel A does not have a production-volume variance because the amount of variable overhead allocated is always the same as the flexible-budget amount. Variable costs never have any unused capacity. When production and sales decline from 12,000 jackets to 10,000 jackets, budgeted variable overhead costs proportionately decline. Fixed costs are different. Panel B has a production-volume variance (see Exhibit 8-3) because Webb did not use some of the fixed overhead capacity it had acquired when it planned to produce 12,000 jackets.

4-Variance Analysis

When all of the overhead variances are presented together as in Exhibit 8-4, we refer to it as a 4-variance analysis:

	4-Variance Analysis		
	Spending Variance	**Efficiency Variance**	**Production-Volume Variance**
Variable overhead	$4,500 F	$15,000 U	Never a variance
Fixed overhead	$9,000 U	Never a variance	$46,000 U

The 4-variance analysis provides the same level of information as the variance analysis carried out earlier for variable overhead and fixed overhead separately (in Exhibits 8-1 and 8-2, respectively), but does so in a unified presentation that also indicates those variances that are never present.

As with other variances, the variances in Webb's 4-variance analysis are not necessarily independent of each other. For example, Webb may purchase lower-quality machine fluids (leading to a favorable variable overhead spending variance), which results in the machines taking longer to operate than budgeted (causing an unfavorable variable overhead efficiency variance), and producing less than budgeted output (causing an unfavorable production-volume variance).

Combined Variance Analysis

To keep track of all that is happening within their areas of responsibility, managers in large, complex businesses, such as General Electric and Disney, use detailed 4-variance analysis. Doing so helps them identify and focus attention on the areas not operating as expected. Managers of small businesses understand their operations better based on personal

LEARNING OBJECTIVE 5

Show how the 4-variance analysis approach reconciles the actual overhead incurred with the overhead amounts allocated during the period

…the 4-variance analysis approach identifies spending and efficiency variances for variable overhead costs and spending and production-volume variances for fixed overhead costs

EXHIBIT 8-4 Columnar Presentation of Integrated 4-Variance Analysis: Webb Company for April 2017[a]

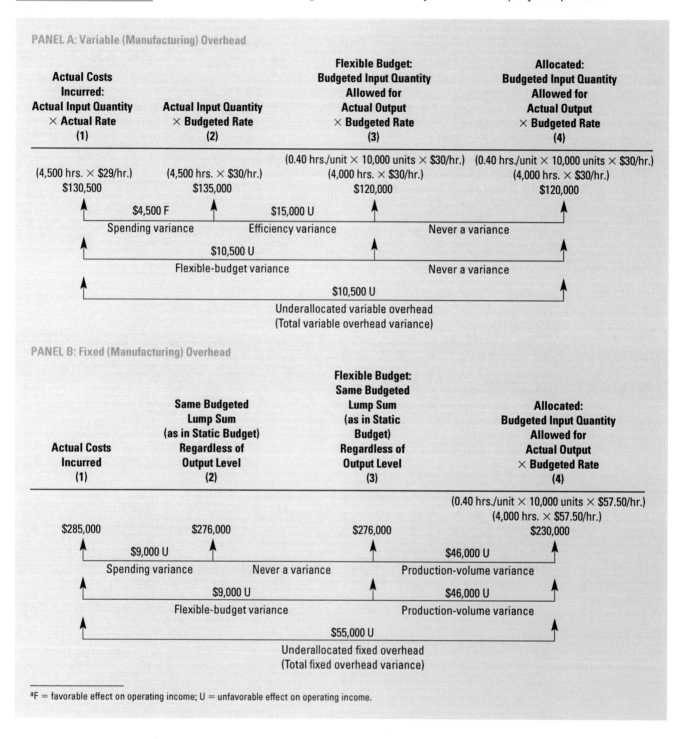

PANEL A: Variable (Manufacturing) Overhead

Actual Costs Incurred: Actual Input Quantity × Actual Rate (1)	Actual Input Quantity × Budgeted Rate (2)	Flexible Budget: Budgeted Input Quantity Allowed for Actual Output × Budgeted Rate (3)	Allocated: Budgeted Input Quantity Allowed for Actual Output × Budgeted Rate (4)
(4,500 hrs. × $29/hr.) $130,500	(4,500 hrs. × $30/hr.) $135,000	(0.40 hrs./unit × 10,000 units × $30/hr.) (4,000 hrs. × $30/hr.) $120,000	(0.40 hrs./unit × 10,000 units × $30/hr.) (4,000 hrs. × $30/hr.) $120,000

$4,500 F — Spending variance
$15,000 U — Efficiency variance
Never a variance

$10,500 U — Flexible-budget variance
Never a variance

$10,500 U
Underallocated variable overhead
(Total variable overhead variance)

PANEL B: Fixed (Manufacturing) Overhead

Actual Costs Incurred (1)	Same Budgeted Lump Sum (as in Static Budget) Regardless of Output Level (2)	Flexible Budget: Same Budgeted Lump Sum (as in Static Budget) Regardless of Output Level (3)	Allocated: Budgeted Input Quantity Allowed for Actual Output × Budgeted Rate (4)
$285,000	$276,000	$276,000	(0.40 hrs./unit × 10,000 units × $57.50/hr.) (4,000 hrs. × $57.50/hr.) $230,000

$9,000 U — Spending variance
Never a variance
$46,000 U — Production-volume variance

$9,000 U — Flexible-budget variance
$46,000 U — Production-volume variance

$55,000 U
Underallocated fixed overhead
(Total fixed overhead variance)

[a]F = favorable effect on operating income; U = unfavorable effect on operating income.

observations and nonfinancial measures. They find less value in doing the additional measurements required for 4-variance analyses. For example, to simplify their costing systems, small companies may not distinguish variable overhead incurred from fixed overhead incurred because making this distinction is often not clear-cut. As we saw in Chapter 2 and will see in Chapter 10, many costs such as supervision, quality control, and materials handling have both variable- and fixed-cost components that may not be easy to separate. Managers may therefore use a less detailed analysis that *combines* the variable overhead and fixed overhead into a single total overhead cost.

When a single total overhead cost category is used, it can still be analyzed in depth. The variances are now the sums of the variable overhead and fixed overhead variances for that level, as computed in Exhibit 8-4. The combined variance analysis looks as follows:

	Combined 3-Variance Analysis		
	Spending Variance	**Efficiency Variance**	**Production-Volume Variance**
Total overhead	$4,500 U	$15,000 U	$46,000 U

The accounting for 3-variance analysis is simpler than for 4-variance analysis, but some information is lost because the variable and fixed overhead spending variances are combined into a single total overhead spending variance.

Finally, the overall **total-overhead variance** is given by the sum of the preceding variances. In the Webb example, this equals $65,500 U. Note that this amount, which aggregates the flexible-budget and production-volume variances, equals the total amount of underallocated (or underapplied) overhead costs. (Recall our discussion of underallocated overhead costs in normal costing from Chapter 4, pages 148–149.) Using figures from Exhibit 8-4, the $65,500 U total-overhead variance is the difference between (a) the total actual overhead incurred ($130,500 + $285,000 = $415,500) and (b) the overhead allocated ($120,000 + $230,000 = $350,000) to the actual output produced. If the total-overhead variance were favorable, it would have corresponded instead to the amount of overapplied overhead costs.

DECISION POINT

What is the most detailed way for a company to reconcile actual overhead incurred with the amount allocated during a period?

You are given the following information about Proton Equipment, Inc.

8-3 TRY IT!

Variances	Spending	Efficiency	Production-Volume
Variable manufacturing overhead	$ 7,500 F	$30,000 U	(B)
Fixed manufacturing overhead	$28,000 U	(A)	$80,000 U

a. What are the amounts (A) and (B) in the above table?
b. In a combined 3-variance analysis, what is the total spending variance?
c. What is the total overhead variance?

Production-Volume Variance and Sales-Volume Variance

As we complete our study of variance analysis for Webb Company, it is helpful to step back to see the "big picture" and to link the accounting and performance evaluation functions of standard costing. Exhibit 7-1, page 272, first identified a static-budget variance of $93,100 U as the difference between the static budget operating income of $108,000 and the actual operating income of $14,900. Exhibit 7-2, page 274, then subdivided the static-budget variance of $93,100 U into a flexible-budget variance of $29,100 U and a sales-volume variance of $64,000 U. In both Chapter 7 and this chapter, we presented more detailed variances that subdivided, whenever possible, individual flexible-budget variances for the selling price, direct materials, direct manufacturing labor, and variable overhead. For the fixed overhead, we noted that the flexible-budget variance is the same as the spending variance. Where does the production-volume variance belong then? As you shall see, the production-volume variance is a component of the sales-volume variance. Under our assumption of actual production and sales of 10,000 jackets, Webb's costing system debits to Work-in-Process Control the standard

LEARNING OBJECTIVE 6

Explain the relationship between the sales-volume variance and the production-volume variance

…the production-volume and operating-income volume variances together comprise the sales-volume variance

costs of the 10,000 jackets produced. These amounts are then transferred to Finished Goods and finally to Cost of Goods Sold:

Direct materials (Chapter 7, page 282, entry 1b)	
($60 per jacket × 10,000 jackets)	$ 600,000
Direct manufacturing labor (Chapter 7, page 283, entry 2)	
($16 per jacket × 10,000 jackets)	160,000
Variable overhead (Chapter 8, page 316, entry 2)	
($12 per jacket × 10,000 jackets)	120,000
Fixed overhead (Chapter 8, page 320, entry 2)	
($23 per jacket × 10,000 jackets)	230,000
Cost of goods sold at standard cost	
($111 per jacket × 10,000 jackets)	$1,110,000

Webb's costing system also records the revenues from the 10,000 jackets sold at the budgeted selling price of $120 per jacket. The net effect of these entries on Webb's budgeted operating income is as follows:

Revenues at budgeted selling price	
($120 per jacket × 10,000 jackets)	$1,200,000
Cost of goods sold at standard cost	
($111 per jacket × 10,000 jackets)	1,110,000
Operating income based on budgeted profit per jacket	
($9 per jacket × 10,000 jackets)	$ 90,000

A crucial point to keep in mind is that under standard costing, fixed overhead costs are treated as if they are a variable cost. That is, in determining the budgeted operating income of $90,000, only $230,000 ($23 per jacket × 10,000 jackets) of the fixed overhead costs are considered, whereas the budgeted fixed overhead costs are $276,000. Webb's accountants then record the $46,000 unfavorable production-volume variance (the difference between the budgeted fixed overhead costs, $276,000, and allocated fixed overhead costs, $230,000, page 320, entry 2), as well as the various flexible-budget variances (including the fixed overhead spending variance) that total $29,100 unfavorable (see Exhibit 7-2, page 274). This results in actual operating income of $14,900 as follows:

Operating income based on budgeted profit per jacket	
($9 per jacket × 10,000 jackets)	$ 90,000
Unfavorable production-volume variance	(46,000)
Flexible-budget operating income (Exhibit 7-2)	44,000
Unfavorable flexible-budget variance for operating income (Exhibit 7-2)	(29,100)
Actual operating income (Exhibit 7-2)	$ 14,900

In contrast, the static-budget operating income of $108,000 (page 272) is not entered in Webb's costing system because standard costing records budgeted revenues, standard costs, and variances only for the 10,000 jackets actually produced and sold, not for the 12,000 jackets that were *planned* to be produced and sold. As a result, the sales-volume variance of $64,000 U, which is the difference between the static-budget operating income of $108,000 and the flexible-budget operating income of $44,000 (Exhibit 7-2, page 274), is never actually recorded under standard costing. Nevertheless, the sales-volume variance is useful because it helps managers understand the lost contribution margin from selling 2,000 fewer jackets (the sales-volume variance assumes fixed costs remain at the budgeted level of $276,000).

The sales-volume variance has two components. They are as follows:

1. A difference between the static-budget operating income of $108,000 for 12,000 jackets and the budgeted operating income of $90,000 for 10,000 jackets. This is the **operating-income volume variance** of $18,000 U ($108,000 − $90,000). It reflects the fact that Webb produced and sold 2,000 fewer units than budgeted.

| EXHIBIT 8-5 | Summary of Levels 1, 2, and 3 Variance Analysis: Webb Company for April 2017 |

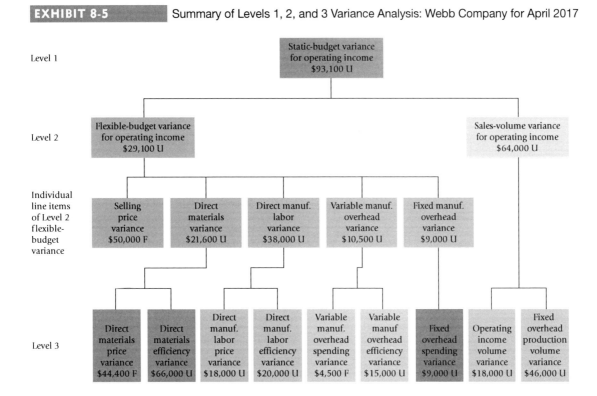

2. A difference between the budgeted operating income of $90,000 and the flexible-budget operating income of $44,000 (Exhibit 7-2, page 274) for the 10,000 actual units. This difference arises because Webb's costing system treats fixed costs as if they behave in a variable manner and assumes fixed costs equal the allocated amount of $230,000, rather than the budgeted fixed costs of $276,000. Of course, this difference is precisely the production-volume variance of $46,000 U.

In summary, we have the following:

	Operating-income volume variance	$18,000 U
(+)	Production-volume variance	46,000 U
Equals	Sales-volume variance	$64,000 U

We can now provide a summary (see Exhibit 8-5) that formally disaggregates the static-budget variance of $93,100 U into its components. Note how the comprehensive chart incorporates all of the variances you have studied in Chapters 7 and 8.

We next describe the use of variance analysis in activity-based costing systems.

DECISION POINT

What is the relationship between the sales-volume variance and the production-volume variance?

Variance Analysis and Activity-Based Costing

Activity-based costing (ABC) systems focus on individual activities as the fundamental cost objects. ABC systems classify the costs of various activities into a cost hierarchy—output unit-level costs, batch-level costs, product-sustaining costs, and facility-sustaining costs (see pages 182–183). In this section, we show how a company that has an ABC system and batch-level costs can benefit from variance analysis. Batch-level costs are the costs of activities related to a group of units of products or services rather than to each individual unit of product or service. We illustrate variance analysis for variable batch-level direct costs and fixed batch-level overhead costs.[4]

LEARNING OBJECTIVE 7

Calculate variances in activity-based costing

...compare budgeted and actual overhead costs of activities

---

[4] The techniques we demonstrate can be applied to analyze variable batch-level overhead costs as well.

Consider Lyco Brass Works, which manufactures many different types of faucets and brass fittings. Because of the wide range of products it produces, Lyco uses an activity-based costing system. In contrast, Webb uses a simple costing system because it makes only one type of jacket. One of Lyco's products is Elegance, a decorative brass faucet for home spas. Lyco produces Elegance in batches.

For each product Lyco makes, it uses dedicated materials-handling labor to bring materials to the production floor, transport items in process from one work center to the next, and take the finished goods to the shipping area. Therefore, materials-handling labor costs for Elegance are direct costs of Elegance. Because the materials for a batch are moved together, materials-handling labor costs vary with the number of batches rather than with the number of units in a batch. Materials-handling labor costs are variable direct batch-level costs.

To manufacture a batch of Elegance, Lyco must set up the machines and molds. Employees must be highly skilled to set up the machines and molds. Hence, a separate setup department is responsible for setting up the machines and molds for different batches of products. Setup costs are overhead costs. For simplicity, assume that setup costs are fixed with respect to the number of setup-hours. The costs consist of salaries paid to engineers and supervisors and the costs of leasing setup equipment.

Information regarding Elegance for 2017 follows:

	Actual Result	Static-Budget Amount
1. Units of Elegance produced and sold	151,200	180,000
2. Batch size (units per batch)	140	150
3. Number of batches (Line 1 ÷ Line 2)	1,080	1,200
4. Materials-handling labor-hours per batch	5.25	5
5. Total materials-handling labor-hours (Line 3 × Line 4)	5,670	6,000
6. Cost per materials-handling labor-hour	$ 14.50	$ 14
7. Total materials-handling labor costs (Line 5 × Line 6)	$ 82,215	$ 84,000
8. Setup-hours per batch	6.25	6
9. Total setup-hours (Line 3 × Line 8)	6,750	7,200
10. Total fixed setup overhead costs	$220,000	$216,000

Flexible Budget and Variance Analysis for Direct Materials-Handling Labor Costs

To prepare the flexible budget for the materials-handling labor costs, Lyco starts with the actual units of output produced, 151,200 units, and proceeds with the following steps.

Step 1: Using the Budgeted Batch Size, Calculate the Number of Batches that Should Have Been Used to Produce the Actual Output. At the budgeted batch size of 150 units per batch, Lyco should have produced the 151,200 units of output in 1,008 batches (151,200 units ÷ 150 units per batch).

Step 2: Using the Budgeted Materials-Handling Labor-Hours per Batch, Calculate the Number of Materials-Handling Labor-Hours that Should Have Been Used. At the budgeted quantity of 5 hours per batch, 1,008 batches should have required 5,040 materials-handling labor-hours (1,008 batches × 5 hours per batch).

Step 3: Using the Budgeted Cost per Materials-Handling Labor-Hour, Calculate the Flexible-Budget Amount for the Materials-Handling Labor-Hours. The flexible-budget amount is 5,040 materials-handling labor-hours × the $14 budgeted cost per materials-handling labor-hour = $70,560.

Note how the flexible-budget calculations for the materials-handling labor costs focus on batch-level quantities (materials-handling labor-hours per batch rather than per unit). The flexible-budget quantity computations focus at the appropriate level of the cost hierarchy. For example, because materials handling is a batch-level cost, the flexible-budget quantity calculations are made at the batch level—the quantity of materials-handling labor-hours that Lyco should have used based on the number of batches it should have used to produce the actual quantity of 151,200 units. If a cost had been a product-sustaining cost—such as product design cost—the flexible-budget quantity computations would focus at the product-sustaining level by, for example, evaluating the actual complexity of the product's design relative to the budget.

The flexible-budget variance for the materials-handling labor costs can now be calculated as follows:

$$
\begin{aligned}
\frac{\text{Flexible-budget}}{\text{variance}} &= \text{Actual costs } - \text{ Flexible-budget costs} \\
&= (5{,}670 \text{ hours} \times \$14.50 \text{ per hour}) - (5{,}040 \text{ hours} \times \$14 \text{ per hour}) \\
&= \$82{,}215 - \$70{,}560 \\
&= \$11{,}655 \text{ U}
\end{aligned}
$$

The unfavorable variance indicates that materials-handling labor costs were $11,655 higher than the flexible-budget target. We can get some insight into the possible reasons for this unfavorable outcome by examining the price and efficiency components of the flexible-budget variance. Exhibit 8-6 presents the variances in columnar form.

$$
\begin{aligned}
\frac{\text{Price}}{\text{variance}} &= \left(\begin{array}{c} \text{Actual price} \\ \text{of input} \end{array} - \begin{array}{c} \text{Budgeted price} \\ \text{of input} \end{array}\right) \times \begin{array}{c} \text{Actual quantity} \\ \text{of input} \end{array} \\
&= (\$14.50 \text{ per hour} - \$14 \text{ per hour}) \times 5{,}670 \text{ hours} \\
&= \$0.50 \text{ per hour} \times 5{,}670 \text{ hours} \\
&= \$2{,}835 \text{ U}
\end{aligned}
$$

The unfavorable price variance for materials-handling labor indicates that the $14.50 actual cost per materials-handling labor-hour exceeds the $14.00 budgeted cost per materials-handling labor-hour. This variance could be the result of Lyco's human resources manager negotiating wage rates less skillfully or of wage rates increasing unexpectedly due to a scarcity of labor.

$$
\begin{aligned}
\frac{\text{Efficiency}}{\text{variance}} &= \left(\begin{array}{c} \text{Actual} \\ \text{quantity of} \\ \text{input used} \end{array} - \begin{array}{c} \text{Budgeted quantity} \\ \text{of input allowed} \\ \text{for actual output} \end{array}\right) \times \begin{array}{c} \text{Budgeted price} \\ \text{of input} \end{array} \\
&= (5{,}670 \text{ hours} - 5{,}040 \text{ hours}) \times \$14 \text{ per hour} \\
&= 630 \text{ hours} \times \$14 \text{ per hour} \\
&= \$8{,}820 \text{ U}
\end{aligned}
$$

EXHIBIT 8-6 Columnar Presentation of Variance Analysis for Direct Materials-Handling Labor Costs: Lyco Brass Works for 2017[a]

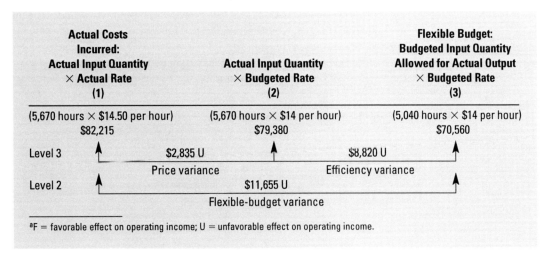

Actual Costs Incurred: Actual Input Quantity × Actual Rate (1)	Actual Input Quantity × Budgeted Rate (2)	Flexible Budget: Budgeted Input Quantity Allowed for Actual Output × Budgeted Rate (3)
(5,670 hours × $14.50 per hour) $82,215	(5,670 hours × $14 per hour) $79,380	(5,040 hours × $14 per hour) $70,560
Level 3 ↑ $2,835 U ↑ Price variance	$8,820 U ↑ Efficiency variance	↑
Level 2 ↑ $11,655 U Flexible-budget variance	↑	

[a]F = favorable effect on operating income; U = unfavorable effect on operating income.

The unfavorable efficiency variance indicates that the 5,670 actual materials-handling labor-hours exceeded the 5,040 budgeted materials-handling labor-hours for the actual output. Possible reasons for the unfavorable efficiency variance are as follows:

- Smaller actual batch sizes of 140 units, instead of the budgeted batch sizes of 150 units, resulted in Lyco producing the 151,200 units in 1,080 batches instead of 1,008 (151,200 ÷ 150) batches
- The actual materials-handling labor-hours per batch (5.25 hours) were higher than the budgeted materials-handling labor-hours per batch (5 hours)

Reasons for smaller-than-budgeted batch sizes could include quality problems when batch sizes exceed 140 faucets and high costs of carrying inventory.

Possible reasons for the larger actual materials-handling labor-hours per batch are as follows:

- Inefficient layout of the Elegance production line
- Materials-handling labor having to wait at work centers before picking up or delivering materials
- Unmotivated, inexperienced, and underskilled employees
- Very tight standards for materials-handling time

Identifying the reasons for the efficiency variance helps Lyco's managers develop a plan for improving its materials-handling labor efficiency and take corrective action that will be incorporated into future budgets.

We now consider fixed setup overhead costs.

Flexible Budget and Variance Analysis for Fixed Setup Overhead Costs

Exhibit 8-7 presents the variances for fixed setup overhead costs in columnar form.

Lyco's fixed setup overhead flexible-budget variance is calculated as follows:

$$\begin{array}{l} \text{Fixed-setup} \\ \text{overhead} \\ \text{flexible-budget} \\ \text{variance} \end{array} = \begin{array}{c} \text{Actual costs} \\ \text{incurred} \end{array} - \begin{array}{c} \text{Flexible-budget} \\ \text{costs} \end{array}$$

$$= \$220{,}000 - \$216{,}000$$

$$= \$4{,}000 \ U$$

Note that the flexible-budget amount for the fixed setup overhead costs equals the static-budget amount of $216,000. That's because there is no "flexing" of fixed costs. Moreover, because the fixed overhead costs have no efficiency variance, the fixed setup overhead spending variance is the same as the fixed overhead flexible-budget variance. The spending variance could be unfavorable because of higher leasing costs of new setup equipment or higher salaries paid to engineers and supervisors. Lyco may have incurred these costs to alleviate some of the difficulties it was having in setting up machines.

To calculate the production-volume variance, Lyco first computes the budgeted cost-allocation rate for the fixed setup overhead costs using the same four-step approach described on page 311.

Step 1: Choose the Period to Use for the Budget. Lyco uses a period of 12 months (the year 2017).

Step 2: Select the Cost-Allocation Base to Use in Allocating the Fixed Overhead Costs to the Output Produced. Lyco uses budgeted setup-hours as the cost-allocation base for fixed setup overhead costs. Budgeted setup-hours in the static budget for 2017 are 7,200 hours.

Step 3: Identify the Fixed Overhead Costs Associated with the Cost-Allocation Base. Lyco's fixed setup overhead cost budget for 2017 is $216,000.

EXHIBIT 8-7 Columnar Presentation of Fixed Setup Overhead Variance Analysis: Lyco Brass Works for 2017[a]

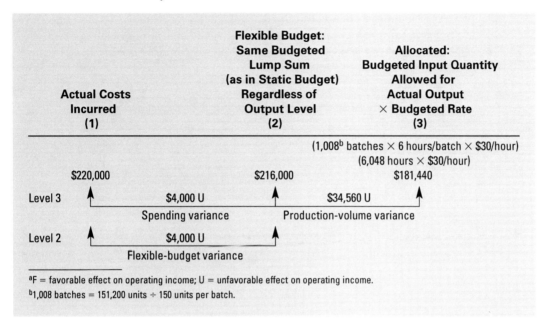

[a]F = favorable effect on operating income; U = unfavorable effect on operating income.
[b]1,008 batches = 151,200 units ÷ 150 units per batch.

Step 4: Compute the Rate per Unit of the Cost-Allocation Base Used to Allocate the Fixed Overhead Costs to the Output Produced. Dividing the $216,000 from Step 3 by the 7,200 setup-hours from Step 2, Lyco estimates a fixed setup overhead cost rate of $30 per setup-hour:

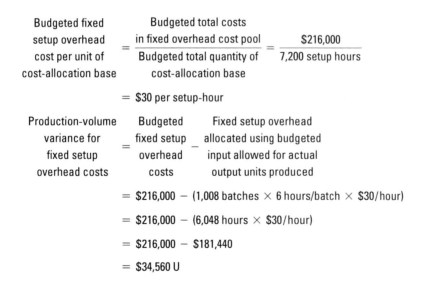

During 2017, Lyco planned to produce 180,000 units of Elegance but actually produced 151,200 units. The unfavorable production-volume variance measures the amount of extra fixed setup costs Lyco incurred for setup capacity it did not use. One interpretation is that the unfavorable $34,560 production-volume variance represents an inefficient use of the company's setup capacity. However, Lyco may have earned higher operating income by selling 151,200 units at a higher price than 180,000 units at a lower price. As a result, Lyco's managers should interpret the production-volume variance cautiously because it does not consider the effect of output on selling prices and operating income.

DECISION POINT

How can variance analysis be used in an activity-based costing system?

TRY IT! 8-4

Matterhorn, Inc., produces a special line of toy racing cars. Matterhorn produces the cars in batches. To manufacture each batch of the cars, Matterhorn must set up the machines and molds. Setup costs are batch-level costs and are fixed with respect to the number of setup-hours. A separate Setup Department is responsible for setting up machines and molds for each style of car. The following information pertains to July 2017:

	Actual Amounts	Static-budget Amounts
Units produced and sold	15,000	11,250
Batch size (number of units per batch)	250	225
Setup-hours per batch	5	5.25
Total fixed setup overhead costs	$12,000	$9,975

Calculate the following:

a. the spending variance for fixed setup overhead costs;

b. the budgeted fixed setup overhead rate; and

c. the production-volume variance for fixed overhead setup costs.

Overhead Variances in Nonmanufacturing Settings

LEARNING
OBJECTIVE 8

Examine the use of overhead variances in nonmanufacturing settings

...analyze nonmanufacturing variable overhead costs for decision making and cost management; fixed overhead variances are especially important in service settings

Our Webb Company example examined variable and fixed manufacturing overhead costs. Managers can also use variance analysis to examine the overhead costs of the nonmanufacturing areas of the company and to make decisions about (1) pricing, (2) managing costs, and (3) the mix of products to make. For example, when product distribution costs are high, as they are in the automobile, consumer durables, cement, and steel industries, standard costing can provide managers with reliable and timely information on variable distribution overhead spending variances and efficiency variances.

What about service-sector companies such as airlines, hospitals, hotels, and railroads? How can they benefit from variance analyses? The output measures these companies commonly use are passenger-miles flown, patient-days provided, room-days occupied, and tonmiles of freight hauled, respectively. Few costs can be traced to these outputs in a cost-effective way. Most of the costs are fixed overhead costs, such as the costs of equipment, buildings, and staff. Using capacity effectively is the key to profitability, and fixed overhead variances can help managers in this task. Retail businesses, such as Kmart, also have high-capacity–related fixed costs (lease and occupancy costs). In the case of Kmart, sales declines resulted in unused capacity and unfavorable fixed-cost variances. Kmart reduced its fixed costs by closing some of its stores, but it also had to file for Chapter 11 bankruptcy.

Consider the following data for United Airlines for selected years from the past 15 years. Available seat miles (ASMs) are the actual seats in an airplane multiplied by the distance the plane traveled.

Year	Total ASMs (Millions) (1)	Operating Revenue per ASM (2)	Operating Cost per ASM (3)	Operating Income per ASM (4) = (2) − (3)
2000	175,493	10.2 cents	10.0 cents	0.2 cents
2003	136,566	8.6 cents	9.8 cents	−1.2 cents
2006	143,085	10.6 cents	10.8 cents	−0.2 cents
2008	135,859	11.9 cents	13.6 cents	−1.7 cents
2011	118,973	13.1 cents	13.5 cents	−0.4 cents
2015	219,956	13.1 cents	12.2 cents	0.9 cents

When air travel declined after the events of September 11, 2001, United's revenues fell. However, most of the company's fixed costs—for its airport facilities, equipment, personnel, and so on—did not. United had a large unfavorable production-volume variance because its capacity was underutilized. As column 1 of the table indicates, United responded by reducing its capacity substantially. Available seat miles (ASMs) declined from 175,493 million in 2000 to 136,566 million in 2003. Yet United was unable to fill even the planes it had retained, so its revenue per ASM declined (column 2) and its cost per ASM stayed roughly the same (column 3). United filed for Chapter 11 bankruptcy in December 2002 and began seeking government guarantees to obtain the loans it needed. Subsequently, strong demand for airline travel, as well as productivity improvements resulting from the more efficient use of resources and networks, led to increased traffic and higher average ticket prices. By maintaining a disciplined approach to capacity and tight control over growth, United saw over a 20% increase in its revenue per ASM between 2003 and 2006. The improvement in performance allowed United to come out of bankruptcy on February 1, 2006. Subsequently, however, the global recession and soaring jet fuel prices had a significant negative impact on United's performance, as reflected in the continued negative operating incomes and the further decline in capacity. In May 2010, a merger agreement was reached between United and Continental Airlines. Continental was formally dissolved in 2012. The merger is reflected in the 85% growth in United's ASM between 2011 and 2015. The revenue benefits from this greater scale and the recent plunge in fuel prices have led United to new heights of profitability.

Financial and Nonfinancial Performance Measures

The overhead variances discussed in this chapter are examples of financial performance measures. As the preceding examples illustrate, nonfinancial measures such as those related to capacity utilization and physical measures of input usage also provide useful information. The nonfinancial measures that managers of Webb would likely find helpful in planning and controlling its overhead costs include the following:

1. Quantity of actual indirect materials used per machine-hour, relative to the quantity of budgeted indirect materials used per machine-hour

2. Actual energy used per machine-hour, relative to the budgeted energy used per machine-hour

3. Actual machine-hours per jacket, relative to the budgeted machine-hours per jacket

These performance measures, like the financial variances discussed in this chapter and Chapter 7, alert managers to problems and probably would be reported daily or hourly on the production floor. The overhead variances we discussed in this chapter capture the financial effects of items such as the three factors listed, which in many cases first appear as nonfinancial performance measures. An especially interesting example along these lines comes from Japan: Some Japanese companies have begun reining in their CO_2 emissions in part by doing a budgeted-to-actual variance analysis of the emissions. The goal is to make employees aware of the emissions and reduce them in advance of greenhouse-gas reduction plans being drawn up by the Japanese government.

Finally, both financial and nonfinancial performance measures are used to evaluate the performance of managers. Exclusive reliance on either is always too simplistic because each gives a different perspective on performance. Nonfinancial measures (such as those described previously) provide feedback on individual aspects of a manager's performance, whereas financial measures evaluate the overall effect of and the tradeoffs among different nonfinancial performance measures. We provide further discussion of these issues in Chapters 12, 19, and 23.

DECISION POINT

How are overhead variances useful in nonmanufacturing settings?

PROBLEM FOR SELF-STUDY

Nina Garcia is the newly appointed president of Laser Products. She is examining the May 2017 results for the Aerospace Products Division. This division manufactures solar arrays for satellites. Garcia's current concern is with manufacturing overhead costs at the Aerospace Products Division. Both variable and fixed overhead costs are allocated to the solar arrays on the basis of laser-cutting-hours. The following budget information is available:

Budgeted variable overhead rate	$200 per hour
Budgeted fixed overhead rate	$240 per hour
Budgeted laser-cutting time per solar array	1.5 hours
Budgeted production and sales for May 2017	5,000 solar arrays
Budgeted fixed overhead costs for May 2017	$1,800,000

Actual results for May 2017 are as follows:

Solar arrays produced and sold	4,800 units
Laser-cutting-hours used	8,400 hours
Variable overhead costs	$1,478,400
Fixed overhead costs	$1,832,200

Required

1. Compute the spending variance and the efficiency variance for variable overhead.
2. Compute the spending variance and the production-volume variance for fixed overhead.
3. Give two explanations for each of the variances calculated in requirements 1 and 2.

Solution

1 and 2. See Exhibit 8-8.

3. a. Variable overhead spending variance, $201,600 F. One possible reason for this variance is that the actual prices of individual items included in variable overhead (such as cutting fluids) are lower than budgeted prices. A second possible reason is that the percentage increase in the actual quantity usage of individual items in the variable overhead cost pool is less than the percentage increase in laser-cutting-hours compared to the flexible budget.

   b. Variable overhead efficiency variance, $240,000 U. One possible reason for this variance is inadequate maintenance of laser machines, causing them to take more laser-cutting time per solar array. A second possible reason is use of undermotivated, inexperienced, or underskilled workers operating the laser-cutting machines, resulting in more laser-cutting time per solar array.

   c. Fixed overhead spending variance, $32,200 U. One possible reason for this variance is that the actual prices of individual items in the fixed-cost pool unexpectedly increased from the prices budgeted (such as an unexpected increase in the cost of leasing each machine). A second possible reason is that the Aerospace Products Division had to lease more machines or hire more supervisors than had been budgeted.

   d. Production-volume variance, $72,000 U. Actual production of solar arrays is 4,800 units, compared with 5,000 units budgeted. One possible reason for this variance is demand factors, such as a decline in an aerospace program that led to a decline in demand for satellites. A second possible reason is supply factors, such as a production stoppage due to labor problems or machine breakdowns.

EXHIBIT 8-8 Columnar Presentation of Integrated Variance Analysis: Laser Products for May 2017[a]

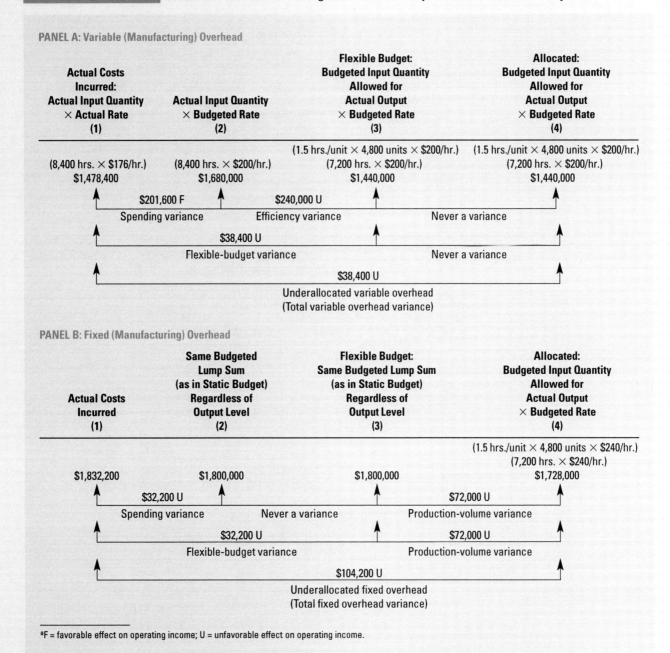

PANEL A: Variable (Manufacturing) Overhead

Actual Costs Incurred: Actual Input Quantity × Actual Rate (1)	Actual Input Quantity × Budgeted Rate (2)	Flexible Budget: Budgeted Input Quantity Allowed for Actual Output × Budgeted Rate (3)	Allocated: Budgeted Input Quantity Allowed for Actual Output × Budgeted Rate (4)
(8,400 hrs. × $176/hr.) $1,478,400	(8,400 hrs. × $200/hr.) $1,680,000	(1.5 hrs./unit × 4,800 units × $200/hr.) (7,200 hrs. × $200/hr.) $1,440,000	(1.5 hrs./unit × 4,800 units × $200/hr.) (7,200 hrs. × $200/hr.) $1,440,000

$201,600 F Spending variance | $240,000 U Efficiency variance | Never a variance

$38,400 U Flexible-budget variance | Never a variance

$38,400 U
Underallocated variable overhead
(Total variable overhead variance)

PANEL B: Fixed (Manufacturing) Overhead

Actual Costs Incurred (1)	Same Budgeted Lump Sum (as in Static Budget) Regardless of Output Level (2)	Flexible Budget: Same Budgeted Lump Sum (as in Static Budget) Regardless of Output Level (3)	Allocated: Budgeted Input Quantity Allowed for Actual Output × Budgeted Rate (4)
$1,832,200	$1,800,000	$1,800,000	(1.5 hrs./unit × 4,800 units × $240/hr.) (7,200 hrs. × $240/hr.) $1,728,000

$32,200 U Spending variance | Never a variance | $72,000 U Production-volume variance

$32,200 U Flexible-budget variance | $72,000 U Production-volume variance

$104,200 U
Underallocated fixed overhead
(Total fixed overhead variance)

[a]F = favorable effect on operating income; U = unfavorable effect on operating income.

Source: Republished with permission of Strategic Finance by Paul Sherman. Copyright 2003 by Institute of Management Accountants. Permission conveyed through Copyright Clearance Center, Inc.

DECISION **POINTS**

The following question-and-answer format summarizes the chapter's learning objectives. Each decision presents a key question related to a learning objective. The guidelines are the answer to that question.

Decision	Guidelines
1. How do managers plan variable overhead costs and fixed overhead costs?	Planning of both variable and fixed overhead costs involves undertaking only activities that add value and then being efficient in that undertaking. The key difference is that for variable-cost planning, ongoing decisions during the budget period play a much larger role; for fixed-cost planning, most key decisions are made before the start of the period.
2. How are budgeted variable overhead and fixed overhead cost rates calculated?	The budgeted variable (fixed) overhead cost rate is calculated by dividing the budgeted variable (fixed) overhead costs by the denominator level of the cost-allocation base.
3. What variances can be calculated for variable overhead costs?	When the flexible budget for variable overhead is developed, an overhead efficiency variance and an overhead spending variance can be computed. The variable overhead efficiency variance focuses on the difference between the actual quantity of the cost-allocation base used relative to the budgeted quantity of the cost-allocation base. The variable overhead spending variance focuses on the difference between the actual variable overhead cost per unit of the cost-allocation base relative to the budgeted variable overhead cost per unit of the cost-allocation base.
4. What variances can be calculated for fixed overhead costs?	For fixed overhead, the static and flexible budgets coincide. The difference between the budgeted and actual amount of fixed overhead is the flexible-budget variance, also referred to as the spending variance. The production-volume variance measures the difference between the budgeted fixed overhead and the fixed overhead allocated on the basis of actual output produced.
5. What is the most detailed way for a company to reconcile actual overhead incurred with the amount allocated during a period?	A 4-variance analysis presents spending and efficiency variances for variable overhead costs and spending and production-volume variances for fixed overhead costs. By analyzing these four variances together, managers can reconcile the actual overhead costs with the amount of overhead allocated to the output produced during a period.
6. What is the relationship between the sales-volume variance and the production-volume variance?	The production-volume variance is a component of the sales-volume variance. The production-volume and operating-income volume variances together comprise the sales-volume variance.
7. How can variance analysis be used in an activity-based costing system?	Flexible budgets in ABC systems give insight into why actual activity costs differ from budgeted activity costs. Using output and input measures for an activity, a comprehensive variance analysis can be conducted.
8. How are overhead variances useful in nonmanufacturing settings?	Managers can analyze variances for all variable overhead costs, including those outside the manufacturing function. The analysis can be used to make pricing and product-mix decisions and to manage costs. Fixed overhead variances are especially important in service settings, where using capacity effectively is the key to profitability. In all cases, the information provided by variances can be supplemented by the use of suitable nonfinancial metrics.

TERMS TO LEARN

The chapter and the Glossary at the end of the book contain definitions of the following important terms:

denominator level (**p. 311**)
denominator-level variance (**p. 318**)
fixed overhead flexible-budget variance
(**p. 317**)
fixed overhead spending variance
(**p. 317**)

operating-income volume variance
(**p. 326**)
production-volume variance
(**p. 318**)
standard costing (**p. 310**)
total-overhead variance (**p. 325**)

variable overhead efficiency variance
(**p. 313**)
variable overhead flexible-budget
variance (**p. 312**)
variable overhead spending variance
(**p. 314**)

ASSIGNMENT MATERIAL

Questions

Pearson MyLab Accounting

8-1 How do managers plan for variable overhead costs?

8-2 How does the planning of fixed overhead costs differ from the planning of variable overhead costs?

8-3 How does standard costing differ from actual costing?

8-4 What are the steps in developing a budgeted variable overhead cost-allocation rate?

8-5 What are the factors that affect the spending variance for variable manufacturing overhead?

8-6 Assume variable manufacturing overhead is allocated using machine-hours. Give three possible reasons for a favorable variable overhead efficiency variance.

8-7 Describe the difference between a direct materials efficiency variance and a variable manufacturing overhead efficiency variance.

8-8 What are the steps in developing a budgeted fixed overhead rate?

8-9 Why is the flexible-budget variance the same amount as the spending variance for fixed manufacturing overhead?

8-10 Explain how the analysis of fixed manufacturing overhead costs differs for (a) planning and control and (b) inventory costing for financial reporting.

8-11 Provide one caveat that will affect whether a production-volume variance is a good measure of the economic cost of unused capacity.

8-12 "The production-volume variance should always be written off to Cost of Goods Sold." Do you agree? Explain.

8-13 What are the variances in a 4-variance analysis?

8-14 "Overhead variances should be viewed as interdependent rather than independent." Give an example.

8-15 Describe how flexible-budget variance analysis can be used in the control of costs of activity areas.

Pearson MyLab Accounting

Multiple-Choice Questions

In partnership with:
BECKER
PROFESSIONAL EDUCATION®

8-16 Each of the following statements is correct regarding overhead variances except:

a. Actual overhead greater than applied overhead is unfavorable.

b. The efficiency overhead variance ignores the standard variable overhead rate.

c. Variable overhead rates are not a factor in the production-volume variance calculation.

d. Favorable spending and efficiency variances imply that the flexible budget variance must be favorable.

8-17 Steed Co. budgets production of 150,000 units in the next year. Steed's CFO expects that each unit will take 8 hours to produce at an hourly wage rate of $10 per hour. If factory overhead is applied on the basis of direct labor hours at $6 per hour, the budget for factory overhead will total:

a. $7,200,000.   c. $12,000,000.
b. $9,000,000.   d. $19,200,000.

8-18 As part of her annual review of her company's budgets versus actuals, Mary Gerard isolates unfavorable variances with the hope of getting a better understanding of what caused them and how to avoid them next year. The variable overhead efficiency variance was the most unfavorable over the previous year, which Gerard will specifically be able to trace to:

a. Actual overhead costs below applied overhead costs.
b. Actual production units below budgeted production units.
c. Standard direct labor hours below actual direct labor hours.
d. The standard variable overhead rate below the actual variable overhead rate.

8-19 Culpepper Corporation had the following inventories at the beginning and end of the month of January:

	January 1	January 31
Finished goods	$125,000	$117,000
Work-in-process	235,000	251,000
Direct materials	134,000	124,000

The following additional manufacturing data was available for the month of January.

Direct materials purchased	$189,000
Transportation in	3,000
Direct labor	400,000
Actual factory overhead	175,000

Culpepper Corporation applies factory overhead at a rate of 40% of direct labor cost, and any overapplied or underapplied factory overhead is deferred until the end of the year.
Culpepper's balance in its factory overhead control account at the end of January was:

1. $15,000 overapplied.   3. $5,000 underapplied.
2. $15,000 underapplied.   4. $5,000 overapplied.

8-20 Fordham Corporation produces a single product. The standard costs for one unit of its Concourse product are as follows:

Direct materials (6 pounds at $0.50 per pound)	$ 3
Direct labor (2 hours at $10 per hour)	20
Variable manufacturing overhead (2 hours at $5 per hour)	10
Total	33

During November Year 2, 4,000 units of Concourse were produced. The costs associated with November operations were as follows:

Material purchased (36,000 pounds at $0.60 per pound)	$21,600
Material used in production (28,000 pounds)	
Direct labor (8,200 hours at $9.75 per hour)	79,950
Variable manufacturing overhead incurred	41,820

What is the variable overhead efficiency variance for Concourse for November Year 2?

1. $2,000 favorable.   3. $1,000 favorable.
2. $2,000 unfavorable.   4. $1,000 unfavorable.

Exercises

8-21 Variable manufacturing overhead, variance analysis. Omega Arts is a manufacturer of designer vases. The cost of each vase is the sum of three variable costs (direct material costs, direct manufacturing labor costs, and manufacturing overhead costs) and one fixed-cost category (manufacturing overhead costs). Variable manufacturing overhead cost is allocated to each vase on the basis of budgeted direct manufacturing labor-hours per vase. For June 2017, each vase is budgeted to take 4 labor-hours. Budgeted variable manufacturing overhead cost per labor-hour is $14. The budgeted number of vases to be manufactured in June 2017 is 1,100.

Actual variable manufacturing costs in June 2017 were $65,205 for 1,150 vases started and completed. There were no beginning inventories or ending inventories for the vases. Actual direct manufacturing labor-hours for June were 4,830.

1. Compute the flexible-budget variance, the spending variance, and the efficiency variance for variable manufacturing overhead.
2. Comment on the results.

Required

8-22 Fixed-manufacturing overhead, variance analysis (continuation of 8-21). Omega Arts allocates fixed manufacturing overhead to each vase using budgeted direct manufacturing labor-hours per vase. Data pertaining to fixed manufacturing overhead costs for June 2017, are budgeted $70,400 and actual $72,200.

1. Compute the spending variance for fixed manufacturing overhead. Comment on the results.
2. Compute the production-volume variance for June 2017. What inferences can Omega Arts draw from this variance?

Required

8-23 Variable manufacturing overhead variance analysis. The French Bread Company bakes baguettes for distribution to upscale grocery stores. The company has two direct-cost categories: direct materials and direct manufacturing labor. Variable manufacturing overhead is allocated to products on the basis of standard direct manufacturing labor-hours. Following is some budget data for the French Bread Company:

Direct manufacturing labor use	0.02 hours per baguette
Variable manufacturing overhead	$10.00 per direct manufacturing labor-hour

The French Bread Company provides the following additional data for the year ended December 31, 2017:

Planned (budgeted) output	3,200,000 baguettes
Actual production	2,800,000 baguettes
Direct manufacturing labor	50,400 hours
Actual variable manufacturing overhead	$680,400

1. What is the denominator level used for allocating variable manufacturing overhead? (That is, for how many direct manufacturing labor-hours is French Bread budgeting?)
2. Prepare a variance analysis of variable manufacturing overhead. Use Exhibit 8-4 (page 324) for reference.
3. Discuss the variances you have calculated and give possible explanations for them.

Required

8-24 Fixed manufacturing overhead variance analysis (continuation of 8-23). The French Bread Company also allocates fixed manufacturing overhead to products on the basis of standard direct manufacturing labor-hours. For 2017, fixed manufacturing overhead was budgeted at $4.00 per direct manufacturing labor-hour. Actual fixed manufacturing overhead incurred during the year was $272,000.

1. Prepare a variance analysis of fixed manufacturing overhead cost. Use Exhibit 8-4 (page 324) as a guide.
2. Is fixed overhead underallocated or overallocated? By what amount?
3. Comment on your results. Discuss the variances and explain what may be driving them.

Required

8-25 Manufacturing overhead, variance analysis. The Principles Corporation is a manufacturer of centrifuges. Fixed and variable manufacturing overheads are allocated to each centrifuge using budgeted assembly-hours. Budgeted assembly time is 2 hours per unit. The following table shows the budgeted amounts and actual results related to overhead for June 2017.

		Home	Insert	Page Layout	Formulas	Data	Review	View
	A	B	C	D	E	F	G

	The Principles Corporation (June 2017)	Actual Results	Static Budget
1			
2	Number of centrifuges assembled and sold	225	110
3	Hours of assembly time	360	
4	Variable manufacturing overhead cost per hour of assembly time		$32.00
5	Variable manufacturing overhead costs	$11,933	
6	Fixed manufacturing overhead costs	$12,180	$10,780

Required

1. Prepare an analysis of all variable manufacturing overhead and fixed manufacturing overhead variances using the columnar approach in Exhibit 8-4 (page 324).
2. Prepare journal entries for Principles' June 2017 variable and fixed manufacturing overhead costs and variances; write off these variances to cost of goods sold for the quarter ending June 30, 2017.
3. How does the planning and control of variable manufacturing overhead costs differ from the planning and control of fixed manufacturing overhead costs?

8-26 4-variance analysis, fill in the blanks. Healthy Limited is a pharmaceutical and biotechnology company. It has the following data for manufacturing overhead costs during August 2018:

	Variable	Fixed
Actual costs incurred	$36,000	$20,000
Costs allocated to products	38,000	16,500
Flexible budget	–	15,000
Actual input × budgeted rate	35,600	–

Fill in the blanks. Use F for favorable and U for unfavorable:

	Variable	Fixed
(1) Spending variance	$_____	$_____
(2) Efficiency variance	_____	_____
(3) Production-volume variance	_____	_____
(4) Flexible-budget variance	_____	_____
(5) Underallocated (overallocated) manufacturing overhead	_____	_____

8-27 Straightforward 4-variance overhead analysis. The Lopez Company uses standard costing in its manufacturing plant for auto parts. The standard cost of a particular auto part, based on a denominator level of 4,000 output units per year, included 6 machine-hours of variable manufacturing overhead at $8 per hour and 6 machine-hours of fixed manufacturing overhead at $15 per hour. Actual output produced was 4,400 units. Variable manufacturing overhead incurred was $245,000. Fixed manufacturing overhead incurred was $373,000. Actual machine-hours were 28,400.

Required

1. Prepare an analysis of all variable manufacturing overhead and fixed manufacturing overhead variances, using the 4-variance analysis in Exhibit 8-4 (page 324).
2. Prepare journal entries using the 4-variance analysis.
3. Describe how individual fixed manufacturing overhead items are controlled from day to day.
4. Discuss possible causes of the fixed manufacturing overhead variances.

8-28 Straightforward coverage of manufacturing overhead, standard-costing system. The Singapore division of a Canadian telecommunications company uses standard costing for its machine-paced production of telephone equipment. Data regarding production during June are as follows:

Variable manufacturing overhead costs incurred	$618,840
Variable manufacturing overhead cost rate	$8 per standard machine-hour
Fixed manufacturing overhead costs incurred	$145,790
Fixed manufacturing overhead costs budgeted	$144,000
Denominator level in machine-hours	72,000
Standard machine-hour allowed per unit of output	1.2
Units of output	65,500
Actual machine-hours used	76,400
Ending work-in-process inventory	0

1. Prepare an analysis of all manufacturing overhead variances. Use the 4-variance analysis framework illustrated in Exhibit 8-4 (page 324).
2. Prepare journal entries for manufacturing overhead costs and their variances.
3. Describe how individual variable manufacturing overhead items are controlled from day to day.
4. Discuss possible causes of the variable manufacturing overhead variances.

8-29 Overhead variances, service sector. Hot Meals Now (HMN) operates a meal home-delivery service. It has agreements with 20 restaurants to pick up and deliver meals to customers who phone or fax orders to HMN. HMN allocates variable and fixed overhead costs on the basis of delivery time. HMN's owner, Asha Ahuja, obtains the following information for May 2017 overhead costs:

	Home	Insert	Page Layout	Formulas	Data	Review
	A				B	C
1	Easy Meals Now (May 2017)				Actual Results	Static Budget
2	Output units (number of deliveries)				8,600	12,000
3	Hours per delivery					0.70
4	Hours of delivery time				5,600	
5	Variable overhead cost per hour of delivery time					$1.75
6	Variable overhead costs				$11,320	
7	Fixed overhead costs				$39,600	$33,600

1. Compute spending and efficiency variances for HMN's variable overhead in May 2017.
2. Compute the spending variance and production-volume variance for HMN's fixed overhead in May 2017.
3. Comment on HMN's overhead variances and suggest how Asha Ahuja might manage HMN's variable overhead differently from its fixed overhead costs.

8-30 Total overhead, 3-variance analysis. XYZ automobiles, Inc. makes accessories primarily for cars. For 2017, budgeted variable overhead is $90,000 for 12,000 direct labor-hours. Budgeted total overhead is $110,000 at 8,000 direct labor-hours. The standard costs allocated to the production of these accessories included a total overhead rate of 80 percent of standard direct labor costs.

In May 2017, XYZ automobiles incurred total overhead of $160,000 and direct labor costs of $255,000. The direct labor efficiency variance was $9,000 unfavorable. The direct labor flexible-budget variance was $6,000 favorable. The standard labor price was $18 per hour. The production-volume variance was $50,050 favorable.

1. Compute the direct labor price variance.
2. Compute the denominator level and the spending and efficiency variances for total overhead.
3. Describe how individual variable overhead items are controlled from day to day. Also, describe how individual fixed overhead items are controlled.

8-31 Production-volume variance analysis and sales-volume variance. Marissa Designs, Inc., makes jewelry in the shape of geometric patterns. Each piece is handmade and takes an average of 1.5 hours to produce because of the intricate design and scrollwork. Marissa uses direct labor-hours to allocate the overhead cost to production. Fixed overhead costs, including rent, depreciation, supervisory salaries, and other production expenses, are budgeted at $10,800 per month. These costs are incurred for a facility large enough to produce 1,200 pieces of jewelry a month.

During the month of February, Marissa produced 720 pieces of jewelry and actual fixed costs were $11,400

1. Calculate the fixed overhead spending variance and indicate whether it is favorable (F) or unfavorable (U).
2. If Marissa uses direct labor-hours available at capacity to calculate the budgeted fixed overhead rate, what is the production-volume variance? Indicate whether it is favorable (F) or unfavorable (U).
3. An unfavorable production-volume variance could be interpreted as the economic cost of unused capacity. Why would Marissa be willing to incur this cost?
4. Marissa's budgeted variable cost per unit is $25, and it expects to sell its jewelry for $55 apiece. Compute the sales-volume variance and reconcile it with the production-volume variance calculated in requirement 2. What does each concept measure?

8-32 Overhead variances, service setting. Alpha Capital Company provides financial services to their clients. Recently, Alpha has experienced rapid growth rate due to expansion and is becoming concerned as to their rising costs, particularly their technology overhead costs.

Alpha had determined the cost driver of both their variable and fixed technology overhead costs to be the number of CPU units of their computer usage. Alpha's measure of "production" is the number of client interactions.

The technology budget for Alpha for the first quarter of 2017 are as follows:

Client interactions	13,000
Variable overhead	0.5 CPU units @ $3 per CPU unit
Fixed overhead	$19,500

The actual results for the first quarter of 2017 are:

Client interactions	14,500
Variable overhead	$22,000
Fixed overhead	$19,200
CPU units used	7,300

1. Calculate the variable overhead spending and efficiency variances, and indicate whether each is favorable (F) or unfavorable (U).
2. Calculate the fixed overhead spending and production volume variances, and indicate whether each is favorable (F) or unfavorable (U).
3. Comment on Alpha Capital's overhead variances. In your view, is the firm right to be worried about its control over technology spending?

8-33 Identifying favorable and unfavorable variances. Alma, Inc., manufactures high-pressure cleaners for large transportation companies. It uses standard costing and allocates variable and fixed manufacturing overhead based on machine-hours. For each independent scenario given, indicate whether each of the manufacturing variances will be favorable or unfavorable or, in case of insufficient information, indicate "CBD" (cannot be determined).

Scenario	Variable Overhead Spending Variance	Variable Overhead Efficiency Variance	Fixed Overhead Spending Variance	Fixed Overhead Production-Volume Variance
Production output is 6% less than budgeted, and actual fixed manufacturing overhead costs are 5% more than budgeted				
Production output is 13% less than budgeted; actual machine-hours are 7% more than budgeted				
Production output is 10% more than budgeted				
Actual machine-hours are 20% less than flexible-budget machine-hours				
Relative to the flexible budget, actual machine-hours are 15% less, and actual variable manufacturing overhead costs are 20% greater				

8-34 Flexible-budget variances, review of Chapters 7 and 8. Michael Roberts is a cost accountant and business analyst for Darby Design Company (DDC), which manufactures expensive brass doorknobs. DDC uses two direct-cost categories: direct materials and direct manufacturing labor. Roberts feels that manufacturing overhead is most closely related to material usage. Therefore, DDC allocates manufacturing overhead to production based upon pounds of materials used.

At the beginning of 2017, DDC budgeted annual production of 410,000 doorknobs and adopted the following standards for each doorknob:

	Input	Cost/Doorknob
Direct materials (brass)	0.3 lb. @ $9/lb.	$ 2.70
Direct manufacturing labor	1.2 hours @ $16/hour	19.20
Manufacturing overhead:		
Variable	$4/lb. × 0.3 lb.	1.20
Fixed	$14/lb. × 0.3 lb.	4.20
Standard cost per doorknob		$27.30

Actual results for April 2017 were as follows:

Production	32,000 doorknobs
Direct materials purchased	12,900 lb. at $10/lb.
Direct materials used	9,000 lbs.
Direct manufacturing labor	29,600 hours for $621,600
Variable manufacturing overhead	$ 64,900
Fixed manufacturing overhead	$160,000

1. For the month of April, compute the following variances, indicating whether each is favorable (F) or unfavorable (U):
   a. Direct materials price variance (based on purchases)
   b. Direct materials efficiency variance
   c. Direct manufacturing labor price variance
   d. Direct manufacturing labor efficiency variance
   e. Variable manufacturing overhead spending variance
   f. Variable manufacturing overhead efficiency variance
   g. Production-volume variance
   h. Fixed manufacturing overhead spending variance
2. Can Roberts use any of the variances to help explain any of the other variances? Give examples.

Required

Problems

Pearson MyLab Accounting

8-35 Comprehensive variance analysis. Chef Whiz manufactures premium food processors. The following are some manufacturing overhead data for Chef Whiz for the year ended December 31, 2017:

Manufacturing Overhead	Actual Results	Flexible Budget	Allocated Amount
Variable	$ 51,480	$ 79,950	$ 79,950
Fixed	350,210	343,980	380,250

Budgeted number of output units: 588

Planned allocation rate: 3 machine-hours per unit

Actual number of machine-hours used: 1,170

Static-budget variable manufacturing overhead costs: $72,324

Compute the following quantities (you should be able to do so in the prescribed order):

Required

1. Budgeted number of machine-hours planned
2. Budgeted fixed manufacturing overhead costs per machine-hour
3. Budgeted variable manufacturing overhead costs per machine-hour
4. Budgeted number of machine-hours allowed for actual output produced
5. Actual number of output units
6. Actual number of machine-hours used per output unit

8-36 Journal entries (continuation of 8-35).

1. Prepare journal entries for variable and fixed manufacturing overhead (you will need to calculate the various variances to accomplish this).
2. Overhead variances are written off to the Cost of Goods Sold (COGS) account at the end of the fiscal year. Show how COGS is adjusted through journal entries.

Required

8-37 Graphs and overhead variances. Best Around, Inc., is a manufacturer of vacuums and uses standard costing. Manufacturing overhead (both variable and fixed) is allocated to products on the basis of budgeted machine-hours. In 2017, budgeted fixed manufacturing overhead cost was $17,000,000. Budgeted variable manufacturing overhead was $10 per machine-hour. The denominator level was 1,000,000 machine-hours.

1. Prepare a graph for fixed manufacturing overhead. The graph should display how Best Around, Inc.'s fixed manufacturing overhead costs will be depicted for the purposes of (a) planning and control and (b) inventory costing.
2. Suppose that 1,125,000 machine-hours were allowed for actual output produced in 2017, but 1,200,000 actual machine-hours were used. Actual manufacturing overhead was $12,075,000, variable, and $17,100,000, fixed. Compute (a) the variable manufacturing overhead spending and efficiency variances and (b) the fixed manufacturing overhead spending and production-volume variances. Use the columnar presentation illustrated in Exhibit 8-4 (page 324).

Required

3. What is the amount of the under- or overallocated variable manufacturing overhead and the under- or overallocated fixed manufacturing overhead? Why are the flexible-budget variance and the under- or overallocated overhead amount always the same for variable manufacturing overhead but rarely the same for fixed manufacturing overhead?

4. Suppose the denominator level was 1,700,000 rather than 1,000,000 machine-hours. What variances in requirement 2 would be affected? Recompute them.

8-38 Overhead variance, missing information. Consider the following two situations—cases A and B—independently. Data refer to operations for April 2017. For each situation, assume standard costing. Also assume the use of a flexible budget for control of variable and fixed manufacturing overhead based on machine-hours.

		Cases	
		A	B
(1)	Fixed manufacturing overhead incurred	$ 84,920	$ 23,180
(2)	Variable manufacturing overhead incurred	$120,400	—
(3)	Denominator level in machine-hours	—	1,000
(4)	Standard machine-hours allowed for actual output achieved	6,200	—
(5)	Fixed manufacturing overhead (per standard machine-hour)	—	—
Flexible-Budget Data:			
(6)	Variable manufacturing overhead (per standard machine-hour)	—	$ 42.00
(7)	Budgeted fixed manufacturing overhead	$ 88,200	$ 20,000
(8)	Budgeted variable manufacturing overhead[a]	—	—
(9)	Total budgeted manufacturing overhead[a]	—	—
Additional Data:			
(10)	Standard variable manufacturing overhead allocated	$124,000	—
(11)	Standard fixed manufacturing overhead allocated	$ 86,800	—
(12)	Production-volume variance	—	$ 4,000 F
(13)	Variable manufacturing overhead spending variance	$ 5,000 F	$ 2,282 F
(14)	Variable manufacturing overhead efficiency variance	—	$ 2,478 F
(15)	Fixed manufacturing overhead spending variance	—	—
(16)	Actual machine-hours used	—	—

[a]For standard machine-hours allowed for actual output produced.

Required

Fill in the blanks under each case. [*Hint*: Prepare a worksheet similar to that in Exhibit 8-4 (page 324). Fill in the knowns and then solve for the unknowns.]

8-39 Flexible budgets, 4-variance analysis. (CMA, adapted) Wilson Products uses standard costing. It allocates manufacturing overhead (both variable and fixed) to products on the basis of standard direct manufacturing labor-hours (DLH). Wilson Products develops its manufacturing overhead rate from the current annual budget. The manufacturing overhead budget for 2017 is based on budgeted output of 672,000 units, requiring 3,360,000 DLH. The company is able to schedule production uniformly throughout the year.

A total of 72,000 output units requiring 321,000 DLH was produced during May 2017. Manufacturing overhead (MOH) costs incurred for May amounted to $355,800. The actual costs, compared with the annual budget and 1/12 of the annual budget, are as follows:

Annual Manufacturing Overhead Budget 2017

	Total Amount	Per Output Unit	Per DLH Input Unit	Monthly MOH Budget May 2017	Actual MOH Costs for May 2017
Variable MOH					
Indirect manufacturing labor	$1,008,000	$1.50	$0.30	$ 84,000	$ 84,000
Supplies	672,000	1.00	0.20	56,000	117,000
Fixed MOH					
Supervision	571,200	0.85	0.17	47,600	41,000
Utilities	369,600	0.55	0.11	30,800	55,000
Depreciation	705,600	1.05	0.21	58,800	88,800
Total	$3,326,400	$4.95	$0.99	$277,200	$355,800

Calculate the following amounts for Wilson Products for May 2017:

Required

1. Total manufacturing overhead costs allocated
2. Variable manufacturing overhead spending variance
3. Fixed manufacturing overhead spending variance
4. Variable manufacturing overhead efficiency variance
5. Production-volume variance
   Be sure to identify each variance as favorable (F) or unfavorable (U).

8-40 Activity-based costing, batch-level variance analysis. Omega's Fleet Feet, Inc., produces dance shoes for stores all over the world. While the pairs of shoes are boxed individually, they are crated and shipped in batches. The shipping department records both variable direct batch-level costs and fixed batch-level overhead costs. The following information pertains to shipping department costs for 2017.

	Static-Budget Amounts	Actual Results
Pairs of shoes shipped	300,000	270,000
Average number of pairs of shoes per crate	15	10
Packing hours per crate	1 hour	1.2 hours
Variable direct cost per hour	$20	$18
Fixed overhead cost	60,000	62,000

Required

1. What is the static budget number of crates for 2017?
2. What is the flexible budget number of crates for 2017?
3. What is the actual number of crates shipped in 2017?
4. Assuming fixed overhead is allocated using crate-packing hours, what is the predetermined fixed over-head allocation rate?
5. For variable direct batch-level costs, compute the price and efficiency variances.
6. For fixed overhead costs, compute the spending and the production-volume variances.

8-41 Overhead variances and sales-volume variance. The Roller Bag Company manufactures extremely light and rolling suitcases. It was one of the first companies to produce rolling suitcases and sales have increased for the past several years. In 2017, Roller Bag budgeted to sell 150,000 suitcases for $80 each.

The budgeted standard machine hours for production in 2017 were 375,000 machine hours. Budgeted fixed overhead costs are $525,000, and variable overhead cost was budgeted at $1.75 per machine-hour.

In 2017, Roller Bag experienced a drop in sales due to increased competition for rolling suitcases. Roller Bag used 310,000 machine-hours to produce the 120,000 suitcases it sold in 2017. Actual variable overhead costs were $488,000 and actual fixed overhead costs were $532,400. The average selling price of the suitcases sold in 2017 was $72.

Actual direct materials and direct labor costs were the same as standard costs, which were $20 per unit and $18 per unit, respectively.

Required

1. Calculate the variable overhead and fixed overhead variances (spending, efficiency, spending, and volume).
2. Create a chart like that in Exhibit 7-2 showing Flexible Budget Variances and Sales-Volume Variances for revenues, costs, contribution margin, and operating income.
3. Calculate the operating income based on budgeted profit per suitcase.
4. Reconcile the budgeted operating income from requirement 3 to the actual operating income from your chart in requirement 2.
5. Calculate the operating income volume variance and show how the sales-volume variance is composed of the production-volume variance and the operating income volume variance.

8-42 Activity-based costing, batch-level variance analysis. The Saluki Company specializes in making fraternity and sorority T-shirts for the college market. Due to the high setup costs for each batch printed, Saluki holds the T-shirt requests until demand is approximately 100 shirts. At that point Saluki will schedule the setup and production of the shirts. For rush orders, Saluki will produce smaller batches for an additional charge of $175 per setup.

Budgeted and actual costs for the production process for 2017 were as follows:

	Static-Budget Amounts	Actual Results
Number of shirts produced	125,000	114,000
Average number of shirts per setup	100	95
Hours to set up machines	5	5.20
Direct variable cost per setup-hour	$ 30	$ 32
Total fixed setup overhead costs	$56,250	$56,000

Required

1. What is the static budget number of setups for 2017?
2. What is the flexible-budget number of setups for 2017?
3. What is the actual number of setups in 2017?
4. Assuming fixed setup overhead costs are allocated using setup-hours, what is the predetermined fixed setup overhead allocation rate?
5. Does Saluki's charge of $175 cover the budgeted direct variable cost of an order? The budgeted total cost?
6. For direct variable setup costs, compute the price and efficiency variances.
7. For fixed setup overhead costs, compute the spending and the production-volume variances.
8. What qualitative factors should Saluki consider before accepting or rejecting a special order?

8-43 Comprehensive review of Chapters 7 and 8, working backward from given variances. The Gallo Company uses a flexible budget and standard costs to aid planning and control of its machining manufacturing operations. Its costing system for manufacturing has two direct-cost categories (direct materials and direct manufacturing labor—both variable) and two overhead-cost categories (variable manufacturing overhead and fixed manufacturing overhead, both allocated using direct manufacturing labor-hours).

At the 50,000 budgeted direct manufacturing labor-hour level for August, budgeted direct manufacturing labor is $1,250,000, budgeted variable manufacturing overhead is $500,000, and budgeted fixed manufacturing overhead is $1,000,000.

The following actual results are for August:

Direct materials price variance (based on purchases)	$179,300 F
Direct materials efficiency variance	75,900 U
Direct manufacturing labor costs incurred	535,500
Variable manufacturing overhead flexible-budget variance	10,400 U
Variable manufacturing overhead efficiency variance	18,100 U
Fixed manufacturing overhead incurred	957,550

The standard cost per pound of direct materials is $11.50. The standard allowance is 6 pounds of direct materials for each unit of product. During August, 20,000 units of product were produced. There was no beginning inventory of direct materials. There was no beginning or ending work in process. In August, the direct materials price variance was $1.10 per pound.

In July, labor unrest caused a major slowdown in the pace of production, resulting in an unfavorable direct manufacturing labor efficiency variance of $40,000. There was no direct manufacturing labor price variance. Labor unrest persisted into August. Some workers quit. Their replacements had to be hired at higher wage rates, which had to be extended to all workers. The actual average wage rate in August exceeded the standard average wage rate by $0.50 per hour.

Required

1. Compute the following for August:
   a. Total pounds of direct materials purchased
   b. Total number of pounds of excess direct materials used
   c. Variable manufacturing overhead spending variance
   d. Total number of actual direct manufacturing labor-hours used
   e. Total number of standard direct manufacturing labor-hours allowed for the units produced
   f. Production-volume variance
2. Describe how Gallo's control of variable manufacturing overhead items differs from its control of fixed manufacturing overhead items.

8-44 Review of Chapters 7 and 8, 3-variance analysis. (CPA, adapted) The Beal Manufacturing Company's costing system has two direct-cost categories: direct materials and direct manufacturing labor. Manufacturing overhead (both variable and fixed) is allocated to products on the basis of standard direct manufacturing labor-hours (DLH). At the beginning of 2017, Beal adopted the following standards for its manufacturing costs:

	Input	Cost per Output Unit
Direct materials	5 lb. at $4 per lb.	$ 20.00
Direct manufacturing labor	4 hrs. at $16 per hr.	64.00
Manufacturing overhead:		
Variable	$8 per DLH	32.00
Fixed	$9 per DLH	36.00
Standard manufacturing cost per output unit		$152.00

The denominator level for total manufacturing overhead per month in 2017 is 37,000 direct manufacturing labor-hours. Beal's budget for January 2017 was based on this denominator level. The records for January indicated the following:

Direct materials purchased	40,300 lb. at $3.80 per lb.
Direct materials used	37,300 lb.
Direct manufacturing labor	31,400 hrs. at $16.25 per hr.
Total actual manufacturing overhead (variable and fixed)	$650,000
Actual production	7,600 output units

1. Prepare a schedule of total standard manufacturing costs for the 7,600 output units in January 2017.
2. For the month of January 2017, compute the following variances, indicating whether each is favorable (F) or unfavorable (U):
   a. Direct materials price variance, based on purchases
   b. Direct materials efficiency variance
   c. Direct manufacturing labor price variance
   d. Direct manufacturing labor efficiency variance
   e. Total manufacturing overhead spending variance
   f. Variable manufacturing overhead efficiency variance
   g. Production-volume variance

8-45 Nonfinancial variances. Kathy's Kettle Potato Chips produces gourmet chips distributed to chain sub shops throughout California. To ensure that their chips are of the highest quality and have taste appeal, Kathy has a rigorous inspection process. For quality control purposes, Kathy has a standard based on the number of pounds of chips inspected per hour and the number of pounds that pass or fail the inspection.

Kathy expects that for every 1,000 pounds of chips produced, 200 pounds of chips will be inspected. Inspection of 200 pounds of chips should take 1 hour. Kathy also expects that 1% of the chips inspected will fail the inspection. During the month of May, Kathy produced 113,000 pounds of chips and inspected 22,300 pounds of chips in 120 hours. Of the 22,300 pounds of chips inspected, 215 pounds of chips failed to pass the inspection.

1. Compute two variances that help determine whether the time spent on inspections was more or less than expected. (Follow a format similar to the one used for the variable overhead spending and efficiency variances, but without prices.)
2. Compute two variances that can be used to evaluate the percentage of the chips that fails the inspection.

8-46 Overhead variances, service sector. Cavio is a cloud service provider that offers computing resources to handle enterprise-wide applications. For March 2017, Cavio estimates that it will provide 18,000 RAM hours of services to clients. The budgeted variable overhead rate is $6 per RAM hour.

At the end of March, there is a $500 favorable spending variance for variable overhead and a $1,575 unfavorable spending variance for fixed overhead. For the services actually provided during the month, 14,850 RAM hours are budgeted and 15,000 RAM hours are actually used. Total actual overhead costs are $119,875.

1. Compute efficiency and flexible-budget variances for Cavio's variable overhead in March 2017. Will variable overhead be over- or underallocated? By how much?
2. Compute production-volume and flexible-budget variances for Cavio's fixed overhead in March 2017. Will fixed overhead be over- or underallocated? By how much?

8-47 Direct-cost and overhead variances, income statement. The Delta Company started business on January 1, 2017. The company adopted a standard absorption costing system for the production of ergonomic backpacks. Delta chose direct labor as the application base for overhead and decided to use the proration method to account for variances at year-end.

In 2017, Delta expected to make and sell 180,000 backpacks; each was budgeted to use 2 yards of fabric and require 0.5 hours of direct labor work. The company expected to pay $3 per yard for fabric and compensate workers at an hourly wage of $18. Delta has no variable overhead costs, but expected to spend $400,000 on fixed manufacturing overhead in 2017.

In 2017, Delta actually made 200,000 backpacks and sold 160,000 of them for a total revenue of $4,000,000. The costs incurred were as follows:

Fixed manufacturing costs	$ 450,000
Fabric costs (410,000 yards bought and used)	$1,250,500
Direct labor costs (100,000 hours)	$1,795,000

1. Compute the following variances for 2017, and indicate whether each is favorable (F) or unfavorable (U):
   a. Direct materials efficiency variance
   b. Direct materials price variance
   c. Direct labor efficiency variance
   d. Direct labor price variance
   e. Total manufacturing overhead spending variance
   f. Fixed overhead flexible budget variance
   g. Fixed overhead production-volume variance
2. Compute Delta Company's gross margin for its first year of operation.

8-48 Overhead variances, ethics. BlueBox Company uses standard costing. The company has two manufacturing plants, one in Shanghai and the other in Shenzhen. For the Shanghai plant, BlueBox has budgeted annual output of 2,000,000 units. Standard labor-hours per unit are 0.50, and the variable overhead rate for the Shanghai plant is $3.30 per direct labor-hour. Fixed overhead for the Shanghai plant is budgeted at $2,400,000 for the year.

For the Shenzhen plant, BlueBox has budgeted annual output of 2,100,000 units with standard labor-hours also 0.50 per unit. However, the variable overhead rate for the Shenzhen plant is $3.10 per hour, and the budgeted fixed overhead for the year is only $2,205,000.

Firm management has always used variance analysis as a performance measure for the two plants and has compared the results of the two plants.

Ken Wooi Keong has just been hired as a new controller for BlueBox. Ken is good friends with the Shenzhen plant manager and wants him to get a favorable review. Ken suggests allocating the firm's budgeted common fixed costs of $3,150,000 to the two plants, but on the basis of one-third to the Shenzhen plant and two-thirds to the Shanghai plant. His explanation for this allocation base is that Shanghai is a more expensive state than Shenzhen.

At the end of the year, the Shanghai plant reported the following actual results: output of 1,950,000 using 1,020,000 labor-hours in total, at a cost of $3,264,000 in variable overhead and $2,440,000 in fixed overhead.

Actual results for the Shenzhen plant are an output of 2,175,000 units using 1,225,000 labor-hours with a variable cost of $3,920,000 and fixed overhead cost of $2,300,000. The actual common fixed costs for the year were $3,075,000.

1. Compute the budgeted fixed cost per labor-hour for the fixed overhead separately for each plant:
   a. Excluding allocated common fixed costs
   b. Including allocated common fixed costs
2. Compute the variable overhead spending variance and the variable overhead efficiency variance separately for each plant.
3. Compute the fixed overhead spending and volume variances for each plant:
   a. Excluding allocated common fixed costs
   b. Including allocated common fixed costs
4. Did Ken Wooi Keong's attempt to make the Shenzhen plant look better than the Shanghai plant by allocating common fixed costs work? Why or why not?
5. Should common fixed costs be allocated in general when variances are used as performance measures? Why or why not?
6. What do you think of Ken Wooi Keong's behavior overall?

11 ▶ Decision Making and Relevant Information

How many decisions have you made today?

Maybe you made a big decision, such as investing in a mutual fund. Or maybe your decision was as simple as buying a coffee maker or choosing a restaurant for dinner. Regardless of whether decisions are significant or routine, the decision process often includes evaluating the costs and benefits of each choice. For decisions that involve costs, some costs are irrelevant. For example, once you purchase a coffee maker, its cost is irrelevant when calculating how much money you save each time you brew coffee at home versus buy it at Starbucks. You incurred the cost of the coffee maker in the past, and you can't recoup that cost. This chapter will explain which costs and benefits are relevant and which are not—and how you should think of them when choosing among alternatives.

RELEVANT COSTS AND BROADWAY SHOWS[1]

The incremental cost to a Broadway producer for an additional customer to attend a Broadway musical like "Hamilton" is incredibly small. Most of the costs (actor fees, performance sets, theater rental, and publicity and marketing) are fixed weeks and months in advance of the performance. An orchestra ticket for "Hamilton" sells for $177. But because incremental costs are so small, is it worthwhile for the show's producer to sell tickets considerably below this price to avoid having empty seats that earning nothing?

If demand is high and the show is sold out, the producer would not sell tickets for anything less than $177 because there are theatergoers willing to pay full price to see the show. But if on the day before the show, it appears as though the venue will not be full, the producer may be willing to lower ticket prices significantly in hopes of attracting more theatergoers and earning a profit on the unfilled seats.

Enter TKTS. The famous discount ticket booth in Times Square sells same-day tickets to Broadway musicals, plays, and dance productions for up to 50% of face value. Ticket availability changes every day depending on demand and theatergoers can browse real-time listings on the TKTS mobile app.

Francis Vachon/Alamy Stock Photo

[1] Haley Goldberg, "You won't believe what these fans are doing for 'Hamilton' tickets," *New York Post*, November 13, 2015 (http://nypost.com/2015/11/13/you-wont-believe-what-these-fans-are-doing-for-hamilton-tickets/); Pia Catton, "For Broadway, 2015 Was a Mixed Bag," *The Wall Street Journal*, January 4, 2016 (http://www.wsj.com/articles/for-broadway-2015-was-a-mixed-bag-1451958995); Musical Workshop, "Production Costs and ROI of Theatrical Shows—From Broadway to West End," (http://www.musicalworkshop.org/workshop/production-costs-and-roi-of-theatrical-shows-from-broadway-to-west-end/), accessed March 2016; Theatre Development Fund, "TKTS Ticket Booths" (https://www.tdf.org/nyc/7/TKTS-Overview), accessed March 2016.

Just like on Broadway, managers at corporations around the world use their deep understanding of costs to make decisions. Managers at JPMorgan Chase gather information about financial markets, consumer preferences, and economic trends before determining whether to offer new services to customers. Managers at Macy's examine all the relevant information related to domestic and international clothing manufacturing before selecting vendors. Managers at Porsche gather cost information to decide whether to manufacture a component part or purchase it from a supplier. The decision process may not always be easy, but as Peter Drucker said, "Wherever you see a successful business, someone once made a courageous decision."

Information and the Decision Process

Managers usually follow a *decision model* for choosing among different courses of action. A **decision model** is a formal method of making a choice that often involves both quantitative and qualitative analyses. Management accountants analyze and present relevant data to guide managers' decisions.

Consider a strategic decision facing managers at Precision Sporting Goods, a manufacturer of golf clubs: Should the company reorganize its manufacturing operations to reduce manufacturing labor costs? Precision Sporting Goods has only two alternatives: do not reorganize or reorganize.

Reorganization will eliminate all manual handling of materials. Current manufacturing labor consists of 20 workers: 15 workers operate machines and 5 workers handle materials. The 5 materials-handling workers have been hired on contracts that permit layoffs without additional payments. Each worker works 2,000 hours annually. Reorganization is predicted to cost $90,000 each year (mostly for new equipment leases). The reorganization will not affect the production output of 25,000 units, the selling price of $250, the direct material cost per unit of $50, manufacturing overhead of $750,000, or marketing costs of $2,000,000.

Managers use the five-step decision-making process presented in Exhibit 11-1 and first introduced in Chapter 1 to make this decision. Study the sequence of steps in this exhibit and note how managers make no reference to information about production volumes, selling price, and costs that are unaffected by the decision. Step 5 evaluates performance to provide feedback about actions taken in the previous steps. This feedback might affect future predictions, the prediction methods used, the way choices are made, or the implementation of the decision.

LEARNING OBJECTIVE 1

Use the five-step decision-making process

...the five steps are identifying the problem and uncertainties; obtaining information; making predictions about the future; making decisions by choosing among alternatives; and implementing the decision, evaluating performance, and learning

DECISION POINT

What is the five-step process that managers can use to make decisions?

The Concept of Relevance

Much of this chapter focuses on Step 4 in Exhibit 11-1 and on the concepts of relevant costs and relevant revenues when choosing among alternatives.

LEARNING OBJECTIVE 2

Distinguish relevant from irrelevant information in decision situations

...only costs and revenues that are expected to occur in the future and differ among alternative courses of action are relevant

Relevant Costs and Relevant Revenues

Relevant costs are *expected future costs* and **relevant revenues** are *expected future revenues* that differ among the alternative courses of action being considered. Costs and revenues that are *not relevant* are called *irrelevant*. It is important to recognize that relevant costs and relevant revenues *must*:

- **Occur in the future**—every decision deals with a manager selecting a course of action based on its expected future results.
- **Differ among the alternative courses of action**—future costs and revenues that do not differ will not matter and, therefore, will have no bearing on the decision being made.

The question is always, "What difference will a particular action make?"

Exhibit 11-2 presents the financial data underlying the choice between the do-not-reorganize and reorganize alternatives for Precision Sporting Goods. Managers can analyze the data in two ways: by considering "all costs and revenues" or considering only "relevant costs and revenues."

EXHIBIT 11-1

Five-Step Decision-Making
Process for Precision
Sporting Goods

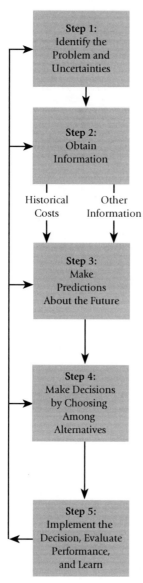

Should Precision Sporting Goods reorganize its
manufacturing operations to reduce manufacturing
labor costs? An important uncertainty is how the
reorganization will affect employee morale.

Step 1:
Identify the
Problem and
Uncertainties

Historical hourly wage rates are $14 per hour. However, a
recently negotiated increase in employee benefits of $2 per
hour will increase wages to $16 per hour. The reorganization
of manufacturing operations is expected to reduce the number
of workers from 20 to 15 by eliminating all 5 workers who
handle materials. The reorganization is likely to have negative
effects on employee morale.

Step 2:
Obtain
Information

Historical   Other
Costs   Information

Managers use information from Step 2 as a basis for predicting
future manufacturing labor costs. Under the existing do-not-
reorganize alternative, costs are predicted to be $640,000
(20 workers × 2,000 hours per worker per year × $16 per
hour), and under the reorganize alternative, costs are predicted
to be $480,000 (15 workers × 2,000 hours per worker per
year × $16 per hour). Recall, the reorganization is predicted
to cost $90,000 per year.

Step 3:
Make
Predictions
About the Future

Managers compare the predicted benefits calculated in Step 3
($640,000 − $480,000 = $160,000—that is, savings from
eliminating materials-handling labor costs, 5 workers × 2,000
hours per worker per year × $16 per hour = $160,000) against
the cost of the reorganization ($90,000) along with other
considerations (such as likely negative effects on employee
morale). Management chooses the reorganize alternative
because the financial benefits are significant and the effects on
employee morale are expected to be temporary and relatively small.

Step 4:
Make Decisions
by Choosing
Among
Alternatives

Evaluating performance after the decision is implemented
provides critical feedback for managers, and the five-step
sequence is then repeated in whole or in part. Managers
learn from actual results that the new manufacturing labor
costs are $540,000, rather than the predicted $480,000, because
of lower-than-expected manufacturing labor productivity. They
also learn about the effects on employee morale. This (now)
historical information can help managers make better subsequent
predictions. Managers will also try to improve implementation
via employee training, increased employee engagement,
and better supervision.

Step 5:
Implement the
Decision, Evaluate
Performance,
and Learn

The first two columns describe the first way and present *all data*. The last two columns
describe the second way and present *only relevant costs*: the $640,000 and $480,000 expected
future manufacturing labor costs and the $90,000 expected future reorganization costs that dif-
fer between the two alternatives. Managers can ignore the revenues, direct materials, manufacturing overhead, and marketing items because these costs will remain the same whether or not
Precision Sporting Goods reorganizes. These costs do not differ between the alternatives and,
therefore, are irrelevant.

Notice that the past (historical) manufacturing hourly wage rate of $14 and total past
(historical) manufacturing labor costs of $560,000 (20 workers × 2,000 hours per worker
per year × $14 per hour) do not appear in Exhibit 11-2. *Although they may be a useful basis
for making informed predictions of the expected future manufacturing labor costs of $640,000
and $480,000, historical costs themselves are past costs that, therefore, are irrelevant to deci-
sion making.* Past costs are also called **sunk costs** because they are unavoidable and cannot be
changed no matter what action is taken.

The analysis in Exhibit 11-2 indicates that reorganizing the manufacturing operations
will increase predicted operating income by $70,000 each year. Note that the managers at

EXHIBIT 11-2   Determining Relevant Revenues and Relevant Costs
for Precision Sporting Goods

	All Revenues and Costs		Relevant Revenues and Costs	
	Alternative 1: Do Not Reorganize	**Alternative 2:** Reorganize	**Alternative 1:** Do Not Reorganize	**Alternative 2:** Reorganize
Revenues[a]	$6,250,000	$6,250,000	—	—
Costs:				
Direct materials[b]	1,250,000	1,250,000	—	—
Manufacturing labor	640,000[c]	480,000[d]	$ 640,000[c]	$ 480,000[d]
Manufacturing overhead	750,000	750,000	—	—
Marketing	2,000,000	2,000,000	—	—
Reorganization costs	—	90,000	—	90,000
Total costs	4,640,000	4,570,000	640,000	570,000
Operating income	$1,610,000	$1,680,000	$(640,000)	$(570,000)

$70,000 Difference $70,000 Difference

[a]25,000 units × $250 per unit = $6,250,000   [c]20 workers × 2,000 hours per worker × $16 per hour = $640,000
[b]25,000 units × $50 per unit = $1,250,000   [d]15 workers × 2,000 hours per worker × $16 per hour = $480,000

Precision Sporting Goods reach the same conclusion whether they use all data or include only relevant data in the analysis. By confining the analysis to only relevant data, managers can clear away the clutter of potentially confusing irrelevant data. Focusing on relevant data is especially helpful when all the information needed to prepare a detailed income statement is unavailable. Understanding which costs are relevant and which are irrelevant helps the decision maker concentrate on obtaining only the pertinent data.

Qualitative and Quantitative Relevant Information

Managers divide the outcomes of decisions into two broad categories: *quantitative* and *qualitative*. **Quantitative factors** are outcomes that are measured in numerical terms. Some quantitative factors are financial; they can be expressed in monetary terms. Examples include the cost of direct materials, direct manufacturing labor, and marketing. Other quantitative factors are nonfinancial; they can be measured numerically, but they are not expressed in monetary terms. Examples include reduction in new product-development time for companies such as Microsoft and the percentage of on-time flight arrivals for companies such as JetBlue. **Qualitative factors** are outcomes that are difficult to measure accurately in numerical terms. Employee morale is an example.

Relevant-cost analysis generally emphasizes quantitative factors that can be expressed in financial terms. *Although quantitative nonfinancial factors and qualitative factors are difficult to measure in financial terms, they are important for managers to consider.* In the Precision Sporting Goods example, managers carefully considered the negative effect on employee morale of laying off materials-handling workers, a qualitative factor, before choosing the reorganize alternative. It is often difficult for managers to consider and trade off nonfinancial and financial considerations. For example, the benefits of decisions to reduce environmental impacts include the reputation benefits of these actions with consumers, employees, and investors. These benefits are not easy to measure but are relevant and important for managers to evaluate and weigh against the costs of reducing harmful environmental effluents. Managers must consider all the consequences of their decisions and not focus on financial factors alone.

Exhibit 11-3 summarizes the key features of relevant information that apply to all decision situations. We present some of these decision situations in this chapter. Later chapters describe other decision situations that require managers to apply the relevance concept, such as joint

| **EXHIBIT 11-3** | Key Features of Relevant Information |

- Past (historical) costs may be helpful as a basis for making *predictions*. However, past costs themselves are always irrelevant when making *decisions*.
- Different alternatives can be compared by examining differences in expected total future revenues and expected total future costs.
- Not all expected future revenues and expected future costs are relevant. Expected future revenues and expected future costs that do not differ among alternatives are irrelevant and, therefore, can be eliminated from the analysis. The key question is always, "What difference will an action make?"
- Appropriate weight must be given to qualitative factors and quantitative nonfinancial factors.

costs (Chapter 16); quality and timeliness (Chapter 19); inventory management and supplier evaluation (Chapter 20); capital investment (Chapter 21); and transfer pricing (Chapter 22). We start our discussion on relevance by considering a decision that affects output levels, such as whether to introduce a new product or to try to sell more units of an existing product.

One-Time-Only Special Orders

One type of decision that affects output levels involves accepting or rejecting special orders when there is idle production capacity and the special orders have no long-run implications. We use the term **one-time-only special order** to describe these conditions.

> **Example 1:** Surf Gear manufactures quality beach towels at its highly auto-mated Burlington, North Carolina, plant. The plant has a production capacity of 45,000 towels each month. Current monthly production is 30,000 towels. Retail department stores account for all existing sales. Exhibit 11-4 shows the expected results for the coming month (August). (These amounts are predictions based on past costs.) We assume that in the short run all costs can be classified as either fixed or variable for a single cost driver (units of output).
>
> Azelia is a luxury hotel chain that purchases towels from Mugar Corporation. The workers at Mugar are on strike, so Azelia must find a new supplier. In August, Azelia contacts Surf Gear and offers to buy 5,000 towels from them at $11 per towel. Based on the following facts, should Surf Gear's managers accept Azelia's offer?

The management accountant gathers the following additional information.

- No subsequent sales to Azelia are anticipated.
- Fixed manufacturing costs are based on the 45,000-towel production capacity. That is, fixed manufacturing costs relate to the production capacity available and not the actual capacity used. If Surf Gear accepts the special order, it will use existing idle capacity to produce the 5,000 towels and fixed manufacturing costs will not change.
- No marketing costs will be necessary for the 5,000-unit one-time-only special order.
- Accepting this special order is not expected to affect the selling price or the quantity of towels sold to regular customers.

The management accountant prepares the data shown in Exhibit 11-4 on an absorption-costing basis (that is, as required by Generally Accepted Accounting Principles (GAAP), both variable and fixed manufacturing costs are included in inventoriable costs and cost of goods sold). In this exhibit, therefore, the manufacturing cost of $12 per unit and the marketing cost of $7 per unit include both variable and fixed costs. The sum of all costs (variable and fixed) in a particular business function of the value chain, such as manufacturing costs or marketing costs, are called **business function costs**. **Full costs of the product**, in this case $19 per unit, are the sum of all variable and fixed costs in all business functions of the value chain (R&D,

	A	B	C	D
1		Total	Per Unit	
2	Units sold	30,000		
3				
4	Revenues	$600,000	$20.00	
5	Cost of goods sold (manufacturing costs)			
6	Variable manufacturing costs	225,000	7.50[b]	
7	Fixed manufacturing costs	135,000	4.50[c]	
8	Total cost of goods sold	360,000	12.00	
9	Marketing costs[a]			
10	Variable marketing costs	150,000	5.00	
11	Fixed marketing costs	60,000	2.00	
12	Total marketing costs	210,000	7.00	
13	Full costs of the product	570,000	19.00	
14	Operating income	$ 30,000	$ 1.00	
15				
16	[a]Surf Gear incurs no R&D, product-design, distribution, or customer-service costs			
17	[b]Variable manufacturing	Direct material	Variable direct manufacturing	Variable manufacturing
18	cost per unit −	cost per unit +	labor cost per unit +	overhead cost per unit
19	= $6.00 + $0.50 + $1.00 = $7.50			
20	[c]Fixed manufacturing	Fixed direct manufacturing	Fixed manufacturing	
21	cost per unit =	labor cost per unit +	overhead cost per unit	
22	= $1.50 + $3.00 = $4.50			

design, production, marketing, distribution, and customer service). For Surf Gear, full costs of the product consist of costs in manufacturing and marketing because these are the only business functions. Because no marketing costs are necessary for the special order, the manager of Surf Gear will focus only on manufacturing costs. Based on the manufacturing cost per unit of $12, which is greater than the $11-per-unit price Azelia offered, the manager might decide to reject the offer.

In Exhibit 11-5, the management accountant separates manufacturing and marketing costs into their variable- and fixed-cost components and presents data in the format of a contribution income statement. The relevant revenues and costs are the expected future revenues and costs that differ as a result of Surf Gear accepting the special offer: revenues of $55,000 ($11 per unit × 5,000 units) and variable manufacturing costs of $37,500 ($7.50 per unit × 5,000 units). The fixed manufacturing costs and all marketing costs (*including variable marketing costs*) are irrelevant in this case because these costs will not change in total whether the special order is accepted or rejected. Surf Gear would gain an additional $17,500 (relevant revenues, $55,000 − relevant costs, $37,500) in operating income by accepting the special order. In this example, by comparing total amounts for 30,000 units versus 35,000 units or focusing only on the relevant amounts in the difference column in Exhibit 11-5, the manager avoids a misleading implication: to reject the special order because the $11-per-unit selling price is lower than the manufacturing cost per unit of $12 (Exhibit 11-4), which includes both variable and fixed manufacturing costs.

The assumption of no long-run or strategic implications is crucial to a manager's analysis of the one-time-only special-order decision. Suppose the manager concludes that the retail department stores (Surf Gear's regular customers) will demand a lower price if Surf Gear sells towels at $11 apiece to Azelia. In this case, revenues from regular customers will be relevant. Why? Because the future revenues from regular customers will differ depending on whether Surf Gear accepts the special order. The Surf Gear manager would need to modify the relevant-revenue and relevant-cost analysis of the Azelia order to consider both the short-run benefits from accepting the order and the long-run consequences on profitability if Surf Gear lowered prices to all regular customers.

One-Time-Only Special-Order Decision for Surf Gear: Comparative Contribution Income Statements

	Home	Insert	Page Layout	Formulas	Data	Review	View	
	A	B	C	D	E	F	G	H
1				Without the Special Order		With the Special Order		Difference: Relevant Amounts
2				30,000		35,000		for the
3				Units to Be Sold		Units to Be Sold		5,000
4		Per Unit		Total		Total		Units Special Order
5		(1)		(2) = (1) × 30,000		(3)		(4) = (3) − (2)
6	Revenues	$20.00		$600,000		$655,000		$55,000[a]
7	Variable costs:							
8	Manufacturing	7.50		225,000		262,500		37,500[b]
9	Marketing	5.00		150,000		150,000		0[c]
10	Total variable costs	12.50		375,000		412,500		37,500
11	Contribution margin	7.50		225,000		242,500		17,500
12	Fixed costs:							
13	Manufacturing	4.50		135,000		135,000		0[d]
14	Marketing	2.00		60,000		60,000		0[d]
15	Total fixed costs	6.50		195,000		195,000		0
16	Operating income	$ 1.00		$ 30,000		$ 47,500		$17,500
17								
18	[a]5,000 units × $11.00 per unit = $55,000.							
19	[b]5,000 units × $7.50 per unit = $37,500.							
20	[c]No variable marketing costs would be incurred for the 5,000-unit one-time-only special order.							
21	[d]Fixed manufacturing costs and fixed marketing costs would be unaffected by the special order.							

TRY IT! 11-1

The Rainier Company provides landscaping services to corporations and businesses. All its landscaping work requires Rainier to use landscaping equipment. Its landscaping equipment has the capacity to do 10,000 hours of landscaping work. It is currently utilizing 9,000 hours of equipment time. Rainier charges $80 per hour for landscaping work. Cost information for the current activity level is as follows:

Revenues ($80 × 9,000 hours)	$720,000
Variable landscaping costs (including materials and labor), which vary with the number of hours worked ($50 per hour × 9,000 hours)	450,000
Fixed landscaping costs	108,000
Variable marketing costs (5% of revenues)	36,000
Fixed marketing costs	72,000
Total costs	666,000
Operating income	$ 54,000

Rainier has just received a one-time only special order for landscaping work from Lasell Corporation at $60 per hour that would require 1,000 hours of equipment time. Should Rainier accept the offer even though revenue per hour is less than Rainier's landscaping cost of $62 per hour [($450,000 + $108,000) ÷ 9,000 hours)]? No marketing costs will be necessary for the one-time only special order.

Potential Problems in Relevant-Cost Analysis

Managers should avoid two potential problems in relevant-cost analysis. First, they must watch for incorrect general assumptions, such as all variable costs are relevant and all fixed costs are irrelevant. In the Surf Gear example, the variable marketing cost of $5 per unit is irrelevant because Surf Gear will incur no extra marketing costs by accepting the special order. But fixed manufacturing costs could be relevant. The extra production of 5,000 towels per month from 30,000 towels to 35,000 towels does not affect fixed manufacturing costs because we assumed that the existing level of fixed manufacturing cost can support any level of production in the relevant range from 30,000 to 45,000 towels per month. In some cases, however, producing the extra 5,000 towels might increase fixed manufacturing costs (and also increase variable manufacturing cost per unit). Suppose Surf Gear would need to run three shifts of 15,000 towels per shift to achieve full capacity of 45,000 towels per month. Increasing monthly production from 30,000 to 35,000 would require a partial third shift (or overtime payments) because two shifts could produce only 30,000 towels. The partial shift would increase fixed manufacturing costs, thereby making these additional fixed manufacturing costs relevant for this decision.

Second, unit-fixed-cost data can potentially mislead managers in two ways:

1. **When irrelevant costs are included.** Consider the $4.50 of fixed manufacturing cost per unit (direct manufacturing labor, $1.50 per unit, plus manufacturing overhead, $3.00 per unit) included in the $12-per-unit manufacturing cost in the one-time-only special-order decision (see Exhibits 11-4 and 11-5). This $4.50-per-unit cost is irrelevant because this cost will not change if the one-time-only special order is accepted, and so managers should not consider it.

2. **When the same unit fixed costs are used at different output levels.** Generally, managers should use total fixed costs rather than unit fixed costs because total fixed costs are easier to work with and reduce the chance for erroneous conclusions. Then, if desired, the total fixed costs can be unitized. In the Surf Gear example, total fixed manufacturing costs remain at $135,000 even if the company accepts the special order and produces 35,000 towels. Including the fixed manufacturing cost per unit of $4.50 as a cost of the special order would lead managers to the erroneous conclusion that total fixed manufacturing costs would increase to $157,500 ($4.50 per towel × 35,000 towels).

The best way for managers to avoid these two potential problems is to keep focusing on (1) total fixed costs (rather than unit fixed cost) and (2) the relevance concept. Managers should always require all items included in an analysis to be expected total future revenues and expected total future costs that differ among the alternatives.

Short-Run Pricing Decisions

In the one-time-only special-order decision in the previous section, Surf Gear's managers had to decide whether to accept or reject Azelia's offer to supply towels at $11 each. Sometimes managers must decide how much to bid on a one-time-only special order. This is an example of a short-run pricing decision—decisions that have a time horizon of only a few months.

Consider a short-run pricing decision facing managers at Surf Gear. Cranston Corporation has asked Surf Gear to bid on supplying 5,000 towels in September after Surf Gear has fulfilled its obligation to Azelia in August. Cranston is unlikely to place any future orders with Surf Gear. Cranston will sell Surf Gear's towels under its own brand name in regions and markets where Surf Gear does not sell its towels. Whether Surf Gear accepts or rejects this order will not affect Surf Gear's revenues—neither the units sold nor the selling price—from existing sales channels.

Relevant Costs for Short-Run Pricing Decisions

As before, Surf Gear's managers estimate how much it will cost to supply the 5,000 towels. There are no incremental marketing costs, so the relevant costs are the variable manufacturing costs of $7.50 calculated in the previous section. As before, the extra production of 5,000 towels in September from 30,000 to 35,000 towels does not affect fixed manufacturing costs because the relevant range is from 30,000 to 45,000 towels per month. Any selling price above $7.50 will improve Surf Gear's profitability in the short run. What price should Surf Gear's managers bid for the order of 5,000 towels?

Strategic and Other Factors in Short-Run Pricing

Based on market intelligence, Surf Gear's managers believe that competing bids will be between $10 and $11 per towel, so they decide to bid $10 per towel. If Surf Gear wins this bid, operating income will increase by $12,500 (relevant revenues, $10 × 5,000 = $50,000 − relevant costs, $7.50 × 5,000 = $37,500). In light of the extra capacity and strong competition, management's strategy is to bid as high above $7.50 as possible while remaining lower than competitors' bids. Note how Surf Gear chooses the price after looking at the problem through the eyes of its competitors, not based on just its own costs.

What if Surf Gear was the only supplier and Cranston could undercut Surf Gear's selling price in Surf Gear's current markets? The relevant cost of the bidding decision would then include the contribution margin lost on sales to existing customers. What if there were many parties eager to bid and win the Cranston contract? In this case, the contribution margin lost on sales to Surf Gear's existing customers would be irrelevant to the decision because Cranston would undercut the existing business regardless of whether Surf Gear wins the contract.

In contrast to the Surf Gear case, in some short-run situations, a company may experience strong demand for its products or have limited capacity. In these circumstances, managers will strategically increase prices in the short run to as much as the market will bear. We observe high short-run prices in the case of new products or new models of older products, such as microprocessors, computer chips, cell phones, and software.

DECISION POINT

When is a revenue or cost item relevant for a particular decision and what potential problems should managers avoid in relevant-cost analysis?

Insourcing-Versus-Outsourcing and Make-or-Buy Decisions

LEARNING OBJECTIVE 3

Explain the concept of opportunity cost and why managers should consider it when making insourcing-versus-outsourcing decisions

...in all decisions, it is important to consider the contribution to income forgone by choosing a particular alternative and rejecting others

We now apply the concept of relevance to another strategic decision: whether a company should make a component part or buy it from a supplier. We again assume idle capacity.

Outsourcing and Idle Facilities

Outsourcing is purchasing goods and services from outside vendors rather than **insourcing**, producing the same goods or providing the same services within an organization. For example, Kodak prefers to manufacture its own motion-picture film (insourcing), but has IBM do its data processing (outsourcing). Honda relies on outside vendors to supply some component parts (outsourcing) but chooses to manufacture other parts internally (insourcing).

Decisions about whether a producer of goods or services will insource or outsource are called **make-or-buy decisions**. Surveys of companies indicate that managers consider quality, dependability of suppliers to deliver according to a schedule, and costs as the most important factors in the make-or-buy decision. Sometimes, however, qualitative factors dominate management's make-or-buy decision. For example, Dell Computer buys the Intel Core i7 processor for its computers from Intel because Dell does not have the know-how and technology to make the processor itself. In contrast, to maintain the secrecy of its formula, Coca-Cola does not outsource the manufacture of its concentrate.

> **Example 2:** The Soho Company manufactures a two-in-one video system consisting of a DVD player and a digital media receiver (that downloads movies and video from Internet sites such as Netflix). Columns 1 and 2 of the following table show the expected total and per-unit costs for manufacturing the DVD player. Soho plans to manufacture the 250,000 units in 2,000 batches of 125 units each. Variable batch-level costs of $625 per batch vary with the number of batches, not the total number of units produced.
>
> Broadfield, Inc., a manufacturer of DVD players, offers to sell Soho 250,000 DVD players next year for $64 per unit on Soho's preferred delivery schedule. Assume that financial factors will be the basis of this make-or-buy decision. Should Soho's managers make or buy the DVD player?

	Expected Total Costs of Producing 250,000 Units in 2,000 Batches Next Year (1)	Expected Cost per Unit (2) = (1) ÷ 250,000
Direct materials ($36 per unit × 250,000 units)	$ 9,000,000	$36.00
Variable direct manufacturing labor ($10 per unit × 250,000 units)	2,500,000	10.00
Variable manufacturing overhead costs of power and utilities ($6 per unit × 250,000 units)	1,500,000	6.00
Mixed (variable and fixed) batch-level manufacturing overhead costs of materials handling and setup [$750,000 + ($625 per batch × 2,000 batches)]	2,000,000	8.00
Fixed manufacturing overhead costs of plant lease, insurance, and administration	3,000,000	12.00
Total manufacturing cost	$18,000,000	$72.00

Columns 1 and 2 of the preceding table indicate the expected total costs and expected cost per unit of producing 250,000 DVD players next year. The expected manufacturing cost per unit for next year is $72. At first glance, it appears that Soho's managers should buy DVD players because the expected $72-per-unit cost of making the DVD player is more than the $64 per unit to buy it. But a make-or-buy decision is rarely obvious. To make a decision, managers need to consider the question, "What is the difference in relevant costs between the alternatives?"

For the moment, suppose (1) the capacity now used to make the DVD players will become idle next year if the DVD players are purchased; (2) the $3,000,000 of fixed manufacturing overhead will continue to be incurred next year regardless of the decision made; and (3) the $750,000 in fixed salaries to support materials handling and setup will not be incurred if the manufacture of DVD players is completely shut down.

Exhibit 11-6 presents the relevant-cost computations, which show that Soho will *save* $1,000,000 by making the DVD players rather than buying them from Broadfield. Based on this analysis, Soho's managers decide to make the DVD players.

EXHIBIT 11-6   Relevant (Incremental) Items for Make-or-Buy Decision for DVD Players at Soho Company

Relevant Items	Total Relevant Costs		Relevant Cost Per Unit	
	Make	Buy	Make	Buy
Outside purchase of parts ($64 × 250,000 units)		$16,000,000		$64
Direct materials	$ 9,000,000		$36	
Direct manufacturing labor	2,500,000		10	
Variable manufacturing overhead	1,500,000		6	
Mixed (variable and fixed) materials-handling and setup overhead	2,000,000		8	
Total relevant costs[a]	$15,000,000	$16,000,000	$60	$64
Difference in favor of making DVD players	$1,000,000		$4	

[a]The $3,000,000 of plant-lease, plant-insurance, and plant-administration costs could be included under both alternatives. Conceptually, they do not belong in a listing of relevant costs because these costs are irrelevant to the decision. Practically, some managers may want to include them in order to list all costs that will be incurred under each alternative.

Note how the key concepts of relevance presented in Exhibit 11-3 apply here:

- Exhibit 11-6 compares differences in expected total future revenues and expected total future costs. Past costs are always irrelevant when making decisions.

- Exhibit 11-6 shows $2,000,000 of future materials-handling and setup costs under the make alternative but not under the buy alternative. Why? Because Soho will incur these future variable costs per batch and avoidable fixed costs only if it manufactures DVD players and not if it buys them. The $2,000,000 represents future costs that differ between the alternatives and so are relevant to the make-or-buy decision.

- Exhibit 11-6 excludes the $3,000,000 of plant-lease, plant-insurance, and plant-administration costs under both alternatives. Why? Because these future costs will not differ between the alternatives, so they are irrelevant.

A common term in decision making is *incremental cost*. An **incremental cost** is the additional total cost incurred for an activity. In Exhibit 11-6, the incremental cost of making DVD players is the additional total cost of $15,000,000 that Soho will incur if it decides to make DVD players. The $3,000,000 of fixed manufacturing overhead is not an incremental cost because Soho will incur these costs whether or not it makes DVD players. Similarly, the incremental cost of buying DVD players from Broadfield is the additional total cost of $16,000,000 that Soho will incur if it decides to buy DVD players. A **differential cost** is the difference in total (relevant) cost between two alternatives. In Exhibit 11-6, the differential cost between the make-DVD-players and buy-DVD-players alternatives is $1,000,000 ($16,000,000 − $15,000,000). Note that *incremental cost* and *differential cost* are sometimes used interchangeably in practice. When faced with these terms, always be sure to clarify what they mean.

We define *incremental revenue* and *differential revenue* similarly to incremental cost and differential cost. **Incremental revenue** is the additional total revenue from an activity. **Differential revenue** is the difference in total revenue between two alternatives.

Strategic and Qualitative Factors

Strategic and qualitative factors affect outsourcing decisions. For example, Soho's managers may prefer to manufacture DVD players in-house to retain control over design, quality, reliability, and delivery schedules. Conversely, despite the cost advantages documented in Exhibit 11-6, Soho's managers may prefer to outsource, become a leaner organization, and focus on areas of its core competencies, the manufacture and sale of video systems. For example, advertising companies, such as J. Walter Thompson, only focus on the creative and planning aspects of advertising (their core competencies) and outsource production activities, such as film, photographs, and illustrations.

Outsourcing is risky. As a company's dependence on its suppliers increases, suppliers could increase prices and let quality and delivery performance slip. To minimize these risks, managers generally enter into long-run contracts specifying costs, quality, and delivery schedules with their suppliers. Wise managers go so far as to build close partnerships or alliances with a few key suppliers. For example, Toyota sends its own engineers to improve the processes of its suppliers. Suppliers of companies such as Ford, Hyundai, Panasonic, and Sony have researched and developed innovative products, met demands for increased quantities, maintained quality and on-time delivery, and lowered costs—actions that the companies themselves would not have had the competencies to achieve.

Outsourcing decisions invariably have a long-run horizon in which the financial costs and benefits of outsourcing become more uncertain. Almost always, strategic and qualitative factors become important determinants of the outsourcing decision. Weighing all these factors requires considerable managerial judgment and care.

International Outsourcing

What additional factors would Soho's managers have to consider if the DVD-player supplier was based in Mexico? One important factor would be exchange-rate risk. Suppose the Mexican supplier offers to sell Soho 250,000 DVD players for 320,000,000 pesos. Should Soho make or buy? The answer depends on the exchange rate that Soho's managers expect next year. If they forecast an exchange rate of 20 pesos per $1, Soho's expected purchase cost equals $16,000,000 (320,000,000 pesos ÷ 20 pesos per $), greater than the $15,000,000 relevant costs for making the DVD players in Exhibit 11-6, so Soho's managers would prefer to make DVD players rather than buy them. If, however, Soho's managers anticipate an exchange rate of 22 pesos per $1, Soho's expected purchase cost equals $14,545,454 (320,000,000 pesos ÷ 22 pesos per $), which is less than the $15,000,000 relevant costs for making the DVD players, so Soho's managers would prefer to buy rather than make the DVD players.

Soho's managers have yet another option. Soho could enter into a forward contract to purchase 320,000,000 pesos. A forward contract allows Soho to contract today to purchase pesos next year at a predetermined, fixed cost, thereby protecting itself against exchange-rate risk. If Soho's managers choose this route, they would make (buy) DVD players if the cost of the contract is greater (less) than $15,000,000.

International outsourcing requires managers to evaluate manufacturing and transportation costs, exchange-rate risks, and the other strategic and qualitative factors discussed earlier such as quality, reliability, and efficiency of the supply chain. Concepts in Action: "Starbucks Brews Up Domestic Production" describes how Starbucks brought back production to the United States.

The Total Alternatives Approach

In the simple make-or-buy decision in Exhibit 11-6, we assumed that the capacity currently used to make DVD players will remain idle if Soho purchases DVDs from Broadfield. Often, however, the released capacity can be used for other, profitable purposes. In this case, Soho's managers must choose whether to make or buy based on how best to use available production capacity.

CONCEPTS IN ACTION ▶ Starbucks Brews Up Domestic Production

Andrew Winning/Reuters/Alamy Stock Photo

After years of outsourcing production to lower-cost countries around the world, many American-based companies are relocating their manufacturing activities within the United States. Starbucks, the world's largest coffee chain, is a leader in the domestic outsourcing movement. In 2012, the company began sourcing its coffee mugs from American Mug and Stein, a reopened ceramics factory in northeastern Ohio. Starbucks also "re-shored" some its own production back to the United States. For example, the company built a new $172 million facility in Georgia to produce its ready-brew VIA coffee and the coffee base for its Frappuccino blended beverages.

While labor costs at the Ohio and Georgia plants are higher than in many offshore locations, Stephen Lovejoy, senior vice president of global supply chain at Starbucks, identified several cost-savings benefits from domestic production. These include:

- Access to highly-skilled labor, which helps with production efficiency
- Reduced transportation and warehousing costs, since more than 50% of Starbucks' retail stores are in the United States
- Greater speed to market, which cuts lead time and inventory carrying costs

While many companies continue to benefit from the global supply chain, Starbucks is among many United States-based companies, including American Apparel and Ralph Lauren, who have benefited from having domestic manufacturing and outsourcing as part of their production mix.

Sources: Zachary Hines, "Case Study: Starbucks' New Manufacturing in the USA," University of San Diego Reshoring Institute (San Diego: University of San Diego, 2015) (http://www.reshoringinstitute.org/wp-content/uploads/2015/05/Starbucks-Casestudy.pdf); Shan Li, Tifany Hsu, and Andrea Chang, "American Apparel, others try to profit from domestic production," *Los Angeles Times*, August 10, 2014 (http://www.latimes.com/business/la-fi-american-apparel-made-in-usa-20140810-story.html); Adrienne Selko, "Starbucks Chooses Domestic Production," *Industry Week*, July 13, 2012 (http://www.industryweek.com/expansion-management/starbucks-chooses-domestic-production).

Example 3: If Soho decides to buy DVD players for its video systems from Broadfield, then Soho's best use of the capacity that becomes available is to produce 100,000 Digiteks, a portable, stand-alone DVD player. From a manufacturing standpoint, Digiteks are similar to DVD players made for the video system. With help from operating managers, Soho's management accountant estimates the following future revenues and costs if Soho decides to manufacture and sell Digiteks:

Incremental future revenues		$8,000,000
Incremental future costs		
Direct materials	$3,400,000	
Variable direct manufacturing labor	1,000,000	
Variable overhead (such as power, utilities)	600,000	
Materials-handling and setup overheads	500,000	
Total incremental future costs		5,500,000
Incremental future operating income		$2,500,000

Because of capacity constraints, Soho can make either DVD players for its video-system unit or Digiteks, but not both. Which of the two alternatives should Soho's managers choose: (1) make video-system DVD players and do not make Digiteks or (2) buy video-system DVD players and make Digiteks?

Exhibit 11-7, Panel A, summarizes the "total-alternatives" approach, the future costs and revenues for *all* products. Soho's managers will choose Alternative 2, buy video-system DVD players, and use the available capacity to make and sell Digiteks. The future incremental costs of buying video-system DVD players from an outside supplier ($16,000,000) exceed the future incremental costs of making video-system DVD players in-house ($15,000,000). But Soho can use the capacity freed up by buying video-system DVD players to gain $2,500,000 in operating income (incremental future revenues of $8,000,000 minus total incremental future costs of $5,500,000) by making and selling Digiteks. The *net relevant* costs of buying video-system DVD players and making and selling Digiteks are $16,000,000 − $2,500,000 = $13,500,000.

The Opportunity-Cost Approach

Deciding to use a resource one way means a manager must forgo the opportunity to use the resource in any other way. This lost opportunity is a cost that the manager must consider when making a decision. **Opportunity cost** is the contribution to operating income that is forgone by not using a limited resource in its next-best alternative use. For example, the (relevant) cost of going to school for a BS in accounting degree is not only the cost of tuition, books, lodging, and food, but also the income sacrificed (opportunity cost) by not working. Presumably, however, the estimated future benefits of obtaining a BS in accounting (such as a higher-paying career) will exceed these out-of-pocket and opportunity costs.

Exhibit 11-7, Panel B, displays the opportunity-cost approach for analyzing the alternatives Soho faces. *Note that the alternatives are defined differently under the two approaches*:

In the total alternatives approach:	In the opportunity cost approach:
1. Make video-system DVD players and do not make Digiteks	1. Make video-system DVD players
2. Buy video-system DVD players and make Digiteks	2. Buy video-system DVD players

The opportunity-cost approach does not reference Digiteks. Under the opportunity-cost approach, the cost of each alternative includes (1) the incremental costs and (2) the opportunity cost, the profit forgone from not making Digiteks. This opportunity cost arises because Digiteks is excluded from formal consideration in the alternatives.

| EXHIBIT 11-7 | Total-Alternatives Approach and Opportunity-Cost Approach to Make-or-Buy Decisions for Soho Company |

Relevant Items	Alternatives for Soho	
	1. Make Video-System DVD Players and Do Not Make Digiteks	2. Buy Video-System DVD Players and Make Digiteks
PANEL A Total-Alternatives Approach to Make-or-Buy Decisions		
Total incremental future costs of making/buying video-system DVD players (from Exhibit 11-6)	$15,000,000	$16,000,000
Deduct excess of future revenues over future costs from Digiteks	0	(2,500,000)
Total relevant costs under total-alternatives approach	$15,000,000	$13,500,000

	1. Make Video-System DVD Players	2. Buy Video-System DVD Players
PANEL B Opportunity-Cost Approach to Make-or-Buy Decisions		
Total incremental future costs of making/buying video-system DVD players (from Exhibit 11-6)	$15,000,000	$16,000,000
Opportunity cost: Profit contribution forgone because capacity will not be used to make Digiteks, the next-best alternative	2,500,000	0
Total relevant costs under opportunity-cost approach	$17,500,000	$16,000,000

Note that the differences in costs across the columns in Panels A and B are the same: The cost of alternative 2 is $1,500,000 less than the cost of alternative 1.

Consider alternative 1, making video-system DVD players. What are all the costs of making video-system DVD players? Certainly Soho will incur $15,000,000 of incremental costs to make video-system DVD players, but is this the entire cost? No, because by deciding to use limited manufacturing resources to make video-system DVD players, Soho will give up the opportunity to earn $2,500,000 by not using these resources to make Digiteks. Therefore, the relevant costs of making video-system DVD players are the incremental costs of $15,000,000 plus the opportunity cost of $2,500,000.

Next, consider alternative 2, buying video-system DVD players. The incremental cost of buying video-system DVD players is $16,000,000. The opportunity cost is zero. Why? Because by choosing this alternative, Soho will not forgo the profit it can earn from making and selling Digiteks.

Panel B leads managers to the same conclusion as Panel A: buying video-system DVD players and making Digiteks is the preferred alternative.

Panels A and B in Exhibit 11-7 describe two consistent approaches to decision making with capacity constraints. The total-alternatives approach in Panel A includes all future incremental costs and revenues. For example, under alternative 2, the additional future operating income from *using capacity to make and sell Digiteks* ($2,500,000) is subtracted from the future incremental cost of buying video-system DVD players ($16,000,000). The opportunity-cost analysis in Panel B takes the opposite approach. It focuses only on video-system DVD players. Whenever capacity is not going to be used to make and sell Digiteks, the future forgone operating income is added as an opportunity cost of making video-system DVD players, as in alternative 1. (Note that when Digiteks are made, as in alternative 2, there is no "opportunity cost of not making Digiteks.") Therefore, whereas Panel A *subtracts* $2,500,000 under alternative 2, Panel B *adds* $2,500,000 under alternative 1. *Panel B highlights the idea that when capacity is constrained, the relevant revenues and costs of any alternative equal (1) the incremental future revenues and costs plus (2) the opportunity cost.* However, when managers are considering more than two alternatives simultaneously, it is generally easier for them to use the total-alternatives approach.

Opportunity costs are not recorded in financial accounting systems. Why? Because historical recordkeeping is limited to transactions involving alternatives that managers *actually selected* rather than alternatives that they rejected. Rejected alternatives do not produce transactions and are not recorded. If Soho makes video-system DVD players, it will not make Digiteks, and it will not record any accounting entries for Digiteks. Yet the opportunity cost of making video-system DVD players, which equals the operating income that Soho forgoes by not making Digiteks, is a crucial input into the make-or-buy decision. Consider again Exhibit 11-7, Panel B. On the basis of only the incremental costs that are systematically recorded in accounting systems, it is less costly for Soho to make rather than buy video-system DVD players. Recognizing the opportunity cost of $2,500,000 leads to a different conclusion: buying video-system DVD players is preferable to making them.

Suppose Soho has sufficient capacity to make Digiteks even if it makes video-system DVD players. In this case, the opportunity cost of making video-system DVD players is $0 because Soho does not give up the $2,500,000 operating income from making and selling Digiteks even if it chooses to make video-system DVD players. The relevant costs are $15,000,000 (incremental costs of $15,000,000 plus opportunity cost of $0). Under these conditions, Soho's managers would prefer to make video-system DVD players, rather than buy them, and also make Digiteks.

Besides quantitative considerations, managers also consider strategic and qualitative factors in make-or-buy decisions. In deciding to buy video-system DVD players from an outside supplier, Soho's managers consider factors such as the supplier's reputation for quality and timely delivery. They also consider the strategic consequences of selling Digiteks. For example, will selling Digiteks take Soho's focus away from its video-system business?

TRY IT! 11-2 ▶

The Rainier Company provides landscaping services to corporations and businesses. All its landscaping work requires Rainier to use landscaping equipment. Its landscaping equipment has the capacity to do 10,000 hours of landscaping work. It currently anticipates getting orders that would utilize 9,000 hours of equipment time from existing customers. Rainier charges $80 per hour for landscaping work. Cost information for the current expected activity level is as follows:

Revenues ($80 × 9,000 hours)	$720,000
Variable landscaping costs (including materials and labor), which vary with the number of hours worked ($50 per hour × 9,000 hours)	450,000
Fixed landscaping costs	108,000
Variable marketing costs (5% of revenue)	36,000
Fixed marketing costs	72,000
Total costs	666,000
Operating income	$ 54,000

Rainier has received an order for landscaping work from Victoria Corporation at $60 per hour that would require 2,000 hours of equipment time. Variable landscaping costs for the Victoria Corporation order are $50 per hour and variable marketing costs are 5% of revenues. Rainier can either accept the Victoria offer in whole or reject it. Should Rainier accept the offer?

Carrying Costs of Inventory

To see another example of an opportunity cost, consider the following data for Soho's DVD player purchasing decision:

Estimated video-system DVD player requirements for next year	250,000 units
Cost per unit when each purchase is equal to 2,500 units	$64.00
Cost per unit when each purchase is equal to or greater than 30,000 units ($64 − 0.5% discount)	$63.68
Cost of a purchase order	$150

Soho's managers are evaluating the following alternatives:

A. Make 100 purchases (twice a week) of 2,500 units each during next year

B. Make 8 purchases (twice a quarter) of 31,250 units during the year

Average investment in inventory:

A. (2,500 units × $64.00 per unit) ÷ 2[a]	$80,000
B. (31,250 units × $ 63.68 per unit) ÷ 2[a]	$995,000
Annual rate of return if cash is invested elsewhere (for example, bonds or stocks) at the same level of risk as investment in inventory	12%

[a] The example assumes that video-system-DVD-player purchases will be used uniformly throughout the year. The average investment in inventory during the year is the cost of the inventory when a purchase is received plus the cost of inventory just before the next purchase is delivered (in our example, zero) divided by 2.

Soho will pay cash for the video-system DVD players it buys. Which purchasing alternative is more economical for Soho?

The management accountant presents the following analysis to the company's managers using the total alternatives approach, recognizing that Soho has, on average, $995,000 of cash available to invest. If Soho invests only $80,000 in inventory as in alternative A, it will have $915,000 ($995,000 − $80,000) of cash available to invest elsewhere, which at a 12% rate of return will yield a total return of $109,800. This income is subtracted from the ordering and purchasing costs incurred under alternative A. If Soho invests all $995,000 in inventory as in alternative B, it will have $0 ($995,000 − $995,000) available to invest elsewhere and will earn no return on the cash.

	Alternative A: Make 100 Purchases of 2,500 Units Each During the Year and Invest Any Excess Cash (1)	**Alternative B:** Make 8 Purchases of 31,250 Units Each During the Year and Invest Any Excess Cash (2)	**Difference** (3) = (1) − (2)
Annual purchase-order costs (100 purch. orders × $150/purch. order; 8 purch. orders × $150/purch. order)	$ 15,000	$ 1,200	$ 13,800
Annual purchase costs (250,000 units × $64.00/unit; 250,000 units × $63.68/unit)	16,000,000	15,920,000	80,000
Deduct annual rate of return earned by investing cash not tied up in inventory elsewhere at the same level of risk [0.12 × ($995,000 − $80,000); 0.12 × ($995,000 − $995,000)]	(109,800)	0	(109,800)
Relevant costs	$15,905,200	$15,921,200	$ (16,000)

Consistent with the trends toward holding smaller inventories, it is more economical (by $16,000) for Soho's managers to purchase smaller quantities of 2,500 units 100 times a year than to purchase 31,250 units 8 times a year.

The following table presents the management accountant's analysis of the two alternatives using the opportunity-cost approach. Each alternative is defined only in terms of the two purchasing choices with no explicit reference to investing the excess cash.

	Alternative A: Make 100 Purchases of 2,500 Units Each During the Year (1)	Alternative B: Make 8 Purchases of 31,250 Units Each During the Year (2)	Difference (3) = (1) − (2)
Annual purchase-order costs (100 purch. orders × $150/purch. order; 8 purch. orders × $150/purch. order)	$ 15,000	$ 1,200	$ 13,800
Annual purchase costs (250,000 units × $64.00/unit; 250,000 units × $63.68/unit)	16,000,000	15,920,000	80,000
Opportunity cost: Annual rate of return that could be earned if investment in inventory were invested elsewhere at the same level of risk (0.12 × $80,000; 0.12 × $995,000)	9,600	119,400	(109,800)
Relevant costs	$16,024,600	$16,040,600	$ (16,000)

Recall that under the opportunity-cost approach, the relevant cost of any alternative is (1) the incremental cost of the alternative plus (2) the opportunity cost of the profit forgone from choosing that alternative. The opportunity cost of holding inventory is the income forgone by tying up money in inventory and not investing it elsewhere. The opportunity cost would not be recorded in the accounting system because, once the money is invested in inventory, there is no money available to invest elsewhere and so no return related to this investment to record. On the basis of the costs recorded in the accounting system (purchase-order costs and purchase costs), Soho's managers would erroneously conclude that making eight purchases of 31,250 units each is the less costly alternative. Column 3, however, indicates that, as in the total-alternatives approach, purchasing smaller quantities of 2,500 units 100 times a year is more economical than purchasing 31,250 units eight times during the year by $16,000. Why? Because the lower opportunity cost of holding smaller inventory exceeds the higher purchase and ordering costs. If the opportunity cost of money tied up in inventory were greater than 12% per year, or if other incremental benefits of holding lower inventory were considered, such as lower insurance, materials-handling, storage, obsolescence, and breakage cost, making 100 purchases would be even more economical.

DECISION POINT

What is an opportunity cost and why should managers consider it when making insourcing-versus-outsourcing decisions?

Product-Mix Decisions with Capacity Constraints

LEARNING OBJECTIVE 4

Know how to choose which products to produce when there are capacity constraints

...select the product with the highest contribution margin per unit of the limiting resource

We now examine how the concept of relevance applies to **product-mix decisions**, the decisions managers make about which products to sell and in what quantities. These decisions usually have only a short-run focus because they typically arise in the context of capacity constraints that can be relaxed in the long run. In the short run, for example, BMW, the German car manufacturer, continually adapts the mix of its different models of cars (for example, 328i, 528i, and 750i) to fluctuations in selling prices and demand.

To determine product mix, managers maximize operating income, subject to constraints such as capacity and demand. Throughout this section, we assume that as short-run changes in product mix occur, the only costs that change are costs that are variable with the number of units produced (and sold). Under this assumption, the analysis of individual product contribution margins provides insight into the product mix that maximizes operating income.

Example 4: Power Recreation assembles two engines, a snowmobile engine and a boat engine, at its Lexington, Kentucky, plant. The following table shows the selling prices, costs, and contribution margins of these two engines:

	Snowmobile Engine	Boat Engine
Selling price	$800	$1,000
Variable cost per unit	560	625
Contribution margin per unit	$240	$ 375
Contribution-margin percentage ($240 ÷ $800; $375 ÷ $1,000)	30%	37.5%

Only 600 machine-hours are available daily for assembling engines. Additional capacity cannot be obtained in the short run. Power Recreation can sell as many engines as it produces. The constraining resource, then, is machine-hours. It takes two machine-hours to produce one snowmobile engine and five machine-hours to produce one boat engine. What product mix should Power Recreation's managers choose to maximize operating income?

In terms of contribution margin per unit and contribution-margin percentage, the data in Example 4 shows that boat engines are more profitable than snowmobile engines. The product that Power Recreation should produce and sell, however, is not necessarily the product with the higher individual contribution margin per unit or contribution-margin percentage. As the following table shows, managers should choose the product with *the highest contribution margin per unit of the constraining resource (factor)*. That's the resource that restricts or limits the production or sale of products.

	Snowmobile Engine	Boat Engine
Contribution margin per unit	$240	$375
Machine-hours required to produce one unit	2 machine-hours	5 machine-hours
Contribution margin per machine-hour		
$240 per unit ÷ 2 machine-hours/unit	$120/machine-hour	
$375 per unit ÷ 5 machine-hours/unit		$75/machine-hour
Total contribution margin for 600 machine-hours		
$120/machine-hour × 600 machine-hours	$72,000	
$75/machine-hour × 600 machine-hours		$45,000

The number of machine-hours is the constraining resource in this example, and snowmobile engines earn more contribution margin per machine-hour ($120/machine-hour) compared with boat engines ($75/machine-hour). Therefore, choosing to produce and sell snowmobile engines maximizes *total* contribution margin ($72,000 vs. $45,000 from producing and selling boat engines) and operating income. Other constraints in manufacturing settings can be the availability of direct materials, components, or skilled labor, as well as financial and sales factors. In a retail department store, the constraining resource may be linear feet of display space. Regardless of the specific constraining resource, managers should always focus on maximizing *total* contribution margin by choosing products that give the highest contribution margin per unit of the constraining resource.

In many cases, a manufacturer or retailer has the challenge of trying to maximize total operating income for a variety of products, each with more than one constraining resource. Some constraints may require a manufacturer or retailer to stock minimum quantities of products even if these products are not very profitable. For example, supermarkets must stock less-profitable products, such as paper towels and toilet paper, because customers will be willing to shop at a supermarket only if it carries a wide range of products. To determine the most profitable production schedule and the most profitable product mix, the manufacturer or retailer needs to determine the maximum total contribution margin in the face of many constraints. Optimization techniques, such as linear programming, discussed in the appendix to this chapter, help solve these more complex problems.

Finally, there is the question of managing the bottleneck constraint to increase output and, therefore, contribution margin. Can the available machine-hours for assembling engines be increased beyond 600, for example, by reducing idle time? Can the time needed to assemble each snowmobile engine (two machine-hours) or each boat engine (five machine-hours) be reduced, for example, by reducing setup time and processing time of assembly? Can some of the assembly operations be outsourced to allow more engines to be built?

In the following section, we examine how managers can deal with the bottleneck constraint to increase output and, therefore, the contribution margin when some operations are bottlenecks and others are not.

TRY IT! 11-3

The Rainier Company provides landscaping services to corporations and businesses. All its landscaping work requires Rainier to use landscaping equipment. Its landscaping equipment has the capacity to do 10,000 hours of landscaping work. It currently anticipates getting orders that would utilize 9,000 hours of equipment time. Rainier charges $80 per hour for landscaping work. Cost information for the current expected activity level is as follows:

Revenues ($80 × 9,000 hours)	$720,000
Variable landscaping costs (including materials and labor), which vary with the number of hours worked ($50 per hour × 9,000 hours)	450,000
Fixed landscaping costs	108,000
Variable marketing costs (5% of revenue)	36,000
Fixed marketing costs	72,000
Total costs	666,000
Operating income	$ 54,000

In order to fill its available capacity, Rainier's salespersons are trying to find new business. Hudson Corporation wants Rainier to do 4,000 hours of landscaping work for $70 per hour. Variable servicing costs for the Hudson Corporation order are $45 per hour and variable marketing costs are 5% of revenues. Rainier can accept as much or as little of the 4,000 hours of Hudson's landscaping work. What should Rainier Corporation do?

Bottlenecks, Theory of Constraints, and Throughput-Margin Analysis

Suppose Power Recreation's snowmobile engine must go through a forging operation before it goes to the assembly operation. The company has 1,200 hours of daily forging capacity dedicated to the manufacture of snowmobile engines. The company takes 3 hours to forge each snowmobile engine, so Power Recreation can forge 400 snowmobile engines per day (1,200 hours ÷ 3 hours per snowmobile engine). Recall that it can assemble only 300 snowmobile engines per day (600 machine-hours ÷ 2 machine-hours per snowmobile engine). The production of snowmobile engines is constrained by the assembly operation, not the forging operation.

The **theory of constraints (TOC)** describes methods to maximize operating income when faced with some bottleneck and some nonbottleneck operations.[2] To implement TOC, we define and use three measures:

1. **Throughput margin** equals revenues minus the direct material costs of the goods sold.

2. *Investments* equal the sum of (a) material costs in direct materials, work-in-process, and finished-goods inventories; (b) R&D costs; and (c) capital costs of equipment and buildings.

---

[2] See Eliyahu M. Goldratt and Jeff Cox, *The Goal* (New York: North River Press, 1986); Eliyahu M. Goldratt, *The Theory of Constraints* (New York: North River Press, 1990); Eric W. Noreen, Debra A. Smith, and James T. Mackey, *The Theory of Constraints and Its Implications for Management Accounting* (New York: North River Press, 1995); and Mark J. Woeppel, *Manufacturers' Guide to Implementing the Theory of Constraints* (Boca Raton, FL: Lewis Publishing, 2000).

3. *Operating costs* equal all costs of operations (other than direct materials) incurred to earn throughput margin. Operating costs include costs such as salaries and wages, rent, utilities, and depreciation.

The objective of the TOC is to increase throughput margin while decreasing investments and operating costs. *The TOC considers a short-run time horizon of a few months and assumes operating costs are fixed and direct material costs are the only variable costs. In a situation where some of the operating costs are also variable in the short run, throughput margin is replaced by contribution margin—revenues minus direct material costs minus other variable operating costs.* In the Power Recreation example, each snowmobile engine sells for $800. We assume that the variable costs of $560 consist only of direct material costs (incurred in the forging department), so throughput margin equals contribution margin. For ease of exposition and consistency with the previous section, we use the term *contribution margin* instead of *throughput margin* throughout this section.

TOC focuses on managing bottleneck operations, as explained in the following steps:

Step 1: Recognize that the bottleneck operation determines the contribution margin of the entire system. In the Power Recreation example, output in the assembly operation determines the output of snowmobile engines.

Step 2: Identify the bottleneck operation by identifying operations with large quantities of inventory waiting to be worked on. As snowmobile engines are produced at the forging operation, inventories will build up at the assembly operation because daily assembly capacity of 300 snowmobile engines is less than the daily forging capacity of 400 snowmobile engines.

Step 3: Keep the bottleneck operation busy and subordinate all nonbottleneck operations to the bottleneck operation. That is, the needs of the bottleneck operation determine the production schedule of the nonbottleneck operations. To maximize operating income, the manager must maximize contribution margin of the constrained or bottleneck resource. The bottleneck assembly operation must always be kept running; the workers should not be waiting to assemble engines. To achieve this objective, Power Recreation's managers maintain a small buffer inventory of snowmobile engines that have gone through the forging operation and are waiting to be assembled. The bottleneck assembly operation sets the pace for the nonbottleneck forging operations. Operating managers maximize contribution margin by ensuring the assembly operation is operating at capacity by developing a detailed production schedule at the forging operation to ensure that the assembly operation is not waiting for work. At the same time, forging more snowmobile engines that cannot be assembled does not increase output or contribution margin; it only creates excess inventory of unassembled snowmobile engines.

Step 4: Take actions to increase the efficiency and capacity of the bottleneck operation as long as the incremental contribution margin exceeds the incremental costs of increasing efficiency and capacity.

We illustrate Step 4 using data from the forging and assembly operations of Power Recreation.

	Forging	Assembly
Capacity per day	400 units	300 units
Daily production and sales	300 units	300 units
Other fixed operating costs per day (excluding direct materials)	$24,000	$18,000
Other fixed operating costs per unit produced ($24,000 ÷ 300 units; $ 18,000 ÷ 300 units)	$80 per unit	$60 per unit

Power Recreation's output is constrained by the capacity of 300 units in the assembly operation. What can Power Recreation's managers do to relieve the bottleneck constraint of the assembly operation?

Desirable actions include the following:

1. **Eliminate idle time at the bottleneck operation (time when the assembly machine is neither being set up to assemble nor actually assembling snowmobile engines).** Power Recreation's manager is evaluating permanently positioning two workers at the assembly operation to unload snowmobile engines as soon as they are assembled and to set up the machine to begin

assembling the next batch of snowmobile engines. This action will cost $320 per day and bottleneck output will increase by 3 snowmobile engines per day. Should Power Recreation's managers incur the additional costs? Yes, because Power Recreation's contribution margin will increase by $720 per day ($240 per snowmobile engine × 3 snowmobile engines), which is greater than the incremental cost of $320 per day. All other costs are irrelevant.

2. **Shift products that do not have to be made on the bottleneck machine to nonbottleneck machines or to outside processing facilities.** Suppose Spartan Corporation, an outside contractor, offers to assemble 5 snowmobile engines each day at $75 per snowmobile engine from engines that have gone through the forging operation at Power Recreation. Spartan's quoted price is greater than Power Recreation's own operating costs in the assembly department of $60 per snowmobile engine. Should Power Recreation's managers accept the offer? Yes, because assembly is the bottleneck operation. Getting Spartan to assemble additional snowmobile engines will increase contribution margin by $1,200 per day ($240 per snowmobile engine × 5 snowmobile engines), while the relevant cost of increasing capacity will be $375 per day ($75 per snowmobile engine × 5 snowmobile engines). The fact that Power Recreation's unit cost is less than Spartan's quoted price is irrelevant.

   Suppose Gemini Industries, another outside contractor, offers to do the forging operation for 8 snowmobile engines per day for $65 per snowmobile engine from direct materials supplied by Power Recreation. Gemini's price is lower than Power Recreation's operating cost of $80 per snowmobile engine in the forging department. Should Power Recreation's managers accept Gemini's offer? No, because other operating costs are fixed costs. Power Recreation will not save any costs by subcontracting the forging operations. Instead, its costs will increase by $520 per day ($65 per snowmobile engine × 8 snowmobile engines) with no increase in contribution margin, which is constrained by assembly capacity.

3. **Reduce setup time and processing time at bottleneck operations (for example, by simplifying the design or reducing the number of parts in the product).** Suppose Power Recreation can assemble 10 more snowmobile engines each day at a cost of $1,000 per day by reducing setup time at the assembly operation. Should Power Recreation's managers incur this cost? Yes, because the contribution margin will increase by $2,400 per day ($240 per snowmobile engine × 10 snowmobile engines), which is greater than the incremental costs of $1,000 per day. Will Power Recreation's managers find it worthwhile to incur costs to reduce machining time at the nonbottleneck forging operation? No. Other operating costs will increase, while the contribution margin will remain unchanged because bottleneck capacity of the assembly operation will not increase.

4. **Improve the quality of parts or products manufactured at the bottleneck operation.** Poor quality is more costly at a bottleneck operation than at a nonbottleneck operation. The cost of poor quality at a nonbottleneck operation is the cost of materials wasted. If Power Recreation produces 5 defective snowmobile engines at the forging operation, the cost of poor quality is $2,800 (direct material cost per snowmobile engine, $560 × 5 snowmobile engines). No contribution margin is forgone because forging has unused capacity. Despite the defective production, forging can produce and transfer 300 good-quality snowmobile engines to the assembly operation. At a bottleneck operation, the cost of poor quality is the cost of materials wasted *plus* the opportunity cost of lost contribution margin. Bottleneck capacity not wasted in producing defective snowmobile engines could be used to generate additional contribution margin. If Power Recreation produces 5 defective units at the assembly operation, the cost of poor quality is the lost revenue of $4,000 ($800 per snowmobile engine × 5 snowmobile engines) or, alternatively stated, direct material costs of $2,800 (direct material cost per snowmobile engine, $560 × 5 snowmobile engines) plus the forgone contribution margin of $1,200 ($240 per snowmobile engine × 5 snowmobile engines).

   The high cost of poor quality at the bottleneck operation means that bottleneck time should not be wasted processing units that are defective. That is, engines should be inspected before the bottleneck operation to ensure that only good-quality parts are processed at the bottleneck operation. Furthermore, quality-improvement programs should place special emphasis on minimizing defects at bottleneck machines.

If successful, the actions in Step 4 will increase the capacity of the assembly operation until it eventually exceeds the capacity of the forging operation. The bottleneck will then shift to the forging operation. Power Recreation would then focus continuous-improvement actions on increasing forging operation efficiency and capacity. For example, the contract with Gemini Industries to forge 8 snowmobile engines per day at $65 per snowmobile engine from direct material supplied by Power Recreation will become attractive because the contribution margin will increase by $1,920 per day ($240 per snowmobile engine × 8 snowmobile engines), which is greater than the incremental costs of $520 ($65 per snowmobile engine × 8 snowmobile engines).

The experience of the Apple Watch illustrates many of the issues discussed in this section. During final testing, the company found that the "taptic engine" motor (designed by Apple to produce the sensation of being tapped on the wrist) made by one of its two suppliers started to break down. As a result, Apple had to scrap some completed watches and move the production of this component to a second supplier. While the second supplier's part did not experience the same problems, it took time for that supplier to increase production. Consequently, Apple asked other component suppliers to align their production to the output of the taptic engine bottleneck.

The theory of constraints emphasizes management of bottleneck operations as the key to improving performance of production operations as a whole. It focuses on short-run maximization of contribution margin. Because TOC regards operating costs as difficult to change in the short run, it does not identify individual activities and drivers of costs. Therefore, TOC is less useful for the long-run management of costs. In contrast, activity-based costing (ABC) systems take a long-run perspective and focus on improving processes by eliminating non-value-added activities and reducing the costs of performing value-added activities. ABC systems are therefore more useful than TOC for long-run pricing, cost control, and capacity management. The short-run TOC emphasis on maximizing contribution margin by managing bottlenecks complements the long-run strategic-cost-management focus of ABC.[3]

DECISION POINT

What steps can managers take to manage bottlenecks?

Customer Profitability and Relevant Costs

We have seen how managers make choices about which products and how much of each product to produce. In addition, managers must often make decisions about adding or dropping a product line or a business segment. Similarly, if the cost object is a customer, managers must decide about adding or dropping customers (analogous to a product line) or a branch office (analogous to a business segment or division). We illustrate relevant-revenue and relevant-cost analysis for these decisions using customers rather than products as the cost object.

LEARNING OBJECTIVE 6

Discuss the factors managers must consider when adding or dropping customers or business units

...managers should focus on how total revenues and costs differ among alternatives and ignore allocated overhead costs

> **Example 5:** Allied West, the West Coast sales office of Allied Furniture, a wholesaler of specialized furniture, supplies furniture to three local retailers: Vogel, Brenner, and Wisk. Exhibit 11-8 presents expected revenues and costs of Allied West by customer for the upcoming year using its activity-based costing system. Allied West's management accountant assigns costs to customers based on the activities needed to support each customer. Information on Allied West's costs for different activities at various levels of the cost hierarchy are:
>
> ▪ Furniture-handling labor costs vary with the number of units of furniture shipped to customers.
>
> ▪ Allied West reserves different areas of the warehouse to stock furniture for different customers. For simplicity, we assume that furniture-handling equipment in an area and depreciation costs on the equipment that Allied West has already acquired are identified with individual customers (customer-level costs). Any unused equipment remains idle. The equipment has a one-year useful life and zero disposal value.

---

[3] For an excellent evaluation of TOC, operations management, cost accounting, and the relationship between TOC and activity-based costing, see Anthony Atkinson, *Cost Accounting, the Theory of Constraints, and Costing* (Issue Paper, CMA Canada, December 2000).

EXHIBIT 11-8   Customer Profitability Analysis for Allied West

	Customer			
	Vogel	**Brenner**	**Wisk**	**Total**
Revenues	$500,000	$300,000	$400,000	$1,200,000
Cost of goods sold	370,000	220,000	330,000	920,000
Furniture-handling labor	41,000	18,000	33,000	92,000
Furniture-handling equipment cost written off as depreciation	12,000	4,000	9,000	25,000
Rent	14,000	8,000	14,000	36,000
Marketing support	11,000	9,000	10,000	30,000
Sales order and delivery processing	13,000	7,000	12,000	32,000
General administration	20,000	12,000	16,000	48,000
Allocated corporate-office costs	10,000	6,000	8,000	24,000
Total costs	491,000	284,000	432,000	1,207,000
Operating income	$ 9,000	$ 16,000	$ (32,000)	$ (7,000)

- Allied West allocates its fixed rent costs to each customer on the basis of the amount of warehouse space reserved for that customer.
- Marketing support costs vary with the number of sales visits made to customers.
- Sales-order costs are batch-level costs that vary with the number of sales orders received from customers. Delivery-processing costs are batch-level costs that vary with the number of shipments made.
- Allied West allocates fixed general-administration costs (facility-level costs) to customers on the basis of customer revenues.
- Allied Furniture allocates its fixed corporate-office costs to sales offices on the basis of the budgeted costs of each sales office. Allied West then allocates these costs to customers on the basis of customer revenues.

In the following sections, we consider several decisions that Allied West's managers face: Should Allied West drop the Wisk account? Should it add a fourth customer, Loral? Should Allied Furniture close down Allied West? Should it open another sales office, Allied South, whose revenues and costs are identical to those of Allied West?

Relevant-Revenue and Relevant-Cost Analysis of Dropping a Customer

Exhibit 11-8 indicates a loss of $32,000 on the Wisk account. Allied West's managers believe the reason for the loss is that Wisk places low-margin orders with Allied and has relatively high sales-order, delivery-processing, furniture-handling, and marketing costs. Allied West's managers are considering several possible actions for the Wisk account: reducing the costs of supporting Wisk by becoming more efficient; cutting back on some of the services Allied West offers Wisk; asking Wisk to place larger, less frequent orders; charging Wisk higher prices; or dropping the Wisk account. The following analysis focuses on the operating-income effect of dropping the Wisk account for the year.

Allied West's managers and management accountants first focus on relevant revenues and relevant costs. Dropping the Wisk account will:

- Save cost of goods sold, furniture-handling labor, marketing support, sales-order and delivery-processing costs incurred on the account.

EXHIBIT 11-9 Relevant-Revenue and Relevant-Cost Analysis for Dropping the Wisk Account and Adding the Loral Account

	(Incremental Loss in Revenues) and Incremental Savings in Costs from Dropping Wisk Account (1)	Incremental Revenues and (Incremental Costs) from Adding Loral Account (2)
Revenues	$(400,000)	$400,000
Cost of goods sold	330,000	(330,000)
Furniture-handling labor	33,000	(33,000)
Furniture-handling equipment cost written off as depreciation	0	(9,000)
Rent	0	0
Marketing support	10,000	(10,000)
Sales order and delivery processing	12,000	(12,000)
General administration	0	0
Corporate-office costs	0	0
Total costs	385,000	(394,000)
Effect on operating income (loss)	$ (15,000)	$ 6,000

- Leave idle the warehouse space and furniture-handling equipment currently used to supply products to Wisk.
- Not affect the fixed rent costs, general-administration costs, or corporate-office costs.

Exhibit 11-9, column 1, presents the relevant-revenue and relevant-cost analysis using data from the Wisk column in Exhibit 11-8. The $385,000 cost savings from dropping the Wisk account will not be enough to offset the $400,000 loss in revenues. Because Allied West's operating income will be $15,000 lower if it drops the Wisk account, Allied West's managers decide to keep the Wisk account. They will, of course, continue to find ways to become more efficient, change Wisk's ordering patterns, or charge higher prices.

Depreciation on equipment that Allied West has already acquired is a past cost and therefore irrelevant. Rent, general-administration, and corporate-office costs are future costs that will not change if Allied West drops the Wisk account and are also irrelevant.

Overhead costs allocated to the sales office and individual customers are always irrelevant. The only question is, will expected total corporate office costs decrease as a result of dropping the Wisk account? In our example, they will not, so these costs are irrelevant. *If expected total corporate-office costs* were to decrease by dropping the Wisk account, those savings would be relevant even if *the amount allocated to Wisk did not change.*

Note that there is no opportunity cost of using warehouse space and equipment for Wisk because there is no alternative use for them. That is, the space and equipment will remain idle if managers drop the Wisk account. But suppose Allied West could lease the available extra space and equipment to Sanchez Corporation for $20,000 per year. Then $20,000 would be Allied West's opportunity cost of continuing to use the warehouse to service Wisk. Allied West would gain $5,000 by dropping the Wisk account ($20,000 from lease revenue minus lost operating income of $15,000). Under the total alternatives approach, the revenue loss from dropping the Wisk account would be $380,000 ($400,000 − $20,000) versus the savings in costs of $385,000 (Exhibit 11-9, column 1). Before reaching a decision, Allied West's managers must examine whether Wisk can be made more profitable so that supplying products to Wisk earns more than the $20,000 from leasing to Sanchez. The managers must also consider strategic factors such as the effect of dropping the Wisk account on Allied West's reputation for developing stable, long-run business relationships with its customers.

Relevant-Revenue and Relevant-Cost Analysis of Adding a Customer

Suppose that Allied West's managers are evaluating the profitability of adding another customer, Loral, to its existing customer base of Vogel, Brenner, and Wisk. There is no other alternative use of the Allied West facility. Loral has a customer profile much like Wisk's. Suppose Allied West's managers predict revenues and costs of doing business with Loral to be the same as the revenues and costs described under the Wisk column in Exhibit 11-8. In particular, Allied West would have to acquire furniture-handling equipment for the Loral account costing $9,000, with a one-year useful life and zero disposal value. If Loral is added as a customer, warehouse rent costs ($36,000), general-administration costs ($48,000), and *actual total* corporate-office costs will not change. Should Allied West's managers add Loral as a customer?

Exhibit 11-9, column 2, shows relevant revenues exceed relevant costs by $6,000. The opportunity cost of adding Loral is $0 because there is no alternative use of the Allied West facility. On the basis of this analysis, Allied West's managers would recommend adding Loral as a customer. Rent, general-administration, and corporate-office costs are irrelevant because these costs will not change if Loral is added as a customer. However, the cost of new equipment to support the Loral order (written off as depreciation of $9,000 in Exhibit 11-9, column 2) is relevant. That's because this cost can be avoided if Allied West decides not to add Loral as a customer. Note the critical distinction here: *Depreciation cost is irrelevant in deciding whether to drop Wisk as a customer because depreciation on equipment that has already been purchased is a past cost, but the cost of purchasing new equipment in the future that will then be written off as depreciation is relevant in deciding whether to add Loral as a customer.*

Relevant-Revenue and Relevant-Cost Analysis of Closing or Adding Branch Offices or Business Divisions

Companies periodically confront decisions about closing or adding branch offices or business divisions. For example, given Allied West's expected loss of $7,000 (see Exhibit 11-8), should Allied Furniture's managers close Allied West for the year? Closing Allied West will save all costs currently incurred at Allied West. Recall that there is no disposal value for the equipment that Allied West has already acquired. Closing Allied West will have no effect on total corporate-office costs and there is no alternative use for the Allied West space.

Exhibit 11-10, column 1, presents the relevant-revenue and relevant-cost analysis using data from the "Total" column in Exhibit 11-8. The revenue losses of $1,200,000 will exceed the cost savings of $1,158,000, leading to a decrease in operating income of $42,000. Allied West should not be closed. The key reasons are that closing Allied West will not save depreciation cost or actual total corporate-office costs. Depreciation cost is past or sunk because it represents the cost of equipment that Allied West has already purchased. Corporate-office costs allocated to various sales offices will change, *but the total amount of these costs will not decline.* The $24,000 no longer allocated to Allied West will be allocated to other sales offices. But because total corporate office costs will not be saved as a result of closing Allied West, the $24,000 of allocated corporate-office costs are irrelevant.

Finally suppose Allied Furniture has the opportunity to open another sales office, Allied South, whose revenues and costs are identical to Allied West's costs, including a cost of $25,000 to acquire furniture-handling equipment with a one-year useful life and zero disposal value. Opening this office will have no effect on total corporate-office costs. Should Allied Furniture's managers open Allied South? Exhibit 11-10, column 2, indicates that they should because opening Allied South will increase operating income by $17,000. As before, the cost of new equipment to be purchased in the future (and written off as depreciation) is relevant and *allocated* corporate-office costs are irrelevant because total corporate-office costs will not change if Allied South is opened.

DECISION POINT

In deciding to add or drop customers or to add or discontinue branch offices or business divisions, what should managers focus on and how should they take into account allocated overhead costs?

EXHIBIT 11-10 Relevant-Revenue and Relevant-Cost Analysis for Closing Allied West and Opening Allied South

	(Incremental Loss in Revenues) and Incremental Savings in Costs from Closing Allied West (1)	Incremental Revenues and (Incremental Costs) from Opening Allied South (2)
Revenues	$(1,200,000)	$1,200,000
Cost of goods sold	920,000	(920,000)
Furniture-handling labor	92,000	(92,000)
Furniture-handling equipment cost written off as depreciation	0	(25,000)
Rent	36,000	(36,000)
Marketing support	30,000	(30,000)
Sales order and delivery processing	32,000	(32,000)
General administration	48,000	(48,000)
Corporate-office costs	0	0
Total costs	1,158,000	(1,183,000)
Effect on operating income (loss)	$ (42,000)	$ 17,000

Irving Corporation runs two stores, one in Medfield and one in Oakland. Operating income for each store in 2017 is as follows:

11-4 TRY IT!

	Medfield Store	Oakland Store
Revenues	$2,100,000	$1,700,000
Operating costs		
Cost of goods sold	1,500,000	1,310,000
Variable operating costs (labor, utilities)	180,000	170,000
Lease rent (renewable each year)	160,000	155,000
Depreciation of equipment	50,000	40,000
Allocated corporate overhead	90,000	75,000
Total operating costs	1,980,000	1,750,000
Operating income (loss)	$ 120,000	$ (50,000)

The equipment has zero disposal value.

1. By closing down the Oakland store, Irving can reduce overall corporate overhead costs by $85,000. Should Irving Corporation close down the Oakland store?

2. Instead of closing down the Oakland store, Irving Corporation is thinking of opening another store with revenues and costs identical to the Oakland store (including a cost of $40,000 to acquire equipment with a one-year useful life and zero disposal value). Opening this store will increase corporate overhead costs by $10,000. Should Irving Corporation open another store like the Oakland store? Explain.

Irrelevance of Past Costs and Equipment-Replacement Decisions

LEARNING OBJECTIVE 7

Explain why book value of equipment is irrelevant to managers making equipment-replacement decisions

...it is a past cost

At several points in this chapter, we reasoned that past (historical or sunk) costs are irrelevant to decision making. That's because a decision cannot change something that has already happened. We now apply this concept to decisions about replacing equipment. We stress the idea that **book value**—original cost minus accumulated depreciation—of existing equipment is a past cost that is irrelevant.

Example 6: Toledo Company, a manufacturer of aircraft components, is considering replacing a metal-cutting machine with a newer model. The new machine is more efficient than the old machine, but has a shorter life. Revenues from aircraft parts ($1.1 million per year) will be unaffected by the replacement decision. The management accountant prepares the following data for the existing (old) machine and the replacement (new) machine:

	Old Machine	New Machine
Original cost	$1,000,000	$600,000
Useful life	5 years	2 years
Current age	3 years	0 years
Remaining useful life	2 years	2 years
Accumulated depreciation	$ 600,000	Not acquired yet
Book value	$ 400,000	Not acquired yet
Current disposal value (in cash)	$ 40,000	Not acquired yet
Terminal disposal value (in cash 2 years from now)	$ 0	$ 0
Annual operating costs (maintenance, energy, repairs, coolants, and so on)	$ 800,000	$460,000

Toledo Corporation uses straight-line depreciation. To focus on relevance, we ignore the time value of money and income taxes.[4] Should Toledo's managers replace its old machine?

Exhibit 11-11 presents a cost comparison of the two machines. Consider why each of the following four items in Toledo's equipment-replacement decision are relevant or irrelevant:

1. **Book value of old machine, $400,000.** Irrelevant, because it is a past or sunk cost. All past costs are "down the drain." Nothing can change what the company has already spent or what has already happened.

2. **Current disposal value of old machine, $40,000.** Relevant, because it is an expected future benefit that will only occur if the company replaces the machine.

EXHIBIT 11-11 Operating Income Comparison: Replacement of Machine, Relevant, and Irrelevant Items for Toledo Company

	Two Years Together		
	Keep (1)	Replace (2)	Difference (3) = (1) – (2)
Revenues	$2,200,000	$2,200,000	—
Operating costs			
Cash operating costs ($800,000/yr. × 2 years; $460,000/yr. × 2 years)	1,600,000	920,000	$ 680,000
Book value of old machine			
Periodic write-off as depreciation or	400,000	—	—
Lump-sum write-off	—	400,000[a]	
Current disposal value of old machine	—	(40,000)[a]	40,000
New machine cost, written off periodically as depreciation	—	600,000	(600,000)
Total operating costs	2,000,000	1,880,000	120,000
Operating income	$ 200,000	$ 320,000	$(120,000)

[a]In a formal income statement, these two items would be combined as "loss on disposal of machine" of $360,000.

[4] See Chapter 21 for a discussion of time-value-of-money and income-tax considerations in capital investment decisions.

| EXHIBIT 11-12 | Cost Comparison: Replacement of Machine, Relevant Items Only, for Toledo Company | | |

| | Two Years Together | | |
	Keep (1)	Replace (2)	Difference (3) = (1) − (2)
Cash operating costs	$1,600,000	$ 920,000	$680,000
Current disposal value of old machine	—	(40,000)	40,000
New machine, written off periodically as depreciation	—	600,000	(600,000)
Total relevant costs	$1,600,000	$1,480,000	$120,000

3. **Loss on disposal, $360,000.** This is the difference between amounts in items 1 and 2. This amount is a meaningless combination blurring the distinction between the irrelevant book value and the relevant disposal value. Managers should consider each value separately, as was done in items 1 and 2.

4. **Cost of new machine, $600,000.** Relevant, because it is an expected future cost that will only occur if the company purchases the machine.

Exhibit 11-11 should clarify these four assertions. Column 3 in Exhibit 11-11 shows that the book value of the old machine does not differ between the alternatives and could be ignored for decision-making purposes. No matter what the timing of the write-off—whether a lump-sum charge in the current year or depreciation charges over the next 2 years—the total amount is still $400,000 because it is a past (historical) cost. In contrast, the $600,000 cost of the new machine and the current disposal value of $40,000 for the old machine are relevant because they would not arise if Toledo's managers decided not to replace the machine. Considering the cost of replacing the machine and savings in cash operating costs, Toledo's managers should replace the machine because the operating income from replacing it is $120,000 higher for the 2 years together.

Exhibit 11-12 concentrates only on relevant items and leads to the same answer—replacing the machine leads to lower costs and higher operating income of $120,000—even though book value is omitted from the calculations. The only relevant items are the cash operating costs, the disposal value of the old machine, and the cost of the new machine, which is represented as depreciation in Exhibit 11-12.

DECISION POINT

Is book value of existing equipment relevant in equipment-replacement decisions?

Decisions and Performance Evaluation

Consider our equipment-replacement example in light of the five-step sequence in Exhibit 11-1 (page 448):

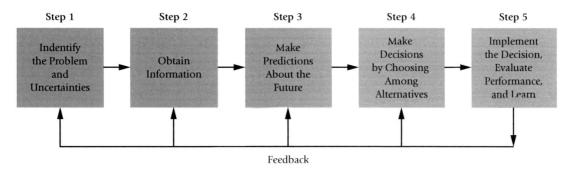

The decision model (Step 4), which is presented in Exhibits 11-11 and 11-12, dictates replacing the machine rather than keeping it. In the real world, however, would the manager

LEARNING OBJECTIVE 8

Explain how conflicts can arise between the decision model a manager uses and the performance-evaluation model top management uses to evaluate managers

...tell managers to take a multiple-year view in decision making but judge their performance only on the basis of the current year's operating income

replace the machine? An important factor in replacement decisions is the manager's perception of whether the decision model is consistent with how the company will judge his or her performance after the decision is implemented (the performance-evaluation model in Step 5).

From the perspective of their own careers, it is no surprise that managers tend to favor the alternative that makes their performance look better. In our examples throughout this chapter, the decision model and the performance-evaluation model were consistent. If, however, the performance-evaluation model conflicts with the decision model, the performance-evaluation model often prevails in influencing managers' decisions. The following table compares Toledo's accrual accounting income for the first year and the second year when the manager decides to keep the machine versus when the manager decides to replace the machine.

	Accrual Accounting First-Year Results		Accrual Accounting Second-Year Results	
	Keep	**Replace**	**Keep**	**Replace**
Revenues	$1,100,000	$1,100,000	$1,100,000	$1,100,000
Operating costs				
Cash-operating costs	800,000	460,000	800,000	460,000
Depreciation	200,000	300,000	200,000	300,000
Loss on disposal	—	360,000	—	—
Total operating costs	1,000,000	1,120,000	1,000,000	760,000
Operating income (loss)	$ 100,000	$ (20,000)	$ 100,000	$ 340,000

Total accrual accounting income for the 2 years together is $120,000 higher if the machine is replaced, as in Exhibit 11-11. But if the promotion or bonus of the manager at Toledo hinges on his or her first year's operating-income performance under accrual accounting, the manager would be very tempted to keep the old machine. Why? Because the accrual accounting model for measuring performance will show a first-year operating income of $100,000 if the old machine is kept versus an operating loss of $20,000 if the machine is replaced. Even though top management's goals encompass the 2-year period (consistent with the decision model), the manager will focus on first-year results if top management evaluates his or her performance on the basis of short-run measures such as the first-year's operating income.

Managers frequently find it difficult to resolve the conflict between the decision model and the performance-evaluation model. In theory, resolving the difficulty seems obvious: Managers should design models that are consistent. Consider our replacement example. Year-by-year effects on operating income of replacement can be budgeted for the 2-year planning horizon. The manager then would be evaluated on the expectation that the first year would be poor and the next year would be much better. Doing this for every decision, however, makes the performance-evaluation model very cumbersome. As a result of these practical difficulties, accounting systems rarely track each decision separately. Performance evaluation focuses on responsibility centers for a specific period, not on projects or individual items of equipment over their useful lives. Thus, the effects of many different decisions are combined in a single performance report and evaluation measure, say operating income. Lower-level managers make decisions to maximize operating income, and top management—through the reporting system—is rarely aware of particular desirable alternatives that lower-level managers did *not* choose because of conflicts between the decision and performance-evaluation models.

Consider another conflict between the decision model and the performance-evaluation model. Suppose a manager buys a particular machine only to discover shortly afterward that he or she could have purchased a better machine instead. The decision model may suggest replacing the machine that was just bought with the better machine, but will the manager do so? Probably not. Why? Because replacing the machine so soon after its purchase will reflect badly on the manager's capabilities and performance. If the manager's bosses have no knowledge of the better machine, the manager may prefer to keep the recently purchased machine rather than alert them to the better machine.

DECISION POINT

How can conflicts arise between the decision model a manager uses and the performance evaluation model top management uses to evaluate that manager?

Many managers consider it unethical to take actions that make their own performance look good when these actions are not in the best interests of the firm. Critics believe that it was precisely these kinds of behaviors that contributed to the recent global financial crisis. To discourage such behaviors, managers develop codes of conduct, emphasize values, and build cultures that focus on doing the right things. Chapter 23 discusses performance-evaluation models, ethics, and ways to reduce conflict between the decision model and the performance-evaluation model in more detail.

PROBLEM FOR SELF-STUDY

Wally Lewis is manager of the engineering development division of Goldcoast Products. Lewis has just received a proposal signed by all 15 of his engineers to replace the workstations with networked personal computers (networked PCs). Lewis is not enthusiastic about the proposal.

Data on workstations and networked PCs are:

	Workstations	Networked PCs
Original cost	$ 300,000	$ 135,000
Useful life	5 years	3 years
Current age	2 years	0 years
Remaining useful life	3 years	3 years
Accumulated depreciation	$ 120,000	Not acquired yet
Current book value	$ 180,000	Not acquired yet
Current disposal value (in cash)	$ 95,000	Not acquired yet
Terminal disposal value (in cash 3 years from now)	$ 0	$ 0
Annual computer-related cash operating costs	$ 40,000	$ 10,000
Annual revenues	$1,000,000	$1,000,000
Annual non-computer-related cash operating costs	$ 880,000	$ 880,000

Lewis's annual bonus includes a component based on division operating income. He has a promotion possibility next year that would make him a group vice president of Goldcoast Products.

1. Compare the costs of workstations and networked PCs. Consider the cumulative results for the 3 years together, ignoring the time value of money and income taxes.
2. Why might Lewis be reluctant to purchase the networked PCs?

Required

Solution

1. The following table considers all cost items when comparing future costs of workstations and networked PCs:

	Three Years Together		
All Items	Workstations (1)	Networked PCs (2)	Difference (3) = (1) − (2)
Revenues	$3,000,000	$3,000,000	—
Operating costs			
Non-computer-related cash operating costs ($880,000 per year × 3 years)	2,640,000	2,640,000	—
Computer-related cash operating costs ($40,000 per year; $10,000 per year × 3 years)	120,000	30,000	$ 90,000

| All Items | Three Years Together | | |
	Workstations (1)	Networked PCs (2)	Difference (3) = (1) − (2)
Workstations' book value			
Periodic write-off as depreciation or	180,000	—	—
Lump-sum write-off	—	180,000	
Current disposal value of workstations	—	(95,000)	95,000
Networked PCs, written off periodically as depreciation	—	135,000	(135,000)
Total operating costs	2,940,000	2,890,000	50,000
Operating income	$ 60,000	$ 110,000	$(50,000)

Alternatively, the analysis could focus on only those items in the preceding table that differ between the alternatives.

| Relevant Items | Three Years Together | | |
	Workstations	Networked PCs	Difference
Computer-related cash operating costs ($40,000 per year × 3 years; $10,000 per year × 3 years)	$120,000	$ 30,000	$ 90,000
Current disposal value of workstations	—	(95,000)	95,000
Networked PCs, written off periodically as depreciation	—	135,000	(135,000)
Total relevant costs	$120,000	$ 70,000	$ 50,000

The analysis suggests that it is cost-effective to replace the workstations with the networked PCs.

2. The accrual-accounting operating incomes *for the first year* under the alternatives of "keep workstations" versus the "buy networked PCs" are:

	Keep Workstations		Buy Networked PCs	
Revenues		$1,000,000		$1,000,000
Operating costs				
Non-computer-related operating costs	$880,000		$880,000	
Computer-related cash operating costs	40,000		10,000	
Depreciation	60,000		45,000	
Loss on disposal of workstations	—		85,000[a]	
Total operating costs		980,000		1,020,000
Operating income (loss)		$ 20,000		$ (20,000)

[a] $85,000 = Book value of workstations, $180,000 − Current disposal value, $95,000.

Lewis would be less happy with the expected operating loss of $20,000 if the networked PCs are purchased than he would be with the expected operating income of $20,000 if the workstations are kept. Buying the networked PCs would eliminate the component of his bonus based on operating income. He might also perceive the $20,000 operating loss as reducing his chances of being promoted to group vice president.

DECISION **POINTS**

The following question-and-answer format summarizes the chapter's learning objectives. Each decision presents a key question related to a learning objective. The guidelines are the answer to that question.

Decision	Guidelines
1. What is the five-step process that managers can use to make decisions?	The five-step decision-making process is (a) identify the problem and uncertainties, (b) obtain information, (c) make predictions about the future, (d) make decisions by choosing among alternatives, and (e) implement the decision, evaluate performance, and learn.
2. When is a revenue or cost item relevant for a particular decision and what potential problems should managers avoid in relevant-cost analysis?	To be relevant for a particular decision, a revenue or cost item must meet two criteria: (a) It must be an expected future revenue or expected future cost and (b) it must differ among alternative courses of action. Relevant-revenue and relevant-cost analysis only consider quantitative outcomes that can be expressed in financial terms. But managers must also consider nonfinancial quantitative factors and qualitative factors, such as employee morale, when making decisions. Two potential problems to avoid in relevant-cost analysis are (a) making incorrect general assumptions—such as all variable costs are relevant and all fixed costs are irrelevant—and (b) losing sight of total fixed costs and focusing instead on unit fixed costs.
3. What is an opportunity cost and why should managers consider it when making insourcing-versus-outsourcing decisions?	Opportunity cost is the contribution to income that is forgone by not using a limited resource in its next-best alternative use. Opportunity cost is included in decision making because the relevant cost of any decision is (a) the incremental cost of the decision plus (b) the opportunity cost of the profit forgone from making that decision. When capacity is constrained, managers must consider the opportunity cost of using the capacity when deciding whether to produce the product in-house versus outsourcing it.
4. When a resource is constrained, how should managers choose which of multiple products to produce and sell?	When a resource is constrained, managers should select the product that yields the highest contribution margin per unit of the constraining or limiting resource (factor). In this way, total contribution margin will be maximized.
5. What steps can managers take to manage bottlenecks?	Managers can take four steps to manage bottlenecks: (a) recognize that the bottleneck operation determines throughput (contribution) margin, (b) identify the bottleneck, (c) keep the bottleneck busy and subordinate all nonbottleneck operations to the bottleneck operation, and (d) increase bottleneck efficiency and capacity.
6. In deciding to add or drop customers or to add or discontinue branch offices or business divisions, what should managers focus on and how should they take into account allocated overhead costs?	When making decisions about adding or dropping customers or adding or discontinuing branch offices and business divisions, managers should focus on only those costs that will change and any opportunity costs. Managers should ignore allocated overhead costs.
7. Is book value of existing equipment relevant in equipment-replacement decisions?	Book value of existing equipment is a past (historical or sunk) cost and, therefore, is irrelevant in equipment-replacement decisions.
8. How can conflicts arise between the decision model a manager uses and the performance-evaluation model top management uses to evaluate that manager?	Top management faces a persistent challenge: making sure that the performance-evaluation model of lower-level managers is consistent with the decision model. A common inconsistency is to tell these managers to take a multiple-year view in their decision making but then to judge their performance only on the basis of the current year's operating income.

APPENDIX

Linear Programming

In this chapter's Power Recreation example (pages 462–464), suppose both the snowmobile and boat engines must be tested on a very expensive machine before they are shipped to customers. The available machine-hours for testing are limited. Production data are:

Department	Available Daily Capacity in Hours	Use of Capacity in Hours per Unit of Product		Daily Maximum Production in Units	
		Snowmobile Engine	Boat Engine	Snowmobile Engine	Boat Engine
Assembly	600 machine-hours	2.0 machine-hours	5.0 machine-hours	300[a] snowmobile engines	120 boat engines
Testing	120 testing-hours	1.0 machine-hour	0.5 machine-hour	120 snowmobile engines	240 boat engines

[a] For example, 600 machine-hours ÷ 2.0 machine-hours per snowmobile engine = 300, the maximum number of snowmobile engines that the assembly department can make if it works exclusively on snowmobile engines.

Exhibit 11-13 summarizes these and other relevant data. In addition, as a result of material shortages for boat engines, Power Recreation cannot produce more than 110 boat engines per day. How many engines of each type should Power Recreation's managers produce and sell daily to maximize operating income?

Because there are multiple constraints, managers can use a technique called *linear programming (LP)* to determine the number of each type of engine to produce. LP models typically assume that all costs are either variable or fixed for a single cost driver (units of output). We will see that LP models also require certain other linear assumptions to hold. When these assumptions fail, managers should consider other decision models.[5]

Steps in Solving an LP Problem

We use the data in Exhibit 11-13 to illustrate the three steps in solving an LP problem. Throughout this discussion, S equals the number of snowmobile engines produced and sold, and B equals the number of boat engines produced and sold.

Step 1: Determine the Objective Function. The **objective function** of a linear program expresses the objective or goal to be maximized (say, operating income) or minimized (say, operating costs). In our example, the objective is to find the combination of snowmobile engines and boat engines that maximizes total contribution margin. Fixed costs remain the same regardless of the product-mix decision and are irrelevant. The linear function expressing the objective for the total contribution margin (TCM) is:

$$TCM = \$240S + \$375B$$

EXHIBIT 11-13   Operating Data for Power Recreation

	Department Capacity (per Day) in Product Units		Selling Price	Variable Cost per Unit	Contribution Margin per Unit
	Assembly	Testing			
Only snowmobile engines	300	120	$ 800	$560	$240
Only boat engines	120	240	$1,000	$625	$375

---

[5] Other decision models are described in Barry Render, Ralph M. Stair, and Michael E. Hanna, *Quantitative Analysis for Management*, 11th ed. (Upper Saddle River, NJ: Prentice Hall, 2012); and Steven Nahmias, *Production and Operations Analysis*, 6th ed. (New York: McGraw-Hill/Irwin, 2008).

EXHIBIT 11-14

Linear Programming:
Graphic Solution for
Power Recreation

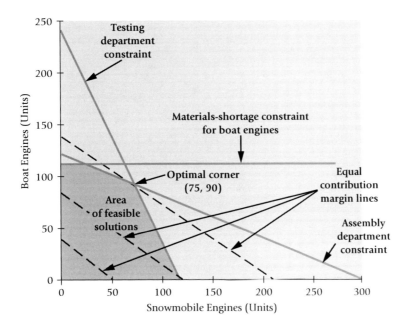

Step 2: Specify the Constraints.

A **constraint** is a mathematical inequality or equality that must be satisfied by the variables in a mathematical model. The following linear inequalities express the relationships in our example:

Assembly department constraint	$2S + 5B \leq 600$
Testing department constraint	$1S + 0.5B \leq 120$
Materials-shortage constraint for boat engines	$B \leq 110$
Negative production is impossible	$S \geq 0$ and $B \geq 0$

The three solid lines on the graph in Exhibit 11-14 show the existing constraints for assembly and testing and the materials-shortage constraint.[6] The feasible or technically possible alternatives are those combinations of quantities of snowmobile engines and boat engines that satisfy all the constraining resources or factors. The shaded "area of feasible solutions" in Exhibit 11-14 shows the boundaries of those product combinations that are feasible.

Step 3: Compute the Optimal Solution.

Linear programming (LP) is an optimization technique used to maximize the *objective function* when there are multiple *constraints*. We present two approaches for finding the optimal solution using LP: trial-and-error approach and graphic approach. These approaches are easy to use in our example because there are only two variables in the objective function and a small number of constraints. Understanding these approaches provides insight into LP. In most real-world LP applications, managers use computer software packages to calculate the optimal solution.[7]

Trial-and-Error Approach

Managers can find the optimal solution by trial and error, by working with coordinates of the corners of the area of feasible solutions. As we will see, the optimal solution always lies at an extreme point of the feasible region.

First, select any set of corner points and compute the total contribution margin. Five corner points appear in Exhibit 11-14. It is helpful to use simultaneous equations to obtain the

---

[6] As an example of how the lines are plotted in Exhibit 11-14, use equal signs instead of inequality signs and assume for the assembly department that $B = 0$; then $S = 300$ (600 machine-hours ÷ 2 machine-hours per snowmobile engine). Assume that $S = 0$; then $B = 120$ (600 machine-hours ÷ 5 machine-hours per boat engine). Connect those two points with a straight line.

[7] Standard computer software packages rely on the *simplex method*, which is an iterative step-by-step procedure for determining the optimal solution to an LP problem. This method starts with a specific feasible solution and then tests it by substitution to see whether the result can be improved. These substitutions continue until no further improvement is possible and the optimal solution is obtained.

exact coordinates in the graph. To illustrate, the corner point ($S = 75$, $B = 90$) can be derived by solving the two pertinent constraint inequalities as simultaneous equations:

$$2S + 5B = 600 \quad (1)$$
$$1S + 0.5B = 120 \quad (2)$$

Multiplying (2) by 2:
$$2S + B = 240 \quad (3)$$

Subtracting (3) from (1):
$$4B = 360$$

Therefore,
$$B = 360 \div 4 = 90$$

Substituting for B in (2):
$$1S + 0.5(90) = 120$$
$$S = 120 - 45 = 75$$

Given $S = 75$ snowmobile engines and $B = 90$ boat engines, $TCM = (\$240$ per snowmobile engine $\times$ 75 snowmobile engines$) + (\$375$ per boat engine $\times$ 90 boat engines$) = \$51,750$.

Second, move from corner point to corner point and compute the total contribution margin at each corner point.

Trial	Corner Point (S, B)	Snowmobile Engines (S)	Boat Engines (B)	Total Contribution Margin		
1	(0, 0)	0	0	$240(0)	+ $375(0)	= $0
2	(0, 110)	0	110	$240(0)	+ $375(110)	= $41,250
3	(25,110)	25	110	$240(25)	+ $375(110)	= $47,250
4	(75, 90)	75	90	$240(75)	+ $375(90)	= $51,750[a]
5	(120, 0)	120	0	$240(120)	+ $375(0)	= $28,800

[a] The optimal solution.

The optimal product mix is the mix that yields the highest total contribution: 75 snowmobile engines and 90 boat engines. To understand the solution, consider what happens when moving from the point (25, 110) to (75, 90). Power Recreation gives up $7,500 [$375 $\times$ (110 − 90)] in contribution margin from boat engines while gaining $12,000 [$240 $\times$ (75 − 25)] in contribution margin from snowmobile engines. This results in a net increase in contribution margin of $4,500 ($12,000 − $7,500), from $47,250 to $51,750.

Graphic Approach

Consider all possible combinations that will produce the same total contribution margin of, say, $12,000. That is,

$$\$240S + \$375B = \$12,000$$

This set of $12,000 contribution margins is a straight dashed line through [$S = 50$ ($12,000 ÷ $240); $B = 0$] and [$S = 0$; $B = 32$ ($12,000 ÷ $375)] in Exhibit 11-14. Other equal total contribution margins can be represented by lines parallel to this one. In Exhibit 11-14, we show three dashed lines. Lines drawn farther from the origin represent more sales of both products and higher amounts of equal contribution margins.

The optimal line is the one farthest from the origin but still passing through a point in the area of feasible solutions. This line represents the highest total contribution margin. The optimal solution—the number of snowmobile engines and boat engines that will maximize the objective function, total contribution margin—is the corner point ($S = 75$, $B = 90$). This solution will become apparent if you put a straight-edge ruler on the graph and move it outward from the origin and parallel with the $12,000 contribution margin line. Move the ruler as far away from the origin as possible—that is, increase the total contribution margin—without leaving the area of feasible solutions. In general, the optimal solution in a maximization problem lies at the corner where the dashed line intersects an extreme point of the area of feasible solutions. Moving the ruler out any farther puts it outside the area of feasible solutions.

Sensitivity Analysis

What are the implications of uncertainty about the accounting or technical coefficients used in the objective function (such as the contribution margin per unit of snowmobile engines or boat engines) or the constraints (such as the number of machine-hours it takes to make a snowmobile engine or a boat engine)? Consider how a change in the contribution margin of snowmobile engines from $240 to $300 per unit would affect the optimal solution. Assume the contribution margin for boat engines remains unchanged at $375 per unit. The revised objective function will be:

$$TCM = \$300S + \$375B$$

Using the trial-and-error approach to calculate the total contribution margin for each of the five corner points described in the previous table, the optimal solution is still ($S = 75$, $B = 90$). What if the contribution margin of snowmobile engines falls to $160 per unit? The optimal solution remains the same ($S = 75$, $B = 90$). Thus, big changes in the contribution margin per unit of snowmobile engines have no effect on the optimal solution in this case. That's because, although the slopes of the equal contribution margin lines in Exhibit 11-14 change as the contribution margin of snowmobile engines changes from $240 to $300 to $160 per unit, the farthest point at which the equal contribution margin lines intersect the area of feasible solutions is still ($S = 75$, $B = 90$).

TERMS TO LEARN

This chapter and the Glossary at the end of the book contain definitions of the following important terms:

book value (**p. 471**)	incremental revenue (**p. 456**)	product-mix decisions (**p. 462**)
business function costs (**p. 450**)	insourcing (**p. 454**)	qualitative factors (**p. 449**)
constraint (**p. 479**)	linear programming (LP) (**p. 479**)	quantitative factors (**p. 449**)
decision model (**p. 447**)	make-or-buy decisions (**p. 454**)	relevant costs (**p. 447**)
differential cost (**p. 456**)	objective function (**p. 478**)	relevant revenues (**p. 447**)
differential revenue (**p. 456**)	one-time-only special order (**p. 450**)	sunk costs (**p. 448**)
full costs of the product (**p. 450**)	opportunity cost (**p. 458**)	theory of constraints (TOC) (**p. 464**)
incremental cost (**p. 456**)	outsourcing (**p. 454**)	throughput margin (**p. 464**)

ASSIGNMENT MATERIAL

Questions

Pearson MyLab Accounting

11-1 Outline the five-step sequence in a decision process.

11-2 Define relevant costs. Why are historical costs irrelevant?

11-3 "All future costs are relevant." Do you agree? Why?

11-4 Distinguish between quantitative and qualitative factors in decision making.

11-5 Describe two potential problems that should be avoided in relevant-cost analysis.

11-6 "Variable costs are always relevant, and fixed costs are always irrelevant." Do you agree? Why?

11-7 "A component part should be purchased whenever the purchase price is less than its total manufacturing cost per unit." Do you agree? Why?

11-8 Define opportunity cost.

11-9 "Managers should always buy inventory in quantities that result in the lowest purchase cost per unit." Do you agree? Why?

11-10 "Management should always maximize sales of the product with the highest contribution margin per unit." Do you agree? Why?

11-11 "A branch office or business segment that shows negative operating income should be shut down." Do you agree? Explain briefly.

11-12 "Cost written off as depreciation on equipment already purchased is always irrelevant." Do you agree? Why?

11-13 "Managers will always choose the alternative that maximizes operating income or minimizes costs in the decision model." Do you agree? Why?

11-14 Describe the three steps in solving a linear programming problem.

11-15 How might the optimal solution of a linear programming problem be determined?

Pearson MyLab Accounting

Multiple-Choice Questions

11-16 Qualitative and quantitative factors. Which of the following is not a qualitative factor that Atlas Manufacturing should consider when deciding whether to buy or make a part used in manufacturing their product?
a. Quality of the outside producer's product.
b. Potential loss of trade secrets.
c. Manufacturing deadlines and special orders.
d. Variable cost per unit of the product.

11-17 Special order, opportunity cost. Chade Corp. is considering a special order brought to it by a new client. If Chade determines the variable cost to be $9 per unit, and the contribution margin of the next best alternative of the facility to be $5 per unit, then if Chade has:
a. Full capacity, the company will be profitable at $4 per unit.
b. Excess capacity, the company will be profitable at $6 per unit.
c. Full capacity, the selling price must be greater than $5 per unit.
d. Excess capacity, the selling price must be greater than $9 per unit.

11-18 Special order, opportunity cost. In order to determine whether a special order should be accepted at full capacity, the sales price of the special order must be compared to the per unit:
a. Contribution margin of the special order.
b. Variable cost and contribution margin of the special order.
c. Variable cost and contribution margin of the next best alternative.
d. Variable cost of current production and the contribution margin of the next best alternative.

11-19 Keep or drop a business segment. Lees Corp. is deciding whether to keep or drop a small segment of its business. Key information regarding the segment includes:

Contribution margin: 35,000
Avoidable fixed costs: 30,000
Unavoidable fixed costs: 25,000

Given the information above, Lees should:
a. Drop the segment because the contribution margin is less than total fixed costs.
b. Drop the segment because avoidable fixed costs exceed unavoidable fixed costs.
c. Keep the segment because the contribution margin exceeds avoidable fixed costs.
d. Keep the segment because the contribution margin exceeds unavoidable fixed costs.

11-20 Relevant costs. Ace Cleaning Service is considering expanding into one or more new market areas. Which costs are relevant to Ace's decision on whether to expand?

	Sunk Costs	Variable Costs	Opportunity Costs
a.	No	Yes	Yes
b.	Yes	Yes	Yes
c.	No	Yes	No
d.	Yes	No	Yes

Exercises

11-21 Disposal of assets. Answer the following questions.

1. A company has an inventory of 1,250 assorted parts for a line of missiles that has been discontinued. The inventory cost is $76,000. The parts can be either (a) remachined at total additional costs of $26,500 and then sold for $33,500 or (b) sold as scrap for $2,500. Which action is more profitable? Show your calculations.

2. A truck, costing $100,500 and uninsured, is wrecked on its first day in use. It can be either (a) disposed of for $18,000 cash and replaced with a similar truck costing $103,000 or (b) rebuilt for $88,500 and thus be brand new as far as operating characteristics and looks are concerned. Which action is less costly? Show your calculations.

11-22 Relevant and irrelevant costs. Answer the following questions.

1. DeCesare Computers makes 5,200 units of a circuit board, CB76, at a cost of $280 each. Variable cost per unit is $190 and fixed cost per unit is $90. Peach Electronics offers to supply 5,200 units of CB76 for $260. If DeCesare buys from Peach it will be able to save $10 per unit in fixed costs but continue to incur the remaining $80 per unit. Should DeCesare accept Peach's offer? Explain.

2. LN Manufacturing is deciding whether to keep or replace an old machine. It obtains the following information:

	Old Machine	New Machine
Original cost	$10,700	$9,000
Useful life	10 years	3 years
Current age	7 years	0 years
Remaining useful life	3 years	3 years
Accumulated depreciation	$7,490	Not acquired yet
Book value	$3,210	Not acquired yet
Current disposal value (in cash)	$2,200	Not acquired yet
Terminal disposal value (3 years from now)	$0	$0
Annual cash operating costs	$17,500	$15,500

LN Manufacturing uses straight-line depreciation. Ignore the time value of money and income taxes. Should LN Manufacturing replace the old machine? Explain.

11-23 Multiple choice. (CPA) Choose the best answer.

1. The Dalton Company manufactures slippers and sells them at $12 a pair. Variable manufacturing cost is $5.00 a pair, and allocated fixed manufacturing cost is $1.25 a pair. It has enough idle capacity available to accept a one-time-only special order of 5,000 pairs of slippers at $6.25 a pair. Dalton will not incur any marketing costs as a result of the special order. What would the effect on operating income be if the special order could be accepted without affecting normal sales: (a) $0, (b) $6,250 increase, (c) $28,750 increase, or (d) $31,250 increase? Show your calculations.

2. The Sacramento Company manufactures Part No. 498 for use in its production line. The manufacturing cost per unit for 30,000 units of Part No. 498 is as follows:

Direct materials	$ 5
Direct manufacturing labor	22
Variable manufacturing overhead	8
Fixed manufacturing overhead allocated	15
Total manufacturing cost per unit	$50

The Counter Company has offered to sell 30,000 units of Part No. 498 to Sacramento for $47 per unit. Sacramento will make the decision to buy the part from Counter if there is an overall savings of at least $30,000 for Sacramento. If Sacramento accepts Counter's offer, $8 per unit of the fixed overhead allocated would be eliminated. Furthermore, Sacramento has determined that the released facilities could be used to save relevant costs in the manufacture of Part No. 575. For Sacramento to achieve an overall savings of $30,000, the amount of relevant costs that would have to be saved by using the released facilities in the manufacture of Part No. 575 would be which of the following: (a) $90,000, (b) $150,000, (c) $180,000, or (d) $210,000? Show your calculations. What other factors might Sacramento consider before outsourcing to Counter?

11-24 Special order, activity-based costing. (CMA, adapted) The Gold Plus Company manufactures medals for winners of athletic events and other contests. Its manufacturing plant has the capacity to produce 11,000 medals each month. Current production and sales are 10,000 medals per month. The company normally charges $150 per medal. Cost information for the current activity level is as follows:

Variable costs that vary with number of units produced	
Direct materials	$ 350,000
Direct manufacturing labor	375,000
Variable costs (for setups, materials handling, quality control, and so on) that vary with number of batches, 200 batches × $500 per batch	100,000
Fixed manufacturing costs	300,000
Fixed marketing costs	275,000
Total costs	$1,400,000

Gold Plus has just received a special one-time-only order for 1,000 medals at $100 per medal. Accepting the special order would not affect the company's regular business. Gold Plus makes medals for its existing customers in batch sizes of 50 medals (200 batches × 50 medals per batch = 10,000 medals). The special order requires Gold Plus to make the medals in 25 batches of 40 medals.

Required

1. Should Gold Plus accept this special order? Show your calculations.
2. Suppose plant capacity were only 10,500 medals instead of 11,000 medals each month. The special order must either be taken in full or be rejected completely. Should Gold Plus accept the special order? Show your calculations.
3. As in requirement 1, assume that monthly capacity is 11,000 medals. Gold Plus is concerned that if it accepts the special order, its existing customers will immediately demand a price discount of $10 in the month in which the special order is being filled. They would argue that Gold Plus's capacity costs are now being spread over more units and that existing customers should get the benefit of these lower costs. Should Gold Plus accept the special order under these conditions? Show your calculations.

11-25 Make versus buy, activity-based costing. The Svenson Corporation manufactures cellular modems. It manufactures its own cellular modem circuit boards (CMCB), an important part of the cellular modem. It reports the following cost information about the costs of making CMCBs in 2017 and the expected costs in 2018:

	Current Costs in 2017	Expected Costs in 2018
Variable manufacturing costs		
Direct material cost per CMCB	$ 180	$ 170
Direct manufacturing labor cost per CMCB	50	45
Variable manufacturing cost per batch for setups, materials handling, and quality control	1,600	1,500
Fixed manufacturing cost		
Fixed manufacturing overhead costs that can be avoided if CMCBs are not made	320,000	320,000
Fixed manufacturing overhead costs of plant depreciation, insurance, and administration that cannot be avoided even if CMCBs are not made	800,000	800,000

Svenson manufactured 8,000 CMCBs in 2017 in 40 batches of 200 each. In 2018, Svenson anticipates needing 10,000 CMCBs. The CMCBs would be produced in 80 batches of 125 each.

The Minton Corporation has approached Svenson about supplying CMCBs to Svenson in 2018 at $300 per CMCB on whatever delivery schedule Svenson wants.

Required

1. Calculate the total expected manufacturing cost per unit of making CMCBs in 2018.
2. Suppose the capacity currently used to make CMCBs will become idle if Svenson purchases CMCBs from Minton. On the basis of financial considerations alone, should Svenson make CMCBs or buy them from Minton? Show your calculations.

3. Now suppose that if Svenson purchases CMCBs from Minton, its best alternative use of the capacity currently used for CMCBs is to make and sell special circuit boards (CB3s) to the Essex Corporation. Svenson estimates the following incremental revenues and costs from CB3s:

Total expected incremental future revenues	$2,000,000
Total expected incremental future costs	$2,150,000

On the basis of financial considerations alone, should Svenson make CMCBs or buy them from Minton? Show your calculations.

11-26 Inventory decision, opportunity costs. Best Trim, a manufacturer of lawn mowers, predicts that it will purchase 204,000 spark plugs next year. Best Trim estimates that 17,000 spark plugs will be required each month. A supplier quotes a price of $9 per spark plug. The supplier also offers a special discount option: If all 204,000 spark plugs are purchased at the start of the year, a discount of 2% off the $9 price will be given. Best Trim can invest its cash at 10% per year. It costs Best Trim $260 to place each purchase order.

1. What is the opportunity cost of interest forgone from purchasing all 204,000 units at the start of the year instead of in 12 monthly purchases of 17,000 units per order?
2. Would this opportunity cost be recorded in the accounting system? Why?
3. Should Best Trim purchase 204,000 units at the start of the year or 17,000 units each month? Show your calculations.
4. What other factors should Best Trim consider when making its decision?

11-27 Relevant costs, contribution margin, product emphasis. The Beach Comber is a take-out food store at a popular beach resort. Sara Miller, owner of the Beach Comber, is deciding how much refrigerator space to devote to four different drinks. Pertinent data on these four drinks are as follows:

	Cola	Lemonade	Punch	Natural Orange Juice
Selling price per case	$19.10	$20.25	$27.10	$39.50
Variable cost per case	$14.40	$15.90	$21.50	$29.80
Cases sold per foot of shelf space per day	10	24	25	22

Miller has a maximum front shelf space of 12 feet to devote to the four drinks. She wants a minimum of 1 foot and a maximum of 6 feet of front shelf space for each drink.

1. Calculate the contribution margin per case of each type of drink.
2. A coworker of Miller's recommends that she maximize the shelf space devoted to those drinks with the highest contribution margin per case. Do you agree with this recommendation? Explain briefly.
3. What shelf-space allocation for the four drinks would you recommend for the Beach Comber? Show your calculations.

11-28 Selection of most profitable products. Isochlorine is produced in a chemical process that is very threatening to the environment. As a result of this, the government has limited the yearly production. Company Soleil uses isochlorine to produce four cosmetic products A, B, C, and D. Soleil has an inventory of 2,000 kg of isochlorine at a value of $20,000.

As a result of production restrictions imposed on their supplier, Soleil will not be able to purchase additional isochlorine during the coming period.

Although Soleil, by means of its commercial campaign, suggests that its main goal is to let people experience the sanitary effects of its cosmetic products, the management is only interested in profit maximization.

The management of Soleil must decide how to use the scarce material. The following information is available concerning the next period:

Product	Sales	Selling Price per Unit	Labor-Hours per Unit	Material per Unit (Grams)
A	3,000	$ 70	1.0	500
B	8,000	$ 60	1.2	300
C	4,000	$100	2.0	600
D	5,000	$ 80	1.0	800

The labor tariff per hour is $30. Labor costs are linear variable. Sales provision is 10% of the selling price. Which products must Soleil produce during the next period? What is the contribution margin for the next period? Show your calculations.

11-29 Theory of constraints, throughput margin, relevant costs. The Pierce Corporation manufactures filing cabinets in two operations: machining and finishing. It provides the following information:

	Machining	**Finishing**
Annual capacity	110,000 units	90,000 units
Annual production	90,000 units	90,000 units
Fixed operating costs (excluding direct materials)	$540,000	$270,000
Fixed operating costs per unit produced ($540,000 ÷ 90,000; $270,000 ÷ 90,000)	$6 per unit	$3 per unit

Each cabinet sells for $70 and has direct material costs of $30 incurred at the start of the machining operation. Pierce has no other variable costs. Pierce can sell whatever output it produces. The following requirements refer only to the preceding data. There is no connection between the requirements.

1. Pierce is considering using some modern jigs and tools in the finishing operation that would increase annual finishing output by 1,150 units. The annual cost of these jigs and tools is $35,000. Should Pierce acquire these tools? Show your calculations.
2. The production manager of the Machining Department has submitted a proposal to do faster setups that would increase the annual capacity of the Machining Department by 9,000 units and would cost $4,000 per year. Should Pierce implement the change? Show your calculations.
3. An outside contractor offers to do the finishing operation for 9,500 units at $9 per unit, triple the $3 per unit that it costs Pierce to do the finishing in-house. Should Pierce accept the subcontractor's offer? Show your calculations.
4. The Hammond Corporation offers to machine 5,000 units at $3 per unit, half the $6 per unit that it costs Pierce to do the machining in-house. Should Pierce accept Hammond's offer? Show your calculations.
5. Pierce produces 1,700 defective units at the machining operation. What is the cost to Pierce of the defective items produced? Explain your answer briefly.
6. Pierce produces 1,700 defective units at the finishing operation. What is the cost to Pierce of the defective items produced? Explain your answer briefly.

11-30 Closing and opening stores. Sanchez Corporation runs two convenience stores, one in Connecticut and one in Rhode Island. Operating income for each store in 2017 is as follows:

	Connecticut Store	**Rhode Island Store**
Revenues	$1,070,000	$ 860,000
Operating costs		
Cost of goods sold	750,000	660,000
Lease rent (renewable each year)	90,000	75,000
Labor costs (paid on an hourly basis)	42,000	42,000
Depreciation of equipment	25,000	22,000
Utilities (electricity, heating)	43,000	46,000
Allocated corporate overhead	50,000	40,000
Total operating costs	1,000,000	885,000
Operating income (loss)	$ 70,000	$ (25,000)

The equipment has a zero disposal value. In a senior management meeting, Maria Lopez, the management accountant at Sanchez Corporation, makes the following comment, "Sanchez can increase its profitability by closing down the Rhode Island store or by adding another store like it."

1. By closing down the Rhode Island store, Sanchez can reduce overall corporate overhead costs by $44,000. Calculate Sanchez's operating income if it closes the Rhode Island store. Is Maria Lopez's statement about the effect of closing the Rhode Island store correct? Explain.
2. Calculate Sanchez's operating income if it keeps the Rhode Island store open and opens another store with revenues and costs identical to the Rhode Island store (including a cost of $22,000 to acquire equipment with a one-year useful life and zero disposal value). Opening this store will increase corporate overhead costs by $4,000. Is Maria Lopez's statement about the effect of adding another store like the Rhode Island store correct? Explain.

11-31 Choosing customers. Rodeo Printers operates a printing press with a monthly capacity of 4,000 machine-hours. Rodeo has two main customers: Trent Corporation and Julie Corporation. Data on each customer for January are:

	Trent Corporation	Julie Corporation	Total
Revenues	$210,000	$140,000	$350,000
Variable costs	84,000	85,000	169,000
Contribution margin	126,000	55,000	181,000
Fixed costs (allocated)	102,000	68,000	170,000
Operating income	$ 24,000	$ (13,000)	$ 11,000
Machine-hours required	3,000 hours	1,000 hours	4,000 hours

Julie Corporation indicates that it wants Rodeo to do an *additional* $140,000 worth of printing jobs during February. These jobs are identical to the existing business Rodeo did for Julie in January in terms of variable costs and machine-hours required. Rodeo anticipates that the business from Trent Corporation in February will be the same as that in January. Rodeo can choose to accept as much of the Trent and Julie business for February as its capacity allows. Assume that total machine-hours and fixed costs for February will be the same as in January.

What action should Rodeo take to maximize its operating income? Show your calculations. What other factors should Rodeo consider before making a decision?

Required

11-32 Relevance of equipment costs. Papa's Pizza is considering replacement of its pizza oven with a new, more energy-efficient model. Information related to the old and new pizza ovens follows:

Old oven—original cost	$60,000
Old oven—book value	$50,000
Old oven—current market value	$42,000
Old oven—annual operating cost	$14,000
New oven—purchase price	$75,000
New oven—installation cost	$ 2,000
New oven—annual operating cost	$ 6,000

The old oven had been purchased a year ago. Papa's Pizza estimates that either oven has a remaining useful life of five years. At the end of five years, either oven would have a zero salvage value.

Ignore the effect of income taxes and the time value of money.

Required

1. Which of the costs and benefits above are relevant to the decision to replace the oven?
2. What information is irrelevant? Why is it irrelevant?
3. Should Papa's Pizza purchase the new oven? Provide support for your answer.
4. Is there any conflict between the decision model and the incentives of the manager who has purchased the "old" oven and is considering replacing it a year later?
5. At what purchase price would Papa's Pizza be indifferent between purchasing the new oven and continuing to use the old oven?

11-33 Equipment upgrade versus replacement. (A. Spero, adapted) The TechGuide Company produces and sells 7,500 modular computer desks per year at a selling price of $750 each. Its current production equipment, purchased for $1,800,000 and with a five-year useful life, is only two years old. It has a terminal disposal value of $0 and is depreciated on a straight-line basis. The equipment has a current disposal price of $450,000. However, the emergence of a new molding technology has led TechGuide to consider either upgrading or replacing the production equipment. The following table presents data for the two alternatives:

	A	B	C
		Upgrade	Replace
1			
2	One-time equipment costs	$3,000,000	$4,800,000
3	Variable manufacturing cost per desk	$ 150	$ 75
4	Remaining useful life of equipment (in years)	3	3
5	Terminal disposal value of equipment	$ 0	$ 0

All equipment costs will continue to be depreciated on a straight-line basis. For simplicity, ignore income taxes and the time value of money.

Required

1. Should TechGuide upgrade its production line or replace it? Show your calculations.
2. Now suppose the one-time equipment cost to replace the production equipment is somewhat negotiable. All other data are as given previously. What is the maximum one-time equipment cost that TechGuide would be willing to pay to replace rather than upgrade the old equipment?
3. Assume that the capital expenditures to replace and upgrade the production equipment are as given in the original exercise, but that the production and sales quantity is not known. For what production and sales quantity would TechGuide (i) upgrade the equipment or (ii) replace the equipment?
4. Assume that all data are as given in the original exercise. Dan Doria is TechGuide's manager, and his bonus is based on operating income. Because he is likely to relocate after about a year, his current bonus is his primary concern. Which alternative would Doria choose? Explain.

Pearson MyLab Accounting

Problems

11-34 Special order, short-run pricing. GamesAhoy Corporation produces cricket bats for kids that it sells for $36 each. At capacity, the company can produce 50,000 bats a year. The costs of producing and selling 50,000 bats are as follows:

	Cost per Bat	Total Costs
Direct materials	$13	$ 650,000
Direct manufacturing labor	5	250,000
Variable manufacturing overhead	2	100,000
Fixed manufacturing overhead	6	300,000
Variable selling expenses	3	150,000
Fixed selling expenses	2	100,000
Total costs	$31	$1,550,000

Required

1. Suppose GamesAhoy is currently producing and selling 40,000 bats. At this level of production and sales, its fixed costs are the same as given in the preceding table. FieldTactics Corporation wants to place a one-time special order for 10,000 bats at $23 each. GamesAhoy will incur no variable selling costs for this special order. Should GamesAhoy accept this one-time special order? Show your calculations.
2. Now suppose GamesAhoy is currently producing and selling 50,000 bats. If GamesAhoy accepts FieldTactics' offer it will have to sell 10,000 fewer bats to its regular customers. (a) On financial considerations alone, should GamesAhoy accept this one-time special order? Show your calculations. (b) On financial considerations alone, at what price would GamesAhoy be indifferent between accepting the special order and continuing to sell to its regular customers at $36 per bat. (c) What other factors should GamesAhoy consider in deciding whether to accept the one-time special order?

11-35 Short-run pricing, capacity constraints. Fashion Fabrics makes pants from a special material. The fabric is special because of the way it fits many body types. The pants sell for $142. A well-known retail establishment has asked Fashion Fabrics to produce 3,000 shorts from the same fabric. The factory has unused capacity, so Barbara Brooks, the owner of Fashion Fabrics, calculates the cost of making a pair of shorts from the fabric. Costs for the pants and shorts are as follows:

	Pants	Shorts
Fabric (6 yds. × $12; 3 yds. × $12)	$ 72	36
Variable direct manufacturing labor	20	10
Variable manufacturing overhead	8	4
Fixed manufacturing cost allocated	15	9
Total manufacturing cost	$115	$59

Required

1. Suppose Fashion Fabrics can acquire all the fabric that it needs. What is the minimum price the company should charge for the shorts?
2. Now suppose that the fabric is in short supply. Every yard of fabric Fashion Fabrics uses to make shorts will reduce the pants that it can make and sell. What is the minimum price the company should charge for the shorts?

11-36 International outsourcing. Cuddly Critters, Inc., manufactures plush toys in a facility in Queensland, Brisbane. Recently, the company designed a group of collectible resin figurines to go with the plush toy line. Management is trying to decide whether to manufacture the figurines themselves in existing space in the Queensland facility or to accept an offer from a manufacturing company in Indonesia. Data concerning the decision are:

Expected annual sales of figurines (in units)	400,000
Average selling price of a figurine	$5
Price quoted by Indonesian company, in Indonesian Rupiah (IDR), for each figurine	27,300 IDR
Current exchange rate	9,100 IDR = $1
Variable manufacturing costs	$2.85 per unit
Incremental annual fixed manufacturing costs associated with the new product line	$200,000
Variable selling and distribution costs[a]	$0.50 per unit
Annual fixed selling and distribution costs[a]	$285,000

[a] Selling and distribution costs are the same regardless of whether the figurines are manufactured in Cleveland or imported.

Required

1. Should Cuddly Critters manufacture the 400,000 figurines in the Queensland facility or purchase them from the Indonesian supplier? Explain.
2. Cuddly Critters believes that the dollar may weaken in the coming months against the Indonesian rupiah and does not want to face any currency risk. Assume that Cuddly Critters can enter into a forward contract today to purchase 27,300 IDRs for $3.40. Should Cuddly Critters manufacture the 400,000 figurines in the Queensland facility or purchase them from the Indonesian supplier? Explain.
3. What are some of the qualitative factors that Cuddly Critters should consider when deciding whether to outsource the figurine manufacturing to Indonesia?

11-37 Relevant costs, opportunity costs. Gavin Martin, the general manager of Oregano Software, must decide when to release the new version of Oregano's spreadsheet package, Easyspread 2.0. Development of Easyspread 2.0 is complete; however, the diskettes, compact discs, and user manuals have not yet been produced. The product can be shipped starting July 1, 2017.

The major problem is that Oregano has overstocked the previous version of its spreadsheet package, Easyspread 1.0. Martin knows that once Easyspread 2.0 is introduced, Oregano will not be able to sell any more units of Easyspread 1.0. Rather than just throwing away the inventory of Easyspread 1.0, Martin is wondering if it might be better to continue to sell Easyspread 1.0 for the next three months and introduce Easyspread 2.0 on October 1, 2017, when the inventory of Easyspread 1.0 will be sold out.

The following information is available:

	Easyspread 1.0	Easyspread 2.0
Selling price	$165	$215
Variable cost per unit of diskettes, compact discs, user manuals	24	38
Development cost per unit	60	95
Marketing and administrative cost per unit	31	41
Total cost per unit	115	174
Operating income per unit	$ 50	$ 41

Development cost per unit for each product equals the total costs of developing the software product divided by the anticipated unit sales over the life of the product. Marketing and administrative costs are fixed costs in 2017, incurred to support all marketing and administrative activities of Oregano Software. Marketing and administrative costs are allocated to products on the basis of the budgeted revenues of each product. The preceding unit costs assume Easyspread 2.0 will be introduced on October 1, 2017.

Required

1. On the basis of financial considerations alone, should Martin introduce Easyspread 2.0 on July 1, 2017, or wait until October 1, 2017? Show your calculations, clearly identifying relevant and irrelevant revenues and costs.
2. What other factors might Gavin Martin consider in making a decision?

11-38 Opportunity costs and relevant costs. Jason Wu operates Exclusive Limousines, a fleet of 10 limousines used for weddings, proms, and business events in Washington, D.C. Wu charges customers a flat fee of $250 per car taken on contract plus an hourly fee of $80. His income statement for May follows:

Revenue (200 contracts × $250) + (1,250 hours × $80)	$150,000
Operating expenses:	
Driver wages and benefits ($35 per hour × 1,250 hours)	43,750
Depreciation on limousines	19,000
Fuel costs ($12.80 per hour × 1,250 hours)	16,000
Maintenance	18,400
Liability and casualty insurance	2,500
Advertising	10,500
Administrative expenses	24,200
Total expenses	134,350
Operating income	$ 15,650

All expenses are fixed, with the exception of driver wages and benefits and fuel costs, which are both variable per hour. During May, the company's limousines were fully booked. In June, Wu expects that Exclusive Limousines will be operating near capacity. Shelly Worthington, a prominent Washington socialite, has asked Wu to bid on a large charity event she is hosting in late June. The limousine company she had hired has canceled at the last minute, and she needs the service of five limousines for four hours each. She will only hire Exclusive Limousines if they take the entire job. Wu checks his schedule and finds that he only has three limousines available that day.

1. If Wu accepts the contract with Worthington, he would either have to (a) cancel two prom contracts each for one car for six hours or (b) cancel one business event for three cars contracted for two hours each. What are the relevant opportunity costs of accepting the Worthington contract in each case? Which contract should he cancel?
2. Wu would like to win the bid on the Worthington job because of the potential for lucrative future business. Assume that Wu cancels the contract in requirement 1 with the lowest opportunity cost, and assume that the three currently available cars would go unrented if the company does not win the bid. What is the lowest amount he should bid on the Worthington job?
3. Another limousine company has offered to rent Exclusive Limousines two additional cars for $300 each per day. Wu would still need to pay for fuel and driver wages on these cars for the Worthington job. Should Wu rent the two cars to avoid canceling either of the other two contracts?

11-39 Opportunity costs. (H. Schaefer, adapted) The Wild Orchid Corporation is working at full production capacity producing 13,000 units of a unique product, Everlast. Manufacturing cost per unit for Everlast is:

Direct materials	$10
Variable direct manufacturing labor	2
Manufacturing overhead	14
Total manufacturing cost	$26

Manufacturing overhead cost per unit is based on variable cost per unit of $8 and fixed costs of $78,000 (at full capacity of 13,000 units). Marketing cost per unit, all variable, is $4, and the selling price is $52.

A customer, the Apex Company, has asked Wild Orchid to produce 3,500 units of Stronglast, a modification of Everlast. Stronglast would require the same manufacturing processes as Everlast. Apex has offered to pay Wild Orchid $40 for a unit of Stronglast and share half of the marketing cost per unit.

1. What is the opportunity cost to Wild Orchid of producing the 3,500 units of Stronglast? (Assume that no overtime is worked.)
2. The Chesapeake Corporation has offered to produce 3,500 units of Everlast for Wild Orchid so that Wild Orchid may accept the Apex offer. That is, if Wild Orchid accepts the Chesapeake offer, Wild Orchid would manufacture 9,500 units of Everlast and 3,500 units of Stronglast and purchase 3,500 units of Everlast from Chesapeake. Chesapeake would charge Wild Orchid $36 per unit to manufacture Everlast. On the basis of financial considerations alone, should Wild Orchid accept the Chesapeake offer? Show your calculations.
3. Suppose Wild Orchid had been working at less than full capacity, producing 9,500 units of Everlast, at the time the Apex offer was made. Calculate the minimum price Wild Orchid should accept for Stronglast under these conditions. (Ignore the previous $40 selling price.)

11-40 Make or buy, unknown level of volume. (A. Atkinson, adapted) Denver Engineering manufactures small engines that it sells to manufacturers who install them in products such as lawn mowers. The company currently manufactures all the parts used in these engines but is considering a proposal from an external supplier who wishes to supply the starter assemblies used in these engines.

The starter assemblies are currently manufactured in Division 3 of Denver Engineering. The costs relating to the starter assemblies for the past 12 months were as follows:

Direct materials	$ 400,000
Variable direct manufacturing labor	300,000
Manufacturing overhead	800,000
Total	$1,500,000

Over the past year, Division 3 manufactured 150,000 starter assemblies. The average cost for each starter assembly is $10 ($1,500,000 ÷ 150,000).

Further analysis of manufacturing overhead revealed the following information. Of the total manufacturing overhead, only 25% is considered variable. Of the fixed portion, $300,000 is an allocation of general overhead that will remain unchanged for the company as a whole if production of the starter assemblies is discontinued. A further $200,000 of the fixed overhead is avoidable if production of the starter assemblies is discontinued. The balance of the current fixed overhead, $100,000, is the division manager's salary. If Denver Engineering discontinues production of the starter assemblies, the manager of Division 3 will be transferred to Division 2 at the same salary. This move will allow the company to save the $80,000 salary that would otherwise be paid to attract an outsider to this position.

Required

1. Tutwiler Electronics, a reliable supplier, has offered to supply starter-assembly units at $8 per unit. Because this price is less than the current average cost of $10 per unit, the vice president of manufacturing is eager to accept this offer. On the basis of financial considerations alone, should Denver Engineering accept the outside offer? Show your calculations. (*Hint:* Production output in the coming year may be different from production output in the past year.)
2. How, if at all, would your response to requirement 1 change if the company could use the vacated plant space for storage and, in so doing, avoid $100,000 of outside storage charges currently incurred? Why is this information relevant or irrelevant?

11-41 Make versus buy, activity-based costing, opportunity costs. The Lexington Company produces gas grills. This year's expected production is 20,000 units. Currently, Lexington makes the side burners for its grills. Each grill includes two side burners. Lexington's management accountant reports the following costs for making the 40,000 burners:

	Cost per Unit	Costs for 40,000 Units
Direct materials	$8.00	$320,000
Variable direct manufacturing labor	4.00	160,000
Variable manufacturing overhead	2.00	80,000
Inspection, setup, materials handling		8,000
Machine rent		12,000
Allocated fixed costs of plant administration, taxes, and insurance		80,000
Total costs		$660,000

Lexington has received an offer from an outside vendor to supply any number of burners Lexington requires at $14.80 per burner. The following additional information is available:

a. Inspection, setup, and materials-handling costs vary with the number of batches in which the burners are produced. Lexington produces burners in batch sizes of 1,000 units. Lexington will produce the 40,000 units in 40 batches.
b. Lexington rents the machine it uses to make the burners. If Lexington buys all of its burners from the outside vendor, it does not need to pay rent on this machine.

Required

1. Assume that if Lexington purchases the burners from the outside vendor, the facility where the burners are currently made will remain idle. On the basis of financial considerations alone, should Lexington accept the outside vendor's offer at the anticipated volume of 40,000 burners? Show your calculations.
2. For this question, assume that if the burners are purchased outside, the facilities where the burners are currently made will be used to upgrade the grills by adding a rotisserie attachment. (*Note:* Each grill contains two burners and one rotisserie attachment.) As a consequence, the selling price of grills will

be raised by $48. The variable cost per unit of the upgrade would be $38, and additional tooling costs of $160,000 per year would be incurred. On the basis of financial considerations alone, should Lexington make or buy the burners, assuming that 20,000 grills are produced (and sold)? Show your calculations.

3. The sales manager at Lexington is concerned that the estimate of 20,000 grills may be high and believes that only 16,000 grills will be sold. Production will be cut back, freeing up work space. This space can be used to add the rotisserie attachments whether Lexington buys the burners or makes them in-house. At this lower output, Lexington will produce the burners in 32 batches of 1,000 units each. On the basis of financial considerations alone, should Lexington purchase the burners from the outside vendor? Show your calculations.

11-42 Product mix, constrained resource. Wechsler Company produces three products: A130, B324, and C587. All three products use the same direct material, Brac. Unit data for the three products are:

	Product		
	A130	**B324**	**C587**
Selling price	$252	$168	$210
Variable costs			
Direct materials	$ 72	$ 45	$ 27
Labor and other costs	$ 84	$ 81	$120
Quantity of Brac per unit	8 lb.	5 lb.	3 lb.

The demand for the products far exceeds the direct materials available to produce the products. Brac costs $9 per pound, and a maximum of 5,000 pounds is available each month. Wechsler must produce a minimum of 200 units of each product.

Required

1. How many units of product A130, B324, and C587 should Wechsler produce?
2. What is the maximum amount Wechsler would be willing to pay for another 1,200 pounds of Brac?

11-43 Product mix, special order. (N. Melumad, adapted) Gormley Precision Tools makes cutting tools for metalworking operations. It makes two types of tools: A6, a regular cutting tool, and EX4, a high-precision cutting tool. A6 is manufactured on a regular machine, but EX4 must be manufactured on both the regular machine and a high-precision machine. The following information is available:

	A6	**EX4**
Selling price	$ 200	$ 300
Variable manufacturing cost per unit	$ 120	$ 200
Variable marketing cost per unit	$ 30	$ 70
Budgeted total fixed overhead costs	$700,000	$1,100,000
Hours required to produce one unit on the regular machine	1.0	0.5

Additional information includes the following:

a. Gormley faces a capacity constraint on the regular machine of 50,000 hours per year.
b. The capacity of the high-precision machine is not a constraint.
c. Of the $1,100,000 budgeted fixed overhead costs of EX4, $600,000 are lease payments for the high-precision machine. This cost is charged entirely to EX4 because Gormley uses the machine exclusively to produce EX4. The company can cancel the lease agreement for the high-precision machine at any time without penalties.
d. All other overhead costs are fixed and cannot be changed.

Required

1. What product mix—that is, how many units of A6 and EX4—will maximize Gormley's operating income? Show your calculations.
2. Suppose Gormley can increase the annual capacity of its regular machines by 15,000 machine-hours at a cost of $300,000. Should Gormley increase the capacity of the regular machines by 15,000 machine-hours? By how much will Gormley's operating income increase or decrease? Show your calculations.
3. Suppose that the capacity of the regular machines has been increased to 65,000 hours. Gormley has been approached by Clark Corporation to supply 20,000 units of another cutting tool, V2, for $240 per unit. Gormley must either accept the order for all 20,000 units or reject it totally. V2 is exactly like A6 except that its variable manufacturing cost is $140 per unit. (It takes 1 hour to produce one unit of V2 on the regular machine, and variable marketing cost equals $30 per unit.) What product mix should Gormley choose to maximize operating income? Show your calculations.

11-44 Theory of constraints, throughput margin, and relevant costs. Rush Industries manufactures electronic testing equipment. Rush also installs the equipment at customers' sites and ensures that it functions smoothly. Additional information on the manufacturing and installation departments is as follows (capacities are expressed in terms of the number of units of electronic testing equipment):

	Equipment Manufactured	Equipment Installed
Annual capacity	310 units per year	275 units per year
Equipment manufactured and installed	275 units per year	275 units per year

Rush manufactures only 275 units per year because the installation department has only enough capacity to install 275 units. The equipment sells for $45,000 per unit (installed) and has direct material costs of $20,000. All costs other than direct material costs are fixed. The following requirements refer only to the preceding data. There is no connection between the requirements.

Required

1. Rush's engineers have found a way to reduce equipment manufacturing time. The new method would cost an additional $50 per unit and would allow Rush to manufacture 20 additional units a year. Should Rush implement the new method? Show your calculations.
2. Rush's designers have proposed a change in direct materials that would increase direct material costs by $2,000 per unit. This change would enable Rush to install 310 units of equipment each year. If Rush makes the change, it will implement the new design on all equipment sold. Should Rush use the new design? Show your calculations.
3. A new installation technique has been developed that will enable Rush's engineers to install seven additional units of equipment a year. The new method will increase installation costs by $55,000 each year. Should Rush implement the new technique? Show your calculations.
4. Rush is considering how to motivate workers to improve their productivity (output per hour). One proposal is to evaluate and compensate workers in the manufacturing and installation departments on the basis of their productivities. Do you think the new proposal is a good idea? Explain briefly.

11-45 Theory of constraints, contribution margin, sensitivity analysis. Talking Toys (TT) produces dolls in two processes: molding and assembly. TT is currently producing two models: Chatty Chelsey and Talking Tanya. Production in the molding department is limited by the amount of materials available. Production in the assembly department is limited by the amount of trained labor available. The only variable costs are materials in the molding department and labor in the assembly department. Following are the requirements and limitations by doll model and department:

	Molding Materials	Assembly Time	Selling Price
Chatty Chelsey	2 pounds per doll	15 minutes per doll	$39 per doll
Talking Tanya	3 pounds per doll	20 minutes per doll	$50 per doll
Materials/Labor Available	36,000 pounds	8,500 hours	
Cost of materials and labor	$8 per pound	$12 per hour	

The following requirements refer only to the preceding data. There is no connection between the requirements.

Required

1. If there were enough demand for either doll, which doll would TT produce? How many of these dolls would it make and sell?
2. If TT sells three Chatty Chelseys for each Talking Tanya, how many dolls of each type would it produce and sell? What would be the total contribution margin?
3. If TT sells three Chatty Chelseys for each Talking Tanya, how much would production and contribution margin increase if the molding department could buy 900 more pounds of materials for $8 per pound?
4. If TT sells three Chatty Chelseys for each Talking Tanya, how much would production and contribution margin increase if the assembly department could get 65 more labor-hours at $12 per hour?

11-46 Closing down divisions. Ainsley Corporation has four operating divisions. The budgeted revenues and expenses for each division for 2017 follows:

	Division			
	A	B	C	D
Sales	$504,000	$ 948,000	$960,000	$1,240,000
Cost of goods sold	440,000	930,000	765,000	925,000
Selling, general, and administrative expenses	96,000	202,500	144,000	210,000
Operating income/loss	$ (32,000)	$(184,500)	$ 51,000	$ 105,000

Further analysis of costs reveals the following percentages of variable costs in each division:

Cost of goods sold	90%	80%	90%	85%
Selling, general, and administrative expenses	50%	50%	60%	60%

Closing down any division would result in savings of 40% of the fixed costs of that division. Top management is very concerned about the unprofitable divisions (A and B) and is considering closing them for the year.

Required

1. Calculate the increase or decrease in operating income if Ainsley closes division A.
2. Calculate the increase or decrease in operating income if Ainsley closes division B.
3. What other factors should the top management of Ainsley consider before making a decision?

11-47 Dropping a product line, selling more tours. Mechum River Anglers, a division of Old Dominion Travel, offers two types of guided fly fishing tours, Basic and Deluxe. Operating income for each tour type in 2017 is as follows:

	Basic	Deluxe
Revenues (500 × $900; 400 × $1,650)	$450,000	$660,000
Operating costs		
Administrative salaries	120,000	100,000
Guide wages	130,000	380,000
Supplies	50,000	100,000
Depreciation of equipment	25,000	60,000
Vehicle fuel	30,000	24,000
Allocated corporate overhead	45,000	66,000
Total operating costs	400,000	730,000
Operating income (loss)	$ 50,000	$(70,000)

The equipment has a zero disposal value. Guide wages, supplies, and vehicle fuel are variable costs with respect to the number of tours. Administrative salaries are fixed costs with respect to the number of tours. Brad Barrett, Mechum River Anglers' president, is concerned about the losses incurred on the deluxe tours. He is considering dropping the deluxe tour and offering only the basic tour.

Required

1. If the deluxe tours are discontinued, one administrative position could be eliminated, saving the company $50,000. Assuming no change in the sales of basic tours, what effect would dropping the deluxe tour have on the company's operating income?
2. Refer back to the original data. If Mechum River Anglers drops the deluxe tours, Barrett estimates that sales of basic tours would increase by 50%. He believes that he could still eliminate the $50,000 administrative position. Equipment currently used for the deluxe tours would be used by the additional basic tours. Should Barrett drop the deluxe tour? Explain.
3. What additional factors should Barrett consider before dropping the deluxe tours?

11-48 Optimal product mix. (CMA adapted) Della Simpson, Inc., sells two popular brands of cookies: Della's Delight and Bonny's Bourbon. Della's Delight goes through the Mixing and Baking departments, and Bonny's Bourbon, a filled cookie, goes through the Mixing, Filling, and Baking departments.

Michael Shirra, vice president for sales, believes that at the current price, Della Simpson can sell all of its daily production of Della's Delight and Bonny's Bourbon. Both cookies are made in batches of 3,000. In each department, the time required per batch and the total time available each day are as follows:

	Home	Insert	Page Layout	Formulas	Data	Review

	A	B	C	D
1		Department Minutes		
2		Mixing	Filling	Baking
3	Della's Delight	30	0	10
4	Bonny's Bourbon	15	15	15
5	Total available per day	660	270	300

Revenue and cost data for each type of cookie are as follows:

	A	B	C
7		Della's	Bonny's
8		Delight	Bourbon
9	Revenue per batch	$ 475	$ 375
10	Variable cost per batch	175	125
11	Contribution margin per batch	$ 300	$ 250
12	Monthly fixed costs		
13	(allocated to each product)	$18,650	$22,350

Required

1. Using D to represent the batches of Della's Delight and B to represent the batches of Bonny's Bourbon made and sold each day, formulate Shirra's decision as an LP model.
2. Compute the optimal number of batches of each type of cookie that Della Simpson, Inc., should make and sell each day to maximize operating income.

11-49 Dropping a customer, activity-based costing, ethics. Justin Anders is the management accountant for Carey Restaurant Supply (CRS). Sara Brinkley, the CRS sales manager, and Justin are meeting to discuss the profitability of one of the customers, Donnelly's Pizza. Justin hands Sara the following analysis of Donnelly's activity during the last quarter, taken from CRS's activity-based costing system:

Sales	$43,680
Cost of goods sold (all variable)	26,180
Order processing (50 orders processed at $280 per order)	14,000
Delivery (5,000 miles driven at $0.70 per mile)	3,500
Rush orders (6 rush orders at $154 per rush order)	924
Customer sales visits (6 sales calls at $140 per call)	840
Total costs	45,444
Profits	$ (1,764)

Sara looks at the report and remarks, "I'm glad to see all my hard work is paying off with Donnelly's. Sales have gone up 10% over the previous quarter!"

Justin replies, "Increased sales are great, but I'm worried about Donnelly's margin, Sara. We were showing a profit with Donnelly's at the lower sales level, but now we're showing a loss. Gross margin percentage this quarter was 40%, down five percentage points from the prior quarter. I'm afraid that corporate will push hard to drop them as a customer if things don't turn around."

"That's crazy," Sara responds. "A lot of that overhead for things like order processing, deliveries, and sales calls would just be allocated to other customers if we dropped Donnelly's. This report makes it look like we're losing money on Donnelly's when we're not. In any case, I am sure you can do something to make its profitability look closer to what we think it is. No one doubts that Donnelly's is a very good customer."

Required

1. Assume that Sara is partly correct in her assessment of the report. Upon further investigation, it is determined that 10% of the order processing costs and 20% of the delivery costs would not be avoidable if CRS were to drop Donnelly's. Would CRS benefit from dropping Donnelly's? Show your calculations.
2. Sara's bonus is based on meeting sales targets. Based on the preceding information regarding gross margin percentage, what might Sara have done last quarter to meet her target and receive her bonus? How might CRS revise its bonus system to address this?
3. Should Justin rework the numbers? How should he respond to Sara's comments about making Donnelly's look more profitable?

11-50 Equipment replacement decisions and performance evaluation. Susan Smith manages the Wexford plant of Sanchez Manufacturing. A representative of Darnell Engineering approaches Smith about replacing a large piece of manufacturing equipment that Sanchez uses in its process with a more efficient model. While the representative made some compelling arguments in favor of replacing the 3-year-old equipment, Smith is hesitant. Smith is hoping to be promoted next year to manager of the larger Detroit plant, and she knows that the accrual-basis net operating income of the Wexford plant will be evaluated closely as part of the promotion decision. The following information is available concerning the equipment-replacement decision:

	Old Machine	New Machine
Original cost	$900,000	$540,000
Useful life	5 years	2 years
Current age	3 years	0 years
Remaining useful life	2 years	2 years
Accumulated depreciation	$540,000	Not acquired yet
Book value	$360,000	Not acquired yet
Current disposal value (in cash)	$216,000	Not acquired yet
Terminal disposal value (in cash 2 years from now)	$0	$0
Annual operating costs (maintenance, energy, repairs, coolants, and so on)	$995,000	$800,000

Sanchez uses straight-line depreciation on all equipment. Annual depreciation expense for the old machine is $180,000 and will be $270,000 on the new machine if it is acquired. For simplicity, ignore income taxes and the time value of money.

Required

1. Assume that Smith's priority is to receive the promotion and she makes the equipment-replacement decision based on the next one year's accrual-based net operating income. Which alternative would she choose? Show your calculations.
2. What are the relevant factors in the decision? Which alternative is in the best interest of the company over the next 2 years? Show your calculations.
3. At what cost would Smith be willing to purchase the new equipment? Explain.

13 Pricing Decisions and Cost Management

LEARNING OBJECTIVES

1 Discuss the three major factors that affect pricing decisions

2 Understand how companies make long-run pricing decisions

3 Price products using the target-costing approach

4 Apply the concepts of cost incurrence and locked-in costs

5 Price products using the cost-plus approach

6 Use life-cycle budgeting and costing when making pricing decisions

7 Describe two pricing practices in which non-cost factors are important

8 Explain the effects of antitrust laws on pricing

Most companies carefully analyze their input costs and the prices of their products.

They know if the price is too high, customers will go to competitors; if the price is too low, the company won't be able to cover the cost of making the product. A company must also know how its customers will react to particular pricing strategies. Understanding these factors has been a key factor in IKEA's success.

EXTREME PRICING AND COST MANAGEMENT AT IKEA[1]

IKEA is a global furniture retailing industry phenomenon. Known for products named after Swedish towns, modern design, flat packaging, and do-it-yourself instructions, IKEA has grown into the world's largest furniture retailer with 343 stores worldwide. How did this happen? Through aggressive pricing, coupled with relentless cost management.

When IKEA decides to create a new product, product developers survey competitors to determine how much they charge for similar items and then select a target price that is 30% to 50% lower than competitors' prices. With a product and price established, IKEA determines the materials to be used and selects one of its 1,800 suppliers to manufacture the item through a competitive-bidding process. It also identifies cost efficiencies throughout design and production. All IKEA products are shipped unassembled in flat packages, because shipping costs are at least six times greater if products are assembled before shipping.

IKEA applies the same cost management techniques to existing products. For example, one of IKEA's best-selling products, the Lack bedside table, has retailed for the same low price since 1981 despite increases in raw material prices and wage rates. Since hitting store shelves, more than 100 technical development projects have been performed on the Lack table to reduce product and distribution costs and maintain profitability.

Steve Allen/Allen Creative/Alamy Stock Photo

---

[1] *Sources:* Lisa Margonelli, "How IKEA Designs Its Sexy Price Tags," *Business 2.0*, October 2002; Daniel Terdiman, "Anatomy of an IKEA Product," CNET News.com, April 19, 2008 (http://news.cnet.com/8301-13772_3-9923315-52.html), accessed June 2013; and Anna Ringstrom, "Ikea Founder to Leave Board," *The New York Times*, June 5, 2013; IKEA Annual Report, 2015.

As founder Ingvar Kamprad once summarized, "Waste of resources is a mortal sin at IKEA. Expensive solutions are a sign of mediocrity, and an idea without a price tag is never acceptable."

Like IKEA, managers at many companies, such as Microsoft, Unilever, and Walmart, are strategic in their pricing decisions. This chapter describes how managers evaluate demand at different prices and manage customers and costs across the value chain and over a product's life cycle to achieve profitability.

Major Factors that Affect Pricing Decisions

Consider for a moment how managers at Adidas might price their newest line of sneakers or how decision makers at Comcast would determine how much to charge for a monthly subscription for Internet service. How managers price a product or a service ultimately depends on demand and supply. Three influences on demand and supply are customers, competitors, and costs.

LEARNING OBJECTIVE 1

Discuss the three major factors that affect pricing decisions

…customers, competitors, and costs

Customers

Customers influence price through their effect on the demand for a product or service. The demand is affected by factors such as the features of a product and its quality. Managers always examine pricing decisions through the eyes of their customers and then manage costs to earn a profit.

Competitors

No business operates in a vacuum. Managers must always be aware of the actions of their competitors. At one extreme, for companies such as Home Depot or Texas Instruments, alternative or substitute products of competitors hurt demand and cause them to lower prices. At the other extreme, companies such as Apple and Porsche have distinctive products and limited competition and are free to set higher prices. When there are competitors, managers try to learn about competitors' technologies, plant capacities, and operating strategies to estimate competitors' costs—valuable information when setting prices because it helps managers understand how low competitors are willing to go on price without making a loss.

Because competition spans international borders, fluctuations in exchange rates between different countries' currencies affect costs and pricing decisions. For example, if the yuan weakens against the U.S. dollar, Chinese producers receive more yuan for each dollar of sales. These producers can lower prices and still make a profit; Chinese products become cheaper for American consumers and, consequently, more competitive in U.S. markets.

Costs

Costs influence prices because they affect supply. The lower the cost of producing a product, such as a Toyota Prius or a Nokia cell phone, the greater the quantity of product the company is willing to supply. As companies increase supply, the cost of producing an additional unit initially declines but eventually increases. Companies supply products as long as the revenue from selling additional units exceeds the cost of producing them. Managers who understand the cost of producing products set prices that make the products attractive to customers while maximizing operating income.

Weighing Customers, Competitors, and Costs

Surveys indicate that managers weigh customers, competitors, and costs differently when making pricing decisions. At one extreme, companies operating in a perfectly competitive market sell very similar commodity products, such as wheat, rice, steel, and aluminum. The managers at these companies have no control over setting prices and must accept the price determined by a market consisting of many participants. Cost information helps managers decide the quantity of output to produce that will maximize operating income.

In less competitive markets, such as those for cameras, televisions, and cellular phones, products are differentiated, and all three factors affect prices: The value customers place on a product and the prices charged for competing products affect demand, and the costs of producing and delivering the product affect supply.

As competition lessens even more, such as in microprocessors and operating software, the key factor affecting pricing decisions is the customer's willingness to pay based on the value that customers place on the product or service, not costs or competitors. In the extreme, there are monopolies. A monopolist has no competitors and has much more leeway to set high prices. Nevertheless, there are limits. The higher the price a monopolist sets, the lower the demand for the monopolist's product because customers will either seek substitute products or forgo buying the product.

DECISION POINT

What are the three major factors affecting pricing decisions?

LEARNING OBJECTIVE 2

Understand how companies make long-run pricing decisions

...consider all future variable and fixed costs and earn a target return on investment

Costing and Pricing for the Long Run

Long-run pricing is a strategic decision designed to build long-run relationships with customers based on stable and predictable prices. Managers prefer a stable price because it reduces the need for continuous monitoring of prices, improves planning, and builds long-run buyer–seller relationships. McDonald's maintains a stable price with its Dollar Menu of fast-food items, as does Apple, which always prices its new entry-level iPad at $499. But to charge a stable price and earn the target long-run return, managers must know and manage long-run costs of supplying products to customers, which includes *all* future direct and indirect costs. Recall that *indirect costs* of a particular cost object are costs that are related to that cost object, but cannot be traced to it in an economically feasible (cost-effective) way. These costs often comprise a large percentage of the overall costs assigned to cost objects such as products, customers, and distribution channels.

Consider cost-allocation issues at Astel Computers. Astel manufactures two products: a high-end computer called Deskpoint and an Intel Core i5 chip–based laptop computer called Provalue. The following figure illustrates six business functions in Astel's value chain.

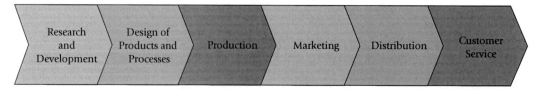

Exhibit 13-1 illustrates four purposes of cost allocation. Different sets of costs are appropriate for different purposes described in the exhibit. When making pricing decisions for Deskpoint and Provalue, Astel's managers allocate indirect costs from all six business functions. Why? Because in the long run, it is only worthwhile to sell a product if the price customers are willing to pay for the product exceeds all costs incurred to produce and sell it while earning a reasonable return on invested capital.

Cost allocations and product profitability analyses affect the products promoted by a company. To increase profits, managers focus on high-margin products. They compensate salespersons based on product profitability, in addition to revenues, to motivate the sales staff to sell products that increase operating income and not just revenues. Cost allocations also influence managers' cost management decisions. For example, identifying all costs of purchasing and ordering prompts Astel's managers to design Provalue with fewer components to reduce these costs.

Cost allocations are sometimes used for cost reimbursements. Astel's contract to supply computers to the U.S. government is based on costs plus a profit margin. The cost reimbursement rules for the U.S. government allow fully allocated manufacturing and design costs, but explicitly exclude marketing costs.

Inventory valuation for income and asset measurement requires costs to be allocated to calculate the cost of manufacturing inventory. For this purpose, Astel allocates only manufacturing costs to products and no costs from other parts of the value chain such as R&D, marketing, or distribution.

Cost allocation is another example of the different costs for different purposes theme of the book. We will discuss cost allocation in the next several chapters. In this chapter, we focus on the role of cost allocation when making long-run pricing decisions based on costs incurred throughout the value chain.

EXHIBIT 13-1

Purposes of Cost Allocation

Purpose	Examples
1. To provide information for economic decisions	To decide on the selling price for a product or service To decide whether to add a new product feature
2. To motivate managers and other employees	To encourage the design of products that are simpler to manufacture or less costly to service To encourage sales representatives to emphasize high-margin products or services
3. To justify costs or compute reimbursement amounts	To cost products at a "fair" price, often required by law and government contracts To compute reimbursement for a consulting firm based on a percentage of the cost savings resulting from the implementation of its recommendations
4. To measure income and assets	To cost inventories for reporting to external parties To cost inventories for reporting to tax authorities

Calculating Product Costs for Long-Run Pricing Decisions

Astel's market research indicates that the market for Provalue is becoming increasingly competitive. Astel's managers face an important decision about the price to charge for Provalue.

Managers first review data for the year just ended—2016. Astel has no beginning or ending inventory of Provalue and manufactures and sells 150,000 units during the year. Astel uses activity-based costing (ABC) to allocate costs and calculate the manufacturing cost of Provalue. Astel's ABC system has:

- Three direct manufacturing costs: direct materials, direct manufacturing labor, and direct machining costs.

- Three manufacturing overhead cost pools: ordering and receiving components, testing and inspection of final products, and rework (correcting and fixing errors and defects).

Astel considers machining costs as a direct cost of Provalue because these machines are dedicated to manufacturing Provalue.[2]

Astel uses a long-run time horizon (one year) to price Provalue. Over this horizon, Astel's managers observe the following:

- Direct material costs vary with the number of units of Provalue produced.

- Direct manufacturing labor costs vary with the number of direct manufacturing labor-hours used.

- Direct machining costs are fixed costs of leasing 300,000 machine-hours of capacity each year for multiple years. These costs do not vary with the number of machine-hours used each year. Each unit of Provalue requires 2 machine-hours. In 2016, Astel uses the entire machining capacity to manufacture Provalue (2 machine-hours per unit × 150,000 units = 300,000 machine-hours).

- Ordering and receiving, testing and inspection, and rework costs vary with the quantity of their respective cost drivers. For example, ordering and receiving costs vary with the number of orders. In the long run, staff members responsible for placing orders can be reassigned or laid off if fewer orders need to be placed or increased if more orders need to be processed.

The following Excel spreadsheet summarizes manufacturing cost information to produce 150,000 units of Provalue in 2016. As described in Chapter 5, management accountants calculate the indirect cost per unit of the cost driver in column (6) by dividing Astel's total costs in each cost pool by the total quantity of the cost driver for that cost pool. (Calculations not shown.)

---

[2] Recall that Astel makes a high-end computer, Deskpoint, and a laptop computer, Provalue. If Deskpoint and Provalue were manufactured using the same machines, Astel would have allocated machining costs on the basis of the budgeted machine-hours used to manufacture the two products and would have treated these costs as fixed manufacturing overhead costs.

	Home	Insert	Page Layout		Formulas	Data	Review	View		
	A	B	C	D		E	F	G	H
1				**Manufacturing Cost Information**					
2				**to Produce 150,000 Units of Provalue**					
3	**Cost Category**	**Cost Driver**		**Details of Cost Driver Quantities**				**Total Quantity of Cost Driver**	**Cost per Unit of Cost Driver**
4	(1)	(2)		(3)			(4)	(5) = (3) × (4)	(6)
5	**Direct Manufacturing Costs**								
6	Direct materials	No. of kits	1	kit per unit		150,000	units	150,000	$460
7	Direct manufacturing labor (DML)	DML-hours	3.2	DML-hours per unit		150,000	units	480,000	$ 20
8	Direct machining (fixed)	Machine-hours						300,000	$ 38
9	**Manufacturing Overhead Costs**								
10	Ordering and receiving	No. of orders	50	orders per component		450	components	22,500	$ 80
11	Testing and inspection	Testing-hours	30	testing-hours per unit		150,000	units	4,500,000	$ 2
12	Rework					8%	defect rate		
13		Rework-hours	2.5	rework-hours per defective unit		12,000[a]	defective units	30,000	$ 40
14									
15	[a]8% defect rate × 150,000 units = 12,000 defective units								

Exhibit 13-2 shows the total cost of manufacturing Provalue in 2016 of $102 million by various categories of direct costs and indirect costs. The manufacturing cost per unit in Exhibit 13-2 is $680. Manufacturing, however, is just one business function in the value chain. To set long-run prices, Astel's managers must calculate the *full cost* of producing and selling Provalue by allocating costs in all functions of the value chain.

For each nonmanufacturing business function, Astel's managers trace direct costs to products and allocate indirect costs using cost pools and cost drivers that measure cause-and-effect relationships (supporting calculations not shown). Exhibit 13-3 summarizes Provalue's 2016 operating income and shows that Astel earned $15 million from Provalue, or $100 per unit sold in 2016.

Alternative Long-Run Pricing Approaches

How should managers at Astel use product cost information to price Provalue in 2017? Two different approaches for pricing decisions are

1. Market-based

2. Cost-based, which is also called cost-plus

The market-based approach to pricing starts by asking, "Given what our customers want and how our competitors will react to what we do, what price should we charge?" Based on this price, managers control costs to earn a target return on investment. The cost-based approach to pricing starts by asking, "Given what it costs us to make this product, what price should we charge that will recoup our costs and achieve a target return on investment?"

Companies operating in *competitive* markets (for example, commodities such as steel, oil, and natural gas) use the market-based approach. The products produced or services

	A	B	C
		Total Manufacturing	
1		**Costs for**	**Manufacturing**
2		**150,000 Units**	**Cost per Unit**
3		**(1)**	**(2) = (1) ÷ 150,000**
4			
5	Direct manufacturing costs		
6	Direct material costs		
7	(150,000 kits × $460 per kit)	$ 69,000,000	$460
8	Direct manufacturing labor costs		
9	(480,000 DML-hours × $20 per hour)	9,600,000	64
10	Direct machining costs		
11	(300,000 machine-hours × $38 per machine-hour)	11,400,000	76
12	Direct manufacturing costs	90,000,000	600
13			
14	Manufacturing overhead costs		
15	Ordering and receiving costs		
16	(22,500 orders × $80 per order)	1,800,000	12
17	Testing and inspection costs		
18	(4,500,000 testing-hours × $2 per hour)	9,000,000	60
19	Rework costs		
20	(30,000 rework-hours × $40 per hour)	1,200,000	8
21	Manufacturing overhead cost	12,000,000	80
22	Total manufacturing costs	$102,000,000	$680

	A	B	C
		Total Amounts	
1		**for 150,000 Units**	**Per Unit**
2		**(1)**	**(2) = (1) ÷ 150,000**
3			
4	Revenues	$150,000,000	$1,000
5	Costs of goods sold[a] (from Exhibit 13-2)	102,000,000	680
6	Operating costs[b]		
7	R&D costs	2,400,000	16
8	Design costs of product and proces	3,000,000	20
9	Marketing and administration costs	15,000,000	100
10	Distribution costs	9,000,000	60
11	Customer-service costs	3,600,000	24
12	Operating costs	33,000,000	220
13	Full cost of the product	135,000,000	900
14	Operating income	$ 15,000,000	$ 100
15			
16	[a]Cost of goods sold = Total manufacturing costs because there is no beginning or ending inventory		
17	of Provalue in 2016		
18	[b]Numbers for operating cost line-items are assumed without supporting calculations		

TRY IT! 13-1

Gonzalo Inc. is a small distributor of mechanical pencils. Gonzalo identifies its three major activities and cost pools as ordering, receiving and storage, and shipping, and it reports the following details for 2016:

Activity	Cost Driver	Quantity of Cost Driver	Cost per Unit of Cost Driver
1. Placing and paying for orders of pencil packs	Number of orders	500	$100 per order
2. Receiving and storage	Loads moved	4,000	$ 60 per load
3. Shipping of pencil packs to retailers	Number of shipments	1,500	$ 80 per shipment

For 2016, Gonzalo buys 250,000 pencil packs at an average cost of $6 per pack and sells them to retailers at an average price of $8 per pack. Assume Gonzalo has no fixed costs and no inventories.

Calculate Gonzalo's operating income for 2016.

provided by one company are very similar to products produced or services provided by others. Companies in these markets must accept the prices set by the market.

Companies operating in *less competitive* markets offer products or services that differ from each other (for example, automobiles, computers, management consulting, and legal services) and can use either the market-based or cost-based approach as the starting point for pricing decisions. Some companies use the cost-based approach: They first look at costs because cost information is more easily available and then consider customers and competitors. Other companies use the market-based approach: They first look at customers and competitors and then look at costs. Both approaches consider customers, competitors, and costs. Only their starting points differ. Managers must always keep in mind market forces, regardless of which pricing approach they use. For example, building contractors often bid on a cost-plus basis but then reduce their prices during negotiations to respond to other lower-cost bids.

Companies operating in markets that are *not competitive* (for example electric utilities) follow cost-based approaches. That's because these companies do not need to respond or react to competitors' prices. The margin they add to costs to determine price depends on the ability and willingness of customers to pay for the product or service. In many of these noncompetitive markets, though, regulators intervene to set prices to limit the profits that companies can earn.

We consider first the market-based approach.

DECISION POINT

How do companies make long-run pricing decisions?

Market-Based Approach: Target Costing for Target Pricing

LEARNING OBJECTIVE 3

Price products using the target-costing approach

…target costing identifies an estimated price customers are willing to pay and then computes a target cost to earn the desired profit

Market-based pricing starts with a **target price**, which is the estimated price for a product or service that potential customers are willing to pay. Managers base this estimate on an understanding of customers' perceived value for a product or service and how competitors will price competing products or services. Managers need to understand customers and competitors for three reasons:

1. Lower-cost competitors continually restrain prices.

2. Products have shorter lives, which leaves companies less time and opportunity to recover from pricing mistakes, loss of market share, and loss of profitability.

3. Customers are more knowledgeable because they have easy access to price and other information online and demand high-quality products at low prices.

Understanding Customers' Perceived Value

A company's sales and marketing organization, through close contact and interaction with customers, identifies customer needs and perceptions of product value. Companies also conduct market research on what customers want and the prices they are willing to pay.

Competitor Analysis

To gauge how competitors might react to a prospective price, a manager must understand competitors' technologies, products or services, costs, and financial conditions. In general, the more distinctive a product or service, the higher the price a company can charge. Where do companies obtain information about their competitors? Usually from former customers, suppliers, and employees of competitors. Some companies *reverse-engineer*—disassemble and analyze competitors' products to determine product designs and materials and understand their technologies. At no time should a manager resort to illegal or unethical means to obtain information about competitors. For example, a manager should never bribe current employees or pose as a supplier or customer to obtain competitor information.

Implementing Target Pricing and Target Costing

We use the Provalue example to illustrate the four steps in developing target prices and target costs.

Step 1: Develop a Product That Satisfies the Needs of Potential Customers. Astel's managers use customer feedback and information about competitors' products to change product features and designs of Provalue in 2017. Their market research indicates that customers do not value Provalue's extra features, such as special audio elements and designs that make the PC run faster. Instead, customers want Astel to redesign Provalue into a basic, reliable and low-priced PC.

Step 2: Choose a Target Price. Competitors are expected to lower the prices of PCs to $850. Astel's managers want to respond aggressively by reducing the price of Provalue by 20%, from $1,000 to $800 per unit. At this lower price, the marketing manager forecasts an increase in annual sales from 150,000 to 200,000 units.

CONCEPTS IN ACTION ▶ H&M Uses Target Pricing to Bring Fast Fashion to Stores Worldwide

Doug Houghton/Alamy Stock Photo

H&M is the worldwide leader in fast fashion, bringing trendy, affordable clothes from the runway to stores in a matter of weeks. Famous for offering Alexander Wang–designed dresses for $4.95 and trench coats for $20, the Swedish-based company is now the world's second-largest clothing retailer, with more than 3,900 stores across 61 countries and $25.3 billion in 2015 sales. How did this happen? Aggressive target pricing, coupled with "cost-consciousness" across the company.

When H&M decides to produce an item, its 160 in-house designers set out to strike the right balance between fashion, quality, and price. Concept teams of designers, buyers, pattern makers, and a controller work together to set a target price. H&M outsources to suppliers throughout Europe and Asia to manufacture the item. High-volume items such as basics and children's wear are ordered far in advance to ensure volume-based cost efficiencies. Trendy items in small quantities are produced at shorter notice. Once produced, the items are shipped to H&M's logistics centers for distribution to stores. H&M stores carry no backup stocks. Stores are replenished directly from the logistic centers, allowing stores to be restocked quickly with only the best-selling products.

H&M has incorporated sustainability into its target pricing and cost management practices. Around 90% of H&M's products are transported from suppliers to distribution centers via sea or rail to avoid fossil fuel–intensive air and road shipping. Additionally, certified organic cotton and environmentally conscious materials, such as organic hemp and recycled wool, make up 14% of the company's total material use.

Sources: Andrew Hoffman, et al., "H&M's Global Supply Chain Management Sustainability: Factories and Fast Fashion," University of Michigan Erb Institute No. 1-429-373 (Ann Arbor, MI: University of Michigan, 2014); "Sales Development in 2015," H&M AB press release (Stockholm, Sweden, December 15, 2015, http://about.hm.com/en/news/newsroom/news.html/en/financial-reports/2015/12/2065879.html); H&M AB, "From Idea to Store" (http://about.hm.com/en/About/Facts-About-HM/Idea-to-Store, accessed March 2016); Clara Lu, "Behind H&M's Fashion Forward Retail Inventory Control," *TradeGecko* blog, August 12, 2014 (https://www.tradegecko.com/blog/hm-retail-inventory-control).

Step 3: Derive a Target Cost per Unit by Subtracting Target Operating Income per Unit from the Target Price. Target operating income per unit is the operating income that a company aims to earn per unit of a product or service sold. **Target cost per unit** is the estimated long-run cost per unit of a product or service that enables the company to achieve its target operating income per unit when selling at the target price.[3] *Target cost per unit* is the target price minus *target operating income per unit*. It is often lower than the existing *full cost of the product*. Target cost per unit is really just that—a target—something the company must strive to achieve.

To earn the target return on capital, Astel needs to earn 10% target operating income per unit on the 200,000 units of Provalue it plans to sell.

Total target revenues	= $800 per unit × 200,000 units = $160,000,000
Total target operating income	= 10% × $160,000,000 = $16,000,000
Target operating income per unit	= $16,000,000 ÷ 200,000 units = $80 per unit
Target cost per unit	= Target price − Target operating income per unit
	= $800 per unit − $80 per unit = $720 per unit
Total current full costs of Provalue	= $135,000,000 (from Exhibit 13-3)
Current full cost per unit of Provalue	= $135,000,000 ÷ 150,000 units = $900 per unit

Provalue's $720 target cost per unit is $180 below its existing $900 unit cost. To achieve the target cost, Astel must reduce costs in all parts of the value chain, from R&D to customer service.

Target costs include *all* future costs, variable costs as well as costs that are fixed in the short run, because in the long run a company's prices and revenues must exceed its total costs if it is to remain in business. In contrast, for short-run pricing or one-time-only special-order decisions, managers only consider costs that vary in the short run.

Step 4: Perform Value Engineering to Achieve Target Cost. Value engineering is a systematic evaluation of all aspects of the value chain, with the objective of reducing costs and achieving a quality level that satisfies customers. Value engineering entails improvements in product designs, changes in materials specifications, and modifications in process methods. The Concepts in Action: H&M Uses Target Pricing to Bring Fast Fashion to Stores Worldwide describes H&M's approach to target pricing and target costing.

DECISION POINT

How do companies determine target costs?

TRY IT! 13-2

Gonzalo Inc. is a small distributor of mechanical pencils. Gonzalo identifies its three major activities and cost pools as ordering, receiving and storage, and shipping, and it reports the following details for 2016:

Activity	Cost Driver	Quantity of Cost Driver	Cost per Unit of Cost Driver
1. Placing and paying for orders of pencil packs	Number of orders	500	$100 per order
2. Receiving and storage	Loads moved	4,000	$ 60 per load
3. Shipping of pencil packs to retailers	Number of shipments	1,500	$ 80 per shipment

For 2016, Gonzalo buys 250,000 pencil packs at an average cost of $6 per pack and sells them to retailers at an average price of $8 per pack. Assume Gonzalo has no fixed costs and no inventories. For 2017, retailers are demanding a 5% discount off the 2016 price. Gonzalo's suppliers are only willing to give a 4% discount. Gonzalo expects to sell the same quantity of pencil packs in 2017 as it did in 2016.

If all other costs and cost-driver information remain the same, by how much must Gonzalo reduce its total cost and cost per unit if it is to earn the same target operating income in 2017 as it earned in 2016 (and thereby earn its required rate of return on investment)?

---

[3] For a more detailed discussion of target costing, see Shahid L. Ansari, Jan E. Bell, and the CAM-I Target Cost Core Group, *Target Costing: The Next Frontier in Strategic Cost Management* (Martinsville, IN: Mountain Valley Publishing, 2009). For implementation information, see Shahid L. Ansari, Dan Swenson, and Jan E. Bell, "A Template for Implementing Target Costing," *Cost Management* (September–October 2006): 20–27.

Value Engineering, Cost Incurrence, and Locked-in Costs

To implement value engineering, managers distinguish value-added activities and costs from non-value-added activities and costs. A **value-added cost** is a cost that, if eliminated, would reduce the actual or perceived value or utility (usefulness) customers experience from using the product or service. In the Provalue example, value-added costs are specific product features and attributes desired by customers, such as reliability, adequate memory, preloaded software, clear images, and prompt customer service.

A **non-value-added cost** is a cost that, if eliminated, would not reduce the actual or perceived value or utility (usefulness) customers gain from using the product or service. Examples of non-value-added costs are the costs of defective products and machine breakdowns. Companies seek to minimize non-value-added costs because they do not provide benefits to customers.

Activities and costs do not always fall neatly into value-added or non-value-added categories, so managers often have to apply judgment to classify costs. Several costs, such as supervision and production control, have both value-added and non-value-added components. When in doubt, some managers prefer to classify costs as non-value-added to focus organizational attention on cost reduction. The risk with this approach is that an organization may cut some costs that are value-adding, leading to poor customer experiences.

Despite these difficult gray areas, managers find it useful to distinguish value-added from non-value-added costs for value engineering. In the Provalue example, direct materials, direct manufacturing labor, and direct machining costs are value-added costs; ordering, receiving, testing, and inspection costs have both value-added and non-value-added components; and rework costs are non-value-added costs.

Astel's managers next distinguish cost incurrence from locked-in costs. **Cost incurrence** describes when a resource is consumed (or benefit forgone) to meet a specific objective. Costing systems measure cost incurrence. For example, Astel recognizes direct material costs of Provalue only when Provalue is assembled and sold. But Provalue's direct material cost per unit is *locked in*, or *designed in*, much earlier, when product designers choose the specific components in Provalue. **Locked-in costs**, or **designed-in costs**, are costs that have not yet been incurred, but will be incurred in the future based on decisions that have already been made.

The best opportunity to manage costs is before costs are locked in, so Astel's managers model the effect of different product design choices on costs such as scrap and rework that will only be incurred later during manufacturing. They then control these costs by making wise design choices. Similarly, managers in the software industry reduce costly and difficult-to-fix errors that appear during coding and testing through better software design and analysis.

Exhibit 13-4 illustrates the locked-in cost curve and the cost-incurrence curve for Provalue. The bottom curve uses information from Exhibit 13-3 to plot the cumulative cost per unit incurred in different business functions of the value chain. The top curve plots cumulative locked-in costs. (The specific numbers underlying this curve are not presented.) Total cumulative cost per unit for both curves is $900, but there is *wide divergence between locked-in costs and costs incurred*. For example, product design decisions lock in more than 86% ($780 ÷ $900) of the unit cost of Provalue (including costs of direct materials, ordering, testing, rework, distribution, and customer service), when Astel incurs only about 4% ($36 ÷ 900) of the unit cost!

Value-Chain Analysis and Cross-Functional Teams

A cross-functional value-engineering team consisting of marketing managers, product designers, manufacturing engineers, purchasing managers, suppliers, dealers, and management accountants redesign Provalue—called Provalue II—to reduce costs while retaining features that customers value. Some of the team's ideas are:

- Use a simpler, more reliable motherboard without complex features to reduce manufacturing and repair costs.

- Snap-fit rather than solder parts together to decrease direct manufacturing labor-hours and related costs.

LEARNING OBJECTIVE **4**

Apply the concepts of cost incurrence

…when resources are consumed

and locked-in costs

…when resources are committed to be incurred in the future

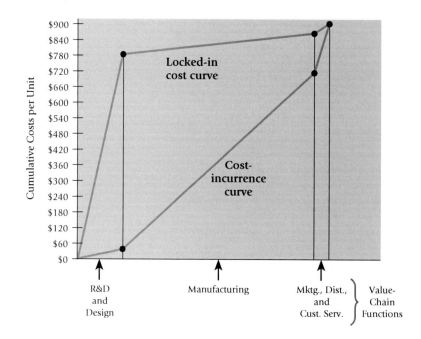

EXHIBIT 13-4

Pattern of Cost Incurrence
and Locked-In Costs for
Provalue

- Use fewer components to decrease ordering, receiving, testing, and inspection costs.
- Make Provalue lighter and smaller to reduce distribution and packaging costs.

Management accountants use their understanding of the value chain to estimate cost savings.

The team focuses on design decisions to reduce costs before costs get locked in. However, not all costs are locked in at the design stage. Managers also use *kaizen,* or *continuous improvement* techniques, to reduce the time it takes to complete a task, eliminate waste, and improve operating efficiency and productivity. To summarize, the key steps in value-engineering are:

1. Understanding customer requirements and value-added and non-value-added costs.

2. Anticipating how costs are locked in before they are incurred.

3. Using cross-functional teams to redesign products and processes to reduce costs while meeting customer needs.

Achieving the Target Cost per Unit for Provalue

Exhibit 13-5 uses an activity-based approach to compare cost-driver quantities and rates for the 150,000 units of Provalue manufactured and sold in 2016 and the 200,000 units of Provalue II budgeted for 2017. Value engineering decreases both value-added costs (by designing Provalue II to reduce direct materials costs, direct manufacturing labor-hours, the number of components and testing-hours) and non-value-added costs (by simplifying Provalue II's design to reduce rework). Value engineering also reduces the machine-hours required to manufacture Provalue II to 1.5 hours per unit. Astel can now use the 300,000 machine-hours of capacity to make 200,000 units of Provalue II (vs. 150,000 units for Provalue), reducing machining cost per unit. For simplicity, we assume that value engineering will not reduce the $20 cost per direct manufacturing labor-hour, the $80 cost per order, the $2 cost per testing-hour, or the $40 cost per rework-hour. (The Problem for Self-Study, pages 565–567, explores how value engineering can also reduce these cost-driver rates.)

Exhibit 13-6 presents the target manufacturing costs of Provalue II, using cost driver and cost-driver rate data from Exhibit 13-5. For comparison, Exhibit 13-6 also shows the actual 2016 manufacturing cost per unit of Provalue from Exhibit 13-2. Astel's managers expect the new design to reduce total manufacturing cost per unit by $140 (from $680 to $540) and cost per unit in other business functions from $220 (Exhibit 13-3) to $180 (calculations not shown)

EXHIBIT 13-5	Cost-Driver Quantities and Rates for Provalue in 2016 and Provalue II for 2017 Using Activity-Based Costing

	Home	Insert		Page Layout		Formulas		Data		Review		View		
	A	B	C	D	E	F	G	H	I	J	K	L	M	N
1														
2				**Manufacturing Cost Information for 150,000 Units of Provalue in 2016**						**Manufacturing Cost Information for 200,000 Units of Provalue II for 2017**				
3	**Cost Category**	**Cost Driver**	**Details of Actual Cost Driver Quantities**				**Actual Total Quantity of Cost Driver**	**Actual Cost per Unit of Cost Driver (p. 528)**	**Details of Budgeted Cost Driver Quantities**				**Budgeted Total Quantity of Cost Driver**	**Budgeted Cost per Unit of Cost Driver (Given)**
4	(1)	(2)	(3)		(4)		(5)=(3)×(4)	(6)	(7)		(8)		(9)=(7)×(8)	(10)
5	**Direct Manufacturing Costs**													
6	Direct materials	No. of kits	1	kit per unit	150,000	units	150,000	$460	1	kit per unit	200,000	units	200,000	$385
7	Direct manuf. labor (DML)	DML hours	3.2	DML hours per unit	150,000	units	480,000	$ 20	2.65	DML hours per unit	200,000	units	530,000	$ 20
8	Direct machining (fixed)	Machine-hours					300,000	$ 38					300,000	$ 38
9	**Manufacturing Overhead Costs**													
10	Ordering and receiving	No. of orders	50	orders per component	450	components	22,500	$ 80	50	orders per component	425	components	21,250	$ 80
11	Testing and inspection	Testing-hours	30	testing-hours per unit	150,000	units	4,500,000	$ 2	15	testing hours per unit	200,000	units	3,000,000	$ 2
12	Rework				8%	defect rate					6.5%	defect rate		
13		Rework-hours	2.5	rework-hours per defective unit	12,000[a]	defective units	30,000	$ 40	2.5	rework-hours per defective unit	13,000[b]	defective units	32,500	$ 40
14														
15	[a]8% defect rate × 150,000 units = 12,000 defective units													
16	[b]6.5% defect rate × 200,000 units = 13,000 defective units													

at the budgeted sales quantity of 200,000 units. The budgeted full unit cost of Provalue II is $720 ($540 + $180), the target cost per unit. At the end of 2017, Astel's managers will compare actual costs and target costs to understand improvements they can make in subsequent target-costing efforts.

Unless managed properly, value engineering and target costing can have undesirable effects:

- Employees may feel frustrated if they fail to attain target costs.
- The cross-functional team may add too many features just to accommodate the different wishes of team members.
- A product may be in development for a long time as the team repeatedly evaluates alternative designs.

EXHIBIT 13-6 Target Manufacturing Costs of Provalue II for 2017

		PROVALUE II				PROVALUE
		Budgeted		Budgeted		Actual Manufacturing
		Manufacturing Costs		Manufacturing		Cost per Unit
		for 200,000 Units		Cost per Unit		(Exhibit 13-2)
		(1)		(2) = (1) ÷ 200,000		(3)
6	Direct manufacturing costs					
7	Direct material costs					
8	(200,000 kits × $385 per kit)	$ 77,000,000		$385.00		$460.00
9	Direct manufacturing labor costs					
10	(530,000 DML-hours × $20 per hour)	10,600,000		53.00		64.00
11	Direct machining costs					
12	(300,000 machine-hours × $38 per machine-hour)	11,400,000		57.00		76.00
13	Direct manufacturing costs	99,000,000		495.00		600.00
14	Manufacturing overhead costs					
15	Ordering and receiving costs					
16	(21,250 orders × $80 per order)	1,700,000		8.50		12.00
17	Testing and inspection costs					
18	(3,000,000 testing-hours × $2 per hour)	6,000,000		30.00		60.00
19	Rework costs					
20	(32,500 rework-hours × $40 per hour)	1,300,000		6.50		8.00
21	Manufacturing overhead costs	9,000,000		45.00		80.00
22	Total manufacturing costs	$108,000,000		$540.00		$ 680.00

- Organizational conflicts may develop as the burden of cutting costs falls unequally on different business functions in the company's value chain, for example, more on manufacturing than on marketing.

To avoid these pitfalls, target-costing efforts should always (1) encourage employee participation and celebrate small improvements toward achieving the target cost, (2) focus on the customer, (3) pay attention to schedules, and (4) set cost-cutting targets for all value-chain functions to encourage a culture of teamwork and cooperation.

The target-pricing approach is another illustration of the five-step decision-making process introduced in Chapter 1.

1. *Identify the problem and uncertainties.* The problem is the price to charge for Provalue in 2017. The uncertainties are identifying what customers want, how competitors will respond, and how to manage costs.

2. *Obtain information.* Astel's managers do market research to identify customer needs, the prices that competitors are likely to charge, and the opportunities to reduce costs.

3. *Make predictions about the future.* Managers make predictions about the effect of different prices on sales volumes and how much they can reduce costs through value engineering and product redesign.

4. *Make decisions by choosing among alternatives.* Managers decide to reduce Provalue's price from $1,000 to $800, anticipating sales to increase from 150,000 units to 200,000 units in 2017.

DECISION POINT

Why is it important for managers to distinguish cost incurrence from locked-in costs?

5. *Implement the decision, evaluate performance, and learn.* Cross-functional value-engineering teams redesign Provalue to achieve a target cost of $720 per unit, considerably lower than the current cost of $900. At the end of 2017, managers will compare actual and target costs to evaluate performance and to identify ways to reduce costs even further.

Gonzalo Inc. is a small distributor of mechanical pencils. Gonzalo identifies its three major activities and cost pools as ordering, receiving and storage, and shipping, and it reports the following details for 2016:

13-3 TRY IT!

Activity	Cost Driver	Quantity of Cost Driver	Cost per Unit of Cost Driver
1. Placing and paying for orders of pencil packs	Number of orders	500	$100 per order
2. Receiving and storage	Loads moved	4,000	$ 60 per load
3. Shipping of pencil packs to retailers	Number of shipments	1,500	$ 80 per shipment

For 2016, Gonzalo buys 250,000 pencil packs at an average cost of $6 per pack and sells them to retailers at an average price of $8 per pack. Assume Gonzalo has no fixed costs and no inventories. For 2017, retailers are demanding a 5% discount off the 2016 price. Gonzalo's suppliers are only willing to give a 4% discount. Gonzalo expects to sell the same quantity of pencil packs in 2017 as it did in 2016.

Using value engineering, Gonzalo decides to make changes in its ordering and receiving-and-storing practices. By placing long-run orders with its key suppliers, Gonzalo expects to reduce the number of orders to 400 and the cost per order to $75. By redesigning the layout of the warehouse and reconfiguring the crates in which the pencil packs are moved, Gonzalo expects to reduce the number of loads moved to 3,500 and the cost per load moved to $50.

Will Gonzalo achieve its target operating income of $90,000 and its target operating income per unit of $0.36 per pencil pack in 2017? Show your calculations.

Cost-Plus Pricing

Instead of using the market-based approach for long-run pricing decisions, managers sometimes use a cost-based approach. The general formula for setting a cost-based selling price adds a markup component to the cost base. Because a markup is added, cost-based pricing is often called cost-plus pricing, where the plus refers to the markup component. Managers use the cost-plus pricing formula as a starting point. The markup component is usually flexible, depending on the behavior of customers and competitors. In other words, market conditions ultimately determine the markup component.[4] Consider, for example, Costco, the large warehouse store. Costco uses cost-plus pricing when setting product prices. Costco's managers, however, will reduce prices if competitors such as Sam's Club offer similar products at lower prices.

LEARNING OBJECTIVE 5

Price products using the cost-plus approach

...cost-plus pricing is based on some measure of cost plus a markup

Cost-Plus Target Rate of Return on Investment

Suppose Astel uses a 12% markup on the full unit cost of Provalue II to compute the selling price. The cost-plus price is:

Cost base (full unit cost of Provalue II)	$720.00
Markup component of 12% (0.12 × $720)	86.40
Prospective selling price	$806.40

How do managers determine the markup percentage of 12%? One way is to choose a markup to earn a **target rate of return on investment**, which is the target annual operating income divided by invested capital. Invested capital can be defined in many ways. In this chapter, we define it as total assets—that is, long-term assets plus current assets. Suppose Astel's (pretax)

---

[4] Exceptions are pricing of electricity and natural gas in many countries, where prices are set by the government on the basis of costs plus a return on invested capital. In these situations, products are not subject to competitive forces and cost accounting techniques substitute for markets as the basis for setting prices.

target rate of return on investment is 15%, and Provalue II's capital investment is $115.2 million. The target annual operating income for Provalue II is:

Invested capital	$115,200,000
Target rate of return on investment	15%
Target annual operating income (0.15 × $115,200,000)	$ 17,280,000
Target operating income per unit of Provalue II ($17,280,000 ÷ 200,000 units)	$ 86.40

This calculation indicates that Astel needs to earn a target operating income of $86.40 on each unit of Provalue II. The markup ($86.40) expressed as a percentage of the full unit cost of the product ($720) equals 12% ($86.40 ÷ $720).

Do not confuse the 15% target rate of return on investment with the 12% markup percentage.

■ The 15% target rate of return on investment expresses Astel's expected annual operating income as a percentage of investment.

■ The 12% markup expresses operating income per unit as a percentage of the full product cost per unit.

Astel uses the target rate of return on investment to calculate the markup percentage.

Alternative Cost-Plus Methods

Computing the specific amount of capital invested in a product is challenging because it requires difficult and arbitrary allocations of investments in equipment and buildings to individual products. The following table uses alternative cost bases (without supporting calculations) and assumed markup percentages to set prospective selling prices for Provalue II without explicitly calculating invested capital to set prices.

Cost Base	Estimated Cost per Unit (1)	Markup Percentage (2)	Markup Component (3) = (1) × (2)	Prospective Selling Price (4) = (1) + (3)
Variable manufacturing cost	$475.00	65%	$308.75	$783.75
Variable cost of the product	547.00	45	246.15	793.15
Manufacturing cost	540.00	50	270.00	810.00
Full cost of the product	720.00	12	86.40	806.40

The different cost bases and markup percentages give four prospective selling prices that are close to each other. The markup percentages in the preceding table vary a great deal, from a high of 65% on variable manufacturing cost to a low of 12% on full cost of the product. Why the wide variation? When determining a prospective selling price, a cost base such as variable manufacturing cost that includes fewer costs requires a higher markup percentage because the price needs to be set to earn a profit margin *and* to recover costs (fixed manufacturing costs and all nonmanufacturing costs) that have been excluded from the base. A company chooses a reliable cost base and markup percentage to recover its costs and earn a return on investment.

Surveys indicate that many managers use the full cost of the product for cost-based pricing decisions—that is, they include variable costs and costs that are fixed in the short run when calculating the cost per unit. Managers include the fixed cost per unit in the cost base for several reasons:

1. **Full recovery of all costs of the product.** In the long run, the price of a product must exceed the full cost of the product if a company is to remain in business. Using just the variable cost as a base may tempt managers to cut prices as long as prices are above variable cost and generate a positive contribution margin. As the experience in the airline industry has shown, price wars, when airline companies cut prices as long as they exceed variable costs, have caused airlines to lose money because revenues are too low to recover the full cost of the product. Using the full cost of the product as a basis for pricing reduces the temptation to cut prices below full costs.

2. **Price stability.** Limiting the ability and temptation of salespeople to cut prices by using the full cost of a product as the basis for pricing decisions also promotes price stability. Stable prices facilitate more accurate forecasting and planning for both sellers and buyers.

3. **Simplicity.** A full-cost formula for pricing does not require the management accountant to perform a detailed analysis of cost-behavior patterns to separate product costs into variable and fixed components. Variable and fixed cost components are difficult to identify for many costs such as testing, inspection, and setups, and in many service businesses such as accounting and management consulting.

Including fixed cost per unit in the cost base for pricing can be challenging. Allocating fixed costs to products can be arbitrary. Also, calculating fixed cost per unit requires a denominator level that is based on an estimate of capacity or expected units of future sales. Errors in these estimates will cause actual full cost per unit of the product to differ from the estimated amount. Despite these challenges, managers generally include fixed costs when making cost-based pricing decisions.

Gonzalo Inc. is a small distributor of mechanical pencils. Gonzalo identifies its three major activities and cost pools as ordering, receiving and storage, and shipping, and it reports the following details for 2017:   **13-4 TRY IT!**

Activity	Cost Driver	Quantity of Cost Driver	Cost per Unit of Cost Driver
1. Placing and paying for orders of pencil packs	Number of orders	400	$75 per order
2. Receiving and storage	Loads moved	3,500	$50 per load
3. Shipping of pencil packs to retailers	Number of shipments	1,500	$80 per shipment

For 2017, Gonzalo buys 250,000 pencil packs at an average cost of $5.76 per pack. Gonzalo plans to use cost-plus pricing.

Calculate the prospective selling price (1) if Gonzalo marks up the purchase costs of the pencil packs by 33% and (2) if Gonzalo marks up the full cost of the pencil packs by 7%.

Cost-Plus Pricing and Target Pricing

The selling prices computed under cost-plus pricing are *prospective* prices. Suppose Astel's initial product design results in a $750 full cost for Provalue II. Assuming a 12% markup, Astel sets a prospective price of $840 [$750 + (0.12 × $750)]. In the competitive personal computer market, customer and competitor reactions to this price may force Astel to reduce the markup percentage and lower the price to, say, $800. Astel may then want to redesign Provalue II to reduce the full cost to $720 per unit, as in our example, and achieve a markup close to 12% while keeping the price at $800. The eventual design and cost-plus price must balance cost, markup, and customer reactions.

The target-pricing approach reduces the need to go back and forth among prospective cost-plus prices, customer reactions, and design modifications. In contrast to cost-plus pricing, the target pricing approach first determines product characteristics and target price on the basis of customer preferences and expected competitor responses and then computes a target cost.

Companies that provide many distinctive products and services to their customers, such as accountants and management consultants, usually use cost-plus pricing. Each job that professional service firms do for their clients is unique. They set prices based on hourly cost-plus billing rates of partners, managers, and associates. These prices are, however, lowered in competitive situations. Professional service firms also take a multiple-year client perspective when deciding prices because clients prefer to work with the same firm over multiple periods. Certified public accountants, for example, sometimes charge a client a low price initially to get the account and recover the lower profits or losses in the initial years by charging higher prices in later years.

Service companies such as home repair services, automobile repair services, and architectural firms use a cost-plus pricing method called the *time-and-materials method*. Individual jobs are priced based on materials and labor time. The price charged for materials equals the cost of materials plus a markup. The price charged for labor represents the cost of labor plus a markup. That is, the price charged for each direct cost item includes its own markup. Companies choose the markups to recover overhead costs and to earn a profit.

DECISION POINT

How do companies price products using the cost-plus approach?

Life-Cycle Product Budgeting and Costing

Managers sometimes need to consider target prices and target costs over a multiple-year product life cycle. The **product life cycle** spans the time from initial R&D on a product to when customer service and support is no longer offered for that product. For automobile companies such as BMW, Ford, and Nissan, the product life cycle is 12 to 15 years to design, introduce, sell, and service different car models. For pharmaceutical products, the life cycle for a successful new medicine at companies such as Pfizer, Merck, and GlaxoSmithKline may be 15 to 20 years. For banks such as Bank of America and Chase, a product such as a newly designed savings account with specific privileges can have a life cycle of 10 to 20 years. Personal computers have a shorter life cycle of 2 to 3 years because rapid innovations in the computing power and speed of microprocessors that run the computers make older models obsolete.

In **life-cycle budgeting**, managers estimate the revenues and business function costs across the entire value chain from a product's initial R&D to its final customer service and support. **Life-cycle costing** tracks and accumulates business function costs across the entire value chain from a product's initial R&D to its final customer service and support. Life-cycle budgeting and life-cycle costing span several years.

Life-Cycle Budgeting and Pricing Decisions

Budgeted life-cycle costs provide useful information for strategically evaluating pricing decisions. Consider Insight, Inc., a computer software company, which is developing a new business accounting package, "General Ledger." Assume the following budgeted amounts for General Ledger over a 6-year product life cycle:

Years 1 and 2

	Total Fixed Costs
R&D costs	$240,000
Design costs	160,000

Years 3 to 6

	Total Fixed Costs	Variable Cost per Package
Production costs	$100,000	$25
Marketing costs	70,000	24
Distribution costs	50,000	16
Customer-service costs	80,000	30

Exhibit 13-7 presents the 6-year life-cycle budget for General Ledger for three alternative-selling-price/sales-quantity combinations.

Some features of costs make life-cycle budgeting particularly important:

1. **The development period for R&D and design is long and costly.** When a company incurs a large percentage of total life-cycle costs before any production begins and any revenues are received, as in the General Ledger example, managers need to evaluate revenues and costs over the life cycle of the product in order to decide whether to begin the costly R&D and design activities.

2. **Many costs are locked in at R&D and design stages, even if R&D and design costs themselves are small.** In our General Ledger example, design and quality decisions about the accounting software package will affect marketing, distribution, and customer-service costs in several subsequent years. A life-cycle revenue-and-cost budget prevents Insight's managers from overlooking these multiple-year relationships among business-function costs. Life-cycle budgeting highlights costs throughout the product's life cycle and, in doing so, facilitates target pricing, target costing, and value engineering at the design stage before costs are locked in. The amounts presented in Exhibit 13-7 are the outcome of value engineering.

Insight's managers decide to sell the General Ledger package for $480 per package because this price maximizes life-cycle operating income. They then compare actual costs to life-cycle

	Alternative-Selling-Price/ Sales-Quantity Combinations		
	A	**B**	**C**
Selling price per package	$400	$480	$600
Sales quantity in units	5,000	4,000	2,500
Life-cycle revenues			
($400 × 5,000; $480 × 4,000; $600 × 2,500)	$2,000,000	$1,920,000	$1,500,000
Life-cycle costs			
R&D costs	240,000	240,000	240,000
Design costs of product/process	160,000	160,000	160,000
Production costs			
$100,000 + ($25 × 5,000); $100,000 +			
($25 × 4,000); $100,000 + ($25 × 2,500)	225,000	200,000	162,500
Marketing costs			
$70,000 + ($24 × 5,000); $70,000 +			
($24 × 4,000); $70,000 + ($24 × 2,500)	190,000	166,000	130,000
Distribution costs			
$50,000 + ($16 × 5,000); $50,000 +			
($16 × 4,000); $50,000 + ($16 × 2,500)	130,000	114,000	90,000
Customer-service costs			
$80,000 + ($30 × 5,000); $80,000 +			
($30 × 4,000); $80,000 + ($30 × 2,500)	230,000	200,000	155,000
Total life-cycle costs	1,175,000	1,080,000	937,500
Life-cycle operating income	$ 825,000	$ 840,000	$ 562,500

EXHIBIT 13-7

Budgeting Life-Cycle Revenues and Costs for "General Ledger" Software Package of Insight, Inc.[a]

[a]This exhibit does not take into consideration the time value of money when computing life-cycle revenues or life-cycle costs. Chapter 21 outlines how this important factor can be incorporated into such calculations.

Winchester Manufacturing, Inc., plans to develop a new industrial motor. The product will take 6 months to design and test. The company expects the motor to sell 10,000 units during the first 6 months of sales; 20,000 units per year over the following 2 years; and 5,000 units over the final 6 months of the product's life cycle. The company expects the following costs:

13-5 TRY IT!

Period	Cost	Total Fixed Cost for the Period	Variable Cost per Unit
Months 0–6	Design costs	$ 500,000	
Months 7–12	Production	$1,300,000	$90 per unit
	Marketing	$1,000,000	
	Distribution	$ 200,000	$10 per unit
Months 13–36	Production	$4,900,000	$70 per unit
	Marketing	$2,325,000	
	Distribution	$ 700,000	$ 8 per unit
Months 37–42	Production	$ 800,000	$60 per unit
	Marketing	$ 475,000	
	Distribution	$ 100,000	$ 7 per unit

Ignore the time value of money.

1. If Winchester prices the motors at $375 each, how much operating income will the company make over the product's life cycle? What is the operating income per unit?
2. Winchester is concerned about the operating income it will report in the first sales phase. It is considering pricing the motor at $425 for the first 6 months and decreasing the price to $375 thereafter. With this pricing strategy, Winchester expects to sell 9,500 units instead of 10,000 units in the first 6 months, 19,000 each year over the next 2 years, and 5,000 over the last 6 months. Assuming the same cost structure given in the problem, which pricing strategy would you recommend? Explain.

budgets to obtain feedback and to learn about how to better estimate costs for subsequent products. Exhibit 13-7 assumes that the selling price per package is the same over the entire life cycle. For strategic reasons, however, Insight's managers may decide to *skim the market* by charging higher prices to eager customers when General Ledger is first introduced and lowering prices later as the product matures. Managers may also decide to add new features in later years to differentiate the product to achieve higher prices and sales. The life-cycle budget will then incorporate the revenues and costs of these strategies.

Managing Environmental and Sustainability Costs

Managing environmental costs is a critical area where managers apply life-cycle costing and value engineering. Environmental laws like the U.S. Clean Air Act and the U.S. Superfund Amendment and Reauthorization Act have introduced tougher environmental standards, imposed stringent cleanup requirements, and introduced severe penalties for polluting the air and contaminating subsurface soil and groundwater. In some countries, such as Sweden, the government levies a carbon tax, a fee or surcharge on carbon-based fuels and other sources of pollution. A carbon tax puts a monetary price on greenhouse gas emissions. Other regions such as the European Union use a cap-and-trade system, where the government puts a limit or cap on the overall level of carbon pollution and conducts a market auction for pollution quotas. Companies pay for the right to pollute and can then either sell (or buy) these rights to (or from) other companies if they pollute less (or more) than their quotas.

Environmental costs that are incurred over several years of the product's life cycle are often locked in at the product- and process-design stage. To avoid environmental liabilities, reduce carbon taxes, or cost of buying pollution quotas, managers in industries such as oil refining, chemical processing, and automobile manufacturing value engineer and design products and processes to prevent and reduce pollution over the product's life cycle. For example, laptop computer manufacturers like Hewlett-Packard and Apple have introduced recycling programs to ensure that chemicals from nickel-cadmium batteries do not leak hazardous chemicals into the soil. The carbon tax has spurred innovation in the design of energy-efficient products and clean energy solutions, such as solar and wind power.[5]

What is the effect of sustainability investments on overall financial performance in subsequent periods? A new organization, the Sustainability Accounting Standards Board (SASB) has begun defining standards for environmental, social, and governance (ESG) performance for different industries. The relevant (or material) ESG standards vary across industries based on financial impact and interest of user groups. For example, the relevant ESG standards in the oil and gas industry include greenhouse gas emissions and water and wastewater management while the relevant ESG standards in the technology and communications industry include life-cycle impacts of products and services and energy management. When measured over multiple periods, companies that have higher relevant ESG ratings have higher future profitability and financial performance, perhaps because of customer loyalty and satisfaction, employee engagement, or brand and reputation.[6]

Customer Life-Cycle Costing

In the previous section, we considered life-cycle costs from the perspective of a product or service. **Customer life-cycle costs** focus on the total costs incurred by a customer to acquire, use, maintain, and dispose of a product or service. Customer life-cycle costs influence the prices a company can charge for its products. For example, Ford can charge a higher price and/or gain market share if its cars require minimal maintenance for 100,000 miles. Similarly, Maytag charges higher prices for appliances that save electricity and have low maintenance costs. Boeing Corporation justifies a higher price for the Boeing 777 because the plane's design allows mechanics easier access to different areas of the plane to perform routine maintenance, reduces the time and cost of maintenance, and significantly decreases the life-cycle cost of owning the plane.

DECISION POINT

Describe life-cycle budgeting and life-cycle costing and when should companies use these techniques?

---

[5] Although Sweden has one of the highest carbon taxes at $140 per ton of carbon pollution, its economy has continued to grow strongly since the tax was introduced in 1991.

[6] M. Khan, G. Serafeim, and A. Yoon, "Corporate Sustainability: First Evidence on Materiality," *The Accounting Review* (September 2016).

Non-Cost Factors in Pricing Decisions

LEARNING
OBJECTIVE 7

Describe two pricing
practices in which non-
cost factors are important

...price discrimination—
charging different
customers different
prices for the same
product—and peak-load
pricing—charging higher
prices when demand ap-
proaches capacity limits

In some cases, cost is *not* a major factor in setting prices. We explore some of the ways that ability to pay, capacity limits, and purchasing power of customers influence price-setting independent of cost.

Price Discrimination

Consider the prices airlines charge for a round-trip flight from New York to London. A coach-class ticket for a flight with a 7-day advance purchase is $1,100 if the passenger stays in London over a Saturday night. The ticket is $2,000 if the passenger returns without staying over a Saturday night. Can this price difference be explained by the difference in the cost to the airline of these round-trip flights? No, because it costs the same amount to transport the passenger from Boston to London and back, regardless of whether the passenger stays in London over a Saturday night. This difference in price is due to *price discrimination.*

Price discrimination is the practice of charging different customers different prices for the same product or service. How does price discrimination work in the airline example? The demand for airline tickets comes from two main sources: business travelers and pleasure travelers. Business travelers must travel to conduct business for their organizations, so their demand for air travel is relatively insensitive to price. Airlines can earn higher operating incomes by charging business travelers higher prices. Insensitivity of demand to price changes is called *demand inelasticity*. Also, business travelers generally go to their destinations, complete their work, and return home without staying over a Saturday night. Pleasure travelers, in contrast, usually don't need to return home during the week and prefer to spend weekends at their destinations. Because they pay for their tickets themselves, pleasure travelers' demand is price-elastic; lower prices stimulate demand while higher prices restrict demand. Airlines can earn higher operating incomes by charging pleasure travelers lower prices.

How can airlines keep fares high for business travelers while keeping fares low for pleasure travelers? Requiring a Saturday night stay discriminates between the two customer segments. The airlines price-discriminate by taking advantage of different sensitivities to prices exhibited by business travelers and pleasure travelers. Prices differ even though there is no difference in cost in serving the two customer segments.

What if economic conditions weaken such that business travelers become more sensitive to price? The airlines may then need to lower the prices they charge to business travelers. Following the global financial crisis in 2009, airlines started offering discounted fares on several routes without requiring a Saturday night stay to stimulate business travel. Business travel picked up and airlines started filling more seats than they otherwise would have. Unfortunately, travel did not pick up enough, and the airline industry as a whole suffered severe losses for a few years.

Peak-Load Pricing

In addition to price discrimination, other non-cost factors such as capacity constraints affect pricing decisions. **Peak-load pricing** is the practice of charging a higher price for the same product or service when demand approaches the physical limit of the capacity to produce that product or service. When demand is high and production capacity and therefore supply are limited, customers are willing to pay more to get the product or service. In contrast, slack or excess capacity leads companies to lower prices in order to stimulate demand and utilize capacity. Peak-load pricing occurs in the telephone, telecommunications, hotel, car rental, and electric-utility industries. During the 2016 Summer Olympics in Rio de Jeneiro, for example, hotels charged very high rates and required multiple-night stays. Airlines charged high fares for flights into and out of many cities in the region for roughly a month around the time of the Games. Demand far exceeded capacity and the hospitality industry and airlines employed peak-load pricing to increase their profits.

International Pricing

Another example of factors other than costs affecting prices occurs when the same product is sold in different countries. Consider software, books, and medicines produced in one country and sold globally. The prices charged in each country vary much more than the costs of

DECISION
POINT

What is price
discrimination and peak
load pricing and why are
there price differences
across countries?

delivering the product to each country. These price differences arise because of differences in the purchasing power of consumers in different countries (a form of price discrimination) and government restrictions that may limit the prices that companies can charge.

Antitrust Laws and Pricing Decisions

LEARNING OBJECTIVE 8

Explain the effects of antitrust laws on pricing

…antitrust laws attempt to counteract pricing below costs to drive out competitors or fixing prices artificially high to harm consumers

Legal considerations also affect pricing decisions. Companies are not always free to charge whatever price they like. For example, under the U.S. Robinson-Patman Act of 1936, a manufacturer cannot price-discriminate between two customers if the intent is to lessen or prevent competition for customers. Two key features of price-discrimination laws are:

1. Price discrimination is permissible if differences in prices can be justified by differences in costs.

2. Price discrimination is illegal only if the intent is to lessen or prevent competition.

The price discrimination by airline companies described earlier is legal because their practices do not hinder competition.

Predatory Pricing

To comply with U.S. antitrust laws, such as the Sherman Act, the Clayton Act, the Federal Trade Commission Act, and the Robinson-Patman Act, pricing must not be predatory.[7] A company engages in **predatory pricing** when it deliberately prices below its costs in an effort to drive competitors out of the market to restrict supply and then recoups its losses by raising prices or enlarging demand.[8]

The U.S. Supreme Court established the following conditions to prove that predatory pricing has occurred:

- The predator company charges a price below an appropriate measure of its costs.
- The predator company has a reasonable prospect of recovering in the future, through larger market share or higher prices, the money it lost by pricing below cost.

The Supreme Court has not specified the "appropriate measure of costs."[9]

Most courts in the United States have defined the "appropriate measure of costs" as the short-run marginal or average variable costs.[10] In the case of *Adjustor's Replace-a-Car v. Agency Rent-a-Car*, Adjustor's (the plaintiff) claimed that it was forced to withdraw from the Austin and San Antonio, Texas, markets because Agency had engaged in predatory pricing.[11] To prove predatory pricing, Adjustor pointed to "the net loss from operations" in Agency's income statement, calculated after allocating Agency's headquarters overhead. The judge, however, ruled that Agency had not engaged in predatory pricing because the price it charged for a rental car never dropped below its average variable costs.

The Supreme Court decision in *Brooke Group v. Brown & Williamson Tobacco* (BWT) made it more difficult for companies to prove predatory pricing. The Court ruled that pricing below average variable costs is not predatory if the company does not have a reasonable

---

[7] Discussion of the Sherman Act and the Clayton Act is in Arnold I. Barkman and John D. Jolley, "Cost Defenses for Antitrust Cases," *Management Accounting* 67, No. 10 (1986): 37–40.

[8] For more details, see W. Kip Viscusi, John M. Vernon, and Joseph E. Harrington, *Economics of Regulation and Antitrust*, 4th ed. (Cambridge, MA: MIT Press, 2006); and Jessica L. Goldstein, "Single Firm Predatory Pricing in Antitrust Law: The Rose Acre Recoupment Test and the Search for an Appropriate Judicial Standard," *Columbia Law Review* 91 (1991): 1557–1592.

[9] *Brooke Group v. Brown & Williamson Tobacco*, 113 S. Ct. (1993); Timothy J. Trujillo, "Predatory Pricing Standards Under Recent Supreme Court Decisions and Their Failure to Recognize Strategic Behavior as a Barrier to Entry," *Iowa Journal of Corporation Law* (Summer 1994): 809–831.

[10] An exception is *McGahee v. Northern Propane Gas Co.* [858 F, 2d 1487 (1988)], in which the Eleventh Circuit Court held that prices below average total cost constitute evidence of predatory intent. For more discussion, see Phillip Areeda and Donald F. Turner, "Predatory Pricing and Related Practices under Section 2 of Sherman Act," *Harvard Law Review* 88 (1975): 697–733. For an overview of case law, see W. Kip Viscusi, John M. Vernon, and Joseph E. Harrington, *Economics of Regulation and Antitrust*, 4th ed. (Cambridge, MA: MIT Press, 2006). See also the "Legal Developments" section of the *Journal of Marketing* for summaries of court cases.

[11] *Adjustor's Replace-a-Car, Inc. v. Agency Rent-a-Car*, 735 2d 884 (1984).

chance of later increasing prices or market share to recover its losses.[12] The defendant, BWT, a cigarette manufacturer, sold brand-name cigarettes and had 12% of the cigarette market. The introduction of generic cigarettes threatened BWT's market share. BWT responded by introducing its own version of generics priced below average variable cost, thereby making it difficult for generic manufacturers to continue in business. The Supreme Court ruled that BWT's action was a competitive response and not predatory pricing. That's because, given BWT's small 12% market share and the existing competition within the industry, it would be unable to later charge a higher price or enlarge demand to recoup its losses.

Dumping

Closely related to predatory pricing is dumping. Under U.S. laws, **dumping** occurs when a non-U.S. company sells a product in the United States at a price below the market price in the country where it is produced, and this lower price materially injures or threatens to materially injure an industry in the United States. If dumping is proven, an antidumping duty can be imposed under U.S. tariff laws equal to the amount by which the foreign price exceeds the U.S. price. Cases related to dumping have occurred in the cement, computer, lumber, paper, semiconductor, solar panel, steel, sweater, and tire industries. In March 2016, the U.S. Department of Commerce announced it would place import duties up to 266% on imports of cold-rolled steel (used in auto parts, appliances, and shipping containers) from China and six other countries. The U.S. International Trade Commission ruled that U.S. steel manufacturers had lost market share in the United States as a result of companies from these seven countries selling cold-rolled steel in the U.S. market below the market prices in their home countries. The United States already had anti-dumping duties in place on 19 other categories of Chinese steel.[13]

Collusive Pricing

Another violation of antitrust laws is **collusive pricing**, which occurs when companies in an industry conspire in their pricing and production decisions to achieve a price above the competitive price and so restrain trade. In 2016, for example, a federal judge determined that lawsuits could proceed against 16 major banks—including J.P. Morgan Chase, Bank of America, and Citigroup—accused of collusion in manipulating the London interbank offered rate, or LIBOR, to the detriment of the banks' customers.[14]

DECISION POINT

How do antitrust laws affect pricing?

---

[12] *Brooke Group v. Brown & Williamson Tobacco*, 113 S. Ct. (1993).

[13] John Miller and William Mauldin, "U.S. Imposes 266% Duty on Some Chinese Steel Imports," *The Wall Street Journal*, March 1, 2016.

[14] Nicole Hong, "Banks Dealt Blow in Libor Lawsuits," *The Wall Street Journal*, May 23, 2016.

PROBLEM FOR SELF-STUDY

Reconsider the Astel Computer example (pages 547–550). Astel's marketing manager realizes that a further reduction in price is necessary to sell 200,000 units of Provalue II. To maintain a target profitability of $16 million, or $80 per unit, Astel will need to reduce costs of Provalue II by $6 million, or $30 per unit. Astel targets a reduction of $4 million, or $20 per unit, in manufacturing costs, and $2 million, or $10 per unit, in marketing, distribution, and customer-service costs. The cross-functional team assigned to this task proposes the following changes to manufacture a different version of Provalue, called Provalue III:

1. Reduce direct materials and ordering costs by purchasing subassembled components rather than individual components.
2. Reengineer ordering and receiving to reduce ordering and receiving costs per order.
3. Reduce testing time and the labor and power required per hour of testing.
4. Develop new rework procedures to reduce rework costs per hour.

No changes are proposed in direct manufacturing labor cost per unit and in total machining costs. The following table summarizes the cost-driver quantities and the cost per unit of each cost driver for Provalue III compared with Provalue II.

	Home	Insert	Page Layout		Formulas	Data	Review	View						
	A	B	C	D	E	F	G	H	I	J	K	L	M	N
1				Manufacturing Cost Information						Manufacturing Cost Information				
2				for 200,000 Units of Provalue II for 2017						for 200,000 Units of Provalue III for 2017				
3	Cost Category	Cost Driver	Details of Budgeted Cost Driver Quantities				Budgeted Total Quantity of Cost Driver	Budgeted Cost per Unit of Cost Driver	Details of Budgeted Cost Driver Quantities				Budgeted Total Quantity of Cost Driver	Budgeted Cost per Unit of Cost Driver
4	(1)	(2)	(3)		(4)		(5)=(3)×(4)	(6)	(7)		(8)		(9)=(7)×(8)	(10)
5	Direct materials	No. of kits	1	kit per unit	200,000	units	200,000	$385	1	kit per unit	200,000	units	200,000	$375
6	Direct manuf. labor (DML)	DML hours	2.65	DML hours per unit	200,000	units	530,000	$ 20	2.65	DML hours per unit	200,000	units	530,000	$ 20
7	Direct machining (fixed)	Machine-hours					300,000	$ 38					300,000	$ 38
8	Ordering and receiving	No. of orders	50	orders per component	425	compo-nents	21,250	$ 80	50	orders per component	400	compo-nents	20,000	$ 60
9	Test and inspection	Testing-hours	15	testing-hours per unit	200,000	units	3,000,000	$ 2	14	testing-hours per unit	200,000	units	2,800,000	$1.70
10	Rework				6.5%	defect rate					6.5%	defect rate		
11		Rework-hours	2.5	rework-hours per defective unit	13,000[a]	defec-tive units	32,500	$ 40	2.5	rework-hours per defective unit	13,000[a]	defec-tive units	32,500	$ 32
12														
13	[a]6.5% defect rate × 200,000 units = 13,000 defective units													

Required

Will the proposed changes achieve Astel's targeted reduction of $4 million, or $20 per unit, in manufacturing costs for Provalue III? Show your computations.

Solution

Exhibit 13-8 presents the manufacturing costs for Provalue III based on the proposed changes. Manufacturing costs will decline from $108 million, or $540 per unit (Exhibit 13-6), to $104 million, or $520 per unit (Exhibit 13-8), and will achieve the target reduction of $4 million, or $20 per unit.

EXHIBIT 13-8   Target Manufacturing Costs of Provalue III for 2017 Based on Proposed Changes

	Home	Insert	Page Layout	Formulas	Data	Review	View			
	A					B		C	D	
1						**Budgeted**			**Budgeted**	
2						**Manufacturing Costs**			**Manufacturing**	
3						**for 200,000 Units**			**Cost per Unit**	
4						**(1)**			**(2) = (1) ÷ 200,000**	
5	Direct manufacturing costs									
6	Direct material costs									
7	(200,000 kits × $375 per kit)					$ 75,000,000			$375.00	
8	Direct manufacturing labor costs									
9	(530,000 DML-hours × $20 per hour)					10,600,000			53.00	
10	Direct machining costs									
11	(300,000 machine-hours × $38 per machine-hour)					11,400,000			57.00	
12	Direct manufacturing costs					97,000,000			485.00	
13										
14	Manufacturing overhead costs									
15	Ordering and receiving costs									
16	(20,000 orders × $60 per order)					1,200,000			6.00	
17	Testing and inspection costs									
18	(2,800,000 testing-hours × $1.70 per hour)					4,760,000			23.80	
19	Rework costs									
20	(32,500 rework-hours × $32 per hour)					1,040,000			5.20	
21	Manufacturing overhead costs					7,000,000			35.00	
22	Total manufacturing costs					$104,000,000			$520.00	

DECISION POINTS

The following question-and-answer format summarizes the chapter's learning objectives. Each decision presents a key question related to a learning objective. The guidelines are the answers to that question.

Decision	Guidelines
1. What are the three major factors affecting pricing decisions?	Customers, competitors, and costs influence prices through their effects on demand and supply; customers and competitors affect demand; and costs affect supply.
2. How do companies make long-run pricing decisions?	Companies consider all future costs (whether variable or fixed in the short run) and use a market-based or a cost-based pricing approach to earn a target return on investment.
3. How do companies determine target cost?	One approach to long-run pricing is to determine a target price. Target price is the estimated price that potential customers are willing to pay for a product or service. Target cost per unit equals target price minus target operating income per unit. Target cost per unit is the estimated long-run cost of a product or service that, when sold, enables the company to achieve target operating income per unit. Value-engineering methods help a company make the cost improvements necessary to achieve target cost.

Decision	Guidelines
4. Why is it important for managers to distinguish cost incurrence from locked-in costs?	Cost incurrence describes when a resource is sacrificed. Locked-in costs are costs that have not yet been incurred but, based on decisions that have already been made, will be incurred in the future. Value engineering techniques are most effective for reducing costs *before* costs are locked in.
5. How do companies price products using the cost-plus approach?	The cost-plus approach to pricing adds a markup component to a cost base as the starting point for pricing decisions. Many different costs, such as full cost of the product or manufacturing cost, can serve as the cost base for applying the cost-plus formula. Prices are then modified on the basis of customers' reactions and competitors' responses, that is, the size of the "plus" is determined by the marketplace.
6. Describe life-cycle budgeting and life-cycle costing and when should companies use these techniques?	Life-cycle budgeting estimates and life-cycle costing tracks and accumulates the costs (and revenues) attributable to a product from its initial R&D to its final customer service and support. These life-cycle techniques are particularly important when (a) a high percentage of total life-cycle costs are incurred before production begins while revenues are earned over several years or (b) a high fraction of life-cycle costs are locked in at the R&D and design stages.
7. What is price discrimination and peak load pricing and why are there price differences across countries?	Price discrimination is charging some customers a higher price for a given product or service than other customers. Peak-load pricing is charging a higher price for the same product or service when demand approaches physical-capacity limits. Under price discrimination and peak-load pricing, prices differ among different types of customers and across time periods even though the cost of providing the product or service is approximately the same. Prices for the same product differ across countries because of differences in the purchasing power of consumers and government restrictions.
8. How do antitrust laws affect pricing?	To comply with antitrust laws, a company must not engage in predatory pricing, dumping, or collusive pricing, which lessens competition; puts another company at an unfair competitive disadvantage; or harms consumers.

TERMS TO LEARN

The chapter and the Glossary at the end of the book contain definitions of the following important terms:

collusive pricing (**p. 565**)
cost incurrence (**p. 553**)
customer life-cycle costs (**p. 562**)
designed-in costs (**p. 553**)
dumping (**p. 565**)
life-cycle budgeting (**p. 560**)
life-cycle costing (**p. 560**)

locked-in costs (**p. 553**)
non-value-added cost (**p. 553**)
peak-load pricing (**p. 563**)
predatory pricing (**p. 564**)
price discrimination (**p. 563**)
product life cycle (**p. 560**)
target cost per unit (**p. 552**)

target operating income per
  unit (**p. 552**)
target price (**p. 550**)
target rate of return on
  investment (**p. 557**)
value-added cost (**p. 553**)
value engineering (**p. 552**)

ASSIGNMENT MATERIAL

Questions

13-1 What are the three major influences on pricing decisions?

13-2 "Relevant costs for pricing decisions are full costs of the product." Do you agree? Explain.

13-3 Describe four purposes of cost allocation.

13-4 How is activity-based costing useful for pricing decisions?

13-5 Describe two alternative approaches to long-run pricing decisions.

13-6 What is a target cost per unit?

13-7 Describe value engineering and its role in target costing.

13-8 Give two examples of a value-added cost and two examples of a non-value-added cost.

13-9 "It is not important for a company to distinguish between cost incurrence and locked-in costs." Do you agree? Explain.

13-10 What is cost-plus pricing?

13-11 Describe three alternative cost-plus pricing methods.

13-12 Give two examples in which the difference in the costs of two products or services is much smaller than the difference in their prices.

13-13 What is life-cycle budgeting?

13-14 What are three benefits of using a product life-cycle reporting format?

13-15 Define predatory pricing, dumping, and collusive pricing.

Multiple-Choice Questions

In partnership with:

BECKER
PROFESSIONAL EDUCATION®

13-16 Which of the following statements regarding price elasticity is incorrect?

a. A product with a perfectly inelastic demand would have the same demand even as prices change.

b. A product with a perfectly inelastic demand would see demand change as prices change.

c. When demand is price elastic, lower prices stimulate demand.

d. When demand is price elastic, higher prices reduce demand.

Exercises

13-17 Value-added, non-value-added costs. The Magill Repair Shop repairs and services machine tools. A summary of its costs (by activity) for 2017 is as follows:

a.	Materials and labor for servicing machine tools	$1,100,000
b.	Rework costs	90,000
c.	Expediting costs caused by work delays	65,000
d.	Materials-handling costs	80,000
e.	Materials-procurement and inspection costs	45,000
f.	Preventive maintenance of equipment	55,000
g.	Breakdown maintenance of equipment	75,000

Required

1. Classify each cost as value-added, non-value-added, or in the gray area between.
2. For any cost classified in the gray area, assume 60% is value-added and 40% is non-value-added. How much of the total of all seven costs is value-added and how much is non-value-added?
3. Magill is considering the following changes: (a) introducing quality-improvement programs whose net effect will be to reduce rework and expediting costs by 40% and materials and labor costs for servicing machine tools by 5%; (b) working with suppliers to reduce materials-procurement and inspection costs by 20% and materials-handling costs by 30%; and (c) increasing preventive-maintenance costs by 70% to reduce breakdown-maintenance costs by 50%. Calculate the effect of programs (a), (b), and (c) on value-added costs, non-value-added costs, and total costs. Comment briefly.

13-18 Target operating income, value-added costs, service company. Europa Associates prepares architectural drawings to conform to local structural-safety codes. Its income statement for 2017 is as follows:

Revenues	$701,250
Salaries of professional staff (7,500 hours × $52 per hour)	390,000
Travel	15,000
Administrative and support costs	171,600
Total costs	576,600
Operating income	$124,650

The percentage of time spent by professional staff on various activities follows:

Making calculations and preparing drawings for clients	77%
Checking calculations and drawings	3
Correcting errors found in drawings (not billed to clients)	8
Making changes in response to client requests (billed to clients)	5
Correcting own errors regarding building codes (not billed to clients)	7
Total	100%

Assume administrative and support costs vary with professional-labor costs. Consider each requirement independently.

Required

1. How much of the total costs in 2017 are value-added, non-value-added, or in the gray area between? Explain your answers briefly. What actions can Europa take to reduce its costs?
2. What are the consequences of misclassifying a non-value-added cost as a value-added cost? When in doubt, would you classify a cost as a value-added or non-value-added cost? Explain briefly.
3. Suppose Europa could eliminate all errors so that it did not need to spend any time making corrections and, as a result, could proportionately reduce professional-labor costs. Calculate Europa's operating income for 2017.
4. Now suppose Europa could take on as much business as it could complete, but it could not add more professional staff. Assume Europa could eliminate all errors so that it does not need to spend any time correcting errors. Assume Europa could use the time saved to increase revenues proportionately. Assume travel costs will remain at $15,000. Calculate Europa's operating income for 2017.

13-19 Target prices, target costs, activity-based costing. Snappy Tiles is a small distributor of marble tiles. Snappy identifies its three major activities and cost pools as ordering, receiving and storage, and shipping, and it reports the following details for 2016:

Activity	Cost Driver	Quantity of Cost Driver	Cost per Unit of Cost Driver
1. Placing and paying for orders of marble tiles	Number of orders	500	$50 per order
2. Receiving and storage	Loads moved	4,000	$30 per load
3. Shipping of marble tiles to retailers	Number of shipments	1,500	$40 per shipment

For 2016, Snappy buys 250,000 marble tiles at an average cost of $3 per tile and sells them to retailers at an average price of $4 per tile. Assume Snappy has no fixed costs and no inventories.

Required

1. Calculate Snappy's operating income for 2016.
2. For 2017, retailers are demanding a 5% discount off the 2016 price. Snappy's suppliers are only willing to give a 4% discount. Snappy expects to sell the same quantity of marble tiles in 2017 as in 2016. If all other costs and cost-driver information remain the same, calculate Snappy's operating income for 2017.
3. Suppose further that Snappy decides to make changes in its ordering and receiving-and-storing practices. By placing long-run orders with its key suppliers, Snappy expects to reduce the number of orders to 200 and the cost per order to $25 per order. By redesigning the layout of the warehouse and reconfiguring the crates in which the marble tiles are moved, Snappy expects to reduce the number of loads moved to 3,125 and the cost per load moved to $28. Will Snappy achieve its target operating income of $0.30 per tile in 2017? Show your calculations.

13-20 Target costs, effect of product-design changes on product costs. Neuro Instruments uses a manufacturing costing system with one direct-cost category (direct materials) and three indirect-cost categories:

a. Setup, production-order, and materials-handling costs that vary with the number of batches
b. Manufacturing-operations costs that vary with machine-hours
c. Costs of engineering changes that vary with the number of engineering changes made

In response to competitive pressures at the end of 2016, Neuro Instruments used value-engineering techniques to reduce manufacturing costs. Actual information for 2016 and 2017 is as follows:

	2016	2017
Setup, production-order, and materials-handling costs per batch	$ 8,900	$8,000
Total manufacturing-operations cost per machine-hour	$ 64	$ 48
Cost per engineering change	$16,000	$8,000

The management of Neuro Instruments wants to evaluate whether value engineering has succeeded in reducing the target manufacturing cost per unit of one of its products, HJ6, by 5%.
   Actual results for 2016 and 2017 for HJ6 are:

	Actual Results for 2016	Actual Results for 2017
Units of HJ6 produced	2,700	4,600
Direct material cost per unit of HJ6	$ 1,400	$ 1,300
Total number of batches required to produce HJ6	60	70
Total machine-hours required to produce HJ6	20,000	30,000
Number of engineering changes made	24	7

1. Calculate the manufacturing cost per unit of HJ6 in 2016.
2. Calculate the manufacturing cost per unit of HJ6 in 2017.
3. Did Neuro Instruments achieve the target manufacturing cost per unit for HJ6 in 2017? Explain.
4. Explain how Neuro Instruments reduced the manufacturing cost per unit of HJ6 in 2017.
5. What challenges might managers at Neuro Instruments encounter in achieving the target cost? How might they overcome these challenges?

Required

13-21 Target costs, effect of process-design changes on service costs. Sun Systems provides energy audits in residential areas of southern Ohio. The energy audits provide information to homeowners on the benefits of solar energy. A consultant from Sun Systems educates the homeowner about federal and state rebates and tax credits available for purchases and installations of solar heating systems. A successful energy audit results in the homeowner purchasing a solar heating system. Sun Systems does not install the solar heating system, but arranges for the installation with a local company. Sun Systems completes all necessary paperwork related to the rebates, tax credits, and financing. The company has identified three major activities that drive the cost of energy audits: identifying new contacts (that varies with the number of new contacts); traveling to and between appointments (that varies with the number of miles driven); and preparing and filing rebates and tax forms (that varies with the number of clerical hours). Actual costs for each of these activities in 2016 and 2017 are:

	2016	2017
Consultant labor cost per hour	$35.00	$35.00
Average cost per new contact	9.00	7.00
Travel cost per mile	0.55	0.65
Preparing and filing cost per clerical hour	9.10	9.50

In 2017, Sun Systems used value engineering to reduce the cost of the energy audits. Managers at Sun Systems want to evaluate whether value engineering has succeeded in reducing the target cost per audit by 5%.
   Actual results for 2016 and 2017 for Sun Systems are:

	Actual Results for 2016	Actual Results for 2017
Successful audits performed	150	178
Number of new contracts	215	275
Miles driven	1,756	1,327
Total clerical hours	1,218	1,367
Consultant labor-hours per audit	2.2	2

1. Calculate the cost per audit in 2016.
2. Calculate the cost per audit in 2017.
3. Did Sun Systems achieve the target cost per audit in 2016? Explain.
4. What challenges might managers at Sun Systems encounter in achieving the target cost and how might they overcome these challenges?

Required

13-22 Cost-plus target return on investment pricing. John Branch is the managing partner of a business that has just finished building a 60-room motel. Branch anticipates that he will rent these rooms for 16,000 nights next year (or 16,000 room-nights). All rooms are similar and will rent for the same price. Branch estimates the following operating costs for next year:

Variable operating costs	$4 per room-night
Fixed costs	
Salaries and wages	$170,000
Maintenance of building and pool	48,000
Other operating and administration costs	122,000
Total fixed costs	$340,000

The capital invested in the motel is $1,000,000. The partnership's target return on investment is 20%. Branch expects demand for rooms to be uniform throughout the year. He plans to price the rooms at full cost plus a markup on full cost to earn the target return on investment.

1. What price should Branch charge for a room-night? What is the markup as a percentage of the full cost of a room-night?
2. Branch's market research indicates that if the price of a room-night determined in requirement 1 is reduced by 10%, the expected number of room-nights Branch could rent would increase by 10%. Should Branch reduce prices by 10%? Show your calculations.

13-23 Cost-plus, target pricing, working backward. TinRoof, Inc., manufactures and sells a do-it-yourself storage shed kit. In 2016, it reported the following:

Units produced and sold	3,200
Investment	$2,400,000
Markup percentage on full cost	8%
Rate of return on investment	12%
Variable cost per unit	$500

1. What was TinRoof's operating income in 2016? What was the full cost per unit? What was the selling price? What was the percentage markup on variable cost?
2. TinRoof is considering increasing the annual spending on advertising by $175,000. The managers believe that the investment will translate into a 10% increase in unit sales. Should the company make the investment? Show your calculations.
3. Refer back to the original data. In 2017, TinRoof believes that it will only be able to sell 2,900 units at the price calculated in requirement 1. Management has identified $125,000 in fixed cost that can be eliminated. If TinRoof wants to maintain an 8% markup on full cost, what is the target variable cost per unit?

13-24 Life-cycle budgeting and costing. Jurgensen Manufacturing, Inc., plans to develop a new industrial-powered vacuum sweeper for household use that runs exclusively on rechargeable batteries. The product will take 6 months to design and test. The company expects the vacuum sweeper to sell 10,000 units during the first six months of sales; 20,000 units per year over the following two years; and 5,000 units over the final 6 months of the product's life cycle. The company expects the following costs:

Period	Cost	Total Fixed Cost for the Period	Variable Cost per Unit
Months 0–6	Design costs	$500,000	
Months 7–12	Production	$1,300,000	$90 per unit
	Marketing	$1,000,000	
	Distribution	$200,000	$10 per unit
Months 13–36	Production	$4,900,000	$70 per unit
	Marketing	$2,325,000	
	Distribution	$700,000	$ 8 per unit
Months 37–42	Production	$800,000	$60 per unit
	Marketing	$475,000	
	Distribution	$100,000	$ 7 per unit

Ignore time value of money.

Required

1. If Jurgensen prices the sweepers at $375 each, how much operating income will the company make over the product's life cycle? What is the operating income per unit?
2. Excluding the initial product design costs, what is the operating income in each of the three sales phases of the product's life cycle, assuming the price stays at $375?
3. How would you explain the change in budgeted operating income over the product's life cycle? What other factors does the company need to consider before developing the new vacuum sweeper?
4. Jurgensen is concerned about the operating income it will report in the first sales phase. It is considering pricing the vacuum sweeper at $425 for the first six months and decreasing the price to $375 thereafter. With this pricing strategy, Jurgensen expects to sell 9,500 units instead of 10,000 units in the first six months, 19,000 each year over the next two years, and 5,000 over the last six months. Assuming the same cost structure given in the problem, which pricing strategy would you recommend? Explain.

13-25 Considerations other than cost in pricing decisions. Fun Stay Express operates a 100-room hotel near a busy amusement park. During June, a 30-day month, Fun Stay Express experienced a 65% occupancy rate from Monday evening through Thursday evening (weeknights). On Friday through Sunday evenings (weekend nights), however, occupancy increases to 90%. (There were 18 weeknights and 12 weekend nights in June.) Fun Stay Express charges $85 per night for a suite. The company recently hired Gina Johnson to manage the hotel to increase the hotel's profitability. The following information relates to Fun Stay Express' costs:

	Fixed Cost	Variable Cost
Depreciation	$25,000 per month	
Administrative costs	$38,000 per month	
Housekeeping and supplies	$16,000 per month	$30 per room-night
Breakfast	$12,000 per month	$6 per breakfast served

Fun Stay Express offers free breakfast to guests. In June, there were an average of two breakfasts served per room-night on weeknights and 4 breakfasts served per room-night on weekend nights.

Required

1. Calculate the average cost per room-night for June. What was Fun Stay Express' operating income or loss for the month?
2. Gina Johnson estimates that if Fun Stay Express decreases the nightly rates to $75, weeknight occupancy will increase to 75%. She also estimates that if the hotel increases the nightly rate on weekend nights to $105, occupancy on those nights will remain at 90%. Would this be a good move for Fun Stay Express? Show your calculations.
3. Why would the guests tolerate a $30 price difference between weeknights and weekend nights?
4. A discount travel clearinghouse has approached Fun Stay Express with a proposal to offer last-minute deals on empty rooms on both weeknights and weekend nights. Assuming that there will be an average of three breakfasts served per night per room, what is the minimum price that Fun Stay Express could accept on the last-minute rooms?

Pearson MyLab Accounting

Problems

13-26 Cost-plus, target pricing, working backward. The new CEO of Rusty Manufacturing has asked for information about the operations of the firm from last year. The CEO is given the following information, but with some data missing:

Total sales revenue	?
Number of units produced and sold	500,000 units
Selling price	?
Operating income	$180,000
Total investment in assets	$2,250,000
Variable cost per unit	$4.00
Fixed costs for the year	$2,500,000

Required

1. Find (a) total sales revenue, (b) selling price, (c) rate of return on investment, and (d) markup percentage on full cost for this product.
2. The new CEO has a plan to reduce fixed costs by $225,000 and variable costs by $0.30 per unit while continuing to produce and sell 500,000 units. Using the same markup percentage as in requirement 1, calculate the new selling price.
3. Assume the CEO institutes the changes in requirement 2 including the new selling price. However, the reduction in variable cost has resulted in lower product quality resulting in 5% fewer units being sold compared with before the change. Calculate operating income (loss).
4. What concerns, if any, other than the quality problem described in requirement 3, do you see in implementing the CEO's plan? Explain briefly.

13-27 Value engineering, target pricing, and target costs. Tiffany Cosmetics manufactures and sells a variety of makeup and beauty products. The company has come up with its own patented formula for a new anti-aging cream The company president wants to make sure the product is priced competitively because its purchase will also likely increase sales of other products. The company anticipates that it will sell 400,000 units of the product in the first year with the following estimated costs:

Product design and licensing	$ 1,000,000
Direct materials	1,800,000
Direct manufacturing labor	1,200,000
Variable manufacturing overhead	600,000
Fixed manufacturing overhead	2,000,000
Fixed marketing	3,000,000

Required

1. The company believes that it can successfully sell the product for $38 a bottle. The company's target operating income is 40% of revenue. Calculate the target full cost of producing the 400,000 units. Does the cost estimate meet the company's requirements? Is value engineering needed?
2. A component of the direct materials cost requires the nectar of a specific plant in South America. If the company could eliminate this special ingredient, the materials cost would drop by 45%. However, this would require design changes of $300,000 to engineer a chemical equivalent of the ingredient. Will this design change allow the product to meet its target cost?
3. The company president does not believe that the formula should be altered for fear it will tarnish the company's brand. She prefers that the company spend more on marketing and increase the price. The company's accountants believe that if marketing costs are increase by $400,000 then the company can achieve a selling price of $42 per bottle without losing any sales. At this price, will the company achieve its target operating income of 40% of revenue?
4. What are the advantages and disadvantages of pursuing alternatives 2 and 3 above?

13-28 Target service costs, value engineering, and activity-based costing. Lagoon is an amusement park that offers family-friendly entertainment and attractions. The park boasts more than 25 acres of fun. The admission price to enter the park, which includes access to all attractions, is $35. At this entrance price, Lagoon's target profit is 35% of revenues. Lagoon's managers have identified the major activities that drive the cost of operating the park. The activity cost pools, the cost driver for each activity, and the cost per unit of the cost driver for each pool are:

Activity	Description of Activity	Cost Driver	Cost per Unit of Cost Driver
1. Ticket sales	Selling tickets on-site for entry into the park	Number of tickets sold on-site	$2 per ticket sold
2. Ticket verification	Verifying tickets purchased at park and online ticket purchases	Number of patrons	$1.50 per patron
3. Operating attractions	Loading, monitoring, off-loading patrons on attraction	Number of runs	$90 per run
4. Litter patrol	Roaming the park and cleaning up waste as necessary	Number of litter patrol hours	$20 per hour

The park operates from 10:00 a.m.–8:00 p.m. everyday. The average number of patrons per week is 55,000. Its Web site is maintained by an external company that charges $1 per ticket sold. Only 15% of the tickets are purchased online. Lagoon has 27 attractions and each can make 6 runs an hour on an average. Cleaning crew members are assigned to 1-acre areas. One person can cover approximately 1 acre per hour.

In response to competitive pressures and to continue to attract 55,000 patrons per week, Lagoon has decided to lower ticket prices to $33 per patron. To maintain the same level of profits as before, Lagoon is looking to make the following improvements to reduce operating costs:

a. Spend $1,000 per week on advertising to promote awareness of the available online ticket purchase. Lagoon's managers expect that this advertising will increase online purchases to 40% of total ticket sales. At this volume, the cost per online ticket sold will decrease to $0.75.
b. Reduce the operating hours for eight of the attractions that are not very popular from 10 hours per day to 7 hours per day.
c. Increase the number of refuse containers in the park at an additional cost of $250 per week. Litter patrol employees will be able to cover 1.25 acres per hour.

The cost per unit of cost driver for all other activities will remain the same.

Required

1. Does Lagoon currently achieve its target profit of 35% of sales?
2. Will the new changes and improvements allow Lagoon to achieve the same target profit in dollars? Show your calculations.

3. What challenges might managers at Lagoon encounter in achieving the target cost? How might they overcome these challenges?

13-29 Cost-plus, target return on investment pricing. Zoom-o-licious makes candy bars for vending machines and sells them to vendors in cases of 30 bars. Although Zoom-o-licious makes a variety of candy, the cost differences are insignificant, and the cases all sell for the same price.

Zoom-o-licious has a total capital investment of $15,000,000. It expects to produce and sell 300,000 cases of candy next year. Zoom-o-licious requires a 10% target return on investment.

Expected costs for next year are:

Variable production costs	$4.00 per case
Variable marketing and distribution costs	$1.00 per case
Fixed production costs	$300,000
Fixed marketing and distribution costs	$400,000
Other fixed costs	$200,000

Zoom-o-licious prices the cases of candy at full cost plus markup to generate profits equal to the target return on capital.

Required

1. What is the target operating income?
2. What is the selling price Zoom-o-licious needs to charge to earn the target operating income? Calculate the markup percentage on full cost.
3. Zoom-o-licious's closest competitor has just increased its candy case price to $16, although it sells 36 candy bars per case. Zoom-o-licious is considering increasing its selling price to $15 per case. Assuming production and sales decrease by 4%, calculate Zoom-o-licious' return on investment. Is increasing the selling price a good idea?

13-30 Cost-plus, time and materials, ethics. A & L Mechanical sells and services plumbing, heating, and air-conditioning systems. A & L's cost accounting system tracks two cost categories: direct labor and direct materials. A & L uses a time-and-materials pricing system, with direct labor marked up 80% and direct materials marked up 60% to recover indirect costs of support staff, support materials, and shared equipment and tools and to earn a profit.

During a hot summer day, the central air conditioning in Michelle Lowry's home stops working. A & L technician Tony Dickenson arrives at Lowry's home and inspects the air conditioner. He considers two options: replace the compressor or repair it. The cost information available to Dickenson follows:

	Labor	Materials
Repair option	7 hours	$120
Replace option	4 hours	$230
Labor rate	$45 per hour	

Required

1. If Dickenson presents Lowry with the replace or repair options, what price would he quote for each?
2. If the two options were equally effective for the three years that Lowry intends to live in the home, which option would she choose?
3. If Dickenson's objective is to maximize profits, which option would he recommend to Lowry? What would be the ethical course of action?

13-31 Cost-plus and market-based pricing. Georgia Temps, a large labor contractor, supplies contract labor to building-construction companies. For 2017, Georgia Temps has budgeted to supply 84,000 hours of contract labor. Its variable costs are $13 per hour, and its fixed costs are $168,000. Roger Mason, the general manager, has proposed a cost-plus approach for pricing labor at full cost plus 20%.

Required

1. If Dickenson presents Lowry with the replace or repair options, what price would he quote for each.
2. If the two options were equally effective for the 3 years that Lowry intends to live in the home, which option would she choose:

Price per Hour	Demand (Hours)
$16	124,000
17	104,000
18	84,000
19	74,000
20	61,000

Georgia Temps can meet any of these demand levels. Fixed costs will remain unchanged for all the demand levels. On the basis of this additional information, calculate the price per hour that Georgia Temps should charge to maximize operating income.

3. Comment on your answers to requirements 1 and 2. Why are they the same or different?

13-32 Cost-plus and market-based pricing. (CMA, adapted) Quick Test Laboratories evaluates the reaction of materials to extreme increases in temperature. Much of the company's early growth was attributable to government contracts, but recent growth has come from expansion into commercial markets. Two types of testing at Quick Test are Heat Testing (HTT) and Arctic-Condition Testing (ACT). Currently, all of the budgeted operating costs are collected in a single overhead pool. All of the estimated testing-hours are also collected in a single pool. One rate per test-hour is used for both types of testing. This hourly rate is marked up by 30% to recover administrative costs and taxes and to earn a profit.

George Barton, Quick Test's controller, believes that there is enough variation in the test procedures and cost structure to establish separate costing rates and billing rates at a 30% markup. He also believes that the inflexible rate structure the company is currently using is inadequate in today's competitive environment. After analyzing the company data, he has divided operating costs into the following three cost pools:

Labor and supervision	$ 436,800
Setup and facility costs	351,820
Utilities	435,600
Total budgeted costs for the period	$1,224,220

George Barton budgets 112,000 total test-hours for the coming period. Test-hours is also the cost driver for labor and supervision. The budgeted quantity of cost driver for setup and facility costs is 700 setup-hours. The budgeted quantity of cost driver for utilities is 12,000 machine-hours.

George has estimated that HTT uses 70% of the test-hours, 20% of the setup-hours, and half the machine-hours.

Required

1. Find the single rate for operating costs based on test-hours and the hourly billing rate for HTT and ACT.
2. Find the three activity-based rates for operating costs.
3. What will the billing rate for HTT and ACT be based on the activity-based costing structure? State the rates in terms of test-hours. Referring to both requirements 1 and 2, which rates make more sense for Quick Test?
4. If Quick Test's competition all charge $23 per hour for arctic testing, what can Quick Test do to stay competitive?

13-33 Life-cycle costing. Maximum Metal Recycling and Salvage receives the opportunity to salvage scrap metal and other materials from an old industrial site. The current owners of the site will sign over the site to Maximum at no cost. Maximum intends to extract scrap metal at the site for 24 months and then will clean up the site, return the land to useable condition, and sell it to a developer. Projected costs associated with the project follow:

		Fixed	Variable
Months 1–24	Metal extraction and processing	$2,000 per month	$80 per ton
Months 1–27	Rent on temporary buildings	$1,000 per month	—
	Administration	$6,000 per month	—
Months 25–27	Clean-up	$20,000 per month	—
	Land restoration	$23,000 total	—
	Cost of selling land	$80,000 total	—

Ignore the time value of money.

Required

1. Assuming that Maximum expects to salvage 70,000 tons of metal from the site, what is the total project life-cycle cost?
2. Suppose Maximum can sell the metal for $110 per ton and wants to earn a profit (before taxes) of $30 per ton. At what price must Maximum sell the land at the end of the project to achieve its target profit per ton?
3. Now suppose Maximum can only sell the metal for $100 per ton and the land at $110,000 less than what you calculated in requirement 2. If Maximum wanted to maintain the same markup percentage on total project life-cycle cost as in requirement 2, by how much would the company have to reduce its total project life-cycle cost?

13-34 Airline pricing, considerations other than cost in pricing. Europa Airways is about to introduce a daily round-trip flight from Madrid, Spain, to Cairo, Egypt, and is determining how to price its round-trip tickets.

The market research group at Europa Airways segments the market into business and pleasure travelers. It provides the following information on the effects of two different prices on the number of seats expected to be sold and the variable cost per ticket, including the commission paid to travel agents:

		Number of Seats Expected to Be Sold	
Price Charged	Variable Cost per Ticket	Business	Pleasure
$800	$85	300	150
1,800	195	285	30

Pleasure travelers start their travel during one week, spend at least one weekend at their destination, and return the following week or thereafter. Business travelers usually start and complete their travel within the same work week. They do not stay over weekends. Assume that round-trip fuel costs are fixed costs of $24,700 and that fixed costs allocated to the round-trip flight for airplane-lease costs, ground services, and flight-crew salaries total $183,000.

Required

1. If you could charge different prices to business travelers and pleasure travelers, would you? Show your computations.
2. Explain the key factor (or factors) for your answer in requirement 1.
3. How might Europa Airways implement price discrimination? That is, what plan could the airline formulate so that business travelers and pleasure travelers each pay the price the airline desires?

13-35 Anti-trust laws and pricing. Global Airlines is a major low-price airline carrier for both domestic and international travel. The company guarantees the "lowest price" ticket for travel within the United States. The "lowest price" ticket guarantee does not apply for travel on Monday mornings and Friday evenings, which are busy travel times for business travelers.

Required

1. Do these pricing practices of Global Airlines violate any anti-trust laws? Why or why not?
2. Why is Global Airlines not offering a price guarantee for flights on Monday mornings and Friday evenings? Do you agree with this policy? Explain briefly.
3. What other factors should Global Airlines consider before implementing these pricing policies?

13-36 Ethics and pricing. Instyle Interior Designs has been requested to prepare a bid to decorate four model homes for a new development. Winning the bid would be a big boost for sales representative Jim Doogan, who works entirely on commission. Sara Groom, the cost accountant for Instyle, prepares the bid based on the following cost information:

Direct costs		
Design costs		$ 20,000
Furniture and artwork		70,000
Direct labor		10,000
Delivery and installation		20,000
Overhead costs		
Design software	5,200	
Furniture handling	4,800	
General and administration	8,000	
Total overhead costs		18,000
Full product costs		$138,000

Based on the company policy of pricing at 120% of full cost, Groom gives Doogan a figure of $165,600 to submit for the job. Doogan is very concerned. He tells Groom that at that price, Instyle has no chance of winning the job. He confides in her that he spent $600 of company funds to take the developer to a basketball playoff game where the developer disclosed that a bid of $156,000 would win the job. He hadn't planned to tell Groom because he was confident that the bid she developed would be below that amount. Doogan reasons that the $600 he spent will be wasted if Instyle doesn't capitalize on this valuable information. In any case, the company will still make money if it wins the bid at $156,000 because it is higher than the full cost of $138,000.

Required

1. Is the $600 spent on the basketball tickets relevant to the bid decision? Why or why not?
2. Groom suggests that if Doogan is willing to use cheaper furniture and artwork, he can achieve a bid of $156,000. The designs have already been reviewed and accepted and cannot be changed without additional cost, so the entire amount of reduction in cost will need to come from furniture and artwork. What is the target cost of furniture and artwork that will allow Doogan to submit a bid of $156,000 assuming a target markup of 20% of full cost?
3. Evaluate whether Groom's suggestion to Doogan to use the developer's tip is unethical. Would it be unethical for Doogan to reduce the cost of furniture and artwork to arrive at a lower bid? What steps should Doogan and Groom take to resolve this situation?

13-37 Value engineering, target pricing, and locked-in costs. Wood Creations designs, manufactures, and sells modern wood sculptures. Sally Jensen is an artist for the company. Jensen has spent much of the past month working on the design of an intricate abstract piece. Jim Smoot, product development manager, likes the design. However, he wants to make sure that the sculpture can be priced competitively. Alexis Nampa, Wood's cost accountant, presents Smoot with the following cost data for the expected production of 75 sculptures:

Design cost	$ 8,000
Direct materials	32,000
Direct manufacturing labor	38,000
Variable manufacturing overhead	32,000
Fixed manufacturing overhead	26,000
Marketing	14,000

Required

1. Smoot thinks that Wood Creations can successfully market each piece for $2,500. The company's target operating income is 25% of revenue. Calculate the target full cost of producing the 75 sculptures. Does the cost estimate Nampa developed meet Wood's requirements? Is value engineering needed?
2. Smoot discovers that Jensen has designed the sculpture using the highest-grade wood available, rather than the standard grade of wood that Wood Creations normally uses. Replacing the grade of wood will lower the cost of direct materials by 60%. However, the redesign will require an additional $1,100 of design cost, and the sculptures will be sold for $2,400 each. Will this design change allow the sculpture to meet its target cost? Is the cost of wood a locked-in cost?
3. Jensen insists that the higher-grade wood is a necessity in terms of the sculpture's design. She believes that spending an additional $3,000 on better marketing will allow Wood Creations to sell each sculpture for $2,700. If this is the case, will the sculptures' target cost be achieved without any value engineering?
4. Compare the total operating income on the 75 sculptures for requirements 2 and 3. What do you recommend Wood Creations do, based solely on your calculations? Explain briefly?
5. What challenges might managers at Wood Creations encounter in achieving the target cost and how might they overcome these challenges?

Allocation of Support-Department Costs, Common Costs, and Revenues

15

How a company allocates its overhead and internal support costs—costs related to information systems, production control, and other internal services—among its various production departments or projects can have a big impact on the profitability of those departments or projects.

While the allocation may not affect the firm's profit as a whole, if the allocation isn't done properly, it can make the profitability of some departments and projects (and their managers) look better or worse than they should. In other cases, the allocations can affect the decisions of managers and, as the following article shows, the prices paid by consumers.

COST ALLOCATION AND "SMART GRID" ENERGY INFRASTRUCTURE[1]

The United States is moving toward a "Smart Grid"—that is, making transmission and power lines operate and communicate in a more effective and efficient manner using technology, computers, and software. This system also integrates with clean-energy sources, such as wind and solar farms, to help create a more sustainable electric supply that reduces carbon emissions.

According to the Electric Power Resource Institute, an independent nonprofit organization, it will cost between $338 billion and $476 billion—in infrastructure, technology, and power lines—to build out the "Smart Grid" by 2030. These costs will need to be recouped over time from energy consumers.

The U.S. government debated two cost allocation methods for charging consumers. One method was interconnection-wide cost allocation. Under this system, for example, if new power lines and "smart" energy meters were deployed in Seattle, Washington, everybody in Washington would help pay for them to lessen the costs to the Seattle consumers for the significant investments in new technology. A competing proposal would allocate costs only to utility ratepayers who actually benefited from the new "Smart Grid" system. In the previous example, consumers in Seattle would pay for the new power lines and energy meters and not be subsidized by those not receiving any benefits.

LEARNING OBJECTIVES

1 Distinguish the single-rate method from the dual-rate method

2 Understand how the choice between allocation based on budgeted and actual rates and between budgeted and actual usage can affect the incentives of division managers

3 Allocate multiple support-department costs using the direct method, the step-down method, and the reciprocal method

4 Allocate common costs using the stand-alone method and the incremental method

5 Explain the importance of explicit agreement between contracting parties when the reimbursement amount is based on costs incurred

6 Understand how bundling of products causes revenue allocation issues and the methods managers use to allocate revenues

iurii/Shutterstock

---

[1] *Sources*: United States Federal Energy Regulatory Commission, Order No. 1000, July 11, 2011 (http://www.ferc .gov/whats-new/comm-meet/2011/072111/E-6.pdf); "Electric Power Monthly" United States Energy Information Administration press release, Washington, D.C., March 25, 2016 (http://www.eia.gov/electricity/monthly/epm_ table_grapher.cfm?t=epmt_1_1).

Ultimately, the government decided to only charge the consumers who benefited. These customers would see their average monthly electricity bill increase by $9 to $12, but Smart Grid technology would provide greater grid reliability, integration of solar rooftop generation and plug-in vehicles, reductions in electricity demand, and stronger cybersecurity. With greater "Smart Grid" access, alternative energy made up more than 13% of U.S. energy production in 2015, up from 9% in 2006.

The same allocation dilemmas apply when costs of corporate support departments are allocated across multiple divisions or operating departments at manufacturing companies such as Nestle, service companies such as Comcast, merchandising companies such as Trader Joe's, and academic institutions such as Auburn University. This chapter focuses on several challenges that managers face when making decisions about cost and revenue allocations and the consequences of those allocations.

Allocating Support Department Costs Using the Single-Rate and Dual-Rate Methods

LEARNING OBJECTIVE 1

Distinguish the single-rate method

...one rate for allocating costs in a cost pool

from the dual-rate method

...two rates for allocating costs in a cost pool—one for variable costs and one for fixed costs

Companies distinguish operating departments (and operating divisions) from support departments. An **operating department**, also called a **production department**, directly adds value to a product or service. Examples are manufacturing departments where products are made. A **support department**, also called a **service department**, provides the services that assist other internal departments (operating departments and other support departments) in the company. Examples of support departments are information systems, production control, materials management, and plant maintenance. Managers face two questions when allocating the costs of a support department to operating departments or divisions: (1) Should fixed costs of support departments, such as the salary of the department manager, be allocated to operating divisions? (2) If fixed costs are allocated, should variable and fixed costs of the support department be allocated in the same way? With regard to the first question, most companies believe that fixed costs of support departments should be allocated because the support department needs to incur these fixed costs to provide operating divisions with the services they require. Depending on the answer to the first question, there are two approaches to allocating support-department costs: the *single-rate cost-allocation method* and the *dual-rate cost-allocation method*.

Single-Rate and Dual-Rate Methods

The **single-rate method** does not distinguish between fixed and variable costs. It allocates costs in each cost pool (support department in this section) to cost objects (operating divisions in this section) using the same rate per unit of a single allocation base. By contrast, the **dual-rate method** partitions the cost of each support department into two pools, a variable-cost pool and a fixed-cost pool, and allocates each pool using a different cost-allocation base. When using either the single-rate method or the dual-rate method, managers can allocate support-department costs to operating divisions based on either a *budgeted* rate or the eventual *actual* cost rate. The latter approach is neither conceptually preferred nor widely used in practice (we explain why in the next section). Accordingly, we illustrate the single-rate and dual-rate methods next based on the use of *budgeted* rates.

We continue the Robinson Company example first presented in Chapter 4. Recall that Robinson manufactures and installs specialized machinery for the paper-making industry. In Chapter 4 we used a single manufacturing overhead cost pool with direct manufacturing labor-hours as the cost-allocation base to allocate all manufacturing overhead costs to jobs. In this chapter, we present a more detailed accounting system to take into account the different operating and service departments within Robinson's manufacturing department.

Robinson has two operating departments—the Machining Department and the Assembly Department—where production occurs and three support departments—Plant Administration, Engineering and Production Control, and Materials Management—that provide essential services to the operating departments for manufacturing the specialized machinery.

- The Plant Administration Department is responsible for managing all activities in the plant. That is, its costs are incurred to support the supervision costs of the other departments.

- The Engineering and Production Control Department supports all the engineering activity in the other departments. In other words, its costs are incurred to support the engineering costs of the other departments.

- The Materials Management Department is responsible for managing and moving materials and components required for different jobs. Each job at Robinson is different and requires small quantities of unique components to be machined and assembled. Materials Management Department costs vary with the number of material-handling labor-hours incurred to support each department.

The specialized machinery that Robinson manufactures does not go through the service departments and so the costs of the service departments must be allocated to the operating departments to determine the full cost of making the specialized machinery. Once costs are accumulated in the operating departments, they can be absorbed into the different specialized machines that Robinson manufactures. Different jobs need different amounts of machining and assembly resources. Each operating department has a different overhead cost driver to absorb overhead costs to machines produced: machine-hours in the Machining Department and assembly labor-hours in the Assembly Department.

We first focus on the allocation of the Materials Management Department costs to the Machining Department and the Assembly Department. The following data relate to the 2017 budget for the Materials Management Department:

Practical capacity	4,000 hours
Fixed costs of the Materials Management Department in the 3,000 labor-hour to 4,000 labor-hour relevant range	$144,000
Budgeted usage (quantity) of materials management labor-hours required to support the productions departments:	
Machining Department	800 hours
Assembly Department	2,800 hours
Total	3,600 hours
Budgeted variable cost per materials-handling labor-hour in the 3,000 labor-hour to 4,000 labor-hour relevant range	$30 per hour used
Actual usage (quantity) of materials management labor-hours required to support the productions departments:	
Machining Department	1,200 hours
Assembly Department	2,400 hours
Total	3,600 hours

The budgeted rates for Materials Management Department costs can be computed based on either the demand for materials-handling services or the supply of materials-handling services. We consider the allocation of Materials Management Department costs based first on the demand for (or usage of) materials-handling services and then on the supply of materials-handling services.

Allocation Based on the Demand for (or Usage of) Materials-Handling Services

We present the single-rate method followed by the dual-rate method.

Single-Rate Method

In this method, a combined budgeted rate is used for fixed and variable costs. The rate is calculated as follows:

Budgeted usage of materials-handling labor-hours	3,600 hours
Budgeted total cost pool: $144,000 + (3,600 hours × $30/hour)	$252,000
Budgeted total rate per hour: $252,000 ÷ 3,600 hours	$70 per hour used

The rate of $70 per hour is used to allocate Materials Management Department costs to the Machining and Assembly Departments. Note that the budgeted rate of $70 per hour is substantially higher than the $30 budgeted *variable* cost per hour. That's because the $70 rate includes an allocated amount of $40 per hour (budgeted fixed costs, $144,000 ÷ budgeted usage, $3,600 hours) for the *fixed* costs of operating the facility.

Under the single-rate method, departments are charged the budgeted rate for each hour of *actual* use of the central facility. Applying this to our example, Robinson allocates Materials Management Department costs based on the $70 per hour budgeted rate and the actual hours the operating departments use. The support costs allocated to the two departments under this method are as follows:

Machining Department: $70 per hour × 1,200 hours	$ 84,000
Assembly Department: $70 per hour × 2,400 hours	$168,000

Dual-Rate Method

When a company uses the dual-rate method, managers must choose allocation bases for both the variable and fixed-cost pools of the Materials Management Department. As in the single-rate method, variable costs are assigned based on the *budgeted* variable cost per hour of $30 for *actual* hours each department uses. However, fixed costs are assigned based on *budgeted* fixed costs per hour and the *budgeted* number of hours for each department. Given the budgeted usage of 800 hours for the Machining Department and 2,800 hours for the Assembly Department, the budgeted fixed-cost rate is $40 per hour ($144,000 ÷ 3,600 hours). Because this rate is charged on the basis of the *budgeted* usage, however, the fixed costs are effectively allocated in advance as a lump sum based on the relative proportions of the materials management facilities the operating departments are budgeted to use. Under the dual-rate method:

The costs allocated to the Machining Department in 2017 equal:

Fixed costs: $40 per hour × 800 (budgeted) hours	$32,000
Variable costs: $30 per hour × 1,200 (actual) hours	36,000
Total costs	$68,000

The costs allocated to the Assembly Department in 2017 equal:

Fixed costs: $40 per hour × 2,800 (budgeted) hours	$112,000
Variable costs: $30 per hour × 2,400 (actual) hours	72,000
Total costs	$184,000

Note that each operating department is charged the same amount for variable costs under the single-rate and dual-rate methods ($30 per hour multiplied by the actual hours of use). However, the overall assignment of costs differs under the two methods because the single-rate method allocates fixed costs of the Materials Management Department based on actual usage of materials-handling resources by the operating departments, whereas the dual-rate method allocates fixed costs based on budgeted usage.

We next consider the alternative approach of allocating Materials Management Department costs based on the capacity of materials-handling services supplied.

Allocation Based on the Supply of Capacity

We illustrate this approach using the 4,000 hours of practical capacity of the Materials Management Department. The budgeted rate is then determined as follows:

Budgeted fixed-cost rate per hour, $144,000 ÷ 4,000 hours	$36 per hour
Budgeted variable-cost rate per hour	30 per hour
Budgeted total-cost rate per hour	$66 per hour

Using the same procedures for the single-rate and dual-rate methods as in the previous section, the Materials Management Department costs allocated to the operating departments are as follows:

Single-Rate Method

Machining Department: $66 per hour $\times$ 1,200 (actual) hours	$ 79,200
Assembly Department: $66 per hour $\times$ 2,400 (actual) hours	158,400
Fixed costs of unused Materials Management Department capacity:	
$36 per hour $\times$ 400 hours[a]	14,400

[a]400 hours = Practical capacity of 4,000 $-$ (1,200 hours used by Machining Department + 2,400 hours used by Assembly Department).

Dual-Rate Method

Machining Department	
Fixed costs: $36 per hour $\times$ 800 (budgeted) hours	$ 28,800
Variable costs: $30 per hour $\times$ 1,200 (actual) hours	36,000
Total costs	$ 64,800
Assembly Department	
Fixed costs: $36 per hour $\times$ 2,800 (budgeted) hours	$100,800
Variable costs: $30 per hour $\times$ 2,400 (actual) hours	72,000
Total costs	$172,800
Fixed costs of unused Materials Management Department capacity:	
$36 per hour $\times$ 400 hours[b]	$ 14,400

[b]400 hours = Practical capacity of 4,000 hours $-$ (800 hours budgeted to be used by Machining Department + 2,800 hours budgeted to be used by Assembly Department).

When a company uses practical capacity to allocate costs, the single-rate method allocates only the *actual* fixed-cost resources used by the Machining and Assembly Departments, while the dual-rate method allocates the *budgeted* fixed-cost resources to be used by the operating departments. Unused Materials Management Department resources are highlighted but usually not allocated to the departments.[2]

The advantage of using practical capacity to allocate costs is that it focuses management's attention on managing unused capacity (described in Chapter 9, pages 366–367, and Chapter 12, pages 524–526). Using practical capacity also avoids burdening the user departments with the cost of unused capacity of the Materials Management Department. In contrast, when costs are allocated on the basis of the demand for materials-handling services, all $144,000 of budgeted fixed costs, including the cost of unused capacity, are allocated to user departments. If costs are used as a basis for pricing, then charging user departments for unused capacity could result in the downward demand spiral (see page 367–368).

Recently, the dual-rate method has been receiving more attention. Resource Consumption Accounting (RCA), an emerging management accounting system, employs an allocation procedure similar to a dual-rate system. For each cost/resource pool, cost assignment rates for fixed costs are based on practical capacity supplied, while rates for proportional costs (i.e., costs that vary with regard to the output of the resource pool) are based on planned quantities.[3]

There are advantages and disadvantages of using the single-rate and dual-rate methods. We discuss these next.

---

[2] In our example, the costs of unused capacity under the single rate and the dual-rate methods are the same (each equals $14,400). This occurs because the total actual usage of the facility matches the total budgeted usage of 3,600 hours. The budgeted cost of unused capacity (in the dual-rate method) can be either greater or lower than the actual cost (in the single-rate method), depending on whether the total actual usage is lower or higher than the budgeted usage.

[3] Other important features of Resource Consumption Accounting (RCA) include (1) the selective use of activity-based costing, (2) the nonassignment of fixed costs when causal relationships cannot be established, and (3) the depreciation of assets based on their replacement cost. RCA has its roots in the nearly 50-year-old German cost accounting system called Grenzplankostenrechnung (GPK), which is used by organizations such as Mercedes-Benz, Porsche, and Stihl. For further details, as well as illustrations of the use of RCA and GPK in organizations, see Sally Webber and Douglas B. Clinton, "Resource Consumption Accounting Applied: The Clopay Case," *Management Accounting Quarterly* (Fall 2004); and Brian Mackie, "Merging GPK and ABC on the Road to RCA," *Strategic Finance* (November 2006).

Advantages and Disadvantages of Single-Rate Method

Advantages: (1) The single-rate method is less costly to implement because it avoids the often expensive analysis necessary to classify the individual cost items of a department into fixed and variable categories. **(2) It offers user departments some operational control over the charges they bear** by conditioning the final allocations on the actual usage of support services, rather than basing them solely on uncertain forecasts of expected demand.

Disadvantage: The single-rate method may lead operating department managers to make suboptimal decisions that are in their own best interest but that may be inefficient from the standpoint of the organization as a whole. This occurs because under the single-rate method, the allocated fixed costs of the support department appear as variable costs to the operating departments. Consider the setting where managers make allocations based on the demand for materials-handling services. In this case, each user department is charged $70 per hour (or $66 per hour based on practical capacity) under the single-rate method where $40 relates to the allocated fixed costs of the Materials Management Department. Suppose an external provider offers the Machining Department materials-handling labor services at a rate of $55 per hour, at a time when the Materials Management Department has unused capacity. The Machining Department's managers would be tempted to use this vendor because it would lower the department's costs ($55 per hour instead of the $70 per hour internal charge for materials-handling services). In the short run, however, the fixed costs of the Materials Management Department remain unchanged in the relevant range (between 3,000 hours of usage and the practical capacity of 4,000 hours). Robinson will therefore incur an additional cost of $25 per hour if the managers were to take this offer—the difference between the $55 external purchase price and the internal variable cost of $30 of using the Materials Management Department.

Advantages and Disadvantages of Dual-Rate Method

Advantages: (1) The dual-rate method guides department managers to make decisions that benefit both the organization as a whole and each department because it signals to department managers how variable costs and fixed costs behave differently. For example, using an external provider of materials-handling services that charges more than $30 per hour would result in Robinson's being worse off than if it uses its own Materials Management Department, which has a variable cost of $30 per hour. By charging the fixed costs of resources budgeted to be used by the operating departments as a lump sum, the dual-rate method succeeds in removing fixed costs from the operating department managers' consideration when making marginal decisions to outsource services. The dual-rate method therefore avoids the potential conflict of interest that can arise under the single-rate method. **(2) Allocating fixed costs based on budgeted usage helps user departments with both short-run and long-run planning because user departments know the costs allocated to them in advance.** Companies commit to infrastructure costs (such as the fixed costs of a support department) on the basis of a long-run planning horizon; budgeted usage measures the long-run demands of the user departments for support-department services.

Disadvantages: (1) The dual-rate method requires managers to distinguish variable costs from fixed costs, which is often a challenging task. (2) The dual-rate method does not indicate to operating managers the cost of fixed support department resources used because fixed costs are allocated to operating departments based on budgeted rather than actual usage. Thus, the Machining Department manager is allocated fixed costs of the Materials Management Department based on the budgeted usage of 800 labor-hours even though the Machining Department actually uses 1,200 labor-hours. **(3) Allocating fixed costs on the basis of budgeted long-run usage may tempt some managers to underestimate their budgeted usage.** Underestimating budgeted usage leads to departments bearing a lower percentage of fixed costs (assuming all other operating department managers do not similarly underestimate their usage). If all user department managers underestimate usage, it might also lead to Robinson underestimating its total support department needs. To discourage such underestimates, some companies reward managers who make accurate forecasts of long-run usage—the "carrot" approach. Other companies impose cost penalties—the "stick" approach—for underestimating long-run usage. For instance, a higher cost rate is charged after an operating department exceeds its budgeted usage.

DECISION POINT

When should managers use the dual-rate method over the single-rate method?

Aberdeen Corporation has one support department, Engineering Services, and two production departments, Machining and Assembly. The following data relate to the 2017 budget for the Engineering Services Department:

15-1 TRY IT!

Practical capacity	8,000 hours
Fixed costs of the Engineering Services Department in the 6,000 labor-hour to 8,000 labor-hour relevant range	$280,000
Budgeted usage (quantity) of engineering services labor-hours required to support the productions departments:	
Machining department	2,500 hours
Assembly department	4,500 hours
Total	7,000 hours
Budgeted variable cost per engineering services labor-hour in the 6,000 labor-hour to 8,000 labor-hour relevant range	$25 per hour used
Actual usage (quantity) of Engineering Services labor-hours required to support the production departments:	
Machining department	2,000 hours
Assembly department	4,000 hours
Total	6,000 hours

1. Using the single-rate method, calculate the cost to be allocated to the Machining and Assembly Departments if the allocation rate is based on budgeted costs and budgeted quantity of Engineering Services and allocated based on actual Engineering Services hours used in each department.
2. Using the dual-rate method, calculate the cost to be allocated to the Machining and Assembly Departments if (a) variable costs are allocated based on the budgeted variable cost per hour for actual hours used in each department and (b) fixed costs are allocated based on budgeted fixed costs per hour and the budgeted number of hours for each department.
3. Using the single-rate method, calculate the cost to be allocated to the Machining and Assembly Departments if the allocation rate is based on budgeted costs and practical capacity of the Engineering Services Department and allocated based on actual Engineering Services hours used in each department.
4. Using the dual-rate method, calculate the cost to be allocated to the Machining and Assembly Departments if (a) variable costs are allocated based on the budgeted variable cost per hour for actual hours used in each department and (b) the fixed-cost allocation rate is based on budgeted costs and practical capacity of Engineering Services Department and fixed costs are allocated based on budgeted Engineering Service hours used in each department.

Budgeted Versus Actual Costs and the Choice of Allocation Base

The allocation methods previously outlined follow specific procedures in terms of the support department costs that are considered as well as the manner in which costs are assigned to the operating departments. In this section, we examine these choices in greater detail and consider the impact of alternative approaches. We show that the decision whether to use actual or budgeted costs, as well as the choice between actual and budgeted usage as allocation base, has a significant impact on the cost allocated to each operating department and the incentives of the operating department managers.

Budgeted Versus Actual Rates

In both the single-rate and dual-rate methods, Robinson uses budgeted rates to assign support department costs (fixed as well as variable costs). An alternative approach would involve using the actual rates based on the support costs realized during the period. This method is much less

LEARNING OBJECTIVE 2

Understand how the choice between allocation based on budgeted and actual rates

...budgeted rates provide certainty to users about charges and motivate the support division to control costs

and between budgeted and actual usage can affect the incentives of division managers

...budgeted usage helps in planning and efficient utilization of fixed resources; actual usage controls consumption of variable resources

common because of the level of uncertainty it imposes on user departments. When allocations are made using budgeted rates, managers of departments to which costs are allocated know with certainty the rates to be used in that budget period. Users can then determine the amount of the service to request and—if company policy allows—whether to use the internal resource or an external vendor. In contrast, when actual rates are used for cost allocation, user department managers do not know the costs allocated to the departments until the end of the budget period.

Budgeted rates also help motivate the manager of the support (or supplier) department (for example, the materials management department) to improve efficiency. During the budget period, the support department, not the user departments, bears the risk of any unfavorable cost variances. That's because user departments do not pay for any costs or inefficiencies of the supplier department that cause actual rates to exceed budgeted rates.

The manager of the supplier department would likely view the budgeted rates negatively if unfavorable cost variances occur due to price increases outside of his or her control. Some organizations try to identify these uncontrollable factors and relieve the support department manager of responsibility for these variances. In other organizations, the supplier department and the user department agree to share the risk (through an explicit formula) of a large, uncontrollable increase in the prices of inputs used by the supplier department. This procedure avoids imposing the risk completely on either the supplier department (as when budgeted rates are used) or the user department (as when actual rates are used).

For the rest of this chapter, we focus only on allocation methods based on budgeted rates.

Budgeted Versus Actual Usage

In both the single-rate and dual-rate methods, the variable costs are assigned on the basis of budgeted rates and actual usage. Because the variable costs are directly and causally linked to usage, charging them as a function of the actual usage is appropriate. Moreover, allocating variable costs on the basis of budgeted usage would provide the user departments with no incentive to control their consumption of support services.

What about fixed costs? Consider the budget of $144,000 fixed costs at the Materials Management Department of Robinson Company. Recall that budgeted usage is 800 hours for the Machining Department and 2,800 hours for the Assembly Department. Assume that actual usage by the Machining Department is always equal to budgeted usage. We consider three cases:

Case 1: When actual usage by the Assembly Department equals budgeted usage.

Case 2: When actual usage by the Assembly Department is greater than budgeted usage.

Case 3: When actual usage by the Assembly Department is lower than budgeted usage.

Fixed-Cost Allocation Based on Budgeted Rates and Budgeted Usage

This is the dual-rate procedure discussed earlier in the chapter. When budgeted usage is the allocation base, regardless of the actual usage of facilities (i.e., whether Case 1, 2, or 3 occurs), user departments receive a preset lump-sum fixed-cost charge. If rates are calculated based on budgeted usage at $40 per hour ($144,000 ÷ 3,600 hours), the Machining Department is assigned $32,000 ($40 per hour × 800 hours) and the Assembly Department, $112,000 ($40 per hour × 2,800 hours). If rates are set using practical capacity at $36 per hour ($144,000 ÷ 4,000 hours), the Machining Department is charged $28,800 ($36 per hour × 800 hours), the Assembly Department is allocated $100,800 ($36 per hour × 2,800 hours), and the remaining $14,400 ($36 per hour × 400 hours) is the unallocated cost of excess capacity.

Fixed-Cost Allocation Based on Budgeted Rates and Actual Usage

Column 2 of Exhibit 15-1 shows the allocations when the budgeted rate is based on budgeted usage ($40 per hour), while column 3 shows the allocations when practical capacity is used to derive the budgeted rate ($36 per hour). Note that each operating department's fixed-cost allocation varies based on its actual usage of support facilities. However, variations in

| EXHIBIT 15-1 | | Effect of Variations in Actual Usage on Fixed-Cost Allocation to Operating Divisions |

	(1) Actual Usage		(2) Budgeted Rate Based on Budgeted Usage[a]		(3) Budgeted Rate Based on Practical Capacity[b]		(4) Allocation of Budgeted Total Fixed Cost	
Case	**Mach. Dept.**	**Assmb. Dept.**	**Mach. Dept.**	**Assmb. Dept.**	**Mach. Dept.**	**Assmb. Dept.**	**Mach. Dept.**	**Assmb. Dept.**
1	800 hours	2,800 hours	$ 32,000	$ 112,000	$ 28,800	$ 100,800	$ 32,000[c]	$ 112,000[d]
2	800 hours	3,200 hours	$ 32,000	$ 128,000	$ 28,800	$ 115,200	$ 28,800[e]	$ 115,200[f]
3	800 hours	2,400 hours	$ 32,000	$ 96,000	$ 28,800	$ 86,400	$ 36,000[g]	$ 108,000[h]

$a \dfrac{\$144{,}000}{(800 + 2{,}800)\ \text{hours}} = \$40\ \text{per hour}$ $\quad b \dfrac{\$144{,}000}{4{,}000\ \text{hours}} = \$36\ \text{per hour}$ $\quad c \dfrac{800}{(800 + 2{,}800)} \times \$144{,}000$ $\quad d \dfrac{2{,}800}{(800 + 2{,}800)} \times \$144{,}000$

$e \dfrac{800}{(800 + 3{,}200)} \times \$144{,}000$ $\quad f \dfrac{3{,}200}{(800 + 3{,}200)} \times \$144{,}000$ $\quad g \dfrac{800}{(800 + 2{,}400)} \times \$144{,}000$ $\quad h \dfrac{2{,}400}{(800 + 2{,}400)} \times \$144{,}000$

actual usage in one department do not affect the costs allocated to the other department. The Machining Department is allocated either $32,000 or $28,800, depending on the budgeted rate chosen, independent of the Assembly Department's actual usage.

This allocation procedure for fixed costs is exactly the same as the allocation procedure under the single-rate method. The procedure therefore shares the advantages of the single-rate method, such as advanced knowledge of budgeted rates, as well as control over the costs charged to the operating departments based on actual usage.[4]

The procedure in column (2) also shares the disadvantages of the single-rate method discussed in the previous section. When the budgeted rate (of $40 per hour) is calculated based on budgeted usage, user departments are charged for the cost of unused capacity. Consider Case 1 when actual usage equals budgeted usage of 3,600 materials-handling labor-hours and is less than the practical capacity of 4,000 labor-hours. In this case, all $144,000 of fixed costs of the Materials Management Department are allocated to the operating departments even though the Materials Management Department has idle capacity. On the other hand, when actual usage (4,000 labor-hours) is more than the budgeted amount (3,600 labor-hours) as in Case 2, a total of $160,000 is allocated, which is more than the fixed costs of $144,000. This results in overallocation of fixed costs requiring end-of period adjustments, as discussed in Chapters 4 and 8. If, however, practical capacity is used to calculate the budgeted rate (of $36 per hour), as in column (3), user departments are only charged for the actual resources of the Materials Management Department used by the operating departments and not for the costs of unused capacity.

As noted earlier, allocating fixed costs based on actual usage induces conflicts of interest when evaluating outsourcing possibilities. The Machining and Assembly Departments can reduce fixed costs allocated to them by reducing the actual usage of Materials Management Department services. That's because the allocated fixed costs of the Materials Management Department appear as variable costs to the operating departments. From the point of view of the company as a whole, however, the fixed costs of the Materials Management Department will not be saved if the operating departments do not use the services of the Materials Management Department and so are irrelevant to the outsourcing decision.

Allocating Budgeted Fixed Costs Based on Actual Usage

In this case, a budgeted fixed-cost rate is not calculated. Instead, the budgeted fixed costs of $144,000 of the Materials Management Department are allocated to the Machining and

---

[4] The total amount of fixed costs allocated to divisions will in general not equal the actual realized costs. Adjustments for overallocations and underallocations would then be made using the methods discussed previously in Chapters 4, 7, and 8.

Assembly Departments based on the actual labor-hours used by the Machining and Assembly Departments as shown in Exhibit 15-1, column 4.

- In Case 1, the fixed costs allocated to the Machining Department equal the amount in column (2) calculated based on a budgeted rate and budgeted usage.

- In Case 2, the fixed costs allocated to the Machining Department are $3,200 less than the amount in column (2) calculated based on a budgeted rate and budgeted usage ($28,800 versus $32,000).

- In Case 3, the fixed costs allocated to the Machining Department are $4,000 more than the amount in column (2) calculated based on a budgeted rate and budgeted usage ($36,000 versus $32,000).

Why is the Machining Department allocated $4,000 more of the fixed costs of the Materials Management Department in Case 3, even though its actual usage equals its budgeted usage? Because the total fixed costs of $144,000 are now spread over 400 fewer hours of actual total usage. In other words, the lower usage by the Assembly Department leads to an increase in the fixed costs allocated to the Machining Department. When budgeted fixed costs are allocated based on actual usage, user departments will not know their fixed-cost allocations until the end of the budget period. This method therefore shares the same flaw as those methods that rely on the use of actual cost rates rather than budgeted cost rates.

To summarize, there are strong economic and motivational reasons to justify the precise forms of the single-rate and dual-rate methods considered in the previous section and, in particular, to support the use of the dual-rate allocation procedure.

DECISION POINT

What factors should managers consider when deciding between allocation based on budgeted and actual rates, and budgeted and actual usage?

Allocating Costs of Multiple Support Departments

LEARNING OBJECTIVE 3

Allocate multiple support-department costs using the direct method,

...allocates support-department costs directly to operating departments

the step-down method,

...partially allocates support-department costs to other support departments

and the reciprocal method

...fully allocates support-department costs to other support departments

In the previous section, we examined general issues that arise when allocating costs from one support department to operating departments. In this section, we examine the special cost-allocation problems that arise when two or more of the support departments whose costs are being allocated provide reciprocal support to each other as well as to operating departments. An example of reciprocal support is Robinson's Materials Management Department providing materials-handling labor services to all other departments, including the Engineering and Production Control Department, while also utilizing the services of the Engineering and Production Control Department for managing materials-handling equipment and scheduling materials movement to the production floor. More accurate support-department cost allocations result in more accurate product, service, and customer costs.

Exhibit 15-2, column 6, provides details of Robinson's total budgeted manufacturing overhead costs of $1,120,000 for 2017 (see page 631), for example, supervision salaries, $200,000; depreciation and maintenance, $193,000; indirect labor, $195,000; and rent, utilities, and insurance, $160,000. Robinson allocates the $1,120,000 of total budgeted manufacturing overhead costs to the Machining and Assembly Departments in several steps.

Step A: Trace or Allocate Each Cost to Various Support and Operating Departments. Exhibit 15-2, columns (1) through (5), show calculations for this step. For example, supervision salaries are traced to the departments in which the supervisors work. As described in Chapter 2 (see page 51), supervision costs are an indirect cost of individual jobs because supervisory costs cannot be traced to individual jobs. They are a direct cost of the different departments, however, because they can be identified with each department in an economically feasible way. Rent, utilities, and insurance costs cannot be traced to each department because these costs are incurred for all of Robinson's manufacturing facility. These costs are therefore allocated to different departments on the basis of the square feet area—the cost driver for rent, utilities, and insurance costs.

Step B: Allocate Plant Administration Costs to Other Support Departments and Operating Departments. Plant administration supports supervisors in each department, so plant administration costs are allocated to departments on the basis of supervision costs.

EXHIBIT 15-2   Details of Budgeted Manufacturing Overhead at Robinson Company for 2017 and Allocation of Plant Administration Department Costs

	Support Departments			Operating Departments		
	Plant Administration Department	**Engineering and Production Control Department**	**Materials Management Department**	**Machining Department**	**Assembly Department**	**Total**
Step A	(1)	(2)	(3)	(4)	(5)	(6)
Plant manager's salary	$ 92,000					$ 92,000
Supervision salaries (traced to each department)		$ 48,000	$ 40,000	$ 52,000	$ 60,000	200,000
Engineering salaries (traced to each department)		110,000	36,000	60,000	24,000	230,000
Depreciation and maintenance (traced to each department)		39,000	55,000	79,000	20,000	193,000
Indirect materials (traced to each department)		20,000	12,000	11,000	7,000	50,000
Indirect labor (traced to each department)		43,000	77,000	37,000	38,000	195,000
Rent, utilities, and insurance (allocated to each department based on square feet area; $8^1 × 1,000; 2,000; 3,000; 8,000; 6,000 sq. ft.)	8,000	16,000	24,000	64,000	48,000	160,000
Total	$ 100,000	$276,000	$244,000	$303,000	$197,000	$1,120,000
Step B						
Allocation of plant administration costs $0.50^2 × $48,000; $40,000; $52,000; $60,000	(100,000)	24,000	20,000	26,000	30,000	
	$ 0	$300,000	$264,000	$329,000	$227,000	

^{1}$160,000 ÷ 20,000 total square feet area = $8 per square foot

$$\text{Plant administration cost-allocation rate} = \frac{\text{Total plant administration costs}}{\text{Total supervision salaries}} = \frac{\$100,000}{\$200,000} = 0.50$$

Some companies prefer not to allocate plant administration costs to jobs, products, or customers because these costs are fixed and independent of the level of activity in the plant. However, most companies, like Robinson, allocate plant administration costs to departments and jobs, products, or customers because allocating all costs allows companies to calculate the full manufacturing costs of products. Robinson calculates the plant administration cost-allocation rate as follows:

$$\text{Plant administration cost-allocation rate} = \frac{\text{Total plant administration costs}}{\text{Total supervision salaries}} = \frac{\$100,000}{\$200,000} = 0.50$$

The bottom part of Exhibit 15-2 shows how Robinson uses the 0.50 cost-allocation rate and supervision salaries to allocate plant administration costs to the other support and operating departments.

Step C: Allocate Engineering and Production Control and Materials Management Costs to the Machining and Assembly Operating Departments. Note that the two support departments whose costs are being allocated—Engineering and Production Control and Materials Management—provide reciprocal support to each other as well as support to the operating departments. That is, the Engineering and Production Control Department provides services to the Materials Management Department (for example, engineering services for materials-handling equipment and scheduling material movement to the production floor), while the Materials Management Department provides services to the Engineering and Production Control Department (for example, delivering materials).

Consider again the Materials Management Department. From Exhibit 15-2, the total budgeted cost of the Materials Management Department equals $264,000. We can also calculate this cost using the fixed and variable cost classification of the previous section. The Materials Management Department is budgeted to provide 800 hours of materials-handling labor services to the Machining Department and 2,800 hours of materials-handling labor services to the Assembly Department. In this section, we further assume that the Materials Management Department will provide an additional 400 hours of materials-handling labor services to the Engineering and Production Control Department. Recall from the previous section that the Materials Management Department has budgeted fixed costs (for example, plant administration, depreciation, and rent) of $144,000 and budgeted variable costs (for example, indirect materials, indirect labor, and maintenance) of $30 per labor-hour. Thus, for the analysis in this section the total budgeted costs of the Materials Management Department can also be calculated as $264,000 [$144,000 + $30 per labor-hour × (800 + 2,800 + 400) labor-hours] as shown in Exhibit 15-2.[5]

Exhibit 15-3 displays the data for budgeted overhead costs from Exhibit 15-2 after allocating Plant Administration Department costs but before any further interdepartment cost allocations and the services provided by each support department to the other departments. To understand the percentages in this exhibit, consider the Engineering and Production Control Department. This department supports the engineering activity in the other departments and so the budgeted costs of this department are allocated based on budgeted engineering salaries in each of the other departments. From Exhibit 15-2, budgeted engineering salaries are $36,000 in the Materials Management Department, $60,000 in the Machining Department, and $24,000 in the Assembly Department for a total of $120,000 ($36,000 + $60,000 + $24,000). Thus, the Engineering and Production Control Department is budgeted to provide support of 30% ($36,000 ÷ $120,000 = 0.30) to the Materials Management Department, 50% ($60,000 ÷ $120,000 = 0.50) to the Machining Department, and 20% ($24,000 ÷ $120,000 = 0.20) to the Assembly Department. Similarly, the Materials Management Department is budgeted to provide a total of 4,000 material handling labor-hours of support work: 10% (400 ÷ 4,000 = 0.10) for the Engineering and Production Control Department, 20% (800 ÷ 4,000 = 0.20) for the Machining Department, and 70% (2,800 ÷ 4,000 = 0.70) for the Assembly Department.

EXHIBIT 15-3 Data for Allocating Support Department Costs at Robinson Company for 2017

| | SUPPORT DEPARTMENTS | | | OPERATING DEPARTMENTS | | |
	Engineering and Production Control	Materials Management		Machining	Assembly	Total
Budgeted overhead costs						
before any interdepartment cost allocations	$300,000	$264,000		$329,000	$227,000	$1,120,000
Support work furnished:						
By Engineering and Production Control						
Budgeted engineering salaries	—	$ 36,000		$ 60,000	$ 24,000	$ 120,000
Percentage	—	30%		50%	20%	100%
By Materials Management						
Budgeted material-handling labor-hours	400	—		800	2,800	4,000
Percentage	10%	—		20%	70%	100%

[5] The previous section assumed that the Materials Management Department only provided services to the Machining and Assembly Departments and not to the Engineering and Production Control Department, resulting in total budgeted costs of $252,000 [$144,000 + $30 per labor-hour × (800 + 2,800) labor-hours].

We describe three methods of allocating budgeted overhead costs from the support departments to the Machining Department and the Assembly Department: *direct*, *step-down*, and *reciprocal*. Throughout this section, we use budgeted costs and budgeted hours. Why? Because our goal is to determine the budgeted costs of the operating departments (Machining and Assembly) after Robinson allocates the budgeted costs of the support departments (Materials Management and Engineering and Production Control) to the operating departments. The budgeted costs of the Machining Department will be divided by the budgeted machine-hours in the Machining Department (the cost driver of Machining Department costs) and the budgeted costs of the Assembly Department will be divided by the budgeted direct manufacturing labor-hours in the Assembly Department (the cost driver of Assembly Department costs) to calculate the budgeted overhead allocation rates for each operating department. These overhead rates will be used to allocate overhead costs to each job as it passes through an operating department based on the actual number of machine-hours used in the Machining Department and the actual number of direct manufacturing labor-hours used in the Assembly Department. To simplify the explanation and to focus on concepts, we use the single-rate method to allocate the costs of each support department. (The Problem for Self-Study (p. 649) illustrates the dual-rate method for allocating reciprocal support-department costs.)

Direct Method

The **direct method** allocates each support-department's budgeted costs to operating departments only. The direct method does not allocate support department costs to other support departments. Exhibit 15-4 illustrates this method using the data in Exhibit 15-3. The base used to allocate Engineering and Production Control costs to the operating departments is the budgeted engineering salaries in the operating departments: $60,000 + $24,000 = $84,000. This amount excludes the $36,000 of budgeted engineering salaries representing services to be provided

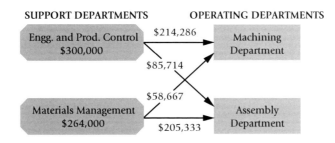

EXHIBIT 15-4

Direct Method of Allocating Support-Department Costs at Robinson Company for 2017

A	B	C	D	E	F	G
	SUPPORT DEPARTMENTS			**OPERATING DEPARTMENTS**		
	Engineering and Production Control	Materials Management		Machining	Assembly	Total
3 Budgeted overhead costs						
4 before any interdepartment cost allocations	$300,000	$264,000		$329,000	$227,000	$1,120,000
5 Allocation of Engg. And Prod. Control (5/7, 2/7)[a]	(300,000)			214,286	85,714	
6 Allocation of Materials Management (2/9, 7/9)[b]		(264,000)		58,667	205,333	
7						
8 Total budgeted overhead of operating departments	$ 0	$ 0		$601,953	$518,047	$1,120,000
9						
10 [a] Base is ($60,000 + $24,000), or $84,000; $60,000 ÷ $84,000 = 5/7; $24,000 ÷ $84,000 = 2/7.						
11 [b] Base is (800 + 2,800), or 3,600 hours; 800 ÷ 3,600 = 2/9; 2,800 ÷ 3,600 = 7/9.						

by Engineering and Production Control to Materials Management. The budgeted cost of the Engineering and Production Control Department of $300,000 is allocated to the Machining Department and the Assembly Department in the ratio ($60,000 ÷ $84,000, $24,000 ÷ 84,000) or (5/7, 2/7). As a result, the Machining Department is allocated 5/7 × $300,000 = $214,286 and the Assembly Department is allocated 2/7 × $300,000 = $85,714. Similarly, the base used for allocating the budgeted cost of the Materials Management Department to the operating departments is 800 + 2,800 = 3,600 budgeted materials-handling labor-hours, which excludes the 400 hours of budgeted materials-handling labor-hours provided by Materials Management to Engineering and Production Control.

An equivalent approach to implementing the direct method involves calculating a budgeted rate for each support department. For example, the budgeted cost rate for the Engineering and Production Control Department is ($300,000 ÷ $84,000), or 357.143%. The Machining Department is then allocated $214,286 (357.143% × $60,000), while the Assembly Department is allocated $85,714 (357.143% × $24,000). For ease of computation and explanation throughout this section, we will allocate support department costs using the fraction of the support department services used by other departments, rather than by calculating budgeted rates.

Most managers adopt the direct method because it is simple and easy to use. Managers do not need to predict the usage of support department services by other support departments. A disadvantage of the direct method is that it ignores information about reciprocal services provided among support departments and can therefore lead to inaccurate estimates of the cost of operating departments. We now examine a second approach, which partially recognizes the services provided among support departments.

Step-Down Method

Some organizations use the **step-down method**—also called the **sequential allocation method**—which allocates support-department costs to other support departments and to operating departments in a sequential manner that partially recognizes the mutual services provided among all support departments.

Exhibit 15-5 shows the step-down method. The Engineering and Production Control budgeted costs of $300,000 are allocated first. Exhibit 15-3 shows that the Engineering and Production Control Department provides 30% of its services to the Materials Management Department, 50% to the Machining Department, and 20% to the Assembly Department. Therefore, $90,000 is allocated to Materials Management (30% of $300,000), $150,000 to Machining (50% of $300,000), and $60,000 to Assembly (20% of $300,000). The Materials Management Department budgeted costs now total $354,000: budgeted costs of the Materials Management Department before any interdepartmental cost allocations, $264,000, plus $90,000 from the allocation of Engineering and Production Control Department costs to the Materials Management Department. The $354,000 is then only allocated between the two operating departments based on the proportion of the Materials Management Department services provided to the Machining Department and the Assembly Department. From Exhibit 15-3, the Materials Management Department provides 20% of its services to the Machining Department and 70% to the Assembly Department, so $78,667 (2/9 × $354,000) is allocated to Machining and $275,333 (7/9 × $354,000) is allocated to Assembly.

Note that this method requires managers to rank (sequence) the support departments in the order that the step-down allocation is to proceed. In our example, the budgeted costs of the Engineering and Production Control Department were allocated first to all other departments, including the Materials Management Department. The budgeted costs of the Materials Management Support Department were allocated second, but only to the two operating departments—Machining and Assembly. Different sequences will result in different allocations of support-department costs to operating departments as, for example, if the Materials Management Department costs had been allocated first and the Engineering and Production Control Department costs had been allocated second. A popular step-down sequence begins with the support department that renders the highest percentage of its total services to *other support departments*. The sequence continues with the department that renders the

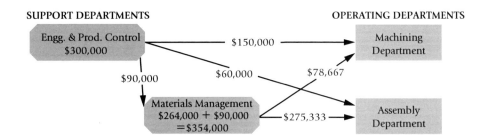

SUPPORT DEPARTMENTS   OPERATING DEPARTMENTS

EXHIBIT 15-5

Step-Down Method
of Allocating Support-
Department Costs at
Robinson Company
for 2017

	SUPPORT DEPARTMENTS			OPERATING DEPARTMENTS		
A	Engineering and Production Control	Materials Management		Machining	Assembly	Total
3 Budgeted overhead costs before any						
4 interdepartment cost allocations	$300,000	$264,000		$329,000	$227,000	$1,120,000
5 Allocation of Engg. and Prod. Control (3/10, 5/10, 2/10) [a]	(300,000)	90,000		150,000	60,000	
6		354,000				
7 Allocation of Materials Management (2/9, 7/9) [b]		(354,000)		78,667	275,333	
8						
9 Total budgeted overhead of operating departments	$ 0	$ 0		$557,667	$562,333	$1,120,000
10						
11 [a] Base is ($36,000 + $60,000 + $24,000), or $120,000 ; $36,000 ÷ $120,000 = 3/10; $60,000 ÷ $120,000 = 5/10; $24,000 ÷ $120,000 = 2/10.						
12 [b] Base is (800 + 2,800), or 3,600 hours; 800 ÷ 3,600 = 2/9; 2,800 ÷ 3,600 = 7/9.						

next-highest percentage, and so on, ending with the support department that renders the lowest percentage.[6] In our example, budgeted costs of the Engineering and Production Control Department were allocated first because it provides 30% of its services to the Materials Management Department, whereas the Materials Management Department provides only 10% of its services to the Engineering and Production Control Department (see Exhibit 15-3).

Under the step-down method, once a support department's costs have been allocated, no subsequent support-department costs are allocated back to it. Once the Engineering and Production Control Department costs are allocated, it receives no further allocation from other (lower-ranked) support departments. The result is that the step-down method does not recognize the total services that support departments provide to each other. The reciprocal method fully recognizes all such services, as we will see next.

Reciprocal Method

The **reciprocal method** allocates support-department costs to operating departments by fully recognizing the mutual services provided among all support departments. For example, the Engineering and Production Control Department provides engineering services to the Materials Management Department. Similarly, the Materials Management Department handles materials for the Engineering and Production Control Department. The reciprocal method fully incorporates interdepartmental relationships into the support-department cost allocations.

---

[6] An alternative approach to selecting the sequence of allocations is to begin with the support department that renders the highest dollar amount of services to other support departments. The sequence ends with the allocation of the costs of the department that renders the lowest dollar amount of services to other support departments.

Exhibit 15-6 presents one way to understand the reciprocal method as an extension of the step-down method. First, Engineering and Production Control Department budgeted costs are allocated to all other departments, including the Materials Management Support Department (Materials Management, 30%; Machining, 50%; Assembly, 20%). The budgeted costs of the Materials Management Department then total $354,000 ($264,000 + $90,000 from the first-round allocation), as in Exhibit 15-5. The $354,000 is then allocated to all other departments that the Materials Management Department supports, including the Engineering and Production Control Support Department—Engineering and Production Control, 10%; Machining, 20%; and Assembly, 70% (see Exhibit 15-3). The Engineering and Production Control Department budgeted costs that had been brought down to $0 now have $35,400 from the Materials Management Department allocation. These costs are again reallocated to all other departments, including Materials Management Department, in the same ratio that the Engineering and Production Control Department costs were previously allocated. Now the Materials Management Department budgeted costs that had been brought down to $0 have $10,620 from the Engineering and Production Control Department allocations. These costs are again allocated in the same ratio that the Materials Management Department costs were previously allocated. Successive rounds result in smaller and smaller amounts being allocated to and reallocated from the support departments until eventually all support-department costs are allocated to the Machining Department and the Assembly Department.

An alternative way to implement the reciprocal method is to formulate and solve linear equations. This implementation requires three steps.

EXHIBIT 15-6   Reciprocal Method of Allocating Support-Department Costs Using Repeated Iterations at Robinson Company for 2017

	A	B	C	D	E	F	G
1/2		Engineering and Production Control	Materials Management		Machining Department	Assembly Department	Total
3	Budgeted overhead costs before any						
4	interdepartment cost allocations	$300,000	$264,000		$329,000	$227,000	$1,120,000
5	1st Allocation of Engg. and Prod. Control (3/10,5/10,2/10)[a]	(300,000)	90,000		150,000	60,000	
6			354,000				
7	1st Allocation of Materials Management (1/10,2/10,7/10)[b]	35,400	(354,000)		70,800	247,800	
8	2nd Allocation of Engg. and Prod. Control (3/10,5/10,2/10)[a]	(35,400)	10,620		17,700	7,080	
9	2nd Allocation of Materials Management (1/10,2/10,7/10)[b]	1,062	(10,620)		2,124	7,434	
10	3rd Allocation of Engg. and Prod. Control (3/10,5/10,2/10)[a]	(1,062)	319		531	212	
11	3rd Allocation of Materials Management (1/10,2/10,7/10)[b]	32	(319)		63	224	
12	4th Allocation of Engg. and Prod. Control (3/10,5/10,2/10)[a]	(32)	10		16	6	
13	4th Allocation of Materials Management (1/10,2/10,7/10)[b]	1	(10)		2	7	
14	5th Allocation of Engg. and Prod. Control (3/10,5/10,2/10)[a]	(1)	0		1	0	
15							
16	Total budgeted overhead of operating departments	$ 0	$ 0		$570,237	$549,763	$1,120,000
17							
18	Total support department amounts allocated and reallocated (the numbers in parentheses in the first two columns):						
19	Engineering and Production Control: $300,000 + $35,400 + $1,062 + $32 + $1 = $336,495						
20	Materials Management: $354,000 + $10,620 + $319 + $10 = $364,949						
21							
22	[a]Base is $36,000 + $60,000 + $24,000 = $120,000; $36,000 ÷ $120,000 = 3/10; $60,000 ÷ $120,000 = 5/10; $24,000 ÷ $120,000 = 2/10
23	[b]Base is 400 + 800 + 2,800 = 4,000 labor-hours; 400 ÷ 4,000 = 1/10; 800 ÷ 4,000 = 2/10; 2,800 ÷ 4,000 = 7/10

Step 1: Express Support-Department Budgeted Costs and Reciprocal Relationships in the Form of Linear Equations. Let *EPC* be the *complete reciprocated costs* of the Engineering and Production Control Department and *MM* be the *complete reciprocated costs* of the Materials Management Department. By **complete reciprocated costs**, we mean the support department's own costs plus any interdepartmental cost allocations. We then express the data in Exhibit 15-3 as follows:

$$EPC = \$300,000 + 0.1\,MM \quad (1)$$
$$MM = \$264,000 + 0.3\,EPC \quad (2)$$

The 0.1 *MM* term in equation (1) is the budgeted percentage of the Materials Management Department services *used by* the Engineering and Production Control Department. The 0.3 *EPC* term in equation (2) is the budgeted percentage of Engineering and Production Control Department services *used by* the Materials Management Department. The complete reciprocated costs in equations (1) and (2) are sometimes called the **artificial costs** of the support departments.

Step 2: Solve the Set of Linear Equations to Obtain the Complete Reciprocated Budgeted Costs of Each Support Department. Substituting equation (1) into (2):

$$MM = \$264,000 + [0.3\,(\$300,000 + 0.1\,MM)]$$
$$MM = \$264,000 + \$90,000 + 0.03\,MM$$
$$0.97\,MM = \$354,000$$
$$MM = \$364,949$$

Substituting this into equation (1):

$$EPC = \$300,000 + 0.1\,(\$364,949)$$
$$EPC = \$300,000 + \$36,495 = \$336,495$$

The complete reciprocated costs or artificial costs are budgeted to be $364,949 for the Materials Management Department and $336,495 for the Engineering and Production Control Department. The complete-reciprocated-cost figures also appear at the bottom of Exhibit 15-6 as the total amounts allocated and reallocated from the Materials Management Department and the Engineering and Production Control Department. When there are more than two support departments with reciprocal relationships, managers can use software such as Excel to calculate the complete reciprocated costs of each support department. Because the calculations involve finding the inverse of a matrix, the reciprocal method is also sometimes referred to as the **matrix method.**[7]

Step 3: Allocate the Complete Reciprocated Budgeted Costs of Each Support Department to All Other Departments (Both Support Departments and Operating Departments) on the Basis of the Budgeted Usage Percentages (Based on Total Units of Service Provided to All Departments). Consider the Materials Management Department. The complete reciprocated budgeted costs of $364,949 are allocated as follows:

To Engineering and Production Control Department (1/10) × $364,949 =	$ 36,495
To Machining Department (2/10) × $364,949	= $ 72,990
To Assembly Department (7/10) × $364,949	= $255,464
Total	$364,949

Similarly, the $336,495 in reciprocated budgeted costs of the Engineering and Production Control Department are allocated to the Materials Management Department (3/10), Machining Department (5/10), and Assembly Department (2/10).

Exhibit 15-7 presents summary data based on the reciprocal method.

---

[7] If there are *n* support departments, then Step 1 will yield *n* linear equations. Solving the equations to calculate the complete reciprocated costs then requires finding the inverse of an $n \times n$ matrix.

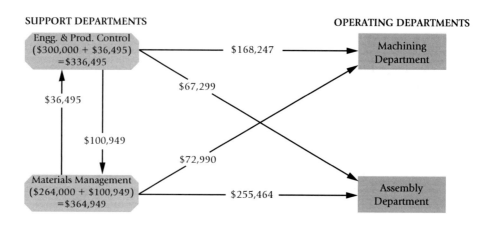

EXHIBIT 15-7

Reciprocal Method
of Allocating Support-
Department Costs
Using Linear Equations
at Robinson Company
for 2017

	SUPPORT DEPARTMENTS			OPERATING DEPARTMENTS		
A	B	C	D	E	F	G
1	**SUPPORT DEPARTMENTS**			**OPERATING DEPARTMENTS**		
2		Engineering and Production Control	Materials Management		Machining	Assembly	Total
3 Budgeted overhead costs before any						
4 interdepartment cost allocations	$300,000	$264,000		$329,000	$227,000	$1,120,000
5 Allocation of Engg. & Prod. Control (3/10, 5/10, 2/10)ᵃ	(336,495)	100,949		168,247	67,299	
6 Allocation of Materials Management (1/10, 2/10, 7/10)ᵇ	36,495	(364,949)		72,990	255,464	
7						
8 Total budgeted overhead of operating departments	$ 0	$ 0		$570,237	$549,763	$1,120,000
9						
10 ᵃBase is ($36,000 + $60,000 + $24,000), or $120,000 ; $36,000 ÷ $120,000 = 3/10; $60,000 ÷ $120,000 = 5/10; $24,000 ÷ $120,000 = 2/10.						
11 ᵇBase is (400 + 800 + 2,800), or 4,000 hours; 400 ÷ 4,000 = 1/10; 800 ÷ 4,000 = 2/10; 2,800 ÷ 4,000 = 7/10.						

Robinson's $701,444 complete reciprocated budgeted costs of the support departments exceed the budgeted amount of $564,000.

Support Department	Complete Reciprocated Budgeted Costs	Budgeted Costs	Difference
Engineering and Production Control	$336,495	$300,000	$ 36,495
Materials Management	364,949	264,000	100,949
Total	$701,444	$564,000	$137,444

Each support department's complete reciprocated budgeted cost is greater than the budgeted amount because it takes into account that support costs are allocated to all departments using its services and not just to operating departments. This step ensures that the reciprocal method fully recognizes all interrelationships among support departments, as well as relationships between support and operating departments. The difference between complete reciprocated budgeted costs and budgeted costs for each support department reflects the costs allocated among support departments. The total budgeted costs allocated to the operating departments under the reciprocal method are still only $564,000 ($168,247 + $67,299 allocated from the Engineering and Production Control Department and $72,990 + $255,464 allocated from the Materials Management Department, see Exhibit 15-7).

Overview of Methods

The amount of budgeted manufacturing overhead costs allocated to the Machining and Assembly Departments will differ depending on the method used to allocate support-department costs. Differences among costs allocated to the operating departments using the three methods increase (1) if the reciprocal allocations are large and (2) if operating departments use each support department's service in different proportions. Note that while the final allocations under the reciprocal method are in between those under the direct and step-down methods in our example (see page 640), in general, there is no relationship between the amount of costs allocated to the operating departments under the different methods. The method of allocation becomes particularly important in the case of cost-reimbursement contracts that require allocation of support-department costs. To avoid disputes, managers should always clarify the method to be used for allocation. For example, Medicare reimbursements and federal government research contracts with universities that allow for the recovery of indirect costs typically mandate use of the step-down method, with explicit requirements about the order and the costs that can be included in the indirect-cost pools.

The reciprocal method is conceptually the most precise method because it considers the mutual services provided among all support departments. The advantage of the direct and step-down methods is that they are simple for managers to compute and understand relative to the reciprocal method. If the costs allocated to the operating departments using the direct or step-down methods closely approximate the costs allocated using the reciprocal method, managers should use the simpler direct or step-down methods. However, as computing power to perform repeated iterations (as in Exhibit 15-6) or to solve sets of simultaneous equations (as on page 637) increases, more companies will find the reciprocal method easier to implement.

Another advantage of the reciprocal method is that it highlights the complete reciprocated costs of support departments and how these costs differ from the budgeted or actual costs of the departments. Knowing the complete reciprocated costs of a support department is a key input for decisions about whether to outsource all the services that the support department provides.

Suppose all of Robinson's support-department costs are variable over the period of a possible outsourcing contract. Consider a third party's bid to provide, say, all services currently provided by the Materials Management Department. Do not compare the bid to the expected (budgeted) $264,000 costs of the Materials Management Department. The complete reciprocated costs of the Materials Management Department, which include the services the Engineering and Production Control Department provides the Materials Management Department, are $364,949 to deliver 4,000 hours of materials-handling labor to other departments at Robinson. The complete reciprocated cost for materials-handling labor is $91.24 per hour ($364,949 ÷ 4,000 hours). Other things being equal, an external provider's bid to supply the same materials management services as Robinson's internal department at less than $364,949, or $91.24 per hour (even if much greater than $264,000) would improve Robinson's operating income.

To see this point, note that the relevant savings from shutting down the Materials Management Department are $264,000 of Materials Management Department costs *plus* $100,949 of expected Engineering and Production Control Department costs (see Exhibit 15-7). By closing down the Materials Management Department, Robinson will no longer incur the 30% of reciprocated Engineering and Production Control Department costs (equal to $100,949) that were incurred to support the Materials Management Department. Therefore, the total expected cost savings are $364,949 ($264,000 + 100,949).[8] Neither the direct nor the step-down method can provide this relevant information for outsourcing decisions.

Calculating the Cost of Job WPP 298

Robinson uses the budgeted costs of each operating department (Machining and Assembly) to compute the rate per unit of each cost-allocation base used to allocate the indirect costs to a job (Step 5 in a job-costing system, see Chapter 4). Robinson budgets 20,000 direct manufacturing

---

[8] Technical issues when using the reciprocal method in outsourcing decisions are discussed in Robert S. Kaplan and Anthony A. Atkinson, *Advanced Management Accounting*, 3rd ed. (Upper Saddle River, NJ: Prentice Hall, 1998), pp. 73–81.

labor-hours for the Assembly Department (of the 28,000 total budgeted direct manufacturing labor-hours) and 10,000 machine-hours for the Machining Department.

The budgeted overhead allocation rates for each operating department by allocation method are:

Support Department Cost-Allocation Method	Total Budgeted Overhead Costs After Allocation of All Support-Department Costs		Budgeted Overhead Rate per Hour for Product-Costing Purposes	
	Machining	Assembly	Machining (10,000 budgeted machine-hours)	Assembly (20,000 budgeted labor-hours)
Direct	$601,953	$518,047	$60.20	$25.90
Step-down	557,667	562,333	55.77	28.12
Reciprocal	570,237	549,763	57.02	27.49

The next step in a job-costing system (Step 6, see Chapter 4) is to compute the indirect costs allocated to a job. For the WPP 298 job, Robinson actually uses 40 machine-hours in the Machining Department and 55 labor-hours in the Assembly Department (out of 88 direct manufacturing labor-hours). The overhead costs allocated to the WPP 298 job under the three methods would be

Direct: $3,833 ($60.20 × 40 + $25.90 × 55)

Step-down: $3,777 ($55.77 × 40 + $28.12 × 55)

Reciprocal: $3,793 ($57.02 × 40 + $27.49 × 55)

The manufacturing overhead costs allocated to WPP 298 differ only a little under the three methods because the WPP 298 job requires roughly equal amounts of machine-hours and assembly labor-hours. These differences would be larger if a job required many more machine-hours than assembly hours or vice versa.

Using normal costing and multiple cost-allocation bases results in higher indirect manufacturing costs allocated to Job WPP 298, $3,793 (under the reciprocal method) compared to $3,520 allocated using direct manufacturing labor-hours as the sole allocation base in Chapter 4 (page 136). By using two cost-allocation bases—machine-hours and assembly labor-hours—Robinson is better able to model the drivers of manufacturing overhead costs.

The final step (Step 7, see Chapter 4) computes the total cost of the job by adding all direct and indirect costs assigned to the job. Under the reciprocal method, the total manufacturing costs of the WPP 298 job are as follows:

Direct manufacturing costs		
Direct materials	$4,606	
Direct manufacturing labor	1,579	$6,185
Manufacturing overhead costs		
Machining Department		
($57.02 per machine-hour × 40 machine-hours)	2,281	
Assembly Department		
($27.49 per labor-hour × 55 labor-hours)	1,512	3,793
Total manufacturing costs of job WPP 298		$9,978

Note that the costs in Step 7 have four dollar amounts, each corresponding respectively to the two direct-cost and two indirect-cost categories in the costing system.

At the end of the year, actual manufacturing overhead costs of the Machining Department and the Assembly Department would be compared to the manufacturing overhead allocated for each department. To calculate the actual manufacturing overhead costs of the Machining and Assembly Departments, Robinson would need to allocate the *actual* (rather than budgeted) costs of the Materials Management and Engineering and Production Control Departments to the *actual* costs of the Machining and Assembly Departments using the methods described in this chapter. Management accountants would then make end-of-year adjustments (pages 148–153) separately for each cost pool for under- or overallocated overhead costs.

We now consider common costs, another special class of costs for which management accountants have developed specific allocation methods.

DECISION POINT

What methods can managers use to allocate costs of multiple support departments to operating departments?

Montvale Tours provides guided educational tours to college alumni associations. The company is divided into two operating divisions: domestic tours and world tours. Each of the tour divisions uses the services of the company's two support departments: Administration and Information Technology. Additionally, the Administration and Information Technology departments use the services of each other. Data concerning the past year are as follows:

◀ **15-2 TRY IT!**

	Support Departments		Operating Departments		
	Administration	Information Technology	Domestic Tours	World Tours	Total
Budgeted overhead costs before any interdepartment cost allocations	$400,000	$250,000	$1,300,000	$1,840,000	$3,790,0000
Support work furnished:					
By Administration					
Budgeted Administration salaries	—	$88,000	$55,000	$77,000	$220,000
Percentage	—	40%	25%	35%	100%
By Information Technology					
Budgeted IT service hours	600	—	2,200	1,200	4,000
Percentage	15%	—	55%	30%	100%

What are the total overhead costs of the operating departments (domestic and world tours) *after* the support department costs of Administration and Information Technology have been allocated using (a) the direct method, (b) the step-down method (allocate Administration first), (c) the step-down method (allocate Information Technology first), and (d) the reciprocal method using the method of repeated iterations and linear equations?

Allocating Common Costs

A **common cost** is the cost of operating a facility, activity, or cost object when that facility, activity, or cost object is shared by two or more users. Common costs arise because each user incurs a lower cost by sharing a facility or activity than operating the facility or performing the activity independently. The cost accounting challenge is how to allocate common costs to each user in a reasonable way.

Consider Jason Stevens, a graduating senior in Seattle who has been invited to a job interview with an employer in Albany. The round-trip Seattle–Albany airfare costs $1,200. A week later, Stevens is also invited to an interview with an employer in Chicago. The Seattle–Chicago round-trip airfare costs $800. Stevens decides to combine the two recruiting trips into a Seattle–Albany–Chicago–Seattle trip that will cost $1,500 in airfare. The prospective employers will reimburse Stevens for the airfare. The $1,500 is a common cost that benefits both prospective employers because it is less than the $2,000 ($1,200 + $800) that the employers would have to pay if Stevens interviewed with them independently.

What is a reasonable way to allocate the common costs of $1,500? Two methods of allocating the common cost between the two employers are the stand-alone method and the incremental method.

Stand-Alone Cost-Allocation Method

The **stand-alone cost-allocation method** determines the weights for cost allocation by considering each user of the common cost facility or activity as a separate entity. For the

LEARNING OBJECTIVE 4

Allocate common costs using the stand-alone method

…uses cost information of each user as a separate entity to allocate common costs

and the incremental method

…allocates common costs primarily to one user and the remainder to other users

common-cost airfare of $1,500, information about the separate (stand-alone) round-trip air-fares ($1,200 and $800) is used to determine the allocation weights:

$$\text{Albany employer: } \frac{\$1,200}{\$1,200 + \$800} \times \$1,500 = 0.60 \times \$1,500 = \$900$$

$$\text{Chicago employer: } \frac{\$800}{\$800 + \$1,200} \times \$1,500 = 0.40 \times \$1,500 = \$600$$

Advocates of this method often emphasize the fairness or equity criterion described in Exhibit 13-1 (page 547). The method is viewed as reasonable because each employer bears a proportionate share of total costs in relation to the individual stand-alone costs.

Incremental Cost-Allocation Method

The **incremental cost-allocation method** ranks the individual users of a cost object in the order of users most responsible for the common cost and then uses this ranking to allocate cost among those users. The first-ranked user of the cost object is the *primary user* (also called the *primary party*) and is allocated costs up to the costs of the primary user as a stand-alone user. The second-ranked user is the *first-incremental user* (*first-incremental party*) and is allocated the additional cost that arises from two users instead of only the primary user. The third-ranked user is the *second-incremental user* (*second-incremental party*) and is allocated the additional cost that arises from three users instead of two users, and so on.

To see how this method works, consider again Jason Stevens and his $1,500 airfare cost. Assume the Albany employer is viewed as the primary party. Stevens's rationale is that he had already committed to go to Albany before accepting the invitation to interview in Chicago. The cost allocations would be as follows:

Party	Costs Allocated	Cumulative Costs Allocated
Albany (primary)	$1,200	$1,200
Chicago (incremental)	300 ($1,500 − $1,200)	$1,500
Total	$1,500	

The Albany employer is allocated the full Seattle–Albany airfare. The unallocated part of the total airfare is then allocated to the Chicago employer. If the Chicago employer had been chosen as the primary party, the cost allocations would have been Chicago $800 (the stand-alone round-trip Seattle–Chicago airfare) and Albany $700 ($1,500 − $800). When there are more than two parties, this method requires them to be ranked from first to last (such as by the date on which each employer invited the candidate to interview).

Under the incremental method, the primary party typically receives the highest allocation of the common costs. If the incremental users are newly formed companies or subunits, such as a new product line or a new sales territory, the incremental method may enhance their chances for short-run survival by assigning them a low allocation of the common costs. The difficulty with the method is that, particularly if a large common cost is involved, every user would prefer to be viewed as the incremental party!

One approach managers can use to avoid disputes in such situations is to use the stand-alone cost-allocation method. Another approach is to use the *Shapley value method*, which considers each party as first the primary party and then the incremental party. From the calculations shown earlier, the Albany employer is allocated $1,200 as the primary party and $700 as the incremental party, for an average of $950 [($1,200 + $700) ÷ 2]. The Chicago employer is allocated $800 as the primary party and $300 as the incremental party, for an average of $550 [($800 + 300) ÷ 2]. The Shapley value method allocates, to each employer, the average of the costs allocated as the primary party and as the incremental party: $950 to the Albany employer and $550 to the Chicago employer.[9]

---

[9] For further discussion of the Shapley value method, see Joel S. Demski, "Cost Allocation Games," in *Joint Cost Allocations*, ed. Shane Moriarity (University of Oklahoma Center for Economic and Management Research, 1981); Lech Krus´ and Piotr Bronisz, "Cooperative Game Solution Concepts to a Cost Allocation Problem," *European Journal of Operational Research* 122:2 (April 16, 2000): 258–271.

As our discussion suggests, allocating common costs is not clear-cut and can cause disputes. Whenever feasible, managers should specify the rules for such allocations in advance. If this is not done, then, rather than blindly follow one method or another, managers should exercise judgment when allocating common costs by thinking carefully about allocation methods that appear fair to each party. For instance, Stevens must choose an allocation method for his airfare cost that is acceptable to each prospective employer and does not exceed the maximum reimbursable amount of airfare for either employer. The next section discusses the role of cost data in various types of contracts, another area where disputes about cost allocation frequently occur.

DECISION POINT

What methods can managers use to allocate common costs to two or more users?

Taylor Inc. and Victor Inc. are two small clothing companies that are considering leasing a dyeing machine together. The companies estimated that in order to meet production, Taylor needs the machine for 600 hours and Victor needs it for 400 hours. If each company rents the machine on its own, the fee will be $60 per hour of usage. If they rent the machine together, the fee will decrease to $54 per hour of usage.

15-3 TRY IT!

1. Calculate Taylor's and Victor's respective share of fees under the stand-alone cost-allocation method.
2. Calculate Taylor's and Victor's respective share of fees using the incremental cost-allocation method assuming (a) Taylor ranked as the primary party and (b) Victor ranked as the primary party.
3. Calculate Taylor's and Victor's respective share of fees using the Shapley value method.
4. Which method would you recommend Taylor and Victor use to share the fees?

Cost Allocations and Contract Disputes

Many commercial contracts include clauses based on cost accounting information. Examples include the following:

LEARNING OBJECTIVE 5

Explain the importance of explicit agreement between contracting parties when the reimbursement amount is based on costs incurred

…to avoid disputes regarding allowable cost items and how indirect costs should be allocated

- A contract between the Department of Defense and a company designing and assembling a new fighter plane specifies that the price paid for the plane will be based on the contractor's direct and overhead costs plus a fixed fee.

- A contract between a consulting firm and a hospital specifies that the consulting firm receives a fixed fee plus a share of the cost savings that arise from implementing the consulting firm's recommendations.

Contract disputes often arise over cost computations, for example, what costs should be included to calculate the costs specified under the two contracts above. Managers can reduce the areas of dispute between contracting parties by making the "rules of the game" explicit and writing them into the contract. Such rules of the game include the definition of allowable cost items; the definitions of terms used, such as what constitutes direct labor; the permissible cost-allocation bases; and how to account for differences between budgeted and actual costs.

The U.S. government reimburses most contractors in one of two main ways:

1. **The contractor is paid a set price without analysis of actual contract cost data.** This approach is used, for example, when there is competitive bidding, when there is adequate price competition, or when there is an established catalog with prices quoted for items sold in substantial quantities to the general public.

2. **The contractor is paid based on an analysis of actual contract cost data.** In some cases, there is great uncertainty about the cost to complete a job because of the nature of the task, for example, a new weapon system. Such contracts, which often involve billions of dollars, are rarely subject to competitive bidding because no contractor is willing to assume all the risk of receiving a fixed price for the contract and subsequently incurring high costs to fulfill it. Setting a market-based fixed price for the contract either will not

attract contractors or will require a contract price that is very high from the government's standpoint. To address this issue, the government typically assumes a major share of the risk of the potentially high costs of completing the contract. Rather than relying on selling prices as ordinarily set by suppliers in the marketplace, the government negotiates contracts on the basis of *costs plus a fixed fee*. This arrangement is called a *cost-plus contract*.

For a cost to be reimbursed as part of a contract, it must be allowable. An **allowable cost** is a cost that the contract parties agree to include in the costs to be reimbursed. Some contracts specify how allowable costs are to be determined. For example, only economy-class airfares are allowable in many U.S. government contracts. Other contracts identify cost categories that are unallowable. For example, the costs of lobbying activities and alcoholic beverages are not allowable costs in U.S. government contracts. However, the set of allowable costs is not always clear-cut. Contract disputes and allegations about overcharging the government arise from time to time (see Concepts in Action: Contract Disputes over Reimbursable Costs with the U.S. Government).

Some allowable overhead costs, such as supervision costs, support many different contracts and activities. Government regulations stipulate that supervision costs would be allocable to a specific contract on a cause-and-effect or benefits received basis. Other allowable overhead costs, such as general administration costs, that support many contracts may be difficult to allocate on the basis of any cause-and-effect or benefits received reasoning. Nonetheless, the contracting parties may still view it as "reasonable" or "fair" to allocate these costs in some manner to help establish a contract amount. The general rule for government cost-plus contracts is that the reimbursement amount is based on actual allocable costs plus a fixed fee.[10]

DECISION
POINT

How can contract disputes over reimbursement amounts based on costs be reduced?

All contracts with U.S. government agencies must comply with cost accounting standards issued by the **Cost Accounting Standards Board (CASB)**. For government contracts, the CASB has the exclusive authority to make, put into effect, amend, and rescind cost accounting standards and interpretations. The standards are designed to achieve *uniformity* and *consistency* in the measurement, assignment, and allocation of costs to government contracts within the United States.[11] The standards represent the complex interplay of political considerations and accounting principles. Terms such as *fairness* and *equity*, as well as cause and effect and benefits received, are relevant to and a part of government contracts.

Bundled Products and Revenue Allocation Methods

**LEARNING
OBJECTIVE** 6

Understand how bundling of products

...two or more products sold for a single price

causes revenue allocation issues

...need to allocate revenues to each product in the bundle to evaluate managers of individual products

and the methods managers use to allocate revenues

...the stand-alone method, the incremental method, or the Shapley value method

Allocation issues can also arise when revenues from multiple products (for example, different software programs or cable and Internet packages) are bundled together and sold at a single price. The methods for revenue allocation parallel those described for common-cost allocations.

Bundling and Revenue Allocation

Revenues are inflows of assets (almost always cash or accounts receivable) received for products or services provided to customers. Similar to cost allocation, **revenue allocation** occurs when

---

[10] The Federal Acquisition Regulation (FAR), issued in March 2005 (see www.acquisition.gov/far/current/pdf/FAR.pdf) includes the following definition of *allocability* (in FAR 31.201-4): "A cost is allocable if it is assignable or chargeable to one or more cost objectives on the basis of relative benefits received or other equitable relationship. Subject to the foregoing, a cost is allocable to a Government contract if it:
(a) Is incurred specifically for the contract;
(b) Benefits both the contract and other work, and can be distributed to them in reasonable proportion to the benefits received; or
(c) Is necessary to the overall operation of the business, although a direct relationship to any particular cost objective cannot be shown."

[11] Details on the Cost Accounting Standards Board are available at www.whitehouse.gov/omb/procurement/casb.html. The CASB is part of the Office of Federal Procurement Policy, U.S. Office of Management and Budget.

CONCEPTS IN ACTION

Contract Disputes over Reimbursable Costs with the U.S. Government

David Coleman/Alamy Stock Photo

The U.S. government spends billions of dollars with private companies to carry out specific contracted services. In recent years, the government has pursued cases against several contractors for overcharging for services. The following examples are from cases pursued by the U.S. Department of Justice's Civil Division on behalf of the federal government.

1. Hewlett-Packard Co. (HP) agreed to pay $32.5 million to settle charges that it overcharged the U.S. Postal Service (USPS) for its products from 2001 through 2010. Specifically, HP was accused of failing to comply with pricing terms of its USPS contract, including a requirement that the company provide prices that were no greater than those offered to other customers with similar-sized contracts.

2. United Technologies Corporation was found liable for more than $473 million arising out of a contract to provide the Air Force with F-15 and F-16 aircraft engines. The company excluded discounts that it received from suppliers in its proposed prices, which led to the Department of Defense paying more than it otherwise would have paid for the engines.

Source: Press releases from the U.S. Department of Justice, Civil Division (2011–2015).

revenues are related to a particular *revenue object* but cannot be traced to it in an economically feasible (cost-effective) way. A **revenue object** is anything for which a separate measurement of revenue is desired. Examples of revenue objects include products, customers, and divisions. We illustrate revenue-allocation issues for Dynamic Software Corporation, which develops, sells, and supports three software programs:

1. WordMaster, a word-processing program, released 36 months ago

2. DataMaster, a spreadsheet program, released 18 months ago

3. FinanceMaster, a budgeting and cash-management program, released six months ago with a lot of favorable media attention

Dynamic Software sells these three products individually as well as together as bundled products.

A **bundled product** is a package of two or more products (or services) that is sold for a single price but whose individual components may be sold as separate items at their own "stand-alone" prices. The price of a bundled product is typically less than the sum of the prices of the individual products sold separately. For example, banks often provide individual customers with a bundle of services from its different departments (checking, safe-deposit box, and investment advisory) for a single fee. A resort hotel may offer, for a single amount per customer, a weekend package that includes services from its lodging (the room), food (the restaurant), and recreational (golf and tennis) departments. When department managers have revenue or profit responsibilities for individual products, the bundled revenue must be allocated among the individual products in the bundle.

Dynamic Software allocates revenues from its bundled product sales (called "suite sales") to individual products. Individual-product profitability is used to compensate software engineers, developers, and product managers responsible for developing and managing each product.

How should Dynamic Software allocate suite revenues to individual products? Consider information pertaining to the three "stand-alone" and "suite" products in 2016:

	Selling Price	Manufacturing Cost per Unit
Stand-alone		
WordMaster	$125	$18
DataMaster	150	20
FinanceMaster	225	25
Suite		
Word + Data	$220	
Word + Finance	280	
Finance + Data	305	
Word + Finance + Data	380	

Just as we saw in the section on common-cost allocations, the two main revenue-allocation methods are the stand-alone method and the incremental method.

Stand-Alone Revenue-Allocation Method

The **stand-alone revenue-allocation method** uses product-specific information on the products in the bundle as weights for allocating the bundled revenues to the individual products. The term *stand-alone* refers to the product as a separate (nonsuite) item. Consider the Word + Finance suite, which sells for $280 and assume Dynamic Software sells equal quantities of WordMaster and FinanceMaster. Three types of weights for the stand-alone method are as follows:

1. **Selling prices.** Using the individual selling prices of $125 for WordMaster and $225 for FinanceMaster, the weights for allocating the $280 suite revenues between the products are as follows:

$$\text{WordMaster:} \frac{\$125}{\$125 + \$225} \times \$280 = 0.357 \times \$280 = \$100$$

$$\text{FinanceMaster:} \frac{\$225}{\$125 + \$225} \times \$280 = 0.643 \times \$280 = \$180$$

2. **Unit costs.** This method uses the costs of the individual products (in this case, manufacturing cost per unit) to determine the weights for the revenue allocations.

$$\text{WordMaster:} \frac{\$18}{\$18 + \$25} \times \$280 = 0.419 \times \$280 = \$117$$

$$\text{FinanceMaster:} \frac{\$25}{\$18 + \$25} \times \$280 = 0.581 \times \$280 = \$163$$

3. **Physical units.** This method gives each product unit in the suite the same weight when allocating suite revenue to individual products. Therefore, with two products in the Word + Finance suite, each product is allocated 50% of the suite revenues.

$$\text{WordMaster:} \frac{1}{1 + 1} \times \$280 = 0.50 \times \$280 = \$140$$

$$\text{FinanceMaster:} \frac{1}{1 + 1} \times \$280 = 0.50 \times \$280 = \$140$$

These three approaches to determining weights for the stand-alone method result in very different revenue allocations to the individual products:

Revenue-Allocation Weights	WordMaster	FinanceMaster
Selling prices	$100	$180
Unit costs	117	163
Physical units	140	140

Which method do managers prefer? The selling prices method is best because the weights explicitly consider the prices customers are willing to pay for the individual products. Weighting approaches that use revenue information better capture "benefits received" by customers than unit costs or physical units.[12] The physical-units revenue-allocation method is used when managers cannot use any of the other methods (such as when selling prices are unstable or unit costs are difficult to calculate for individual products).[13]

Incremental Revenue-Allocation Method

The **incremental revenue-allocation method** ranks individual products in a bundle according to criteria determined by management and then uses this ranking to allocate bundled revenues to individual products. The first-ranked product is the *primary product* in the bundle. The second-ranked product is the *first-incremental product*, the third-ranked product is the *second-incremental product*, and so on.

How do companies decide on product rankings under the incremental revenue-allocation method? Some organizations survey customers about the importance of each of the individual products in their purchase decision. For example, if one product in the bundle is an established product and the second product in the bundle is a new product, managers would rank the established product as the primary product and the new product as the first-incremental product. Other managers rank products on the basis of the recent stand-alone revenues of the individual products in the bundle. In a third approach, top managers use their knowledge or intuition to decide the rankings.

Consider again the Word + Finance suite and assume Dynamic Software sells equal quantities of WordMaster and FinanceMaster. Assume WordMaster is designated as the primary product and FinanceMaster as the first-incremental product. WordMaster is allocated 100% of its *stand-alone* revenue of $125 and FinanceMaster is allocated the remaining revenue of $155 ($280 − $125):

Product	Revenue Allocated	Cumulative Revenue Allocated
WordMaster	$125	$125
FinanceMaster	155 ($280 − $125)	$280
Total	$280	

If the suite price is less than or equal to the stand-alone price of the primary product, the primary product is allocated 100% of the *suite* revenue. All other products in the suite receive no allocation of revenue.

---

[12] Revenue-allocation issues also arise in external reporting. The AICPA's Statement of Position 97-2 (Software Revenue Recognition) states that with bundled products, revenue allocation "based on vendor-specific objective evidence (VSOE) of fair value" is required. The "price charged when the element is sold separately" is said to be "objective evidence of fair value" (see "Statement of Position 97-2," Jersey City, NJ: AICPA, 1998). In September 2009, the FASB ratified Emerging Issues Task Force (EITF) Issue 08-1, specifying that with no VSOE or third-party evidence of selling price for all units of accounting in an arrangement, the consideration received for the arrangement should be allocated to the separate units based upon their estimated relative selling prices. Revenue allocation is an important issue in the new revenue recognition standards that will become effective in 2018.

[13] If Dynamic Software sells 80,000 units of WordMaster and 20,000 units of FinanceMaster in the most recent quarter and Dynamic Software's managers believe that sales of the Word + Finance suite are four times more likely to be driven by WordMaster than FinanceMaster (80,000 ÷ 20,000), the revenue-allocation methods can be adapted to put four times more weight on WordMaster compared to Finance Master. Using selling prices results in the following allocations:

$$\text{WordMaster}: \frac{\$125 \times 4}{\$125 \times 4 + \$225 \times 1} \times \$280 = 0.690 \times \$280 = \$193$$

$$\text{FinanceMaster}: \frac{\$225 \times 1}{\$125 \times 4 + \$225 \times 1} \times \$280 = 0.310 \times \$280 = \$87$$

Note that the allocations in this case are equivalent to using revenues rather than prices as the weights. Revenues of WordMaster = $125 × 80,000 units = $10,000,000 and revenues of FinanceMaster = $225 × 20,000 units = $4,500,000.

$$\text{WordMaster}: \frac{\$10,000,000}{\$10,000,000 + \$4,500,000} \times \$280 = 0.690 \times \$280 = \$193$$

$$\text{FinanceMaster}: \frac{\$4,500,000}{\$10,000,000 + \$4,500,000} \times \$280 = 0.310 \times \$280 = \$87$$

Now suppose FinanceMaster is designated as the primary product and WordMaster as the first-incremental product. Then the incremental revenue-allocation method allocates revenues of the Word + Finance suite as follows:

Product	Revenue Allocated	Cumulative Revenue Allocated
FinanceMaster	$225	$225
WordMaster	55 ($280 − $225)	$280
Total	$280	

The Shapley value method allocates to each product the average of the revenues allocated as the primary and first-incremental products:

WordMaster:	($125 + $55) ÷ 2 = $180 ÷ 2 =	$ 90
FinanceMaster:	($225 + $155) ÷ 2 = $380 ÷ 2 =	190
Total		$280

The incremental revenue-allocation methods can be adapted if Dynamic Software sells many more units of one product relative to another.[14]

When there are more than two products in the suite, the incremental revenue-allocation method allocates suite revenues sequentially. Assume WordMaster is the primary product in Dynamic Software's three-product suite, Word + Finance + Data. FinanceMaster is the first-incremental product, and DataMaster is the second-incremental product and Dynamic Software sells equal quantities of WordMaster, FinanceMaster, and DataMaster. The suite sells for $380. The allocation of the $380 suite revenues proceeds as follows:

Product	Revenue Allocated	Cumulative Revenue Allocated
WordMaster	$125	$125
FinanceMaster	155 ($280 − $125)	$280 (price of Word + Finance suite)
DataMaster	100 ($380 − $280)	$380 (price of Word + Finance + Data suite)
Total	$380	

Now suppose WordMaster is the primary product, DataMaster is the first-incremental product, and FinanceMaster is the second-incremental product.

Product	Revenue Allocated	Cumulative Revenue Allocated
WordMaster	$125	$125
DataMaster	95 ($220 − $125)	$220 (price of Word + Data suite)
FinanceMaster	160 ($380 − $220)	$380 (price of Word + Data + Finance suite)
Total	$380	

The ranking of the individual products in the suite determines the revenues allocated to them. Product managers at Dynamic Software likely would have different views of how their individual products contribute to sales of the suite products. In fact, each product manager would claim to be responsible for the primary product in the Word + Finance + Data suite![15] Because the stand-alone revenue-allocation method does not require rankings of individual products in the suite, this method is less likely to cause debates among product managers.[16]

---

[14] Suppose Dynamic Software sells 80,000 units of WordMaster and 20,000 units of FinanceMaster in the most recent quarter and its managers believe that the sales of the Word + Finance suite are four times more likely to be driven by WordMaster as the primary product. The *weighted Shapley value method* assigns four times as much weight to the revenue allocations when WordMaster is the primary product as when FinanceMaster is the primary product, resulting in the following allocations:

WordMaster:	($125 × 4 + $55 × 1) ÷ (4 + 1) = $555 ÷ 5 =	$111
FinanceMaster:	($225 × 1 + $155 × 4) ÷ (4 + 1) = $845 ÷ 5 =	169
Total		$280

[15] Calculating the Shapley value method mitigates this problem because each product is considered as a primary, first-incremental, and second-incremental product. Assuming equal weights on all products, the revenue allocated to each product is an average of the revenues calculated for the product under these different assumptions. In the preceding example, the interested reader can verify that this will result in the following revenue allocations: FinanceMaster, $180; WordMaster, $87.50; and DataMaster, $112.50.

[16] To avoid the challenges of revenue allocations and to encourage departments to work together to achieve sales of bundled products, some companies credit all departments with the full revenues from the bundled product when evaluating each department's performance. Besides the problem of double-counting revenues, the issue here is that different departments may have contributed unequally to achieving the bundled revenue, yet will get credit for the same total revenue.

Revenue allocations are also important for tax reasons. For example, Verizon Communications Inc., the second-largest provider of telecommunications and cable services in the United States, sells each of its services—telephone, cable television, and broadband—separately and in bundled arrangements. State and local tax laws often stipulate that if a bundle is sold and the price for each line item is not split out on the consumer's bill, then all services are taxed as telephone services, which generally carries the highest tax rate. To preclude consumers from paying higher taxes on the entire package, Verizon allocates bundled service revenue to its telephone, cable television, and broadband services based on the stand-alone selling prices of these services. Consumers then pay taxes on the amounts billed for each service. Specialized software packages, such as CCH SureTax, help companies such as Verizon to properly recognize revenue according to the laws of each state.[16]

> ### DECISION POINT
>
> What is product bundling, and how can managers allocate revenues of a bundled product to individual products in the bundle?

> **15-4 TRY IT!**
>
> Essence Company blends and sells designer fragrances. It has a Men's Fragrances Division and a Women's Fragrances Division, each with different sales strategies, distribution channels, and product offerings. Essence is now considering the sale of a bundled product called Sync, consisting of one bottle of Him, a men's cologne, and one bottle of Her, a women's perfume, two of Essence's very successful products. Essence sells equal quantities of Him and Her perfume. For the most recent year, Essence reported the following:
>
> | Product | Retail Price |
> |---|---|
> | Him | $25.00 |
> | Her | $50.00 |
> | Sync (Him and Her) | $60.00 |
>
> 1. Allocate revenue from the sale of each unit of Sync to Him and Her using the following:
>   a. The stand-alone revenue-allocation method based on selling price of each product
>   b. The incremental revenue-allocation method, with Him ranked as the primary product
>   c. The incremental revenue-allocation method, with Her ranked as the primary product
>   d. The Shapley value method
> 2. Of the four methods in requirement 1, which one would you recommend for allocating Sync's revenues to Him and Her? Explain.

---

[16] CCH Incorporated, "CCH SureTax Communications," http://www.suretax.com/solutions/suretax-telecom, accessed July 2016; Verizon Communications Inc., 2015 Annual Reports (New York: Verizon Communications Inc., 2016).

PROBLEM FOR SELF-STUDY

This problem illustrates how costs of two corporate support departments are allocated to operating divisions using the dual-rate method. Fixed costs are allocated using budgeted costs and budgeted hours used by other departments. Variable costs are allocated using actual costs and actual hours used by other departments.

Computer Horizons reports the following budgeted and actual amounts for its two central corporate support departments (legal and personnel) for supporting each other and the two manufacturing divisions: the laptop division (LTD) and the work station division (WSD):

	A	B	C	D	E	F	G
1		**SUPPORT**			**OPERATING**		
2		**Legal Department**	**Personnel Department**		**LTD**	**WSD**	**Total**
3	**BUDGETED USAGE**						
4	Legal (hours)	—	250		1,500	750	2,500
5	(Percentages)	—	10%		60%	30%	100%
6	Personnel (hours)	2,500	—		22,500	25,000	50,000
7	(Percentages)	5%	—		45%	50%	100%
8							
9	**ACTUAL USAGE**						
10	Legal (hours)	—	400		400	1,200	2,000
11	(Percentages)	—	20%		20%	60%	100%
12	Personnel (hours)	2,000	—		26,600	11,400	40,000
13	(Percentages)	5%	—		66.5%	28.5%	100%
14	Budgeted fixed overhead costs before any						
15	interdepartment cost allocations	$360,000	$475,000		—	—	$835,000
16	Actual variable overhead costs before any						
17	interdepartment cost allocations	$200,000	$600,000		—	—	$800,000

Required

What amount of support-department costs for legal and personnel will be allocated to LTD and WSD using (a) the direct method, (b) the step-down method (allocating the legal department costs first), and (c) the reciprocal method using linear equations?

Solution

Exhibit 15-8 presents the computations for allocating the fixed and variable support-department costs. A summary of these costs follows:

	Laptop Division (LTD)	Work Station Division (WSD)
(a) Direct Method		
Fixed costs	$465,000	$370,000
Variable costs	470,000	330,000
	$935,000	$700,000
(b) Step-Down Method		
Fixed costs	$458,053	$376,947
Variable costs	488,000	312,000
	$946,053	$688,947
(c) Reciprocal Method		
Fixed costs	$462,513	$372,487
Variable costs	476,364	323,636
	$938,877	$696,123

EXHIBIT 15-8 Alternative Methods of Allocating Corporate Support-Department Costs to Operating Divisions of Computer Horizons: Dual-Rate Method

	Home	Insert	Page Layout	Formulas	Data	Review	View

	A	B	C	D	E	F	G
20		CORPORATE SUPPORT DEPARTMENTS			OPERATING DIVISIONS		
21	**Allocation Method**	Legal Department	Personnel Department		LTD	WSD	Total
22	**A. DIRECT METHOD**						
23	Fixed costs	$360,000	$475,000				
24	Legal (1,500 ÷ 2,250; 750 ÷ 2,250)	(360,000)			$240,000	$120,000	
25	Personnel (22,500 ÷ 47,500; 25,000 ÷ 47,500)		(475,000)		225,000	250,000	
26	Fixed support dept. cost allocated to operating divisions	$ 0	$ 0		$465,000	$370,000	$835,000
27	Variable costs	$200,000	$600,000				
28	Legal (400 ÷ 1,600; 1,200 ÷ 1,600)	(200,000)			$ 50,000	$150,000	
29	Personnel (26,600 ÷ 38,000; 11,400 ÷ 38,000)		(600,000)		420,000	180,000	
30	Variable support dept. cost allocated to operating divisions	$ 0	$ 0		$470,000	$330,000	$800,000
31	**B. STEP-DOWN METHOD**						
32	(Legal department first)						
33	Fixed costs	$360,000	$475,000				
34	Legal (250 ÷ 2,500; 1,500 ÷ 2,500; 750 ÷ 2,500)	(360,000)	36,000		$216,000	$108,000	
35	Personnel (22,500 ÷ 47,500; 25,000 ÷ 47,500)		(511,000)		242,053	268,947	
36	Fixed support dept. cost allocated to operating divisions	$ 0	$ 0		$458,053	$376,947	$835,000
37	Variable costs	$200,000	$600,000				
38	Legal (400 ÷ 2,000; 400 ÷ 2,000; 1,200 ÷ 2,000)	(200,000)	40,000		$ 40,000	$120,000	
39	Personnel (26,600 ÷ 38,000; 11,400 ÷ 38,000)		(640,000)		448,000	192,000	
40	Variable support dept. cost allocated to operating divisions	$ 0	$ 0		$488,000	$312,000	$800,000
41	**C. RECIPROCAL METHOD**						
42	Fixed costs	$360,000	$475,000				
43	Legal (250 ÷ 2,500; 1,500 ÷ 2,500; 750 ÷ 2,500)	(385,678)[a]	38,568		$231,407	$115,703	
44	Personnel (2,500 ÷ 50,000; 22,500 ÷ 50,000; 25,000 ÷ 50,000)	25,678	(513,568)[a]		231,106	256,784	
45	Fixed support dept. cost allocated to operating divisions	$ 0	$ 0		$462,513	$372,487	$835,000
46	Variable costs	$200,000	$600,000				
47	Legal (400 ÷ 2,000; 400 ÷ 2,000; 1,200 ÷ 2,000)	(232,323)[b]	46,465		$ 46,465	$139,393	
48	Personnel (2,000 ÷ 40,000; 26,600 ÷ 40,000; 11,400 ÷ 40,000)	32,323	(646,465)[b]		429,899	184,243	
49	Variable support dept. cost allocated to operating divisions	$ 0	$ 0		$476,364	$323,636	$800,000
50							
51	[a] FIXED COSTS	[b] VARIABLE COSTS					
52	Letting LF = Legal department fixed costs, and PF = Personnel department fixed costs, the simultaneous equations for the reciprocal method for fixed costs are	Letting LV = Legal department variable costs, and PV = Personnel department variable costs, the simultaneous equations for the reciprocal method for variable costs are					
53	$LF = \$360,000 + 0.05\,PF$	$LV = \$200,000 + 0.05\,PV$					
54	$PF = \$475,000 + 0.10\,LF$	$PV = \$600,000 + 0.20\,LV$					
55	$LF = \$360,000 + 0.05\,(\$475,000 + 0.10\,LF)$	$LV = \$200,000 + 0.05\,(\$600,000 + 0.20\,LV)$					
56	$LF = \$385,678$	$LV = \$232,323$					
57	$PF = \$475,000 + 0.10\,(\$385,678) = \$513,568$	$PV = \$600,000 + 0.20\,(\$232,323) = \$646,465$					

DECISION **POINTS**

The following question-and-answer format summarizes the chapter's learning objectives. Each decision presents a key question related to a learning objective. The guidelines are the answer to that question.

Decision	Guidelines
1. When should managers use the dual-rate method over the single-rate method?	The single-rate method aggregates fixed and variable costs and allocates them to objects using a single allocation base and rate. Under the dual-rate method, costs are grouped into separate variable-cost and fixed-cost pools; each pool uses a different cost-allocation base and rate. If costs can be easily separated into variable and fixed costs, managers should use the dual-rate method because it provides better information for making decisions.
2. What factors should managers consider when deciding between allocation based on budgeted and actual rates and budgeted and actual usage?	Using budgeted rates enables managers of user departments to have certainty about the costs allocated to them and insulates users from inefficiencies in the supplier department. Charging budgeted variable-cost rates to users based on actual usage charges users for the resources consumed and promotes control of resource consumption. Charging fixed-cost rates on the basis of budgeted usage helps user divisions with planning and leads to goal congruence when considering outsourcing decisions.
3. What methods can managers use to allocate costs of multiple support departments to operating departments?	The three methods managers can use are the direct, the step-down, and the reciprocal methods. The direct method allocates each support department's costs to operating departments without allocating a support department's costs to other support departments. The step-down method allocates support-department costs to other support departments and to operating departments in a sequential manner that partially recognizes the mutual services provided among all support departments. The reciprocal method fully recognizes mutual services provided among all support departments.
4. What methods can managers use to allocate common costs to two or more users?	Common costs are the costs of a cost object (such as operating a facility or performing an activity) that are shared by two or more users. The stand-alone cost-allocation method uses information pertaining to each user of the cost object to determine cost-allocation weights. The incremental cost-allocation method ranks individual users of the cost object and allocates common costs first to the primary user and then to the other incremental users. The Shapley value method considers each user, in turn, as the primary and the incremental user.
5. How can contract disputes over reimbursement amounts based on costs be reduced?	Disputes can be reduced by making the cost-allocation rules as explicit as possible and including them in the contract. These rules should include details such as the allowable cost items, the acceptable cost-allocation bases, and how differences between budgeted and actual costs will be accounted for.
6. What is product bundling, and how can managers allocate revenues of a bundled product to individual products in the bundle?	Bundling occurs when a package of two or more products (or services) is sold for a single price. Revenue allocation of the bundled price is required when managers of the individual products in the bundle are evaluated on product revenue or product operating income. Revenues can be allocated for a bundled product using the stand-alone method, the incremental method, or the Shapley value method.

TERMS TO LEARN

This chapter and the Glossary at the end of the book contain definitions of the following important terms:

allowable cost (**p. 644**)
artificial costs (**p. 637**)
bundled product (**p. 645**)
common cost (**p. 641**)
complete reciprocated
  costs (**p. 637**)
Cost Accounting Standards Board
  (CASB) (**p. 644**)
direct method (**p. 633**)
dual-rate method (**p. 622**)

incremental cost-allocation
  method (**p. 642**)
incremental revenue-allocation
  method (**p. 647**)
matrix method (**p. 637**)
operating department (**p. 622**)
production department (**p. 622**)
reciprocal method (**p. 635**)
revenue allocation (**p. 644**)
revenue object (**p. 645**)

service department (**p. 622**)
single-rate method (**p. 622**)
sequential allocation
  method (**p. 634**)
stand-alone cost-allocation
  method (**p. 641**)
stand-alone revenue-allocation
  method (**p. 646**)
step-down method (**p. 634**)
support department (**p. 622**)

ASSIGNMENT MATERIAL

Questions

Pearson MyLab Accounting

15-1 Distinguish between the single-rate and the dual-rate methods.

15-2 Describe how the dual-rate method is useful to division managers in decision making.

15-3 How do budgeted cost rates motivate the support-department manager to improve efficiency?

15-4 Give examples of allocation bases used to allocate support-department cost pools to operating departments.

15-5 Why might a manager prefer that budgeted rather than actual cost-allocation rates be used for costs being allocated to his or her department from another department?

15-6 "To ensure unbiased cost allocations, fixed costs should be allocated on the basis of estimated long-run use by user-department managers." Do you agree? Why?

15-7 Distinguish among the three methods of allocating the costs of support departments to operating departments.

15-8 What is conceptually the most defensible method for allocating support-department costs? Why?

15-9 Distinguish between two methods of allocating common costs.

15-10 What are the challenges of using the incremental cost allocation method when allocating common costs and how might they be overcome?

15-11 What role does the Cost Accounting Standards Board play when companies contract with the U.S. government?

15-12 What is one key way to reduce cost-allocation disputes that arise with government contracts?

15-13 Describe how companies are increasingly facing revenue-allocation decisions.

15-14 Distinguish between the stand-alone and the incremental revenue-allocation methods.

15-15 Identify and discuss arguments that individual product managers may put forward to support their preferred revenue-allocation method.

Exercises

Pearson MyLab Accounting

15-16 **Single-rate versus dual-rate methods, support department.** The Ukraine power plant that services all manufacturing departments of CC Engineering has a budget for the coming year. This budget has been expressed in the following monthly terms:

Manufacturing Department	Needed at Practical Capacity Production Level (Kilowatt-Hours)	Average Expected Monthly Usage (Kilowatt-Hours)
Livonia	16,000	12,000
Warren	22,000	10,000
Dearborn	23,000	8,000
Westland	19,000	10,000
Total	80,000	40,000

The expected monthly costs for operating the power plant during the budget year are $21,600: $4,000 variable and $17,600 fixed.

Required

1. Assume that a single cost pool is used for the power plant costs. What budgeted amounts will be allocated to each manufacturing department if (a) the rate is calculated based on practical capacity and costs are allocated based on practical capacity and (b) the rate is calculated based on expected monthly usage and costs are allocated based on expected monthly usage?

2. Assume the dual-rate method is used with separate cost pools for the variable and fixed costs. Variable costs are allocated on the basis of expected monthly usage. Fixed costs are allocated on the basis of practical capacity. What budgeted amounts will be allocated to each manufacturing department? Why might you prefer the dual-rate method?

15-17 Single-rate method, budgeted versus actual costs and quantities. Chocolat Inc. is a producer of premium chocolate based in Palo Alto. The company has a separate division for each of its two products: dark chocolate and milk chocolate. Chocolat purchases ingredients from Wisconsin for its dark chocolate division and from Louisiana for its milk chocolate division. Both locations are the same distance from Chocolat's Palo Alto plant.

Chocolat Inc. operates a fleet of trucks as a cost center that charges the divisions for variable costs (drivers and fuel) and fixed costs (vehicle depreciation, insurance, and registration fees) of operating the fleet. Each division is evaluated on the basis of its operating income. For 2017, the trucking fleet had a practical capacity of 50 round-trips between the Palo Alto plant and the two suppliers. It recorded the following information:

	Home	Insert	Page Layout	Formulas	Data	Review	View
	A					B	C
1						**Budgeted**	**Actual**
2	Costs of truck fleet					$115,000	$96,750
3	Number of round-trips for dark chocolate division (Palo Alto plant—Wisconsin)					30	30
4	Number of round-trips for milk chocolate division (Palo Alto plant—Louisiana)					20	15

Required

1. Using the single-rate method, allocate costs to the dark chocolate division and the milk chocolate division in these three ways.
   a. Calculate the budgeted rate per round-trip and allocate costs based on round-trips budgeted for each division.
   b. Calculate the budgeted rate per round-trip and allocate costs based on actual round-trips used by each division.
   c. Calculate the actual rate per round-trip and allocate costs based on actual round-trips used by each division.

2. Describe the advantages and disadvantages of using each of the three methods in requirement 1. Would you encourage Chocolat Inc. to use one of these methods? Explain and indicate any assumptions you made.

15-18 Dual-rate method, budgeted versus actual costs and quantities (continuation of 15-17). Chocolat Inc. decides to examine the effect of using the dual-rate method for allocating truck costs to each round-trip. At the start of 2017, the budgeted costs were:

Variable cost per round-trip	$ 1,350
Fixed costs	$47,500

The actual results for the 45 round-trips made in 2017 were:

Variable costs	$58,500
Fixed costs	38,250
	$96,750

Assume all other information to be the same as in Exercise 15-17.

Required

1. Using the dual-rate method, what are the costs allocated to the dark chocolate division and the milk chocolate division when (a) variable costs are allocated using the budgeted rate per round-trip and actual round-trips used by each division and when (b) fixed costs are allocated based on the budgeted rate per round-trip and round-trips budgeted for each division?

2. From the viewpoint of the dark chocolate division, what are the effects of using the dual-rate method rather than the single-rate method?

15-19 Support-department cost allocation; direct and step-down methods. Phoenix Partners provides management consulting services to government and corporate clients. Phoenix has two support departments—administrative services (AS) and information systems (IS)—and two operating departments—government consulting (GOVT) and corporate consulting (CORP). For the first quarter of 2017, Phoenix's cost records indicate the following:

	A	B	C	D	E	F	G
		SUPPORT			OPERATING		
1							
2		AS	IS		GOVT	CORP	Total
3	Budgeted overhead costs before any						
4	interdepartment cost allocations	$600,000	$2,400,000		$8,756,000	$12,452,000	$24,208,000
5	Support work supplied by AS (budgeted head count)	—	25%		40%	35%	100%
6	Support work supplied by IS (budgeted computer time)	10%	—		30%	60%	100%

Required

1. Allocate the two support departments' costs to the two operating departments using the following methods:
   a. Direct method
   b. Step-down method (allocate AS first)
   c. Step-down method (allocate IS first)
2. Compare and explain differences in the support-department costs allocated to each operating department.
3. What approaches might be used to decide the sequence in which to allocate support departments when using the step-down method?

15-20 Support-department cost allocation, reciprocal method (continuation of 15-19). Refer to the data given in Exercise 15-19.

Required

1. Allocate the two support departments' costs to the two operating departments using the reciprocal method. Use (a) linear equations and (b) repeated iterations.
2. Compare and explain differences in requirement 1 with those in requirement 1 of Exercise 15-19. Which method do you prefer? Why?

15-21 Direct and step-down allocation. E-books, an online book retailer, has two operating departments—corporate sales and consumer sales—and two support departments—human resources and information systems. Each sales department conducts merchandising and marketing operations independently. E-books uses number of employees to allocate human resources costs and processing time to allocate information systems costs. The following data are available for September 2017:

	A	B	C	D	E	F
1		SUPPORT DEPARTMENTS			OPERATING DEPARTMENTS	
2		Human Resources	Information Systems		Corporate Sales	Consumer Sales
3	Budgeted costs incurred before any					
4	interdepartment cost allocations	$72,700	$234,400		$998,270	$489,860
5	Support work supplied by human resources department					
6	Budgeted number of employees	—	21		42	28
7	Support work supplied by information systems department					
8	Budgeted processing time (in minutes)	320	—		1,920	1,600

Required

1. Allocate the support departments' costs to the operating departments using the direct method.
2. Rank the support departments based on the percentage of their services provided to other support departments. Use this ranking to allocate the support departments' costs to the operating departments based on the step-down method.
3. How could you have ranked the support departments differently?

15-22 Reciprocal cost allocation (continuation of 15-21). Consider E-books again. The controller of E-books reads a widely used textbook that states that "the reciprocal method is conceptually the most defensible." He seeks your assistance.

Required

1. Describe the key features of the reciprocal method.
2. Allocate the support departments' costs (human resources and information systems) to the two operating departments using the reciprocal method. Use (a) linear equations and (b) repeated iterations.
3. In the case presented in this exercise, which method (direct, step-down, or reciprocal) would you recommend? Why?

15-23 Allocation of common costs. Evan and Brett are students at Berkeley College. They share an apartment that is owned by Brett. Brett is considering subscribing to an Internet provider that has the following packages available:

Package	Per Month
A. Internet access	$75
B. Phone services	25
C. Internet access + phone services	90

Evan spends most of his time on the Internet ("everything can be found online now"). Brett prefers to spend his time talking on the phone rather than using the Internet ("going online is a waste of time"). They agree that the purchase of the $90 total package is a "win–win" situation.

Required

1. Allocate the $90 between Evan and Brett using (a) the stand-alone cost-allocation method, (b) the incremental cost-allocation method, and (c) the Shapley value method.
2. Which method would you recommend they use and why?

15-24 Allocation of common costs. Barbara Richardson, a self-employed consultant near Sacramento, received an invitation to visit a prospective client in Baltimore. A few days later, she received an invitation to make a presentation to a prospective client in Chicago. She decided to combine her visits, traveling from Sacramento to Baltimore, Baltimore to Chicago, and Chicago to Sacramento.

Richardson received offers for her consulting services from both companies. Upon her return, she decided to accept the engagement in Chicago. She is puzzled over how to allocate her travel costs between the two clients. She has collected the following data for regular round-trip fares with no stopovers:

Sacramento to Baltimore	$900
Sacramento to Chicago	$600

Richardson paid $1,200 for her three-leg flight (Sacramento–Baltimore, Baltimore–Chicago, Chicago–Sacramento). In addition, she paid $30 each way for limousines from her home to Sacramento Airport and back when she returned.

Required

1. How should Richardson allocate the $1,600 airfare between the clients in Baltimore and Chicago using (a) the stand-alone cost-allocation method, (b) the incremental cost-allocation method, and (c) the Shapley value method?
2. Which method would you recommend Richardson use and why?
3. How should Richardson allocate the $60 limousine charges between the clients in Baltimore and Chicago?

15-25 Revenue allocation, bundled products. Essence Company blends and sells designer fragrances. It has a Men's Fragrances Division and a Women's Fragrances Division, each with different sales strategies, distribution channels, and product offerings. Essence is now considering the sale of a bundled product called Sync consisting of one bottle of Him, a men's cologne, and one bottle of Her, a women's perfume. For the most recent year, Essence reported the following:

	Home	Insert	Page Layout	Formulas
	A			B
1	**Product**			**Retail Price**
2	Him			$ 25.00
3	Her			$ 50.00
4	Sync (Him and Her)			$ 60.00

Required

1. Allocate revenue from the sale of each unit of Sync to Him and Her using the following:
   a. The stand-alone revenue-allocation method based on selling price of each product
   b. The incremental revenue-allocation method, with Him ranked as the primary product
   c. The incremental revenue-allocation method, with Her ranked as the primary product
   d. The Shapley value method, assuming equal unit sales of Him and Her
2. Of the four methods in requirement 1, which one would you recommend for allocating Sync's revenues to Him and Her? Explain.

15-26 Allocation of common costs. Hall Auto Sales uses all types of media to advertise its products (television, radio, newspaper, and so on). At the end of 2016, the company president, Tina Hall, decided that all advertising costs would be incurred by corporate headquarters and allocated to each of the company's four sales locations based on number of vehicles sold. Tina was confident that her corporate purchasing manager could negotiate better advertising contracts on a corporate-wide basis than each of the sales managers could on their own. Tina budgeted total advertising cost for 2017 to be $1.7 million. She introduced the new plan to her sales managers just before the New Year. The manager of the east sales location, Lee Chan, was not happy. He complained that the new allocation method was unfair and would increase his advertising costs significantly over the prior year. The east location sold high volumes of low-priced used cars and most of the corporate advertising budget was related to new car sales. Following Lee's complaint, Tina decided to take another hard look at what each of the divisions was paying for advertising before the new allocation plan. The results were as follows:

Sales Location	Actual Number of Cars Sold in 2016	Actual Advertising Cost Incurred in 2016
East	4,620	$ 261,600
West	1,120	392,400
North	3,220	697,600
South	5,040	828,400
	14,000	$2,180,000

1. Using 2016 data as the cost bases, show the amount of the 2017 advertising cost ($1,700,000) that would be allocated to each of the divisions under the following criteria:
   a. Davenport's allocation method based on number of cars sold
   b. The stand-alone method
   c. The incremental-allocation method, with divisions ranked on the basis of dollars spent on advertising in 2016
2. Which method do you think is most equitable to the divisional sales managers? What other options might President Tina Hall have for allocating the advertising costs?

Required

Problems

Pearson MyLab Accounting

15-27 Single-rate, dual-rate, and practical capacity allocation. Preston Department Store has a new promotional program that offers a free gift-wrapping service for its customers. Preston's customer-service department has practical capacity to wrap 5,000 gifts at a budgeted fixed cost of $4,950 each month. The budgeted variable cost to gift-wrap an item is $0.35. During the most recent month, the department budgeted to wrap 4,500 gifts. Although the service is free to customers, a gift-wrapping service cost allocation is made to the department where the item was purchased. The customer-service department reported the following for the most recent month:

	A	B	C
1	Department	Budgeted Items Wrapped	Actual Items Wrapped
2	Giftware	1,000	1,200
3	Women's Apparel	850	650
4	Fragrances	1,000	900
5	Men's Apparel	750	450
6	Domestics	900	800
7	Total	4,500	4,000

1. Using the single-rate method, allocate gift-wrapping costs to different departments in these three ways:
   a. Calculate the budgeted rate based on the budgeted number of gifts to be wrapped and allocate costs based on the budgeted use (of gift-wrapping services).
   b. Calculate the budgeted rate based on the budgeted number of gifts to be wrapped and allocate costs based on actual usage.
   c. Calculate the budgeted rate based on the practical gift-wrapping capacity available and allocate costs based on actual usage.

Required

2. Using the dual-rate method, compute the amount allocated to each department when (a) the fixed-cost rate is calculated using budgeted fixed costs and the practical gift-wrapping capacity, (b) fixed costs are allocated based on budgeted fixed costs and budgeted usage of gift-wrapping services, and (c) variable costs are allocated using the budgeted variable-cost rate and actual usage.

3. Comment on your results in requirements 1 and 2. Discuss the advantages of the dual-rate method.

15-28 Revenue allocation. Yang Inc. produces and sells DVDs to business people and students who are planning extended stays in China. It has been very successful with two DVDs: Beginning Mandarin and Conversational Mandarin. It is introducing a third DVD, Reading Chinese Characters. It has decided to market its new DVD in two different packages grouping the Reading Chinese Characters DVD with each of the other two languages DVDs. Information about the separate DVDs and the packages follow.

DVD	Selling Price
Beginning Mandarin (BegM)	$ 72
Conversational Mandarin (ConM)	$112
Reading Chinese Characters (RCC)	$ 48
BegM + RCC	$100
ConM + RCC	$140

Required

1. Using the selling prices, allocate revenues from the BegM + RCC package to each DVD in that package using (a) the stand-alone method; (b) the incremental method, in either order; and (c) the Shapley value method.

2. Using the selling prices, allocate revenues from the ConM + RCC package to each DVD in that package using (a) the stand-alone method; (b) the incremental method, in either order; and (c) the Shapley value method.

3. Which method is most appropriate for allocating revenues among the DVDs? Why?

15-29 Fixed-cost allocation. Baker University completed construction of its newest administrative building at the end of 2017. The University's first employees moved into the building on January 1, 2018. The building consists of office space, common meeting rooms (including a conference center), a cafeteria, and even a workout room for its exercise enthusiasts. The total 2018 building space of 250,000 square feet was utilized as follows:

Usage of Space	% of Total Building Space
Office space (occupied)	52%
Vacant office space	8%
Common meeting space	25%
Workout room	5%
Cafeteria	10%

The new building cost the university $60 million and was depreciated using the straight-line method over 20 years. At the end of 2018 three departments occupied the building: executive offices of the president, accounting, and human resources. Each department's usage of its assigned space was as follows:

Department	Actual Office Space Used (sq. ft.)	Planned Office Space (sq. ft.)	Practical Capacity Office Space (sq. ft.)
Executive	32,500	24,800	36,000
Accounting	52,000	52,080	66,000
Human resources	45,500	47,120	48,000

Required

1. How much of the total building cost will be allocated in 2018 to each of the departments, if the total cost is allocated to each department on the basis of the following?
   a. Actual usage of the three departments
   b. Planned usage of the three departments
   c. Practical capacity of the three departments

2. Assume that Baker University allocates the total annual building cost in the following manner:
   a. All vacant office space is absorbed by the university and is not allocated to the departments.
   b. All occupied office space costs are allocated on the basis of actual square footage used.
   c. All common area costs are allocated on the basis of a department's practical capacity. Calculate the cost allocated to each department in 2018 under this plan. Do you think the allocation method used here is appropriate? Explain.

15-30 Allocating costs of support departments; step-down and direct methods. The Central Valley Company has prepared department overhead budgets for budgeted-volume levels before allocations as follows:

Support departments:		
Building and grounds	$45,000	
Personnel	300	
General plant administration	37,320	
Cafeteria: operating loss	970	
Storeroom	9,990	$ 93,580
Operating departments:		
Machining	$36,600	
Assembly	46,000	82,600
Total for support and operating departments		$176,180

Management has decided that the most appropriate inventory costs are achieved by using individual department overhead rates. These rates are developed after support-department costs are allocated to operating departments. Bases for allocation are to be selected from the following:

Department	Direct Manufacturing Labor-Hours	Number of Employees	Square Feet of Floor Space Occupied	Manufacturing Labor-Hours	Number of Requisitions
Building and grounds	0	0	0	0	0
Personnel[a]	0	0	2,500	0	0
General plant administration	0	40	12,000	0	0
Cafeteria: operating loss	0	10	5,000	3,000	0
Storeroom	0	5	6,000	2,000	0
Machining	8,000	55	22,000	13,000	6,000
Assembly	32,000	140	202,500	26,000	4,000
Total	40,000	250	250,000	44,000	10,000

[a]Basis used is number of employees.

Required

1. Using the step-down method, allocate support-department costs. Develop overhead rates per direct manufacturing labor-hour for machining and assembly. Allocate the costs of the support departments in the order given in this problem. Use the allocation base for each support department you think is most appropriate.
2. Using the direct method, rework requirement 1.
3. Based on the following information about two jobs, determine the total overhead costs for each job by using rates developed in (a) requirement 1 and (b) requirement 2.

	Direct Manufacturing Labor-Hours	
	Machining	**Assembly**
Job 88	17	7
Job 89	9	20

4. The company evaluates the performance of the operating department managers on the basis of how well they managed their total costs, including allocated costs. As the manager of the Machining Department, which allocation method would you prefer from the results obtained in requirements 1 and 2? Explain.

15-31 Support-department cost allocations; single-department cost pools; direct, step-down, and reciprocal methods. The Milton Company has two products. Product 1 is manufactured entirely in department X. Product 2 is manufactured entirely in department Y. To produce these two products, the Milton Company has two support departments: A (a materials-handling department) and B (a power-generating department).

An analysis of the work done by departments A and B in a typical period follows:

	Used by			
Supplied by	**A**	**B**	**X**	**Y**
A	—	200	500	300
B	750	—	125	375

The work done in department A is measured by the direct labor-hours of materials-handling time. The work done in department B is measured by the kilowatt-hours of power. The budgeted costs of the support departments for the coming year are as follows:

	Department A (Materials Handling)	Department B (Power Generation)
Variable indirect labor and indirect materials costs	$150,000	$15,000
Supervision	45,000	25,000
Depreciation	15,000	50,000
	$210,000	$90,000
	+ Power costs	+ Materials-handling costs

The budgeted costs of the operating departments for the coming year are $1,250,000 for department X and $950,000 for department Y. Supervision costs are salary costs. Depreciation in department B is the straight-line depreciation of power-generation equipment in its 19th year of an estimated 25-year useful life; it is old, but well-maintained, equipment.

Required

1. What are the allocations of costs of support departments A and B to operating departments X and Y using (a) the direct method, (b) the step-down method (allocate department A first), (c) the step-down method (allocate department B first), and (d) the reciprocal method?
2. An outside company has offered to supply all the power needed by the Milton Company and to provide all the services of the present power department. The cost of this service will be $80 per kilowatt-hour of power. Should Milton accept? Explain.

15-32 Common costs. Ema Inc. and Gold Inc. are two small clothing companies that are considering leasing a dyeing machine together. The companies estimated that in order to meet production, Ema needs the machine for 600 hours and Gold needs it for 400 hours. If each company rents the machine on its own, the fee will be $60 per hour of usage. If they rent the machine together, the fee will decrease to $54 per hour of usage.

Required

1. Calculate Ema's and Gold's respective share of fees under the stand-alone cost-allocation method.
2. Calculate Ema's and Gold's respective share of fees using the incremental cost-allocation method. Assume Taylor to be the primary party.
3. Calculate Ema's and Gold's respective share of fees using the Shapley value method.
4. Which method would you recommend Ema and Gold use to share the fees?

15-33 Stand-alone revenue allocation. Office Magic, Inc., sells computer hardware to end consumers. Its most popular model, the CX30 is sold as a "bundle," which includes three hardware products: a personal computer (PC) tower, a 26-inch monitor, and a color laser printer. Each of these products is made in a separate manufacturing division of Office Magic and can be purchased individually as well as in a bundle. The individual selling prices and per unit costs are as follows:

Computer Component	Individual Selling Price per Unit	Cost per Unit
PC tower	$1,140	$376
Monitor	$ 260	$200
Color laser printer	$ 600	$224
Computer bundle purchase price	$1,500	

Required

1. Allocate the revenue from the computer bundle purchase to each of the hardware products using the stand-alone method based on the individual selling price per unit.
2. Allocate the revenue from the computer bundle purchase to each of the hardware products using the stand-alone method based on cost per unit.
3. Allocate the revenue from the computer bundle purchase to each of the hardware products using the standalone method based on physical units (that is, the number of individual units of product sold per bundle).
4. Which basis of allocation makes the most sense in this situation? Explain your answer.

15-34 Support-department cost allocations; single-department cost pools; direct, step-down, and reciprocal methods. Sportz, Inc., manufactures athletic shoes and athletic clothing for both amateur and professional athletes. The company has two product lines (clothing and shoes), which are produced in separate manufacturing facilities; however, both manufacturing facilities share the same support services for information technology and human resources. The following shows total costs for each manufacturing facility and for each support department.

	Variable Costs	Fixed Costs	Total Costs by Department (in thousands)
Information technology (IT)	$ 600	$ 2,000	$ 2,600
Human resources (HR)	$ 400	$ 1,000	$ 1,400
Clothing	$2,500	$ 8,000	$10,500
Shoes	$3,000	$ 4,500	$ 7,500
Total costs	$6,500	$15,500	$22,000

The total costs of the support departments (IT and HR) are allocated to the production departments (clothing and shoes) using a single rate based on the following:

Information technology: Number of IT labor-hours worked by department
Human resources: Number of employees supported by department

Data on the bases, by department, are given as follows:

Department	IT Hours Used	Number of Employees
Clothing	5,040	220
Shoes	3,960	88
Information technology	—	92
Human resources	3,000	—

Required

1. What are the total costs of the production departments (clothing and shoes) after the support department costs of information technology and human resources have been allocated using (a) the direct method, (b) the step-down method (allocate information technology first), (c) the step-down method (allocate human resources first), and (d) the reciprocal method?
2. Assume that all of the work of the IT department could be outsourced to an independent company for $97.50 per hour. If Sportz no longer operated its own IT department, 30% of the fixed costs of the IT department could be eliminated. Should Sportz outsource its IT services?

15-35 Revenue allocation, bundled products. Premier Resorts (PR) operates a five-star hotel with a championship golf course. PR has a decentralized management structure, with three divisions:

- Lodging (rooms, conference facilities)
- Food (restaurants and in-room service)
- Recreation (golf course, tennis courts, swimming pool, and so on)

Starting next month, PR will offer a two-day, two-person "getaway package" for $800.
This deal includes the following:

	As Priced Separately
Two nights' stay for two in an ocean-view room	$ 640 ($320 per night)
Two spa treatments (can be used by either guest)	$ 300 ($150 per round)
Candlelight dinner for two at BR's finest restaurant	$ 160 ($80 per person)
Total package value	$1,100

Jenny Lee, president of the recreation division, recently asked the CEO of PR how her division would share in the $800 revenue from the getaway package. The golf course was operating at 100% capacity. Currently, anyone booking the package was guaranteed access to the golf course. Lee noted that every "getaway" booking would displace $300 of other golf bookings not related to the package. She emphasized that the high demand reflected the devotion of her team to keeping the golf course rated one of the "Best 10 Courses in the World" by Golf Monthly. As an aside, she also noted that the lodging and food divisions had to turn away customers during only "peak-season events such as the New Year's period."

Required

1. Using selling prices, allocate the $800 getaway-package revenue to the three divisions using:
   a. The stand-alone revenue-allocation method
   b. The incremental revenue-allocation method (with recreation first, then lodging, and then food)
2. What are the pros and cons of the two methods in requirement 1?
3. Because the recreation division is able to book the golf course at 100% capacity, the company CEO has decided to revise the getaway package to only include the lodging and food offerings shown previously. The new package will sell for $720. Allocate the revenue to the lodging and food divisions using the following:
   a. The Shapley value method
   b. The weighted Shapley value method, assuming that lodging is three times as likely to sell as the food

15-36 Support-department cost allocations; direct, step-down, and reciprocal methods. Ballantine Corporation has two operating departments: Eastern Department and Western Department. Each of the operating departments uses the services of the company's two support departments: Engineering and Information Technology. Additionally, the Engineering and Information Technology departments use the services of each other. Data concerning the past year are as follows:

	Support Departments		Operating Departments		
	Engineering	Information Technology	Eastern Department	Western Department	Total
Budgeted overhead costs before any interdepartment cost allocations	$300,000	$250,000	$650,000	$920,000	$2,120,000
Support work furnished:					
By Engineering					
Budgeted Engineering salaries	—	$60,000	$50,000	$90,000	$200,000
Percentage	—	30%	25%	45%	100%
By Information Technology					
Budgeted IT service hours	450	—	1,500	1,050	3,000
Percentage	15%	—	50%	35%	100%

1. What are the total overhead costs of the operating departments (Eastern and Western) *after* the support-department costs of Engineering and Information Technology have been allocated using (a) the direct method, (b) the step-down method (allocate Engineering first), (c) the step-down method (allocate Information Technology first), and (d) the reciprocal method?
2. Which method would you recommend that Ballantine Corporation use to allocate service-department costs? Why?

Performance Measurement, Compensation, and Multinational Considerations

23

When you complete this course, you'll receive a grade that represents a measure of your performance in it.

Your grade will likely consist of four elements—homework, quizzes, exams, and class participation. Do some of these elements better reflect your knowledge of the material than others? Would the relative weights placed on the various elements when determining your final grade influence how much effort you expend to improve your performance on the different elements? Would it be fair if you received a good grade regardless of your performance? The following article about Viacom chief executive Philippe Dauman examines that very situation in a corporate context.

EXECUTIVE COMPENSATION AT VIACOM[1]

A substantial part of American chief executive officers' pay is now tied to company performance. But that doesn't mean their compensation follows their results in lock step.

In 2016, Viacom Inc. revealed that 2015 compensation for its CEO Philippe Dauman rose by 22% over the year before, even though the value of its shareholders' investment in the company fell dramatically. Dauman, regularly one of the highest paid CEOs among publicly traded companies, made $54.2 million in 2015 (up from $44.3 million the year before) despite the company's stock plunging more than 40% due to ratings troubles at Viacom's cable channels such as Nickelodeon, MTV, and Comedy Central.

While Viacom said its board and management were "completely focused on delivering long-term value" for shareholders, some investors disagreed. Proxy advisory firm Institutional Shareholder Services issued a rare recommendation against re-election of all five Viacom board members on the company's compensation committee due to the disconnect between pay and performance. The situation at Viacom shows that companies face heightened risks of conflict with their investors when pay is out of line with performance.

Companies measure and reward performance to motivate managers to work toward organizational goals. As the Viacom example illustrates, if rewards are inappropriate or not

LEARNING OBJECTIVES

1. Select financial and nonfinancial performance measures to use in a balanced scorecard

2. Examine accounting-based measures for evaluating a business unit's performance, including return on investment (ROI), residual income (RI), and economic value added (EVA®)

3. Analyze the key measurement choices in the design of each performance measure

4. Study the choice of performance targets and design of feedback mechanisms

5. Indicate the difficulties that occur when the performance of divisions operating in different countries is compared

6. Understand the roles of salaries and incentives when rewarding managers

7. Describe the four levers of control and why they are necessary

Ringo Chiu/ZUMA Press, Inc./Alamy Stock Photo

[1] *Sources:* Joann S. Lublin, "How Much the Best-Performing and Worst-Performing CEOs Got Paid," *The Wall Street Journal* (June 25, 2015); Clair Atkinson, "Viacom boss Philippe Dauman Gets Hefty Raise While Profits Dip," *New York Post* (January 22, 2016); Kim Masters, "Viacom CEO Dauman's $54M Payday? Meet the Five Board Members Who Signed Off on It," *The Hollywood Reporter* (February 3, 2016).

connected to sustained performance, managers can increase their compensation without supporting the company's objectives. This chapter discusses the general design, implementation, and uses of performance measures, which are part of the final step in the decision-making process.

Financial and Nonfinancial Performance Measures

LEARNING
OBJECTIVE 1

Select financial performance measures

…such as return on investment and residual income

and nonfinancial performance measures

…such as customer satisfaction and number of defects

to use in a balanced scorecard

As you have learned, many organizations record financial and nonfinancial performance measures for their subunits on a *balanced scorecard*. The scorecards of different organizations emphasize different measures, but the measures are always derived from a company's strategy. Consider the case of Hospitality Inns, a chain of hotels. Hospitality Inns' strategy is to provide excellent customer service and to charge a higher room rate than its competitors. Hospitality Inns uses the following measures in its balanced scorecard:

1. **Financial perspective**—the firm's stock price, net income, return on sales, return on investment, and residual income
2. **Customer perspective**—market share in different geographic locations, customer satisfaction, brand image, and average number of repeat visits
3. **Internal-business-process perspective**—customer-service time for making reservations, check-in, and restaurant services; cleanliness of the hotels and rooms; time taken to clean rooms; room-service and restaurant quality; reductions in waste output and energy and water consumption; number of new services, such as wireless Internet, provided to customers; and the time taken to plan and build new hotels
4. **Learning-and-growth perspective**—the education, skills, and satisfaction levels of the firm's employees; employee turnover and hours of employee training; and the company's achievement of ISO 14001:2015 certification for environment management

As in all balanced scorecard implementations, the goal is to make improvements in the learning-and-growth perspective that will lead to enhancements in the internal-business-process perspective that, in turn, will result in improvements in the customer and financial perspectives. Hospitality Inns also uses balanced scorecard measures to evaluate and reward the performance of its managers.

Some performance measures, such as the time it takes to plan and build new hotels, have a long time horizon. Other measures, such as time taken to check in or quality of room service, have a short time horizon. In this chapter, we focus on *organization subunits'* most widely used performance measures that cover an intermediate to long time horizon. These are internal financial measures based on accounting numbers routinely reported by organizations. In later sections, we describe why companies use both financial and nonfinancial measures to evaluate performance.

Designing accounting-based performance measures requires several steps:

Step 1: Choose Performance Measures That Align with the Firm's Financial Goals. For example, is operating income, net income, return on assets, or revenues the best measure of a subunit's financial performance?

Step 2: Choose the Details of Each Performance Measure in Step 1. Once a firm has chosen a specific performance measure, it must make a variety of decisions about the precise way in which various components of the measure are to be calculated. For example, if the chosen performance measure is return on assets, should it be calculated for one year or for a multiyear period? Should assets be defined as total assets or net assets (total assets minus total liabilities)? Should assets be measured at historical cost or current cost?

Step 3: Choose a Target Level of Performance and Feedback Mechanism for Each Performance Measure in Step 1. For example, should all subunits have identical targets, such as the same required rate of return on assets? Should performance reports be sent to top managers daily, weekly, or monthly?

The decisions made in these steps don't have to be sequential. The issues considered in each step are interdependent, and top managers will often proceed through these steps several times before deciding on one or more accounting-based performance measures. At each step, the answers to the questions raised depend on top management's beliefs about how well each measure fulfills the behavioral criteria of promoting goal congruence, motivating management effort, evaluating subunit performance, and preserving subunit autonomy (see Chapter 22).

Accounting-Based Measures for Business Units

Companies commonly use four measures to evaluate the economic performance of their subunits. We illustrate these measures for Hospitality Inns.

Hospitality Inns owns and operates three hotels: one each in San Francisco, Chicago, and New Orleans. Exhibit 23-1 summarizes data for each hotel for 2017. At present, Hospitality Inns does not allocate the total long-term debt of the company to the three separate hotels. The exhibit indicates that the New Orleans hotel generates the highest operating income, $510,000, compared with Chicago's $300,000 and San Francisco's $240,000. But does this comparison mean the New Orleans hotel is the most "successful"? The main weakness of comparing operating incomes alone is that it ignores the differences in *the size of the investment* in each hotel. **Investment** refers to the resources or assets used to generate income. The real question is whether a division generates sufficient operating income relative to the investment made to earn it.

Three of the approaches to measuring performance include a measure of investment: return on investment, residual income, and economic value added. A fourth approach, return on sales, does not measure investment.

DECISION POINT

What financial and nonfinancial performance measures do companies use in their balanced scorecards?

LEARNING OBJECTIVE 2

Examine accounting-based measures for evaluating a business unit's performance, including return on investment (ROI),

…return on sales times investment turnover

residual income (RI),

…income minus a dollar amount for required return on investment

and economic value added (EVA®)

…a variation of residual income

EXHIBIT 23-1 Financial Data for Hospitality Inns for 2017 (in thousands)

	Home	Insert	Page Layout	Formulas	Data	Review	View	
	A			B	C	D	E	
1				San Francisco Hotel	Chicago Hotel	New Orleans Hotel	Total	
2	Hotel revenues			$1,200,000	$1,400,000	$3,185,000	$5,785,000	
3	Hotel variable costs			310,000	375,000	995,000	1,680,000	
4	Hotel fixed costs			650,000	725,000	1,680,000	3,055,000	
5	Hotel operating income			$ 240,000	$ 300,000	$ 510,000	1,050,000	
6	Interest costs on long-term debt at 10%						450,000	
7	Income before income taxes						600,000	
8	Income taxes at 30%						180,000	
9	Net income						$ 420,000	
10	Net book value at the end of 2017:							
11	Current assets			$ 400,000	$ 500,000	$ 660,000	$1,560,000	
12	Long-term assets			600,000	1,500,000	2,340,000	4,440,000	
13	Total assets			$1,000,000	$2,000,000	$3,000,000	$6,000,000	
14	Current liabilities			$ 50,000	$ 150,000	$ 300,000	$ 500,000	
15	Long-term debt						4,500,000	
16	Stockholders' equity						1,000,000	
17	Total liabilities and stockholders' equity						$6,000,000	
18								

Return on Investment

Return on investment (ROI) is an accounting measure of income divided by an accounting measure of investment.

$$\text{Return on investment} = \frac{\text{Income}}{\text{Investment}}$$

Return on investment is the most popular approach to measure performance for two reasons: (1) It blends all the ingredients of profitability—revenues, costs, and investment—into a single percentage and (2) it can be compared with the rate of return on opportunities elsewhere, inside or outside the company. As with any single performance measure, however, managers should use ROI cautiously and in conjunction with other measures.

ROI is also called the *accounting rate of return* or the *accrual accounting rate of return* (Chapter 21, pages 850–851). Managers usually use the term *ROI* when evaluating the performance of an organization's subunit and the term *accrual accounting rate of return* when using an ROI measure to evaluate a project. Companies vary in the way they define income in the numerator and investment in the denominator of the ROI calculation. Some companies use operating income for the numerator; others prefer to calculate ROI on an after-tax basis and use net income. Some companies use total assets in the denominator; others prefer to focus on only those assets financed by long-term debt and stockholders' equity and use total assets minus current liabilities.

Consider the ROIs of each of the three Hospitality hotels in Exhibit 23-1. For our calculations, we use the operating income of each hotel for the numerator and the total assets of each hotel for the denominator.

Using these ROI figures, the San Francisco hotel appears to make the best use of its total assets.

Hotel	Operating Income	÷	Total Assets	=	ROI
San Francisco	$240,000	÷	$1,000,000	=	24%
Chicago	$300,000	÷	$2,000,000	=	15%
New Orleans	$510,000	÷	$3,000,000	=	17%

Each manager can increase his or her hotel's ROI by increasing its revenues or decreasing its costs (each of which increases the numerator) or by decreasing the investment in the hotel (which decreases the denominator). Even when a hotel's operating income falls, the manager can increase its ROI by reducing its total assets by a greater percentage. Suppose, for example, that the operating income of the Chicago hotel decreases by 4% from $300,000 to $288,000 and its total assets decrease by 10% from $2,000,000 to $1,800,000. The ROI of the Chicago hotel would then increase from 15% to 16% ($288,000 ÷ $1,800,000).

ROI can provide more insight into performance when it is represented as two components:

$$\frac{\text{Income}}{\text{Investment}} = \frac{\text{Income}}{\text{Revenues}} \times \frac{\text{Revenues}}{\text{Investment}}$$

which is also written as

$$ROI = \text{Return on sales} \times \text{Investment turnover}$$

This approach is known as the *DuPont method of profitability analysis.* The DuPont method recognizes the two basic ingredients in profit making: increasing the income per dollar of revenues and using assets to generate more revenues. An improvement in either ingredient without changing the other increases the ROI.

Assume Hospitality Inns' top managers adopt a 30% target ROI for the San Francisco hotel. How can this return be attained? Using the DuPont method, the following example shows three ways the managers of the hotel can increase its ROI from 24% to 30%.

	Operating Income (1)	Revenues (2)	Total Assets (3)	$\dfrac{\text{Operating Income}}{\text{Revenues}}$ $(4) = (1) \div (2)$	$\times$	$\dfrac{\text{Revenues}}{\text{Total Assets}}$ $(5) = (2) \div (3)$	$=$	$\dfrac{\text{Operating Income}}{\text{Total Assets}}$ $(6) = (4) \times (5)$
Current ROI	$240,000	$1,200,000	$1,000,000	20%	$\times$	1.2	$=$	24%
Alternatives								
A. Decrease assets (such as receivables), keeping revenues and operating income per dollar of revenue constant	$240,000	$1,200,000	$ 800,000	20%	$\times$	1.5	$=$	30%
B. Increase revenues (via higher occupancy rate), keeping assets and operating income per dollar of revenue constant	$300,000	$1,500,000	$1,000,000	20%	$\times$	1.5	$=$	30%
C. Decrease costs (via, say, efficient maintenance) to increase operating income per dollar of revenue, keeping revenue and assets constant	$300,000	$1,200,000	$1,000,000	25%	$\times$	1.2	$=$	30%

Other alternatives, such as increasing the selling price per room, could increase both the revenues per dollar of total assets and the operating income per dollar of revenues.

ROI makes clear the benefits managers can obtain by reducing their investment in current or long-term assets. Most managers know they need to boost revenues and control costs, but pay less attention to reducing their investment base. Reducing the investment base involves decreasing idle cash, managing credit judiciously, determining proper inventory levels, and spending carefully on long-term assets.

Residual Income

Residual income (RI) is an accounting measure of income minus a dollar amount for required return on an accounting measure of investment.

$$\text{Residual income } (RI) = \text{Income} - (\text{Required rate of return} \times \text{Investment})$$

The required rate of return multiplied by the investment is the *imputed cost of the investment.* The **imputed cost** of the investment is a cost recognized in particular situations but not recorded in financial accounting systems because it is an opportunity cost. In this situation, the imputed cost refers to the return Hospitality Inns could have obtained by making an alternative investment with similar risk characteristics.

Assume that each hotel faces similar risks and that Hospitality Inns has a required rate of return of 12%. The RI for each hotel is calculated as the operating income minus the required rate of return of 12% of total assets:

Hotel	Operating Income	−	Required Rate of Return	$\times$	Investment	$=$	Residual Income
San Francisco	$240,000	−	(12%	$\times$	$1,000,000)	$=$	$120,000
Chicago	$300,000	−	(12%	$\times$	$2,000,000)	$=$	$ 60,000
New Orleans	$510,000	−	(12%	$\times$	$3,000,000)	$=$	$150,000

Note that the New Orleans hotel has the best RI. In general, RI is influenced by size: For a given level of performance, larger divisions generate higher RI.

Some companies favor the RI measure because managers will concentrate on maximizing an absolute amount, such as dollars of RI, rather than a percentage, such as ROI. The objective of maximizing RI means that as long as a subunit earns a return in excess of the required return for investments, that subunit should continue to invest.

The objective of maximizing ROI may give managers of highly profitable subunits the incentive to reject projects that, from the viewpoint of the company as a whole, should be accepted. Suppose Hospitality Inns is considering upgrading room features and furnishings at the San Francisco hotel. The upgrade will increase the operating income of the San Francisco hotel by $70,000 and increase its total assets by $400,000. The ROI for the expansion is 17.5% ($70,000 ÷ $400,000), which is attractive to Hospitality Inns because it exceeds the required rate of return of 12%. By making this expansion, however, the San Francisco hotel's ROI will decrease:

$$\text{Pre-upgrade } ROI = \frac{\$240,000}{\$1,000,000} = 0.24, \text{ or } 24\%$$

$$\text{Post-upgrade } ROI = \frac{\$240,000 + \$70,000}{\$1,000,000 + \$400,000} = \frac{\$310,000}{\$1,400,000} = 0.221, \text{ or } 22.1\%$$

The annual bonus paid to the San Francisco manager may decrease if ROI affects the bonus calculation and the upgrading option is selected. Consequently, the manager may shun the expansion. In contrast, if the annual bonus is a function of RI, the San Francisco manager will favor the expansion:

$$\text{Pre-upgrade } RI = \$240,000 - (0.12 \times \$1,000,000) = \$120,000$$

$$\text{Post-upgrade } RI = \$310,000 - (0.12 \times \$1,400,000) = \$142,000$$

So, it is more likely that a firm will achieve goal congruence if it uses RI rather than ROI to measure the subunit manager's performance.

To see that this is a general result, notice that the post-upgrade ROI is a weighted average of the pre-upgrade ROI and the ROI of the project under consideration. Therefore, whenever a new project has a return higher than the required rate of return (12% in our example) but below the current ROI of the division (24% in our example), the division manager is tempted to reject it even though it is a project shareholders would like to pursue.[2] On the other hand, RI is a measure that aggregates linearly, that is, the post-upgrade RI always equals the pre-upgrade RI plus the RI of the project under consideration. To verify this in the preceding example, observe that the project's RI is $70,000 - (12% \times \$400,000) = \$22,000$, which is the difference between the post-upgrade and pre-upgrade RI amounts. As a result, a manager who is evaluated on residual income will choose a new project only if it has a positive RI. But this is exactly the criterion shareholders want the manager to employ; in other words, RI achieves goal congruence.

TRY IT! 23-1 ▶

Capital Investments has two divisions. Each division's required rate of return is 15%. Planned operating results for 2017 are as follows:

Division	Operating income	Investment
A	$15,000,000	$100,000,000
B	$11,000,000	$ 50,000,000

a. What is the current ROI for each division?
b. What is the current residual income for each division?

Capital is planning an expansion that will require each division to increase its investments by $25,000,000 and its income by $4,500,000.

c. Assuming the managers are evaluated on either ROI or residual income, which division (if either) is pleased with the expansion?

---

[2] Analogously, the manager of an underperforming division with an ROI of 7%, say, may wish to accept projects with returns between 7% and 12% even though these opportunities do not meet the shareholders' required rate of return.

Economic Value Added

Economic value added (EVA®) is a variation of RI used by many companies.[3] It is calculated as follows:

$$\begin{array}{c} \text{Economic value} \\ \text{added (EVA)} \end{array} = \begin{array}{c} \text{After-tax} \\ \text{operating income} \end{array} - \left[\begin{array}{c} \text{Weighted} \\ \text{average} \\ \text{cost of capital} \end{array} \times \left(\begin{array}{c} \text{Total} \\ \text{assets} \end{array} - \begin{array}{c} \text{Current} \\ \text{liabilities} \end{array} \right) \right]$$

That is, EVA substitutes the following numbers in the RI calculation:

1. Income: After-tax operating income,
2. Required rate of return: (After-tax) weighted-average cost of capital, and
3. Investment: Total assets minus current liabilities.[4]

We use the Hospitality Inns' data in Exhibit 23-1 to illustrate the basic EVA calculations. The weighted-average cost of capital (WACC) equals the *after-tax* average cost of all the long-term funds Hospitality Inns uses. The company has two sources of long-term funds: (a) long-term debt with a market value and book value of $4.5 million issued at an interest rate of 10%, and (b) equity capital that also has a market value of $4.5 million (but a book value of $1 million).[5] Because interest costs are tax-deductible and the income tax rate is 30%, the after-tax cost of debt financing is $0.10 \times (1 - \text{Tax rate}) = 0.10 \times (1 - 0.30) = 0.07$, or 7%. The cost of equity capital is the opportunity cost to investors of not investing their capital in another investment that is similar in risk to Hospitality Inns. Hospitality Inns' cost of equity capital is 14%.[6] The WACC computation, which uses market values of debt and equity, is as follows:

$$\begin{aligned} WACC &= \frac{(7\% \times \text{Market value of debt}) + (14\% \times \text{Market value of equity})}{\text{Market value of debt} + \text{Market value of equity}} \\[2mm] &= \frac{(0.07 \times \$4{,}500{,}000) + (0.14 \times \$4{,}500{,}000)}{\$4{,}500{,}000 + \$4{,}500{,}000} \\[2mm] &= \frac{\$945{,}000}{\$9{,}000{,}000} = 0.105, \text{ or } 10.5\% \end{aligned}$$

The company applies the same WACC to all its hotels because each hotel faces similar risks.

Total assets minus current liabilities (see Exhibit 23-1) can also be computed as follows:

$$\text{Total assets} - \text{Current liabilities} = \text{Long-term assets} + \text{Current assets} - \text{Current liabilities}$$

$$= \text{Long-term assets} + \text{Working capital}$$

where

$$\text{Working capital} = \text{Current assets} - \text{Current liabilities}$$

After-tax hotel operating income is:

$$\begin{array}{c} \text{Hotel operating} \\ \text{income} \end{array} \times (1 - \text{Tax rate}) = \begin{array}{c} \text{Hotel operating} \\ \text{income} \end{array} \times (1 - 0.30) = \begin{array}{c} \text{Hotel operating} \\ \text{income} \end{array} \times 0.70$$

---

[3] Stephen F. O'Byrne and S. David Young, *EVA and Value-Based Management: A Practical Guide to Implementation* (New York: McGraw-Hill, 2000); Joel M. Stern, John S. Shiely, and Irwin Ross, *The EVA Challenge: Implementing Value Added Change in an Organization* (New York: John Wiley and Sons, 2001).

[4] When implementing EVA, companies make several adjustments to the operating income and asset numbers reported under Generally Accepted Accounting Principles (GAAP). For example, when calculating EVA, costs such as R&D, restructuring costs, and leases that have long-run benefits are recorded as assets (which are then amortized), rather than as current operating costs. The goal of these adjustments is to obtain a better representation of the economic assets, particularly intangible assets, used to earn income. Of course, the specific adjustments applicable to a company will depend on its individual circumstances.

[5] The market value of Hospitality Inns' equity exceeds book value because book value, based on historical cost, does not measure the current value of the company's assets and because various intangible assets, such as the company's brand name, are not shown in the balance sheet under GAAP.

[6] In practice, the most common method of calculating the cost of equity capital is by applying the capital asset pricing model (CAPM). For details, see Jonathan Berk and Peter DeMarzo, *Corporate Finance*, 3rd ed. (Upper Saddle River, NJ: Prentice Hall, 2013).

EVA calculations for Hospitality Inns are as follows:

Hotel	After-Tax Operating Income	−	[WACC × (Total Assets − Current Liabilities)]	=	EVA
San Francisco	$240,000 × 0.70	−	[10.50% × ($1,000,000 − $ 50,000)]	=	$68,250
Chicago	$300,000 × 0.70	−	[10.50% × ($2,000,000 − $150,000)]	=	$15,750
New Orleans	$510,000 × 0.70	−	[10.50% × ($3,000,000 − $300,000)]	=	$73,500

The New Orleans hotel has the highest EVA. Economic value added, like residual income, charges managers for the cost of their investments in long-term assets and working capital. Value is created only if the subunit's after-tax operating income exceeds the cost of investing the capital. To improve EVA, managers can, for example, (a) earn more after-tax operating income with the same amount of capital, (b) use less capital to earn the same after-tax operating income, or (c) invest capital in high-return projects.[7]

Companies such as Briggs and Stratton (a leading producer of gasoline engines), Coca-Cola, Eli Lilly, and Infosys Limited use EVA to guide their decisions. CSX, a railroad company, credits EVA for decisions such as to run trains with three locomotives instead of four and to schedule arrivals just in time for unloading rather than having trains arrive at their destination several hours in advance. The result? Higher income because of lower fuel costs and lower capital investments in locomotives. Division managers find EVA helpful because it allows them to incorporate the cost of capital, which is generally only available at the company-wide level, into the decisions they make. Comparing the actual EVA achieved to the estimated EVA is useful for evaluating the performance of subunits and their managers.

TRY IT! 23-2 ▶ Chopper City supplies helicopters to corporate clients. Chopper City has two sources of funds: long-term debt with a market and book value of $32 million issued at an interest rate of 10% and equity capital that has a market value of $18 million (book value of $8 million). The cost of equity capital for Chopper City is 15%, and its tax rate is 30%. Chopper City has divisions in two cities that operate autonomously. The company's results for 2017 are as follows:

	Operating Income	Assets	Current Liabilities
New York	$1,750,000	$11,500,000	$2,500,000
Chicago	2,400,000	9,000,000	3,500,000

a. What is Chopper City's weighted average cost of capital?
b. Compute each division's Economic Value Added.

Return on Sales

The income-to-revenues ratio (or sales ratio), often called the *return on sales* (ROS), is a frequently used financial performance measure. As we have seen, ROS is one component of ROI in the DuPont method of profitability analysis. To calculate the ROS for each of Hospitality's hotels, we divide operating income by revenues:

Hotel	Operating Income	÷	Revenues (Sales)	=	ROS
San Francisco	$240,000	÷	$1,200,000	=	20.0%
Chicago	$300,000	÷	$1,400,000	=	21.4%
New Orleans	$510,000	÷	$3,185,000	=	16.0%

The Chicago hotel has the highest ROS, but its performance is rated worse than the other hotels using measures such as ROI, RI, and EVA.

---

[7] Observe that the sum of the divisional after-tax operating incomes used in the EVA calculation, ($240,000 + $300,000 + $510,000) × 0.7 = $735,000, exceeds the firm's net income of $420,000. The difference is due to the firm's after-tax interest expense on its long-term debt, which amounts to $450,000 × 0.7 = $315,000. Because the EVA measure includes a charge for the weighted-average cost of capital, which includes the after-tax cost of debt, the income figure used to compute EVA should reflect the after-tax profit before interest payments on debt are considered. After-tax operating income (often referred to in practice as NOPAT, or net operating profit after taxes) is thus the relevant measure of divisional profit for EVA calculations.

Comparing Performance Measures

The following table summarizes the performance of each hotel and ranks it (in parentheses) under each of the four performance measures:

Hotel	ROI	RI	EVA	ROS
San Francisco	24% (1)	$120,000 (2)	$68,250 (2)	20.0% (2)
Chicago	15% (3)	$ 60,000 (3)	$15,750 (3)	21.4% (1)
New Orleans	17% (2)	$150,000 (1)	$73,500 (1)	16.0% (3)

The RI and EVA rankings are the same. They differ from the ROI and ROS rankings. Consider the ROI and RI rankings for the San Francisco and New Orleans hotels. The New Orleans hotel has a smaller ROI, indicating that its assets are being used relatively less efficiently. Although its operating income is only slightly more than twice the operating income of the San Francisco hotel—$510,000 versus $240,000—its total assets are three times as large—$3 million versus $1 million. However, the New Orleans hotel has a higher RI because it earns a higher income after covering the required rate of return on investment of 12%. Even though each dollar invested in the New Orleans hotel does not yield the same return as the San Francisco hotel, this large investment creates considerable value because its return exceeds the required rate of return. The Chicago hotel has the highest ROS but the lowest ROI. The high ROS indicates that the Chicago hotel has the lowest cost structure per dollar of revenues of all of Hospitality Inns' hotels. Chicago has a low ROI because it generates very low revenues per dollar of assets invested. Is any method better than the others for measuring performance? No, because each evaluates a different aspect of performance.

ROS measures how effectively costs are managed. To evaluate a unit's overall aggregate performance, however, ROI, RI, or EVA measures are more appropriate than ROS because they consider both income and investment. ROI indicates which investment yields the highest return. RI and EVA overcome some of the goal-congruence problems of ROI. Some managers favor EVA because of the accounting adjustments related to the capitalization of investments in intangibles. Other managers favor RI because it is easier to calculate and because, in most cases, it leads to the same conclusions as EVA does. Generally, companies use multiple financial measures to evaluate performance.

DECISION
POINT

What are the relative merits of return on investment (ROI), residual income (RI), and economic value added (EVA) as performance measures for subunit managers?

Choosing the Details of the Performance Measures

It is not sufficient for a company to identify the set of performance measures it wishes to use. The company has to decide how to compute the measures. This includes deciding on the time frame over which the measures are computed, defining key terms such as *investment*, and agreeing on how to calculate the components of each performance measure.

Alternative Time Horizons

An important element in designing accounting-based performance measures is choosing the time horizon of the performance measures. The ROI, RI, EVA, and ROS calculations represent the results for a single period, one year in our example. Managers could take actions that cause short-run increases in these measures but that conflict with the long-run interest of the company. For example, managers might curtail R&D and plant maintenance spending in the last three months of a fiscal year to achieve a target level of annual operating income. For this reason, many companies evaluate subunits on the basis of ROI, RI, EVA, and ROS over multiple years.

Another reason to evaluate subunits over multiple years is that the benefits of actions taken in the current period may not show up in short-run performance measures, such as the current year's ROI or RI. For example, an investment in a new hotel may adversely affect ROI and RI in the short run but positively affect them in the long run.

LEARNING OBJECTIVE 3

Analyze the key measurement choices in the design of each performance measure

...choice of time horizon, alternative definitions, and measurement of assets

A multiyear analysis highlights another advantage of the RI measure: The net present value of all cash flows over the life of an investment equals the net present value of the RIs.[8] This means that if managers use the net present value method to make investment decisions (as Chapter 21 advocates), then using a multiyear RI to evaluate managers' performances achieves goal congruence.

Another way to motivate managers to take a long-run perspective is by compensating them on the basis of changes in the market price of the company's stock because stock prices incorporate the expected future effects of a firm's current decisions.

Alternative Definitions of Investment

Companies use a variety of definitions to measure the investments made in their divisions. Four common alternative definitions used in the construction of accounting-based performance measures are:

1. **Total assets available**—includes all assets, regardless of their intended purpose.

2. **Total assets employed**—total assets available minus the sum of idle assets and assets purchased for future expansion. For example, if the New Orleans hotel in Exhibit 23-1 has unused land set aside for potential expansion, the total assets employed (used) by the hotel would exclude the cost of that land.

3. **Total assets employed minus current liabilities**—total assets employed, excluding assets financed by short-term creditors. One negative feature of defining investment in this way is that it may encourage subunit managers to use an excessive amount of short-term debt because short-term debt reduces the amount of investment.

4. **Stockholders' equity**—calculated by assigning liabilities among subunits and deducting these amounts from the total assets of each subunit. One drawback of this method is that it combines the operating decisions made by hotel managers with the financing decisions made by top management.

Companies that use ROI or RI generally define investment as the total assets available. When a firm directs a subunit manager to carry extra or idle assets, the total assets employed can be more informative than total assets available. Companies that use EVA define investment as the total assets employed minus current liabilities. The rationale for using this definition is that it captures total investment as measured by the sum of working capital (current assets minus current liabilities) and the long-term assets employed in the subunit. Managers are responsible for generating an adequate return on both components.

Alternative Asset Measurements

To design accounting-based performance measures, we must consider different ways to measure the assets included in the investment calculations. Should the assets be measured at

---

[8] This equivalence, referred to as the "conservation property" of residual income, was first articulated by Gabriel Preinreich in 1938. To see the equivalence, suppose the $400,000 investment in the San Francisco hotel increases its operating income by $70,000 per year as follows: Increase in operating cash flows of $150,000 each year for 5 years minus depreciation of $80,000 ($400,000 ÷ 5) per year, assuming straight-line depreciation and $0 terminal disposal value. Depreciation reduces the investment amount by $80,000 each year. Assuming a required rate of return of 12%, the net present values of cash flows and residual incomes are as follows:

Year		0	1	2	3	4	5	Net Present Value
(1)	Cash flow	−$400,000	$150,000	$150,000	$150,000	$150,000	$150,000	
(2)	Present value of $1 discounted at 12%	1	0.89286	0.79719	0.71178	0.63552	0.56743	
(3)	Present value: (1) × (2)	−$400,000	$133,929	$119,578	$106,767	$ 95,328	$ 85,114	$140,716
(4)	Operating income		$ 70,000	$ 70,000	$ 70,000	$ 70,000	$ 70,000	
(5)	Assets at start of year		$400,000	$320,000	$240,000	$160,000	$ 80,000	
(6)	Capital charge: (5) × 12%		$ 48,000	$ 38,400	$ 28,800	$ 19,200	$ 9,600	
(7)	Residual income: (4) − (6)		$ 22,000	$ 31,600	$ 41,200	$ 50,800	$ 60,400	
(8)	Present value of RI: (7) × (2)		$ 19,643	$ 25,191	$ 29,325	$ 32,284	$ 34,273	$140,716

historical cost or current cost? Should gross book value (that is, original cost) or net book value (original cost minus accumulated depreciation) be used for depreciable assets?

Current Cost

Current cost is the cost of purchasing an asset today identical to the one currently held or the cost of purchasing an asset that provides services like the one currently held if an identical asset cannot be purchased. Of course, measuring assets at current costs will result in different ROIs than the ROIs calculated on the basis of historical costs.

We illustrate the current-cost ROI calculations using the data for Hospitality Inns (Exhibit 23-1) and then compare current-cost-based ROIs and historical-cost-based ROIs. Consider the following additional information about the long-term assets of each hotel:

	San Francisco	Chicago	New Orleans
Age of facility in years (at end of 2017)	8	4	2
Gross book value (original cost)	$1,400,000	$2,100,000	$2,730,000
Accumulated depreciation	$ 800,000	$ 600,000	$ 390,000
Net book value (at end of 2017)	$ 600,000	$1,500,000	$2,340,000
Depreciation for 2017	$ 100,000	$ 150,000	$ 195,000

Hospitality Inns assumes its facilities have a 14-year estimated useful life and zero terminal disposal value and uses straight-line depreciation.

An index of construction costs indicating how the cost of construction has changed over the eight-year period Hospitality Inns has been operating (2009 year-end $=$ 100) is as follows:

Year	2010	2011	2012	2013	2014	2015	2016	2017
Construction cost index	110	122	136	144	152	160	174	180

Earlier in this chapter, we computed an ROI of 24% for San Francisco, 15% for Chicago, and 17% for New Orleans (page 914). One possible explanation for the high ROI for the San Francisco hotel is that its long-term assets are expressed in 2009 construction-price levels— prices that prevailed eight years ago—and the long-term assets for the Chicago and New Orleans hotels are expressed in terms of higher, more recent construction-price levels, which depress ROIs for these two hotels.

Exhibit 23-2 illustrates a step-by-step approach for incorporating current-cost estimates of long-term assets and depreciation expense into the ROI calculation. We make these calculations to approximate what it would cost today to obtain assets that would produce the same expected operating income the subunits currently earn. (For RI and EVA calculations, similar adjustments to represent the current costs of capital and depreciation expense can be made.) The current-cost adjustment reduces the ROI of the San Francisco hotel by more than half.

	Historical-Cost ROI	Current-Cost ROI
San Francisco	24%	10.8%
Chicago	15%	11.1%
New Orleans	17%	14.7%

Adjusting assets to recognize current costs negates differences in the investment base caused solely by differences in construction-price levels. The current-cost ROI better measures the current economic returns from the investment than the historical-cost ROI does. If Hospitality Inns were to invest in a new hotel today, investing in one like the New Orleans hotel offers the best ROI.

Current-cost estimates can be difficult to obtain for some assets. Why? Because the estimate requires a company to consider, in addition to increases in price levels, technological advances and process improvements that could reduce the current cost of assets needed to earn today's operating income.

Long-Term Assets: Gross or Net Book Value?

The historical cost of assets is often used to calculate ROI. There has been much discussion about whether managers should use gross book value or net book value of assets. Using the

EXHIBIT 23-2 ROI for Hospitality Inns: Computed Using Current-Cost Estimates as of the End of 2017 for Depreciation Expense and Long-Term Assets

	Home	Insert	Page Layout	Formulas	Data	Review	View			
	A	B	C	D	E	F	G	H	I	J

	A	B	C	D	E	F	G	H	I	J
1	**Step 1:** Restate long-term assets from gross book value at historical cost to gross book value at current cost as of the end of 2017.									
2		**Gross book value of long-term assets at historical cost**	×	**Construction cost index in 2017**	÷	**Construction cost index in year of construction**	=	**Gross book value of long-term assets at current cost at end of 2017**		
3	San Francisco	$1,400,000	×	(180	÷	100)	=	$2,520,000		
4	Chicago	$2,100,000	×	(180	÷	144)	=	$2,625,000		
5	New Orleans	$2,730,000	×	(180	÷	160)	=	$3,071,250		
6										
7	**Step 2:** Derive net book value of long-term assets at current cost as of the end of 2017. (Assume estimated useful life of each hotel is 14 years.)									
8		**Gross book value of long-term assets at current cost at end of 2017**	×	**Estimated remaining useful life**	÷	**Estimated total useful life**	=	**Net book value of long-term assets at current cost at end of 2017**		
9	San Francisco	$2,520,000	×	(6	÷	14)	=	$1,080,000		
10	Chicago	$2,625,000	×	(10	÷	14)	=	$1,875,000		
11	New Orleans	$3,071,250	×	(12	÷	14)	=	$2,632,500		
12										
13	**Step 3:** Compute current cost of total assets in 2017. (Assume current assets of each hotel are expressed in 2017 dollars.)									
14		**Current assets at end of 2017 (from Exhibit 23-1)**	+	**Long-term assets from Step 2**	=	**Current cost of total assets at end of 2017**				
15	San Francisco	$400,000	+	$1,080,000	=	$1,480,000				
16	Chicago	$500,000	+	$1,875,000	=	$2,375,000				
17	New Orleans	$660,000	+	$2,632,500	=	$3,292,500				
18										
19	**Step 4:** Compute current-cost depreciation expense in 2017 dollars.									
20		**Gross book value of long-term assets at current cost at end of 2017 (from Step 1)**	÷	**Estimated total useful life**	=	**Current-cost depreciation expense in 2017 dollars**				
21	San Francisco	$2,520,000	÷	14	=	$180,000				
22	Chicago	$2,625,000	÷	14	=	$187,500				
23	New Orleans	$3,071,250	÷	14	=	$219,375				
24										
25	**Step 5:** Compute 2017 operating income using 2017 current-cost depreciation expense.									
26		**Historical-cost operating income**	−	**Current-cost depreciation expense in 2017 dollars (from Step 4)**	−	**Historical-cost depreciation expense**	=	**Operating income for 2017 using current-cost depreciation expense in 2017 dollars**		
27	San Francisco	$240,000	−	($180,000	−	$100,000)	=	$160,000		
28	Chicago	$300,000	−	($187,500	−	$150,000)	=	$262,500		
29	New Orleans	$510,000	−	($219,375	−	$195,000)	=	$485,625		
30										
31	**Step 6:** Compute ROI using current-cost estimates for long-term assets and depreciation expense.									
32		**Operating income for 2017 using current-cost depreciation expense in 2017 dollars (from Step 5)**	÷	**Current cost of total assets at end of 2017 (from Step 3)**	=	**ROI using current-cost estimate**				
33	San Francisco	$160,000	÷	$1,480,000	=	10.8%				
34	Chicago	$262,500	÷	$2,375,000	=	11.1%				
35	New Orleans	$485,625	÷	$3,292,500	=	14.7%				

data in Exhibit 23-1 (page 913), we calculate ROI using net and gross book values of plant and equipment:

	Operating Income (from Exhibit 23-1) (1)	Net Book Value of Total Assets (from Exhibit 23-1) (2)	Accumulated Depreciation (from page 921) (3)	Gross Book Value of Total Assets (4) = (2) + (3)	2017 ROI Using Net Book Value of Total Assets calculated earlier (5) = (1) ÷ (2)	2017 ROI Using Gross Book Value of Total Assets (6) = (1) ÷ (4)
San Francisco	$240,000	$1,000,000	$800,000	$1,800,000	24%	13.3%
Chicago	$300,000	$2,000,000	$600,000	$2,600,000	15%	11.5%
New Orleans	$510,000	$3,000,000	$390,000	$3,390,000	17%	15.0%

Using gross book value, the 13.3% ROI of the older San Francisco hotel is lower than the 15.0% ROI of the newer New Orleans hotel. Those who favor using gross book value claim it enables a firm to compare ROI across its subunits more accurately. For example, when using gross-book-value calculations, the return on the original plant-and-equipment investment is higher for the newer New Orleans hotel than for the older San Francisco hotel. This difference probably reflects the decline in earning power of the San Francisco hotel. Using the net book value masks this decline in earning power because the constantly decreasing investment base results in a higher ROI for the San Francisco hotel—24% in this example. This higher rate may mislead decision makers into thinking that the earning power of the San Francisco hotel has not decreased.

The proponents of using net book value as an investment base maintain that it is less confusing because (1) it is consistent with the amount of total assets shown in the conventional balance sheet and (2) it is consistent with income computations that include deductions for depreciation expense. Surveys report that the net book value is the measure of assets most commonly used by companies for internal performance evaluation.

DECISION POINT

Over what time frame should companies measure performance, and what are the alternative choices for calculating the components of each performance measure?

Ecowas Products, which exports processed palm oil, operates in a variety of West African countries. The following information relates to its Nigerian division for 2017:

23-3 TRY IT!

Sales revenues	$1,400,000
Plant depreciation	200,000
Other operating costs	760,000
Operating income	$ 440,000

The division has current assets of $500,000 and one long-term asset (the plant) with a net book value of $1,800,000. The plant is 3 years old at the end of 2017 and has an estimated useful life of 12 years. The straight-line method is used for depreciation and no salvage value is assumed.

Over the 10-year period Ecowas has been operating, the index of construction costs in Nigeria is as follows (2007 year-end 100):

2007	2014	2017
100	136	170

a. What is the ROI for the Nigerian division using historical-cost measures?
b. What is the ROI for the Nigerian division using current-cost estimates for depreciation expense and long-term assets?

Target Levels of Performance and Feedback

Now that we have covered the different types of measures and how to choose them, let us turn our attention to how mangers set and measure target levels of performance.

Choosing Target Levels of Performance

Historical-cost-based accounting measures are usually inadequate for evaluating economic returns on new investments and, in some cases, create disincentives for expansion. Despite these problems, managers can use historical-cost ROIs to evaluate current performance by

LEARNING OBJECTIVE 4

Study the choice of performance targets and design of feedback mechanisms

...carefully crafted budgets and sufficient feedback for timely corrective action

establishing *target* ROIs. For Hospitality Inns, we need to recognize that the hotels were built in different years, which means they were built at different construction-price levels. The firm could adjust the target historical-cost-based ROIs accordingly, say, by setting San Francisco's ROI at 26%, Chicago's at 21%, and New Orleans' at 19%.

This useful alternative of comparing actual results with targeted, or budgeted, results is often overlooked, but should not be. *Companies should tailor and negotiate a budget for a particular subunit, a particular accounting system, and a particular performance measure while keeping in mind the pitfalls of using historical-cost accounting.* For example, many problems related to valuing assets and measuring income can be resolved if top managers can get subunit managers to focus on what is attainable in the forthcoming budget period—whether ROI, RI, or EVA is used and whether the financial measures are based on historical costs or some other measure, such as current costs.

A popular way to establish targets is to set continuous improvement targets. If a company is using EVA as a performance measure, the firm can evaluate operations on the year-to-year changes in EVA, rather than on absolute measures of EVA. Evaluating performance on the basis of *improvements* in EVA makes the initial method of calculating it less important.

Companies using balanced scorecards establish targets for financial performance measures, while simultaneously setting targets in the customer, internal-business-process, and learning-and-growth perspectives. For example, Hospitality Inns will establish targets for employee training and satisfaction, customer-service times for reservations and check-in, the quality of room service, and customer satisfaction levels that each hotel must reach to achieve its ROI and EVA targets.

Choosing the Timing of Feedback

A final step in designing accounting-based performance measures is the timing of performance feedback, which depends largely on (1) how critical the information is for the success of the organization, (2) the management level receiving the feedback, and (3) the sophistication of the organization's information technology. For example, hotel managers responsible for room sales want information on the number of rooms sold (rented) on a daily or weekly basis because a large percentage of hotel costs are fixed costs. Achieving high room sales and taking quick action to reverse any declining sales trends are critical to the financial success of each hotel. Supplying managers with daily information about room sales is much easier if Hospitality Inns has a computerized room-reservation and check-in system. The company's top managers, however, might look at information about daily room sales only on a monthly basis unless there is a problem, like the low sales-to-total-assets ratio the Chicago hotel has. In this case, the managers might ask for the information weekly.

Similarly, human resources managers at each hotel measure employee satisfaction annually because satisfaction is best measured over a longer horizon. However, housekeeping department managers measure the quality of room service over much shorter time horizons, such as a week, because poor levels of performance in these areas for even a short period of time can harm a hotel's reputation for a long period. Moreover, managers can detect and resolve housekeeping problems over a short time period.

DECISION POINT

What targets should companies use, and when should they give feedback to managers regarding their performance relative to these targets?

LEARNING OBJECTIVE 5

Indicate the difficulties that occur when the performance of divisions operating in different countries is compared

...adjustments needed for differences in inflation rates and changes in exchange rates

Performance Measurement in Multinational Companies

Our discussion so far has focused on performance evaluation of different divisions of a company operating within a single country. We next discuss the additional difficulties created when managers compare the performance of divisions of a company operating in different countries. Several issues arise.[9]

- The economic, legal, political, social, and cultural environments differ significantly across countries. Operating a division in an open economy like New Zealand is very different

---

[9] See M. Zafar Iqbal, *International Accounting: A Global Perspective* (Cincinnati: South-Western College Publishing, 2002).

from operating in a closed economy such as Venezuela, where many prices are controlled and there is a constant threat of nationalization.

- Import quotas and tariffs range widely from country to country, and it's not unusual for countries to impose custom duties to restrict the imports of certain goods.

- The availability of materials and skilled labor as well as the costs of materials, labor, and infrastructure (power, transportation, and communication) also differ significantly across countries. Companies operating in Indonesia, for example, must spend 30% of their total production costs on transportation, whereas these costs account for just 12% of total spending in China.

- Divisions operating in different countries account for their performance in different currencies, and inflation and fluctuations in foreign-currency exchange rates affect performance measurement. For example, economies such as Kazakhstan, Myanmar, and Nigeria suffer from double-digit inflation, which dampens the performance of divisions in those countries when their results are measured in dollars.

As a result of these differences, adjustments need to be made to accurately compare the performance of divisions in different countries.

Calculating a Foreign Division's ROI in the Foreign Currency

Suppose Hospitality Inns invests in a hotel in Mexico City. The investment consists mainly of the costs of buildings and furnishings. Also assume the following:

- The exchange rate at the time of Hospitality Inns' investment on December 31, 2016, is 10 pesos = $1.

- During 2017, the Mexican peso suffers a steady decline in its value. The exchange rate on December 31, 2017, is 15 pesos = $1.

- The average exchange rate during 2017 is [(10 + 15) ÷ 2] = 12.5 pesos = $1.

- The investment (total assets) in the Mexico City hotel is 30,000,000 pesos.

- The operating income of the Mexico City hotel in 2017 is 6,000,000 pesos.

What is the historical-cost-based ROI for the Mexico City hotel in 2017?

To answer this question, Hospitality Inns' managers first have to determine if they should calculate the ROI in pesos or in dollars. If they calculate the ROI in dollars, what exchange rate should they use? The managers may also be interested in how the ROI of Hospitality Inns Mexico City (HIMC) compares with the ROI of Hospitality Inns New Orleans (HINO), which is also a relatively new hotel of approximately the same size. The answers to these questions yield information that will be helpful when making future investment decisions.

$$\text{HIMC's } ROI \text{ (calculated using pesos)} = \frac{\text{Operating income}}{\text{Total assets}} = \frac{6,000,000 \text{ pesos}}{30,000,000 \text{ pesos}} = 0.20, \text{ or } 20\%$$

HIMC's ROI of 20% is higher than HINO's ROI of 17% (page 914). Does this mean that HIMC outperformed HINO based on the ROI criterion? Not necessarily. That's because HIMC operates in a very different economic environment than HINO.

The peso has declined in value relative to the dollar in 2017. This decline has led to higher inflation in Mexico than in the United States. As a result of the higher inflation in Mexico, HIMC will charge higher prices for its hotel rooms, which will increase HIMC's operating income and lead to a higher ROI. Inflation clouds the real economic returns on an asset and makes historical-cost-based ROI higher. Differences in inflation rates between the two countries make a direct comparison of HIMC's peso-denominated ROI with HINO's dollar-denominated ROI misleading.

Calculating the Foreign Division's ROI in U.S. Dollars

One way to make a comparison of historical-cost-based ROIs more meaningful is to restate HIMC's performance in U.S. dollars. But what exchange rate should the managers use to make the comparison meaningful? Assume HIMC's operating income was earned evenly throughout 2017. Hospitality Inns' managers should use the average exchange rate of 12.5 pesos = $1 to convert the operating income from pesos to dollars: 6,000,000 pesos ÷ 12.5 pesos per dollar = $480,000. The effect of dividing the operating income in pesos by the higher pesos-to-dollar exchange rate prevailing during 2017, rather than the 10 pesos = $1 exchange rate on December 31, 2016, is that any increase in operating income in pesos as a result of inflation during 2017 is eliminated when converting back to dollars.

At what rate should HIMC's total assets of 30,000,000 pesos be converted? They should be converted at the 10 pesos = $1 exchange rate, which was the exchange rate when the assets were acquired on December 31, 2016. Why? Because HIMC's assets are recorded in pesos at the December 31, 2016, cost, and the assets are not revalued as a result of inflation in Mexico in 2017. Since the subsequent inflation does not affect the cost of assets in HIMC's financial accounting records, managers should use the exchange rate prevailing on the date the assets were acquired to convert the assets into dollars. Using exchange rates after December 31, 2016, would be incorrect because these exchange rates incorporate the higher inflation in Mexico in 2017. HIMC's total assets are therefore $3,000,000 (30,000,000 pesos ÷ 10 pesos per dollar).

Then

$$\text{HIMC's } ROI \text{ (calculated using dollars)} = \frac{\text{Operating income}}{\text{Total assets}} = \frac{\$480,000}{\$3,000,000} = 0.16, \text{or } 16\%$$

As we have discussed, these adjustments make the historical-cost-based ROIs of the Mexico City and New Orleans hotels comparable because they negate the effects of any differences in inflation rates between the two countries. Now HIMC's ROI is less than HINO's (16% versus HINO's ROI of 17%).

Calculating residual income in pesos poses the same problems as calculating the ROI does. Calculating HIMC's RI in dollars adjusts for changes in exchange rates and makes for more-meaningful comparisons with Hospitality's other hotels:

$$\text{HIMC's } RI = \$480,000 - (0.12 \times \$3,000,000)$$

$$= \$480,000 - \$360,000 = \$120,000$$

which is also less than HINO's RI of $150,000.

Keep in mind that HIMC's and HINO's ROIs and RIs are historical-cost-based calculations. However, both hotels are relatively new, so this is less of a concern.

DECISION POINT

How can companies compare the performance of divisions operating in different countries?

TRY IT! 23-4

Patricof Corporation has a division in the United States, and another in France. The investment in the French assets was made when the exchange rate was $1.20 per euro. The average exchange rate for the year was $1.30 per euro. The exchange rate at the end of the fiscal year was $1.38 per euro. Income and investment for the two divisions are:

	United States	France
Investment in assets	$3,490,000	2,400,000 euros
Income for current year	$ 383,900	266,400 euros

The required return for Patricof is 10%. Calculate ROI and RI for the two divisions in their local currencies. For the French division, also calculate these measures using dollars. Which division is doing better?

Distinguishing the Performance of Managers From the Performance of Their Subunits[10]

Our focus has been on how to evaluate the performance of a subunit of a company, such as a division. However, is evaluating the performance of a subunit manager the same as evaluating the performance of the subunit? If the subunit performed well, does it mean the manager performed well? In this section, we argue that a company should distinguish between the performance evaluation of a *manager* and the performance evaluation of that manager's *subunit*. For example, companies often put the most skillful division manager in charge of the division producing the poorest economic return in an attempt to improve it. But this may take years and the relative underperformance of the division during that time is no reflection of the performance of the manager.

As another example, consider again the Hospitality Inns Mexico City (HIMC) hotel. Suppose, despite the high inflation in Mexico, HIMC could not increase its room prices because of price-control regulations imposed by the government. HIMC's performance in dollar terms would be poor because of the decline in the value of the peso. But should top managers conclude the HIMC manager performed poorly? Probably not. The poor performance of HIMC is largely the result of regulatory and economic factors beyond the manager's control.

In the following sections, we show the basic principles for evaluating the performance of an individual subunit manager. These principles apply to managers at all organization levels. Later sections consider the principles that apply to rank-and-file employees and those that apply to top executives. We illustrate these principles using the RI performance measure.

LEARNING OBJECTIVE 6

Understand the roles of salaries and incentives when rewarding managers

…balancing risk and performance-based rewards

The Basic Tradeoff: Creating Incentives versus Imposing Risk

How companies measure and evaluate the performance of managers and other employees affects their rewards. Compensation arrangements range from a flat salary with no performance-based incentive (or bonus), as in the case of many government employees, to rewards based solely on performance, as in the case of real estate agents who are compensated only via commissions paid on the properties they sell. The total compensation for most managers includes some combination of salary and performance-based incentive. In designing compensation arrangements, we need to consider the *tradeoff between creating incentives and imposing risk.* We illustrate this tradeoff in the context of our Hospitality Inns example.

Indra Chungi owns the Hospitality Inns chain of hotels. Roger Brett manages the Hospitality Inns San Francisco (HISF) hotel. Assume Chungi uses RI to measure performance. To improve the hotel's RI, Chungi would like Brett to increase its sales, control its costs, provide prompt and courteous customer service, and reduce the hotel's working capital. But even if Brett did all those things, a high RI is not guaranteed. HISF's RI is affected by many factors beyond Chungi's and Brett's control, such as a downturn in San Francisco's economy or road construction near the hotel that would make it difficult for customers to get to it.

As an entrepreneur, Chungi expects to bear risk. But Brett does not like being subject to risk. One way of "insuring" Brett against risk is to pay him a flat salary, regardless of the actual amount of RI the hotel earns. Chungi would then bear all of the risk. This arrangement creates a problem, however, because Brett's effort is difficult to monitor. The absence of performance-based compensation means that Brett has no direct incentive to work harder or to undertake extra physical and mental effort beyond what is necessary to hold onto his job.

Moral hazard describes a situation in which an employee prefers to exert less effort compared with the effort the owner desires because the owner cannot accurately monitor and enforce the employee's effort.[11] Moral hazard also occurs when an employee reports inaccurate or distorted information for personal benefit because the owner cannot monitor the validity of the reported information. Repetitive jobs, as in electronic assembly, are relatively

---

[10] The presentations here draw (in part) from teaching notes prepared by S. Huddart, N. Melumad, and S. Reichelstein.

[11] The term *moral hazard* originated in insurance contracts to represent situations in which insurance coverage caused insured parties to take less care of their properties than they might otherwise. One response to moral hazard in insurance contracts is the system of deductibles (that is, the insured parties pay for damages below a specified amount).

straightforward to monitor and so are less subject to moral hazard. However, a manager's job, which is to gather and interpret information and exercise judgment on the basis of the information obtained, is more difficult to monitor.

Paying no salary and rewarding Brett *only* on the basis of some performance measure—RI in our example—raises different concerns. In this case, Brett would be motivated to strive to increase the hotel's RI because his rewards would increase. But compensating Brett on RI also subjects him to risk because HISF's RI depends not only on Brett's effort, but also on factors such as local economic conditions over which Brett has no control.

Brett does not like being subject to risk. To compensate Brett for taking risk, Chungi must pay him extra compensation. That is, using performance-based bonuses will cost Chungi more money, *on average*, than paying Brett a flat salary. Why "on average"? Because Chungi's compensation payment to Brett will vary with RI outcomes. When averaged over these outcomes, the RI-based compensation will cost Chungi more than paying Brett a flat salary. The motivation for having some salary and some performance-based compensation is to balance the benefit of incentives against the extra cost of imposing risk on a manager.

Intensity of Incentives and Financial and Nonfinancial Measurements

What affects the intensity of incentives? That is, how large should the incentive component of a manager's compensation be relative to the salary component? To answer these questions, we need to understand how much the performance measure is affected by the actions the manager takes to further the owner's objectives.

Preferred performance measures are those that are sensitive to or that change significantly with the manager's performance. They do not change much with changes in factors that are beyond the manager's control. Sensitive performance measures motivate the manager and limit the manager's exposure to risk, reducing the cost of providing incentives. Less-sensitive performance measures are not affected by the manager's performance and fail to induce the manager to improve. The more owners have access to sensitive performance measures, the more they can rely on incentive compensation for their managers.

The salary component of compensation dominates when performance measures that are sensitive to managers' actions are not available. This is the case, for example, for some corporate staff and government employees. A high salary component, however, does not mean incentives are completely absent. Promotions and salary increases do depend on some overall measure of performance, but the incentives are less direct. The incentive component of compensation is high when sensitive performance measures are available and when monitoring the employee's effort is difficult, such as in real estate agencies.

To evaluate Brett, Chungi uses measures from multiple perspectives of the balanced scorecard because nonfinancial measures on the scorecard—employee satisfaction and the time taken for check-in, cleaning rooms, and providing room service—are more sensitive to Brett's actions. Financial measures such as RI are less sensitive to Brett's actions because they are affected by external factors, such as local economic conditions, beyond Brett's control. Residual income may capture the economic viability of the hotel, but it is only a partial measure of Brett's performance.

In addition to considerations of sensitivity and risk, another reason for using nonfinancial measures is that these measures follow Hospitality Inns' strategy and are drivers of future performance. Evaluating managers on these nonfinancial measures motivates them to take actions that will sustain the long-run performance of the firm's hotels while meeting the company's environmental and social goals. Therefore, evaluating performance in all four perspectives of the balanced scorecard promotes both short- and long-run actions. The relative weight placed on the various measures in the scorecard is ideally aimed at achieving congruence between the extent to which the manager is motivated to maximize each performance metric and its importance in generating the long-run objective the firm wishes to achieve. The tradeoff between considerations of sensitivity and risk, on the one hand, and the congruence of goals, on the other, determines the effective intensity of incentives placed on each measure of performance. Concepts in Action: Performance Measurement at Unilever illustrates the use of multiple measures to motivate a CEO to balance financial and nonfinancial (health and environmental sustainability) goals.

CONCEPTS IN ACTION ▶ Performance Measurement at Unilever

Kristoffer Tripplaar/Alamy Stock Photo

Managers and boards are often pushed to focus intently on a single measure of success, such as shareholder value or profit, and then do everything they can to maximize it. As a result, they can overlook other important measures, which can do long-term damage to a company.

Unilever, the Anglo-Dutch manufacturer of Axe body spray and Lipton tea, has taken a different approach under chief executive officer Paul Polman. On Polman's first day as CEO, Unilever did away with earnings guidance and quarterly reporting in order to refocus the company's metrics on the long-term needs of a full range of stakeholders. And in 2012, Unilever launched an ambitious plan to double revenue by 2020 while halving the company's environmental impact.

Dubbed the *Unilever Sustainable Living Plan*, the company is working to decouple financial growth from its impact on the environment and global health. Unilever's ambitious goals include improving financial performance while slashing its environmental footprint by 50%, sourcing 100% of its raw materials sustainably, and helping more than a billion people improve their health and well-being. Assessing the impact of its commitment means Unilever not only measures success based on its financial performance—including annual revenue, year-over-year revenue growth, and operating margin—but also how many calories it cuts from its ice cream products and how much of its energy use is derived from renewable sources.

Initially, investors took a dim view of Unilever's shift in perspective, punishing the stock price. But it quickly rebounded, after analysts and shareholders accepted Polman's wider lens. By the end of 2015, Unilever's growth found the company with more than 170,000 employees and a market value of nearly $130 billion.

Sources: Graham Kenny, "The False Promise of the Single Metric," *HBR.org*, August 26, 2015; Adi Ignatius, "Captain Planet," *Harvard Business Review*, June 2012; Graham Ruddick, "Unilever CEO Paul Polman–The Optimistic Pessimist," *The Guardian*, January 25, 2016; Andy Boynton and Margareta Barchan, "Unilever's Paul Polman: CEOs Can't Be 'Slaves' to Shareholders," *Forbes*, July 20, 2015.

Benchmarks and Relative Performance Evaluation

Owners often use financial and nonfinancial benchmarks to evaluate the performance of their managers. The benchmarks, which are metrics that correspond to the best practices of organizations, may be available inside or outside of the organization. For HISF, the benchmarks could be from similar hotels, either within or outside of the Hospitality Inns chain. Suppose Brett is responsible for HISF's revenues, costs, and investments. To evaluate Brett's performance, Chungi would want to benchmark a similar-sized hotel—one affected by the same uncontrollable factors, such as location, demographic trends, or economic conditions, that affect HISF. If all these factors were the same or very similar, the *differences* in the performances of the two hotels could, for the most part, be attributed to the differences in the two managers' performances. Benchmarking, which is also called *relative performance evaluation*, filters out the effects of the common uncontrollable factors.

Can the performance of two managers responsible for running similar operations within a company be benchmarked against each other? Yes, but this approach could create a problem: It could reduce the managers' incentives to help one another. When managers do not cooperate, the company suffers. In this case, using internal benchmarks for performance evaluation may not lead to goal congruence.

Performance Measures at the Individual Activity Level

Managers need to do two things when designing the measures used to evaluate the performance of individual employees: (1) design performance measures for activities that require multiple tasks and (2) design performance measures for activities done in teams.

Performing Multiple Tasks

Most employees perform more than one task as part of their jobs. Marketing representatives sell products, provide customer support, and gather market information. Manufacturing workers are responsible for both the quantity and quality of their output. Employers want employees to allocate their time and effort intelligently among various tasks or aspects of their jobs.

Consider mechanics at an auto repair shop. Their jobs have two distinct aspects: repair work—performing more repair work generates more revenues for the shop—and customer satisfaction—the higher the quality of the job, the more likely the customer will be pleased. If the employer wants an employee to focus on both aspects, then the employer must measure and compensate performance on both aspects.

Suppose the employer can easily measure the quantity, but not the quality, of auto repairs. If the employer rewards workers on a by-the-job rate, which pays workers only on the basis of the number of repairs actually performed, mechanics will likely increase the number of repairs they make and quality will suffer. Sears Auto Center experienced this problem when it introduced by-the-job rates for its mechanics. To resolve the problem, Sears took three steps to motivate workers to balance both quantity and quality: (1) The company dropped the by-the-job rate system and paid mechanics an hourly salary, a step that de-emphasized the quantity of repairs. Managers determined mechanics' bonuses, promotions, and pay increases on the basis of an assessment of each mechanic's overall quantity and quality of repairs. (2) Sears evaluated employees, in part, using the number of dissatisfied customers, the number of customer complaints, and data gathered from customer satisfaction surveys. (3) Finally, Sears used staff from an independent outside agency to randomly monitor whether the repairs performed were of high quality.

Team-Based Compensation Arrangements

Many manufacturing, marketing, and design problems can be resolved when employees with multiple skills, knowledge, experiences, and perceptions pool their talents. A team achieves better results than individual employees acting alone.[12] Many companies reward employees on teams based on how well their teams perform. Team-based incentives encourage individuals to help one another as they strive toward a common goal.

The specific forms of team-based compensation vary across companies. Colgate-Palmolive rewards teams based on each team's performance. Novartis, the Swiss pharmaceutical company, rewards teams based on the company's overall performance; some team-based bonuses are paid only if the company reaches certain goals. Eastman Chemical Company rewards team members using a checklist of team-based skills, such as communication and the willingness to help one another. Whether team-based compensation is desirable depends, to a large extent, on the culture and management style of a particular organization. One criticism of team-based compensation is that it diminishes the incentives of individual employees, which can harm a firm's overall performance. Another problem is how to manage team members who are not productive contributors to the team's success but who, nevertheless, share in the team's rewards.

Executive Performance Measures and Compensation

The principles of performance evaluation described in the previous sections also apply to executive compensation plans. These plans are based on both financial and nonfinancial performance measures and consist of a mix of (1) base salary; (2) annual incentives, such as a cash bonus based on achieving a target annual RI; (3) long-run incentives, such as stock options (described later in this section) based on a stock's performance over, say, a five-year period; and (4) other benefits, such as medical benefits, pension plans, and life insurance.

Well-designed plans use a compensation mix that balances risk (the effect of uncontrollable factors on the performance measure and hence compensation) with short-run and long-run incentives. For example, an evaluation based on a firm's annual EVA sharpens an executive's short-run focus. Using EVA and stock option plans over, say, five years motivates the executive to take a long-run view as well.

Stock options give executives the right to buy company stock at a specified price (called the exercise price) within a specified period. Suppose that on July 1, 2016, Hospitality Inns gave its CEO the option to buy 200,000 shares of the company's stock at any time before June 30, 2021, at the July 1, 2016, market price of $49 per share. Let's say Hospitality Inns'

---

[12] *Teams That Click: The Results-Driven Manager Series* (Boston: Harvard Business School Press, 2004).

stock price rises to $69 per share on March 24, 2020, and the CEO exercises his options on all 200,000 shares. The CEO would earn $20 per share ($69 − $49) on 200,000 shares, or $4 million. Alternatively, if Hospitality Inns' stock price stays below $49 during the entire five-year period, the CEO will simply forgo his right to buy the shares. By linking CEO compensation to increases in the company's stock price, the stock option plan motivates the CEO to improve the company's long-run performance and stock price.

The Securities and Exchange Commission (SEC) requires detailed disclosures of the compensation arrangements of top-level executives. For example, in 2016, Wyndham Worldwide, one of the world's largest hospitality companies, disclosed a compensation table showing the salaries, bonuses, stock options, other stock awards, and other compensation earned by its top five executives during the 2013, 2014, and 2015 fiscal years. Wyndham, whose brands include Days Inn, Howard Johnson, Ramada, and Travelodge, also disclosed the peer companies it uses to set the pay for its executives and conduct performance comparisons. These companies include competitors in the hospitality industry, such as Hyatt, Intercontinental, Marriott, and Starwood. The list also includes companies with similar revenues, market values, or business models (e.g., those that have franchise and brand portfolio operations) and firms with whom Wyndham competes for executive talent. Examples are Colgate Palmolive, Disney, Starbucks, and Yum Brands. Investors use this information to evaluate the relationship between compensation and performance across companies generally and across companies operating in similar industries.

SEC rules require companies to disclose the principles underlying their executive compensation plans. In its financial statements, Wyndham describes some of its compensation principles. They include supporting a high-performance environment by linking compensation with performance, attracting and retaining superior management talent, and aligning the interests of executives with those of shareholders. The SEC also compels companies to disclose the performance criteria—such as a firm's profitability, revenue growth, and market share—used to reward executives. Wyndham uses adjusted corporate and business unit EBIT, relative to target, as the basis for cash-based annual incentive pay. The Compensation Committee of the board of directors then reviews each executive's individual contributions and personal leadership together with their performance on strategic objectives, business development, and other initiatives in setting the final pay award. Wyndham also provides long-term incentives based on the company's stock price performance as well as realized earnings per share, relative to target. For fiscal years starting in 2017, the SEC has mandated an additional disclosure for public companies—the ratio of the CEO's annual total compensation to that of the median employee.

The Dodd-Frank law passed in 2010 in response to the financial crisis requires companies to provide shareholders with an advisory (nonbinding) vote on executive compensation. These "say-on-pay" votes must be held at least once every three years. They have reshaped the way companies create, disclose, and communicate their executive compensation policies. To date, however, they have not slowed down growth in executive pay or indicated much shareholder dissatisfaction with compensation plans. As of June, only 4 out of 344 S&P 500 companies had failed their say-on-pay votes in 2016, while 79% of companies received greater than 90% support.

DECISION POINT

Why are managers compensated based on a mix of salary and incentives?

Strategy and Levers of Control[13]

Financial and nonfinancial performance-evaluation measures help managers track their progress toward achieving a company's strategic goals. Because these measures help diagnose whether a company is performing to expectations, they are collectively called **diagnostic control systems**. Companies motivate managers by holding them accountable for and by rewarding them for meeting these goals. It's not unusual for managers to cut corners and misreport numbers to make their performance look better than it is, as happened at companies such as Enron, WorldCom, Tyco, and Health South. To prevent unethical and outright fraudulent behavior, companies need to balance the push for performance resulting from diagnostic control systems, the first of four levers of control, with three other levers: *boundary systems,*

LEARNING OBJECTIVE

Describe the four levers of control and why they are necessary

…boundary, belief, and interactive control systems counterbalance diagnostic control systems

---

[13] For a more detailed discussion, see Robert Simons, *Levers of Control: How Managers Use Innovative Control Systems to Drive Strategic Renewal* (Boston: Harvard Business School Press, 1995).

belief systems, and *interactive control systems*. This will ensure that proper business ethics, inspirational values, and attention to future threats and opportunities are not sacrificed while achieving business results.

Boundary Systems

Boundary systems describe standards of behavior and codes of conduct expected of all employees, especially actions that are off-limits. Ethical behavior on the part of managers is paramount. In particular, numbers that subunit managers' report should not be tainted by "cooking the books." The books should be free of, for example, overstated assets, understated liabilities, fictitious revenues, and understated costs.

Codes of business conduct signal appropriate and inappropriate individual behaviors. The following are excerpts from Caterpillar's "Worldwide Code of Conduct":

> While we conduct our business within the framework of applicable laws and regulations, for us, mere compliance with the law is not enough. We strive for more than that....We must not engage in activities that create, or even appear to create, conflict between our personal interests and the interests of the company.

Division managers who fail to adhere to legal or ethical accounting policies and procedures often rationalize their behavior by claiming they were under enormous pressure from top managers "to make the budget." A healthy amount of motivational pressure is desirable, as long as the "tone from the top" and the firm's code of conduct simultaneously communicate the absolute need for all managers to behave ethically at all times. Managers should also train employees to behave ethically. They should promptly and severely reprimand unethical conduct, regardless of the benefits that might accrue to the company from unethical actions. Some companies, such as Lockheed Martin, emphasize ethical behavior by routinely evaluating employees against the firm's code of ethics.

Many organizations also set explicit boundaries precluding actions that harm the environment. Environmental violations (such as water and air pollution) carry heavy fines and prison terms under the laws of the United States and other countries.

In many companies, the environmental responsibilities of employees extend beyond legal requirements. Some companies, such as DuPont, make environmental performance a line item on every employee's salary appraisal report. Duke Power Company appraises employees on measures such as reducing solid waste, cutting emissions and discharges, and implementing environmental plans. Socially responsible companies such as Best Buy, Campbell Soup, and Intel set aggressive environmental goals and measure and report their performance against them. German, Swiss, and Scandinavian companies report on environmental performance as part of a larger set of social responsibility disclosures (such as employee welfare and community development activities). In 2012, Dutch financial services giant ING began incorporating social, ethical, and environmental objectives as part of its top management's pay structure. Other firms in the Netherlands—including chemical company Akzo Nobel, life sciences group DSM, and mail operator TNT—also tie executive compensation to environmental improvement.

More broadly, there is growing awareness of the empirical business case for embedding sustainability into corporate operations. As a result, companies are integrating sustainability into traditional governance practices, including board oversight, and through corporate policies and management systems. About a quarter of companies link executive pay to some sustainability metrics, with a smaller percent making explicit links between compensation practices and publicly disclosed sustainability targets. At materials company Alcoa, 20 percent of executive compensation is tied to safety, environmental stewardship (including greenhouse gas reductions), energy efficiency, and diversity goals. Energy provider Excelon has an innovative long-term performance share award that, among other nonfinancial goals, rewards executives for engaging stakeholders to help shape the company's public policy positions. Xcel Energy ties compensation to goals achieved in "demand-side management," that is, reductions in energy consumption by its customers.

Belief Systems

Belief systems articulate the mission, purpose, and core values of a company. They describe the accepted norms and patterns of behavior expected of all managers and other employees when interacting with one another, shareholders, customers, and communities. For example, Johnson & Johnson describes its values and norms in a credo statement that is intended to inspire all managers and other employees to do their best.[14] Belief systems play to employees' *intrinsic motivation*, the desire to achieve self-satisfaction for performing well regardless of external rewards such as bonuses or promotion. Intrinsic motivation comes from being given greater responsibility, doing interesting and creative work, having pride in doing that work, making a commitment to the organization, and developing personal bonds with one's coworkers. High intrinsic motivation enhances a firm's performance because managers and workers feel a sense of achievement in doing something important, feel satisfied with their jobs, and see opportunities for personal growth.

Interactive Control Systems

Interactive control systems are formal information systems managers use to focus the company's attention and learning on key strategic issues. Managers use interactive control systems to create an ongoing dialogue around these key issues and to personally involve themselves in the decision-making activities of subordinates. An excessive focus on diagnostic control systems and critical performance variables can cause an organization to ignore emerging threats and opportunities—changes in technology, customer preferences, regulations, and competitors that can undercut a business. Interactive control systems help prevent this problem by highlighting and tracking strategic uncertainties businesses face, such as the emergence of digital imaging in the case of Kodak and Fujifilm, airline deregulation in the case of American Airlines, and the shift in customer preferences toward open-source Android operating systems in the case of BlackBerry. The key to this control lever is frequent face-to-face communications among managers and employees regarding these critical uncertainties. The result is ongoing discussion and debate about assumptions and action plans. New strategies emerge from the dialogue and debate surrounding the interactive process. Interactive control systems force busy managers to step back from the actions needed to manage the business today and to shift their focus forward to positioning the organization for the opportunities and threats of tomorrow.

> **DECISION POINT**
>
> What are the four levers of control, and why does a company need to implement them?

---

[14] A full statement of the credo can be accessed at www.jnj.com/about-jnj/jnj-credo.

PROBLEM FOR SELF-STUDY

The baseball division of Home Run Sports manufactures and sells baseballs. Assume production equals sales. Budgeted data for February 2017 are as follows:

Current assets	$ 400,000
Long-term assets	600,000
Total assets	$1,000,000
Production output	200,000 baseballs per month
Target ROI (Operating income ÷ Total assets)	30%
Fixed costs	$400,000 per month
Variable cost	$4 per baseball

1. Compute the minimum selling price per baseball necessary to achieve the target ROI of 30%.
2. Using the selling price from requirement 1, separate the target ROI into its two components using the DuPont method.
3. Compute the RI of the baseball division for February 2017, using the selling price from requirement 1. Home Run Sports uses a required rate of return of 12% on total division assets when computing division RI.

4. In addition to her salary, Amanda Kelly, the division manager, receives 3% of the monthly RI of the baseball division as a bonus. Compute Kelly's bonus. Why do you think Kelly is rewarded using both salary and a performance-based bonus? Kelly does not like bearing risk.

Solution

1.

$$\text{Target operating income} = 30\% \text{ of } \$1,000,000 \text{ of total assets}$$
$$= \$300,000$$
$$\text{Let } P = \text{Selling price}$$
$$\text{Revenues} - \text{Variable costs} - \text{Fixed costs} = \text{Operating income}$$
$$200,000P - (200,000 \times \$4) - \$400,000 = \$300,000$$
$$200,000P = \$300,000 + \$800,000 + \$400,000$$
$$= \$1,500,000$$
$$P = \$7.50 \text{ per baseball}$$

Proof:		
Revenues, 200,000 baseballs × $7.50/baseball		$1,500,000
Variable costs, 200,000 baseballs × $4/baseball		800,000
Contribution margin		700,000
Fixed costs		400,000
Operating income		$ 300,000

2. The DuPont method describes ROI as the product of two components: return on sales (income ÷ revenues) and investment turnover (revenues ÷ investment).

$$\frac{\text{Income}}{\text{Revenues}} \times \frac{\text{Revenues}}{\text{Investment}} = \frac{\text{Income}}{\text{Investment}}$$

$$\frac{\$300,000}{\$1,500,000} \times \frac{\$1,500,000}{\$1,000,000} = \frac{\$300,000}{\$1,000,000}$$

$$0.2 \times 1.5 = 0.30, \text{ or } 30\%$$

3. $RI = \text{Operating income} - \text{Required return on investment}$

$$= \$300,000 - (0.12 \times \$1,000,000)$$
$$= \$300,000 - \$120,000$$
$$= \$180,000$$

4. Kelly's bonus $= 3\%$ of RI

$$= 0.03 \times \$180,000 = \$5,400$$

The baseball division's RI is affected by many factors, such as general economic conditions, beyond Kelly's control. These uncontrollable factors make the baseball division's profitability uncertain and risky. Because Kelly does not like bearing risk, paying her a flat salary, regardless of RI, would shield her from this risk. But there is a moral-hazard problem with this compensation arrangement. Because Kelly's effort is difficult to monitor, the absence of performance-based compensation will provide her with no incentive to undertake extra physical and mental effort beyond what is necessary to retain her job or to uphold her personal values.

Paying no salary and rewarding Kelly only on the basis of RI provides her with incentives to work hard but also subjects her to excessive risk because of uncontrollable factors that will affect RI and hence Kelly's compensation. A compensation arrangement based only on RI would be costlier for Home Run Sports because it would have to compensate Kelly for taking on uncontrollable risk. A compensation arrangement that consists of both a salary and an RI-based performance bonus balances the benefits of incentives against the extra costs of imposing uncontrollable risk.

DECISION **POINTS**

The following question-and-answer format summarizes the chapter's learning objectives. Each decision presents a key question related to a learning objective. The guidelines are the answer to that question.

Decision	**Guidelines**
1. What financial and nonfinancial performance measures do companies use in their balanced scorecards?	Financial measures such as return on investment and residual income measure aspects of the performance of organizations, their subunits, managers, and employees. In many cases, financial measures are supplemented with nonfinancial measures of performance based on the customer, internal-business-process, and learning-and-growth perspectives of the balanced scorecard—for example, customer satisfaction, quality of products and services, employee satisfaction, and the achievement of environmental objectives.
2. What are the relative merits of return on investment (ROI), residual income (RI), and economic value added (EVA) as performance measures for subunit managers?	Return on investment (ROI) is the product of two components: income divided by revenues (return on sales) and revenues divided by investment (investment turnover). Managers can increase ROI by increasing revenues, decreasing costs, and decreasing the investment. But ROI may induce the managers of highly profitable divisions to reject projects in the firm's best interest because accepting the project reduces the ROI for their divisions.
	Residual income (RI) is income minus a dollar amount of required return on investment. RI is more likely than ROI to promote goal congruence. Evaluating managers on RI is also consistent with using the net present value method to choose long-term projects.
	Economic value added (EVA) is a variation of the RI calculation. It equals after-tax operating income minus the product of the (after-tax) weighted-average cost of capital and total assets minus current liabilities.
3. Over what time frame should companies measure performance, and what are the alternative choices for calculating the components of each performance measure?	A multiyear measure gives managers the incentive to consider the long-term consequences of their actions and prevents a myopic focus on short-run profits. When constructing accounting-based performance measures, firms must first define what constitutes investment. They must also choose whether the assets included in the investment calculations are measured at historical cost or current cost and whether depreciable assets are calculated at gross or net book value.
4. What targets should companies use, and when should they give feedback to managers regarding their performance relative to these targets?	Companies should tailor a budget to a particular subunit, a particular accounting system, and a particular performance measure. In general, asset valuation and income measurement problems can be overcome by emphasizing budgets and targets that stress continuous improvement. Timely feedback enables managers to implement actions that correct deviations from the target performance.
5. How can companies compare the performance of divisions operating in different countries?	Comparing the performance of divisions operating in different countries is difficult because of legal, political, social, economic, and currency differences. ROI and RI calculations for subunits operating in different countries need to be adjusted for differences in inflation between the two countries and changes in exchange rates.
6. Why are managers compensated based on a mix of salary and incentives?	Companies create incentives by rewarding managers on the basis of performance. But managers face risk because factors beyond their control may also affect their performance. Owners choose a mix of salary and incentive compensation to trade off the incentive benefit against the cost of imposing risk.

Decision	**Guidelines**
7. What are the four levers of control, and why does a company need to implement them?	The four levers of control are diagnostic control systems, boundary systems, belief systems, and interactive control systems. Implementing the four levers of control helps a company simultaneously strive for performance, behave ethically, inspire employees, and respond to strategic threats and opportunities.

TERMS TO LEARN

This chapter and the Glossary at the end of the book contain definitions of the following important terms:

belief systems (**p. 933**)
boundary systems (**p. 932**)
current cost (**p. 921**)
diagnostic control systems (**p. 931**)

economic value added
  (EVA®) (**p. 917**)
imputed cost (**p. 915**)
interactive control systems (**p. 933**)

investment (**p. 913**)
moral hazard (**p. 927**)
residual income (RI) (**p. 915**)
return on investment (ROI) (**p. 914**)

ASSIGNMENT MATERIAL

Pearson MyLab Accounting

Questions

23-1 Give examples of financial and nonfinancial performance measures that can be found in each of the four perspectives of the balanced scorecard.

23-2 What are the three steps in designing accounting-based performance measures?

23-3 What factors affecting ROI does the DuPont method of profitability analysis highlight?

23-4 "RI is not identical to ROI, although both measures incorporate income and investment into their computations." Do you agree? Explain.

23-5 Describe EVA.

23-6 Give three definitions of investment used in practice when computing ROI.

23-7 Distinguish between measuring assets based on current cost and historical cost.

23-8 What special problems arise when evaluating performance in multinational companies?

23-9 Why is it important to distinguish between the performance of a manager and the performance of the organization subunit for which the manager is responsible? Give an example.

23-10 Describe moral hazard.

23-11 "Managers should be rewarded only on the basis of their performance measures. They should be paid no salary." Do you agree? Explain.

23-12 Explain the role of benchmarking in evaluating managers.

23-13 Explain the incentive problems that can arise when employees must perform multiple tasks as part of their jobs.

23-14 Describe two disclosures required by the SEC with respect to executive compensation.

23-15 Describe the four levers of control.

Pearson MyLab Accounting

Multiple-Choice Questions

In partnership with:
BECKER PROFESSIONAL EDUCATION·

23-16 During the current year, a strategic business unit (SBU) within Roke Inc. saw costs increase by $2 million, revenues increase by $4 million, and assets decrease by $1 million. SBUs are set up by Roke as follows

  I. Cost SBU   **III.** Profit SBU
  II. Revenue SBU   **IV.** Investment SBU

Given the numbers above, a SBU manager will receive a favorable performance review if she is responsible for a:

a. I or IV only.   **c.** I, II, or IV only.
b. II or III only.   **d.** II, III, or IV only.

23-17 Assuming an increase in price levels over time, which of the following asset valuations will produce the highest return on assets?

a. Net book value
b. Gross book value
c. Replacement cost
d. Depreciated replacement cost

23-18 If ROI is used to evaluate a manager's performance for a relatively new division, which of the following measures for assets (or investment) will increase ROI?

a. Gross book value used instead of net book value.
b. Net book value using accelerated rather than straight-line depreciation.
c. Gross book value used instead of replacement cost, if gross book value is higher.
d. Replacement cost used instead of liquidation value, if replacement cost is higher.

23-19 The Long Haul Trucking Company is developing metrics for its drivers. The company computes variable costs of each load based upon miles driven and allocates fixed costs based upon time consumed. Load costing standards consider safe driving speeds and Department of Transportation regulations on hours of service (the amount of time the driver can be on duty or drive). The most effective metric for driver performance would likely be:

a. Contribution per mile driven.
b. Gross margin per mile driven.
c. Achievement of delivered loads in allowed times.
d. Percentage increase in delivered loads below standard.

23-20 ABC Inc. desires to maintain a capital structure of 80% equity and 20% debt. They currently have an effective tax rate of 30%. The company's cost of equity capital is 12%. To obtain their debt financing, they issue bonds with an interest rate of 10%. What is the company's weighted average cost of capital?

a. 8.0%   **c.** 11.0%
b. 10.4%   **d.** 11.6%

Exercises

Pearson MyLab Accounting

23-21 ROI, comparisons of three companies. (CMA, adapted) Return on investment (ROI) is often expressed as follows:

$$\frac{\text{Income}}{\text{Investment}} = \frac{\text{Income}}{\text{Revenues}} \times \frac{\text{Revenues}}{\text{Investment}}$$

1. What advantages are there in the breakdown of the computation into two separate components?
2. Fill in the blanks for the following table:

Required

	Companies in Same Industry		
	A	**B**	**C**
Revenues	$1,600,000	$1,300,000	?
Income	$ 96,000	$ 78,000	?
Investment	$ 800,000	?	$2,600,000
Income as a percentage of revenues	?	?	1.5%
Investment turnover	?	?	2.0
ROI	?	3%	?

After filling in the blanks, comment on the relative performance of these companies as thoroughly as the data permit.

23-22 Analysis of return on invested assets, comparison of two divisions, DuPont method. Performance Aid, Inc. has two divisions: Test Preparation and Language Arts. Results (in millions) for the past three years are partially displayed here:

	A	B	C	D	E	F	G
1		Operating Income	Operating Revenues	Total Assets	Operating Income/ Operating Revenues	Operating Revenues/ Total Assets	Operating Income/ Total Assets
2	Test Preparation Division						
3	2015	$ 630	$ 7,500	$1,500	?	?	?
4	2016	990	?	?	11%	?	44.0%
5	2017	1,110	?	?	12%	5.0	?
6	Language Arts Division						
7	2015	$ 650	$ 2,600	$1,625	?	?	?
8	2016	?	3,000	1,875	22.5%	?	?
9	2017	?	?	2,500	?	2.0	25.0%
10	Performance Aid, Inc.						
11	2015	$1,280	$10,100	$3,125	?	?	?
12	2016	?	?	?	?	?	?
13	2017	?	?	?	?	?	?

Required

1. Complete the table by filling in the blanks.
2. Use the DuPont method of profitability analysis to explain changes in the operating-income-to-total-assets ratios over the 2015–2017 period for each division and for Performance Aid as a whole. Comment on the results.

23-23 ROI and RI. (D. Kleespie, adapted) The Sports Equipment Company produces a wide variety of sports equipment. Its newest division, Golf Technology, manufactures and sells a single product—AccuDriver, a golf club that uses global positioning satellite technology to improve the accuracy of golfers' shots. The demand for AccuDriver is relatively insensitive to price changes. The following data are available for Golf Technology, which is an investment center for Sports Equipment:

Total annual fixed costs	$26,000,000
Variable cost per AccuDriver	$ 600
Number of AccuDrivers sold each year	170,000
Average operating assets invested in the division	$46,000,000

Required

1. Compute Golf Technology's ROI if the selling price of AccuDrivers is $800 per club.
2. If management requires an ROI of at least 25% from the division, what is the minimum selling price that the Golf Technology Division should charge per AccuDriver club?
3. Assume that Sports Equipment judges the performance of its investment centers on the basis of RI rather than ROI. What is the minimum selling price that Golf Technology should charge per AccuDriver if the company's required rate of return is 20%?

23-24 ROI and RI with manufacturing costs. Excellent Motor Company makes electric cars and has two products, the Simplegreen and the Excellentgreen. To produce the Simplegreen, Excellent Motor employed assets of $10,500,000 at the beginning of 2017 and $14,450,000 of assets at the end of 2017. Other costs to manufacture the Simplegreen include the following:

Direct materials	$5,000 per unit
Setup	$1,500 per setup-hour
Production	$ 415 per machine-hour

General administration and selling costs for Simplegreen total $7,820,000 in 2017. During the year, Excellent Motor produced 11,000 Simplegreen cars using 6,000 setup-hours and 139,000 machine-hours. It sold these cars for $12,000 each.

Required

1. Assuming that Excellent Motor defines investment as average assets during the period, what is the return on investment for the Simplegreen division?
2. Calculate the residual income for Simplegreen if Excellent Motor has a required rate of return of 16% on investments.

23-25 ROI, RI, EVA. Hamilton Corp. is a reinsurance and financial services company. Hamilton strongly believes in evaluating the performance of its stand-alone divisions using financial metrics such as ROI and residual income. For the year ended December 31, 2017, Hamilton's CFO received the following information about the performance of the property/casualty division:

Sales revenues	$ 900,000
Operating income	225,000
Total assets	1,500,000
Current liabilities	300,000
Debt (interest rate: 5%)	400,000
Common equity (book value)	500,000

For the purposes of divisional performance evaluation, Hamilton defines investment as total assets and income as operating income (that is, income before interest and taxes). The firm pays a flat rate of 25% in taxes on its income.

Required

1. What was the net income after taxes of the property/casualty division?
2. What was the division's ROI for the year?
3. Based on Hamilton's required rate of return of 8%, what was the property/casualty division's residual income for 2017?
4. Hamilton's CFO has heard about EVA and is curious about whether it might be a better measure to use for evaluating division managers. Hamilton's four divisions have similar risk characteristics. Hamilton's debt trades at book value while its equity has a market value approximately 150% that of its book value. The company's cost of equity capital is 10%. Calculate each of the following components of EVA for the property/casualty division, as well as the final EVA figure:
   a. Net operating profit after taxes
   b. Weighted-average cost of capital
   c. Investment, as measured for EVA calculations

23-26 Goal incongruence and ROI. Comfy Corporation manufactures furniture in several divisions, including the patio furniture division. The manager of the patio furniture division plans to retire in two years. The manager receives a bonus based on the division's ROI, which is currently 7%.

One of the machines that the patio furniture division uses to manufacture the furniture is rather old, and the manager must decide whether to replace it. The new machine would cost $35,000 and would last 10 years. It would have no salvage value. The old machine is fully depreciated and has no trade-in value. Comfy uses straight-line depreciation for all assets. The new machine, being new and more efficient, would save the company $5,000 per year in cash operating costs. The only difference between cash flow and net income is depreciation. The internal rate of return of the project is approximately 7%. Comfy Corporation's weighted-average cost of capital is 5%. Comfy is not subject to any income taxes.

Required

1. Should Comfy Corporation replace the machine? Why or why not?
2. Assume that "investment" is defined as average net long-term assets (that is, after depreciation) during the year. Compute the project's ROI for each of its first five years. If the patio furniture manager is interested in maximizing his bonus, would he replace the machine before he retires? Why or why not?
3. What can Comfy do to entice the manager to replace the machine before retiring?

23-27 ROI, RI, EVA. Performance Auto Company operates a new car division (that sells high-performance sports cars) and a performance parts division (that sells performance-improvement parts for family cars). Some division financial measures for 2017 are as follows:

	A	B New Car Division	C Performance Parts Division
2	Total assets	$33,000,000	$28,500,000
3	Current liabilities	$ 6,600,000	$ 8,400,000
4	Operating income	$ 2,475,000	$ 2,565,000
5	Required rate of return	12%	12%

Required

1. Calculate return on investment (ROI) for each division using operating income as a measure of income and total assets as a measure of investment.
2. Calculate residual income (RI) for each division using operating income as a measure of income and total assets minus current liabilities as a measure of investment.

3. William Abraham, the new car division manager, argues that the performance parts division has "loaded up on a lot of short-term debt" to boost its RI. Calculate an alternative RI for each division that is not sensitive to the amount of short-term debt taken on by the performance parts division. Comment on the result.

4. Performance Auto Company, whose tax rate is 40%, has two sources of funds: long-term debt with a market value of $18,000,000 at an interest rate of 10% and equity capital with a market value of $12,000,000 and a cost of equity of 15%. Applying the same weighted-average cost of capital (WACC) to each division, calculate EVA for each division.

5. Use your preceding calculations to comment on the relative performance of each division.

23-28 Capital budgeting, RI. Ryan Alcoa, a new associate at Jonas Partners, has compiled the following data for a potential investment for the firm:

Investment: $300,000

Annual sales revenues = $180,000

Annual cash costs = $80,000

4-year useful life, no salvage value

Jonas Partners faces a 30% tax rate on income and is aware that the tax authorities will only permit straight-line depreciation for tax purposes. The firm has an after-tax required rate of return of 8%.

Required

1. Based on net present value considerations, is this a project Jonas Partners would want to take?
2. Jonas Partners use straight-line depreciation for internal accounting and measure investment as the net book value of assets at the start of the year. Calculate the residual income in each year if the project were adopted.
3. Demonstrate that the conservation property of residual income, as described on page 920, holds in this example.
4. If Ryan Alcoa is evaluated on the residual income of the projects he undertakes, would he take this project? Explain.

23-29 Multinational performance measurement, ROI, RI. The Seaside Corporation manufactures similar products in the United States and Norway. The U.S. and Norwegian operations are organized as decentralized divisions. The following information is available for 2017; ROI is calculated as operating income divided by total assets:

	U.S. Division	Norwegian Division
Operating income	?	6,840,000 kroner
Total assets	$7,700,000	72,000,000 kroner
ROI	15.00%	?

Both investments were made on December 31, 2016. The exchange rate at the time of Seaside's investment in Norway on December 31, 2016, was 9 kroner = $1. During 2017, the Norwegian kroner decreased steadily in value so that the exchange rate on December 31, 2017, is 10 kroner = $1. The average exchange rate during 2017 is [(9 + 10) ÷ 2] = 9.5 kroner = $1.

Required

1. **a.** Calculate the U.S. division's operating income for 2017.
   b. Calculate the Norwegian division's ROI for 2017 in kroner.
2. Top management wants to know which division earned a better ROI in 2017. What would you tell them? Explain your answer.
3. Which division do you think had the better RI performance? Explain your answer. The required rate of return on investment (calculated in U.S. dollars) is 11%.

23-30 ROI, RI, EVA, and performance evaluation. Cora Manufacturing makes fashion products and competes on the basis of quality and leading-edge designs. The company has two divisions, clothing and cosmetics. Cora has $5,000,000 invested in assets in its clothing division. After-tax operating income from sales of clothing this year is $1,000,000. The cosmetics division has $12,500,000 invested in assets and an after-tax operating income this year of $2,000,000. The weighted-average cost of capital for Cora is 6%. The CEO of Cora has told the manager of each division that the division that "performs best" this year will get a bonus.

Required

1. Calculate the ROI and residual income for each division of Cora Manufacturing, and briefly explain which manager will get the bonus. What are the advantages and disadvantages of each measure?
2. The CEO of Cora Manufacturing has recently heard of another measure similar to residual income called EVA. The CEO has the accountant calculate adjusted incomes for clothing and cosmetics and finds that the adjusted after-tax operating incomes are $634,200 and $2,181,600, respectively. Also, the clothing division has $470,000 of current liabilities, while the cosmetics division has only $380,000 of

current liabilities. Using the preceding information, calculate the EVA for each division and discuss which manager will get the bonus.

3. What nonfinancial measures could Cora use to evaluate divisional performances?

23-31 Risk sharing, incentives, benchmarking, multiple tasks. Wonkies, Inc. is a large company that owns fast-food restaurants, has a soft drink division, and a snack division. Wonkies, Inc. corporate management gives its division managers considerable operating and investment autonomy in running their divisions. Wonkies, Inc. is considering how it should compensate Mark Hamm, the general manager of the snack division.

- Proposal 1 calls for paying Hamm a fixed salary.
- Proposal 2 calls for paying Hamm no salary and compensating him only on the basis of the division's RI, calculated based on operating income before any bonus payments.
- Proposal 3 calls for paying Hamm some salary and some bonus based on RI.

1. Evaluate the three proposals, specifying the advantages and disadvantages of each.

Required

2. Wonkies, Inc. competes against Galaxy Industries in the snack business. Galaxy is approximately the same size as the Wonkies snack division and operates in a business environment that is similar to Wonkies. The top management of Wonkies, Inc. is considering evaluating Hamm on the basis of his snack division's RI minus Galaxy's RI. Hamm complains that this approach is unfair because the performance of another company, over which he has no control, is included in his performance-evaluation measure. Is Hamm's complaint valid? Why or why not?
3. Now suppose that Hamm has no authority for making capital-investment decisions. Corporate management makes these decisions. Is RI a good performance measure to use to evaluate Hamm? Is RI a good measure to evaluate the economic viability of snack division? Explain.
4. The salespeople for the snack division of Wonkies, Inc. are responsible for selling and providing customer service and support. Sales are easy to measure. Although customer service is important to the snack division in the long run, it has not yet implemented customer-service measures. Hamm wants to compensate his sales force only on the basis of sales commissions paid for each unit of product sold. He cites two advantages to this plan:
   a. It creates strong incentives for the sales force to work hard, and
   b. the company pays salespeople only when the company itself is earning revenues.

Do you agree with this plan? Why or why not?

23-32 Residual income and EVA; timing issues. Doorchime Company makes doorbells. It has a weighted-average cost of capital of 6% and total assets of $5,690,000. Doorchime has current liabilities of $550,000. Its operating income for the year was $630,000. Doorchime does not have to pay any income taxes. One of the expenses for accounting purposes was a $70,000 advertising campaign run in early January. The entire amount was deducted this year, although the Doorchime CEO believes the beneficial effects of this advertising will last 4 years.

1. Calculate residual income, assuming Doorchime defines investment as total assets.

Required

2. Calculate EVA for the year. Adjust both the year-end assets and operating income for advertising assuming that for the purposes of economic value added the advertising is capitalized and amortized on a straight-line basis over 4 years.
3. Discuss the difference between the outcomes of requirements 1 and 2. Which measure would you recommend, and why?

Problems

Pearson MyLab Accounting

23-33 ROI performance measures based on historical cost and current cost. Nature's Juice Corporation operates three divisions that process and bottle natural fruit juices. The historical-cost accounting system reports the following information for 2017:

	Passion Fruit Division	Kiwi Fruit Division	Mango Fruit Division
Revenues	$1,300,000	$1,800,000	$2,400,000
Operating costs			
(excluding plant depreciation)	550,000	1,050,000	900,000
Plant depreciation	270,000	175,000	290,000
Operating income	$ 480,000	$ 575,000	$1,210,000
Current assets	$ 425,000	$ 600,000	$ 700,000
Long-term assets—plant	540,000	1,575,000	3,190,000
Total assets	$ 965,000	$2,175,000	$3,890,000

Nature's Juice estimates the useful life of each plant to be 12 years, with no terminal disposal value. The straight-line depreciation method is used. At the end of 2017, the passion fruit plant is 10 years old, the kiwi fruit plant is 3 years old, and the mango fruit plant is 1 year old. An index of construction costs over the 10-year period that Nature's Juice has been operating (2007 year-end = 100) is as follows:

2007	2014	2016	2017
100	120	185	200

Given the high turnover of current assets, management believes that the historical-cost and current-cost measures of current assets are approximately the same.

Required

1. Compute the ROI ratio (operating income to total assets) of each division using historical-cost measures. Comment on the results.
2. Use the approach in Exhibit 23-2 (page 922) to compute the ROI of each division, incorporating current-cost estimates as of 2017 for depreciation expense and long-term assets. Comment on the results.
3. What advantages might arise from using current-cost asset measures as compared with historical-cost measures for evaluating the performance of the managers of the three divisions?

23-34 ROI, measurement alternatives for performance measures Appleton's owns and operates a variety of casual dining restaurants in three cities: St. Louis, Memphis, and New Orleans. Each geographic market is considered a separate division. The St. Louis division includes four restaurants, each built in early 2007. The Memphis division consists of three restaurants, each built in January 2011. The New Orleans division is the newest, consisting of three restaurants built 4 years ago. Division managers at Appleton's are evaluated on the basis of ROI. The following information refers to the three divisions at the end of 2017:

	Home	Insert	Page Layout	Formulas	Data	Review	View
	A			B	C	D	E
1				St. Louis	Memphis	New Orleans	Total
2	Division revenues			$17,336,000	$12,050,000	$10,890,000	$40,276,000
3	Division expenses			15,890,000	11,042,000	9,958,000	36,890,000
4	Division operating income			1,446,000	1,008,000	932,000	3,386,000
5	Gross book value of long-term assets			9,000,000	7,500,000	8,100,000	24,600,000
6	Accumulated depreciation			6,600,000	3,500,000	2,160,000	12,260,000
7	Current assets			1,999,600	1,536,400	1,649,200	5,185,200
8	Depreciation expense			600,000	500,000	540,000	1,640,000
9	Construction cost index for year of construction			100	110	118	

Required

1. Calculate ROI for each division using net book value of total assets.
2. Using the technique in Exhibit 23-2, compute ROI using current-cost estimates for long-term assets and depreciation expense. The construction cost index for 2017 is 122. Estimated useful life of operational assets is 15 years.
3. How does the choice of long-term asset valuation affect management decisions regarding new capital investments? Why might this choice be more significant to the St. Louis division manager than to the New Orleans division manager?

23-35 Multinational firms, differing risk, comparison of profit, ROI, and RI. Newmann, Inc. has divisions in the United States, France, and Australia. The U.S. division is the oldest and most established of the three and has a cost of capital of 6%. The French division was started four years ago when the exchange rate for the Euro was 1 Euro = $1.34 USD. The French division has a cost of capital of 8%. The division in Australia was started this year, when the exchange rate was 1 Australian Dollar (AUD) = $0.87 USD. Its cost of capital is 11%. Average exchange rates for the current year are 1 euro = $1.07 and 1 AUD = $0.74 USD. Other information for the three divisions includes:

	United States	France	Australia
Long-term assets	$22,048,000	11,422,761 euros	8,798,851 AUD
Operating revenues	$31,826,170	7,023,860 euros	4,509,628 AUD
Operating expenses	$26,738,330	4,980,290 euros	3,216,892 AUD
Income-tax rate	35%	30%	20%

1. Translate the French and Australian information into dollars to make the divisions comparable. Find the after-tax operating income for each division and compare the profits.
2. Calculate ROI using after-tax operating income. Compare among divisions.
3. Use after-tax operating income and the individual cost of capital of each division to calculate residual income and compare.
4. Redo requirement 2 using pretax operating income instead of net income. Why is there a big difference, and what does this mean for performance evaluation?

23-36 ROI, RI, DuPont method, investment decisions, balanced scorecard. News Report Group has two major divisions: Print and Internet. Summary financial data (in millions) for 2016 and 2017 are as follows:

	Home	Insert	Page Layout	Formulas	Data	Review	View		
	A	B	C	D	E	F	G	H	I
1		Operating Income			Revenues			Total Assets	
2		2016	2017		2016	2017		2016	2017
3	Print	$3,720	$4,500		$18,700	$22,500		$18,200	$25,000
4	Internet	525	690		25,000	23,000		11,150	10,000

The two division managers' annual bonuses are based on division ROI (defined as operating income divided by total assets). If a division reports an increase in ROI from the previous year, its management is automatically eligible for a bonus; however, the management of a division reporting a decline in ROI has to present an explanation to the News Report Group board and is unlikely to get any bonus.

Carol Mays, manager of the Print division, is considering a proposal to invest $2,580 million in a new computerized news reporting and printing system. It is estimated that the new system's state-of-the-art graphics and ability to quickly incorporate late-breaking news into papers will increase 2018 division operating income by $360 million. News Report Group uses a 10% required rate of return on investment for each division.

1. Use the DuPont method of profitability analysis to explain differences in 2017 ROIs between the two divisions. Use 2017 total assets as the investment base.
2. Why might Mays be less than enthusiastic about accepting the investment proposal for the new system despite her belief in the benefits of the new technology?
3. John Mendenhall, CEO of News Report Group, is considering a proposal to base division executive compensation on division RI.
   a. Compute the 2017 RI of each division.
   b. Would adoption of an RI measure reduce Mays's reluctance to adopt the new computerized system investment proposal?
4. Mendenhall is concerned that the focus on annual ROI could have an adverse long-run effect on News Report Group's customers. What other measurements, if any, do you recommend that Mendenhall use? Explain briefly.

23-37 Division managers' compensation, levers of control (continuation of 23-36). John Mendenhall seeks your advice on revising the existing bonus plan for division managers of News Report Group. Assume division managers do not like bearing risk. Mendenhall is considering three ideas:

- Make each division manager's compensation depend on division RI.
- Make each division manager's compensation depend on company-wide RI.
- Use benchmarking and compensate division managers on the basis of their division's RI minus the RI of the other division.

1. Evaluate the three ideas Mendenhall has put forth using performance-evaluation concepts described in this chapter. Indicate the positive and negative features of each proposal.
2. Mendenhall is concerned that the pressure for short-run performance may cause managers to cut corners. What systems might Mendenhall introduce to avoid this problem? Explain briefly.
3. Mendenhall is also concerned that the pressure for short-run performance might cause managers to ignore emerging threats and opportunities. What system might Mendenhall introduce to prevent this problem? Explain briefly.

23-38 Executive compensation, balanced scorecard. Acme Company recently introduced a new bonus plan for its corporate executives. The company believes that current profitability and customer satisfaction levels are equally important to the company's long-term success. As a result, the new plan awards a bonus equal to 0.5% of salary for each 1% increase in business unit net income or 1% increase in the business unit's customer satisfaction index. For example, increasing net income from $1 million to $1.1 million (or 10% from its initial value) leads to a bonus of 5% of salary, while increasing the business unit's customer satisfaction index from 50 to 60 (or 20% from its initial value) leads to a bonus of 10% of salary. There is no bonus penalty when net income or customer satisfaction declines. In 2016 and 2017, Acme's three business units reported the following performance results:

	Retail Sales		Online Sales		Wholesale Sales	
	2016	**2017**	**2016**	**2017**	**2016**	**2017**
Net income	$730,000	$811,900	$1,218,000	$1,557,479	$1,062,540	$1,108,123
Customer satisfaction	87	93	78.3	75	65.7	72.9

Required

1. Compute the bonus as a percent of salary earned by each business unit executive in 2017.
2. What factors might explain the differences between improvement rates for net income and those for customer satisfaction in the three units? Are increases in customer satisfaction likely to result in increased net income right away?
3. Acme's board of directors is concerned that the 2017 bonus awards may not accurately reflect the executives' overall performance. In particular, the board is concerned that executives can earn large bonuses by doing well on one performance dimension but underperforming on the other. What changes can it make to the bonus plan to prevent this from happening in the future? Explain briefly.

23-39 Financial and nonfinancial performance measures, goal congruence. (CMA, adapted) Precision Equipment specializes in the manufacture of medical equipment, a field that has become increasingly competitive. Approximately 2 years ago, Pedro Mendez, president of Precision, decided to revise the bonus plan (based, at the time, entirely on operating income) to encourage division managers to focus on areas that were important to customers and that added value without increasing cost. In addition to a profitability incentive, the revised plan includes incentives for reduced rework costs, reduced sales returns, and on-time deliveries. The company calculates and rewards bonuses semiannually on the following basis: A base bonus is calculated at 2% of operating income; this amount is then adjusted as follows:

a. (i) Reduced by excess of rework costs over and above 2% of operating income
   (ii) No adjustment if rework costs are less than or equal to 2% of operating income
b. (i) Increased by $4,000 if more than 98% of deliveries are on time and by $1,500 if 96–98% of deliveries are on time
   (ii) No adjustment if on-time deliveries are below 96%
c. (i) Increased by $2,500 if sales returns are less than or equal to 1.5% of sales
   (ii) Decreased by 50% of excess of sales returns over 1.5% of sales

If the calculation of the bonus results in a negative amount for a particular period, the manager simply receives no bonus, and the negative amount is not carried forward to the next period.

Results for Precision's Central division and Western division for 2017, the first year under the new bonus plan, follow. In 2016, under the old bonus plan, the Central division manager earned a bonus of $20,295 and the Western division manager received a bonus of $15,830.

	Central Division		Western Division	
	Jan. 1, 2017, to June 30, 2017	**July 1, 2017, to Dec. 31, 2017**	**Jan. 1, 2017, to June 30, 2017**	**July 1, 2017, to Dec. 31, 2017**
Revenues	$3,150,000	$3,300,000	$2,137,500	$2,175,000
Operating income	$346,500	$330,000	$256,500	$304,500
On-time delivery	95.4%	97.3%	98.2%	94.6%
Rework costs	$8,625	$8,250	$4,500	$6,000
Sales returns	$63,000	$52,500	$33,560	$31,875

Required

1. Why did Mendez need to introduce these new performance measures? That is, why does Mendez need to use these performance measures in addition to the operating-income numbers for the period?
2. Calculate the bonus earned by each manager for each 6-month period and for 2017 overall.
3. What effect did the change in the bonus plan have on each manager's behavior? Did the new bonus plan achieve what Mendez wanted? What changes, if any, would you make to the new bonus plan?

23-40 RI, decision making. The following data refer to Clear Panes, a division of Global Corporation. Clear Panes makes and sells residential windows that sell for $150 each. Clear Panes expects sales of 150,000 units in 2017. Clear Panes' annual fixed costs are $2,750,000 and their variable cost is $90 per window.

Global evaluates Clear Panes based on residual income. The total investment attributed to Clear Panes is $12 million and the required rate of return on investment is 16%.

Ignore taxes and depreciation expense. Answer each of the following parts *independently*, unless otherwise stated.

Required

1. What is the expected residual income in 2017?
2. Clear Panes receives an external special order for 10,000 units at $120 each. If the order is accepted, Clear Panes will have to incur incremental fixed costs of $250,000 and invest an additional $450,000 in various assets. What is the effect on Clear Panes's residual income of accepting the order?
3. The window latch Clear Panes manufactures for its windows has a variable cost of $20. An outside vendor has offered to supply the 150,000 units required at a cost of $21 per unit. If the component is purchased outside, fixed costs will decline by $100,000 and assets with a book value of $150,000 will be sold at book value. Will Clear Panes decide to make or buy the component? Explain your answer.
4. One of Clear Panes's regular customers asks for a special window with stained glass inserts. The customer requires 2,500 of these windows. Clear Panes estimates its variable cost for these special units at $105 each. Clear Panes will also have to undertake new investment of $300,000 to produce these windows. What is the minimum selling price that will make the deal acceptable to Clear Panes?
5. Assume the same facts as in requirement 4. Also suppose that the customer has offered $130 for each stained glass window. In addition, the customer has indicated that its purchases of the existing product will drop by 1,500 units.
   a. What is the net change in Clear Panes's residual income from taking the offer, relative to its planned 2017 situation?
   b. At what drop in unit sales of the regular window would Clear Panes be indifferent to the offer?

23-41 Ethics, levers of control. Zuzu is a large manufacturer of snack cakes. The company operates distribution centers in Chicago. The distribution center bakes and packages the snack cakes and ships them to grocery warehouses throughout the country. Because of the high standards set for both quality and appearance, there is a reasonable number of "seconds" that do not meet standards and are sold to company outlets for sale at reduced prices. In recent years, the company's average yield has been 90% of first-quality products for sale to grocery warehouses. The remaining 10% is sent to the outlet store. Zuzu's performance-evaluation system pays its distribution center managers substantial bonuses if the company achieves annual budgeted profit numbers. In the last quarter of 2017, Noah Spalding, Zuzu's controller, noted a significant increase in yield percentage of the Chicago distribution center, from 90% to 98%. This increase resulted in a 10% increase in the center's profits.

During a recent trip to the Chicago center, Spalding wandered into the snack cake warehouse. He noticed that most of the snack cake "seconds" were being packed and sent off to grocery warehouses instead of being sent to the outlet stores. When he asked one of the workers, he was told that the center's manager had directed workers to stop sending all the "seconds" to the outlet except for the extremely damaged packages. This practice resulted in the center overreporting both yield and ending inventory of normal, saleable product. The overstatement of Chicago inventory will have a significant impact on Zuzu's financial statements.

Required

1. What should Spalding do? You may want to refer to the *IMA Statement of Ethical Professional Practice*, page 17.
2. Which lever of control is Zuzu emphasizing? What changes, if any, should be made?

23-42 RI, EVA, measurement alternatives, goal congruence. Refresh Resorts, Inc., operates health spas in Key West, Florida; Phoenix, Arizona; and Carmel, California. The Key West spa was the company's first and opened in 1991. The Phoenix spa opened in 2004, and the Carmel spa opened in 2013. Refresh Resorts has previously evaluated divisions based on RI, but the company is considering changing to an EVA approach. All spas are assumed to face similar risks. Data for 2017 are:

	A	B	C	D	E
	Home Insert Page Layout Formulas Data Review View				
		Key West	Phoenix	Carmel	Total
1					
2	Revenues	$4,100,000	$4,380,000	$3,230,000	$11,710,000
3	Variable costs	1,600,000	1,630,000	955,000	4,185,000
4	Fixed costs	1,280,000	1,560,000	980,000	3,820,000
5	Operating income	1,220,000	1,190,000	1,295,000	3,705,000
6	Interest costs on long-term debt at 8%	368,000	416,000	440,000	1,224,000
7	Income before taxes	852,000	774,000	855,000	2,481,000
8	Net income after 35% taxes	553,800	503,100	555,750	1,612,650
9					
10	Net book value at 2017 year-end:				
11	Current assets	$1,280,000	$ 850,000	$ 600,000	$ 2,730,000
12	Long-term assets	4,875,000	5,462,000	6,835,000	17,172,000
13	Total assets	6,155,000	6,312,000	7,435,000	19,902,000
14					
15	Current liabilities	330,000	265,000	84,000	679,000
16	Long-term debt	4,600,000	5,200,000	5,500,000	15,300,000
17	Stockholders' equity	1,225,000	847,000	1,851,000	3,923,000
18	Total liabilities and stockholders' equity	6,155,000	6,312,000	7,435,000	19,902,000
19					
20	Market value of debt				$15,300,000
21	Market value of equity				7,650,000
22	Cost of equity capital				14%
23	Required rate of return				11%
24	Accumulated depreciation on long-term assets	$2,200,000	$1,510,000	$ 220,000	

Required

1. Calculate RI for each of the spas based on operating income and using total assets as the measure of investment. Suppose that the Key West spa is considering adding a new group of saunas from Finland that will cost $225,000. The saunas are expected to bring in operating income of $22,000. What effect would this project have on the RI of the Key West spa? Based on RI, would the Key West manager accept or reject this project? Without resorting to calculations, would the other managers accept or reject the project? Why?

2. Why might Refresh Resorts want to use EVA instead of RI for evaluating the performance of the three spas?

3. Refer back to the original data. Calculate the WACC for Refresh Resorts.

4. Refer back to the original data. Calculate EVA for each of the spas, using net book value of long-term assets. Calculate EVA again, this time using gross book value of long-term assets. Comment on the differences between the two methods.

5. How does the selection of asset measurement method affect goal congruence?

Appendix A

Notes on Compound Interest and Interest Tables

Interest is the cost of using money. It is the rental charge for funds, just as renting a building and equipment entails a rental charge. When the funds are used for a period of time, it is necessary to recognize interest as a cost of using the borrowed ("rented") funds. This requirement applies even if the funds represent ownership capital and if interest does not entail an outlay of cash. Why must interest be considered? Because the selection of one alternative automatically commits a given amount of funds that could otherwise be invested in some other alternative.

Interest is generally important, even when short-term projects are under consideration. Interest looms correspondingly larger when long-run plans are studied. The rate of interest has significant enough impact to influence decisions regarding borrowing and investing funds. For example, $100,000 invested now and compounded annually for 10 years at 8% will accumulate to $215,900; at 20%, the $100,000 will accumulate to $619,200.

Interest Tables

Many computer programs and pocket calculators are available that handle computations involving the time value of money. You may also turn to the following four basic tables to compute interest.

Table 1—Future Amount of $1

Table 1 shows how much $1 invested now will accumulate in a given number of periods at a given compounded interest rate per period. Consider investing $1,000 now for three years at 8% compound interest. A tabular presentation of how this $1,000 would accumulate to $1,259.70 follows:

Year	Interest per Year	Cumulative Interest Called Compound Interest	Total at End of Year
0	$ —	$ —	$1,000.00
1	80.00 (0.08 × $1,000)	80.00	1,080.00
2	86.40 (0.08 × $1,080)	166.40	1,166.40
3	93.30 (0.08 × $1,166.40)	259.70	1,259.70

This tabular presentation is a series of computations that could appear as follows, where S is the future amount and the subscripts 1, 2, and 3 indicate the number of time periods.

$$S_1 = \$1,000\,(1.08)^1 = \$1,080$$

$$S_2 = \$1,080\,(1.08) = \$1,000\,(1.08)^2 = \$1,166.40$$

$$S_3 = \$1,166.40 \times (1.08) = \$1,000\,(1.08)^3 = \$1,259.70$$

The formula for the "future amount of P," often called the "future value of P," or "compound amount of P," can be written as follows:

$$S = P(1 + r)^n$$

S is the future value amount; P is the present value, r is the rate of interest; and n is the number of time periods.

When $P = \$1{,}000$, $n = 3$, $r = 0.08$, $S = \$1{,}000(1 + .08)^3 = \$1{,}259.70$.

Fortunately, tables make key computations readily available. A facility in selecting the *proper* table will minimize computations. Check the accuracy of the preceding answer using Table 1, page 951.

Table 2—Present Value of $1

In the previous example, if $1,000 compounded at 8% per year will accumulate to $1,259.70 in three years, then $1,000 must be the present value of $1,259.70 due at the end of three years. The formula for the present value can be derived by reversing the process of *accumulation* (finding the future amount) that we just finished.

If

$$S = P(1 + r)^n$$

then

$$P = \frac{S}{(1 + r)^n}$$

In our example, $S = \$1{,}259.70$, $n = 3$, $r = 0.08$, so

$$P = \frac{\$1{,}259.70}{(1.08)^3} = \$1{,}000$$

Use Table 2, page 952, to check this calculation.

When accumulating, we advance or roll forward in time. The difference between our original amount and our accumulated amount is called *compound interest*. When discounting, we retreat or roll back in time. The difference between the future amount and the present value is called *compound discount*. Note the following formulas:

$$\text{Compound interest} = P[(1 + r)^n - 1]$$

In our example, $P = \$1{,}000$, $n = 3$, $r = 0.08$, so

$$\text{Compound interest} = \$1{,}000[(1.08)^3 - 1] = \$259.70$$

$$\text{Compound discount} = S\left[1 - \frac{1}{(1 + r)^n}\right]$$

In our example, $S = \$1{,}259.70$, $n = 3$, $r = 0.08$, so

$$\text{Compound discount} = \$1{,}259.70\left[1 - \frac{1}{(1.08)^3}\right] = \$259.70$$

Table 3—Compound Amount (Future Value) of Annuity of $1

An (ordinary) *annuity* is a series of equal payments (receipts) to be paid (or received) at the end of successive periods of equal length. Assume that $1,000 is invested at the end of each of three years at 8%:

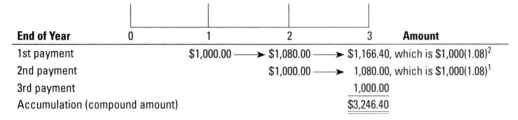

End of Year	0	1	2	3	Amount
1st payment		$1,000.00 ⟶	$1,080.00 ⟶	$1,166.40, which is $1,000(1.08)^2	
2nd payment			$1,000.00 ⟶	1,080.00, which is $1,000(1.08)^1	
3rd payment				1,000.00	
Accumulation (compound amount)				$3,246.40	

The preceding arithmetic may be expressed algebraically as the future value of an ordinary annuity of $1,000 for 3 years $= \$1,000(1 + r^2) + \$1,000(1 + r)^1 + \$1,000$.

We can develop the general formula for S_n, the future value of an ordinary annuity of $1, by using the preceding example as a basis where $n = 3$ and $r = 0.08$:

1. $S_3 = 1 + (1 + r)^1 + (1 + r)^2$
2. Substitute $r = 0.08$: $S_3 = 1 + (1.08)^1 + (1.08)^2$
3. Multiply (2) by $(1 + r)$: $(1.08)\,S_3 = (1.08)^1 + (1.08)^2 + (1.08)^3$
4. Subtract (2) from (3): Note that all terms on the right-hand side are removed except $(1.08)^3$ in equation (3) and 1 in equation (2). $1.08S_3 - S_3 = (1.08)^3 - 1$
5. Factor (4): $S_3(1.08 - 1) = (1.08)^3 - 1$
6. Divide (5) by $(1.08 - 1)$:

$$S_3 = \frac{(1.08)^3 - 1}{1.08 - 1} = \frac{(1.08)^3 - 1}{0.08} = \frac{0.2597}{0.08} = 3.246$$

7. The general formula for the future value of an ordinary annuity of $1 becomes:

$$S_n = \frac{(1 + r)^n - 1}{r} \text{ or } \frac{\text{Compound interest}}{\text{Rate}}$$

This formula is the basis for Table 3, page 953. Check the answer in the table.

Table 4—Present Value of an Ordinary Annuity of $1

Using the same example as for Table 3, we can show how the formula of P_n, the present value of an ordinary annuity, is developed.

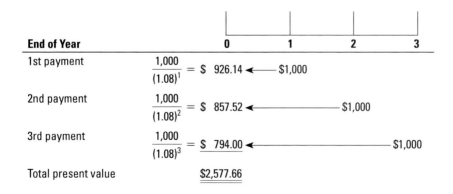

End of Year		0	1	2	3
1st payment	$\dfrac{1,000}{(1.08)^1} = \$ \ 926.14$ ⟵	$1,000			
2nd payment	$\dfrac{1,000}{(1.08)^2} = \$ \ 857.52$ ⟵			$1,000	
3rd payment	$\dfrac{1,000}{(1.08)^3} = \$ \ 794.00$ ⟵				$1,000
Total present value	$2,577.66				

We can develop the general formula for P_n by using the preceding example as a basis where $n = 3$ and $r = 0.08$:

1.

$$P_3 = \frac{1}{1 + r} + \frac{1}{(1 + r)^2} + \frac{1}{(1 + r)^3}$$

2. Substitute $r = 0.08$:

$$P_3 = \frac{1}{1.08} + \frac{1}{(1.08)^2} + \frac{1}{(1.08)^3}$$

3. Multiply (2) by $\frac{1}{1.08}$:

$$P_3 \frac{1}{1.08} = \frac{1}{(1.08)^2} + \frac{1}{(1.08)^3} + \frac{1}{(1.08)^4}$$

4. Subtract (3) from (2):

$$P_3 - P_3 \frac{1}{1.08} = \frac{1}{1.08} - \frac{1}{(1.08)^4}$$

5. Factor (4):

$$P_3\left(1 - \frac{1}{(1.08)}\right) = \frac{1}{1.08}\left[1 - \frac{1}{(1.08)^3}\right]$$

6. or

$$P_3\left(\frac{0.08}{1.08}\right) = \frac{1}{1.08}\left[1 - \frac{1}{(1.08)^3}\right]$$

7. Multiply (6) by $\frac{1.08}{0.08}$:

$$P_3 = \frac{1}{0.08}\left[1 - \frac{1}{(1.08)^3}\right] = \frac{0.2062}{0.08} = 2.577$$

The general formula for the present value of an annuity of $1.00 is as follows:

$$P_n = \frac{1}{r}\left[1 - \frac{1}{(1 + r)^n}\right] = \frac{\text{Compound discount}}{\text{Rate}}$$

The formula is the basis for Table 4, page 954. Check the answer in the table. The present value tables, Tables 2 and 4, are used most frequently in capital budgeting.

The tables for annuities are not essential. With Tables 1 and 2, compound interest and compound discount can readily be computed. It is simply a matter of dividing either of these by the rate to get values equivalent to those shown in Tables 3 and 4.

TABLE 1

Compound Amount of $1.00 (The Future Value of $1.00)

$S = P(1 + r)^n$. In this table $P = \$1.00$

Periods	2%	4%	6%	8%	10%	12%	14%	16%	18%	20%	22%	24%	26%	28%	30%	32%	40%	Periods
1	1.020	1.040	1.060	1.080	1.100	1.120	1.140	1.160	1.180	1.200	1.220	1.240	1.260	1.280	1.300	1.320	1.400	1
2	1.040	1.082	1.124	1.166	1.210	1.254	1.300	1.346	1.392	1.440	1.488	1.538	1.588	1.638	1.690	1.742	1.960	2
3	1.061	1.125	1.191	1.260	1.331	1.405	1.482	1.561	1.643	1.728	1.816	1.907	2.000	2.097	2.197	2.300	2.744	3
4	1.082	1.170	1.262	1.360	1.464	1.574	1.689	1.811	1.939	2.074	2.215	2.364	2.520	2.684	2.856	3.036	3.842	4
5	1.104	1.217	1.338	1.469	1.611	1.762	1.925	2.100	2.288	2.488	2.703	2.932	3.176	3.436	3.713	4.007	5.378	5
6	1.126	1.265	1.419	1.587	1.772	1.974	2.195	2.436	2.700	2.986	3.297	3.635	4.002	4.398	4.827	5.290	7.530	6
7	1.149	1.316	1.504	1.714	1.949	2.211	2.502	2.826	3.185	3.583	4.023	4.508	5.042	5.629	6.275	6.983	10.541	7
8	1.172	1.369	1.594	1.851	2.144	2.476	2.853	3.278	3.759	4.300	4.908	5.590	6.353	7.206	8.157	9.217	14.758	8
9	1.195	1.423	1.689	1.999	2.358	2.773	3.252	3.803	4.435	5.160	5.987	6.931	8.005	9.223	10.604	12.166	20.661	9
10	1.219	1.480	1.791	2.159	2.594	3.106	3.707	4.411	5.234	6.192	7.305	8.594	10.086	11.806	13.786	16.060	28.925	10
11	1.243	1.539	1.898	2.332	2.853	3.479	4.226	5.117	6.176	7.430	8.912	10.657	12.708	15.112	17.922	21.199	40.496	11
12	1.268	1.601	2.012	2.518	3.138	3.896	4.818	5.936	7.288	8.916	10.872	13.215	16.012	19.343	23.298	27.983	56.694	12
13	1.294	1.665	2.133	2.720	3.452	4.363	5.492	6.886	8.599	10.699	13.264	16.386	20.175	24.759	30.288	36.937	79.371	13
14	1.319	1.732	2.261	2.937	3.797	4.887	6.261	7.988	10.147	12.839	16.182	20.319	25.421	31.691	39.374	48.757	111.120	14
15	1.346	1.801	2.397	3.172	4.177	5.474	7.138	9.266	11.974	15.407	19.742	25.196	32.030	40.565	51.186	64.359	155.568	15
16	1.373	1.873	2.540	3.426	4.595	6.130	8.137	10.748	14.129	18.488	24.086	31.243	40.358	51.923	66.542	84.954	217.795	16
17	1.400	1.948	2.693	3.700	5.054	6.866	9.276	12.468	16.672	22.186	29.384	38.741	50.851	66.461	86.504	112.139	304.913	17
18	1.428	2.026	2.854	3.996	5.560	7.690	10.575	14.463	19.673	26.623	35.849	48.039	64.072	85.071	112.455	148.024	426.879	18
19	1.457	2.107	3.026	4.316	6.116	8.613	12.056	16.777	23.214	31.948	43.736	59.568	80.731	108.890	146.192	195.391	597.630	19
20	1.486	2.191	3.207	4.661	6.727	9.646	13.743	19.461	27.393	38.338	53.358	73.864	101.721	139.380	190.050	257.916	836.683	20
21	1.516	2.279	3.400	5.034	7.400	10.804	15.668	22.574	32.324	46.005	65.096	91.592	128.169	178.406	247.065	340.449	1171.356	21
22	1.546	2.370	3.604	5.437	8.140	12.100	17.861	26.186	38.142	55.206	79.418	113.574	161.492	228.360	321.184	449.393	1639.898	22
23	1.577	2.465	3.820	5.871	8.954	13.552	20.362	30.376	45.008	66.247	96.889	140.831	203.480	292.300	417.539	593.199	2295.857	23
24	1.608	2.563	4.049	6.341	9.850	15.179	23.212	35.236	53.109	79.497	118.205	174.631	256.385	374.144	542.801	783.023	3214.200	24
25	1.641	2.666	4.292	6.848	10.835	17.000	26.462	40.874	62.669	95.396	144.210	216.542	323.045	478.905	705.641	1033.590	4499.880	25
26	1.673	2.772	4.549	7.396	11.918	19.040	30.167	47.414	73.949	114.475	175.936	268.512	407.037	612.998	917.333	1364.339	6299.831	26
27	1.707	2.883	4.822	7.988	13.110	21.325	34.390	55.000	87.260	137.371	214.642	332.955	512.867	784.638	1192.533	1800.927	8819.764	27
28	1.741	2.999	5.112	8.627	14.421	23.884	39.204	63.800	102.967	164.845	261.864	412.864	646.212	1004.336	1550.293	2377.224	12347.670	28
29	1.776	3.119	5.418	9.317	15.863	26.750	44.693	74.009	121.501	197.814	319.474	511.952	814.228	1285.550	2015.381	3137.935	17286.737	29
30	1.811	3.243	5.743	10.063	17.449	29.960	50.950	85.850	143.371	237.376	389.758	634.820	1025.927	1645.505	2619.996	4142.075	24201.432	30
35	2.000	3.946	7.686	14.785	28.102	52.800	98.100	180.314	327.997	590.668	1053.402	1861.054	3258.135	5653.911	9727.860	16599.217	130161.112	35
40	2.208	4.801	10.286	21.725	45.259	93.051	188.884	378.721	750.378	1469.772	2847.038	5455.913	10347.175	19426.689	36118.865	66520.767	700037.697	40

TABLE 2 (*Place a clip on this page for your reference.*)

Present Value of $1.00

$P = \dfrac{S}{(1 + r)^n}$. In this table $S = \$1.00$.

Periods	2%	4%	6%	8%	10%	12%	14%	16%	18%	20%	22%	24%	26%	28%	30%	32%	40%	Periods
1	0.980	0.962	0.943	0.926	0.909	0.893	0.877	0.862	0.847	0.833	0.820	0.806	0.794	0.781	0.769	0.758	0.714	1
2	0.961	0.925	0.890	0.857	0.826	0.797	0.769	0.743	0.718	0.694	0.672	0.650	0.630	0.610	0.592	0.574	0.510	2
3	0.942	0.889	0.840	0.794	0.751	0.712	0.675	0.641	0.609	0.579	0.551	0.524	0.500	0.477	0.455	0.435	0.364	3
4	0.924	0.855	0.792	0.735	0.683	0.636	0.592	0.552	0.516	0.482	0.451	0.423	0.397	0.373	0.350	0.329	0.260	4
5	0.906	0.822	0.747	0.681	0.621	0.567	0.519	0.476	0.437	0.402	0.370	0.341	0.315	0.291	0.269	0.250	0.186	5
6	0.888	0.790	0.705	0.630	0.564	0.507	0.456	0.410	0.370	0.335	0.303	0.275	0.250	0.227	0.207	0.189	0.133	6
7	0.871	0.760	0.665	0.583	0.513	0.452	0.400	0.354	0.314	0.279	0.249	0.222	0.198	0.178	0.159	0.143	0.095	7
8	0.853	0.731	0.627	0.540	0.467	0.404	0.351	0.305	0.266	0.233	0.204	0.179	0.157	0.139	0.123	0.108	0.068	8
9	0.837	0.703	0.592	0.500	0.424	0.361	0.308	0.263	0.225	0.194	0.167	0.144	0.125	0.108	0.094	0.082	0.048	9
10	0.820	0.676	0.558	0.463	0.386	0.322	0.270	0.227	0.191	0.162	0.137	0.116	0.099	0.085	0.073	0.062	0.035	10
11	0.804	0.650	0.527	0.429	0.350	0.287	0.237	0.195	0.162	0.135	0.112	0.094	0.079	0.066	0.056	0.047	0.025	11
12	0.788	0.625	0.497	0.397	0.319	0.257	0.208	0.168	0.137	0.112	0.092	0.076	0.062	0.052	0.043	0.036	0.018	12
13	0.773	0.601	0.469	0.368	0.290	0.229	0.182	0.145	0.116	0.093	0.075	0.061	0.050	0.040	0.033	0.027	0.013	13
14	0.758	0.577	0.442	0.340	0.263	0.205	0.160	0.125	0.099	0.078	0.062	0.049	0.039	0.032	0.025	0.021	0.009	14
15	0.743	0.555	0.417	0.315	0.239	0.183	0.140	0.108	0.084	0.065	0.051	0.040	0.031	0.025	0.020	0.016	0.006	15
16	0.728	0.534	0.394	0.292	0.218	0.163	0.123	0.093	0.071	0.054	0.042	0.032	0.025	0.019	0.015	0.012	0.005	16
17	0.714	0.513	0.371	0.270	0.198	0.146	0.108	0.080	0.060	0.045	0.034	0.026	0.020	0.015	0.012	0.009	0.003	17
18	0.700	0.494	0.350	0.250	0.180	0.130	0.095	0.069	0.051	0.038	0.028	0.021	0.016	0.012	0.009	0.007	0.002	18
19	0.686	0.475	0.331	0.232	0.164	0.116	0.083	0.060	0.043	0.031	0.023	0.017	0.012	0.009	0.007	0.005	0.002	19
20	0.673	0.456	0.312	0.215	0.149	0.104	0.073	0.051	0.037	0.026	0.019	0.014	0.010	0.007	0.005	0.004	0.001	20
21	0.660	0.439	0.294	0.199	0.135	0.093	0.064	0.044	0.031	0.022	0.015	0.011	0.008	0.006	0.004	0.003	0.001	21
22	0.647	0.422	0.278	0.184	0.123	0.083	0.056	0.038	0.026	0.018	0.013	0.009	0.006	0.004	0.003	0.002	0.001	22
23	0.634	0.406	0.262	0.170	0.112	0.074	0.049	0.033	0.022	0.015	0.010	0.007	0.005	0.003	0.002	0.002	0.000	23
24	0.622	0.390	0.247	0.158	0.102	0.066	0.043	0.028	0.019	0.013	0.008	0.006	0.004	0.003	0.002	0.001	0.000	24
25	0.610	0.375	0.233	0.146	0.092	0.059	0.038	0.024	0.016	0.010	0.007	0.005	0.003	0.002	0.001	0.001	0.000	25
26	0.598	0.361	0.220	0.135	0.084	0.053	0.033	0.021	0.014	0.009	0.006	0.004	0.002	0.002	0.001	0.001	0.000	26
27	0.586	0.347	0.207	0.125	0.076	0.047	0.029	0.018	0.011	0.007	0.005	0.003	0.002	0.001	0.001	0.001	0.000	27
28	0.574	0.333	0.196	0.116	0.069	0.042	0.026	0.016	0.010	0.006	0.004	0.002	0.002	0.001	0.001	0.000	0.000	28
29	0.563	0.321	0.185	0.107	0.063	0.037	0.022	0.014	0.008	0.005	0.003	0.002	0.001	0.001	0.000	0.000	0.000	29
30	0.552	0.308	0.174	0.099	0.057	0.033	0.020	0.012	0.007	0.004	0.003	0.002	0.001	0.001	0.000	0.000	0.000	30
35	0.500	0.253	0.130	0.068	0.036	0.019	0.010	0.006	0.003	0.002	0.001	0.001	0.000	0.000	0.000	0.000	0.000	35
40	0.453	0.208	0.097	0.046	0.022	0.011	0.005	0.003	0.001	0.001	0.000	0.000	0.000	0.000	0.000	0.000	0.000	40

TABLE 3

Compound Amount of Annuity of $1.00 in Arrears* (Future Value of Annuity)

$$S_n = \frac{(1 + r)^n - 1}{r}$$

Periods	2%	4%	6%	8%	10%	12%	14%	16%	18%	20%	22%	24%	26%	28%	30%	32%	40%	Periods
1	1.000	1.000	1.000	1.000	1.000	1.000	1.000	1.000	1.000	1.000	1.000	1.000	1.000	1.000	1.000	1.000	1.000	1
2	2.020	2.040	2.060	2.080	2.100	2.120	2.140	2.160	2.180	2.200	2.220	2.240	2.260	2.280	2.300	2.320	2.400	2
3	3.060	3.122	3.184	3.246	3.310	3.374	3.440	3.506	3.572	3.640	3.708	3.778	3.848	3.918	3.990	4.062	4.360	3
4	4.122	4.246	4.375	4.506	4.641	4.779	4.921	5.066	5.215	5.368	5.524	5.684	5.848	6.016	6.187	6.362	7.104	4
5	5.204	5.416	5.637	5.867	6.105	6.353	6.610	6.877	7.154	7.442	7.740	8.048	8.368	8.700	9.043	9.398	10.946	5
6	6.308	6.633	6.975	7.336	7.716	8.115	8.536	8.977	9.442	9.930	10.442	10.980	11.544	12.136	12.756	13.406	16.324	6
7	7.434	7.898	8.394	8.923	9.487	10.089	10.730	11.414	12.142	12.916	13.740	14.615	15.546	16.534	17.583	18.696	23.853	7
8	8.583	9.214	9.897	10.637	11.436	12.300	13.233	14.240	15.327	16.499	17.762	19.123	20.588	22.163	23.858	25.678	34.395	8
9	9.755	10.583	11.491	12.488	13.579	14.776	16.085	17.519	19.086	20.799	22.670	24.712	26.940	29.369	32.015	34.895	49.153	9
10	10.950	12.006	13.181	14.487	15.937	17.549	19.337	21.321	23.521	25.959	28.657	31.643	34.945	38.593	42.619	47.062	69.814	10
11	12.169	13.486	14.972	16.645	18.531	20.655	23.045	25.733	28.755	32.150	35.962	40.238	45.031	50.398	56.405	63.122	98.739	11
12	13.412	15.026	16.870	18.977	21.384	24.133	27.271	30.850	34.931	39.581	44.874	50.895	57.739	65.510	74.327	84.320	139.235	12
13	14.680	16.627	18.882	21.495	24.523	28.029	32.089	36.786	42.219	48.497	55.746	64.110	73.751	84.853	97.625	112.303	195.929	13
14	15.974	18.292	21.015	24.215	27.975	32.393	37.581	43.672	50.818	59.196	69.010	80.496	93.926	109.612	127.913	149.240	275.300	14
15	17.293	20.024	23.276	27.152	31.772	37.280	43.842	51.660	60.965	72.035	85.192	100.815	119.347	141.303	167.286	197.997	386.420	15
16	18.639	21.825	25.673	30.324	35.950	42.753	50.980	60.925	72.939	87.442	104.935	126.011	151.377	181.868	218.472	262.356	541.988	16
17	20.012	23.698	28.213	33.750	40.545	48.884	59.118	71.673	87.068	105.931	129.020	157.253	191.735	233.791	285.014	347.309	759.784	17
18	21.412	25.645	30.906	37.450	45.599	55.750	68.394	84.141	103.740	128.117	158.405	195.994	242.585	300.252	371.518	459.449	1064.697	18
19	22.841	27.671	33.760	41.446	51.159	63.440	78.969	98.603	123.414	154.740	194.254	244.033	306.658	385.323	483.973	607.472	1491.576	19
20	24.297	29.778	36.786	45.762	57.275	72.052	91.025	115.380	146.628	186.688	237.989	303.601	387.389	494.213	630.165	802.863	2089.206	20
21	25.783	31.969	39.993	50.423	64.002	81.699	104.768	134.841	174.021	225.026	291.347	377.465	489.110	633.593	820.215	1060.779	2925.889	21
22	27.299	34.248	43.392	55.457	71.403	92.503	120.436	157.415	206.345	271.031	356.443	469.056	617.278	811.999	1067.280	1401.229	4097.245	22
23	28.845	36.618	46.996	60.893	79.543	104.603	138.297	183.601	244.487	326.237	435.861	582.630	778.771	1040.358	1388.464	1850.622	5737.142	23
24	30.422	39.083	50.816	66.765	88.497	118.155	158.659	213.978	289.494	392.484	532.750	723.461	982.251	1332.659	1806.003	2443.821	8032.999	24
25	32.030	41.646	54.865	73.106	98.347	133.334	181.871	249.214	342.603	471.981	650.955	898.092	1238.636	1706.803	2348.803	3226.844	11247.199	25
26	33.671	44.312	59.156	79.954	109.182	150.334	208.333	290.088	405.272	567.377	795.165	1114.634	1561.682	2185.708	3054.444	4260.434	15747.079	26
27	35.344	47.084	63.706	87.351	121.100	169.374	238.499	337.502	479.221	681.853	971.102	1383.146	1968.719	2798.706	3971.778	5624.772	22046.910	27
28	37.051	49.968	68.528	95.339	134.210	190.699	272.889	392.503	566.481	819.223	1185.744	1716.101	2481.586	3583.344	5164.311	7425.699	30866.674	28
29	38.792	52.966	73.640	103.966	148.631	214.583	312.094	456.303	669.447	984.068	1447.608	2128.965	3127.798	4587.680	6714.604	9802.923	43214.343	29
30	40.568	56.085	79.058	113.283	164.494	241.333	356.787	530.312	790.948	1181.882	1767.081	2640.916	3942.026	5873.231	8729.985	12940.859	60501.081	30
35	49.994	73.652	111.435	172.317	271.024	431.663	693.573	1120.713	1816.652	2948.341	4783.645	7750.225	12527.442	20188.966	32422.868	51869.427	325400.279	35
40	60.402	95.026	154.762	259.057	442.593	767.091	1342.025	2360.757	4163.213	7343.858	12936.535	22728.803	39792.982	69377.460	120392.883	207874.272	1750091.741	40

*Payments (or receipts) at the end of each period.

TABLE 4 (*Place a clip on this page for your reference.*)

Present Value of Annuity $1.00 in Arrears*

$$P_n = \frac{1}{r}\left[1 - \frac{1}{(1+r)^n}\right]$$

Periods	2%	4%	6%	8%	10%	12%	14%	16%	18%	20%	22%	24%	26%	28%	30%	32%	40%	Periods
1	0.980	0.962	0.943	0.926	0.909	0.893	0.877	0.862	0.847	0.833	0.820	0.806	0.794	0.781	0.769	0.758	0.714	1
2	1.942	1.886	1.833	1.783	1.736	1.690	1.647	1.605	1.566	1.528	1.492	1.457	1.424	1.392	1.361	1.331	1.224	2
3	2.884	2.775	2.673	2.577	2.487	2.402	2.322	2.246	2.174	2.106	2.042	1.981	1.923	1.868	1.816	1.766	1.589	3
4	3.808	3.630	3.465	3.312	3.170	3.037	2.914	2.798	2.690	2.589	2.494	2.404	2.320	2.241	2.166	2.096	1.849	4
5	4.713	4.452	4.212	3.993	3.791	3.605	3.433	3.274	3.127	2.991	2.864	2.745	2.635	2.532	2.436	2.345	2.035	5
6	5.601	5.242	4.917	4.623	4.355	4.111	3.889	3.685	3.498	3.326	3.167	3.020	2.885	2.759	2.643	2.534	2.168	6
7	6.472	6.002	5.582	5.206	4.868	4.564	4.288	4.039	3.812	3.605	3.416	3.242	3.083	2.937	2.802	2.677	2.263	7
8	7.325	6.733	6.210	5.747	5.335	4.968	4.639	4.344	4.078	3.837	3.619	3.421	3.241	3.076	2.925	2.786	2.331	8
9	8.162	7.435	6.802	6.247	5.759	5.328	4.946	4.607	4.303	4.031	3.786	3.566	3.366	3.184	3.019	2.868	2.379	9
10	8.983	8.111	7.360	6.710	6.145	5.650	5.216	4.833	4.494	4.192	3.923	3.682	3.465	3.269	3.092	2.930	2.414	10
11	9.787	8.760	7.887	7.139	6.495	5.938	5.453	5.029	4.656	4.327	4.035	3.776	3.543	3.335	3.147	2.978	2.438	11
12	10.575	9.385	8.384	7.536	6.814	6.194	5.660	5.197	4.793	4.439	4.127	3.851	3.606	3.387	3.190	3.013	2.456	12
13	11.348	9.986	8.853	7.904	7.103	6.424	5.842	5.342	4.910	4.533	4.203	3.912	3.656	3.427	3.223	3.040	2.469	13
14	12.106	10.563	9.295	8.244	7.367	6.628	6.002	5.468	5.008	4.611	4.265	3.962	3.695	3.459	3.249	3.061	2.478	14
15	12.849	11.118	9.712	8.559	7.606	6.811	6.142	5.575	5.092	4.675	4.315	4.001	3.726	3.483	3.268	3.076	2.484	15
16	13.578	11.652	10.106	8.851	7.824	6.974	6.265	5.668	5.162	4.730	4.357	4.033	3.751	3.503	3.283	3.088	2.489	16
17	14.292	12.166	10.477	9.122	8.022	7.120	6.373	5.749	5.222	4.775	4.391	4.059	3.771	3.518	3.295	3.097	2.492	17
18	14.992	12.659	10.828	9.372	8.201	7.250	6.467	5.818	5.273	4.812	4.419	4.080	3.786	3.529	3.304	3.104	2.494	18
19	15.678	13.134	11.158	9.604	8.365	7.366	6.550	5.877	5.316	4.843	4.442	4.097	3.799	3.539	3.311	3.109	2.496	19
20	16.351	13.590	11.470	9.818	8.514	7.469	6.623	5.929	5.353	4.870	4.460	4.110	3.808	3.546	3.316	3.113	2.497	20
21	17.011	14.029	11.764	10.017	8.649	7.562	6.687	5.973	5.384	4.891	4.476	4.121	3.816	3.551	3.320	3.116	2.498	21
22	17.658	14.451	12.042	10.201	8.772	7.645	6.743	6.011	5.410	4.909	4.488	4.130	3.822	3.556	3.323	3.118	2.498	22
23	18.292	14.857	12.303	10.371	8.883	7.718	6.792	6.044	5.432	4.925	4.499	4.137	3.827	3.559	3.325	3.120	2.499	23
24	18.914	15.247	12.550	10.529	8.985	7.784	6.835	6.073	5.451	4.937	4.507	4.143	3.831	3.562	3.327	3.121	2.499	24
25	19.523	15.622	12.783	10.675	9.077	7.843	6.873	6.097	5.467	4.948	4.514	4.147	3.834	3.564	3.329	3.122	2.499	25
26	20.121	15.983	13.003	10.810	9.161	7.896	6.906	6.118	5.480	4.956	4.520	4.151	3.837	3.566	3.330	3.123	2.500	26
27	20.707	16.330	13.211	10.935	9.237	7.943	6.935	6.136	5.492	4.964	4.524	4.154	3.839	3.567	3.331	3.123	2.500	27
28	21.281	16.663	13.406	11.051	9.307	7.984	6.961	6.152	5.502	4.970	4.528	4.157	3.840	3.568	3.331	3.124	2.500	28
29	21.844	16.984	13.591	11.158	9.370	8.022	6.983	6.166	5.510	4.975	4.531	4.159	3.841	3.569	3.332	3.124	2.500	29
30	22.396	17.292	13.765	11.258	9.427	8.055	7.003	6.177	5.517	4.979	4.534	4.160	3.842	3.569	3.332	3.124	2.500	30
35	24.999	18.665	14.498	11.655	9.644	8.176	7.070	6.215	5.539	4.992	4.541	4.164	3.845	3.571	3.333	3.125	2.500	35
40	27.355	19.793	15.046	11.925	9.779	8.244	7.105	6.233	5.548	4.997	4.544	4.166	3.846	3.571	3.333	3.125	2.500	40

*Payments (or receipts) at the end of each period.

Glossary

Abnormal spoilage. Spoilage that would not arise under efficient operating conditions; it is not inherent in a particular production process. (740)

Absorption costing. Method of inventory costing in which all variable manufacturing costs and all fixed manufacturing costs are included as inventoriable costs. (350)

Account analysis method. Approach to cost function estimation that classifies various cost accounts as variable, fixed, or mixed with respect to the identified level of activity. Typically, qualitative rather than quantitative analysis is used when making these cost-classification decisions. (398)

Accrual accounting rate-of-return (AARR) method. Capital budgeting method that divides an accrual accounting measure of average annual income of a project by an accrual accounting measure of its investment. See also *return on investment (ROI)*. (850)

Activity. An event, task, or unit of work with a specified purpose. (180)

Activity-based budgeting (ABB). Budgeting approach that focuses on the budgeted cost of the activities necessary to produce and sell products and services. (229)

Activity-based costing (ABC). Approach to costing that focuses on individual activities as the fundamental cost objects. It uses the costs of these activities as the basis for assigning costs to other cost objects such as products or services. (180)

Activity-based management (ABM). Method of management decision-making that uses activity-based costing information to improve customer satisfaction and profitability. (192)

Actual cost. Cost incurred (a historical or past cost), as distinguished from a budgeted or forecasted cost. (49)

Actual costing. A costing system that traces direct costs to a cost object by using the actual direct-cost rates times the actual quantities of the direct-cost inputs and allocates indirect costs based on the actual indirect-cost rates times the actual quantities of the cost allocation bases. (131)

Actual indirect-cost rate. Actual total indirect costs in a cost pool divided by the actual total quantity of the cost-allocation base for that cost pool. (139)

Adjusted allocation-rate approach. Restates all overhead entries in the general ledger and subsidiary ledgers using actual cost rates rather than budgeted cost rates. (149)

Allowable cost. Cost that the contract parties agree to include in the costs to be reimbursed. (644)

Appraisal costs. Costs incurred to detect which of the individual units of products do not conform to specifications. (770)

Artificial costs. See *complete reciprocated costs*. (637)

Autonomy. The degree of freedom to make decisions. (878)

Average cost. See *unit cost*. (56)

Average waiting time. The average amount of time that an order will wait in line before the machine is set up and the order is processed. (782)

Backflush costing. Costing system that omits recording some of the journal entries relating to the stages from purchase of direct materials to the sale of finished goods. (816)

Balanced scorecard. A framework for implementing strategy that translates an organization's mission and strategy into a set of performance measures. (501)

Batch-level costs. The costs of activities related to a group of units of products or services rather than to each individual unit of product or service. (183)

Belief systems. Lever of control that articulates the mission, purpose, norms of behaviors, and core values of a company intended to inspire managers and other employees to do their best. (933)

Benchmarking. The continuous process of comparing the levels of performance in producing products and services and executing activities against the best levels of performance in competing companies or in companies having similar processes. (287)

Book value. The original cost minus accumulated depreciation of an asset. (471)

Bottleneck. An operation where the work to be performed approaches or exceeds the capacity available to do it. (781)

Boundary systems. Lever of control that describes standards of behavior and codes of conduct expected of all employees, especially actions that are off-limits. (932)

Breakeven point (BEP). Quantity of output sold at which total revenues equal total costs, that is where the operating income is zero. (93)

Budget. Quantitative expression of a proposed plan of action by management for a specified period and an aid to coordinating what needs to be done to implement that plan. (30)

Budgetary slack. The practice of underestimating budgeted revenues, or overestimating budgeted costs, to make budgeted targets more easily achievable. (240)

Budgeted cost. Predicted or forecasted cost (future cost) as distinguished from an actual or historical cost. (49)

Budgeted indirect-cost rate. Budgeted annual indirect costs in a cost pool divided by the budgeted annual quantity of the cost allocation base. (133)

Budgeted performance. Expected performance or a point of reference to compare actual results. (270)

Bundled product. A package of two or more products (or services) that is sold for a single price, but whose individual components may be sold as separate items at their own "stand-alone" prices. (645)

Business function costs. The sum of all costs (variable and fixed) in a particular business function of the value chain. (450)

Byproducts. Products from a joint production process that have low total sales values compared with the total sales value of the main product or of joint products. (665)

Capital budgeting. The making of long-run planning decisions for investments in projects. (839)

Carrying costs. Costs that arise while holding inventory of goods for sale. (799)

Cash budget. Schedule of expected cash receipts and disbursements. (247)

Cause-and-effect diagram. Diagram that identifies potential causes of defects. Four categories of potential causes of failure are human factors, methods and design factors, machine-related factors, and materials and components factors. Also called a *fishbone diagram*. (775)

Chief financial officer (CFO). Executive responsible for overseeing the financial operations of an organization. Also called *finance director*. (34)

Choice criterion. Objective that can be quantified in a decision model. (111)

Coefficient of determination (r^2). Measures the percentage of variation in a dependent variable explained by one or more independent variables. (420)

Collusive pricing. Companies in an industry conspire in their pricing and production decisions to achieve a price above the competitive price and so restrain trade. (565)

Common cost. Cost of operating a facility, activity, or like cost object that is shared by two or more users. (641)

Complete reciprocated costs. The support department's own costs plus any interdepartmental cost allocations. Also called the *artificial costs* of the support department. (637)

Composite unit. Hypothetical unit with weights based on the mix of individual units. (601)

Conference method. Approach to cost function estimation on the basis of analysis and opinions about costs and their drivers gathered from various departments of a company (purchasing, process engineering, manufacturing, employee relations, and so on). (398)

Conformance quality. Refers to the performance of a product or service relative to its design and product specifications. (769)

Constant. The component of total cost that, within the relevant range, does not vary with changes in the level of the activity. Also called *intercept*. (394)

Constant gross-margin percentage NRV method. Method that allocates joint costs to joint products in such a way that the overall gross-margin percentage is identical for the individual products. (671)

Constraint. A mathematical inequality or equality that must be satisfied by the variables in a mathematical model. (479)

Continuous budget. See *rolling budget*. (222)

Contribution income statement. Income statement that groups costs into variable costs and fixed costs to highlight the contribution margin. (89)

Contribution margin. Total revenues minus total variable costs. (88)

Contribution margin per unit. Selling price minus the variable cost per unit. (88)

Contribution margin percentage. Contribution margin per unit divided by selling price. Also called *contribution margin ratio*. (89)

Contribution margin ratio. See *contribution margin percentage*. (89)

Control. Taking actions that implement the planning decisions, deciding how to evaluate performance, and providing feedback and learning that will help future decision making. (30)

Control chart. Graph of a series of successive observations of a particular step, procedure, or operation taken at regular intervals of time. Each observation is plotted relative to specified ranges that represent the limits within which observations are expected to fall. (774)

Controllability. Degree of influence that a specific manager has over costs, revenues, or related items for which he or she is responsible. (239)

Controllable cost. Any cost that is primarily subject to the influence of a given responsibility center manager for a given period. (239)

Controller. The financial executive primarily responsible for management accounting and financial accounting. Also called *chief accounting officer*. (34)

Conversion costs. All manufacturing costs other than direct materials costs. (65)

Cost. Resource sacrificed or forgone to achieve a specific objective. (49)

Cost accounting. Measures, analyzes, and reports financial and nonfinancial information relating to the costs of acquiring or using resources in an organization. It provides information for both management accounting and financial accounting. (22)

Cost Accounting Standards Board (CASB). Government agency that has the exclusive authority to make, put into effect, amend, and rescind cost accounting standards and interpretations thereof designed to achieve uniformity and consistency in regard to measurement, assignment, and allocation of costs to government contracts within the United States. (644)

Cost accumulation. Collection of cost data in some organized way by means of an accounting system. (49)

Cost allocation. Assignment of indirect costs to a particular cost object. (50)

Cost-allocation base. A factor that links in a systematic way an indirect cost or group of indirect costs to a cost object. (128)

Cost-application base. Cost-allocation base when the cost object is a job, product, or customer. (128)

Cost assignment. General term that encompasses both (1) tracing accumulated costs that have a direct relationship to a cost object and (2) allocating accumulated costs that have an indirect relationship to a cost object. (50)

Cost–benefit approach. Approach to decision-making and resource allocation based on a comparison of the expected benefits from attaining company goals and the expected costs. (32)

Cost center. Responsibility center where the manager is accountable for costs only. (238)

Cost driver. A variable, such as the level of activity or volume, that causally affects costs over a given time span. (54)

Cost estimation. The attempt to measure a past relationship based on data from past costs and the related level of an activity. (396)

Cost function. Mathematical description of how a cost changes with changes in the level of an activity relating to that cost. (393)

Cost hierarchy. Categorization of indirect costs into different cost pools on the basis of the different types of cost drivers, or cost-allocation bases, or different degrees of difficulty in determining cause-and-effect (or benefits received) relationships. (182)

Cost incurrence. Describes when a resource is consumed (or benefit forgone) to meet a specific objective. (553)

Cost leadership. Organization's ability to achieve lower costs relative to competitors through productivity and efficiency improvements, elimination of waste, and tight cost control. (499)

Cost management. The approaches and activities of managers to use resources to increase value to customers and to achieve organizational goals. (23)

Cost object. Anything for which a measurement of costs is desired. (49)

Cost of capital. See *required rate of return (RRR)*. (843)

Cost of goods manufactured. Cost of goods brought to completion, whether they were started before or during the current accounting period. (63)

Cost pool. A grouping of individual cost items. (128)

Cost predictions. Forecasts about future costs. (396)

Cost tracing. Describes the assignment of direct costs to a particular cost object. (50)

Costs of quality (COQ). Costs incurred to prevent, or the costs arising as a result of, the production of a low-quality product. (770)

Cost–volume–profit (CVP) analysis. Examines the behavior of total revenues, total costs, and operating income as changes occur in the units sold, the selling price, the variable cost per unit, or the fixed costs of a product. (87)

Cumulative average-time learning model. Learning curve model in which the cumulative average time per unit declines by a constant percentage each time the cumulative quantity of units produced doubles. (411)

Current cost. Asset measure based on the cost of purchasing an asset today identical to the one currently held, or the cost of purchasing an asset that provides services like the one currently held if an identical asset cannot be purchased. (921)

Customer-cost hierarchy. Hierarchy that categorizes costs related to customers into different cost pools on the basis of different types of cost drivers, or cost-allocation bases, or different degrees of difficulty in determining cause-and-effect or benefits-received relationships. (581)

Customer life-cycle costs. Focuses on the total costs incurred by a customer to acquire, use, maintain, and dispose of a product or service. (562)

Customer-profitability analysis. The reporting and analysis of revenues earned from customers and the costs incurred to earn those revenues. (580)

Customer relationship management (CRM). A strategy that integrates people and technology in all business functions to deepen relationships with customers, partners, and distributors. (25)

Customer-response time. Duration from the time a customer places an order for a product or service to the time the product or service is delivered to the customer. (780)

Customer service. Providing after-sale support to customers. (25)

Decentralization. The freedom for managers at lower levels of the organization to make decisions. (878)

Decision model. Formal method for making a choice, often involving both quantitative and qualitative analyses. (447)

Decision table. Summary of the alternative actions, events, outcomes, and probabilities of events in a decision model. (112)

Degree of operating leverage. Contribution margin divided by operating income at any given level of sales. (103)

Denominator level. The denominator in the budgeted fixed overhead rate computation. (311)

Denominator-level variance. See *production-volume variance*. (318)

Dependent variable. The cost to be predicted. (400)

Design of products and processes. The detailed planning and engineering of products and processes. (25)

Design quality. Refers to how closely the characteristics of a product or service meet the needs and wants of customers. (769)

Designed-in costs. See *locked-in costs*. (553)

Diagnostic control systems. Lever of control that monitors critical performance variables that help managers track progress toward achieving a company's strategic goals. Managers are held accountable for meeting these goals. (931)

Differential cost. Difference in total cost between two alternatives. (456)

Differential revenue. Difference in total revenue between two alternatives. (456)

Direct costing. See *variable costing*. (350)

Direct costs of a cost object. Costs related to the particular cost object that can be traced to that object in an economically feasible (cost-effective) way. (49)

Direct manufacturing labor costs. Include the compensation of all manufacturing labor that can be traced to the cost object (work in process and then finished goods) in an economically feasible way. (59)

Direct manufacturing labor mix variance. The difference between (1) budgeted cost for actual mix of the actual total quantity of direct manufacturing labor used and (2) budgeted cost of budgeted mix of the actual total quantity of direct manufacturing labor used. (293)

Direct manufacturing labor yield variance. The difference between (1) budgeted cost of direct manufacturing labor based on the actual total quantity of direct manufacturing labor used and (2) flexible-budget cost of direct manufacturing labor based on the budgeted total quantity of direct manufacturing labor allowed for actual output produced. (293)

Direct materials costs. Acquisition costs of all materials that eventually become part of the cost object (work in process and then finished goods), and that can be traced to the cost object in an economically feasible way. (59)

Direct materials inventory. Direct materials in stock and awaiting use in the manufacturing process. (58)

Direct method. Cost allocation method that allocates each support department's costs to operating departments only. (633)

Discount rate. See *required rate of return (RRR)*. (843)

Discounted cash flow (DCF) methods. Capital budgeting methods that measure all expected future cash inflows and outflows of a project as if they occurred at the present point in time. (842)

Discounted payback method. Capital budgeting method that calculates the amount of time required for the discounted expected future cash flows to recoup the net initial investment in a project. (849)

Discretionary costs. Arise from periodic (usually annual) decisions regarding the maximum amount to be incurred and have no measurable cause-and-effect relationship between output and resources used. (525)

Distribution. Delivering products or services to customers. (25)

Downsizing. An integrated approach of configuring processes, products, and people to match costs to the activities that need to be performed to operate effectively and efficiently in the present and future. Also called *rightsizing*. (525)

Downward demand spiral. Pricing context where prices are raised to spread capacity costs over a smaller number of output units. Continuing reduction in the demand for products that occurs when the prices of competitors' products are not met and, as demand drops further, higher and higher unit costs result in more and more reluctance to meet competitors' prices. (367)

Dual pricing. Approach to transfer pricing using two separate transfer-pricing methods to price each transfer from one subunit to another. (891)

Dual-rate method. Allocation method that classifies costs in each cost pool into two pools (a variable-cost pool and a fixed-cost pool) with each pool using a different cost-allocation base. (622)

Dumping. Under U.S. laws, it occurs when a non-U.S. company sells a product in the United States at a price below the market value in the country where it is produced, and this lower price materially injures or threatens to materially injure an industry in the United States. (565)

Dysfunctional decision making. See *suboptimal decision making*. (880)

Economic order quantity (EOQ). Decision model that calculates the optimal quantity of inventory to order under a set of assumptions to minimize the sum of ordering and carrying costs. (800)

Economic value added (EVA®). After-tax operating income minus the (after-tax) weighted-average cost of capital multiplied by total assets minus current liabilities. (917)

Effectiveness. The degree to which a predetermined objective or target is met. (286)

Efficiency. The relative amount of inputs used to achieve a given output level. (286)

Efficiency variance. The difference between actual input quantity used and budgeted input quantity allowed for actual output, multiplied by budgeted price. Also called *usage variance*. (279)

Effort. Exertion toward achieving a goal. (878)

Engineered costs. Costs that result from a cause-and-effect relationship between the cost driver, output, and the (direct or indirect) resources used to produce that output. (524)

Enterprise resource planning (ERP) system. An integrated set of software modules covering a company's accounting, distribution, manufacturing, purchasing, human resources, and other functions. (814)

Equivalent units. Derived amount of output units that (a) takes the quantity of each input (factor of production) in units completed and in incomplete units of work in process and (b) converts the quantity of input into the amount of completed output units that could be produced with that quantity of input. (699)

Event. A possible relevant occurrence in a decision model. (112)

Expected monetary value. See *expected value*. (113)

Expected value. Weighted average of the outcomes of a decision with the probability of each outcome serving as the weight. Also called *expected monetary value*. (113)

Experience curve. Function that measures the decline in cost per unit in various business functions of the value chain, such as manufacturing, marketing, distribution, and so on, as the amount of these activities increases. (411)

External failure costs. Costs incurred on defective products after they are shipped to customers. (771)

Facility-sustaining costs. The costs of activities that cannot be traced to individual products or services but support the organization as a whole. (183)

Factory overhead costs. See *indirect manufacturing costs*. (59)

Favorable variance. Variance that has the effect of increasing operating income relative to the budgeted amount. Denoted F. (271)

Finance director. See *chief financial officer (CFO)*. (34)

Financial accounting. Measures and records business transactions and provides financial statements that are based on generally accepted accounting principles. It focuses on reporting to external parties such as investors and banks. (22)

Financial budget. Part of the master budget that focuses on how operations and planned capital outlays affect cash. It is made up of the capital expenditures budget, the cash budget, the budgeted balance sheet, and the budgeted statement of cash flows. (223)

Financial planning models. Mathematical representations of the relationships among operating activities, financial activities, and other factors that affect the master budget. (235)

Finished goods inventory. Goods completed but not yet sold. (58)

First-in, first-out (FIFO) process-costing method. Method of process costing that assigns the cost of the previous accounting period's equivalent units in beginning work-in-process inventory to the first units completed and transferred out of the process, and assigns the cost of equivalent units worked on during the current period first to complete beginning inventory, next to start and complete new units, and finally to units in ending work-in-process inventory. (707)

Fixed cost. Cost that remains unchanged in total for a given time period, despite wide changes in the related level of total activity or volume. (52)

Fixed overhead flexible-budget variance. The difference between actual fixed overhead costs and fixed overhead costs in the flexible budget. (317)

Fixed overhead spending variance. Same as the fixed overhead flexible-budget variance. The difference between actual fixed overhead costs and fixed overhead costs in the flexible budget. (317)

Flexible budget. Budget developed using budgeted revenues and budgeted costs based on the actual output in the budget period. (273)

Flexible-budget variance. The difference between an actual result and the corresponding flexible-budget amount based on the actual output level in the budget period. (274)

Full costs of the product. The sum of all variable and fixed costs in all business functions of the value chain (R&D, design, production, marketing, distribution, and customer service). (450)

Goal congruence. Exists when individuals and groups work toward achieving the organization's goals. Managers working in their own best interest take actions that align with the overall goals of top management. (878)

Gross margin percentage. Gross margin divided by revenues. (109)

Growth component. Change in operating income attributable solely to the change in the quantity of output sold between one period and the next. (517)

High-low method. Method used to estimate a cost function that uses only the highest and lowest observed values of the cost driver within the relevant range and their respective costs. (402)

Homogeneous cost pool. Cost pool in which all the costs have the same or a similar cause-and-effect or benefits-received relationship with the cost-allocation base. (598)

Hurdle rate. See *required rate of return (RRR).* (843)

Hybrid-costing system. Costing system that blends characteristics from both job-costing systems and process-costing systems. (717)

Idle time. Wages paid for unproductive time caused by lack of orders, machine breakdowns, material shortages, poor scheduling, and the like. (67)

Imputed cost. Costs recognized in particular situations but not incorporated in financial accounting records. (915)

Incongruent decision making. See *suboptimal decision making.* (880)

Incremental cost. Additional total cost incurred for an activity. (456)

Incremental cost-allocation method. Method that ranks the individual users of a cost object in the order of users most responsible for the common cost and then uses this ranking to allocate cost among those users. (642)

Incremental revenue. Additional total revenue from an activity. (456)

Incremental revenue-allocation method. Method that ranks individual products in a bundle according to criteria determined by management (for example, sales), and then uses this ranking to allocate bundled revenues to the individual products. (647)

Incremental unit-time learning model. Learning curve model in which the incremental time needed to produce the last unit declines by a constant percentage each time the cumulative quantity of units produced doubles. (412)

Independent variable. Level of activity or cost driver used to predict the dependent variable (costs) in a cost estimation or prediction model. (400)

Indirect costs of a cost object. Costs related to the particular cost object that cannot be traced to that object in an economically feasible (cost-effective) way. (50)

Indirect manufacturing costs. All manufacturing costs that are related to the cost object (work in process and then finished goods) but that cannot be traced to that cost object in an economically feasible way. Also called *manufacturing overhead costs* and *factory overhead costs.* (59)

Industrial engineering method. Approach to cost function estimation that analyzes the relationship between inputs and outputs in physical terms. Also called *work measurement method.* (398)

Inflation. The decline in the general purchasing power of the monetary unit, such as dollars. (863)

Insourcing. Process of producing goods or providing services within the organization rather than purchasing those same goods or services from outside vendors. (454)

Inspection point. Stage of the production process at which products are examined to determine whether they are acceptable or unacceptable units. (741)

Interactive control systems. Formal information systems that managers use to focus organization attention and learning on key strategic issues. (933)

Intercept. See *constant.* (394)

Intermediate product. Product transferred from one subunit to another subunit of an organization. This product may either be further worked on by the receiving subunit or sold to an external customer. (882)

Internal failure costs. Costs incurred on defective products before they are shipped to customers. (771)

Internal rate-of-return (IRR) method. Capital budgeting discounted cash flow (DCF) method that calculates the discount rate at which the present value of expected cash inflows from a project equals the present value of its expected cash outflows. (844)

Inventoriable costs. All costs of a product that are considered as assets in the balance sheet when they are incurred and that become cost of goods sold only when the product is sold. (59)

Inventory management. Planning, coordinating, and controlling activities related to the flow of inventory into, through, and out of an organization. (799)

Investment. Resources or assets used to generate income. (913)

Investment center. Responsibility center where the manager is accountable for investments, revenues, and costs. (238)

Job. A unit or multiple units of a distinct product or service. (129)

Job-cost record. Source document that records and accumulates all the costs assigned to a specific job, starting when work begins. Also called *job-cost sheet.* (133)

Job-cost sheet. See *job-cost record.* (133)

Job-costing system. Costing system in which the cost object is a unit or multiple units of a distinct product or service called a job. (129)

Joint costs. Costs of a production process that yields multiple products simultaneously. (664)

Joint products. Two or more products that have high total sales values compared with the total sales values of other products yielded by a joint production process. (665)

Just-in-time (JIT) production. Demand-pull manufacturing system in which each component in a production line is produced as soon as, and only when, needed by the next step in the production line. Also called *lean production.* (812)

Just-in-time (JIT) purchasing. The purchase of materials (or goods) so that they are delivered just as needed for production (or sales). (807)

Kaizen budgeting. Budgetary approach that explicitly incorporates continuous improvement anticipated during the budget period into the budget numbers. (242)

Labor-time sheet. Source document that contains information about the amount of labor time used for a specific job in a specific department. (133)

Lean accounting. Costing method that supports creating value for the customer by costing the entire value stream, not individual products or departments, thereby eliminating waste in the accounting process. (825)

Lean production. See *just-in-time (JIT) production.* (812)

Learning. Involves managers examining past performance and systematically exploring alternative ways to make better-informed decisions and plans in the future. (31)

Learning curve. Function that measures how labor-hours per unit decline as units of production increase because workers are learning and becoming better at their jobs. (410)

Life-cycle budgeting. Budget that estimates the revenues and business function costs of the value chain attributable to each product from initial R&D to final customer service and support. (560)

Life-cycle costing. System that tracks and accumulates business function costs of the value chain attributable to each product from initial R&D to final customer service and support. (560)

Line management. Managers (for example, in production, marketing, or distribution) who are directly responsible for attaining the goals of the organization. (33)

Linear cost function. Cost function in which the graph of total costs versus the level of a single activity related to that cost is a straight line within the relevant range. (393)

Linear programming (LP). Optimization technique used to maximize an objective function (for example, contribution margin of a mix of products), when there are multiple constraints. (479)

Locked-in costs. Costs that have not yet been incurred but, based on decisions that have already been made, will be incurred in the future. Also called *designed-in costs*. (553)

Main product. Product from a joint production process that has a high total sales value compared with the total sales values of all other products of the joint production process. (665)

Make-or-buy decisions. Decisions about whether a producer of goods or services will insource (produce goods or services within the firm) or outsource (purchase them from outside vendors). (454)

Management accounting. Measures, analyzes, and reports financial and nonfinancial information that helps managers make decisions to fulfill the goals of an organization. It focuses on internal reporting. (22)

Management by exception. Practice of focusing management attention on areas not operating as expected and giving less attention to areas operating as expected. (270)

Management control system. Means of gathering and using information to aid and coordinate the planning and control decisions throughout an organization and to guide the behavior of its managers and employees. (877)

Manufacturing cells. Grouping of all the different types of equipment used to make a given product. (812)

Manufacturing cycle efficiency (MCE). Value-added manufacturing time divided by manufacturing cycle time. (780)

Manufacturing cycle time. See *manufacturing lead time*. (780)

Manufacturing lead time. Duration between the time an order is received by manufacturing to the time a finished good is produced. Also called *manufacturing cycle time*. (780)

Manufacturing overhead allocated. Amount of manufacturing overhead costs allocated to individual jobs (or products or services) based on the budgeted rate multiplied by the actual quantity used of the cost-allocation base used for each job. Also called *manufacturing overhead applied*. (143)

Manufacturing overhead applied. See *manufacturing overhead allocated*. (143)

Manufacturing overhead costs. See *indirect manufacturing costs*. (59)

Manufacturing-sector companies. Companies that purchase materials and components and convert them into various finished goods. (58)

Margin of safety. Amount by which budgeted (or actual) revenues exceed breakeven revenues. (101)

Marketing. Promoting and selling products or services to customers or prospective customers. (25)

Market-share variance. The difference in budgeted contribution margin for actual market size in units caused solely by actual market share being different from budgeted market share. (603)

Market-size variance. The difference in budgeted contribution margin at the budgeted market share caused solely by actual market size in units being different from budgeted market size in units. (603)

Master budget. Expression of management's operating and financial plans for a specified period (usually a fiscal year) including a set of budgeted financial statements. Also called *pro forma statements*. (219)

Master-budget capacity utilization. The expected level of capacity utilization for the current budget period (typically one year). (364)

Materials requirements planning (MRP). Push-through system that manufactures finished goods for inventory on the basis of demand forecasts. (812)

Materials-requisition record. Source document that contains information about the cost of direct materials used on a specific job and in a specific department. (133)

Matrix method. See *reciprocal method*. (637)

Merchandising-sector companies. Companies that purchase and then sell tangible products without changing their basic form. (58)

Mixed cost. A cost that has both fixed and variable elements. Also called a *semivariable cost*. (394)

Moral hazard. Describes situations in which an employee prefers to exert less effort (or to report distorted information) compared with the effort (or accurate information) desired by the owner because the employee's effort (or validity of the reported information) cannot be accurately monitored and enforced. (927)

Motivation. The desire to attain a selected goal (the goal-congruence aspect) combined with the resulting pursuit of that goal (the effort aspect). (878)

Multicollinearity. Exists when two or more independent variables in a multiple regression model are highly correlated with each other. (428)

Multiple regression. Regression model that estimates the relationship between the dependent variable and two or more independent variables. (404)

Net income. Operating income plus nonoperating revenues (such as interest revenue) minus nonoperating costs (such as interest cost) minus income taxes. (96)

Net present value (NPV) method. Capital budgeting discounted cash flow (DCF) method that calculates the expected monetary gain or loss from a project by discounting all expected future cash inflows and outflows to the present point in time, using the required rate of return. (843)

Net realizable value (NRV) method. Method that allocates joint costs to joint products on the basis of final sales value minus separable costs of total production of the joint products during the accounting period. (670)

Nominal rate of return. Made up of three elements: (a) a risk-free element when there is no expected inflation, (b) a business-risk element, and (c) an inflation element. (863)

Nonlinear cost function. Cost function in which the graph of total costs based on the level of a single activity is not a straight line within the relevant range. (409)

Non-value-added cost. A cost that, if eliminated, would not reduce the actual or perceived value or utility (usefulness) customers obtain from using the product or service. (553)

Normal capacity utilization. The level of capacity utilization that satisfies average customer demand over a period (say, two to three years) that includes seasonal, cyclical, and trend factors. (364)

Normal costing. A costing system that traces direct costs to a cost object by using the actual direct-cost rates times the actual quantities of the direct-cost inputs and that allocates indirect costs based on the budgeted indirect-cost rates times the actual quantities of the cost-allocation bases. (133)

Normal spoilage. Spoilage inherent in a particular production process that arises even under efficient operating conditions. (740)

Objective function. Expresses the objective to be maximized (for example, operating income) or minimized (for example, operating costs) in a decision model (for example, a linear programming model). (478)

On-time performance. Delivering a product or service by the time it is scheduled to be delivered. (781)

One-time-only special order. Orders that have no long-run implications. (450)

Operating budget. Budgeted income statement (for operations) and its supporting budget schedules. (223)

Operating department. Department that directly adds value to a product or service. Also called a *production department* in manufacturing companies. (622)

Operating income. Total revenues from operations minus cost of goods sold and operating (period) costs (excluding interest expense and income taxes). (64)

Operating-income volume variance. The difference between static-budget operating income and the operating income based on budgeted profit per unit and actual units of output. (326)

Operating leverage. Effects that fixed costs have on changes in operating income as changes occur in units sold and contribution margin. (103)

Operation. A standardized method or technique that is performed repetitively, often on different materials, resulting in different finished goods. (717)

Operation-costing system. Hybrid-costing system applied to batches of similar, but not identical, products. Each batch of products is often a variation of a single design, and proceeds through a sequence of operations, but each batch does not necessarily move through the same operations as other batches. Within each operation, all product units use identical amounts of the operation's resources. (717)

Opportunity cost. The contribution to operating income that is forgone or rejected by not using a limited resource in its next-best alternative use. (458)

Opportunity cost of capital. See *required rate of return (RRR)*. (843)

Ordering costs. Costs of preparing, issuing, and paying purchase orders, receiving and inspecting the items included in the orders, and matching invoices received, purchase orders, and delivery records to make payments. (799)

Organization structure. Arrangement of lines of responsibility within the organization. (237)

Outcomes. Predicted economic results of the various possible combinations of actions and events in a decision model. (112)

Output unit–level costs. The costs of activities performed on each individual unit of a product or service. (183)

Outsourcing. Process of purchasing goods and services from outside vendors rather than producing the same goods or providing the same services within the organization. (454)

Overabsorbed indirect costs. See *overallocated indirect costs*. (148)

Overallocated indirect costs. Allocated amount of indirect costs in an accounting period is greater than the actual (incurred) amount in that period. Also called *overapplied indirect costs* and *overabsorbed indirect costs*. (148)

Overapplied indirect costs. See *overallocated indirect costs*. (148)

Overtime premium. Wage rate paid to workers (for both direct labor and indirect labor) in excess of their straight-time wage rates. (66)

Pareto diagram. Chart that indicates how frequently each type of defect occurs, ordered from the most frequent to the least frequent. (775)

Partial productivity. Measures the quantity of output produced divided by the quantity of an individual input used. (531)

Payback method. Capital budgeting method that measures the time it will take to recoup, in the form of expected future cash flows, the net initial investment in a project. (847)

Peak-load pricing. Practice of charging a higher price for the same product or service when the demand for it approaches the physical limit of the capacity to produce that product or service. (563)

Perfectly competitive market. Exists when there is a homogeneous product with buying prices equal to selling prices and no individual buyers or sellers can affect those prices by their own actions. (886)

Period costs. All costs in the income statement other than cost of goods sold. (59)

Physical-measure method. Method that allocates joint costs to joint products on the basis of the relative weight, volume, or other physical measure at the splitoff point of total production of these products during the accounting period. (668)

Planning. Selecting organization goals, predicting results under various alternative ways of achieving those goals, deciding how to attain the desired goals, and communicating the goals and how to attain them to the entire organization. (30)

Practical capacity. The level of capacity that reduces theoretical capacity by unavoidable operating interruptions such as scheduled maintenance time, shutdowns for holidays, and so on. (364)

Predatory pricing. Company deliberately prices below its costs in an effort to drive out competitors and restrict supply and then raises prices rather than enlarge demand. (564)

Prevention costs. Costs incurred to preclude the production of products that do not conform to specifications. (770)

Previous-department costs. See *transferred-in costs*. (712)

Price discount. Reduction in selling price below list selling price to encourage increases in customer purchases. (580)

Price discrimination. Practice of charging different customers different prices for the same product or service. (563)

Price-recovery component. Change in operating income attributable solely to changes in prices of inputs and outputs between one period and the next. (517)

Price variance. The difference between actual price and budgeted price multiplied by actual quantity of input. Also called *rate variance*. (278)

Prime costs. All direct manufacturing costs. (65)

Pro forma statements. Budgeted financial statements. (219)

Probability. Likelihood or chance that an event will occur. (112)

Probability distribution. Describes the likelihood (or the probability) that each of the mutually exclusive and collectively exhaustive set of events will occur. (112)

Process-costing system. Costing system in which the cost object is masses of identical or similar units of a product or service. (129)

Product. Any output that has a positive total sales value (or an output that enables an organization to avoid incurring costs). (665)

Product cost. Sum of the costs assigned to a product for a specific purpose. (68)

Product-cost cross-subsidization. Costing outcome where one undercosted (overcosted) product results in at least one other product being overcosted (undercosted). (174)

Product differentiation. Organization's ability to offer products or services perceived by its customers to be superior and unique relative to the products or services of its competitors. (499)

Product life cycle. Spans the time from initial R&D on a product to when customer service and support is no longer offered for that product. (560)

Product-mix decisions. Decisions about which products to sell and in what quantities. (462)

Product overcosting. A product consumes a low level of resources but is reported to have a high cost per unit. (173)

Product-sustaining costs. The costs of activities undertaken to support individual products regardless of the number of units or batches in which the units are produced. (183)

Product undercosting. A product consumes a high level of resources but is reported to have a low cost per unit. (173)

Production. Acquiring, coordinating, and assembling resources to produce a product or deliver a service. (25)

Production department. See *operating department*. (622)

Production-volume variance. The difference between budgeted fixed overhead and fixed overhead allocated on the basis of actual output produced. Also called *denominator-level variance*. (318)

Productivity. Measures the relationship between actual inputs used (both quantities and costs) and actual outputs produced; the lower the inputs for a given quantity of outputs or the higher the outputs for a given quantity of inputs, the higher the productivity. (531)

Productivity component. Change in costs attributable to a change in the quantity of inputs used in the current period relative to the quantity of inputs that would have been used in the prior period to produce the quantity of current period output. (517)

Profit center. Responsibility center where the manager is accountable for revenues and costs. (238)

Proration. The spreading of underallocated manufacturing overhead or overallocated manufacturing overhead among ending work in process, finished goods, and cost of goods sold. (149)

Purchase-order lead time. The time between placing an order and its delivery. (800)

Purchasing costs. Cost of goods acquired from suppliers including incoming freight or transportation costs. (799)

PV graph. Shows how changes in the quantity of units sold affect operating income. (96)

Qualitative factors. Outcomes that are difficult to measure accurately in numerical terms. (449)

Quality. The total features and characteristics of a product made or a service performed according to specifications to satisfy customers at the time of purchase and during use. (769)

Quantitative factors. Outcomes that are measured in numerical terms. (449)

Rate variance. See *price variance*. (278)

Real rate of return. The rate of return demanded to cover investment risk (with no inflation). It has a risk-free element and a business-risk element. (863)

Reciprocal method. Cost allocation method that fully recognizes the mutual services provided among all support departments. Also called *matrix method*. (635)

Reengineering. The fundamental rethinking and redesign of business processes to achieve improvements in critical measures of performance, such as cost, quality, service, speed, and customer satisfaction. (500)

Refined costing system. Costing system that reduces the use of broad averages for assigning the cost of resources to cost objects (jobs, products, services) and provides better measurement of the costs of indirect resources used by different cost objects, no matter how differently various cost objects use indirect resources. (178)

Regression analysis. Statistical method that measures the average amount of change in the dependent variable associated with a unit change in one or more independent variables. (404)

Relevant costs. Expected future costs that differ among alternative courses of action being considered. (447)

Relevant range. Band of normal activity level or volume in which there is a specific relationship between the level of activity or volume and the cost in question. (55)

Relevant revenues. Expected future revenues that differ among alternative courses of action being considered. (447)

Reorder point. The quantity level of inventory on hand that triggers a new purchase order. (802)

Required rate of return (RRR). The minimum acceptable annual rate of return on an investment. Also called the *discount rate*, *hurdle rate*, *cost of capital*, or *opportunity cost of capital*. (842)

Research and development (R&D). Generating and experimenting with ideas related to new products, services, or processes. (25)

Residual income (RI). Accounting measure of income minus a dollar amount for required return on an accounting measure of investment. (915)

Residual term. The vertical difference or distance between actual cost and estimated cost for each observation in a regression model. (404)

Responsibility accounting. System that measures the plans, budgets, actions, and actual results of each responsibility center. (238)

Responsibility center. Part, segment, or subunit of an organization whose manager is accountable for a specified set of activities. (238)

Return on investment (ROI). An accounting measure of income divided by an accounting measure of investment. See also *accrual accounting rate of return method*. (914)

Revenue allocation. The allocation of revenues that are related to a particular revenue object but cannot be traced to it in an economically feasible (cost-effective) way. (644)

Revenue center. Responsibility center where the manager is accountable for revenues only. (238)

Revenue driver. A variable, such as volume, that causally affects revenues. (93)

Revenue object. Anything for which a separate measurement of revenue is desired. (645)

Revenues. Inflows of assets (usually cash or accounts receivable) received for products or services provided to customers. (59)

Rework. Units of production that do not meet the specifications required by customers for finished units that are subsequently repaired and sold as good finished units. (739)

Rightsizing. See *downsizing*. (525)

Rolling budget. Budget or plan that is always available for a specified future period by adding a period (month, quarter, or year) to the period that just ended. Also called *continuous budget or rolling forecast*. (222)

Rolling forecast. See *rolling budget*. (222)

Safety stock. Inventory held at all times regardless of the quantity of inventory ordered using the EOQ model. (803)

Sales mix. Quantities of various products or services that constitute total unit sales. (105)

Sales-mix variance. The difference between (1) budgeted contribution margin for the actual sales mix, and (2) budgeted contribution margin for the budgeted sales mix. (601)

Sales-quantity variance. The difference between (1) budgeted contribution margin based on actual units sold of all products at the budgeted mix and (2) contribution margin in the static budget (which is based on the budgeted units of all products to be sold at the budgeted mix). (602)

Sales value at splitoff method. Method that allocates joint costs to joint products on the basis of the relative total sales value at the splitoff point of the total production of these products during the accounting period. (668)

Sales-volume variance. The difference between a flexible-budget amount and the corresponding static-budget amount. (274)

Scrap. Residual material left over when making a product. (739)

Selling-price variance. The difference between the actual selling price and the budgeted selling price multiplied by the actual units sold. (276)

Semivariable cost. See *mixed cost*. (394)

Sensitivity analysis. A what-if technique that managers use to calculate how an outcome will change if the original predicted data are not achieved or if an underlying assumption changes. (100)

Separable costs. All costs (manufacturing, marketing, distribution, and so on) incurred beyond the splitoff point that are assignable to each of the specific products identified at the splitoff point. (664)

Sequential allocation method. See *step-down method*. (634)

Sequential tracking. Approach in a product-costing system in which recording of the journal entries occurs in the same order as actual purchases and progress in production. (816)

Service department. See *support department*. (622)

Service-sector companies. Companies that provide services or intangible products to their customers. (58)

Service-sustaining costs. The costs of activities undertaken to support individual services regardless of the number of units or batches in which services are provided. (183)

Shrinkage costs. Costs that result from theft by outsiders, embezzlement by employees, misclassifications, or misplacement of inventory. (800)

Simple regression. Regression model that estimates the relationship between the dependent variable and one independent variable. (404)

Single-rate method. Allocation method that allocates costs in each cost pool to cost objects using the same rate per unit of a single allocation base without distinguishing fixed from variable costs. (622)

Slope coefficient. Coefficient term in a cost estimation model that indicates the amount by which total cost changes when a one-unit change occurs in the level of activity within the relevant range. (393)

Source document. An original record that supports journal entries in an accounting system. (133)

Specification analysis. Testing of the assumptions of regression analysis. (423)

Splitoff point. The juncture in a joint-production process when two or more products become separately identifiable. (664)

Spoilage. Units of production that do not meet the specifications required by customers for good units and that are discarded or sold at reduced prices. (739)

Staff management. Staff (such as management accountants and human resources managers) who provide advice and assistance to line management. (33)

Stand-alone cost-allocation method. Method that uses information pertaining to each user of the common cost facility or activity as a separate entity to determine the cost-allocation weights. (641)

Stand-alone revenue-allocation method. Method that uses product-specific information on the products in the bundle as weights for allocating the bundled revenues to the individual products. (646)

Standard. A carefully determined price, cost, or quantity that is used as a benchmark for judging performance. It is usually expressed on a per unit basis. (277)

Standard cost. A carefully determined cost of a unit of output. (278)

Standard costing. Costing system that traces direct costs to output produced by multiplying the standard prices or rates by the standard quantities of inputs allowed for actual outputs produced and allocates overhead costs on the basis of the standard overhead-cost rates times the standard quantities of the allocation bases allowed for the actual outputs produced. (310)

Standard error of the estimated coefficient. Regression statistic that indicates how much the estimated value of the coefficient is likely to be affected by random factors. (421)

Standard error of the regression. Statistic that measures the standard deviation of residuals in a regression analysis. (421)

Standard input. A carefully determined quantity of input required for one unit of output. (277)

Standard price. A carefully determined price that a company expects to pay for a unit of input. (277)

Static budget. Budget based on the level of output planned at the start of the budget period. (271)

Static-budget variance. Difference between an actual result and the corresponding budgeted amount in the static budget. (271)

Step cost function. A cost function in which the cost remains the same over various ranges of the level of activity, but the cost increases by discrete amounts (that is, increases in steps) as the level of activity changes from one range to the next. (409)

Step-down method. Cost allocation method that allocates support department costs to other support departments and to operating departments in a sequential manner that partially recognizes the mutual services provided among all support departments. Also called *sequential allocation method*. (634)

Stockout costs. Costs that result when a company runs out of a particular item for which there is customer demand. The company must act to meet that demand or suffer the costs of not meeting it. (799)

Strategic cost management. Describes cost management that specifically focuses on strategic issues. (24)

Strategy. Specifies how an organization matches its own capabilities with the opportunities in the marketplace to accomplish its objectives. (23)

Strategy map. A diagram that describes how an organization creates value by connecting strategic objectives in explicit cause-and-effect relationships with each other in the financial, customer, internal business process, and learning and growth perspectives. (502)

Suboptimal decision making. Decisions in which the benefit to one subunit is more than offset by the costs or loss of benefits to the organization as a whole. Also called *incongruent decision making* or *dysfunctional decision making*. (880)

Sunk costs. Past costs that are unavoidable because they cannot be changed no matter what action is taken. (448)

Super-variable costing. See *throughput costing*. (361)

Supply chain. Describes the flow of goods, services, and information from the initial sources of materials and services to the delivery of products to consumers, regardless of whether those activities occur in the same organization or in other organizations. (26)

Support department. Department that provides the services that assist other internal departments (operating departments and other support departments) in the company. Also called a *service department*. (622)

Sustainability. The development and implementation of strategies to achieve long-term financial, social, and environmental goals. (27)

Target cost per unit. Estimated long-run cost per unit of a product or service that enables the company to achieve its target operating income per unit when selling at the target price. Target cost per unit is derived by subtracting the target operating income per unit from the target price. (552)

Target operating income per unit. Operating income that a company aims to earn per unit of a product or service sold. (552)

Target price. Estimated price for a product or service that potential customers will pay. (550)

Target rate of return on investment. The target annual operating income that an organization aims to achieve divided by invested capital. (557)

Theoretical capacity. The level of capacity based on producing at full efficiency all the time. (364)

Theory of constraints (TOC). Describes methods to maximize operating income when faced with some bottleneck and some non-bottleneck operations. (464)

Throughput costing. Method of inventory costing in which only variable direct material costs are included as inventoriable costs. Also called *super-variable costing*. (361)

Throughput margin. Revenues minus the direct material costs of the goods sold. (464)

Time driver. Any factor in which a change in the factor causes a change in the speed of an activity. (781)

Time value of money. Takes into account that a dollar (or any other monetary unit) received today is worth more than a dollar received at any future time. (842)

Total factor productivity (TFP). The ratio of the quantity of output produced to the costs of all inputs used, based on current period prices. (532)

Total-overhead variance. The sum of the flexible-budget variance and the production-volume variance. (325)

Total quality management (TQM). An integrative philosophy of management for continuously improving the quality of products and processes. (27)

Transfer price. Price one subunit (department or division) charges for a product or service supplied to another subunit of the same organization. (882)

Transferred-in costs. Costs incurred in previous departments that are carried forward as the product's costs when it moves to a subsequent process in the production cycle. Also called *previous department costs*. (712)

Trigger point. Refers to a stage in the cycle from purchase of direct materials to sale of finished goods at which journal entries are made in the accounting system. (816)

Uncertainty. The possibility that an actual amount will deviate from an expected amount. (101)

Underabsorbed indirect costs. See *underallocated indirect costs*. (148)

Underallocated indirect costs. Allocated amount of indirect costs in an accounting period is less than the actual (incurred) amount in that period. Also called *underapplied indirect costs* or *underabsorbed indirect costs*. (148)

Underapplied indirect costs. See *underallocated indirect costs*. (148)

Unfavorable variance. Variance that has the effect of decreasing operating income relative to the budgeted amount. Denoted U. (271)

Unit cost. Cost computed by dividing total cost by the number of units. Also called *average cost*. (56)

Unused capacity. The amount of productive capacity available over and above the productive capacity employed to meet consumer demand in the current period. (524)

Usage variance. See *efficiency variance*. (279)

Value-added cost. A cost that, if eliminated, would reduce the actual or perceived value or utility (usefulness) customers obtain from using the product or service. (553)

Value chain. The sequence of business functions by which a product is made progressively more useful to customers. (24)

Value engineering. Systematic evaluation of all aspects of the value chain, with the objective of reducing costs and achieving a quality level that satisfies customers. (552)

Value streams. All valued-added activities needed to design, manufacture, and deliver a given product or product line to customers. (824)

Variable cost. Cost that changes in total in proportion to changes in the related level of total activity or volume. (52)

Variable costing. Method of inventory costing in which only all variable manufacturing costs are included as inventoriable costs. Also called *direct costing*. (350)

Variable overhead efficiency variance. The difference between the actual quantity of variable overhead cost-allocation base used and budgeted quantity of variable overhead cost-allocation base that should have been used to produce actual output, multiplied by budgeted variable overhead cost per unit of cost-allocation base. (313)

Variable overhead flexible-budget variance. The difference between actual variable overhead costs incurred and flexible-budget variable overhead amounts. (312)

Variable overhead spending variance. The difference between actual variable overhead cost per unit and budgeted variable overhead cost per unit of the cost-allocation base, multiplied by actual quantity of variable overhead cost-allocation base used for actual output. (314)

Variance. The difference between actual result and expected performance. (270)

Weighted-average process-costing method. Method of process costing that assigns the equivalent-unit cost of the work done to date (regardless of the accounting period in which it was done) to equivalent units completed and transferred out of the process and to equivalent units in ending work-in-process inventory. (704)

Whale curve. A typically backward-bending curve that represents the results from customer profitability analysis by first ranking customers from best to worst and then plotting their cumulative profitability level. (587)

Work-in-process inventory. Goods partially worked on but not yet completed. Also called *work in progress*. (58)

Work in progress. See *work-in-process inventory*. (58)

Work-measurement method. See *industrial engineering method*. (398)

Index

Author

Company

Subject